QlikView® Your Business

An Expert Guide to Business Discovery with QlikView® and Qlik Sense™

Oleg Troyansky

Tammy Gibson

Charlie Leichtweis

QlikView® Your Business: An Expert Guide to Business Discovery with QlikView® and Qlik Sense™

Project Editor Tom Dinse
Technical Editors Dr. Henric Cronström, Rob Wunderlich
Production Manager Kathleen Wisor
Copy Editor Kezia Endsley
Manager of Content Development & Assembly Mary Beth Wakefield
Marketing Director David Mayhew
Marketing Manager Carrie Sherrill
Professional Technology & Strategy Director Barry Pruett
Business Manager Amy Knies
Associate Publisher Jim Minatel
Project Coordinator, Cover Brent Savage
Book Designer and Compositor Maureen Forys, Happenstance Type-O-Rama
Proofreader Jen Larsen, Word One
Indexer Johnna VanHoose Dinse
Cover Designer Michael E. Trent/Wiley
Cover Image Courtesy of Oleg Troyansky

Published by
John Wiley & Sons, Inc.
10475 Crosspoint Boulevard
Indianapolis, IN 46256
www.wiley.com

Copyright © 2015 by John Wiley & Sons, Inc., Indianapolis, Indiana
Published simultaneously in Canada

ISBN: 978-1-118-94955-9
ISBN: 978-1-118-94958-0 (ebk)
ISBN: 978-1-118-94957-3 (ebk)

Manufactured in the United States of America
10 9 8 7 6 5 4 3 2 1

About the Authors

Natural Synergies, Inc.

This book was created by a team of consultants from Natural Synergies, Inc.—a boutique BI consulting firm that specializes in helping QlikView customers maximize the benefits from their BI and ERP investments.

The company was founded in 2007 by a team of devoted QlikView veterans, with the goal of providing high-quality professional services to QlikView customers. Led by Oleg Troyansky, Natural Synergies, Inc. proudly employs a team of seasoned QlikView professionals who provide a full range of services on the QlikView platform:

- Educating QlikView developers and designers
  - Teaching standard and custom QlikView courses for beginners and advanced developers
  - Mentoring and coaching internal teams of QlikView developers and helping them cultivate their knowledge over time
  - Supporting internal teams of QlikView developers with expert help on demand, conveniently packaged as an affordable subscription
- Assisting customers in developing their analytic applications
  - Leveraging industry expertise to coach customers and design powerful and insightful analytic applications
  - Exposing customers to best practices, industry standards, and robust analytics
- Expert services
  - Performance tuning and optimization
  - QlikView application review
  - Architecture and design of customized QlikView environments, as well as individual solutions

If you enjoy the depth of QlikView expertise in this book, please contact Natural Synergies and let them help you *QlikView Your Business*. Visit www.NaturalSynergies.com for more information.

Oleg Troyansky implemented QlikView in 2003 as an IT executive at a mid-size manufacturing company. After falling in love at first sight, Oleg developed several analytic applications to help the company improve management of sales, inventories, profitability, freight costs, and more.

Oleg has been an active supporter and advocate for QlikView, speaking at industry events like the Gartner BI Summit, annual Qonnections meetings, and others. Many of Oleg's success stories from that time are published in several on-line publications.

Since forming Natural Synergies in 2007, Oleg has been helping customers generate value from their QlikView and ERP investments. Advanced Inventory Analysis, Plant Capacity Simulation, and Sales & Operations Planning (S&OP) Dashboard are just a few examples of his advanced analytic development work.

Oleg is one of the most active members and among the first moderators of the Qlik Community forums, where he helps thousands of QlikView developers overcome technical challenges and make the most of the tool.

Oleg Troyansky is one of the four recognized QlikView experts who teach advanced QlikView topics at the Masters Summit for QlikView (www.masterssummit.com)—the most advanced technical venue for experienced QlikView professionals. Additionally, in recognition of his contributions to the field, Oleg has been accredited as a 2014 Qlik Luminary.

Oleg writes a QlikView blog on the company's website at

www.naturalsyenrgies.com.

As an educator and a QlikView advocate, Oleg has educated generations of QlikView professionals and experts through his input on the Qlik Community forums, public and private QlikView classes, sessions of the Masters Summit, and entries on his blog.

Oleg and his family reside in Buffalo Grove, Illinois.

Tammy Gibson is a premier QlikView consultant in the United States, with deep architectural and design experience.

Like Oleg, Tammy first discovered QlikView as a customer in 2004. In her role as director of IT and data integration, she provided marketing and sales analytics to a live entertainment organization. By 2007, she had acquired the skills to become a technical consultant, delivering QlikView applications and data warehouse modeling designs. Tammy is renowned for her ideas and techniques on modern dashboard design, as well as her enterprise deployment strategies.

In addition to her work with Natural Synergies, Tammy is the co-founder and CTO of VenueCube—a provider of SaaS-based software and business intelligence analytics to the live event industry. It's headquartered in Palo Alto, CA. Earlier in her career, Tammy held corporate IT positions in several large organizations, including CIBC World Markets and Akzo-Nobel.

She holds a B.S. in Computer Science from the Missouri University of Science and Technology (Rolla, MO), QlikView Designer/Developer/Server certifications, and MCSE and MCDBA certifications from Microsoft.

Tammy and her family reside in Fort Lauderdale, Florida.

Charlie Leichtweis is Senior Advisor at Phoenix Strategic Advisors where he leads their Manufacturing Practice. He is an experienced business leader with significant successes in change management, strategic planning, general management, mergers/acquisitions, and international business.

Charlie has served as the President and CEO of Testor Corporation, a leading manufacturer of coatings, adhesives, and a variety of injection molded products for the hobby and craft markets.

His diverse career is marked by the ability to build sustainable profitable growth through alignment of strategy with process, brand management, cost containment, margin improvement, structure optimization, and cash management.

Prior to Testor, he was a Group Vice President (Chief Operating Officer) at Blyth North American Wholesale Group. There, he led global manufacturing operations, supply chain, finance, plus enterprise wide reengineering. He also served as

General Manager with full P&L responsibility for the Retail Outlets Division, and led the New Markets group, which identified and developed secondary channel market opportunities.

Previously, Charlie served as CFO at both Rand McNally Book Services and at Rust-Oleum, and held management roles in finance at Abbott Labs. In addition, from 1997 to 2000, he was the Founder and President of Process Solutions, a business process consultancy. He started his career with Deloitte in Detroit, MI.

Charlie has an MBA in Operations Management from Loyola University of Chicago, and a B.S. (Cum Laude) in Accounting from the University of Detroit. He is a CPA and CMA.

He has been an Adjunct Professor at the Lake Forest Graduate School of Management. He also served for four years as the Chairman of the Board of Directors, Junior Achievement of Chicago, Northern Division.

About the Technical Editors

Dr. Henric Cronström is the technical product advocate at Qlik, where he has worked for most of the time since the company was founded. At Qlik, Henric has had several roles. During the first few years in Qlik's history, he was the product manager for QlikView, after which he moved into solution implementation and training. After many years in the field, including a role as manager of the technical staff in QlikTech Germany, he returned to Sweden as deputy manager for the development organization.

His area of expertise is the product itself and includes advanced application development, scripting, and data modelling.

In his current role, his main task is technical product communication. He does this via blogs, in the press, and directly with large accounts and user groups. Henric has a doctorate in elementary particle physics from the University of Lund.

Rob Wunderlich has over 30 years of experience in the IT industry, holding positions as a software developer, manager, and consultant. Rob has been working with QlikView and now Qlik Sense since 2006. He authors a popular QlikView blog and publishes the website QlikViewCookbook.com. Rob currently splits his consulting time between QlikView development and training QlikView developers. He is a co-founder and a featured presenter at the Masters Summit for QlikView.

Acknowledgments

First, we would like to thank the wonderful team of professionals at Qlik for creating and bringing to market a phenomenal tool worth writing about. We thank Lars Björk, Qlik's CEO, for leading the troops and for writing the foreword for this book.

Special thanks to Henric Cronström, Rob Wunderlich, Phil Bishop, and Elif Tutuk, for their valuable input and contributions to the content of the book.

There were a number of people who made this book possible, including Robert Elliot, who approached us about writing the book, and Tom Dinse and others from Wiley who helped shepherd us through the process.

Other well-deserved thanks go to Victorya Slobodetsky, who created most of the electronic content for the book, and to Andrey Konoplyastyy, who developed an elaborate data-generating tool in order to create the data set used in the book.

We'd like to thank all of the QlikView professionals whose questions, issues, and suggestions helped us sharpen our knowledge and ultimately express it in this book. We hope you enjoy the book as much as we do.

I dedicate this book to my beloved family—my parents, my wife Rimma, and our children, Victorya and Eitan, who are both beginning QlikView professionals.

—OLEG

I dedicate this book to my mom, Georgia. She would have been so proud despite not understanding one single word of this book. To my wife, Dayene, and my sons, Cash and Bodhi—thank you for your love, encouragement, and endless patience.

—TAMMY

I would like to dedicate this book to my dad. He was a life-long educator who believed that teaching was one of the most important ways to give back.

—CHARLIE

Contents

PART III Expanding Your Skill Set: Profitability Analysis

Foreword

When Oleg Troyansky told me he was writing a QlikView book, I joked, "Are people writing books anymore?" In our largely digital world, filled with developer forums, blogs, YouTube videos, and Tweets, it seems like our attention span for information is shrinking, leaving little space left for full-size books. Now that I'm holding the manuscript in my hands, I know that *QlikView Your Business* will certainly find its place in the Qlik ecosystem. Now my only question to Oleg is, "What took you so long?"

I remember Oleg as one of the early adopters of QlikView in the United States. He quickly became one of the product's most vocal advocates. When we opened our Qlik Community forum, Oleg was among the first few active experts who happily shared their knowledge with new developers. Eventually he became one of the first official moderators of the forum. With all of his knowledge and passion for Qlik, it was no surprise when Oleg made the transition from a QlikView customer to a full-time QlikView developer, partner, and co-founder of a reputable BI firm, Natural Synergies. If anyone should write the book on QlikView, Oleg is certainly the right man for the job.

QlikView Your Business takes an unconventional approach. Unlike traditional technology books that rarely talk about business or business books that fail to teach readers how to develop complex analytic applications, this book takes a unique approach by combining the two. In a way it's very similar to the way we do business at Qlik. It focuses on the individual—the human behind the analysis—and finds a way to help solve their challenges, regardless of where they sit within an organization.

At Qlik, we value the concept of *simplicity*. We believe that BI shouldn't be complicated, hard, or intimidating. We feel that our products make the job of data analysis *instinctive*. At the same time, QlikView offers tremendous depth for those analytical needs that can't be solved by simply scratching the surface of data. This is where developers' expertise comes into play, and Oleg brings these advanced concepts home very elegantly. After reading this book, you will learn real-life techniques for building scalable data models. You will practice the most advanced aspects of Set Analysis and Advanced Aggregation. You will learn how to build the most intricate visualizations.

Most importantly, you will discover how to use QlikView to ask limitless questions and find innumerable insights.

Last year, we launched a new addition to the Qlik family—Qlik Sense. We believe that Qlik Sense makes the task of data analysis more intuitive, natural, and self-explanatory. It also unlocks new possibilities for developers with its open APIs and powerful analytics engine. I'm pleased to see the detail with which Qlik Sense is covered in this book, as it provides further insight into the possibilities both products present to users. With our growing product portfolio, Qlik ensures that the needs of all users are met, unlocking transformative insights along the way.

In conclusion, let me praise you, the reader, on your decision to read *QlikView Your Business*. I'm confident that you will find it both informative and thought provoking and hope it inspires you to take the time to further explore the information around you. Only by discovering great insights can we inspire more powerful action.

—Lars Björk

CEO, Qlik

Introduction

It's no secret that we live in a rapidly accelerating world. Not too long ago, computers were huge and practically brainless and humans had to crunch the data output for months in pursuit of meaningful insight. Not too long ago, anything related to data processing required employing a team of professional programmers—these mysterious gods of cryptic languages, debuggers, and binary code.

In the last 20 years, several things had changed in this picture. Our computers are now small in size yet very powerful. Our tools are so smart that they offer insights at an amazing speed. Data processing has evolved through a number of generations, from Executive Information Systems through data warehousing, to business intelligence, and now to business discovery, enabling a wide community of developers, analysts, and power users to participate in the analytics process.

The data revolution that we are all experiencing has created a new occupation—data scientist, which was called "The sexiest job of the 21st century" by the *Harvard Business Review*. Data scientists bring together the technical knowledge of the traditional *developers* and the business acumen of the traditional *analysts*.

Similarly, this book combines the business aspects of developing business discovery applications and the specific techniques that we use to develop business analytics using QlikView and Qlik Sense.

This book, written by a data scientist, a programmer, and a businessman, is for the data scientist who wants to analyze data with Qlik tools; the developer who wants to learn the technical and the business aspects of Qlik Business Discovery; the business analyst who wants to learn how to develop Qlik visualizations; and anyone who is trying to determine whether QlikView and Qlik Sense are the right tools for their business needs. As each type of reader might want something different from the book, the "How to Read This Book" section provides guidelines for a custom path through the chapters.

The book will take you through the three common scenarios of business analytics—sales analysis, profitability analysis, and inventory analysis. You will learn the business aspects of these topics, the data modeling techniques that we use to build robust analytic data models, QlikView scripting techniques, and visualizations that can be used for effective, intuitive analytics.

Part V of this book is devoted to Qlik Sense, a new tool in the Qlik family that primarily targets the world of self-service analytics. You will learn how to use Qlik Sense to prepare a self-service analytics environment for your users and how to extend your Qlik Sense apps with extensions.

The book is built as a tutorial, with data sources and supplemental materials available online. Going through the tutorial, you will grasp both basic and advanced techniques of building business analytics with Qlik products.

Overview of the Book and Technology

This book is about business analytics and business discovery, but most of all, it's about QlikView. It wouldn't be an exaggeration to say that QlikView became our passion and the highlight of our professional careers soon after we become acquainted with the tool.

We believe that the secret to QlikView's overwhelming success and almost fanatical following is its focus on *simplicity* and ease of use. In QlikView developers' minds, business intelligence doesn't have to be hard, cumbersome, and expensive. This has been the slogan of all QlikView fans for many years.

At the same time, simplicity shouldn't be confused with a pass to stay ignorant. We still need to know what we're doing when developing an insightful analytical application.

Albert Einstein is believed to have said, "Everything should be made as simple as possible, but not one bit simpler." While most people remember the first part of this sentence, we'd like to reflect on the second. Life is inherently complicated, and business life is no exception. Not every business need can be met with a lightweight, simple solution. We should certainly make every effort to simplify, and yet we need to be prepared to develop something sophisticated and complex when needed.

As a BI tool, QlikView offers it all. It can be simple and lightweight, allowing you to develop a simple solution in hours. At the same time, it offers enough depth and sophistication to let you create something truly unique and remarkable.

Following the same premise, this book starts from describing the basics, and then moves on to more and more advanced techniques, diving deep into the most sophisticated areas of QlikView such as Advanced Aggregation, Set Analysis, and advanced data modeling.

QlikView development methodology has evolved through the years, along with the evolution of the tool and business analytics. We learned how to deal with large data volumes and how to manage the complexity of our environments. As active contributors in the community, we participated in developing the collective set of tips, tricks, and best practices, and we absorbed tips offered by others. These tricks and best practices are available to you in this book.

The book covers the four main parts of any BI development:

- **Business Case**, which describes the subject of the analysis—the main goals and the main metrics that need to be analyzed.

- **Data Modeling**, which is a theoretical exercise that describes how the source data needs to be organized for an effective analysis.

- **Data Load Scripting**, which is the practical implementation of the data modeling exercise. Here, we build the data model and describe how it's done.

- **Building Visualizations**, which is the process of building the visual layout of the analytical application and creating insightful visualizations, based on the requirements that were laid out in the business case.

We will walk you through these four steps over the three business scenarios. Together, we will analyze sales, profitability, and inventory, moving from simple to advanced techniques of QlikView development.

We all know the saying "wearing multiple hats." If you happen to work in a mid-size business, you do it every day. Throughout this book, you will get to wear four different hats—the hats of a business professional, a data architect, a developer, and a designer. The ability to wear these four hats is the core of the QlikView professional skillset, and we hope to help you sharpen this ability with this book.

How This Book Is Organized

This book is divided into five sections:

- **Getting Started (Chapters 1 and 2).** Here we describe the case for business analytics and how Qlik fits in the overall business intelligence landscape.

- **Sales Analysis (Chapters 3–6).** We describe the common business requirements for sales analysis and the basic QlikView techniques that are used for developing a typical sales analysis application. We learn the basics of loading data into QlikView and the basic visualization techniques.

- **Profitability Analysis (Chapters 7–10).** Using the business scenario of profitability analysis, we describe more advanced QlikView techniques:

  - We learn how to organize data structures with multiple fact tables using Link tables.

  - We build a QVD data layer and a library of reusable scripts.

  - We describe more advanced visualization techniques including simple and more advanced Set Analysis.

- **Inventory Analysis (Chapters 11–14).** This section describes the most complex QlikView methodologies that are commonly used for complex analytic solutions, such as inventory analysis:

  - Organizing multiple fact tables into a single Concatenated Fact table.

  - Calculating running totals in the data load process.

  - Using generic link tables and an alternative solution utilizing Set Analysis.

  - Answering advanced analytical questions using Advanced Aggregation and advanced Set Analysis.

  - Adding interactivity using buttons, actions, and show conditions.

- **Qlik Sense (Chapters 15 and 16).** This section describes the new tool in the family, Qlik Sense. We demonstrate how to load data and how to build self-service analytical applications, as well as dashboards, using the tool. In addition, we provide a basic example of integrating a simple extension.

How to Read This Book

You can, of course, read this book straight through from cover to cover. However, depending on your goals, you may skip some sections without losing much context. For example, if you are a data analyst trying to learn how to design QlikView visualizations, you may prefer to skip the technical chapters describing data modeling and scripting. The following are a couple of suggested paths though the book for different reader profiles.

The summary of all possible tracks is presented in Figure I.1 at the end of this section (which is, of course, a QlikView chart). In this table, readers can pick one of the three tracks—Executive, Non-Technical, and Technical. The green checkmark signifies chapters that we recommend to readers who follow the corresponding track. Gray checkmarks mean that we suggest skimming through the chapter. Other chapters can be skipped altogether if you are not interested in their contents.

Data Scientist, Developer, Consultant

If you are a data scientist, a developer with a technical background, or perhaps a QlikView consultant, you are most likely to read the book cover to cover, because you will ultimately need it all—the business cases, the technical aspects of data modeling and scripting, and the advanced visualization techniques. You might decide to skim through the business chapters (1–3, 7, and 11) and focus on more technical chapters. See the Technical track in Figure I.1.

If you are familiar with QlikView fundamentals, you can skim through the first two parts and jump right into more advanced topics in Parts III and IV.

Business Analyst, Designer, Power User

If you are interested mostly in creating QlikView visualizations without worrying too much about the technical aspects of data modeling and scripting, you can read the first two chapters in each part and stop there. The electronic materials are built in a way that allows you to develop the layout of each application without worrying about the data. The most recommended chapters for you are: 1–4, 7–8, 11–12, and 15–16. See the Non-Technical track in Figure I.1.

Executive, Project Manager, Technology Evaluator

If you are reading this book with the goal of understanding what Qlik is all about, or to determine if QlikView is the right tool for your business, we recommend you focus on the business chapters of the book and flip through the visualization chapters, where you will see what kinds of visualizations can be created with the tool for each business problem. The recommended chapters for you are: 1–3, 7, and 11. Glance through Chapters 4, 8, 12, and 16. Also, take a look at the list of additional educational opportunities in the appendix. See the Executive Track in Figure I.1.

FIGURE I.1:
How to read this book. In the column for your chosen track, read the chapters marked in green and skim through those marked in gray

Part/Chapter	Executive Track	Non-Technical Track	Technical Track
Part I: Getting Started			
Chapter 1: Basics of Business Analytics	●	●	●
Chapter 2: Why Use QlikView for Business Analytics?	●	●	●
Part II: Sales Analysis			
Chapter 3: Defining a Business Scenario for Sales Analysis	●	●	●
Chapter 4: Visualizing Sales Analysis in QlikView	●	●	●
Chapter 5: Data Modeling for Sales Analysis			●
Chapter 6: Developing a Data Load Script for Sales Analysis		●	●
Part III: Profitability Analysis			
Chapter 7: Defining a Business Scenario for Profitability Analysis	●	●	●
Chapter 8: Visualizing Profitability Analysis in QlikView	●	●	●
Chapter 9: Data Modeling for Profitability Analysis			●
Chapter 10: Developing a Data Load Script for Profitability Ana...			●
Part IV: Inventory Analysis			
Chapter 11: Defining a Business Scenario for Inventory Analysis	●	●	●
Chapter 12: Visualizing Inventory Analysis in QlikView	●	●	●
Chapter 13: Data Modeling for Inventory Analysis			●
Chapter 14: Developing a Data Load Script for Inventory Analysis			●
Part V: Introducing Qlik Sense			
Chapter 15: Loading Data in Qlik Sense		●	●
Chapter 16: Building Visualizations in Qlik Sense	●	●	●
Appendix: Where Do You Go Next?	●	●	●

Conventions

To help you get the most from the text and keep track of what's happening, we've used a number of conventions throughout the book:

Boxes like this one hold important, not-to-be-forgotten information directly relevant to the surrounding text.

This icon indicates notes, tips, hints, tricks, and asides to the current discussion.

Important Comments and Summary Statements

Here we include important comments and summarizing statements that help to clarify and add important, not to be missed detail to the core topic.

Exercises that you can perform as part of our tutorial appear in a box like this:

Exercise I.1: Develop Something Truly Awsome

These are exercises you should work through, in order to maximize the educational value of the book to you.

1. They usually consist of a set of steps.
2. Each step has a number.
3. Follow the steps in your own QlikView environment.

As for styles in the text:

- We *highlight* important keywords when we introduce them.
- Menu options, buttons, and other texts that you should see on your QlikView screen, are highlighted like this: **File ▶ Open**.
- Text that you need to key in appear highlighted like this: **entered values**.
- We show URLs, database tables and fields, and code within the text in a special monofont typeface, like this: `Customer ID`.

We present code in two different ways:

```
We use a monofont type with no highlighting for most code examples.
We use bold to emphasize code that is particularly important in the
    present
context or to show changes from a previous code snippet.
```

Also, the QlikView script editor provides a rich color scheme to indicate various parts of code syntax. That's a great tool to help you read the script in the editor and to help prevent mistakes as you code. The script examples in this book use colors similar to what you see on your QlikView screen while working with the book's code. In order to optimize print clarity, some colors have a slightly different hue in print than what you see onscreen. But all of the colors for the code in this book should be close enough to the default QlikView colors to give you an accurate representation of the colors.

Preparing Your Work Environment

In this section, we describe the tools and the supplemental materials that you need to download and install in order to use our tutorial. Please take the time to prepare your work environment before you dive into the book materials.

Tools You Need

If you are new to QlikView and/or Qlik Sense Desktop, you need to download and install both tools in order to follow our tutorial. Fortunately,

Personal Editions of these tools are free to use. You simply need to get registered on the Qlik website at www.qlik.com and download the tools there.

At the time when this book was written, we used versions QlikView ver. 11.2 SR9 and Qlik Sense ver. 1.1.0; however, you may use the most current versions of both tools. We don't expect the difference between the versions to impact your experience with the book. If you happen to use an earlier version of QlikView, we recommend installing one of the recent releases of QlikView ver. 11.2.

Once you download the tools, install them with the default settings. The installation process is nothing more than just clicking **Next** at each prompt.

In addition to the Qlik tools, you need the supplemental materials for this book, described in the next section.

Supplemental Materials and Information

The companion website to this book is hosted at http://www.wiley.com/go/qlikview. The site contains information about downloading source code and finding the sample data used throughout the book.

Download and install the data package that contains the electronic materials for the book. We recommend installing the folder in the root of your hard drive C:\. You should find the following subfolders:

- \Apps. This subfolder will contain your new QlikView applications.
- \Data. Here you will find all the data sources that are used in this book.
- \Data Loaders. Here you will store the data load scripts that you will use for building a layer of Transformed QVDs.
- \Data Models. Here you will store the data models that you will create as part of the tutorials.
- \Icons. Here you will find images that will be used in your QlikView applications.
- \Metadata. Here you will find and store text files with expression definitions that we will use in the advanced chapters of the book.
- \Resources. Here you will find additional resources, such as the Open Sans font that we used in our template.

- `\Scripts`. Here you will find and store text files with reusable scripts that can be included in your QlikView applications.

- `\Solutions QlikView`. In this folder, we stored multiple versions of solutions to the exercises. Each version is marked with the exercise number and it corresponds to the expected state of your QlikView document after completing the exercise. This structure allows you to find missing answers when needed or to skip a few exercises and pick up further into the chapter. Whenever you need to continue from a certain point, locate the appropriate solution file and save it with the "main" application name under one of the work folders—`\Apps`, `\Data Loaders`, or `\Data Models`. For example, in order to restore your Sales Analysis application to its expected state after Exercise 5.15, locate the `\Solutions QlikView\5.15 - Sales Analysis.qvw` file and store it in the folder `\Apps\` as `\Apps\Sales Analysis XX.qvw`, where XX is your initials.

  All solution files are stored with no data to decrease the size of the download. After copying one of the solution files, reload the data in the document by using the **Reload** toolbar button.

- `\Solutions Sense`. Similarly, here you can find solutions to the exercises in Qlik Sense. These solutions can be copied into the Qlik Sense standard apps folder:

  `C:\Users\<user>\Documents\Qlik\Sense\Apps`

We highly recommend installing the Open Sans font that we used in our QlikView template. This step is optional; however, it is easier to use our solution files when this font is installed on your computer.

In order to install the font, locate the `\Resources\open-sans` folder and open all the font files one by one. Click on the Install button on top of the window. Repeat for all 10 font files in the folder.

You are now fully prepared for the journey. We are very excited to be sharing this experience with you and hope that you will find it meaningful and beneficial to your particular needs. Let's get started!

Getting Started

The Needs and Challenges of Business Intelligence and Analytics

Every day we are confronted by the challenges of our business, whether we work in the boiler room or the board room. We worry about how to make things work in the best possible way and we worry about avoiding mistakes that can cause things to go wrong. There are a lot of moving parts to any business and it takes a number of people to monitor and manage those moving parts. The fact that there are challenges to managing your enterprise is not a new revelation. Challenges are the main reasons we face some amount of stress in our jobs each time we care enough to "get it right." The question is not just, "What am I supposed to be doing right now?" but, "Where are the current and potential problem areas that will prevent me and my business from succeeding?"

This chapter begins to address those questions and provides some insight into the ways this book will help you answer them. You will learn what business intelligence (BI) is, and the analytics that drive an understanding of the strengths and opportunities that exist in your business.

The Case for Business Intelligence

The issues that keep us up at night include *what we don't know about our business* as much as what we do know. For example, one company experienced a 30% drop in sales in a period of two and a half years. It's true that they knew what customers they lost. In fact, they lost all of their mass channel retail accounts in North America. They were also told by the accounts that they were being dropped because of lack of service and poor unit movement of their products on the shelves of the retailers. The company involved, who shall remain nameless, knew they had a big problem, yet they never saw it coming. They didn't know exactly what the problem was. They didn't know what the root cause of the problem was, and most importantly, they didn't know how to fix it! In this case, a significant problem was service level. The company never calculated service level performance, which is the measure of *on time and complete delivery* to customers.

On Time and Complete Delivery

This metric measures the count of orders delivered complete and on time, divided by the total count of orders. In the example here, this measure was below 40%, which means that 60% of the time the company did not deliver the order with the right quantities or in the time frame required by the customer! The requirement for compliance with mass retailers is a minimum of 98.5% on time and complete.

The company failed to service customers because they did not have proper measurement systems in place for many of the major processes of the business. Data that was needed for proper measurements was buried in functional silos, which meant lack of visibility and communication across functions or to the organization in total. Does this sound familiar? If it does, you are definitely not alone!

The lack of an accurate forecasting process prevented the company from meeting service requirements. Forecasting is an example of a major process that must be connected to other major processes of the organization in order to be successful. When it's based on a good understanding of your customers, forecasting will positively impact your production requirements, inventory accuracy, and purchasing requirements. The company's failure to have the right measurements and its failure to connect the information from these key processes led to blind management and an unacceptably poor customer service level. Poor service in turn led to a catastrophic loss of business.

Your company's situation may not be as severe, but are you sure about what is going on in your business—good and bad—and aware of what needs to be done about it in a timely manner?

NOTE

The question posed in the chapter introduction was, "Where are the current and potential problem areas that will prevent me and my business from succeeding?" This can be very difficult question to answer. And yet, your ability to answer the question positively may be the difference between the success and failure of your company. Running a successful business certainly takes having the right people in the right places in your organization. With that, it is also critical that you have the right data and the ability to access and share that data across your business.

Business intelligence has evolved as a significant segment of the information technologies market by helping companies answer these fundamental questions—How do we know what's going on in the business? What needs to be done about it sooner rather than later? How can we maximize "what we know" and learn more about "what we don't know" about our business?

In the early days, business intelligence was a luxury, only available to the biggest and the richest companies. Today, even midsize and small companies use business intelligence tools and analytics to enable their people to make informed decisions on a timely basis. BI has become a critical component in the mix of tools and processes that companies use to maximize their businesses' potentials and avoid costly pitfalls.

Common Challenges of Business Analytics

Throughout history, businesses have faced significant challenges that threatened their relative success and even their existence. In addition to economic cycles, competition, and regulations, significant challenges frequently faced by businesses include having accurate and timely data about:

- Who their customers are
- What their customers' needs are
- How their customers make purchasing decisions
- How to reduce the cost of products and the cost of servicing their customers

The enterprise that successfully unlocks the data necessary to make timely, accurate decisions about these challenges is better equipped to create sustainable, profitable growth.

Every company, regardless of the segment of the market that they sell to, is challenged to make sense of large amounts of historical and live data across their various data sources. There are a number of barriers that impair a company's ability to effectively connect the dots between mission-critical processes and make timely decisions that positively affect sales, operating income, return on investment (ROI), and cash flow. Because of this reality, business intelligence and analytics are critical areas for technology investment.

There can be significant barriers to successful decision making in a variety of business scenarios, including:

- **Manual processes**—Management reporting using cumbersome spreadsheets that are labor intensive and too slow.
- **Functional and data silos**—The need to integrate information across key functions and multiple locations makes the process even slower.

- **Fragmented view of the business**—There is no ability to easily and accurately create a corporate-level, single-view dashboard of the business in a timely manner.
- **Data quality**—Data correctness across different data sources is in question, resulting in significant time spent reconciling data from various sources.

Do these barriers sound familiar to you? These barriers affect the accuracy and timeliness of connecting critical business processes, which impact customer-facing activities, and ultimately impair the enterprise's ability to optimize sustainable profitable growth.

Perfect Information Costs Too Much!

We all know that perfect information always costs too much! However, being able to access data from a variety of data sources within your IT architecture and the Internet—being able to format it and share it with your associates within research, marketing, product development, sourcing, manufacturing, sales, service, and finance in a timely manner—is priceless!

How Successful Businesses Use Business Intelligence

How do we answer the question, "What information do we need for good decision making"? It starts with identifying the answers to the following questions.

What data do we need? What are the right measurements of performance and measurements of drivers of performance for your business? What are the right tools to analyze your business?

Introducing the Six Process Spheres

To know where to begin identifying data needed to help your associates maximize your results, it is important to understand the six basic groups of processes (we call them *process spheres*). The data from these spheres must be connected in order to maximize and sustain business results:

- *Strategy* is the guiding plan that helps define priorities in each of the mission-critical processes in the other five spheres. The strategy must be aligned with the other five spheres and vice versa in order to optimize business results. To be successful, your strategy needs to be converted into a set of measureable goals and include an action plan of implementation. Business intelligence dashboards play a critical role in communicating the tactics that support the strategy to the organization.

- *Customer-facing activities* involve any process that touches the customer. Included here are sales, marketing, service (orders on time and complete), logistics, product quality, and any other customer interaction. These activities define:

  - How your customers view your company.

  - Whether or not your company "qualifies" as a vendor.

  - If your company provides value to the customers.

  - If your company has a sustainable competitive advantage over your competition.

- *Product development/innovation* is ideally driven by requirements that come from outside of the company, as opposed to internal requirements. Strategy, customer facing-activities, and research are sources for input into product development/innovation activities. Product development/innovation includes marketing, research, trend data, regulatory requirements, customer requirements, and quality.

- *Supply chain activities* are essentially what they sound like. They are the chain of activities that allow the organization to supply products (or services) to its customers. The product must be delivered in accordance with agreed upon product specifications, delivery times, quantities, locations, and logistics. Supply chain activities include manufacturing, finished product and component sourcing, inventory management, warehousing, and shipping. Information from customer-facing activities, product development, and strategy are needed in order to optimize supply chain activities.

- *Financial management* requires accuracy of data transactions and aggregate records to meet the financial requirements of the business. Financial management includes cash flow management, internal controls, financial statement accuracy, and business financing. Without strong financial results, none of the other spheres of mission-critical activities is possible.

- *Associate engagement* may be the most important activity of all. It is critical that all associates understand how their work supports the strategy of the business and the objectives of each of the mission-critical processes embedded in the six spheres. Using BI dashboards to communicate strategic goals and measures of their achievements can help the company establish a culture of transparency and trust. The culture of trust is essential to driving continuous improvement and to creating sustainable profitable growth.

Understanding the measurements of the processes within these spheres is one key dimension of sustainable excellence in performance; the other key dimension is the connection between those spheres of processes. The connection between them is like the electrical system in your home or office. It's the conduit of energy that makes things work. This conduit gives your organization the ability to "turn the lights on and off," if you will. The employees and the technology they use represent the "wiring" in that conduit, and it needs to be in place, maintained, and updated.

Many organizations have what they believe to be the processes they need to manage the business. Every computer system we have seen, no matter how antiquated, has the basic data necessary to enable people to make informed decisions that lead to sustainable profitable growth. Often missing is the technology and the human knowledge necessary for extracting the data from the transactional systems, and the ability to use that data to visualize the six process spheres and the connections between them. Our role, as BI professionals, is to help companies connect the dots between fragmented pieces of information and uncover the "natural synergies" between their processes, their data, and their IT systems.

Figure 1-1 shows that the business world is indeed round, making it a continuum of connectivity that provides feedback to and from each of the six spheres of key business processes. The nucleus of this "world" is the people who interpret and act on the data. The axis around which this world rotates is financial management.

FIGURE 1-1:
The six process spheres

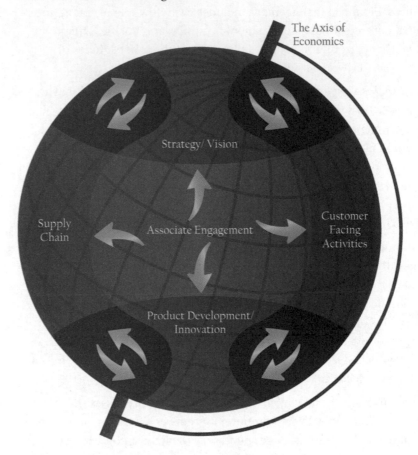

Identifying Business Measures

Even with all the processes and connections in place, it is important to establish the right feedback mechanisms. Those feedback mechanisms include measures of performance and culture. While measurements of culture are extremely important, there is an entire field dedicated to understanding this topic, which is covered in separate literature. This book focuses on the measures of performance.

Business analytics typically look at two types of measures—measures of results and measures of drivers. In the BI jargon, they are called *lagging indicators* and *leading indicators.*

Measures of results, or the lagging indicators, communicate the outcome of what just happened. They are financial results and are focused on components of sales, operating income, return on investment (ROI), and cash flow. These are critical measurements of how a business has done, yet analyzing these measurements alone does not always give you the best answers as to why something happened and what will happen going forward, so that the enterprise can proactively make adjustments.

In contrast, measures of drivers, or leading indicators, are designed to reveal the reasons for certain results (good or bad) and possibly provide insight into future performance. Instead of measuring outcomes, they measure processes and activities that drive the outcomes.

For example, every company measures its sales, or top-line revenue, in comparison to the budget and to the prior year. The measurement is usually communicated as a dollar value and as a percentage. This is the measure of a result (or a lagging indicator). On the other hand, sales growth may be *driven* by many leading indicators, including:

- Change in volume vs. change in pricing
- Acquisition of new customers vs. lost customers
- Revenues driven by new products vs. revenues driven by existing products
- Measures of sales activities, such as the number of sales calls per day, closing ratios, and so on
- Measures of customer satisfaction and customer service

Each item in this list represents one or more of the drivers, or leading indicators, that contribute to the outcome of sales growth. Understanding and communicating those measures can have a significant impact on achieving strategic growth goals.

To give you a feel for the kind of data, the types of measures, and the business spheres that the data and measurements help connect, we have constructed Table 1-1 with some examples.

TABLE 1-1: Some Examples of Spheres Connected, Measurements, and Data Needed

BUSINESS SPHERES CONNECTED	EXAMPLE MEASUREMENT	MEASUREMENT TYPE	EXAMPLE DATA NEEDED
Strategy, customer-facing activities, supply chain, product development, associate engagement, financial management	Sales	Results	Shipments in units and dollars
	POS from customers	Driver and results	Unit take-away by SKU, including color, size, and type
	Average selling price	Results	Unit shipments and net invoiced price
	Number of sales calls	Driver	Call report information by sales person
	Sales forecast	Driver	Sales, forecasted by product and customer
	Service levels	Driver	Units shipped, date shipped, customer order information
Supply chain, product development, associate engagement, financial management	Inventory investment	Results	Units and unit costs
	Inventory days on hand	Driver and results	Units, unit costs, demand by SKU
	Average cost per unit	Driver and results	Units and unit costs
	Inventory accuracy	Driver	Cycle count results

BUSINESS SPHERES CONNECTED	EXAMPLE MEASUREMENT	MEASUREMENT TYPE	EXAMPLE DATA NEEDED
Financial management, associate engagement	Spending levels	Results	Responsibility by department and account
	Activities that drive spending	Driver	Various activities from a variety of sources
Strategy, customer-facing activities, supply chain, product development, associate engagement, financial management	Enterprise direct profitability	Driver and results	Variety of data related to the go-to market tactics of the enterprise defined as variable and fixed

Recall the example of the company that knew something was wrong but didn't know what it was, presented in the "The Case for Business Intelligence" section earlier this chapter. The following list discusses how certain drivers could be measured better:

- The measure of service level drives future sales. For the company in this example, it turned out to be a measure that signaled that the company was not meeting customer requirements and therefore predicted the loss of sales.

- There were also drivers that lead to poor service levels that should have been monitored. Those measurements include forecast accuracy, inventory accuracy, and capacity utilization.

- Another issue that negatively affected the company was cash flow. The cash flow was negative even without significant investment in the assets or resources of the company. It prevented the company from investing in the right inventory, which would have helped timely fulfillment.

- Profitability issues drove the negative cash flow with existing customers. The ability to assess the direct contribution to profitability by product or customer would have been invaluable in avoiding non-profitable product lines and/or customers. It's important that your organization stop doing things it doesn't get paid for. This is very difficult when the company doesn't know which activities it's not getting paid for. Profitability reporting at its most basic level involves using data to calculate the margin.

A new management team implemented a number of these measurements and used analytics to make better business decisions, which began to turn around the business. Service-level measurements allowed the business to understand what was required to reach mass channel customers and retain them, and to identify and implement corrective actions to meet those requirements. They implemented forecasting processes and began to measure forecasting accuracy in order to better forecast demand. These efforts, combined with a focus on inventory management, in turn led to an organized production effort. That in turn led to customer orders being fulfilled completely and in a timely manner. Service levels were improved from below 40% to over 98% in a relatively short period of time, resulting in significant organic growth of the business.

This example is important because it demonstrates that data—combined with the right business intelligence tools and analytical techniques—can be used to help answer the ever-present business questions, *why did something happen* (good or bad) and *what should we do about it.*

What Companies Gain from Implementing BI

When companies consider implementing BI for the first time, they always spend a significant amount of time and energy on comparing costs between different tools, calculating the total cost of ownership, and deciding whether the company can afford such a significant investment. Companies often don't realize what it costs *not* to implement BI. The cost of continuing to act in the dark can often be much higher than the most expensive BI tool.

With the help of BI, your management team can:

- Get a quick snapshot of the entire business.
- Make proactive decisions.

- Free up resources to focus on what truly optimizes the business.

- Achieve significant operational efficiencies across key functional areas of the business.

In order to accomplish this nirvana of analysis, there should not be different versions of the same data in the enterprise. For example, unit cost broken down into its components of labor, material, and overhead that reside in one area of your database cannot add up to something different than the total cost that resides in another "table" or database in the organization. Using business intelligence tools ensures that you can access the correct version of the data even if it resides in a variety of places in your information technology architecture.

Inevitably, different versions of the same data get created in any system. This is particularly true for smaller companies that do not always have the resources to install a new integrated ERP system. You don't need to wait until you have the "perfect" ERP. With BI tools you can begin to build your analysis around the parts of your data that are correct and ignore the incorrect versions in the short term, in order to move forward with a better understanding of your business. If you wait for traffic to clear in each direction for a mile before crossing the road, you will likely never cross!

When BI technology is implemented throughout your company, beyond the top executive level, you can enable your associates to:

- Reach your customers in ways that give you a competitive advantage.

- Measure customer decisions to buy products/services. Understanding your customers' needs can help you predict demand trends that in turn feed product development/innovation activities, production planning, sourcing activities, and working capital projections.

- Ensure that you are meeting customer service requirements so you keep and expand existing customers, at the very least, and create a value-add that allows the enterprise to penetrate new customer/channels, in the best case.

The Business Scenario Used in the Book

The business problems and the QlikView techniques introduced in this book are universal and can be applied to a variety of companies and industry segments. We used a fictional company called *Q-Tee Brands* for the examples in the book.

Q-Tee Brands focuses on manufacturing and distributing high-quality shirts, including dressy shirts, polos, and T-shirts, and it maintains a number of well known brands such as Q-Tee Baby, Q-Tee Mommy, Q-Tee Daddy, and Q-Tee Golf.

The company needs our help in analyzing sales, profitability, and inventory, in order to support their strategic goals of growing revenues and profits.

As with any textile company, Q-Tee Brands is managing their products using the attributes of style, size, and color, and it's essential for them to understand the dynamics of sales, profitability, and inventory based on those key attributes.

Now, let's step back and admit that this book can't possibly represent all the complexities of a real-life business environment and a real-life business system. For the purposes of this educational environment, we built a "straw man" of a company, with a simplified straw man of the data set. This is the classroom version of business analytics. Real life is infinitely more complex and demanding.

The methods and techniques described here, however, are very much real. Understanding and applying these techniques to your real-life environment will enable you and your team to develop powerful analytic solutions to your real-life business challenges.

2

Why Use Qlik for Data Discovery and Analytics?

This chapter gives a short version of the evolution of business intelligence, and how Qlik's disruptive entry into the market has impacted not only the technology that businesses use, but how they actually use data and analytics.

You'll look at how Qlik's products facilitate *data discovery*— a more realistic and natural approach to data analysis than the somewhat outdated notion of business intelligence. And finally, you'll learn about both of Qlik's products, QlikView and Qlik Sense.

To complete the exercises in this chapter, follow the instructions in the Introduction to install QlikView 11 and Qlik Sense.

The Evolution of BI

Software providing *business intelligence* (BI for short) has been around for several decades, but was affordable only to very large enterprises. And while the technology was expensive and labor-intensive, BI systems mostly delivered an underwhelming product: static reports. However, in recent years, fluid changes in economic conditions require that businesses adapt quickly to stay competitive. No longer satisfied with static reports and analysis, businesses increasingly demand more flexibility and insight from BI systems. The success of products like QlikView highlights the fading value of the static reporting system. Why? To fully appreciate the revolutionary change brought by QlikView to the BI market, it's helpful to review where things started.

This story begins with a description of traditional business intelligence.

Traditional Business Intelligence (OLAP)

The term BI describes a system of tools and processes that transform transactional data into meaningful or actionable information for the business. Traditional BI systems are typically proprietary stacks consisting of specialized databases, scripting languages, and report writers—all for the purpose of extracting raw data and presenting some sort of summarized "intelligent" view for analysis purposes.

For many years, BI technology was led by OLAP (On-Line Analytical Processing), which is just a part of the broader category of business intelligence. In a nutshell, OLAP systems are in the business of loading massive amounts of pre-aggregated data into data structures that allow for fast reporting and analysis. The primary feature of all OLAP systems is the *OLAP cube*, which contains the logical definitions for all expected calculations (measures or facts), summarized at their expected levels of aggregation (dimensions).

OLAP systems are further categorized based on how the aggregated data is *physically* stored, whether in relational tables (ROLAP), proprietary multi-dimensional storage arrays (MOLAP), or some hybrid combination. With plenty of resources available that describe the different types and techniques of physical cube storage, we won't go into them here. Suffice it to say that the different types are differentiated by their focus on query flexibility or query speed. For the end user, the type of physical cube storage is transparent. Front-end reporting tools are all somewhat similar, in that reports are based on a query that fetches data from the cube.

The main drawback for all OLAP systems is that the desired levels of detail (dimensions) and the desired calculations (measures) need to be predefined. Also, the labyrinth of architecture layers and supporting technologies make development complex and time consuming. OLAP systems are ideally suited for environments where changes occur relatively infrequently—adding a measure or dimension to a cube can require changes to many components and layers. For these reasons, OLAP projects tend to be very long and expensive.

Figure 2.1 shows a high-level map of a data ecosystem including OLAP BI.

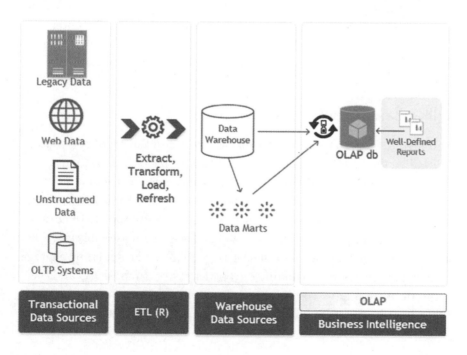

FIGURE 2.1:
OLAP in the data ecosystem

This diagram also shows a *data warehouse*, which is another luxury of the deep-pocketed large enterprise. Organizations that deploy OLAP without a data warehouse might instead use a snapshot copy of the transactional databases to source the BI layer.

With all of their technical complexity and dependencies, traditional BI systems usually find themselves under control of the IT department—and amid an environment of competing priorities, business users compete for often constrained IT resources. The result? BI systems quickly become obsolete—both in technology and in usefulness to the business.

While large enterprises were saddled with BI systems that were expensive and hard to change, small and mid-sized businesses were left out of the BI market altogether. One key difference between a large enterprise and a smaller one is the size and makeup of the IT staff—larger enterprises have highly specialized people managing specialized tools, while smaller enterprises are typically staffed by IT generalists. Another difference is just the sheer size and scale of data applications. Since traditional business intelligence systems were designed for large-scale projects requiring a highly trained and specialized technical staff, smaller businesses could not easily (or affordably) spin up a BI platform. The BI offerings from the stack vendors were not right-priced or right-sized for the less-than-large enterprise, so many opted for PC-based solutions such as Excel add-ons and Access databases. By the mid-2000s, the wait for right-sized BI was over.

Qlik's Disruptive Approach to BI

Founded in Sweden in 1993, Qlik introduced a desktop product (eventually called QlikView) that could extract data from database systems, and then summarize and graphically present the data without requiring pre-aggregations or multi-dimensional cubes. This in itself was revolutionary—without pre-aggregations, how could QlikView complete the heavy computations required for summarized analysis in a reasonable time? It achieved this by loading all of the data into RAM and calculating aggregations on the fly, thereby avoiding the bottleneck of database I/O and the limitations from hard-coding the aggregations. If that wasn't enough, QlikView also presented data in a new, *associative* way. Users unfamiliar with relational data structures could easily discover hierarchies and relationships among data elements, without having any knowledge of the underlying data architecture. This "natural" approach to analytics—more than its in-memory architecture—is what sets Qlik's products far apart from its competitors.

By the mid-2000s, Qlik became a major disrupting force in the business intelligence market. With its rapid-development mantra, along with a new server-based platform, QlikView was uniquely suited to the mid-sized business. With some basic training, IT staff could quickly deploy reporting and analytic solutions to users, without building the over-scaled scaffolding required by other OLAP platforms.

By the late 2000s, more and more large enterprises were taking notice. Largely due to steady improvements in the product platform and a growing sales organization, enterprise adoption of QlikView accelerated. But there were also certain trends in the industry occurring at just the right time to highlight QlikView's appeal:

- An embrace of more agile development practices
- The acceptance that IT, by nature, cannot keep pace with the constant changing needs of the business
- An increase in the demand for user-driven BI
- The prevalence of 64-bit hardware and software

With these trends, the ever-decreasing cost of server hardware and RAM, and a proven stable platform, QlikView was able to show the corporate user that big-company analytics didn't have to be slow, cumbersome, and static. QlikView made it possible for some development to be done out in the business units and departments, instead of IT. This allowed organizations to control the pace of development, to better match the speed at which requirements were changing. The genie was out of the bottle.

Let us clarify some of the technical terms for the non-technical readers.

- *RAM (random-access memory) is a computer component that we commonly call "memory." Performing computations with data that resides in RAM is considerably faster than reading the same data from the hard drive. Qlik pioneered the in memory BI direction, and it remains the leader of in memory BI today.*

- *The term "database I/O" (input-output) refers to the database operations of reading and writing data from and to the database. I/O operations are considered to be the slowest among various computing operations. Therefore database-driven BI systems are comparatively slower than those operating in memory, and they have to build pre-defined OLAP cubes to allow faster processing.*

Data Discovery Is the New Black

In the past, business users had to predict what questions they would ask so that IT could build a report to provide the answers. Lots of resources went in to researching and writing down what the business needed out of the BI system. IT was keen to have the business sign off on exactly what it wanted before the tedious and expensive efforts of development began. Of course, the problem with that approach is that the business was likely communicating requirements that it had in the *past*, not necessarily requirements that it anticipated for the future.

In classic "chicken-or-the-egg" form, IT would ask, "How do you want to see the data in your reports?" and the business would reply, "I don't know; how *can* I see the data in the reports?" Being naturally very risk-averse, IT departments are not in the business of building applications as "suggestions" for the business, just to see what sticks. The risk is too great that the application could be rejected, and the project would be sent back to the drawing board having wasted precious time, resources, and reputations.

But the business has a valid question—"How *can* I see the data in reports?" means "What if my questions are ad hoc?" or "Can the system allow me to follow a path of ad hoc discovery, leading to previously undiscovered insight?" These types of questions require a robust analytical solution. No gigantic binder of month-end reports will serve this need. Static reports from BI systems are, in fact, the *opposite* of what is needed! Instead, analysis must be driven by the user, not the report-writer. This scenario exactly describes the concept of *data discovery*, sometimes referred to as *business discovery*. According to a 2013 report, technology research firm Gartner predicted that "by 2015, the majority of BI vendors will make data discovery their prime BI platform offering, shifting BI emphasis from reporting-centric to analysis-centric." (This report, "Gartner Predicts Business Intelligence and Analytics Will Remain Top Focus for CIOs Through 2017," is available on Gartner's website at http://www.gartner.com/newsroom/id/2637615. More detailed information is available in the report "Predicts 2014: Business Intelligence and Analytics Will Remain CIO's Top Technology Priority" at http://www.gartner.com/document/2629220?ref=QuickSearch&sthkw=schulte%20AND%20BI%20AND%20%22predicts%22.)

Credited for pioneering the data discovery space, Qlik is well positioned to continue as a leader in this new market. With the release of Qlik Sense, Qlik is resetting the bar in offering user-friendly data discovery tools, while providing a well governed and scalable platform.

QlikView 11 Overview

For readers unfamiliar with QlikView or Qlik Sense, this section describes the core elements of the platform, and explains how it differs from traditional BI.

In-Memory Storage Means No Need for Pre-Calculated Cubes

Unlike OLAP systems, QlikView uses RAM as the physical storage medium for data. Since computers can access memory hundreds of times faster than disk, calculations and aggregations can be performed on the fly, with astounding speed. Thus, the limitations of building pre-aggregated cubes are gone! Figure 2.2 shows a data ecosystem with the addition of QlikView. Notice that QlikView can extract from multiple sources and does not require any pre-aggregated cubes.

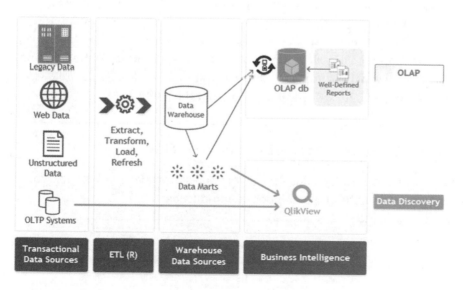

FIGURE 2.2:
QlikView in the data ecosystem

Using QlikView, transactional data can be loaded into RAM and then summarized at runtime, at the user's request. If you're used to the terminology of traditional BI, you can think of QlikView as creating "cubes on-demand," from RAM. Transparent to the user, the aggregations occur seamlessly in the front-end, with each chart essentially creating its own cube. The benefit of loading the granular detail is two-fold: the data can be aggregated up to any level, and the user can drill down to view the details.

For the small or medium-sized organization, QlikView may replace the need for OLAP or other reporting tools. For the enterprise, QlikView is often added as a data discovery/analytics platform that works alongside OLAP systems—particularly if the organization still requires paper-based reporting.

An Interactive User Experience

A user accustomed to the traditional BI report interface knows that you need a game plan going in, before actually seeing any data. Typically, the user must select a specific report and provide the required parameters or filters before the report is run. QlikView completely rejects this approach, and instead presents the user with *all* of the available data, immediately accessible in the interface.

When a user opens a QlikView application, data is visible right away, without specifying any parameters. The user interacts with the interface to step through the data in an exploratory way, to zero in on specific results. Figure 2.3 shows a basic example of QlikView application containing sales data for an apparel company. You'll use this data set, which is available from the book's download site, throughout the book.

Downloading the Electronic Materials for This Book

If you haven't done so yet, please download the electronic materials provided for this book. You can find the detailed instructions at the end of this book's Introduction.

This is a screenshot of a typical QlikView application. Using a tabbed sheet layout, developers place objects on the sheet to allow for searching and selecting data and visualizing measures.

In this app, a few filter objects called list boxes are shown across the top (Year, Quarter, Month) and down the left pane (Channel, Product, Season). Three visualization charts are shown: a pie chart, bar chart, and straight (non-pivot) table. The data in the charts reflect the entire data set, with no filters applied. In QlikView parlance, filters are called *selections*. The current state of the selections can be tracked in the Current Selections box, shown in the upper left.

Using a familiar tabbed sheet layout, this simple QlikView application invites the user to make selections to explore the data and click on the tabs to explore the layout. By default, selections made on one tab are persistent throughout the entire application (this behavior can be changed by the developer, depending on requirements). In Figure 2.4, the app is shown with selections applied for Channel and Season.

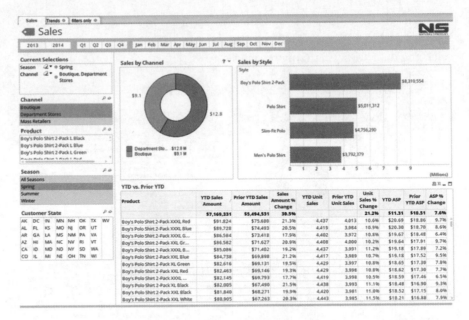

As soon as the user makes selections, the data in the charts dynamically update. No need to press Go, Generate, or Apply—results are rendered immediately. All visual objects in a QlikView app can be interactive in some way. Most obviously, the list boxes allow clicking or searching for attribute values. In addition, the user can click or lasso the slices of a pie chart, or the bars in a bar chart, to make selections within the visualization itself. The table in the bottom-right of Figure 2.4 is also selectable and sortable.

With an attractive and interactive interface, QlikView apps encourage users to ask questions of the data, which may encourage asking questions of each other, which may result in collaboration, which may then lead to true business insight.

Associative Logic Powers Data Discovery

Perhaps the most effective driver of data discovery in QlikView is its patented *associative query logic*. Without going into the details of how it works, let's look at what it *delivers*.

Selected, Associated, and Non-Associated Values

Perhaps the most obvious feature of QlikView's associative logic is the ability to visually see how other pieces of data are associated with your selections. The feature that truly differentiates QlikView is the ability to see the data that is *not* associated.

Figure 2.5 shows list boxes with two explicit selections applied.

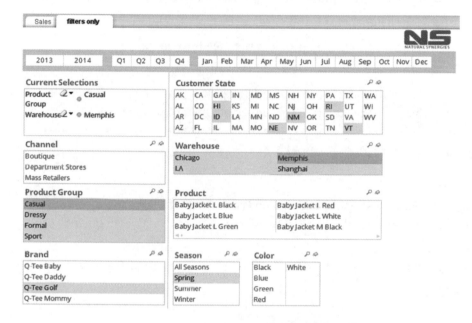

FIGURE 2.5:
Green, white, and gray

Selections are made in the Product Group and Warehouse list boxes for Casual and Memphis, respectively. What can you learn from this simple selection?

Based on QlikView's display defaults:

- Selected values are highlighted in green
- Associated values are highlighted in white
- Excluded values are highlighted in gray

From this, you can infer the following:

- There are no products from the Spring collection in the results

- There are no customers from ID, HI, NE, NM, RI, or VT

- There are no products from the Q-Tee Golf brand in the results

Using only list boxes, QlikView can visually communicate meaningful associations within the data. Seeing which data is associated (and which is not) can confirm a hunch or prompt the user to look under previously un-turned stones. A question of, "Why are there no Q-Tee Golf products shipping out of Memphis?" may lead the user to one of these conclusions:

- The data is wrong and needs to be fixed or cleansed

- There is a business problem that needs to be solved

- There is a valid reason for the results

All of these are valuable outcomes! The power to show you what is related and what is not related is a key feature of Qlik's patented associative logic.

Exercise 2.1: Experience Green, White, and Gray in QlikView 11

1. Open QlikView.

2. To open an existing document, use the menu command File ▶ Open. Navigate to the folder containing the electronic materials for this book, subfolder \Apps, and open the document `Example Sales Analysis.qvw`.

3. From the Sales tab, select three products in the Product list box—Baby Jacket L Black, Blue, and Green, as shown in Figure 2.6.

FIGURE 2.6:
Product selections

3.1. Click on the first product in the list and hold down the left button while dragging down. Let go of the mouse button when you're hovered over the third product in the list. The Product list box should look like the one in Figure 2.6, with the three products highlighted in green.

3.2. Notice the values associated in other fields (in white)—as well as the values *not* associated with your selections (in gray).

4. Explore the data by making other selections and viewing the charts on the Trends tab. Notice that selections are persistent as you navigate tabs.

5. Clear selections by clicking on the Eraser icon in the caption of each list box, or within the Current Selections box.

In addition to the common *green*, *white*, and *gray* selection states, Qlik Sense offers an easier way to handle the lesser-known states of *Alternate* and *Select Excluded*. These states are described in Chapter 16.

Direct and Associative Searches

QlikView's associative logic offers the ability to conduct direct and indirect (associative) searches either within a single field or the entire data set. To demonstrate, let's take a look at the bread-and-butter visualization object in any QlikView application—the list box. List boxes are used to display the values found in a single field in the data model. Values can be selected by directly clicking on them, or by searching. The direct and indirect search capability is illustrated in Figure 2.7.

Let's assume that you want to search for a product in the Product list box. One way to initiate the search is to click on the magnifying glass in the caption of the Product list box and type in a search phrase. In this example, the phrase "jacket" is typed in the search box. The direct search results appear in yellow highlight in the Product list box. Associated results appear when you click on the chevron (>>). Notice that the phrase "jacket" was found in two *other* fields, Style and Style Short Name. You can either click on the exact results in the Product list box or select from the associated results to temporarily limit the products in the Product field.

FIGURE 2.7:

Direct and associative
search results

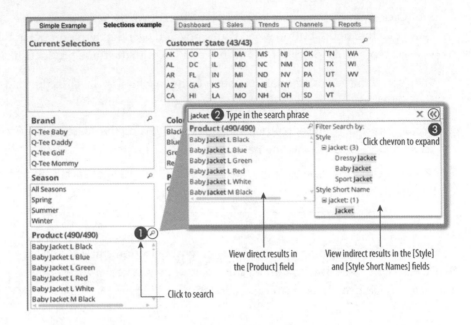

Exercise 2.2 describes the basics of the text search capability in QlikView.

Exercise 2.2: Search and Associative Search in QlikView 11

1. Open QlikView.

2. To open an existing document, use the menu command File ► Open. Navigate to the folder containing the electronic materials for this book, subfolder \Apps, and open the document called `Example Sales Analysis.qvw`.

3. Search for "jacket" in the Product field.

    3.1. Click on the caption (title) of the Product list box and begin typing `jacket` (the string is not case-sensitive). You can also click on the magnifying glass in the caption area of the Product list box

    3.2. Click or Ctrl+click on individual products or press Enter to select all of the products returned in the search. Notice that the contents of the Current Selections box display the filters that are applied.

    3.3. Right-click on the Product list box and select Clear (or click the Eraser icon next to the magnifying glass).

4. Limit the results for "jacket" by using Associative Search.

   4.1. Click on the caption of the Product list box and start typing `jacket`.

   4.2. Click the chevron (>>) in the right corner of the search box to display associated results.

   4.3. Click on Dressy Jacket in the associated results area (see Figure 2.8) and press Enter. Notice that this did not explicitly select Dressy Jacket in the `Style` field, but instead limited the results in the `Product` field to those that also have the `Style` attribute "Dressy Jacket."

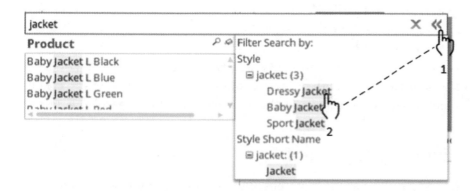

FIGURE 2.8:
Direct and associated search results

5. Based on QlikView's green-white-gray display rules, what can you learn about the Season availability of the Dressy Jacket products? Which states do not have customers with Dressy Jacket sales?

While this exercise described the common text search feature, there are several other search features available, including numeric search, fuzzy search, and an advanced search dialog. For more information on these features, open Help ► Contents from the menu and type `search` on the Index tab.

A Front End with No Queries

Using QlikView's built-in ETL features, data from source systems are modeled, transformed, and loaded into memory. The resulting set of data, in memory, is the source of data for the front-end objects.

Qlik's associative architecture maintains the relationships among all data points in memory, in real time. After each selection that a user makes, the associations in the data model are updated. What does this mean? It means that the front-end objects do no not require SQL-like queries to define the object. In traditional BI systems, a data query must be written for *each* chart to properly fetch data from the cube. In other words, the developer must define, with SQL code, how the data is related each time a chart is created. This makes it almost impossible for non-technical users to design their own applications. In QlikView, the difficult queries are written once, in the ETL layer. The resulting data set is then available to the front end with all of the associations intact. With the data loaded into memory, charts do not require supporting queries — they only need to be configured with a dimension and a measure. With minimal training, non-technical users can create their own dashboard objects without knowing how to write SQL queries.

Right-Sized Analytics

With several deployment options, QlikView offers a right-sized solution for any analytics or data discovery project. The desktop QlikView client allows you to quickly load data and create visualizations, all from your personal computer. Anyone who's ever used Excel to extract data from an external source can easily learn to do the same in QlikView. Analysts can use QlikView to build their own applications to answer ad hoc business questions or create compelling visuals to use in presentations. Try doing that with traditional BI platforms!

On the other end of the scale, QlikView's server platform provides for sharing QlikView applications among teams, or thousands of users within a global organization. With the option of clustering QlikView servers, users can have highly reliable access to applications in a distributed enterprise environment.

Qlik Sense Overview

Introduced in mid-2014, Qlik Sense offers an intuitive development interface and next-generation visualizations to facilitate true self-service business intelligence. Built on the second generation of Qlik's associative data engine, the QIX (Qlik Index) engine delivers powerful data discovery features to a new front-end and ETL interface. This section briefly describes the user interface improvements.

New, Intelligent Visualizations

Built from the ground up with HTML5, Qlik Sense's responsive design offers modern, touch-sensitive visualizations. Whether consuming the app on a laptop, large screen, or mobile device, intelligent visualization objects dynamically adapt themselves to optimize the display based on the available screen size. Figure 2.9 shows the new GUI presentation format of Qlik Sense, using Qlik Sense Desktop.

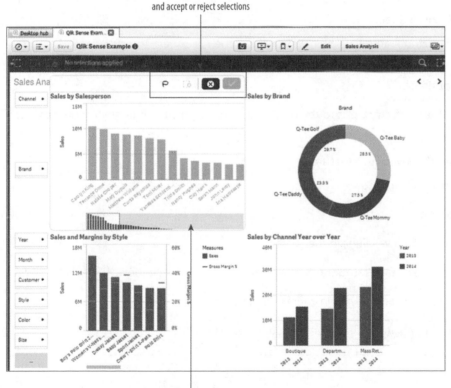

Touch-friendly icons to lasso values and accept or reject selections

Mini chart automatically displays if bar chart is too wide to fit display

FIGURE 2.9:
Smart visualizations automatically adapt to screen size

When a chart has focus (the bar chart in the upper left of Figure 2.9), an icon appears to allow drawing or lassoing to make selections. After lassoing, the other charts dynamically update to reflect the temporary selections, and the user can then choose to cancel or accept the temporary selections.

Exercise 2.3 walks you through opening an app in Qlik Sense, and demonstrates the responsive design of the interface.

Exercise 2.3: Experience the Intelligent Visualizations in Qlik Sense

1. Open Qlik Sense Desktop.

2. Next, open Windows Explorer, navigate to the folder containing the electronic materials for this book, and open the subfolder \Solutions Sense.

3. Drag the file Example Sales Analysis.qvf and drop it onto the window displaying the Qlik Sense hub.

4. Click on the Sales Analysis sheet.

5. Experience the auto-sizing features of the new visualizations.

    5.1. Reduce the size of the display window until you see the mini-chart displayed beneath the bar chart in the upper left.

    5.2. Click and drag the mini-chart lens to the right or use the scroll button on your mouse to scroll through the data.

6. Experience the new touch-sensitive features.

    6.1. Click on any chart visualization.

    6.2. Click the lasso icon.

    6.3. Draw a loop around a few values in the chart.

    6.4. Notice that the other charts temporarily show the results of the selection.

    6.5. Click the red X to cancel or the green checkmark to accept.

    6.6. Your selection appears in the dark gray selections bar at the top.

New Data Stories Add Context to Analytics

Qlik Sense includes a new built-in collaboration feature for telling "data stories." Similar to other presentation tools, users can add text and graphics to slides that add a narrative context to the data. Figure 2.10 shows a slide from a story with that includes a visualization snapshot.

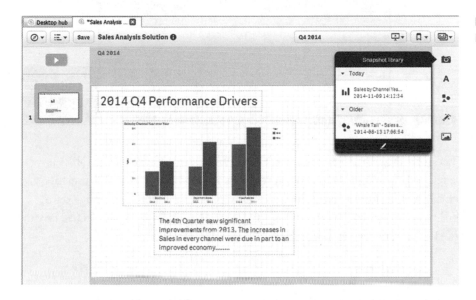

FIGURE 2.10:
Editing a data story

Multiple stories can be created to facilitate different analyses or audiences.

Qlik Sense Desktop is a stand-alone Windows application that is free for personal and business use. An unlimited number of full-featured applications can be shared with other Qlik Sense Desktop users. An enterprise platform is also available, providing access for mobile devices as well as an all-new Qlik Management Console for security and governance.

User-Driven Development Means Self-Serve BI

With Qlik Sense, users of all skill levels can easily create their own applications for data discovery and analysis. Mobile-ready apps are created by using drag-and-drop as well as other easy-to-use features.

Figure 2.11 shows an example of using the drag-and-drop feature to add a dimension to a chart.

The new Data load editor serves the same basic purpose as the QlikView script editor—it is the place to create, edit, and execute the ETL script code. A redesigned layout includes new panes in which to manage data connections as well as the debugging process. Figure 2.12 shows the layout of the Data load editor window.

FIGURE 2.12:
The Data load editor

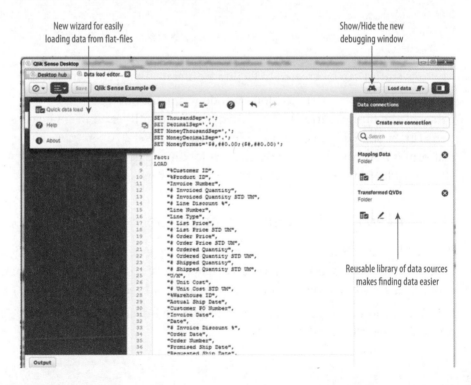

In addition to the full-featured Data load editor, Qlik Sense provides a new wizard for a Quick data load. This new wizard makes loading flat-file data easier than ever before for the non-technical user.

With beautiful visualizations right out of the box, as well as an all-new data load interface, Qlik Sense provides the ability for nearly anyone to quickly create and share beautiful analytic applications.

In Chapters 15 and 16, you'll learn more about how to build applications using Qlik Sense Desktop.

Learning the Core Techniques: Sales Analysis

3

Defining a Business Scenario for Sales Analysis

The metric of sales is one of the most important measurements when evaluating the performance and prospects for success for a business. The growth, profitability, and cash flow of your company rely on the level of sales, and margin on those sales, you can achieve. Understanding the value you receive for the sale—the price someone pays you—is critical to making decisions related to product development, supply chain, working capital investments, and so on. The value you receive affects virtually all aspects of your business.

Many businesses believe that they know the value they are receiving for their products and that that price is essentially their price list. There are, however, decisions made every day that affect the value they actually receive. Those decisions can be in the form of customer programs such as co-op advertising, volume discounts, seasonal discounts, markdowns, and so on. They can also take the form of product promotional discounts, damage allowances, and so on. The effect of each of these decisions can result in different transactions in different parts of your ERP/financial reporting systems. These decisions are drivers of sales and margins in your business. Quantifying and understanding these drivers are part of advanced sales analysis beyond the one line on your financial statement labeled "Sales."

In this chapter, we describe the common characteristics of an advanced sales analysis that can allow your company to better understand the outcomes and the drivers of sales. The data you need for advanced sales analysis can be complicated to identify and access. Business intelligence (BI) tools can accelerate the analytical methods required to access and evaluate that data. The chapters that follow this business case will demonstrate the use of Qlikview business intelligence tools to help you understand more about your business and make better decisions.

"What Do You Mean When You Say Sales?"

This is perhaps the most common question asked at the beginning of every BI project, and the answer is never trivial. When finance people say "sales," they typically mean revenue. Their definition encompasses delivered and invoiced products or services that are ultimately paid for. Operations executives, on the other hand, may be more interested in "shipments." Sales people like to count the number of customer orders written, whether or not the product or service was delivered or charged for.

Depending on the audience, sales numbers may represent any of the above, including or excluding various discounts, returns, liquidations, and more. It is very important to know what you're including in your sales analyses. If you don't have an accurate understanding of what's driving your sales, you run the risk of making incorrect pricing or volume decisions.

We have all heard the saying, "they are so good at sales they could sell ice to an Eskimo." Making a sale is first and foremost a relationship event. After the relationship has been consummated, what is the actual result of the transaction? There are many things to think about when trying to answer this question. The answer to the question will come by analyzing the data associated with the analytical questions posed throughout this chapter.

Many people believe that "sales" analysis is the most understood and straightforward business metric out there. To most, there are only two components to understanding sales—the unit price and how many units shipped. Because of these simplifying assumptions, sales data is too often analyzed only at the aggregate level. This approach can leave many organizations in the dark with respect to significant drivers of their business.

> Sales *commonly represent the amount that a company bills or invoices its customers for goods and/or services. It is known by a number of business labels, including revenue, billings, sales, and so on.*

What Is the Real Value of the Sale?

Consider going to a store to buy a retail item of almost any kind. First, you may have received a coupon. With the coupon in hand, you are feeling good about this form of incentive, which has added to your rationalization to purchase! Then when you get to the store you are bombarded with all kinds of point-of-purchase information about further markdowns, customer loyalty programs, and even "point" systems that can be used against future purchases. The item you set out to purchase may normally have a price tag of $100, but with all the incentives, it costs you only $75. You are now convinced that you just received the deal of the century!

This example raises some basic questions, such as what is the real price of the item you bought and what should it be? A related question is what is the revenue, or sale, to the company that sold you the item?

Do you know the real price of your company's products? Is it the "list" price or list price reduced by terms, discounts, and other programs that you don't have much visibility into?

Another example involves a manufacturer of consumer products that sells to major retail chains in North America. In order to set the stage for this example, it is important to know that retail chains, like most businesses, are constantly challenged with achieving results in terms of sales and margin. To help meet this challenge, retailers have ways to "ask" suppliers for money to increase their margins. These many ways include co-op advertising paid for by the manufacturer, free goods, in some cases as a promotion, and slotting allowances. In addition to the demands placed on suppliers to pay for these programs, suppliers typically have to pay commissions to those who represent their products.

Slotting allowances, for those of you who are not painfully aware of them, are the costs of buying out the competitors' merchandise to make room for your products on store shelves.

The company in question was attempting to understand their sales information and why their margins continued to erode. The company controller was attempting to help so he went to see the sales folks. After a number of well placed questions and intentionally vague answers, the controller believed he finally had an understanding of some of the issues. After verifying with the sales folks that he had heard the facts correctly, he said, "So, we paid sales commissions and we owe the customer advertising money for the privilege of shipping them free product? Is that right?" To which the stunned sales folks replied, "free goods that qualify for sales credit and co-op dollars…yep that's it!" Each individual decision was made for a good cause and may have made sense by itself; however, the sales personnel didn't recognize the cumulative impact of these decisions.

You can see from these examples a number of variables that affect the revenue you receive when you sell a product to someone. These are common sense variables such as:

- Customer allowances with the intent to grow sales over a period of time
- Product promotions to add velocity to new product introductions
- Advertising to grow sales and brand or product awareness
- The payments required by customers to gain shelf space in their outlets
- Payments to reduce price in an attempt to move slow-moving product

The variables in a business to business (B2B) sale may be called something different than the variables in a business to consumer (B2C) sale; however, those variables present the same challenges to understanding the real revenue of the product you are selling.

The revenue you receive should represent the "price" component of your sales. The other component is volume. Regardless of what channel you sell in, it is important to be able to identify the elements that answer the question, "What does the result of a sale tell you about the current state of your business and its future potential?" The analysis starts with some basic questions, which are discussed in the following sections.

What Happened?

Typical sales analysis includes reporting the outcomes of "what happened?" These outcomes are reported in a set of so-called *lagging indicators*, which are measures of results.

Although only part of the story, absolute sales amounts are important to know. You are probably familiar with looking at an absolute amount of sales and comparing it to a history or to some expectation. You might compare the absolute amount of sales to a budget or a sales quota (the two are usually not the same), to the latest estimate, or to the same period from a previous year. Some of the most common time comparisons include:

- Actual year-to-date sales compared to actual prior year-to-date sales
- Actual quarter-to-date sales compared to actual prior year quarter-to-date sales

- Actual month-to-date sales compared to prior year month-to-date sales
- Recent rolling 12-month sales to the previous rolling 12-month sales

Trend analysis is rather important in the effort to understand your business. Trend comparisons can be done at a variety of data levels. In addition to comparisons at an aggregate level, we recommend that an organization have the functionality in their systems to analyze the data at the following levels of detail for both units and dollars:

- Total for the organization
- Customer/channels/geographies
- Product/styles/sizes/color/brand
- New and existing customers
- New and promotional products

Again, this type of analysis is common. However, analyzing lagging indicators won't always help you answers the questions of why it happened and what it means.

Why Did it Happen? What Does It Mean for My Business?

These questions are near and dear to every business leader wanting to know what is happening in the marketplace and what the opportunities are for the future. To answer these analytical questions, you need to go deeper than just looking at measures of *results* (lagging indicators). You need to understand the *drivers* (leading indicators) of your sales.

The Importance of Understanding the Real Drivers of Sales

One company found itself in a situation where raw material costs were skyrocketing (over 25% in one year!). As a result they calculated that they needed to raise their prices by an average of 8% to recover the raw material increases. They even built this expected result into their financial plan. Their customer base was made up primarily of mass retailers who did not want to accept price increases at all. Six months into the year, the company noticed that sales had increased in total by 6%. They believed that price had increased by 8% because they announced the increase at the beginning of the year. They then concluded that volume had decreased 2% since the net total increase was 6%. Based on this level of analysis, the company embarked on a course of action of what to do about losing volume. This in turn led to looking at spending reductions that could ultimately harm their long-term goals.

The real issue was not volume. If the company had been able to look at sales at the detailed level of volume and average selling price (ASP) by customer and product, they would have found some completely different drivers. Volume had actually grown 10% and average price had actually decreased 4%!

There were in fact a number of important drivers that the company could not see:

- Volume was up significantly due to new customers and some new products.

- Some of the invisible price decrease was due to the product mix. The new customers were buying products in categories that were lower priced on average.

- The price increase to existing customers, announced at the beginning of the year, was delayed due to customer timetables to accept the increase.

There was additional critical information that the company could not see. While some new products were contributing to the volume increase, some other new products were not meeting expectations. In the independent channel of distribution of their products, they were losing customers faster than they could add them (as measured by the number of store doors).

Defining Measures of Drivers for Sales Analysis

We recognize that companies may understand their unique drivers of sales. Here are some examples of drivers (leading indicators) of sales that we will use in the QlikView example.

Pricing drivers:

- **Average sales price (ASP)**—Calculated by dividing the sales dollars by units in total. ASP should also be calculated at relevant levels for the business, such as product categories and customer channels. Each channel and category may have its own pricing dynamics that affect ASP.

- **Price mix**—With the calculation of ASP comes the ability to understand the price mix of your products. The mix impact is revealed by calculating the percentage of volume that each category of average price is to the total of all sales. This "weight" is then compared against the same categories of another period to analyze the effect of the change in mix.

Customer drivers:

- **New customer sales**—Calculating the percent of new customers based on ship dates gives you a picture of whether you're meeting organic growth goals or not.

- **New and lost customers**—Measuring the number of new store doors added based on ship to data (your own or that of a distributor) will give you market penetration achievement. Conversely, measuring the number of store doors lost will give you your attrition rate for a given channel. The *net* doors added/lost is a key measurement of the future of a given channel of distribution.

- **Channel mix dynamics**—Like price mix, this measurement will allow you to understand what is happening to your business as the channels that customers use to buy your product change. For example, in many categories the channels where customers buy products have changed from independent local merchants to big box retailers, which are more centrally located. We also see a shift from "brick and mortar" (physical) stores to "virtual" (online) stores. You can calculate channel mix by taking the sales in each channel and dividing it by the total sales across all channels. You can then compare this calculation to other periods to determine trends.

Product drivers:

- **Unit volume**—It is important to be able to analyze unit volume by product categories. These categories are groupings of like products (for example, same sizes, same use, and so on).

- **New products**—Percent of new product sales to total sales will help reveal any issues with acceptance or penetration.

- **The rate of sales**—You can calculate the rate of sales for any product or group of products based on unit movement information. This calculation frequently takes the form of units per week per selling location. The selling location is usually the store where your products are sold. If that information is not available, shipment information out of your warehouse or your distributor's warehouse can be used.

Service-level drivers:

- **Service level**—Defined as percent of orders on time *and* complete. The calculation here is based on actual units shipped versus the original order and the actual ship date versus the original order requirement. If you have three orders and two of them are complete in units and on time while the third order is on time but not complete in units, your service level is 66%. You get zero credit for any orders that are not on time *and* complete.

- **Service level by reason**—Calculating service level is one thing, but being able to understand service level failures requires being able to describe those failures by some relevant reason code. Losing sales because the product was not available is an example that is important to understand at a more detailed level. More detailed levels of understanding for lost sales could reveal that a supplier did not deliver to your business on time, or that your own production issues delayed delivery to your warehouse, or that your inventory system is inaccurate, and so on.

Sales person drivers:

- **Sales per person**—This is a calculation of sales productivity. It is calculated just as it sounds; you divide sales by the number of sales people. The number can be calculated in total for the business as well as for each salesperson for comparison purposes.

- **New accounts closed**—The purpose of this driver is the same as when looking at sales in total. At the individual level, it can be a leading indicator of expected sales growth.

- **Placement of new products**—Like new accounts closed, this metric can be a leading indicator of expected sales growth.

- **Attainment of quota**—This is a measure of actual sales achieved by a salesperson compared to the quota, or goal, set in advance for that person. It should be noted that quota is not always the same as the goal in the published financial plan. This particular driver will not be illustrated in our example analysis in the following chapters.

In order to make this analysis of these and other drivers a reality, you need business intelligence tools.

What Data Is Needed

To lead an organization that can answer the questions about what happened, why it happened, and what it means to the business, you need measures of results *and* measures of drivers of results. QlikView allows you to get at the data to do this. The data elements required to analyze your sales in ways that we have discussed are:

- Invoice information at the line level, including units and amounts
- List price information by product and by customer
- Invoice or line discounts (discounts used to get from list price to invoice) by customer or channel
- Customer master information
- Customer grouping designation (usually by channel or class of trade)
- Product master information
- Product classification (brands, categories, styles, and so on)
- Sales person information and sales hierarchy
- Date dimension, if available, including fiscal calendar data

These data elements can involve data from invoice tables, as well as product and customer master tables. Some information may need to be integrated from spreadsheets.

If your company is managing sales on multiple systems (typically a result of a recent merger or acquisition), you might need to merge data from multiple systems and map the master data from one system to another.

Advanced Sales Analysis Makes the Data Visible and Available

With the information presented in this chapter, when you analyze sales you can determine any or all of the following:

- At the end of the day, am I really getting the value for my product that I should?

- What are the customer, product, or channel dynamics that affect my volume and profitability?

- Do the investments in my customers drive sales?

- What are the trends in customer buying habits that drive sales and that should drive the product development process?

- Are new products selling as well as expected?

- Are new products cannibalizing existing products?

- What should the focal point of the sales incentive program be?

- What is the conversion ratio from leads to prospects to customers (based on CRM data)?

- What is the sales productivity?

Answering these questions will enable you understand why the results are what they are and what it means to your business. That means you can make better decisions about:

- Channel and customer strategies

- Product development

- Pricing implementation with customers

- Investment priorities in the business

The value of improving your ability to make these critical decisions is undeniable. Chapters 4 and 5 of this book demonstrate, in a practical way, how to use QlikView to mine this information from your existing system! Those chapters cover loading data and ways to visualize the data that allows the appropriate associates in your organization to analyze and report information to help answer the questions listed in this chapter.

4

Visualizing Sales Analysis in QlikView

In real life, developing QlikView applications follows an approach that begins with gathering business requirements, then planning the data model, then identifying data sources, and then loading the data into QlikView. The last step is building visualizations.

However, because we believe it's better to learn simple QlikView techniques before proceeding to more advanced ones, this chapter describes the process of building visualizations before you learn data modeling and scripting. We will cover these topics in Chapters 5 and 6.

For this chapter, imagine that you are a business analyst. You need to build a Sales Analysis dashboard, but you don't need to know how to load data into QlikView. We'll assume that you've asked the trusted consultants from Natural Synergies to develop a data model, and you'll use it "as is" for developing the analytic solution.

In the next few sections, you'll build a simple yet effective Sales Analysis application, and in the process of doing so you will learn the following visualization techniques:

- Developing list boxes and multi boxes to allow user selections
- Building a page outline with text objects and line/arrow objects
- Building simple charts
- Comparing current year-to-date with prior year-to-date and applying other conditions to your aggregations
- Building a professional-looking dashboard

Preparing the Environment and Getting Ready

In this section, you open the template document and make some initial preparations. You will learn about the following:

- Opening and saving QlikView documents
- Utilizing user settings to save your work automatically
- Creating and working with sheets
- Defining colors in QlikView

If you haven't installed the book's electronic materials yet, please revisit the Introduction and follow detailed instructions for preparing your work environment for this book's tutorial. You need to download and install QlikView and Qlik Sense, download our electronic materials, and preferably install our font. We described all the necessary preparations at the end of the Introduction.

Opening a Template Document

The first step in developing any QlikView document is opening the QlikView Developer tool from the Windows Start menu. Going forward, we refer to it simply as QlikView, for simplicity.

QlikView opens with a default start page that provides quick access to **Examples, Recent Documents**, and **Favorites**. Other than that, QlikView is a standard Windows application, with the familiar menu, toolbars, and other attributes of Windows applications. QlikView documents can be opened, saved, and managed overall in the same way you manage MS Office documents.

We will highlight now a few specific options within QlikView menus that are important at the beginning. You'll discover more options when they become relevant to your development.

The **View** menu offers a few helpful commands that deal with zooming, sizing the window, and other options. You will use the **View** menu to enable the **Design** toolbar, which is extremely useful for designing visualizations.

The **Settings** menu contains **User Preferences, Document Properties,** and a few other useful commands (some of those commands are only available when a document is opened). For your current purposes, you will use **User Preferences** to define the **Auto Saving** settings, which will help you preserve your work in case of any failures. Feel free to browse other settings on your own. We will just mention that **Document Properties** describe settings for the current document, and they follow the document wherever it needs to go. Conversely, **User Preferences** store settings that describe your individual preferences as a developer and a user of QlikView. Those settings remain local and apply to all the documents that you work with. In the following exercise you set the user preferences for the sales analysis document that you downloaded for this chapter.

Exercise 4.1: Opening the Sales Analysis Document

1. Open QlikView.
2. In QlikView, open an existing document using the menu command File ▶ Open. Navigate to the folder \QlikView Your Business\Apps, and open the document Sales Analysis Template.QVW.
3. Create your own version of the document by using File ▶ Save As... and replacing the word Template with your initials.
4. Navigate to the View ▶ Toolbars menu and enable the Design toolbar. Now you should see a second row of icons added below the Standard toolbar.

5. Navigate to Settings ▶ Document Properties, open the General tab and verify that Sheet Object Style is set to Transparent. In the Presentation tab, verify that Default Theme for New Objects is set to NS_Flat.qvt. If it's set to [None], navigate to the folder \QlikView Your Business\Resources\ Themes\ and select the theme file from there. This might happen if you installed your book materials under a different path.

6. Navigate to Settings ▶ User Preferences, open the Save tab, and check the first three check boxes—Save Before Reload, After Reload, and Every 30 Minutes (see Figure 4.1, points 5-7). If your computer should crash for any reason, you will not lose more than the last 30 minutes of your work. Once you open QlikView again, you will be offered a chance to recover the document from the automatically saved copy.

Figure 4.1 presents some of the basic elements of the QlikView environment—the main menu (1), the main toolbar (2), the **Design** toolbar that you just enabled (3), and the **User Preferences** window, opened on the **Save** tab (4), with the three checkboxes that we recommended you check (5-7).

FIGURE 4.1: QlikView menus, toolbars, and user preferences

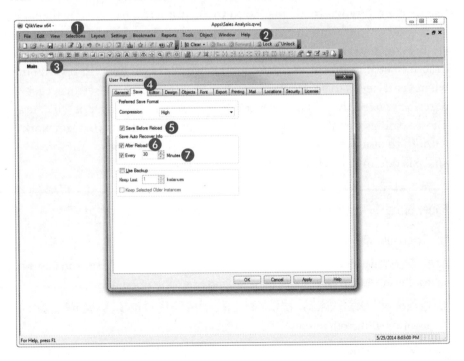

Sheets and Sheet Objects

QlikView visualizations are called *sheet objects*, and they are kept in *sheets*. By default, each new application is created with a single *sheet* called **Main**. Developers can rename the **Main** sheet and add more sheets as needed for the application. There is no technical limitation to the number of sheets, but it's advised to keep the number of sheets manageable, to avoid unnecessary clutter.

Creating a new sheet is simple. You can use **Layout** ▶ **Add Sheet** or simply click on the first icon on the **Design** toolbar. Both options are shown in Figure 4.2.

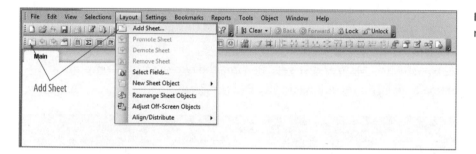

FIGURE 4.2: Adding new sheets

When multiple sheets exist, they can be moved up or down the list using the **Promote Sheet** and **Demote Sheet** options (either in the **Layout** menu or with the toolbar icons).

New sheets are created with a full set of default properties, inherited from the **Document Properties**. The properties can be accessed and modified as needed, by right-clicking on the sheet (any empty space on the screen) and selecting **Properties** from the context menu. For example, the **Title** of the sheet is the first attribute that you need to change, unless you like using default titles Sheet1, Sheet2, and so on. As an alternative, you can access the Sheet Properties by using the toolbar icon **Sheet Properties**, located in the **Design** toolbar, next to the **Promote** and **Demote** buttons.

Fortunately, not too many Sheet Properties need to be adjusted. For the most part, it's recommended to accept the document defaults, in order to keep the look and feel of the sheets consistent. For this reason, we are going to cancel our scheduled 45-minute tour around the detailed list of all Sheet Properties. You will instead discover each setting as it comes up.

About Tabs and Tabrow

Sheet titles appear on the tabs on top of the screen. The area that hosts all the tabs is called the *tabrow*. When you right-click **on the tab of an active sheet, you get a choice of either Tabrow Properties** or **Sheet Properties**. You usually need to access **Sheet Properties**. You may notice that **Sheet Properties** are not available when you right-click on the tab of an inactive sheet, hence you need to activate the sheet before you can access its properties.

Exercise 4.2: Creating and Renaming New Sheets

1. Add a new sheet by clicking on the Add Sheet toolbar icon in the Design toolbar or by selecting the Layout ► Add Sheet menu option.

2. Now you should have two sheets—Main and Sheet1. Rename the two sheets to **Template** and **Sales.** In order to rename a sheet, do the following (see Figure 4.3):

FIGURE 4.3:
Accessing sheet
properties

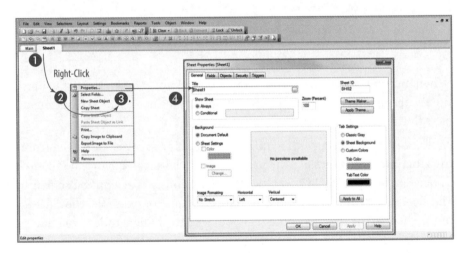

2.1. Click on the sheet label to activate it (1).

2.2. Right-click anywhere on the empty space (2)

2.3. Select Properties from the context menu (3).

2.4. Find the Title field on top of the General tab and replace the default title with the new one (4).

Working with Colors in QlikView

Every pixel on a QlikView sheet is painted in a certain color, and each one of those colors is configurable through dozens of properties—text colors, line colors, background colors, and so on. This section describes the process of defining a color in QlikView, and you will use the same process every time you need to define another color.

All the colors in QlikView are defined in a similar way. Let's examine Figure 4.4, which describes the process of defining a default background color for the document.

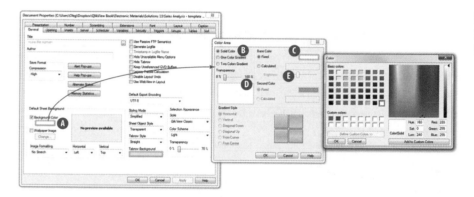

FIGURE 4.4:
Defining a color in QlikView

The **Background Color** setting appears as a button with the same color that it describes (A). Once you click on the button, QlikView opens the **Color Area** window.

Each color area can be defined with a solid color or two types of gradient colors (B). The base color is presented with a similar button (C). Clicking on this button leads to the **Color** window, which allows picking the color itself.

The color can be picked from 48 basic colors or from a continuous palette on the right, or it can be entered manually as a combination of HSL numbers or RGB numbers. Most organizations are very particular about their branding colors, and it's good to identify those and use them in your layouts. To help with this process, QlikView offers a selection of up to 16 custom colors that can be saved for easy retrieval in the future.

As an alternative to selecting the color manually, the color can be also defined as calculated (Figure 4.4, E). You will learn more about calculated colors in Chapters 8 and 12. In the following exercise, you define the default **Background Color** and the **Tab Text Color**.

Exercise 4.3: Defining Colors

1. Open Settings ▶ Document Properties, then click the General tab and locate Background Color.

2. Experiment with the Background Color settings. Set the background to the Two Color Gradient, using your high school's colors as a base.

3. Once you've had enough fun, scratch it off and replace the background color with a solid color of pure white.

4. Open Sheet Properties, select the General tab, and locate the setting for the Tab Text Color. Set the color to RGB(0,100,200). Throughout the book, we will be using this format for red-green-blue color definitions. It corresponds to red: 0, green: 100, and blue: 200. The RGB numbers can be entered in the lower-right corner of the Color dialog.

At this time, the sheets are ready to be filled with sheet objects. Let's begin filling them up, starting from simple objects and continuing on to charts and gauges.

List Boxes, Text Objects, and Other Sheet Objects

Charts carry most of the weight in QlikView, but let's first talk about simpler objects that create the proper environment for charts—list boxes that allow users to make selections; text objects that carry texts, images, and backgrounds; and a few other object types that are commonly used in most QlikView applications.

In this section, you will build the template that will be used throughout this application. The end result is presented in Figure 4.5. In the process, you will learn about the following QlikView objects:

- List boxes and multi boxes
- Table boxes

- Text objects
- Line/arrow objects
- Current selections box and search object

If you are familiar with the basics of QlikView visualizations, feel free to test your knowledge by building the template on your own. You may refer to the exercises in this section to get specific settings such as colors, positions, and sizes of various objects. Then, feel free to skip to the next section, called "Developing Simple Charts in QlikView."

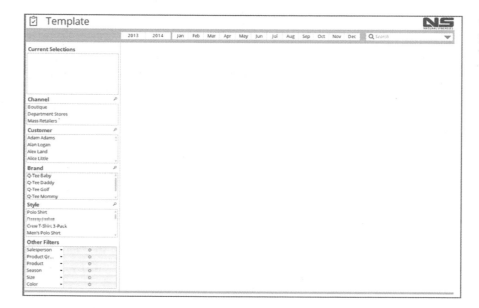

FIGURE 4.5: The end in mind—the finished Template sheet

Introducing List Boxes and Multi Boxes

List boxes and multi boxes serve a similar purpose in QlikView. They allow you to make selections and show selected, associated, and excluded values.

List Box: The Cornerstone of QlikView

List boxes present lists of field values and offer the ability to select certain items of interest. When certain data items are selected, their background turns green. Items that are associated with the selected values appear with the white background, and other items that are not associated are grayed out. The green-white-gray color scheme is one of the fundamentals of QlikView, and it's implemented in list boxes.

Since list boxes are presenting fields (for the most part; you'll see the exceptions later), they are also called "fields" presented on the sheet, and the list of those fields can be managed from the **Sheet Properties** on the **Fields** tab.

A list box can be created in two ways:

- A single list box can be created as any other sheet object can, by right-clicking on the screen and using the **New Sheet Object** option.
- One or more list boxes can be created in the **Fields** tab of the **Sheet Properties**, by selecting the desired fields from the list.

Since list boxes can be created simply by naming the corresponding fields, you can conclude that the only essential setting of a list box is the field that it represents. The rest of the settings are assigned by default (many of those defaults are stored in **Document Properties** and some are permanently defined in the tool).

Exercise 4.4: Creating List Boxes on the Template Sheet

1. Activate the Template sheet and open the Sheet Properties (right-click on the screen and select Properties).

2. Open the Fields tab and select four fields—Brand, Channel, Customer, and Style. Add the fields to the list of Fields Displayed in List Boxes using the Add button. You may add fields one by one, or select a group of fields by using Ctrl+Click.

3. Exit the Properties window. The four list boxes should be created in the upper-left corner of the screen. Grab them by the caption (click and hold the left mouse button) and drag across the screen to position them along the left side of the screen, approximately in the middle between the top and the bottom.

By default, most list boxes show a list of field values in a single column. Sometimes you'll prefer to show values in multiple columns. For example, two-character state abbreviations are best displayed in a multi-column grid. In addition, year and month list boxes are traditionally displayed as single line boxes, positioned across the top of the screen. Those settings are defined in the **List Box Properties**, on the **Presentation** tab (see Figure 4.6).

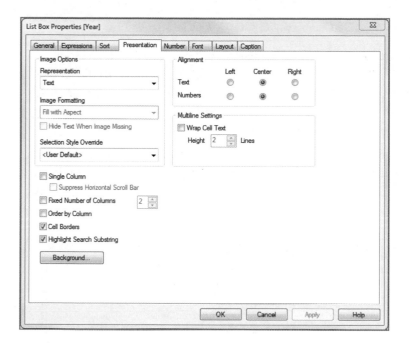

Exercise 4.5: Creating Multi-Column List Boxes for Years and Months

1. Open Sheet Properties, select the Fields tab, and add two more fields—Year and Month.

2. Open the Object Properties (right-click the object and select Properties) for each one of the two new fields and configure the following:

   2.1. Sort tab: Uncheck Sort by State. You want the years and months sorted chronologically, disregarding the selection state.

   2.2. Presentation tab: Uncheck Single Column, uncheck Order by Column, check Cell Borders, and then center-align both Text and Numbers.

   2.3. Layout tab: Set Border Width to 0 pts.

   2.4. Caption tab: Uncheck Show Caption.

You may need to resize the list boxes in order to force all the values into a single line, as displayed on top of the screen in Figure 4.5. Moving objects with no captions is a bit tricky. You need to position your mouse precisely at the top of the object. Alternatively, you can hold the Alt key and drag the object, pointing at its center.

3. Save your work.

Multi Box: A Space-Saving Compromise

List boxes are great for displaying lists of values and unveiling associations between the selected items and other data fields. The only problem is they take a lot of valuable real estate on the screen. You might have more fields than you can fit on the screen, and the **Multi Box** is the solution for allowing more selections in a limited space.

In a multi box, multiple fields share the same object, and each field takes up a single line. The list of fields that should be displayed in a multi box is managed in the **General** tab (see Figure 4.7). Other than that, multi boxes share most of the common settings of the list box.

FIGURE 4.7:

Multi Box Properties, General tab

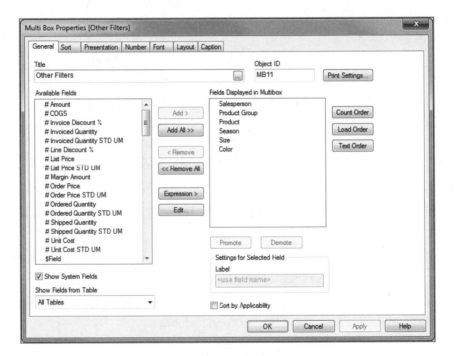

Sizing multi boxes is not as easy as sizing list boxes. Like any other multi-column objects in QlikView, multi boxes can't be stretched by dragging the edges of the object. Each column within a multi-column object needs to be resized individually. Hover over the columns until your pointer turns into a resizing symbol. Drag the columns to the left and to the right as needed.

In the next exercise, you create a multi box with additional fields that couldn't be presented in individual list boxes.

Exercise 4.6: Creating a Multi Box

1. Right-click on the screen and select New Sheet Object ► Multi Box.
2. Type **Other Filters** as the title of the object.
3. Select the following fields to be displayed in the multi box: Salesperson, Product Group, Product, Season, Size, and Color. Press OK to confirm all the changes.
4. Drag the new object across and position it on the left side of the screen, below the list boxes.
5. Save your work.

Table Box and How It Should (Not) Be Used

A **Table Box** is a simple object that shows a table of data values from multiple fields. For example, a table box with customer names, addresses, and phone numbers could serve as a short list of customers to call.

Table boxes are easy to configure. The desired fields are selected from a list of all fields on the General tab of the Table Box Properties (see Figure 4.8). At the same time, the usefulness of the table box is somewhat limited. Unlike the straight table chart, which you learn about later in this chapter, table boxes don't allow you to aggregate the data. Table boxes are also known to perform poorly with large data sets, because they are not as good at memory management as the straight table chart.

Our recommendation is to use table boxes only for "quick and dirty" development needs, like data validation. At the same time, table boxes should not be used in any production applications. Even if you need to show a simple list of data items with no aggregation, a straight table chart with no expressions is a better choice, for its better performance. These comments will be clearer after we introduce the straight table chart later in this chapter. For now, just remember that table boxes are not the best choice for production use.

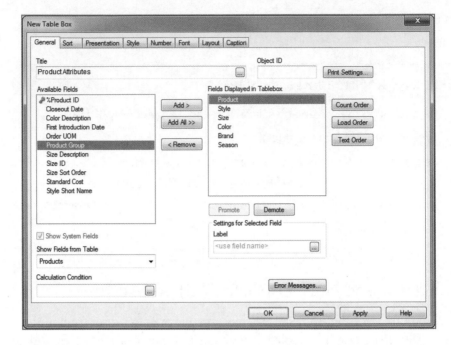

Using Text Objects for Labels, Images, and Backgrounds

Text Objects can play many roles in a QlikView application—they can carry simple texts and calculated texts, show images, or serve as a background for other objects.

In QlikView, all the text in the text object has to carry the same attributes—the same color, font, font size, and so on. In Chapter 16, you will see how it's different in Qlik Sense, but for now you have to stick to the consistent formatting for the text within the text object.

Most of the important properties of the text box are defined in the **General** tab (see Figure 4.9). For most of the text boxes, it's enough to enter the text and/or define the background. Horizontal and vertical alignment options help position the text and align it properly within the boundaries of the object.

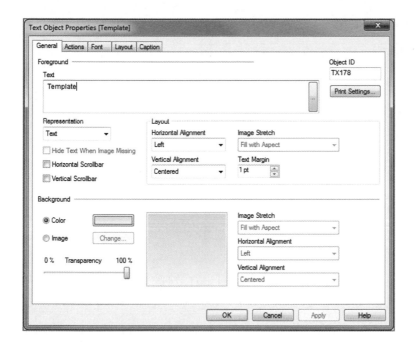

For text objects that carry images, it's important to choose the right **Image Stretch** option. When the object is sized differently than the original image size, this option will determine how the image should fill the size of the object. The most useful option that helps avoiding distortion of the image is **Keep Aspect**.

In the following exercise, you create and configure a number of text objects that are used in the Sales Analysis template.

Exercise 4.7: Creating Text Objects

A number of text objects need to be created for this template. Use Figure 4.5 as the visual guide.

1. Create a new text object that will carry the sheet title (**Right-Click ▶ New Sheet Object**—you know the drill…).

    1.1. Type **Template** in the **Text** box.

    1.2. Make the **Background** fully transparent by sliding the **Transparency** slider fully to 100%.

    1.3. Fonts tab: Use Font Size **22**, color RGB(0, 100, 200).

1.4. Layout tab: Set Border Width to **0** pt. Press OK to confirm.

1.5. Position the object on top of the screen, almost all the way to the left.

2. Create a new text object that will carry the icon next to the sheet title:

   2.1. Leave the Text empty.

   2.2. For the Background, use Image. Click on Change and find an icon image in the subfolder called \Icons. Pick an image of your choice. Under Image Stretch, pick Keep Aspect. Click OK to confirm the changes.

   2.3. Position the image in the upper-left corner, to the left of the sheet heading.

3. Create a new text object that will carry the logo in the upper-right corner of the screen.

   3.1. Leave the Text empty.

   3.2. For the Background, use Image. Click on Change and find the logo image in the subfolder called \Icons. Alternatively, you can use any other logo of your choice. Under Image Stretch, pick Keep Aspect. Click OK to confirm the changes.

   3.3. Position the image in the upper-right corner of the screen.

4. Create a new text object that will provide a gray ribbon outlining the header from the rest of the screen:

   4.1. Leave the Text empty.

   4.2. For the Background, use Color. Open the Color dialog and define the gray color as RGB(200, 200, 200).

   4.3. Layout tab: Border Width=**0**, Layer—Bottom.

   4.4. Caption tab: In order to ensure precise position of the object, enter the exact coordinates and sizes in the bottom-left corner: X-pos=**0**, Y-pos=**41**, Width=**1,240**, and Height=**40**. Click OK to confirm.

   4.5. Ensure that the previous three text boxes fit nicely above the gray ribbon. Position the list boxes for Year and Month on top of the gray ribbon, approximately in the middle.

5. Create another gray text object, which will serve as the bottom outline of the page. It is very similar to the object created in Step 4, with the only difference in size and position. On the Caption tab, set X-pos=**0**, Y-pos=**800**, Width=**1,240**, and Height=**6**.

6. Save your work.

This template is optimized to fit nicely in a screen with the resolution of 1280x1024. If you want to develop a template that works for a different screen size, tweak these suggested sizes and positions accordingly.

Line/Arrow Object

The name says it all—with this object, you can create lines or arrows on the screen, as a simple means of dividing the screen into sections. Figure 4.10 shows the **General** properties of the **Line/Arrow** object.

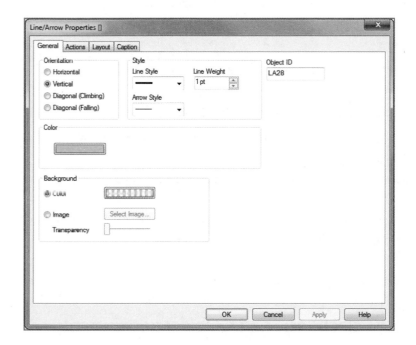

FIGURE 4.10: General properties of the Line/Arrow object

A line can be horizontal, vertical, or diagonal. You can set the **Line Style**, **Line Weight**, and **Arrow Style** properties, along with **Color** and **Background Color** properties, to define the look and feel of the line.

In most cases, the background color should be set to transparent to avoid overlapping with surrounding objects.

Pay attention to the exact size of the Line/Arrow object (**Object Properties**, **Caption** tab). The width of the object defines the length of the line (that is, for a horizontal line). The height appears to be unimportant; however, we recommend leaving it at the default setting (48 pts). Making line objects too narrow leads to visible distortions of the line, so it's best not to make the size too narrow. Keeping the background transparent helps avoid any space issues.

In the following exercise, you add a thin vertical line to separate the list boxes from the charts.

Exercise 4.8: Adding a Vertical Line to the Template Sheet

1. Create a Line/Arrow object. Set the orientation to Vertical. Set the Arrow Style to be a straight line with no arrow heads.

2. Set the color to RGB(200, 200, 200).

3. Set the background color to fully transparent. Open the Color Area window and slide the Transparency slider all the way to 100%.

4. Layout tab: Layer=Custom -5 (this will position the object below Bottom).

5. Caption tab: Enter the position and size manually. X-pos=250, Y-Pos=80, Width=48, and Height=705. Click OK to confirm.

6. Verify that the line connects between the two gray ribbons with no gaps and no overlap. Adjust as needed.

7. Resize and reposition the three list boxes and the multi box to fit nicely on the left of the new line. You set the width and the exact position of these objects later in this chapter.

8. Save your work.

Mind Your Selections: Search Object and Current Selections Box

Search Object and **Current Selections Box** are two commonly used objects. We recommend adding them to every analytical application and finding a prominent place for them in your document templates.

Search Object

The Search object is extremely useful and is easy to configure. It provides users with convenient Google-style search capabilities across multiple fields in the data set. It is especially useful when the user is not sure where to look for certain text. For example, you might have an order number, but you're not sure if it's an original order number, or the customer's order number, or some sort of a reference order number. Typing the number in the search box will reveal a short list of fields that contain the desired text. Then you can make the selection in the field of your choice.

Configuring a search object is extremely simple. In the **General** tab (see Figure 4.11), you can decide if you want to allow search across all fields, provide a list of fields, or manually pick selected fields to be allowed in the search.

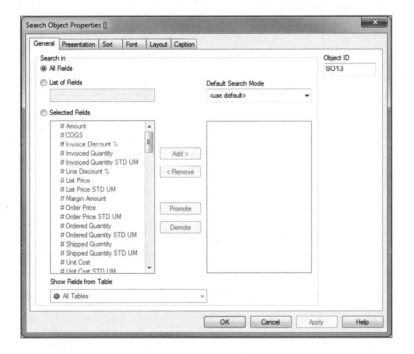

FIGURE 4.11:
General properties of the search object

All Fields is the quickest and the easiest setting, but the search may get confusing in a large application with many fields and cryptic codes that the users may not understand.

The **List of Fields** uses a semicolon as a separator and can include wild-cards. For example, entering `Customer*` will lead to including all the fields that begin with the word Customer, while entering `*Name` will lead to including all the fields that end with the word Name.

Selected Fields may not be as flexible, but in many cases it is the preferred method, due to its simplicity.

In the **Presentation** tab, a few interesting settings are available. For example, you can choose the shape of the search object as rounded or squared.

In the following exercise, you add a **Search Object** to the **Template** sheet.

Exercise 4.9: Adding a Search Object to the Template Sheet

1. Add a new Search Object. Allow the search in All Fields.

2. Presentation tab: Make sure that the appearance is set to Squared.

3. Layout tab: Make sure that the Layer is set to Normal or Top. Click OK to confirm.

4. Position the Search Object on the right side of the gray ribbon. Move Year and Month to the left if needed. Use Figure 4.5 as a visual guide.

5. Save your work.

Current Selections Box

The **Current Selections** box allows users to see the current selections. Since all the numbers on the screen are only relevant in the context of the currently selected items, it's extremely important to know what data is selected. In a way, this is a version of the "You Are Here" sign on a tourist map.

Because of its importance, the Current Selections box should be present in a prominent place in most analytical applications—most commonly in the upper-left corner of the screen, above the list boxes.

The Current Selections box comes predefined with several presentation settings. In most cases, it's good enough to create the object and accept all the defaults.

The Current Selections box consists of three columns with invisible, yet existing, boundaries—**Fields**, **Field Values**, and special **Icons** between them. Each currently selected field will be listed with the corresponding list of values, and the icons allow clearing or modifying the selection. An additional icon, not included by default, allows you to lock and unlock selections from the Current Selections box, which is less common.

Resizing the Current Selections box is a bit tricky. It's easy to make the object wider. In order to make it narrower and to avoid the horizontal scrollbar, you need to resize the three columns individually. The process is similar to resizing individual columns in a multi box. However, in the Current Selections box, you should resize the columns from the top of the column. Dragging the boundaries in the middle of the object doesn't lead to the same effect.

In the next exercise, you add a Current Selections box to the template.

Exercise 4.10: Adding a Current Selections Box

1. Create a new **Current Selections Box**. Accept all the defaults and click **OK**.

2. Position the new object in the upper-left corner, just below the gray ribbon and above the list boxes, as it appears in Figure 4.5. Resize the object as needed to fit nicely in the available space.

3. Save your work.

Organizing and Arranging Objects on the Screen

Now is the time to bring it all together and arrange all the objects neatly on the screen. In this section, you learn everything about moving, arranging, and copying objects in QlikView. You also arrange all the objects on the **Template** screen in a neat organized way, ready for prime time.

Moving and Positioning QlikView Objects On the Screen

The most basic way QlikView objects can be moved around and repositioned on the screen is simply by dragging the Caption bar of the desired object to a new location. Objects without a Caption bar (Year and Month, for example) can be moved by holding the Alt key and dragging the object using its center area.

With a sufficient amount of hand-eye coordination, objects can be dragged to their desired locations and aligned manually. However, professional-looking applications require precise placement of objects.

> ## Get a Mouse!
>
> Our sincere advice to all laptop users—get a mouse! Unless you are a die-hard trackpad expert, you will discover that moving, cloning, and resizing objects involves a lot of dragging and dropping, which can be done much more comfortably with a mouse rather than a trackpad.

When multiple objects are presented on the screen, they should be properly aligned, forming visible horizontal and vertical lines. Our eyes are looking for a sense of order and structure, and if we can't find a well organized set of vertical and horizontal lines, we perceive the presentation as sloppy and unprofessional. For this reason, it's extremely important to keep multiple objects on the screen well aligned and similarly sized. The following techniques can help you get pixel-perfect control over an object's position and alignment:

- Move an object using keyboard shortcuts. Pressing Ctrl and one of the arrow keys will result in moving the object a single pixel at a time. Pressing Ctrl+Shift+Arrow will move the object 10 pixels at a time.

- Specify the exact pixel position and enter itmanually in the **Caption** tab of the **Object Properties** window.

- In order to position a group of objects in a consistent way, use a set of object alignment tools, which you learn about in the next section.

Aligning Multiple Objects

QlikView offers a nice set of alignment tools that become available as soon as multiple objects are activated. Objects can be activated either by clicking the Caption bars of multiple objects one by one while holding the Shift key, or by "lassoing" a group of objects with the mouse. When lassoing, the objects need to be covered by the "lasso" completely, or they won't be included in the multiple selection.

When working on moving, aligning, and resizing objects, it can be helpful to turn on the **Design Grid**. The **Design Grid** is a helper tool that shows a grid on the screen, helping to snap objects into place. When the **Design Grid** is on, active objects are outlined with a visible frame with eight "handles." The frames let you see how much space is allocated for each object. The handles can be used to resize the object vertically, horizontally, and diagonally. In the process of "lassoing" multiple objects, the frames around the active objects help you verify what objects were in fact activated. The **Design Grid** can be turned on from the **View** menu, or using the corresponding icon on the **Design** toolbar, or with the keyboard shortcut Ctrl+G. See Figure 4.12.

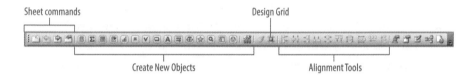

Sheet commands   Design Grid   Create New Objects   Alignment Tools

FIGURE 4.12:
Design toolbar

Once the desired group of objects is activated, you can align them in a variety of ways—align to top, bottom, left, right, or center. You can also distribute the objects in a couple of ways—in a tight line with a few pixels between objects (**Adjust**), or by distributing the available space between the first and the last object in the group (**Space**). Alignment tools can be accessed by right-clicking the group of selected objects and selecting one of the alignment icons from the context menu. The same icons are available in the **Layout** menu and on the **Design** toolbar. See Figure 4.12.

In the following exercise, you will align all the template objects and make the screen look nicely organized.

Exercise 4.11: Aligning the Template Objects

1. Turn on the Design Grid to make it easier to see object sizes.

2. Lasso the three text objects on top of the screen—the icon, the heading, and the logo. Right-click and select Center Vertically.

3. Lasso the gray ribbon and the three objects located on top of it, and also center them vertically. Make sure that the list boxes and the search object have approximately equal height. You may have to resize the search object for that.

4. Select all the list boxes, the multi box, and the Current Selections box (use Shift-Click to select multiple objects). Right-click and select Align Left. Right-click again and select Adjust Top. Resize objects as necessary to fit them nicely together and to ensure that they are aligned on the left and right. Note that when multiple objects are selected, they all get resized together, except for the multi box. If you recall, you have to resize individual columns within the multi box in order to resize the object.

5. Save your work.

Cloning Sheet Objects

There are a number of ways to clone sheet objects in QlikView. Feel free to practice all of them and pick your favorite:

- Right-click on the object and select **Clone** from the context menu. The new object will be created slightly below the source object. You can reposition the new object by dragging it to the new location with your mouse, holding it by the Caption bar.

- You can also clone an object by dragging it while pressing the Ctrl key. The new object will be created in the new location while you release the mouse key.

  This method also allows moving and copying objects between sheets. Dragging the object and dropping it on the other sheet's tab allows moving the object. The same movement combined with pressing the Ctrl key results in cloning the object and placing the new clone in the new tab.

- Right-click on the object, select **Copy to Clipboard ▶ Object**, and then paste it anywhere on the same sheet or on another sheet, or even in another document. Yes, that's right. QlikView objects can be copied between documents. As long as the same data fields exist in both documents, the copied object will function the same way in a different QlikView application.

- Lastly, if you prefer good ol' keyboard shortcuts Ctrl+C and Ctrl+V, those will work too. Just make sure to activate the desired object by clicking on it. Similarly, to copy and paste all the objects on a given sheet, use the combination of shortcuts Ctrl+A (**Select All**), Ctrl+C (**Copy**), and then Ctrl+V (**Paste**) on the new sheet.

Cloning Sheets and Pasting Objects as Links

In the previous section, you finished building the **Template** sheet. Having the main outline of a page saved in a **Template** sheet helps create new sheets with a consistent set of common objects.

For that matter, you need an easy and effective way of cloning the contents of the whole sheet. You can copy all objects and paste them on the new sheet, but there are better ways.

One way is to copy the sheet by right-clicking anywhere on the sheet and selecting **Copy Sheet** from the menu. A new sheet will be created with exact copies of all objects.

The new objects that are created are going to repeat all the settings of the old objects, but they are individual objects, not linked in any way to their originals. That means that if you need to make any changes to your common objects (assign another color or font, or modify a border), these changes will have to be propagated manually in all copies of the same object on different sheets.

QlikView offers a better alternative for objects that need to be repeated many times. Objects can be copied and pasted as links. This way, the objects remain linked and share the same set of properties. Now, a change in one of the objects will affect all the linked objects at once.

Different instances of linked objects may have different positions on different screens. However, it's common to reposition the object in the template and to want all linked objects to follow the same position. For this purpose, linked objects offer a special menu option in the right-click context menu—**Linked Objects ▶ Adjust Position of Linked Objects**. This way, all linked objects can be positioned identically.

The process of creating linked objects is somewhat similar to the regular process of copy and paste. The only difference is that this kind of paste cannot be performed with the **Paste** command or with Ctrl+V. Instead, you right-click on the desired sheet and select **Paste Sheet Object as Link**. Alternatively, you can drag and drop objects while holding Ctrl+Shift to create linked objects.

For the purpose of cloning template objects, using the **Copy** and **Paste Objects as Link** options is preferable to the simple **Copy Sheet**, for easier maintenance.

Notice that once the linked objects are created at least once, **Copy Sheet** will produce the desired result as well. Since all the common objects are already identified as linked objects, the new sheet will contain new instances of the same linked objects.

In the following exercise, you create linked objects for all template objects and then clone the **Template** sheet to create two more sheets.

Exercise 4.12: Cloning Common Objects as Linked Objects

1. Activate all objects on the Template sheet (Ctrl+A) and copy them (Ctrl+C).

2. Open the sheet called Sales. Right-click it and select Paste Sheet Object as Link.

3. IMPORTANT! Sheet title and sheet icon need to be different on every sheet. For this reason, these two objects on top of the sheet need to remain unlinked. Right-click the text object with the sheet title Template and select Link Object ► Unlink This Object. Repeat for the text object that carries the icon in the upper-left corner.

4. Use Copy Sheet to clone the Sales sheet and create two more sheets named **Trends** and **Reports**.

Voila! The application is now ready for the main analytical part—adding charts.

Developing Simple Charts in QlikView

Charts are definitely the heart of QlikView visualizations. Charts carry most of the analytical value in any QlikView dashboard. The other sheet objects serve as accessories and accents, which merely support the main message communicated in charts. Needless to say, mastering the craft of developing insightful charts is a huge part of becoming a QlikView professional.

QlikView 11 supports 13 types of charts—10 types of graphs, 2 textual objects, and a variety of gauges. We will cover all the available chart types throughout this book.

In this section, you learn the basics of QlikView charts and create the following chart types:

- Bar charts
- Line charts

- Pie charts
- Straight tables and Pivot tables

Main Components of QlikView Charts

QlikView charts can be divided into three logical groups:

- Graphical charts, such as bar charts, line charts, and several other graphical chart types.
- Non-graphical charts, such as straight tables and pivot tables (you will discover that these can also include some graphical elements).
- Gauges, such as speedometers and dials, that are used to represent single KPIs in a graphical form.

The various charts may look different from each other, yet they share a set of important common characteristics. For this reason, all of them are called "charts" and are configured in a similar way. The next sections describe the two main characteristics shared by all charts—expressions and dimensions.

Chart Expressions

Charts communicate aggregated information, presented in a variety of forms. The main component of a chart that defines *what* the measure is and *how* it should be calculated is called an *expression*. Simple charts typically visualize a single expression, while more complex charts may have multiple expressions.

Since charts always present aggregated data, a chart expression should always contain one or more aggregation functions. The most commonly used aggregation functions are `sum()`, `count()`, `avg()`, `min()`, and `max()` (many other aggregation functions can be found in QlikView's Help section). All of these functions accept at least one parameter—an expression that will get calculated at each detailed row and then aggregated up. For example, the following expression:

```
sum([# Sales Amount])
```

will simply summarize the values of the field [# Sales Amount] for all available rows of data. This expression:

```
sum([# Sales Amount] - [# COGS])
```

instructs QlikView to subtract the two fields at the detailed level and then summarize the result. Let's compare this expression to the following expressions:

```
sum([# Sales Amount]) - sum([# COGS])
```

This time, the two fields are aggregated separately, and then one summarized result is subtracted from the other. The end result of the two expressions is virtually identical (there might be subtle differences that have to do with missing values, but you can ignore them at the moment).

However, the following two expressions will produce completely different results, despite the similarities:

```
(sum([# Sales Amount]) - sum([# COGS])) / sum([# Sales Amount])
```

versus

```
sum(([# Sales Amount] - [# COGS])/[# Sales Amount])
```

The first expression calculates the average margin percent, and it's accurate—the summarized Cost of Goods Sold (COGS) is subtracted from the summarized Sales Amount, and the result is divided by the summarized Sales Amount. Conversely, the second expression, while valid syntax-wise, is logically incorrect. The margin percent calculation is enclosed in a single aggregation function, therefore it is performed at every detail line, and then the resulting percentages are summarized. Even if you replaced sum() by avg(), the result would be different from the formula above, and most likely be different from the expected result.

To summarize this brief introduction to chart expressions, let's emphasize the two points that you've just seen:

- Chart expressions should always be defined with an aggregation function.

- When multiple fields are involved in a calculation, it's important to determine the order of operations—which calculations need to happen at a detailed level and which calculations need to apply to the aggregated results.

Chart Dimensions

If charts always show aggregated data and chart expressions define what aggregation functions should be used, then *dimensions* describe the *level of aggregation* for the chart.

The task of picking the right fields as chart dimensions is one of the first challenges awaiting new developers. The solution can typically be derived from the verbal definition of the chart.

For example, if the requirement was to produce a bar chart of "Sales by Customer," the first question is, "Do we use the field Sales as a dimension, or the field Customer as a dimension?" In simple cases like this, it's quite easy to make the right choice. Expressions define the "what" that needs to be presented, and dimensions describe "by what fields" or "at what level." So, in this simple case, Sales is the definition of the expression and "by Customer" provides the definition of the dimension. Table 4.1 provides a few other examples.

TABLE 4.1: Deriving the Choice of Dimensions from the Requirements

CHART DEFINITION	EXPRESSIONS	DIMENSIONS
Annual Sales and Profits by Brand	Sales and Profits	Brand, Year
Monthly Sales Trends	Sales	Month or Year-Month
Top 10 Salespeople based on YTD Sales	YTD Sales	Salesperson (Additional condition—top 10 entries)

Dimensions are usually described by fields. Many times, just replacing the dimension of the chart allows you to create a variety of different charts based on the same origin.

Besides dimensions and expressions, charts have a multitude of various attributes that can define and enhance the look and feel of the chart. We will describe the most useful attributes in this chapter, and then you'll learn about more advanced chart attributes in Chapters 8 and 12.

Using Bar Charts to Compare Outcomes Among Brands, Channels, and Salespeople

QlikView has this wonderful quality—many times it's easier to make something happen than to describe how it's done. Hence, the easiest way to present a bar chart is to create one.

Creating a Basic Bar Chart

All QlikView sheet objects, including charts, are created the same way. You begin with right-clicking on the empty space and selecting **New Sheet Object** from the context menu. Then, to create a chart, you select **Chart** from the list of 16 available object types.

Creating Sheet Objects

Right-clicking the empty space is not the only way to create a sheet object. Alternatively, you can select the menu option **Layout ▶ New Sheet Object**, or click the appropriate icon in the **Design** toolbar. Notice the 15 "object" icons following the four sheet-related icons in the **Design** toolbar.

We prefer the "right-clicking" method for one subtle advantage. When you use this method, the new object will be created at the same exact location where you right-clicked on the screen. With all other methods, the new object will be placed in the upper-left corner, where it might overlap with other existing objects.

After you select **Charts** from the context menu, QlikView opens the **Chart Properties** window. For new charts, it acts like a wizard, walking you step by step from one tab to another. At this stage, we will walk through the most essential settings, leaving the rest for later review.

The first tab is **General** (see Figure 4.13). It describes the most basic, general information about the object—its **Title**, **Chart Type**, and a few other settings that are less important at the moment. For new charts, you usually define the chart type (bar chart is always selected as a default) and move on.

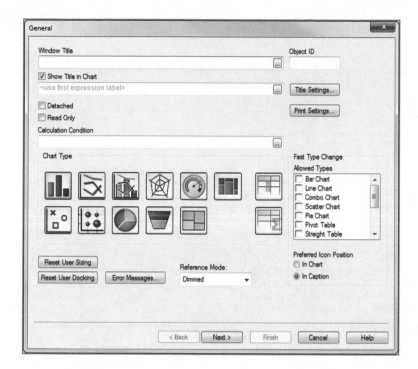

The next tab is **Dimensions**. Here you can define the dimensions for the chart and add a few attributes that have to do with the look and feel of the dimensions. On the screen, you can see the list of all the existing fields on the left and a short list of those fields that are used as dimensions in this chart on the right. You can add or remove dimensions with the **Add** and **Remove** buttons located in the middle. When multiple dimensions are selected, they can be rearranged using the **Promote** and **Demote** buttons. A few settings underneath the list of dimensions allow additional formatting, and you will explore them soon.

For a new bar chart, it's enough to select the desired field(s) and to continue to the next tab. See Figure 4.14.

The next tab should be the **Expressions** tab, but for new charts QlikView initiates the **Expression Editor** to create a new expression (see Figure 4.15). **Expression Editor** is an important tool, and it deserves a separate discussion. For the moment, however, let's stay focused on the job of creating the first bar chart. You type the chart expression here and click **OK** to exit the **Expression Editor**. You will return to the **Expressions** tab, where you can assign a label for the new expression and set many other attributes related to expressions (we will ignore these at the moment).

FIGURE 4.14:
Chart Properties,
Dimensions tab

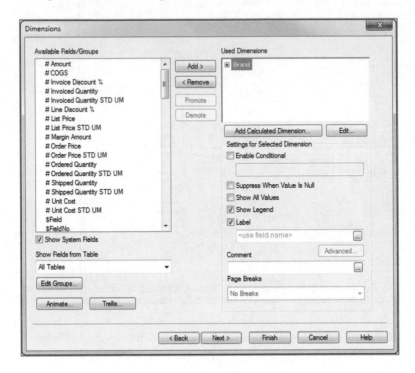

FIGURE 4.14:
Chart Properties,
Dimensions tab

FIGURE 4.15:
Chart Properties,
Expressions editor

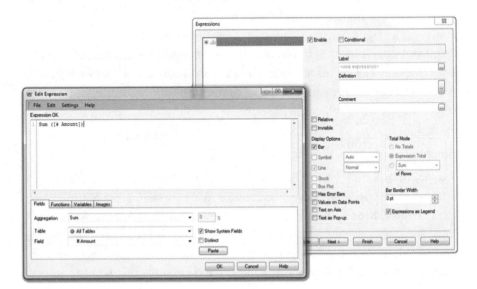

There are nine more tabs of settings that you can access by pressing the **Next** button. Only a few of them are actually relevant for a particular task, so most of the time developers finish the wizard at this point, examine the result, and then re-open the properties to make specific pointed enhancements. Figure 4.16 shows the chart that was created with a few basic settings that we've discussed.

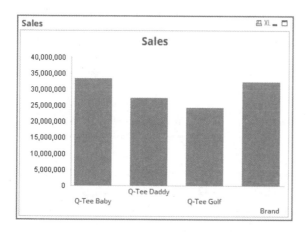

FIGURE 4.16:
Basic bar chart

In the following exercise, you create a basic bar chart, following the process that we just described.

Exercise 4.13: Creating a Basic Bar Chart

In this exercise, you will develop a basic chart showing `Total Sales by Brand`. As you can derive from the name of the chart, `Brand` will be used as a dimension, and `Sales` calculation will be used as an expression. Use the following steps to create the chart:

1. Ensure that you are using the main document called Sales Analysis and activate the Sales sheet.

2. Right-click on an empty space on the screen and select New Sheet Object ▶ Chart from the context menu.

3. On the General tab, confirm Bar Chart as the default chart type and click Next.

4. On the Dimensions tab, locate the Brand field in the list of fields (click in the list and type **B** to get closer). You can double-click the desired field (Brand) or highlight it and click on the Add button. Click Next to proceed.

5. In the Expression Editor, type the following formula, using the auto-complete function (Intel-liSense). Follow these steps:

   5.1. Type `sum()` and step back into the parentheses.

   5.2. Now, type the hash sign `#`.

   5.3. You will see the list of all measures, with the Amount being the first on the list (as you will see in Chapter 6, we took specific steps to simplify the job).

   5.4. Press Enter to confirm the IntelliSense suggestion. Notice that the field name is added with the square brackets, as needed.

   Examine the result. Your expression should look like this:

   ```
   Sum ([# Amount])
   ```

   5.5. Click OK to close the Expression Editor.

6. In the Expressions tab, label the new expression as `Sales` and click on Finish to exit the wizard. Your chart should look similar to the chart displayed in Figure 4.17.

Voila! You created your first chart with just a few basic settings. It's certainly not perfect, but it isn't too bad either. In the next section, you will take a closer look at the various chart properties and learn how to enhance the look and feel of your charts.

Enhancing Bar Chart Look and Feel with Additional Attributes

First of all, let's examine the new chart (see Figure 4.17). It shows vertical bars in the default color, presenting sales by brand. Brands are listed across the x-axis (A). The y-axis contains the numeric scale for the sales amounts (B).

Above the chart itself, there is the caption bar that contains the chart title and some default icons (C), as well as another "Title in Chart" (D). Currently, both titles show **Sales** as the default.

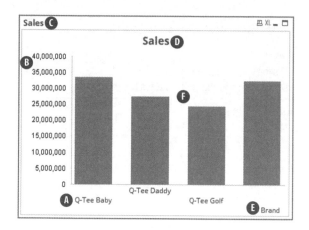

FIGURE 4.17:
Anatomy of the
basic bar chart

The chart can use some improvements, of course. You can easily identify all the flaws of the presentation. We have listed some of them in Table 4.2, in the first column. In the second column, we listed the tabs of the **Chart Properties** dialog that are used for those settings.

TABLE 4.2: Enhancing the Look and Feel of the Basic Bar Chart

ISSUE OR ENHANCEMENT	PROPERTIES TABS AND MAIN FEATURES
You don't need to repeat the default titles (C and D), and you'd rather have a more descriptive title; for example, **Sales by Brand**.	**General Tab:** - Chart Type - Title - Title in Chart - Fast Change
If you stated **Sales by Brand** in the title, you may not want to show the Dimension name **Brand** at the bottom of the chart (E), to reduce unnecessary clutter.	**Dimensions:** - Choice of Dimensions - Dimension Labels - Hiding Labels or Legend
You may want to add values to data points, to be explicitly displayed at all times, without the need in hovering over each value.	**Expressions:** - Definitions of Expressions and their Labels - Representation Options - Show Values on Data points or on Axis
The chart would look better if it were sorted by the descending amount of sales (F).	**Sort:** - Determines sorting rules - Multiple rules are validated from top to bottom

ISSUE OR ENHANCEMENT	PROPERTIES TABS AND MAIN FEATURES
The x-axis labels (A) are not easily associated with the bars and the last label doesn't fit.	**Axes:** - Dimension labels direction - Dimension and Expression Axes look and feel
The chart would look better with visible axis lines and grid lines (A and B).	**Axes:** - Show/hide Axis lines - Enable grid
When you hover over the bars, you can see the actual amounts, but the numbers are not formatted.	**Number:** - Number formatting
The amounts on the y-axis are too long; you could save space if you presented the chart in thousands or in millions.	**Number:** - Special symbols for single units, thousands, millions and billions
You may want to change the default color to match your branding.	**Colors:** - Chart colors - Background color
You may need to disable the Caption bar (C) or change some of the attributes.	**Caption:** - Show/Hide Caption - Colors and fonts for active and inactive captions - Special Icons - Enable Minimize/Maximize, including Auto Minimize

These may not be all of the improvements that you'd like to make to the chart, but it will do the job for now. If you follow the suggested roadmap and modify all the settings accordingly, you should see an improved version of the chart that looks something like Figure 4.18.

FIGURE 4.18:
An enhanced bar chart

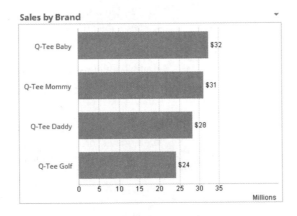

Notice that the horizontal orientation shows the dimension labels in the most natural way, and it also helps to fit the values next to the bars. The Y-axis (which is now horizontal, with the new chart orientation) scales automatically to the appropriate unit of measure—thousands, millions, or billions.

Let's practice the corresponding enhancements, using the roadmap presented in Table 4.2.

Exercise 4.14: Enhancing the Look and Feel of a Bar Chart

Use Table 4.2 as a roadmap and perform the following enhancements to the chart. Examine the effect of each change by accepting the changes with the OK button and re-opening the Properties window again (you can also keep the chart visible and click Apply to see the effect of your changes without exiting the Properties):

1. Open Chart Properties from the General tab. Set Windows Title to **Sales by Brand**. Uncheck Show Title in Chart.

2. Open the Number tab. Format the expression as a currency field (Money) and manually delete the two decimal positions and the decimal point in the Format Pattern. Enter the special symbols at the bottom—your local currency symbol as a Symbol for the single units, **Thousands** for the Thousand Symbol, **Millions** for the Million Symbol, and **Billions** for the Billion Symbol.

3. Open the Axes tab. Experiment with the following settings (see Figure 4.19):

    3.1. Set the axis line width to **1** pixel for the expression (1) and dimension (2) axes. Check Show Grid for the Expression Axes (experiment with the Dimension Axis grid as well).

    3.2. Examine the difference between the horizontal, diagonal, and vertical directions of the dimension labels (4).

    3.3. Experiment with various Grid Styles (5), as well as grid and axes colors and fonts.

4. Open the Sort tab and select the sorting option by Y-Value, Descending.

5. Open the Style tab. Experiment with various chart styles and compare the look of the Vertical and Horizontal orientations. At the end, keep the Horizontal orientation for the chart.

6. Open the Expressions tab. Check the Values on Data Points checkbox.

7. Open the Caption tab (you may need to scroll to the right in the Properties tabrow using the little arrow buttons). Experiment with the following settings:

    7.1. Examine the color settings for inactive and active captions.

    Notice the pixel-precise position and size settings of the object, located at the bottom.

FIGURE 4.19: Chart Properties, Axes tab

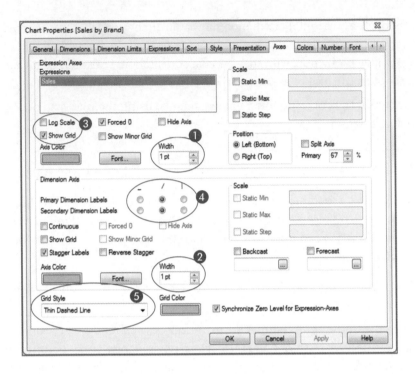

7.2. In the list of Special Icons, disable all the default icons and enable the icon menu.

7.3. Uncheck the Allow Minimize and Allow Maximize checkboxes. Close the Properties window and examine the effects of the recent changes.

7.4. Open Properties again on the Caption tab and type **Hello World!** in the Help Text expression window in the bottom-right corner. Examine the effect of the added Help text.

8. Lastly, open the Dimensions tab and clear the Label checkbox, to eliminate the brand label. You may have to scroll to the left using the little arrow buttons (since version 11, there are more tabs in the Chart Properties window, and they don't fit in the allowed space anymore).

Verify that your chart looks similar to the chart shown in Figure 4.18, earlier in the chapter.

Creating Additional Charts

Well, this was fun! You must admit that creating a decent quality bar chart wasn't that hard. And yet, you probably won't like it if we asked you to repeat the same process three more times, starting from scratch. This reminds us of an old programmer's joke: Programmers really write only one program in their lives. The rest is just copying and pasting.

Similarly, QlikView charts don't have to be created from scratch every time. Once you create a chart of sales by brand, you can easily clone the chart and create similar charts for channels, salespersons, and warehouses.

We've described the process of cloning objects in QlikView earlier in this chapter. Feel free to go back a few pages and get a refresher if you need it.

In the following exercise, you will create three more bar charts by cloning and modifying the existing chart.

Exercise 4.15: Copying, Moving, and Aligning Objects

In this exercise, you will master the techniques of cloning, moving, and aligning objects. All the charts on the **Sales** sheet will show sales amounts compared by different data entities—Brands, Channels, Salespersons, and Warehouses. The charts will be almost identical, except for the choice of the chart dimension and the window title that includes the name of the dimension.

1. Create three copies of the existing bar chart. Experiment with different methods of cloning objects.

2. Reposition the new charts manually, by dragging the charts to their new locations. Position the four charts as four quadrants—two charts on top and the other two charts on the bottom.

3. Open **Properties** of the three new charts one by one and replace the Brand dimension with Channel, Salesperson, and Warehouse, accordingly. Modify the **Window Title** for each chart accordingly (from the **General** tab).

4. For the charts by channel and warehouse, compare the **Horizontal** and **Vertical** orientations of the charts (from the **Style** tab). Pick the preferred orientation.

5. Notice that the chart by salesperson looks too cluttered with too many entries. The chart would look much better with fewer bars displayed at a time. Open **Chart Properties**, **Presentation** tab and locate the **Chart Scrolling** section on the right. Check the **Enable X-Axis Toolbar** checkbox and accept **10** as the default number of Items.

6. Align the charts to the left and to the top accordingly, by activating two charts at a time and then aligning them and adjusting. You will end up selecting, aligning, and adjusting at least three pairs of charts. Notice how alignment tools always pick the first object in the direction of the alignment.

7. **Save** your work.

After all the changes, your sheet should look similar to the one in Figure 4.20.

FIGURE 4.20:
Four bar charts,
formatted and aligned

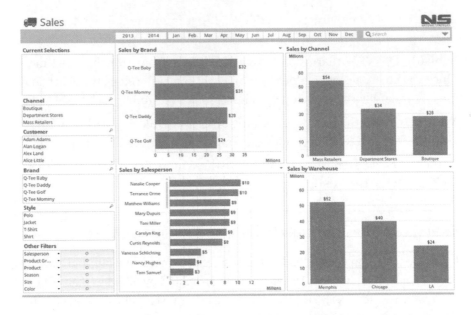

Using Line Charts to Visualize Trends over Time

Trends, or timeline charts, can be presented in bar charts, but it's more common to visualize time trends using lines, especially at detailed levels such as monthly, weekly, or daily.

Line charts are very similar to bar charts in terms of their development and configuration. If you already have a sales bar chart, you can clone it and change the chart type to line chart, to get the job done faster.

Creating the Line Chart by Changing the Chart Type

To get started, you will clone an existing bar chart and change the dimension to one of the calendar fields, such as a Year. Annual bar charts are used quite commonly for visualizing annual trends.

Then, you can simply change the chart type on the **General** tab to a line chart (see Figure 4.21, point A).

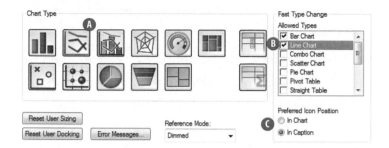

Fast Type Change

Many times, several chart types can be equally helpful for visualizing the same trend. You can allow your users to pick the desired chart type using the technique called **Fast Type Change**. The setting is located on the **General** tab within the chart properties, to the right from the **Chart Type** icons (see Figure 4.21, point B).

When you select a number of available types, QlikView will create another special icon, called **Fast Change**, and the users can pick one of the available chart types by clicking on the icon.

By default, the icon is placed on the Caption bar, but it can also be placed in the chart (C). This is helpful for charts that don't have captions.

Don't Lock Yourself Out with Fast Type Change!

When selecting the available chart types, don't forget to select the "main" chart type as well, or else the user won't be able to return to it.

When using straight tables and pivot tables, avoid placing the Fast Type Change icon in the chart, as those two textual charts don't have the ability to place the icon in the body of the chart. Once the user selects a textual chart with the icon located **in chart**, there is no way to get back to the original chart type.

Let's practice cloning a bar chart and transforming it into a line chart.

Exercise 4.16: Transforming a Bar Chart into a Line Chart

1. Open the application on the **Sales** tab. Clone the chart **Sales by Channel** into the **Trends** sheet.

2. Replace the dimension Channel with Year (from the **Dimensions** tab) and switch the chart type from a bar chart to a line chart (from the **General tab**). Click **OK** to examine the result.

3. Notice that the chart is not sorted by Year. Remember, you sorted the bar charts by y-value in descending order. Well, timeline charts can't be sorted by y-value. You should always sort timeline charts by the date/time field that you use as your dimensions. Open **Chart Properties** (from the **Sort tab**) and disable sorting by y-value.

4. Enable **Fast Change** between **Bar Chart** and **Line Chart** (from the **General** tab). Experiment with the two possible views. Admittedly, when only two values are available, a bar chart might be a better visualization than a line chart.

5. Change the chart title to **Annual Sales** (from the **General** tab).

6. **Save** your work.

What Calendar Fields Do You Use as Dimensions?

This question might sound trivial, yet the answer might not always be obvious. If you open the **Chart Properties** on the **Dimensions** tab and select the MasterCalendar table in the **Show Fields from** the **Table** drop-down list, you will see a short list of all the calendar fields that can be used as dimensions. See Figure 4.22.

Notice that months, quarters, and weeks are represented by a pair of fields—Month and MonthYear, Quarter and QuarterYear, Week and WeekYear. If the goal was to produce a monthly chart, what field should you use, and what's the difference?

If you tried using Month as a dimension, the chart would show sales, aggregated to the month name—so, under January, the chart would show all the sales that happened in January of any year. That's not very insightful, is it? It can become insightful if Year is also used as a dimension—this way, January sales between multiple years can be compared.

The Month, Quarter, and Week fields can be used when only one year of data can be available, or when Year is also used as a dimension in the chart. Conversely, the MonthYear, QuarterYear, and WeekYear fields should be used for charts that show trends that cross multiple years.

In the following exercise, you will create two monthly line charts, using MonthYear as a single dimension and a combination of Month and Year as two different dimensions.

Exercise 4.17: Creating Two Monthly Line Charts

1. Open the Trends sheet and create a new chart. In the General tab of the Chart Properties, name the chart **Monthly Sales**. Disable the Title in Chart. Select Line Chart as the chart type and allow Fast Change between Line Chart and Bar Chart.

2. In the Dimensions tab, select MonthYear as the dimension and disable the label.

3. Type the same expression for Sales—type **sum(#** and accept the field [# Amount] from the IntelliSense list. Close the parenthesis for the sum().

4. Press Next until you arrive at the Number tab and format the number as Money with no decimal digits. Enter the same four symbols for single units, **Thousands**, **Millions**, and **Billions**. Press Finish to exit the wizard. Examine the result (refer to Figure 4.22).

The chart looks rather busy, with 24 month labels jammed up at the bottom. In addition, it would look better with axis lines and a grid.

5. Open the Axis tab (see Figure 4.23) and experiment with diagonal and vertical placement of the labels (A). Then, check the Continuous box (B) and select diagonal labels (A). Also, increase the width to **1** for the Expression Axes (C) and the Dimension Axis (D). Also, enable Show Grid for the Expression Axis (E).

FIGURE 4.23:

Axis settings for continuous axis

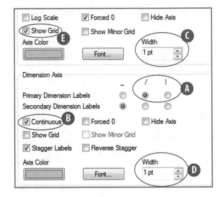

6. In addition, return to the Number tab and format the Continuous X-Axis as a Date, with the **MMM-YY** format pattern. Examine the result.

7. Open the Expressions tab. Notice that there is an additional option, Symbol, in the Display Options section. Symbols help to emphasize the data points and make it easier to hover over them. Experiment with the different shapes of symbols available from the drop-down list and the different line types.

8. In the Presentation tab, there are a few new settings for line charts. You can adjust the line width and the symbol size to match the presentation needs. Set the Line Width to **3** and the Symbol Size to **4** and examine the result.

9. Now, clone the chart. Name the new chart **Monthly Sales Year over Year**. Replace the dimension MonthYear with two dimensions—Month and Year, in this order. Uncheck Continuous in the Axis tab and examine the result.

10. Save your work.

The chart contains two lines now, with a legend on the side. Sales for each year form a separate line. Compare the analytical value of the two charts. The first chart shows a multi-year monthly trend, allowing the user to follow a continuous trend. The second chart allows the user to compare monthly results between the two years. This chart is better for spotting seasonal trends and comparing the effect of calendar events in one year versus the other.

Your two charts should look similar to the charts presented in Figure 4.24.

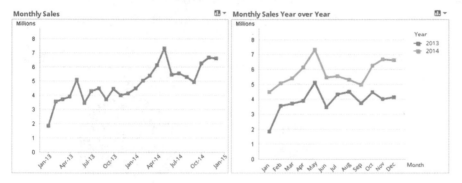

FIGURE 4.24:
Two line charts side by side

Using Pie Charts to Visualize Distribution of the Whole Between its Parts

Pie charts are used to visualize the relations between the parts of a whole. For example, distribution of sales between regions, brands, or market channels. It would be meaningless to use a pie chart to visualize a metric that isn't additive (for example, profit margin percent).

Typically, pie charts have a single dimension and a single expression. (More complex pies can accommodate two dimensions, but the result becomes a bit too complex to be treated as an effective visualization.)

The process of creating a pie chart is very similar. You can create a new chart and follow the same process of configuring the dimension and the expression, or you can clone an existing chart, change the chart type to pie chart, and tweak the settings. In the following exercise, you create a simple pie chart.

Exercise 4.18: Creating a Simple Pie Chart

1. Copy the Template sheet once again and name the new sheet **Channels**. On this sheet, you will explore various visual characteristics of pie charts.

2. Clone the Sales by Channel chart, which you created on the Sales sheet (see Exercise 4.15) and place the new copy in the new sheet called Channels.

3. Change the chart type to Pie Chart (from the General tab) and examine the result.

Your chart should look similar to chart A presented in Figure 4.25. Notice that the pie looks very small, because of the large amounts that are presented as Values on Data Points. The actual size of the pie is always determined by the amount of available space within the boundaries of the object.

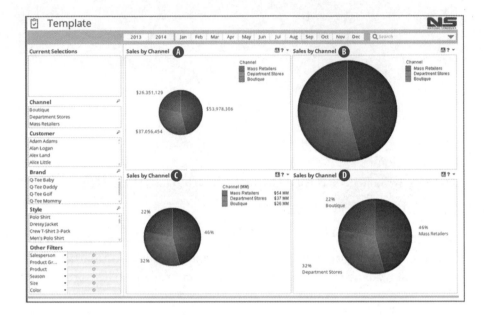

FIGURE 4.25:
Pie charts

Let's examine the other three pie charts in Figure 4.25. All of them present the same picture—distribution of sales by channel.

- Chart B is the same as chart A, only without displaying values on data points. The advantage of this chart is the larger size of the pie within the same boundaries of the object. The drawback is that users have to hover over the slices of the pie in order to see the actual numbers.

- Chart C offers two improvements over chart B. The relative parts for each channel are displayed next to the slices of the pie, and the actual amounts, presented in millions, are displayed in the legend. This presentation offers much more valuable information in the same chart.

- Chart D presents the dimension values (Channels) next to the slices, eliminating the need for a separate legend and making the overall look and feel more natural.

Admittedly, while option A looks too busy with unnecessary detail, all other options can be used effectively in different situations. In the following exercise, you will learn how to configure each of the options.

Exercise 4.19: Configuring Pie Charts

1. Clone the pie chart that was created in Exercise 4.18. Position the new chart to the right of the existing chart—this will be your version of chart B in Figure 4.25.

2. Open Chart Properties on the Expressions tab, and uncheck Show Values on Data Points. Examine the result.

3. Clone chart B and position the new copy in the lower-left corner. This will be your version of chart C. For this chart, perform the following:

    3.1. In the Expressions tab, clone the Sales expression (right-click the expression and select Copy, then right-click on the empty space next to the expression and select Paste).

    3.2. For the second version of the Sales expression, check the Relative and Values on Data Points boxes.

    3.3. In the Presentation tab, locate the Legend section and check the Show Numbers in Legend box.

    3.4. In the Number tab, highlight the first expression and enter shorter symbols for the amounts (we suggest **$** for single numbers, **K** for thousands, **MM** for millions, and **Bn** for billions).

    3.5. Examine the results of these configuration settings.

4. Clone the chart created in Step 3 and perform the following:

    4.1. Add another expression. Use the following formula for the new expression:

    `Only(Channel)`

    4.2. Label the new expression **Channel** and check the Values on Data Points box.

    4.3. In the Presentation tab, uncheck the Show Legend box.

    4.4. Examine the result. The four charts should look similar to the ones presented in Figure 4.25.

5. Save your work.

A Few Words about the Only() Function

We used the Only() function in the chart expression for the channel. The Only() function is a special kind of an aggregation function that returns *only* one value when *only* one value is available. When multiple values are available, the Only() function returns the NULL value. This function is often used in expressions when no aggregation is necessary. In fact, it's the default function that will be assumed implicitly when no other aggregation is specified in a chart expression.

Notice that outside of a chart, multiple values of Channel are available, and Only() would not be applicable. However, it is perfectly valid in a chart with Channel being used as a dimension—obviously, for each value of the dimension Channel, there is only one available channel, hence the function will return a valid value.

You may also notice that if you simply use the Channel field without the Only() function, you get the same result. This is because Only() is presumed by default if no aggregation function is specified. We still recommend using the function in order to be explicit in every way.

Finally, keep in mind that the technique of displaying dimension values next to the pie slices works well with only a few dimension values. When the pie becomes too busy with many small slices, this technique needs some adjustments that require more advanced functions. We will explore these functions in Chapters 8 and 12.

Using Straight Tables and Pivot Tables to Show Details

So far, we described a few simple graphical charts that presented a single expression plotted over a single dimension. More complex charts can plot a few expressions over a single dimension or plot a single expression over several dimensions. It's quite difficult to picture a graph that can effectively visualize several expressions over several dimensions.

Straight tables and pivot tables are the only two chart types that enable virtually unlimited number of expressions and dimensions. These two textual types of charts are sometimes called "reports." While the term is not technically accurate, it describes the resemblance of these tabular objects to the traditional "reports" that we know from any other reporting environment. They are classified as charts because they share most of the logical characteristics with the graphical charts. The only difference is the textual representation of the data. Later, however, you will discover that even these textual objects can present data graphically.

Creating a Straight Table

The process of creating a straight table is no different from creating any other charts. The following steps describe the process; in Exercise 4.20, following this list, you will actually create a straight table.

1. Create a **New Sheet Object** and select **Chart** from the list of all objects.

2. In the **General** tab, specify the **Title** and select **Straight Table** as the chart type.

3. In the **Dimensions** tab, specify all the dimensions for the chart. For straight tables, some of these dimensions may define the level of aggregation, and some dimensions may provide attributes to those levels. For example, picture a straight table that lists sales by customer and product. Since customer and product are independent of each other, both fields specify the level of aggregation—the sales will get aggregated by customer and by product. On the other hand, the chart by customer and channel is somewhat different. Since channel is an attribute of a customer, the true level of aggregation will be customer and the channel will merely serve as an attribute. For that matter, channel could be used in an expression equally well.

4. In the **Expressions** tab, define the expressions for the straight table. Because of the textual representation of the chart, straight tables can effectively present many different measures next to each other—as long as the object remains easy to read.

5. Define sorting rules in the **Sort** tab. Notice that all the dimensions are listed on the left side, and their order will determine sorting priorities. For each dimension, sorting rules are specified on the right.

6. The rest of the tabs and settings are mostly optional, except for the **Number** tab. Definitely remember to format your expressions appropriately.

In Exercise 4.20, you will create a straight table that shows unit sales, sales amounts, average selling price, and gross profit margins by product.

Exercise 4.20: Creating a Straight Table

Following the process described previously, create a new straight table on the Reports sheet:

1. Name the chart **Product Detail**.

2. Specify Product and Product Group as dimensions.

3. Create the following four expressions:

   3.1. Definition: sum([# Invoiced Quantity])
   Label: Unit Sales

   3.2. Definition: sum([# Amount])
   Label: Sales Amount

   3.3. Definition: [Sales Amount] / [Unit Sales]
   Label: Average Selling Price

   3.4. Definition: sum([# Margin Amount]) / [Sales Amount]
   Label: Gross Profit Margin %

4. In the Number tab, format the four expressions accordingly—units should be formatted as integer numbers, amounts as money, and margin % as a percentage with one fixed decimal digit.

Your result should look similar to the straight table shown in Figure 4.26.

FIGURE 4.26:
Simple straight table

Product	Product Group	Unit Sales	Sales Amount	Average Selling Price	Gross Profit Margin %
		11,516,552	$115,892,383.71	$10.06	21.7%
"Boy's Polo Shirt 2-Pack L Bla...	Sport	26,843	$406,226.95	$15.13	-11.0%
"Boy's Polo Shirt 2-Pack L Blue"	Sport	26,830	$421,259.53	$15.70	-11.7%
"Boy's Polo Shirt 2-Pack L Gr...	Sport	26,825	$415,639.69	$15.49	-12.0%
"Boy's Polo Shirt 2-Pack L Red"	Sport	26,836	$421,790.80	$15.72	-13.1%
"Boy's Polo Shirt 2-Pack L Wh...	Sport	26,889	$417,248.38	$15.52	-12.3%
"Boy's Polo Shirt 2-Pack M Bl...	Sport	26,902	$400,323.82	$14.88	-12.1%
"Boy's Polo Shirt 2-Pack M Bl...	Sport	26,832	$411,536.11	$15.34	-10.5%
"Boy's Polo Shirt 2-Pack M G...	Sport	26,885	$402,611.94	$14.98	-10.2%

Notice that we calculated **Unit Sales** and **Sales Amount** as expressions, and then we used the same calculated results in the following two expressions, by referencing the existing expressions by their labels. If you labeled your expressions differently, you need to adjust your expressions accordingly. This method of referring to existing expressions by name is both convenient and efficient—the calculation of sales is being reused multiple times, saving valuable resources, which becomes increasingly important when dealing with large volumes of data.

Noteworthy Properties of Straight Tables

While straight tables share their main characteristics with other charts, many important properties are specific to them. Let's explore together the most noteworthy settings (while staying at a relatively simple level for now).

First, here are a few characteristics of a straight table from the user standpoint:

- Each line of the chart shows the metrics (expressions), aggregated to the level of chart dimensions.

- On top of the list, the same metrics are aggregated at the total level. For first-time users, it may be unusual to see the total on top and not at the bottom. We find it logical—how many times have you scrolled down a long multi-page report just the see the summary at the bottom?

- The list can be sorted dynamically by double-clicking the label of a column. Both expressions and dimensions can be sorted dynamically. Double-click the same label again to switch between ascending and descending sorting.

- Columns can be moved by dragging and dropping. Dimensions can be positioned between expressions and vice versa.

There are many other wonderful features, like easy printing and easy export to Excel, but let's stay focused on exploring the main characteristics. Here are the most interesting settings and properties that deserve your attention at this point:

- **Expressions** tab
    - Notice the **Total Mode** section. Some totals may not be relevant, like the total Sales Units across multiple products. These unnecessary totals can be disabled by selecting **No Totals**. Sometimes, totals need to be calculated differently than by evaluating the same expression at the total level. Instead, you can use **Sum of Rows**, **Avg of Rows**, or any one of 16 available aggregations.
    - Notice the **Relative** checkbox. You already used it briefly in a pie chart. When **Relative** is selected, the column will show the relative share of the calculated metric from the total for the chart.

- Notice the **Accumulation** section. It's not specific to straight tables. It can be useful for certain types of analysis that require accumulating values across multiple rows of a chart.
- **Presentation** tab
  - The **Alignment** section allows you to align the data and the labels for each column. By default, texts are left-justified and numbers are right-justified. It's common to center the labels for all expressions, for a nicer presentation.
  - Any of the columns can be shown, hidden, or conditional.
  - The **Dropdown Select** checkbox allows adding a selection "filter" for a dimension.
  - The **Max Number (1-100)** setting allows you to limit the list to the selected number of rows. This setting can be used as an easy way of creating a "Top 10" report.
  - Totals can be positioned on top or at the bottom (if you insist), and a separate label can be assigned to the total row.
  - **Multiline Settings** allow wrapping headers and/or cells to multiple lines. This is particularly helpful for fitting long field headings nicely.
  - A set of miscellaneous settings in the lower-left corner offer additional presentation controls (feel free to play with these settings and examine the results).
- The **Visual Cues** tab is available only for textual charts—straight tables and pivot tables. It offers an easy way of color-coding some of the expression values, based on comparing the value to upper and lower limits. As an example, a profit margin % that's lower than the target can be marked with red text on a light yellow background.
- The **Style** tab is relatively simple for straight tables.
  - Experiment with various pre-set styles available in the **Current Style** drop-down list. Some of those styles are truly wacky. The default style, called **Light**, is perhaps the most suitable for modern visual trends.
  - **Transparency** options can allow creating tables that can blend well into dark backgrounds (mostly geared toward an iPad experience).

These are some of the simple settings for straight tables that can help you enhance the look and feel, as well as the usefulness, of your charts.

Exercise 4.21: Enhancing the Look of the Straight Table

Using this list of settings, you can enhance the straight table in the following ways:

1. Disable totals for the Unit Sales expression (from the Expressions tab).

2. Centralize labels for all the expressions (from the Presentation tab) and wrap the headers into three lines. Enable Dropdown Select for the two dimensions.

3. Using Visual Cues, color the values of Gross Profit Margin % in red for all values that are less than 20% (the actual value for 20% is 0.2).

Creating a Pareto Report

In the next exercise, you will use the **Accumulation** feature to create a Pareto report. In a nutshell, the Pareto principle states that 80% of outcomes are driven by 20% of efforts. You will create a report that shows customers in terms of the cumulative percent of sales amount they are driving.

Exercise 4.22: Creating a Pareto Report

Clone the straight table that you just enhanced and perform the following transformations:

1. Name the chart **Pareto Report on Sales Volume** (from the General tab).

2. Replace the two existing dimensions with a single dimension called Customer (from the Dimensions tab).

3. Delete the Unit Sales and Average Selling Price expressions, only keeping Sales Amount and Gross Profit Margin (from the Expressions tab).

4. Clone the Sales Amount expression and check the Relative box for the new expression. Label the new expression **Sales % to Total**. Promote it to appear after the Sales Amount expression.

5. Clone the same expression again and check both Relative and Full Accumulation. Label the new expression **Cumulative % to Total**. Promote it to appear after the Sales % to Total expression.

6. Accept all the changes by clicking OK and examine the result. Make sure to sort the report in the order of descending sales. Looking at the Cumulative % to Total, you can see that the first handful

of customers is responsible for about half of the revenues, and that contributions to total are dropping rapidly as you scroll down the list.

7. **Save** your work.

Extra Credit

It would be helpful to see which channel each customer belongs to. Usually, to add another textual attribute, you add the desired field as a dimension.

1. Add `Channel` as the second dimension and examine the result. Notice that the accumulation logic appears to be "broken" now. The accumulation restarts from zero for every channel. Evidently, the accumulation feature only works with a single dimension in the chart. Remove `Channel` from the dimensions (you can use Ctrl+Z to quickly undo the latest change).

    You still want to see which channel each customer belongs to. Since each customer only belongs to a single channel, you can apply the same technique used for a pie chart, using the `ONLY()` function in a chart expression.

2. Add another expression (from the **Expressions** tab) and make it present the channel. Disable totals for this expression and promote it to the first position. It will appear next to the `Customer` dimension.

    You can see the end result on Figure 4.27. Now you can see that the top six lines are taken by mass retailers, followed by department stores, and then independent boutique stores.

FIGURE 4.27:

The Pareto report

Pareto Report on Sales Volume

Customer	Channel	Sales Amount	Sales % to Total	Cumulative % to Total	Gross Profit Margin %
		$115,892,383.71	**100.00%**	**100.00%**	**21.7%**
QV-Max	Mass Retailers	$10,469,008.00	9.03%	9.03%	15.9%
Q&V	Mass Retailers	$10,118,831.04	8.73%	17.76%	16.3%
QVS	Mass Retailers	$8,929,037.98	7.70%	25.47%	13.8%
Qohl's	Mass Retailers	$8,775,413.03	7.57%	33.04%	13.7%
Super-Q	Mass Retailers	$8,348,922.00	7.20%	40.25%	14.1%
Q-Mart	Mass Retailers	$7,708,493.34	6.65%	46.90%	13.9%
DMS Authority	Department Stores	$3,342,111.33	2.88%	49.78%	23.1%
Apples&Oranges	Department Stores	$2,900,509.38	2.50%	52.28%	19.8%
SaqS	Department Stores	$2,885,328.23	2.49%	54.77%	22.1%
Con-Cat	Department Stores	$2,791,382.30	2.41%	57.18%	23.4%
Q-4-Men	Department Stores	$2,661,591.95	2.30%	59.48%	21.3%
SectionAccess	Department Stores	$2,596,762.55	2.24%	61.72%	22.5%
QAP	Department Stores	$2,571,274.71	2.22%	63.94%	24.0%
Quinsy's	Department Stores	$2,549,215.61	2.20%	66.14%	21.7%
QalvinQlein	Department Stores	$2,488,378.65	2.15%	68.28%	19.7%

3. Clone **Pareto Report on Sales Volume** and create the same report, based on profits (using the field [# Margin Amount] instead of the field [# Amount]). Comparing the two reports, what can you learn about the contributions of various customers and channels to revenues and profits?

Creating a Pivot Table

Pivot tables are quite similar to straight tables, with a few key differences.

- Pivot tables allow grouping the data into multiple hierarchy levels with totals and subtotals.

- Each dimension level can be collapsed or expanded, offering flexible view options at multiple levels of detail.

- In addition, pivot tables allow transforming some of the dimensions into running horizontally rather than vertically (this feature is called "pivoting"). The most obvious example is comparing the same results year over year, or period over period.

Once a pivot table is created, multiple dimension levels are collapsed by default. You can expand the dimensions by right-clicking on the dimension and selecting **Expand All** from the context menu. Then, if you need to pivot some of the dimensions, you can "grab" the dimension label and drag it to the right and upward, following an invisible semi-circle. A blue double-sided arrow is showing the new location of the dimension in the process of dragging. Once the desired location is reached, you leave the dimension there by releasing the mouse button. This process can take some getting used to, and is certainly easier with an actual mouse, as opposed to a trackpad.

In the following exercise, you will create a pivot table that analyzes sales, average selling price, and margins, aggregated by product groups, styles, and products, and compared between two years.

Exercise 4.23: Creating a Pivot Table

Clone the first straight table you created, called Product Detail. Perform the following changes to convert it into the desired pivot table:

1. Name the chart **Product Detail Year by Year** and change the chart type to Pivot Table (from the General tab).

2. Replace the existing dimensions by Product Group, Style, Product and Year, in this order.

3. Center the Year Labels and Data (from the Presentation tab) and clear the Wrap Header Text checkbox.

4. Accept the changes by clicking OK and examine the result. Save your work.

You should only see the `Product Group` dimension—this is because all other dimensions are collapsed by default.

5. Right-click on `Product Group` and select **Expand All**. Repeat expanding until all three dimensions are fully expanded.

6. Now, let's pivot the `Year` dimension to run across. Grab the **Year** label and slowly drag the mouse to the right. Notice the blue arrow. Your goal is to turn the blue arrow from vertical to horizontal.

Notice that you can position the `Year` above or below the expressions. Experiment with both options and notice the difference. For the purposes here, it's preferable to position the `Year` below the expressions. This way, annual values for each metric can be conveniently examined side by side.

Your chart should look similar to the pivot table shown in Figure 4.28.

FIGURE 4.28:
Simple pivot table

Product Detail Year by Year

Produ... ▼ Style		Year	Unit Sales		Sales Amount		Average Selling Price		Gross Profit Margin %	
		Product ▼	2013	2014	2013	2014	2013	2014	2013	2014
		Baby Jacket L Black	11,930	16,317	$122,630.55	$187,128.28	$10.28	$11.47	39.0%	40.6%
		Baby Jacket L Blue	11,996	1,151	$130,043.60	$13,897.43	$10.84	$12.07	39.0%	39.8%
		Baby Jacket L Gr...	11,930	16,312	$129,246.35	$193,664.05	$10.83	$11.87	39.1%	39.4%
		Baby Jacket L Red	11,934	16,354	$123,849.73	$184,890.63	$10.38	$11.31	39.0%	38.8%
Casual	Jacket	Baby Jacket L White	11,958	16,395	$125,802.53	$191,079.77	$10.52	$11.65	39.2%	39.0%
		Baby Jacket M Bl...	11,982	16,363	$118,477.70	$180,491.25	$9.89	$11.03	39.0%	40.0%
		Baby Jacket M Blue	11,960	1,138	$123,154.33	$12,708.57	$10.30	$11.17	39.0%	38.7%
		Baby Jacket M G...	11,970	16,281	$121,531.08	$180,820.78	$10.15	$11.11	39.0%	39.6%
		Baby Jacket M Red	11,976	16,306	$123,300.88	$183,469.04	$10.30	$11.25	39.0%	38.4%

Now you can try collapsing and expanding dimensions, to see the same metrics aggregated at different levels.

Most of the properties that are specific for pivot tables are located in the **Presentation** tab:

- **Show Partial Sums** is perhaps the most important of all—it allows you to create totals and subtotals for various dimensions. When this checkbox is enabled for the first dimension, it enables an overall total at the chart level. When it's enabled for any subsequent levels, the values at that level will get summed up and presented at one level above.

- **Allow Pivoting** and **Always Fully Expanded** can enable or disable pivoting, collapsing, and expanding dimensions.

- Notice that pivot tables, in comparison to straight tables, don't allow hiding dimensions (at least not in the same way). Similarly, it's not possible to limit the number of rows for pivot tables.

In addition, the **Style** tab offers an alternative view that can be used for some pivot tables—called **Indent Mode**. With **Indent Mode**, several dimensions can be presented as an indented structure, leveraging the same space. This can be useful when showing outcomes for hierarchical structures. In the following exercise, you enhance the look and feel of the pivot table.

Exercise 4.24: Enhancing the Pivot Table

1. In the Presentation tab, enable Show Partial Sums for the first three dimensions. Examine the result.

2. Experiment with the Allow Pivoting and Always Fully Expanded settings.

3. Compare the look of the pivot table with the totals presented On Top and At Bottom.

4. With totals presented On Top, turn on the Indent Mode (from the Style tab). Resize the dimension columns to make them appear closer to each other. Compare the appearance of the pivot table with and without Indent Mode.

Arranging Multiple Charts on the Screen Using Auto Minimize

Some QlikView sheets, like Dashboards, always show the same set of sheet objects. More detailed sheets that provide analytics and reporting may hold more charts than the available screen space can show. There are several techniques that allow accommodating multiple charts in a limited amount of space. All of them deal with different ways of showing a single chart and hiding all other charts at the same time. In this chapter, you will learn the first and the easiest technique, which uses the **Auto Minimize** setting on the **Caption** tab of the **Chart Properties**.

When the **Auto Minimize** setting is enabled for a number of objects on a given sheet, QlikView will allow you to show one of the objects at a time, while automatically minimizing all other objects.

The minimized objects appear as small icons, which you usually position at the bottom or along the right side of the screen, depending on the desired screen composition. Minimized objects can be restored by double-clicking on the minimized icon. The object is restored, and the previously displayed object becomes minimized. See Figure 4.29.

FIGURE 4.29:
Four charts, arranged with auto minimize

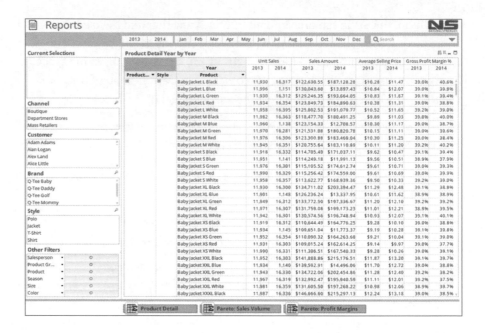

When charts are restored, it's nice to position and size them identically, so that all the charts "land" at the same place on the screen. For this reason, we recommend aligning and sizing all the objects together before applying the Auto Minimize setting. Once all the objects are minimized, the minimized icons also need to be aligned and sized consistently.

In the next exercise, you will arrange all the charts on the **Reports** sheet into a group of charts that shows one report at a time, while keeping all other charts automatically minimized.

Exercise 4.25: Arranging Charts Using Auto Minimize

In the **Reports** sheet, perform the following, using Figure 4.29 as a visual guide:

1. Ensure that the **Design Grid** is activated.

2. Activate all charts on the screen, leaving out the list boxes and text objects.

3. Align the charts to the **Left** and to the **Top** (all the charts will start at the same point).

4. While all the charts are activated together, right-click and open **Properties**. In the **Layout** tab, uncheck **Size to Data**. This setting will allow all the charts to have the same size, regardless of the data size.

5. Resize the charts together by dragging the black "handles" around one of the charts. Try to size them in such a way that they fill up the whole screen, vertically and horizontally.

6. Open Chart Properties again and set Auto Minimize on the Caption tab.

7. Minimize the charts one by one. The minimized icons will appear in the upper-left corner of the screen. Drag them into their place along the bottom of the screen, under the gray line, and resize the icons to show the text as much as possible. Rename the reports to shorten the text, if needed.

8. When all the charts are minimized, align the icons to form a neat horizontal line. Examine the auto-minimizing function by double-clicking icons and making reports get restored and minimized automatically.

9. Save your work.

Your screen should look similar to Figure 4.29.

This exercise concludes the description of basic charts in QlikView 11. We will cover advanced charts in the next section, as well as in Chapters 8 and 12.

First Round of Improvements

This section covers additional features and techniques that can enhance the solution that you've developed so far:

- Using dimension and expression groups
- Three techniques for conditional aggregation:
  - Using the IF() function
  - Using conditional flags
  - Using basic Set Analysis
- Developing text objects with calculated texts
- Building gauges
- Guidelines for building professional-looking dashboards

Gathering Feedback at the First Application Review

If this was your first encounter with QlikView, you can be proud and pleased—you learned a lot in a short time. With just a little bit of work, you developed a fully functioning Sales Analysis application that presents comparisons, trends, and some basic reports. Imagine that you share your accomplishment with your boss and she runs to share the good news with the executive team. Then you are invited to demonstrate your app at the executive staff meeting, to share the exciting news with the bigwigs.

At the meeting, the overall excitement and praise continues, and then you get your first batch of change requests. Once people see what the application is capable of, the light bulbs turn on and people tell you what they really need:

- The president, a former pilot, asked for a "cockpit report," or a dashboard that shows the year-over-year growth in sales and gross margins and some sort of a customer service metric (but he's not sure exactly what he wants this to be).

- The CFO asked for a year-to-date (YTD) comparison of all major metrics to prior YTD numbers—specifically unit sales, sales amounts, margins, and average sales prices (ASP). After a brief moment of hesitation, he asked for the same comparison for the current month-to-date.

- All three vice presidents for sales asked for the ability to present all the same charts by sales managers, regional directors, and VP for sales. They also want to see analysis of "new doors" versus "lost doors," which allows comparing the number of new shipping locations (stores, or "doors") compared to those that were lost.

- The VP for operations asked for the ability to present all the sales charts in units, not only in dollars, and for trend charts that show monthly trends year over year.

- The VP for supply chain would like to see a chart visualizing "on time and complete" measure (he described it as the count of order lines shipped on time and complete, compared to all order lines).

- The VP for marketing wanted to see all the charts by product category, style, size, and color. She also asked to see the mix of sales by brand and by channel, compared year over year.

You leave the meeting, grumpily muttering something about the camel being a horse designed by a committee, but deep inside you are celebrating! Not only did they like your work, but they actually care enough to give you real-world requirements that will improve your application so much more!

Now is the time to learn more about QlikView charts and expressions, in order to enable all the requested functionality.

Using Groups to Add Flexibility to Your Charts

In this section, you will learn about two types of groups that can be used in QlikView to add flexibility and to put your users in control—dimension groups and expression groups.

Dimension Groups

This phenomenon is known to anyone who has developed reports and charts. You develop a chart that compares sales by brand. The user praises your work and asks for exactly the same chart, only by product group. You go back to your office, clone the chart, and replace the dimension to produce the new version of the chart.

Then, the user asks for the same report by style, size, and color, and so on and so on. While it's easy enough to clone the report and generate another version, at some point you just want to be done with it. Ideally, you'd like to let your users select the dimension for the chart.

This can be done with the use of groups as chart dimensions. QlikView offers two types of dimension groups: drill-down groups and cyclic groups.

Drill-down groups can be used to form ad hoc hierarchies. When a drill-down group is used as a dimension, the chart will begin at the very top level (the first field in the group) and drill down to the next level as soon as a single value is selected from the first level. For example, a trend chart can start at the level of years, and then drill down to quarters when a single year is selected. From that level, the user can either go up and reverse the selection of the year, or continue drilling down to the monthly level.

In comparison, cyclic groups offer a simple choice of different dimensions that can be used for the chart. The dimensions are independent of each other. Using cyclic groups, the same chart can be presented by brand, style, size, color, and so on.

The definitions of groups can be accessed from the **Document Properties**, **Groups** tab, or from any **Chart Properties** window, on the **Dimensions** tab. In both cases, you get the list of the existing groups, with the ability to add a new group, or to edit or delete an existing group (see Figure 4.30, A).

FIGURE 4.30:
Managing groups

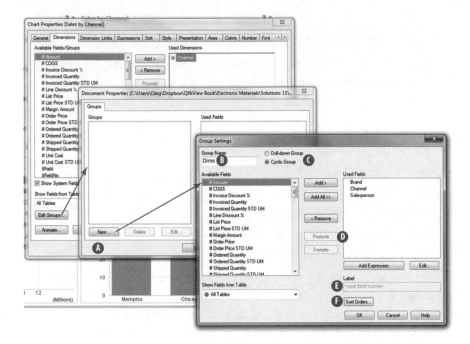

Clicking the **New** button opens the **Group Settings** window, where all the attributes of the new group are configured:

- **Group Name** (B)
- A choice between **Drill-Down** and a **Cyclic Group** (C)
- An ability to select any number of fields from the list of **Available Fields** on the left
- **Used Fields** can be promoted and demoted within the group (D)
- Each field can be renamed with the optional **Label** (E)
- Individual **Sort Orders** can be defined for each field in the group in a separate **Group Sort Order** window (F)
- Notice that you can also use **Add Expression,** to be used as a calculated dimension; however it's way too early to discuss this functionality now

In the following exercise, you create a drill-down group and a cyclic group and use both groups in sales charts.

Exercise 4.26: Creating Groups

1. Using the description provided previously, create a cyclic group for all product-related dimensions.

    1.1. Name the group **ProductDims** and include the following fields: Brand, Product Group, Style, Color, Size, and Product. In addition, include the field Warehouse to the group.

    1.2. Modify the bar chart Sales by Warehouse that we created in Exercise 4.15, and use the new group as a dimension. Notice that the group name appears on top of the field list in the Dimensions tab, highlighted with a light purple background.

    1.3. Examine the look and feel of the chart when different fields are selected from the group.

    1.4. Select Size from the list of fields in the group and notice the sorting of the chart. Notice that the sizes are not sorted from smaller to larger. In order to sort sizes correctly, revisit the definition of the group, click on the Sort Orders button, and configure sorting for the Size by Expression. Use only([Size Sort Order]) as the sorting expression for Size.

2. In a similar way, create a drill-down group for some of the product attributes:

    2.1. Name the drill-down group **ProductDrill** and include the following fields, in this order: Brand, Product Group, Style, and Product.

    2.2. Modify the bar chart Sales by Brand and replace the dimension by the drill-down group. Examine the differences in behavior between the two groups.

3. Save your work.

Expression Groups

In a similar fashion, multiple expressions can be combined into groups, allowing the user to pick the desired metric from a list of available metrics.

For example, the same chart showing top 10 performers can show top 10 salespersons based on sales, or margin, or average selling price, or number of customers, and so on.

The process of creating an expression group is quite simple. Create a number of expressions in the **Expressions** tab, and then highlight the *second* expression in the list and click on the **Group** button. The first two expressions will be included in a group that's signified by an icon with a circular arrow. See Figure 4.31. After the first two expressions are grouped, you can highlight the next expression in the list, to include it in the same group. If you highlight an expression that's further down the list, it will be grouped with the expression above it, forming another group. There is no limitation to the number of groups that you can have; however, offering too many choices in a single chart may create too much complexity and cause confusion, so we recommend using common sense and keeping the number of groups reasonable.

FIGURE 4.31:
Creating expression groups

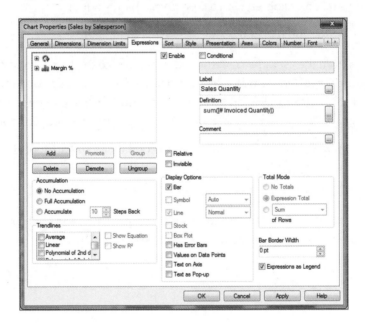

When groups are used in straight tables, the ⟳ icon is displayed in the column heading, which makes it easy to interpret. In graphical charts, the icon is simply placed at the bottom of the chart, with no verbal explanation. We usually use the **Text in Chart** option on the **Presentation** tab to explain what this icon is about.

If this is your first time using the **Text in Chart** option, we need to teach you how to move texts and other parts within a chart. The secret key is activating the chart object and then pressing and holding Ctrl+Shift. Once you do this, notice the little red frames outlining different parts of the chart. Drag the red frame with the new text to the desired position and then release Ctrl+Shift. You can also resize the frame to fit the long text. See Figure 4.32.

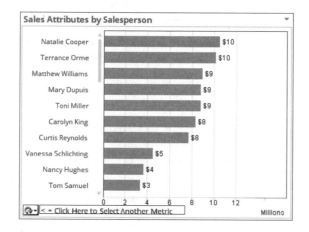

FIGURE 4.32:
Rearranging the internal structure of a chart

If you go too far in the process of resizing and rearranging the internal parts of a chart, you can always start over, using two buttons on the **General** tab of the **Chart Properties** in the lower-left corner: **Reset User Sizing** and **Reset User Docking**. Click on these two buttons to return the chart to its original state.

Exercise 4.27: Creating Expression Groups

In this exercise, you will use one of the bar charts that was created in Exercise 4.15 — Sales by Salesperson.

1. Open the Chart Properties from the Expressions tab and add three new expressions:

    1.1. Unit Sales—Sum of the field [# Invoiced Quantity].

    1.2. Profit Margin Amount—Sum of the field [# Margin Amount].

    1.3. Profit Margin %—Profit Margin Amount, divided by Sales Amount.

2. Group all the expressions in a single group by repeatedly highlighting the second expression in the list and clicking on the Group button.

3. Examine the behavior of the chart with the new group.

4. Notice that the group icon (the circular arrow) is not described in any way. Add Text in Chart (Presentation tab) that states < = **Click Here to Select Another Metric** and position the text next to the button (using Ctrl+Shift).

   Your chart should look similar to the chart presented on Figure 4.32.

This exercise concludes the section about using dimension groups and expression groups to add flexibility to charts. Examine your existing charts and add groups when you find it necessary.

Comparing YTD to Prior YTD or Other Conditions

So far, you've learned that QlikView charts present all of the available data, aggregated to the level of chart dimensions. When you make selections in list boxes, you limit the amount of available data and therefore change the aggregated results. For example, when you select 2014 as the year, the chart will only aggregate data for the year 2014. When you select 2013, the chart will only aggregate data for the year 2013.

Now you face a different need. Only part of the available data needs to be aggregated into the YTD total, and another part of the data needs to be aggregated into the prior YTD total. If you selected year 2014, the data for prior year would become unavailable (or not associated, or grayed out). If you select year 2013, the data for 2014 would become unavailable.

This new need leads to a new kind of aggregation, called *conditional aggregation.* You need to limit the scope of aggregated data to a certain condition. In this case, the condition is that the date (invoice date, to be exact) belongs to the YTD period, for one metric, or to the prior YTD period for the other metric.

Using the Conditional IF() Function

The first technique that's available for conditional aggregation is using the conditional function IF.

You are likely to be familiar with the common logic of the IF statement, as one exists in any programming language:

```
IF <a certain condition is true> THEN
<do something>
ELSE
<do something else>
END IF
```

QlikView scripting language also allows this structure for conditional script processing. In addition, QlikView offers an IF() function that implements a similar logic within a single function and returns a single value that depends on a condition:

```
IF(<condition>, <returned value if true>[, <returned value if false>])
```

This function can receive two or three parameters. The first parameter is the condition that needs to be validated, and the second parameter (separated by a comma) is the value that the function should return if the condition is TRUE. The optional third parameter can list a value that the function should return if the condition is FALSE. When the third parameter is omitted, IF() returns a NULL value if the condition renders FALSE.

Calculating YTD Conditions

If the current challenge is to calculate year-to-date totals, the condition should express something like this: "The Invoiced Date is greater than or equal to the first date of the year and is less than the Current Date." The condition for prior YTD should be something like this: "The Invoiced Date is greater than or equal to the first date of the prior year and is less than the Current Date within the prior year."

Luckily, QlikView offers a function that encapsulates all this logic:

```
YearToDate([Invoice Date])
```

YearToDate returns TRUE if the date belongs to the current YTD period, or FALSE if it doesn't. A set of optional parameters allows you to calculate the same using an alternate start of the year, or calculate the same within a different year (for example, prior year). Open **QlikView Help** ▶ and search for date functions. Locate the function called YearToDate and read about all the parameters of the function.

In our case, however, we need to take into account another complication. The data in our dataset is only available through December 31, 2014. For this reason, comparing invoice dates to the true current date (the date when you read this book) using the YearToDate() function would always return FALSE. We need to "freeze" the current date at December 31, 2014 and calculate the YTD logic based on that date. For this purpose, we can use another QlikView function called InYearToDate():

```
InYearToDate([Invoice Date], '12/31/2014', 0)
```

This function takes three or more parameters. At a minimum, you need to provide the date value that needs to be examined, the comparison date, and the shift in years (0 corresponds to the current year, -1 corresponds to the previous year, and so on).

Use Help to Learn about Functions!

We encourage you to open QlikView Help every time you need to learn about another function. Compared to books, printed manuals, and any other sources, the QlikView Help is the most complete, accessible, accurate, and up-to-date source of information about QlikView functions. Learn about the function types, formats, optional parameters, and so on. Some functions accept field names with quotes and some without. Some functions start counting from 1 and some count from 0. How would you know? From reading the Help. It's a very good habit to consult the Help every time you are in doubt.

Well, after reading the Help article about the InYearToDate() function, you should have no trouble writing the function for prior YTD:

```
InYearToDate([Invoice Date], '12/31/2014', -1)
```

Now you can formulate the conditional aggregation formula for the YTD sales amount:

```
Sum ( IF( InYearToDate([Invoice Date], '12/31/2014', 0) ,[# Amount])   )
```

Let's examine this expression. The SUM() function will summarize the detailed results of the IF() function. IF() tests the YTD condition and returns the Amount when the condition is TRUE.

Notice that you don't need to worry about the exact location of the [Invoice Date] and [# Amount] fields. Whether they are located in the same table or in different tables, QlikView can process the desired logic, using the associations between the different data elements. So, to be precise, we should say that the SUM() function aggregates those amounts that are *associated* with invoice dates that fall within the YTD period.

Similarly, the calculation of the prior YTD sales will be:

```
Sum ( IF( InYearToDate([Invoice Date], '12/31/2014', -1) ,[# Amount])  )
```

In the following exercise you develop a straight table with several expressions that leverage conditional aggregation functions described here.

Exercise 4.28: Create a YTD Comparison Chart

Using the conditional function IF() and the formulas described previously, create a straight table (within the Reports sheet) that shows current YTD results, compared to the prior YTD results for Unit Sales, Sales Amounts, and Average Sales Price (ASP), aggregated by Product. The chart will have three columns for each one of the three metrics—Current YTD, Prior YTD, and % Change. In total, you should create nine expressions.

The end result should look like the chart in Figure 4.33.

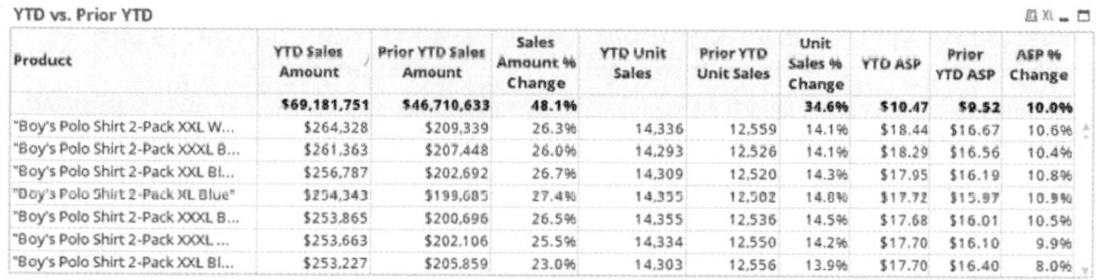

YTD vs. Prior YTD

Product	YTD Sales Amount	Prior YTD Sales Amount	Sales Amount % Change	YTD Unit Sales	Prior YTD Unit Sales	Unit Sales % Change	YTD ASP	Prior YTD ASP	ASP % Change
	$69,181,751	$46,710,633	48.1%			34.6%	$10.47	$9.52	10.0%
"Boy's Polo Shirt 2-Pack XXL W...	$264,328	$209,339	26.3%	14,336	12,559	14.1%	$18.44	$16.67	10.6%
"Boy's Polo Shirt 2-Pack XXXL B...	$261,363	$207,448	26.0%	14,293	12,526	14.1%	$18.29	$16.56	10.4%
"Boy's Polo Shirt 2-Pack XXL Bl...	$256,787	$202,692	26.7%	14,309	12,520	14.3%	$17.95	$16.19	10.8%
"Boy's Polo Shirt 2-Pack XL Blue"	$254,343	$199,685	27.4%	14,355	12,502	14.8%	$17.72	$15.97	10.9%
"Boy's Polo Shirt 2-Pack XXXL B...	$253,865	$200,696	26.5%	14,355	12,536	14.5%	$17.68	$16.01	10.5%
"Boy's Polo Shirt 2-Pack XXXL ...	$253,663	$202,106	25.5%	14,334	12,550	14.2%	$17.70	$16.10	9.9%
"Boy's Polo Shirt 2-Pack XXL Bl...	$253,227	$205,859	23.0%	14,303	12,556	13.9%	$17.70	$16.40	8.0%

FIGURE 4.33: YTD comparison chart

Calculating On Time and Complete Conditions

Similarly, you can use the conditional function IF() to calculate the count of order lines that were shipped on time and complete. The condition should only account for those order lines that were shipped on or before the requested ship date, *and* with the shipped quantity that's equal to the ordered quantity. The total count of lines can be calculated as the following:

```
count([# Amount])
```

Count of Amount?

Don't get confused with the use of the COUNT function on the Amount field. A simple, non-distinct count of any field returns a full count of rows that are being aggregated. Hence, this calculation is accurate only if each line of sales data represents a single order line "one-to-one." Alternatively, you could use a distinct count of the order number, concatenated with line number:

```
count(DISTINCT [Order Number] & '|' & [Line Number])
```

In this formula, you use the pipe symbol as a separator to avoid any accidental combinations of numbers—for example, order number 11, line 11 should not be the same as order number 111, line 1.

Another new feature mentioned here is the DISTINCT keyword. When used in any aggregation function, it means that each distinct value will get counted (aggregated) only once.

For the purpose of this book exercise, however, we will assume that order lines are represented uniquely in the rows of sales data, and that the use of the simple COUNT formula is acceptable.

The number of lines shipped on time and complete will look like this:

```
count( IF([Actual Ship Date]<=[Promised Ship Date] and
[# Shipped Quantity]>=[# Ordered Quantity], [# Amount]))
```

When expressions become too long and tangled, it may help to add a structured look by using multiple lines and tabulating parts of the expression:

```
count(
        IF(
                [Actual Ship Date]<=[Promised Ship Date]
        and
                [# Shipped Quantity]>=[# Ordered Quantity], [# Amount]
        )
)
```

Much easier to read, isn't it?

Now you can combine the two aggregations to produce the desired metric—
the ratio of order lines shipped on time and complete to the total count of lines:

```
count(
        IF(
                [Actual Ship Date]<=[Promised Ship Date]
        and
                [# Shipped Quantity]>=[# Ordered Quantity], [# Amount]
        )
)
/ count([# Amount])
```

Exercise 4.29: Creating a Trend Chart of On Time and Complete Delivery

Using the conditional function IF() and the formulas described previously, create a line chart (within the **Trends** sheet) that shows a monthly trend of % On Time and Complete, comparing the results between different channels.

Your chart will have a single expression. The dimensions will be MonthYear and Channel, in this order (try to swap the two dimensions and see what happens).

Set the grid and the axis settings in the **Axes** tab. Experiment with the **Forced 0** setting for the **Expression Axes**.

Your trend chart should look like the chart in Figure 4.34. Notice the unusual position of the legend at the bottom of the chart. The legend can be docked at the bottom by dragging the legend frame (while holding Ctrl+Shift) and dropping it at the bottom edge of the chart, when the red frame snaps into place and takes up the whole width of the chart at the bottom.

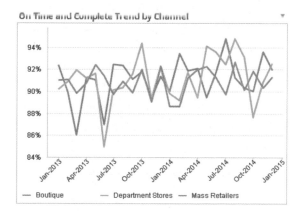

FIGURE 4.34:
Trend chart for % on time and complete

Why Not Use the Conditional Function IF()?

The IF() function is pretty easy to learn and understand, which makes it popular among developers and analysts. At the same time, using IF() can have a negative effect on performance in applications with larger data sets.

IF() comparisons are relatively heavy in terms of performance. When the IF() function is positioned in an aggregation function (such as SUM()), the comparison is being performed at each and every detailed line. In applications that store millions of rows, the IF() function will be performed millions of times for each conditional expression. The application will eventually slow down and become too sluggish. Alphabetic comparisons, as opposed to numeric ones, are known for their especially slow performance.

For this purpose, IF() functions, especially those located inside aggregation functions, should be banned from any application that operates with large volumes of data. In the next two sections, we will present two better alternatives that offer the same functionality with much better performance.

Using Conditional Flags

In QlikView, we differentiate two timeframes. The *runtime* is the time of the interactive analysis with a user in front of the screen, waiting for the next chart to render. This is obviously the most important timeframe, when every split second counts.

The *load time* is the off-line process of loading data, typically at night, when nobody is actively waiting for the results. While we try to be efficient here, the importance of time is secondary at this stage.

The trick of performance optimization is to move the bulk of the "heavy lifting" from the runtime to the load time. With regard to conditional aggregation, it means that the heavy comparisons should be evaluated during the load time, and the results should be saved in such a form that can be used in the runtime for faster processing.

In order to save time in the runtime, we will evaluate the condition in the script and store the result in a field that can hold one of two values:

- When the condition is TRUE, the field will hold 1.
- When the condition is FALSE, the field will hold 0.

Those fields are called *conditional flags*, and they can be used in chart expressions in the following way:

```
Sum ([# Amount]*_CYTD_Flag)
```

The flag equals 1 when the Current Year To Date (CYTD) condition is TRUE. Therefore, the sales amounts associated with CYTD dates will be multiplied by 1 and aggregated. All other amounts will be multiplied by 0 and therefore excluded from the aggregation. This notion may be unusual at first, but it's relatively straightforward.

Chapter 6 offers a detailed discussion about the logic of creating conditional flags in QlikView Script. For now, you can simply use the flags that exist in the data set. Notice that all conditional flags in this book are named consistently—the field name always begins with an underscore _ and ends with the _Flag suffix. When typing your expressions, simply type an underscore to get a short list of all flags from the IntelliSense prompt.

In the following exercise, you replace the IF() conditions that you used earlier, with the conditional flags that were calculated in the data set. The new expressions will perform much faster, especially with a large data set.

Exercise 4.30: Replacing IF() Functions with Flags

Clone the straight table you created in Exercise 4.28 and replace all the instances of the function IF with simplified expressions using conditional flags.

Do the same with the trend chart of **% on Time and Complete**.

Extra Credit

Compare calculation times spent on the two versions of the same chart. For this purpose, save your document, restart QlikView, and re-open the document. Open the charts one by one and make a note of the calculation time that's listed in the **Sheet Properties**, on the **Objects** tab.

Using Set Analysis

In this section, we introduce the basics of *Set Analysis*, a powerful technique that allows unlimited flexibility in transforming the set of aggregated data to fit your analytic needs. The syntax of Set Analysis is a bit quirky, but the power of the solution more than makes up for the trouble of getting used to it.

What's Wrong with Using Conditional Flags

While conditional flags offer substantial performance improvements over the practice of using the IF() function, their usefulness is still somewhat limited.

First of all, it's easy to "break the logic" inherited in the conditional flags, by making selections in related data fields. For example, if the user selects a month of February, the YTD calculation does not show the YTD total anymore. Instead, the total may or may not include the February numbers, depending on the current date, and it will never include any other months, because they become unavailable (not associated, grayed out) with the selection of February.

Speaking more broadly, you can only reduce the subset of aggregated data using conditional flags, but you can never expand the set and aggregate more data, or use a completely different subset of the data.

Consider the following need. When the user selects a certain product, you need to show how that product performs in comparison with all other products. Based on the traditional associative logic, all other products become unavailable (not associated, grayed out) with the selection of a single product. How can you possibly calculate metrics for data that's unavailable?

Set Analysis was introduced to help solve problems of this kind.

Understanding the Basics of Set Analysis

Before you learn the syntax of Set Analysis, let's understand its meaning. Each aggregation function (such as SUM, AVG, MIN, and so on) can be equipped with a set condition, which determines what set of data should be included in the particular aggregation.

The definition of the set is described with various selections that should be made in the data behind the scenes, before the data is aggregated. Picture a little elf that lives behind your screen and makes all sorts of selections for the sake of a specific calculation.

The Set Analysis condition is written within the aggregation function, right after the opening parenthesis, and it's signified by a pair of curly brackets { }:

```
SUM( { … }  [# Amount])
```

Every Set Analysis condition begins with the *Set Identifier*. This is a starting point for the set. There are many various codes that can be used as identifiers. For now, let's remember the basic three:

$ represents the current selections set, or the default data set.

1 represents the whole document, disregarding all selections.

0 represents an empty set (we've never seen a practical use of it)

Current selections ($) is the most commonly used, and it's also the implicit default—when no set ID is specified, $ is assumed (this logic was slightly modified with the introduction of Alternate States, and we describe the subtle difference when we introduce Alternate States in Chapter 12).

Logically, using $ as the starting point means that we mostly respect user selections, but we will tweak them in a certain way. The actual way of tweaking the selections is described in the so-called *set modifier*.

The set modifier is defined as one or more field selections that should be applied to the corresponding set identifier. The set modifier is enclosed in a pair of angled brackets < >. Within the brackets, one or more field selections are listed, separated by comma. Each field selection is presented in the following format:

```
FieldName = {values}
```

Notice another use of the same curly brackets (this is what makes reading Set Analysis conditions so much fun!). The equals sign looks like a comparison operator, but it's not. The precise meaning of it is "replace user selections with the following values." You will learn additional options for modifying field selections in Chapters 8 and 12.

The list of values can include a variety of things—a single value, a list of values separated by commas, or a search condition. A simple search condition can be presented by a wild card; for example, the search string "*Blue*" will cause selecting all the text that includes the word Blue.

Some field conditions may only have the field name and the equals sign, with no list of values. It means that the current selections in those fields need to be disregarded.

Here are a few simple examples of set analysis conditions. This is the sum of Amount across the whole data set (all user selections are ignored):

```
SUM( {1} [# Amount])
```

The is the sum of Amount for the current selections, within the year 2014:

```
SUM( {$<Year={2014}>} [# Amount])
```

This is the sum of Amount for the current selections, only within the year 2014 and only for products that contain the word Baby in the name:

```
SUM( {$<Year={2014}, Product={"*Baby*"}>} [# Amount])
```

This is the sum of Amount for the current selections, only within the year 2014 and disregarding the user selection in the Month field:

```
SUM( {$<Year={2014}, Month=>} [# Amount])
```

Time to Throw Away the Conditional Flags?

If Set Analysis is so much more powerful and flexible than the technique of using conditional flags, that perhaps we should scrap the idea of using the flags altogether? Well, not quite… With the power and flexibility that's offered by Set Analysis, you still need to minimize the amount of runtime computations. Also, the syntax of Set Analysis is quite particular, so it would be even more difficult to maintain complex conditions if you had to calculate all the logic there.

Instead, we recommend using the same conditional flags in combination with Set Analysis. For example, the current YTD calculation could look like this, using Set Analysis:

```
Sum ({$<_CYTD_Flag={1}>}  [# Amount] )
```

This condition is simple, easy to read, and flexible (notice that it will remain valid year over year, as long as the flag is calculated in the script).

This expression, however, carries the same issues as the original expression that was using multiplying by the flag. It's easy to break if the user can select years or months. In order to protect the YTD logic from the date-related selections, you need to add conditions that disregard user selections in these fields.

```
Sum ({$< Year=, Month=, _CYTD_Flag={1}>}  [# Amount] )
```

This Set Analysis condition is protected against accidental glitches caused by user selections in the Year and Month fields.

In the following exercise, you develop a simple chart with YTD comparison implemented using Set Analysis.

Exercise 4.31: Using Basic Set Analysis

Create a straight table showing current YTD unit sales compared to prior YTD unit sales, and a % change aggregated by Product Group. Use Set Analysis in combination with the conditional flags, as presented, for the conditional aggregation.

Use Visual Cues to color % Change green when it's higher than 10%, and red when it's lower than -10%.

This brief explanation of the basics of Set Analysis is just the beginning of a journey that leads you to the point of knowing, understanding, and effectively using all the versatile features that Set Analysis can offer. You will continue this journey throughout the book, especially in Chapters 8 and 12.

Building Dashboards

Now let's talk about satisfying the needs of the ex-pilot, the company president, who requested a "cockpit report." In this section, you will learn the building blocks and techniques for building professional-looking dashboards.

Dashboards—Tools or Toys?

Cockpit reports, or dashboards, are traditionally attributed to the needs of executives. Not surprisingly, the old-fashioned term that pre-dates the term BI was EIS—Executive Information Systems.

We'd argue that dashboards play an important role in any analytic application, not just for upper management. Despite their cartoonish looks and wasteful use of screen space, they serve an important function. They let you know quickly and effectively how you are doing on the vital metrics (KPIs). One glance at a well-designed dashboard will set the tone for the following analysis. Are you going to look for problems or opportunities? Are you looking for top performers who will be praised, or for a few people at the bottom of the list with whom you need to have a serious conversation?

In QlikView, dashboards are commonly built as the "front page" of an analytic application (not to be confused with the Introduction page) and they mainly consist of gauges, in combination with other types of charts and text objects.

It's common to show a small number of major KPIs (usually the measures of outcomes, or "lagging indicators") and a number of leading indicators for each one of the KPIs, typically presenting metrics that influence the outcome in one way or another.

Figure 4.35 shows a sales dashboard that you are going to develop at the end of this section. Notice that the dashboard consists of a few bar charts, a straight table at the bottom right, and of a large number of text objects in a variety of font sizes.

FIGURE 4.35:
The Sales Dashboard

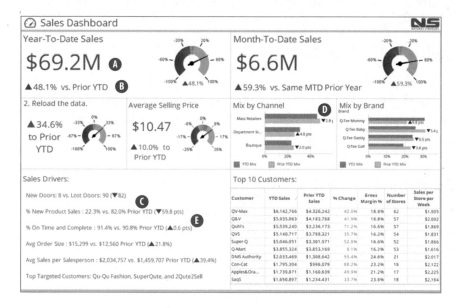

Revisiting Text Objects

In the earlier sections of this chapter, you learned how to use text objects for showing simple texts on the screen. Now you will learn how to present aggregated metrics on a dashboard screen, using text objects that carry calculated texts.

The goal of any dashboard is to show you the big picture in such a way that can be understood as quickly as possible. For this reason, the most important numbers (KPIs) should appear on top of the dashboard in a large font, telling you exactly how things are going.

Numbers of secondary importance should follow the main numbers, in smaller fonts, providing the context for the main number. Most of this information is communicated using text objects.

You can equip text objects with the same aggregated expressions as you use for charts. The text in the text object is treated as an expression if it begins with the equals sign -. The same text without the equal sign in the beginning will simply display the text of the formula.

Another main difference is the need to format the number manually. Since text objects can carry a combination of free text and numbers, the task of formatting the numbers falls completely on the developers. For this purpose, you can use the formatting function num(), which typically receives two parameters—the expression that calculates the number that should be formatted and the format code. In addition, the decimal separator and the thousand separator may be added as the third and the fourth parameters, but those are less common. The format code is the same string as the format pattern used in the **Chart Properties** on the **Number** tab. As a string, the format code needs to be enclosed in single quotes.

Here is an example of a simple expression with a formatted number:

```
=num( sum([# Amount])   , '$#,##0.00')
```

Format patterns use a few simple rules that are not too hard to remember and follow:

- The hash symbol # (often called the pound sign in the US) signifies a possible digit, while zero 0 signifies a mandatory digit. While # and 0 often have the same meaning, # signs are commonly used to signify the beginning digits of the number, while zeros are used for the last digit and all decimal digits: #,##0.0

- $-sign (or any other character) in front of the number may serve as a currency symbol. Generally speaking, any characters can be appended before or after the number.

- %-sign at the end of the format code signifies the number as a percentage. The number will be multiplied by 100.

- Format codes may include an optional second part that will be used for formatting negative numbers. This part is separated by a semicolon (;).

Here are three most commonly used format patterns (the number format corresponds to the U.S. standards):

Whole numbers, with a thousand separator: '#,##0'

Dollar amounts, with two decimals: '$#,##0.00'

Percentages, with one decimal: '#,##0.0%'

Formatted numbers may be concatenated with the corresponding labels to form cohesive texts. The ampersand symbol & serves as a concatenation operator. In order to open a new line in the text, you can use the CHR(10) function. The CHR() function converts an ASCII (or ANSI or Unicode) number to the corresponding character. ASCII code 10 corresponds to "line feed," the character that causes the system to open a new line. Here is a common example of an expression that generates two lines of text in the same text object—YTD sales and prior YTD sales. Notice the structured presentation that makes complex expressions more readable.

```
='Total YTD Sales: ' &
num(
      sum({<Year=, Month=, Quarter=, _CYTD_Flag={1}>}  [# Amount])
, '$#,##0')
& CHR(10) &
'Prior YTD Sales: ' &
num(
      sum({<Year=, Month=, Quarter=, _PYTD_Flag={1}>}  [# Amount])
, '$#,##0')
```

In the following exercise, you create a text object that uses the calculation described above.

Exercise 4.32: Creating a Text Object with Calculated Texts

Using the techniques presented previously, create a text object that shows % change in sales between prior YTD and current YTD.

Advanced Use of Number Formatting for Visualizing Change

Comparing numbers to a prior year is very common, especially for display in dashboards. Many times, % change to a prior year is accompanied by an image of an arrow pointing up or down, depending on the direction of the change.

While this technique is not terribly challenging, it involves calculating the same number one more time, just for the sake of verifying the condition and displaying the corresponding image—IF (<change calculation>) is positive, THEN show one image, ELSE show another image.

Recently, following the modern trend to flatten all the design elements, the arrow images are often being replaced with simplified characters ▲ and ▼ (see Figure 4.35). These characters can be generated using the CHR() function with the Unicode numbers 9650 and 9660, respectively. Since number formatting in QlikView allows you to add any characters to the format pattern, you can add these characters in front of your numbers. Notice that the format pattern can include separate formats for positive and negative numbers. Using this feature, you can use the upward pointing symbol for positive numbers and the downward pointing symbol for negative numbers. For example, % Change of Sales can be formatted using the following format pattern:

```
CHR(9650) & '#,##0.0%' & ';' & CHR(9660) & '#,##0.0%'
```

Notice how we concatenate parts of the format pattern together into a single string. Here is the fully formatted formula for the % Change of Sales (as presented on Figure 4.35, C):

```
=num(
      (sum({<Year=, Month=, Quarter=, _CYTD_Flag={1}>}  [# Amount])
      /
      sum({<Year=, Month=, Quarter=, _PYTD_Flag={1}>}  [# Amount])
      ) - 1
, CHR(9650) & '#,##0.0%' & ';' & CHR(9660) & '#,##0.0%' )
& ' vs. Prior YTD'
```

When it comes to comparing measures that are already presented as percentages, such as profit margin %, it's common to calculate the net change in percentage points, rather than calculating % change between two percentages. So the calculation of the change is slightly different—it's a simple subtraction between the current percentage and the prior percentage. The number formatting is slightly different too—instead of a percentage sign %, you add the abbreviation pts for points. Notice that in absence of the % at the end of the format pattern, it's now up to you to multiply the number by 100. Here is an example of a complex formula that presents % new product sales, including the current YTD number, compared to the prior YTD number, and the change presented in parentheses (as presented in Figure 4.35):

```
= '% New Product Sales : ' &
num(
      sum( {<_NewProduct_Flag={1},
             Year=, Quarter=, Month=, _CYTD_Flag={1}>} [# Amount])/
      sum( {< Year=, Quarter=, Month=, _CYTD_Flag={1}>} [# Amount])
, '#,##0.0%')
& ' vs. ' &
num(
      sum( {<_NewProduct_Flag={1},
             Year=, Quarter=, Month=, _PYTD_Flag={1}>} [# Amount])/
      sum( {< Year=, Quarter=, Month=, _PYTD_Flag={1}>} [# Amount])
, '#,##0.0%')
&
```

```
' Prior YTD (' &
num(
        (
        sum( {<_NewProduct_Flag={1},
                Year=, Quarter=, Month=, _CYTD_Flag={1}>} [# Amount])/
        sum( {< Year=, Quarter=, Month=, _CYTD_Flag={1}>} [# Amount])

        -

        sum( {<_NewProduct_Flag={1},
                Year=, Quarter=, Month=, _PYTD_Flag={1}>} [# Amount])/
        sum( {< Year=, Quarter=, Month=, _PYTD_Flag={1}>} [# Amount])
        ) * 100
, CHR(9650) & '#,##0.0 pts' & ';' & CHR(9660) & '#,##0.0 pts' )
& ')'
```

You can use the same technique in charts, but in a special way. Unfortunately, format patterns that are used in **Chart Properties** on the **Number** tab cannot be calculated by concatenating strings together. This setting in **Chart Properties** can only accept hard-coded literals. The trick is to format the chart expression in the same way as you did above for the text object, and to use the number format called **Expression Default**, which essentially means that the number will not be formatted by the chart. This technique is used in the dashboard on Figure 4.35, to format the % change that's presented as values on data points within the bar charts.

In the following exercise, you practice these techniques while creating a text object that shows a YTD comparison for % on time and complete.

Exercise 4.33: Creating a Text Object Formatted as a % Change

Using the techniques described previously, create a text object with a formatted calculation of % On Time and Complete for the current YTD, compared to the same for the prior YTD and the % change presented in percentage points (see Figure 4.35).

To calculate % On Time and Complete, divide the count of [# Amount] with the flag _OnTimeAndComplete_Flag = 1, by the count of [# Amount] without the same condition. For current YTD, add the YTD conditions to your Set Analysis. For prior YTD, repeat the same and replace the CYTD flag with the PYTD flag.

Creating Gauges

A *gauge* is a type of a QlikView chart that presents a single number in a graphical way, such as a speedometer, a measuring tube, or one of a handful of other visual choices.

Most gauges show the scale of the possible values divided into segments, color-coded in various combinations of green, yellow, and red, to communicate how good, bad, or ugly the outcome is, in relation to some preset targets. In order to enable such a comparison, gauges are typically used for relative numbers and ratios. Typical metrics suitable for gauges could be sales (or any other measure) compared to prior year, sales compared to budget, % on time and complete delivery, or any other measure calculated as a ratio or a percentage.

Since gauges present a single value, they don't require any dimensions and they don't need sorting. In essence, most of the gauge settings are concentrated on three tabs of the object properties:

- **Expressions:** The main expression for the gauge is defined here, in the same way as it is defined for all other charts.

- **Style:** The look for the gauge is selected here, from seven available options (see Figure 4.36). Speedometer is the most commonly used type of gauge, and we will be describing the rest of the settings as they pertain to the speedometer.

- **Presentation:** This is where most of the important settings for the gauge are defined (see Figure 4.37).

  - **Min** and **Max** values (A) define the range of available values for the gauge.

  - **Segments Setup** settings (B) define the number of segments, their colors, and the lower bound for each segment. Notice that the **Lower Bound** setting is grayed out. By default, all gauges are sized identically and there is no need to size each segment individually. This default can be altered by clearing the **Autowidth Segments** checkbox in the lower-left corner of the window (C). Once **Autowidth Segments** is off, the **Lower Bound** becomes available, and the value needs to be entered for each segment. First segment should always start from the **Min** value, then the second segment's **Lower Bound** will signify the end of the first segment, and so on.

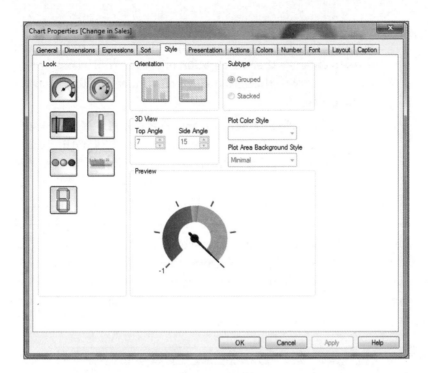

FIGURE 4.36:
Gauge Properties,
Style tab

- The **Indicator** section (D) allows selecting **Mode, Style,** and **Color** of the pointing indicator. An interesting option for the **Mode** is **Fill To Value.** With this setting, the segments of the gauge are only filled up to the actual value, forming unfinished arches of various lengths.

- The **Show Scale** checkbox (E) and the settings within that section describe the look and feel of the scale—those numbers and ticks that form the dial. The number of **Major Units** defines how many major "ticks" will appear on the dial. You can opt to show labels on every tick, on every other tick, and so on. By default, the number zero means that no labels (numbers) are presented.

- **Circular Gauge Settings** (F) allows you to alter the cylinder thickness, angle span, and center angle of the gauge. With these settings, you can create thinner gauges that only span to, let's say, 90 degrees and are turned to a strange angle around their centers.

- **Reference Lines** (G) and **Text in Chart** (H) are similar to the same settings for other charts. They allow you to add lines and texts to enhance the presentation of the chart. It's common to add the text with the actual value of the measure to the bottom of the gauge.

- Finally, the **Hide Segment Boundaries** and **Hide Gauge Outlines** (I) settings allow you to get rid of the black outline that's surrounding the gauge, which offers a better, less cluttered view of the gauge.

Gauges are equipped with the same set of attributes such as borders, a caption bar, chart titles, and so on. The size of the gauge is determined by the size of the object and the available space. Once you play with the gauge object long enough, you will probably agree that it's not too easy to center the gauge and the title within the boundaries of the object. For this reason, we recommend removing all titles, borders, and a caption. You can add the necessary titles in separate text objects.

FIGURE 4.37:
Gauge Properties, Presentation tab

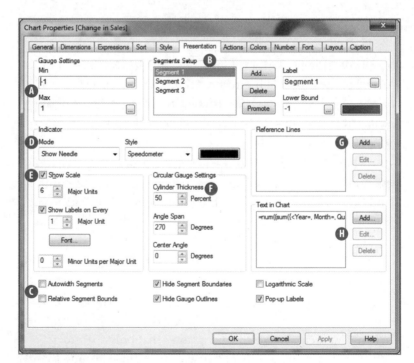

In the following exercise, you create a gauge that presents YTD change in sales.

Exercise 4.34: Creating a Gauge

Open the Dashboard sheet and create a gauge that presents the YTD sales change from prior YTD (as presented on Figure 4.35):

1. In the General tab, select Gauge as the chart type and disable the chart title.

2. Skip Dimensions.

3. In the Expressions tab, enter the expression for % Change in Sales:

```
(sum({<Year=, Month=, Quarter=, _CYTD_Flag={1}>}  [# Amount])
/
sum({<Year=, Month=, Quarter=, _PYTD_Flag={1}>}  [# Amount])
) - 1
```

4. Skip Sort.

5. In the Style tab, pick the speedometer without a plate as the Look.

6. In the Presentation tab, enter the following settings:

    6.1. Gauge Settings: Min=**-1**, Max = **1**

    6.2. Define three segments—Red, Yellow, and Green. Uncheck Autowidth Segments and define the following Lower Bound numbers: **-1** for Segment 1, **-0.05** for Segment 2, and **0.05** for Segment 3.

    6.3. Leave the default settings for Indicator and Circular Gauge.

    6.4. Under Show Scale, define **6** Major Units, with Labels on Every **1** Major Unit.

    6.5. Check Hide Segment Boundaries and Hide Gauge Outlines.

7. Proceed to the Number tab and format the number as Integer, with the setting Show in Percent (%). This setting controls the formatting of the number on the scale.

8. On the Caption tab, disable Show Caption. Finish the wizard and examine the result.

9. Copy the text of the expression and open the Presentation tab again. Create Text in Chart (using the Add button). Similarly to text objects, you will need to add an equals sign in front of the text

and format the number as percentage manually, using the num()function. Once you're finished, accept the changes and examine the result.

10. The new text is created in the upper-left corner of the gauge. In order to move it to the desired place (usually in the middle, underneath the arrow), press and hold Ctrl+Shift. Notice the little red frames outlining different parts of the chart. Drag the red frame with the new text to the desired position and only then release Ctrl+Shift.

11. **Save** your work.

Bringing It All Together

This is the moment of truth. You are building your first full-fledged analytic dashboard on your own. At this point, you know everything you need to in order to build the dashboard presented in Figure 4.35. Instead of giving you step-by-step instructions, this section describes the various components of the dashboard and lets you use the acquired knowledge to build it by yourself.

The dashboard screen is different from other screens because it typically does not include the common selection attributes—the calendar selections, the list boxes, and the Current Selections box. The information on the dashboards is typically pre-packaged into YTD and MTD time frames (your company might use other periods) and the current outcomes are typically compared to the same period of the prior year. The goal of the dashboard is to show users the big picture without too much clicking around.

For this reason, we modified our template structure to keep a thin (6 pt) gray ribbon on top of the screen and the same gray ribbon at the bottom. Those ribbons are implemented as text objects. Then, we divided the screen in half horizontally, using a thin (1 pt) vertical gray line. Another gray line runs along the right side of the screen, creating a visual grid and enclosing the contents of the screen.

We divided the vertical space between the two gray ribbons in half, using a thin gray line, and then we divided the top half of the screen in half again.

The upper-left section of the dashboard shows YTD sales outcome, presented as a large number (font size 48), highlighted in blue. Below it, a smaller text (font size 18) describes the comparison to prior YTD. The gauge on the right shows the visual representation of the year-over-year change.

The upper-right section shows the same information, calculated for the current month-to-date (MTD) period, compared to the same MTD prior year.

The two sections below are divided in half, to present four leading indicators, or drivers, of sales:

- On the left, the two contributors to sales growth are Unit Sales and the Average Sales Price.

  - Since the actual unit quantity is meaningless when aggregated across multiple products, we only show the change to prior year, in a text object and in a gauge.

  - Average Selling Price is presented as an absolute number (as text), and in comparison to prior YTD, in a text object and in a gauge.

- The two bar charts on the right visualize *mix*—the distribution of sales by channel and by brand.

  - YTD Mix and Prior YTD Mix are two expressions that calculate sales amounts. The amounts are turned into relative shares using the **Relative** setting on the **Expressions** tab.

  - The label that shows the change in mix from one year to another is the third expression that's not presented as a bar, but rather displayed using **Values On Data Points**. Unfortunately, the change in mix cannot be calculated using the **Relative** checkbox. The relative shares need to be calculated and subtracted manually, as presented in the following formula:

```
=num(
    (
    sum({<Year=, Quarter=, Month=, _CYTD_Flag={1}>} [# Amount])/
    sum({<Year=, Quarter=, Month=, _CYTD_Flag={1}>} TOTAL [# Amount])
    -
    sum({<Year=, Quarter=, Month=, _PYTD_Flag={1}>} [# Amount])/
    sum({<Year=, Quarter=, Month=, _PYTD_Flag={1}>} TOTAL [# Amount])
    ) * 100
, CHR(9650) & '#,##0.0 pts' & ';' & CHR(9660) & '#,##0.0 pts' )
```

The bottom-left section shows the less significant drivers of sales, represented in text objects.

- New Doors and Lost Doors are calculated as a distinct count of [Ship To Name] using conditional flags :

```
= 'New Doors: ' &
    num(count( {<_NewDoor_Flag={1},
                    Year=, Quarter=, Month=, _CYTD_Flag={1}>}
                distinct [ShipTo Name]), '#,##0')
& ' vs. Lost Doors: ' &
    num(count( {<_LostDoor_Flag={1},
                    Year=, Quarter=, Month=, _CYTD_Flag={1}>}
                distinct [ShipTo Name]), '#,##0')
& ' (' &
    num(
        count( {<_NewDoor_Flag={1},
                    Year=, Quarter=, Month=, _CYTD_Flag={1}>}
                distinct [ShipTo Name])
        -
        count( {<_LostDoor_Flag={1},
                    Year=, Quarter=, Month=, _CYTD_Flag={1}>}
                distinct [ShipTo Name])
    , CHR(9650) & '#,##0' & ';' & CHR(9660) & '#,##0' )
& ')'
```

- New Product Sales is the ratio of the sales attributed to new products (using the corresponding conditional flag) to the total sales for the period. The formula was presented earlier, in the section called "Advanced Use of Number Formatting for Visualizing Change."

- % On Time and Complete is calculated as a ratio of the line count for those order lines that were marked with the OnTimeAndComplete flag, compared to the total count of order lines for the time period:

```
= '% On Time and Complete : ' &
num(
    count( {<_OnTimeAndComplete_Flag={1},
                Year=, Quarter=, Month=,_CYTD_Flag={1}>} [# Amount])/
    count( {<Year=, Quarter=, Month=, _CYTD_Flag={1}>} [# Amount])
, '#,##0.0%')
& ' vs. ' &
```

```
num(
      count( {<_OnTimeAndComplete_Flag={1},
                Year=, Quarter=, Month=, _PYTD_Flag={1}>} [# Amount])/
      count( {<Year=, Quarter=, Month=, _PYTD_Flag={1}>} [# Amount])
, '#,##0.0%')
& ' Prior YTD (' &
num(

      (
      sum( {<_OnTimeAndComplete_Flag={1},
            Year=, Quarter=, Month=, _CYTD_Flag={1}>} [# Amount])/
      sum( {<Year=, Quarter=, Month=, _CYTD_Flag={1}>} [# Amount])

      -

      sum( {<_OnTimeAndComplete_Flag={1},
            Year=, Quarter=, Month=, _PYTD_Flag={1}>} [# Amount])/
      sum( {< Year=, Quarter=, Month=, _PYTD_Flag={1}>} [# Amount])
      ) * 100
, CHR(9650) & '#,##0.0 pts' & ';' & CHR(9660) & '#,##0.0 pts' )
& ')'
```

- Average Order Size is calculated as the total sales amount for the time period, divided by the distinct count of orders for the period. We will let you build this expression on your own, using the other similar calculations listed in this section.

- Similarly, we'll ask you to come up with the formula for the Average Sales per Salesperson—total sales divided by the distinct count of salespersons.

- The text at the bottom is simply a static text listing the top targeted customers. This information is not available through the data, but it is important as an integral part of the sales dashboard.

The bottom-right section hosts a straight table that shows the top 10 customers. For each one of the top customers, the following measures are calculated:

- YTD Sales, Prior YTD Sales, and the % Change are the same calculations you've used before.

- Average Gross Margin % is calculated as the sum of margin amounts, divided by the total sales amounts, calculated for the current YTD period.

- **Number of Stores** is a distinct count of [Ship To ID], calculated for the current YTD period.

- **Sales per Store per Week** is calculated as total sales, divided by the distinct count of stores, calculated by the distinct count of weeks for the current YTD period.

Exercise 4.35: Building the Sales Dashboard

Using Figure 4.35 and the verbal description just provided, build the Sales Dashboard sheet of your Sales Analysis application.

Then, using the key calculations of outcomes and drivers of sales, fill the rest of the sheets with insightful charts that can help users analyze sales at various levels. Here are a few ideas that can guide you:

- Analyze the effectiveness of the sales force, calculating sales and gross margins by salesperson, regional director, and VP sales.

- Analyze monthly trends for each one of the sales drivers.

- Compare channels, brands, and categories by their sales amounts, average selling prices, and gross margins.

This exercise concludes the discussion about building simple visualizations in QlikView. We will return to discussing more advanced visualizations in QlikView in Chapters 8 and 12. In Chapter 16, we will describe the process of building a similar dashboard in Qlik Sense.

5

Data Modeling for Sales Analysis

Now that you've seen how the initial user stories can be visualized, the next step is to begin the data modeling process. Because QlikView makes it so easy to quickly load data and create visualizations, the data modeling step sometimes gets overlooked, or at least skimmed over.

NOTE At the core of every successful QlikView project is a carefully planned and well-designed data model.

A properly designed data model should be:

- **Accurate**—Without confidence in the data, your project will fail.
- **Easy to use**—Developers and analysts who create the visualizations can find data elements easily.
- **Understandable**—A non-technical business person can look at a diagram of the data model and say, "Yep—that's how my business works."
- **Fast**—For the end user, sheet navigation and chart rendering is fast.
- **Scalable**—A developer can add elements and significant row volume without redesigning the entire model.

For the data modeler, these are not trivial goals. How do you make sure that your model delivers on expectations? Understanding the fundamentals of data modeling is key.

So, what exactly *is* a data model, and how does one go about the business of designing it? Generally speaking, a *data model* is the logical representation of how data from multiple tables are related. *Data modeling* describes the process of crafting a database design (what goes in the tables and how they are related) that best serves the applications that use it. In QlikView, you write scripts to extract data from various sources and load the data into memory. The way that data is loaded *and* the data itself is referred to as "the data model."

Before we dive into the details of building data models in QlikView, let's take a step back to gain some perspective. In the first section of this chapter, we'll review the basics of data models and the applications that use them.

Data Modeling Basics

The main goal of a data model is to enable software applications. The design, architecture, and physical implementation of a data model should primarily benefit the application(s) that are using it. We discuss two basic types of software classes in this section:

- **Transactional software class**—Applications in this class emphasize *updating* small amounts of data in a database for record keeping purposes. This class of applications typically uses the entity-relationship model.

- **Analytical software class**—Applications in this class emphasize *retrieving* large amounts of data from a database for aggregation and slice-and-dice purposes. The multi-dimensional model is typically used by analytical applications.

The Transactional Software Class

Transactional systems (accounting systems, point-of-sale systems, and so on) are designed to execute lots of small, basic transactions. The acronym *CRUD* describes the four basic functions of a transaction system: create, read, update, and delete. Any application that requires immediate processing of data entry transactions falls into this category. *OLTP* (online transaction processing) is the generic acronym used to describe such applications.

Almost all businesses use OLTP systems to store their most crucial data. Keeping track of basic business processes is the job of the OLTP application—from simple accounting systems (QuickBooks) to mega-ERP systems (SAP), and everything in between. A data modeler designing a database for OLTP systems must ensure that the bread-and-butter transactions—CRUD functions—are handled as quickly as possible. A single transaction may only impact a small number of rows, perhaps in the tens, but a large system could process millions of transactions per day. Transactions can occur frequently (within milliseconds), and the system must be ready to handle each transaction without delay. To maximize the speed of the transaction, redundant data must be minimized or eliminated.

The original term "online" in OLTP means "interactive processing"—where the transactions are processed immediately—compared to the "batch" transaction processing of an earlier era. These terms were invented at a time when "online" did not refer to being connected to the Internet.

Throughout the book, we use the term "online" to differentiate the interactive user experience at runtime with the batch process of loading data.

Because transactional applications are almost always associated with a normalized database, the term "OLTP" has come to describe the entire system—both the software and the database.

The process of removing redundant data from a database design is called "normalization." A normalized database can be visualized with the entity-relationship data model.

The Entity-Relationship Data Model

The *entity-relationship model* offers the best design to support the transactional class of applications. In this model, each data entity gets its own table, and the attributes become the columns. For example, a customer is an entity with many attributes (name, DOB, phone number, and so on), so a table named [Customer] is created, and columns are added for the attributes.

Similarly, if another entity uses "customer name" as an attribute, a link to the customer row is all that is stored—thereby eliminating the need for the attribute value to be stored in multiple tables. In the simple *ERD* (entity-relationship diagram) shown in Figure 5.1, it's easy to see why the [Invoice] table would have a link to the [Customer] table. Imagine if a simple change of a customer's fax number required updating the row in the [Customer] table AND updating all of the rows of the [Invoice] and [Purchase Order] tables that were related to that customer. The transaction would take far too long. The relational model enables CRUD transactions to happen quickly and efficiently.

The ERD shown in Figure 5.1 was simplified for example purposes. However, many OLTP applications have data models that are vastly more complex. The ERD in Figure 5.2 is an example of the complexity you'll find in many corporate OLTP systems. But even this one is relatively small.

Usually, these complicated ERDs can be spotted hanging on a cubicle wall in an area where database professionals ply their trade. There is not enough space on this page to display some of the largest ones we've spotted. Large OLTP systems sometimes require hundreds or even thousands of tables. Given its purpose of mapping every possible data process as well as reducing data redundancy among tables, the entity-relationship model is inherently complex. As there are plentiful resources available on relational theory and practical implementations, we won't go into further detail here.

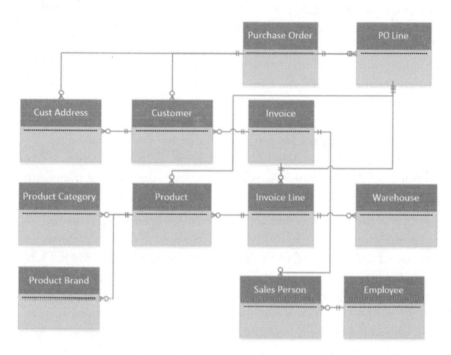

FIGURE 5.1: Simple entity-relationship diagram (ERD)

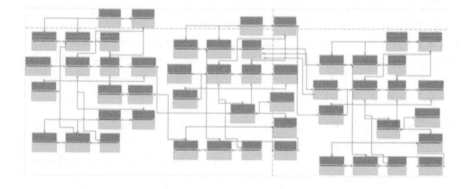

FIGURE 5.2: Complex ERD

The Analytical Software Class

Not long after the first OLTP applications were written to manage data in normalized databases, one thing became immediately clear: while it's very efficient to execute lots of small transactions (CRUD), it can be very inefficient to retrieve and aggregate large amounts of data. Business reporting and analysis requires access to large amounts of data from one or more OLTP systems. A business analyst might need to analyze how a certain product has sold via certain channels over a period of years. In the OLTP system, that data set could include an enormous amount transactional data. To run a seemingly simple report such as "Total Sales by Product by Channel by Year," you must answer a number of questions. Should the total include returns? Chargebacks? Discounts? Orders that haven't shipped? Is the "Channel" defined in the database, or is it derived based on some other attribute or logic? As you can see, even the simplest query can quickly become challenging to define and execute.

The entity-relationship (normalized) model is designed for the transactional application, not the analytical one. Aggregation queries issued on a normalized database tend to be slow, due to the number of rows in each table that may need to be read, the complex relationships among tables, and the number of hops it may take to link one table to the next. An aggregation query may take a *very* long time to run, depending on server resources, and may delay the processing of critical business transactions. For precisely this reason, running reporting queries in a production OLTP environment is usually prohibited (or throttled).

A different data structure is needed for the analytical application: one that is optimized for reporting and analysis. The *multi-dimensional data model* is well suited for this purpose. A dimensional model used by analytical applications is different from the entity-relationship model both in purpose and structure:

- The tables are not intended to contain "live" data, but rather a snapshot of the transactional data. Complex analytical queries can be run against the data without impacting the critical function of the OLTP system.
- Table relationships are designed with an emphasis on simplicity and the speed of aggregation.

Analytical applications depend on the multi-dimensional model to provide an efficient way to execute complex aggregations on vast amounts of data. The next section describes how the multi-dimensional model is structured.

The Multi-Dimensional Data Model

A multi-dimensional model is designed to organize the data that are extracted, transformed, and sometimes aggregated from transactional sources. The dimensional model presents data in a more natural structure tailored for analysis, as opposed to the entity-relationship model, which is designed for data processing. When the data are stored in tables, the structure can be visualized with a star-like model, as shown in Figure 5.3.

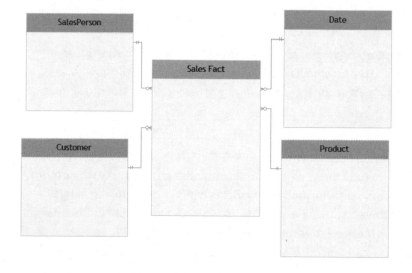

FIGURE 5.3: Basic dimensional model/star schema

The table in the center of the star diagram is called the *fact table*. "Facts" are transactions or events that happen in the business, such as sales, shipments, returns, and so on. The primary components of the fact table are the "measurements" of those transactions and events—typically dollar amounts or quantities that can be summed up or counted. The other fields in a fact table are the key fields that link the fact to the dimension tables. The tables circling the fact table are called the *dimension tables.* These tables contain data that describe how the "fact" happened—the who, what, when, and where of the transaction. You can think of dimensions as the things that we use to slice-and-dice the data in the fact table. For example, a report or chart that shows $ Total Sales by Customer by Month can be thought of as a subtotal of the facts ($ Sales) by the Customer and Month dimensions.

In its design, the multi-dimensional model is inherently simple. All of the measures are stored in one fact table. Each row in the fact table is linked to a dimension table by only one field, whereas multi-column relationships are common in OLTP systems. All of the attributes of each data entity are grouped together in a single dimension table, as opposed to the normalized entity-relationship model. For example, in a normalized model, various attributes for a product could be stored in many tables (Product, Style, Color, Size, and so on). As you will see in Chapter 6, we combine several source tables to create a single product dimension table.

In his seminal book, *The Data Warehouse Toolkit: The Complete Guide to Dimensional Modeling* (Wiley, 2002), Ralph Kimball writes:

> *The central attraction of the dimensional model of a business is its simplicity.... that simplicity is the fundamental key that allows users to understand databases, and allows software to navigate databases efficiently.*

In a perfect star-schema, there is only one ring or layer of dimensions circling the fact table (as shown in Figure 5.3). However, sometimes it may be desirable to include hierarchical dimension tables, or to link two or more fact tables. This semi-normalized model is called a *snowflake schema*. Figure 5.4 shows a snowflake schema, in which a star schema's dimensions have been normalized to some extent.

In this example, the [SalesDirector] and [SalesVP] tables provide the "hierarchy" for the sales organization. To maintain a star schema, denormalize the tables by combining the fields from the hierarchy tables into a single dimension. The resulting dimension table could be called SalesHierarchy. Using a single dimension (instead of snow-flaked tables) retains the one-hop distance from the fact table, and offers a simpler structure in the event that the model is extended. Specific steps for denormalizing tables are described in Chapter 6.

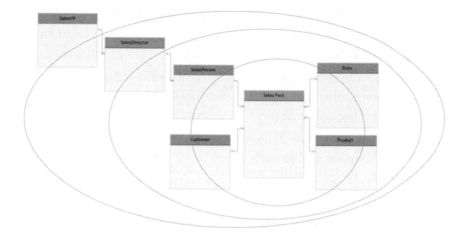

Which Is Better: The Star Schema or the Snowflake Schema?

In theory, QlikView would perform faster using a star schema due to the fact that there is only one hop between any dimension and the fact table. However, empirical tests have shown only marginal differences in performance between the star and snowflake designs. For extensibility, we prefer using the star schema. If the coding required to denormalize your tables is too complex, or if you just prefer the more normalized design, then using a snowflake schema is fine too. However, if performance degrades as your fact table grows, you may need to consider reducing the number of tables in the model. The most important rule to follow is to always keep all the measures in the fact table. Calculations that involve fields from multiple tables can substantially degrade performance in a large dataset.

Since the tables shown in Figures 5.3 and 5.4 are used together for the purpose of analyzing a particular business process—in this case sales—they can be considered a *data mart*. A database that has one or more subject-specific data marts is called a data warehouse. If the data in the data warehouse covers broad categories of a particular business, it's often called an *enterprise data warehouse (EDW)*. Data marts are common implementations of dimensional data models, as are OLAP cubes and some QlikView applications. For relatively small QlikView projects, strict adherence to dimensional modeling techniques is not required. As a best practice, use the dimensional model in your QlikView applications when the data sets are large (to improve performance), or if there are plans to combine data from multiple systems.

We've shown how the dimensional model is simpler than the entity-relationship model, but exactly what makes the dimensional model "optimized" for reporting and analysis?

- All measures are stored in one table (the fact table) and can be easily retrieved and aggregated.

- The fact table is only one "hop" away from any of the dimension tables (in a perfect star schema).

- A single key field defines the relationship between the fact and the dimension table.

- There are no circular references.

These characteristics allow any query to behave in a symmetrical, predictable way. In contrast, the performance of an aggregation query executed on an OLTP database is quite unpredictable: the query might involve only a few tables, or a vast number of tables with complex multi-column relationships.

In summary, all data-driven applications in business can be classified as either *transactional* or *analytical* in nature. Table 5.1 describes the characteristics of each.

TABLE 5.1: Characteristics of Transactional vs. Analytical Applications

	TRANSACTIONAL SOFTWARE	ANALYTICAL SOFTWARE
Examples	ERP systems, POS systems	Reporting/BI systems
Typical data store	RDBMS (relational database management system)	RDBMS, multi-dimensional array storage (cube), RAM
Data model	Entity-relationship	Multi-dimensional
Schema	Normalized	Star schema or Snowflake
Transaction focus	Add/update/insert/delete	Retrieval and aggregation
Transaction size	Small	Large

	TRANSACTIONAL SOFTWARE	ANALYTICAL SOFTWARE
Transaction time horizon	Short (days, weeks, months)	Long (years)
Transaction frequency	Very frequent (data entry frequency)	Occasional (reporting frequency)
User base	Large	Small
User level	Operational only	Operational to strategic

Since QlikView is used to create analytical applications, the multi-dimensional model is the best choice for the data model design. The multi-dimensional model supports the goals that we laid out in the beginning of this chapter for the QlikView data models—it's easy to understand, fast, and scalable.

Next up—a discussion on how data moves from source systems to dimensional structures.

Using ETL to Populate Dimensional Tables

How are tables in a dimensional model populated with data? Complex SQL statements are used to select the correct data elements, perform the required transformations and aggregations (if any), create the new tables, and then insert the data. *ETL* (extract, transform, and load) is the generic term for describing the efforts of moving data from one storage area to another.

Extract, Transform, and Load

The three basic components of ETL are described here.

- **Extract**—The process of selecting the "raw" data from its source, typically a transactional (OLTP) database or other source system, and optionally storing the data in temporary tables to await the "transform" process.

- **Transform**—The process of changing the data to conform to certain rules. Some examples of transformations include:
  - *Cleansing*—Some data elements may require "cleansing" if they contain incorrect or missing data (often called "dirty data" in BI lingo).
  - *Mapping*—Data loaded from multiple sources may need to be conformed to use one set of codes. For example, mapping part numbers to SKU codes.
  - *Additional calculations*—Sometimes called "derived facts," additional metrics may need to be pre-calculated for the purpose of effective analysis at runtime.
- **Load**—The process of inserting the transformed data into the new target tables (or other storage structures).

ETL code is the hammer and nails with which data marts and data warehouses are built. It's possible to use hand-written SQL statements to perform ETL functions, but the code is usually too complex and difficult to maintain. Instead, specialized ETL software can provide the additional benefits of a graphical user interface, extended metadata, data lineage, error recovery, and data validation testing, among others.

To populate the tables in data warehouses (and data marts), ETL procedures are run in "batch" mode (for example, daily or weekly), creating a snapshot of the data in the target tables. The entire ETL process can be managed by one tool and one developer, or in highly complex environments, each step could be controlled by a different developer, or even by a different ETL tool.

As you'll see in the next sections, the work of developing data models in QlikView can vary significantly depending on whether or not the organization's data ecosystem contains a data warehouse.

QlikView in a Data Warehouse Environment

Deploying QlikView in a data warehouse environment can have significant advantages—the ETL processes have already done much of the hard work. Figure 5.5 shows QlikView deployed in a data warehouse environment.

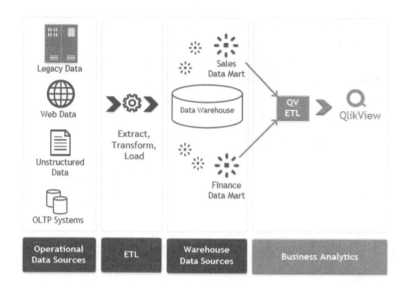

Data available in the data mart tables may have already been mapped and cleansed. Tables that align in a star schema are readily accessible to the QlikView developer to load without much additional transformation. Data management policies often dictate that reporting and analysis be sourced only from the data warehouse, thus restricting developers from accessing the operational data sources directly. This scenario is typical of the large enterprise organization.

The data modeling work can become more complex if the existing tables are not at the correct granularity. If the data in the warehouse has been aggregated up to a certain level, detailed drill-down analysis will not be available. An alternative is to access the data from the source systems, if data management policies allow access. Additional challenges arise if the application requires data from multiple schemas. For example, consider the user story depicted in Figure 5.6.

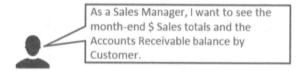

As a Sales Manager, I want to see the month-end $ Sales totals and the Accounts Receivable balance by Customer.

FIGURE 5.6:
A user story requiring data from multiple data marts

Implementing this story could require accessing the $ Sales totals from the Sales data mart, and the Accounts Receivable balance from the Finance data mart. Modeling challenges would include how to correlate month-end $ Sales with the month-end A/R, when sales uses "invoice date," and billing uses "posting date."

QlikView as the Primary ETL Solution

For smaller organizations that do not have the resources to build or manage a data warehouse, the ETL tool built-in to QlikView provides a powerful alternative. Sourcing directly from operational data sources, a developer can use QlikView to perform all of the required ETL processing steps. Figure 5.7 shows QlikView as the primary ETL solution.

FIGURE 5.7:
QlikView in the small-medium business (SMB)

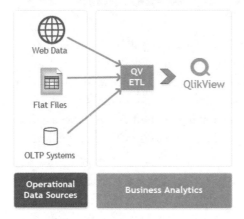

The "start-from-scratch" scenario presents some obvious challenges—complex OLTP systems must be demystified, business rules must be articulated, and dimensional models must be designed—all of which can add significant time to your project.

Faced with these challenges, many developers end up using the same normalized relationships as the ERD. In a small data environment, this may be an easier way to get things done quickly. For larger and more complex applications, using an ERD model can inhibit performance and scalability. To avoid costly rework, we recommend investing the time to create a robust dimensional model for any application that needs to accommodate larger data volumes or more complexity.

Throughout the book, we'll demonstrate data modeling techniques for transforming transactional data into a dimensional star schema.

Designing a Data Model for Sales Analysis

You're finally ready to begin designing the data model for the Sales Analysis application discussed in previous chapters. In this section, you will take a look at how to create each major part of a dimensional model for sales analysis. Based on the user stories, you'll consider the following questions:

- Which part of the sales transaction process is required for the application—orders, invoices, or shipments? All of these? Others?

- Which dimensions and measures are required?

- Where is the data stored? Are there multiple sources?

- Are all the required attributes and measures available in the data source(s)?

As a teaching aide, we're going to "draw" what our model looks like, before we actually write any code. We'll draw the dimension and fact tables and pencil in some of the fields that we'll need for the application. In reality, as you get more familiar with the tools and techniques, you probably won't take such a formal approach. Many developers use QlikView to discover data sources and build the model using trial-and-error techniques. You'll see that QlikView makes it easy to iteratively build your model by offering a straightforward development environment—no logical layers, logical models, or any other tedious metadata scaffolding gets in the way of immediately seeing the results of your script. For demonstration purposes, we'll take the long road and build a straw-man model first, before you start scripting in Chapter 6.

Starting with Stories

Let's consider some of the user stories (similar to use cases) that informed the visualizations that you see in Chapter 4. Figure 5.8 shows three simple user stories.

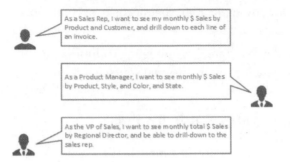

We assume that these are just a few of the user stories collected, and that they have been identified as going into the first release. The first step is to understand and identify the underlying transactions that are the basis of the user stories. In each example, the user wants "$ Sales" grouped by one or more dimensions. What is the "$ Sales" that they're talking about? For the project, we're going to use the Invoice as the core of the model. The next step is to identify the components of the invoice and categorize them as facts or dimensions.

Identify the Dimensions

We know that dimensions are the "who-where-what-when" associated with a business transaction. In general, the concept of an invoice includes a request for payment from a particular customer, for particular products or services, on a specified date. From the stories shown in Figure 5.8, we'll need to sum up the dollar amount requested and group by Dates, Products, Customers, ShipTo Locations, Warehouses, and SalesPersons. The initial model will include dimension tables for each of these components of an invoice. Figure 5.9 shows the beginning stages of the model, with the dimensions placed around a central fact table.

The boxed field names in Figure 5.9 highlight the attributes mentioned in the user stories. Note that the second user story in Figure 5.8 requires additional attributes for Product—so we've added Style, Size, and Color to the dimension.

Each row in the dimension table is identified with a unique value, or "key." In Figure 5.9, notice that each table has an ID field, which acts as the key to link the row in the dimension table to the associated transactions in the fact table.

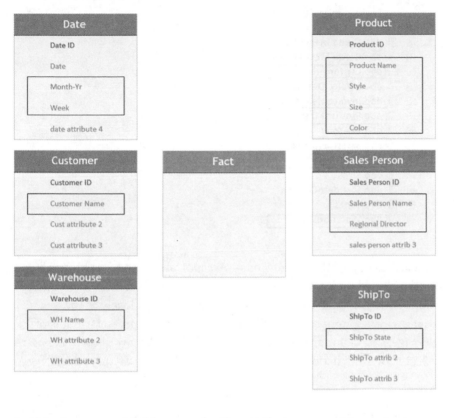

FIGURE 5.9:
Dimensional model—
first draft

In this phase, exact field names for the attributes are not important—generic names are sufficient. At some point in the design process, you'll need to agree on a naming convention and put a strategy in place. Placeholders for possible unknown attributes are shown in each dimension table. As more user stories are included, the attribute fields will begin to get filled in, and more dimension tables may be required.

Now that we've penciled in our initial dimension tables and added a few attributes, let's take a look at the set of source tables that will populate the model. Figure 5.10 shows a list of tables available in the sales database.

FIGURE 5.10: Source tables in the Sales database

It appears that all of the dimensions—except Date—can be easily sourced from the circled tables. Of course, we need to make sure that the required attributes are available in each source table. Looking closely at the [ProductMaster] source table, you'll notice that the required attributes of Style, Size, and Color are not available—only ID fields are shown. Figure 5.11 shows the list of available fields in the [ProductMaster] table.

FIGURE 5.11: Columns in the ProductMaster table

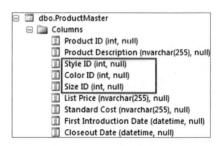

The actual descriptions for Style, Color, and Size are stored elsewhere and the ID fields shown in Figure 5.11 are key fields that point to rows in other tables. In the list of tables previously shown in Figure 5.10, you can see that there are indeed separate tables for Colors, Sizes, and Styles. In Figure 5.12, the tables are shown in a normalized relationship, as stored in the source database.

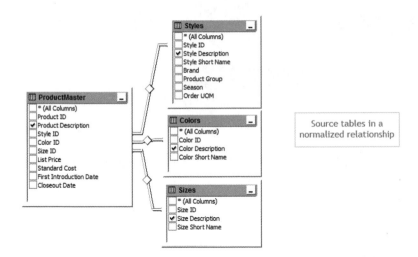

FIGURE 5.12:
Product attributes in
multiple source tables

This is an example of a group of tables that you will "denormalize" (merge) into one target table. In Chapter 6, you'll use code similar to SQL JOIN statements to combine the fields from the four tables into one Product dimension table.

Keep in mind that some of the required attributes may not exist in the OLTP systems. Code tables or other supporting data may be stored outside the system, perhaps in text or Excel files. With QlikView, data can be loaded from multiple sources and formats into a single data model—so there's no need to worry about importing external data into the OLTP system.

We've described the basic tasks of designing the dimension tables: identify the required attributes, find the source data, and determine if any of the source data needs to be merged to complete a dimension. Now on to designing the fact table.

Designing the Fact Table

You now know that fact tables contain the measures of a business transaction and the key fields that link to dimension tables. Since we've already designed the dimension tables, let's start by adding the key fields to the Fact table. Figure 5.13 shows version 2 of the model.

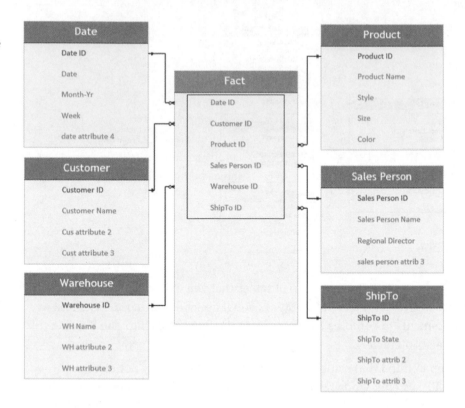

FIGURE 5.13: Data model with keys in the fact table

The next step is the most important part—identifying the required "granularity" of the fact table. The finer the granularity, the more rows in the fact table and the more detail available to the end user. Lower granularity requires fewer rows in the fact table, as transactions are aggregated. From the first user story depicted in Figure 5.8, we'll need to drill down to the individual invoice-line level for sales.

The "line" level is the lowest level for several subject areas of business transactions. The table duo of [Invoice Header] and [Invoice Detail] represent a master/detail table structure that is common among other data processes in the OLTP system. Some other common header/line table pairings are:

- [Order Header] / [Order Lines]
- [Purchase Request Header] / [Purchase Request Lines]
- [Journal Entry Header] / [Journal Entry Lines]
- [Shipment Header] / [Shipment Lines]

In our model, since the lowest level is the individual line item of an invoice, we start by loading the required columns from each row of the [Invoice Detail] table. Columns from the "master" [Invoice Header] table are then added to each row by using a join statement, similar to a standard SQL JOIN (this process is shown in detail in Chapter 6). In this way, the header and lines table are denormalized. The master and detail information that was previously in a one-to-many relationship is merged into one row in the fact table. Figure 5.14 shows the fact table resulting from the [Invoice Header] and [Invoice Detail] tables being merged.

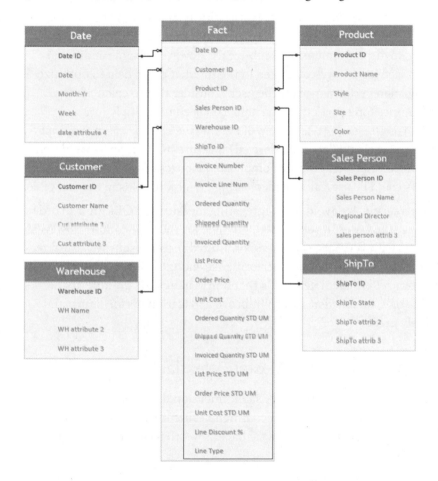

FIGURE 5.14: Invoice Header and Invoice Detail tables merged into the fact table

The fields outlined in red are the measures that already exist in the [Invoice Header] and [Invoice Detail] tables. Remember that the best kind of measures to put in the fact table are numeric and additive. Fields such as [List Price], [Order Price], and [Invoice Quantity] fit that description, but [Invoice Number] and [Invoice Line Num] are a bit peculiar. Neither field is a key that links to a dimension table, and neither field is a cumulative measure. Instead, these fields act as "control" numbers in that they allow you to identify the original lines of an invoice as they appeared in the transaction system.

In this model, aggregations of the measures are unnecessary since we are required to maintain the ability to drill down to invoice line level (based on the user stories). Instead of pre-aggregating the data in the model, we'll use the front-end GUI objects in QlikView to sum up the line-level metrics, on the fly, to display dimensional sub-totals. However, if some additional line-level metrics are pre-calculated in the script, it could help to optimize the application performance for the user. Consider that to calculate the extended price for a particular line item, you need to multiply [Ordered Price] by [Invoice Quantity]. Instead of making the calculation in the front-end, you can pre-calculate this "derived" measure in the script. In addition to "Extended Price," other more complicated metrics involving costs and discounts could be pre-calculated, creating even more fields in the fact table.

As a general rule, we avoid pre-aggregating measures in QlikView in order to preserve the lowest level of detail possible for the application. However, in projects with very large data sets (or limited server resources), the size of the fact table could degrade performance enough to require some pre-aggregations. Pre-calculated fields that don't change the granularity of the fact table offer an efficient way to improve application performance and are widely used.

The Importance of the Master Calendar

As stated earlier, a source for the Date dimension does not exist in the source system. In this case, we recommend generating a Date dimension using the existing dates in the fact table. It's worth a closer look at why this concept is important.

Date dimensions have a special role in analytics. Transactions that make up our data are usually recorded on a daily basis. At the same time, we need to analyze trends using weeks, months, quarters, or years. In order to use those date attributes as chart dimensions, we need to have them represented in our data model as individual fields.

Furthermore, many companies manage their finances using a "Fiscal Calendar"—an alternative calendar with a different beginning for a fiscal year and a different way of managing fiscal periods. In those environments, Fiscal Year, Fiscal Quarter, and Fiscal Period are different than a (Gregorian) Calendar Year, Calendar Quarter, and Calendar Month. Different parts of the business gravitate to one of the two calendars—while corporate management and finance departments live by the fiscal calendar, sales and operations often prefer the regular (Gregorian) calendar because they work with customers, suppliers, and employees who don't have as much interest in the matters of financial reporting.

Date values associated with fiscal calendars also need to be stored as data fields to be used in visualizations. Lastly, many important metrics include comparisons such as current period to prior period, or current period to the same period in a prior year, or comparing the last rolling 12 months to the previous rolling 12 months, and so on. In order to facilitate these comparisons, we recommend using flag fields (the flag is set to 1 when the corresponding condition is true, and it is set to zero or NULL when the condition is false). These flags are typically stored in the Master Calendar.

To summarize, Master Calendar is a Dimension table that consists of the (main) Date field and all the attributes associated with dates—year, month, quarter, and fiscal calendar attributes, as well as special flags that simplify the task of comparing different periods.

Master Calendar can be loaded from an ERP system when it's available, or it can be generated in the load script using the main Date field and a handful of QlikView date functions. The logic for generating a Master Calendar is pretty standard, and it's common for companies to store the "Master Calendar" routine in a standardized external text file for inclusion in QlikView scripts.

Since you are just in the beginning of your QlikView education, you don't know all the techniques that need to be used to generate a Master Calendar. Thankfully, the trusted consultants from Natural Synergies have created a common routine that you can simply use as is. We will describe the process of generating the Master Calendar in Chapter 10, when you learn more about advanced scripting techniques.

Tips Before You Start Scripting

Before you begin to code, or "script," your data model, there are a few tasks that can help the development process go smoothly.

Verify Access to Data Sources

■ Install database query tools if needed.

■ Verify that you have authorization to access the databases and have been granted the appropriate permissions to browse the schema and select rows from tables/views.

■ Install the database driver(s) for your environment.

Find the SMEs (Subject Matter Experts)

■ Identify the people who understand the data sources.

■ Identify the people who understand the business use-cases.

■ Make sure they are available to answer questions during development.

Download the QlikView Manuals

■ QlikView manuals are provided in soft copy only. Look for the PDF files in the installation directory, or download from QlikView's website before you get started—you'll refer to them often.

In Chapter 6, we'll demonstrate the technical steps for implementing a dimensional model in QlikView.

6

Developing a Data Load Script for Sales Analysis

If you are reading this chapter voluntarily, you must be a technical person who enjoys the process of getting your hands dirty and writing code. And if you aren't that sort of person, don't worry! QlikView is not as technical as you may think. In fact, it's non-technical, for the most part.

In this chapter, you look under the hood to see how the magic happens. You'll get to prepare that magical associative data model that allows your users to navigate data with ease. You will build the foundation that allows them to paint the world in green, white, and gray.

At this point, you know the business requirements from Chapter 3. You even know what kind of visualizations you are going to develop, from Chapter 4 (which is, by the way, a luxury that you don't usually have in real life). Now, buckle up and let's load some data!

Load Script and Script Editor

As you know by now, QlikView needs to load data into its associative data model, which in turn will be loaded into memory for visual analysis. The process of loading the data is specified in the QlikView load script, which is managed in the **Script Editor**.

Chapter 5 mentioned the term ETL (extraction, transformation, and load). The QlikView script language covers all three parts of ETL. In a mature QlikView environment, you may choose to separate the three processes into distinct layers (there are merits to doing so, and we will cover those best practices in Chapter 10), or you may choose to perform your data load in a single step, for simplicity. In both cases, you will be using the same script language to describe the processes.

For the purpose of the simple exercises in this chapter, we will be combining our E, T, and L in a single cohesive load script. In Chapter 10 and 14, we demonstrate some of the techniques that are commonly used for separating extraction, transformation, and load into three separate stages.

Script Editor Basics in QlikView

In this section, you learn the first steps of creating a load script in QlikView:

- How to create a new document in QlikView
- How to open the **Script Editor**
- How to connect to a database
- How to load a single table from a database

Creating a New Document

In QlikView, you follow a familiar Microsoft process for creating a new document: using the menu option **File ▶ New** or using the keyboard shortcut Ctrl+N, or using the **New** button on the toolbar.

By default, QlikView offers a **Getting Started** wizard every time a new document is created. New users of QlikView might find the wizard helpful in creating a simple load script and adding basic charts. However, most developers quickly learn the advantages of creating scripts and charts manually—there are far greater options and settings to choose from. Since the **Getting Started** wizard provides limited features, we suggest disabling it from the **Settings ▶ User Preferences** menu. At this point, however, it's sufficient to exit the wizard using the **Cancel** button.

Once the new document is created, it's recommended you name and save it in the appropriate folder right away, before writing the script. This step is important, because it lets you establish the path to your document prior to developing your load script. You will see very soon why this is so important.

Setting Your Saving Preferences

If you haven't done so yet, we recommend setting your saving preferences to avoid losing any of your work. Navigate to the **Save** tab from **Settings ▶ User Preferences**, and check the **Save Before Reload** box. Saving before reload is important because you may easily lose some of your recent changes if your script run fails for any reason.

We also recommend checking both radio buttons in the **Save Auto Recover Info** section, which defaults to saving **After Reload** and **Every 30 Minutes**. You may adjust these settings at any time.

Opening the Script Editor

Next, open the **Script Editor** by opening **File ▶ Edit Script,** or by pressing Ctrl+E, or using the toolbar button **Edit Script**, located to the right of the printer icon.

Script Editor (see Figure 6.1) is a typical Microsoft-style application, with its own menu (A), toolbar (B), and a set of specialized tools at the bottom (D).

This list explains the most important highlights that you should know at this point, without boring you with the exhaustive list of all features:

- The main white area in the middle (C) houses the script. The 10 SET statements are automatically generated for each new document, and they represent your local settings for date, time, and currency formats.

FIGURE 6.1:
QlikView Script Editor

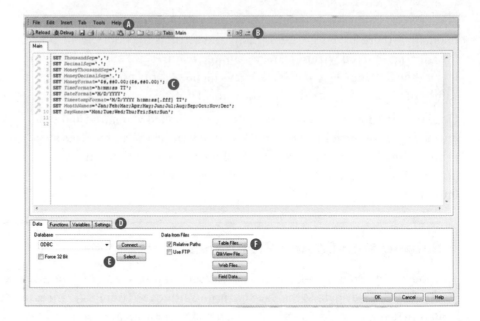

- If you know your syntax and enjoy the process of typing your script manually, you can certainly do it—for hard-core programmers, it offers hours of endless fun. Alternatively, you can generate your LOAD statements using the wizards that can be invoked with the buttons at the bottom of the screen (D).

- The two buttons under the **Database** section on the left (E) can be used to invoke wizards for connecting to a database and selecting data from a database.

- The four buttons on the right (F) offer wizards for loading all other, non-database, types of data—text files of all kinds, QlikView files, web files, and data from previously loaded data fields.

- The other three tabs at the bottom provide easy access to functions, variables, and settings. The importance of these tools is secondary at this point.

We will describe some of the other important features of the **Script Editor** later. Now, let's get ready to connect to the database.

Exercise 6.1: Create a New Document and Open the Script Editor

1. Open QlikView from the Windows Start menu.

2. Select File ▶ New from the menu, or press Ctrl+N, or use the toolbar button New.

3. Cancel out of the Getting Started wizard.

4. Save the new document in the subfolder `\Data Models` and give it a name `Sales Analysis Data XX.QVW`, where XX is your initials.

5. Open the Script Editor, either from the File menu, by pressing Ctrl+E, or by using the toolbar button Edit Script located next to the printer icon.

Extra Credit: Disable the "Getting Started Wizard"

If you feel comfortable navigating the menu unsupervised, go ahead and disable the wizard from popping up every time. This setting is on the main screen of the General tab in Settings ▶ User Preferences. If you are in the Script Editor, you will need to exit it to access this menu. When you are done modifying the settings, you can reopen the Script Editor.

Connecting to a Database

QlikView supports two modes of connecting to databases—using ODBC data sources or using OLE DB data providers. Depending on a specific database, one or the other mechanism can be considered as preferred, but both protocols should perform reasonably well with most common databases. In our practice, we have found that ODBC connections work faster when connecting to an IBM DB2 database running on an iSeries platform. Conversely, OLE DB seems to perform better when connecting to Microsoft databases.

Using an ODBC data source requires an existing system data source that stores the ODBC connection details for your database. System data sources are configured outside of QlikView, in the Windows program **ODBC Data Source Administrator**. You can access this program via

Control Panel ▶ Administrative Tools ▶ Data Sources (ODBC).
QlikView also includes a shortcut to the ODBC Data Source Administrators (for 64-bit and 32-bit), from the **Script Editor** menu: the **Tools** option.

32-Bit or 64-Bit?

Even though 64-bit operating systems have existed for many years and practically dominate today, many database vendors never developed 64-bit ODBC and OLE DB drivers to their databases. For example, MS Access may be equipped with either a 32-bit or a 64-bit ODBC driver, depending on the specific version.

Unfortunately, 64-bit software programs cannot communicate directly with 32-bit drivers, because they operate in different memory spaces. For quite some time, this problem used to be annoying for QlikView users who had to connect to their databases via 32-bit drivers.

Fortunately, QlikView offered an elegant solution that allows "the impossible"—64-bit QlikView software can communicate with a 32-bit driver. You simply need to specify the correct type of connector when defining the connection.

Using OLE DB is somewhat easier, since you only need to select the OLE DB provider from the list of available providers and point to the location of your database. This chapter uses the OLE DB connection and the provider called **Microsoft Jet 4.0 OLE DB Provider**. It's a 32-bit driver, so you need to use the checkbox **Force 32 Bit** (assuming that you are using a 64-bit version of QlikView).

Exercise 6.2: Connect to a Database

1. Open the Script Editor if necessary.

2. Under the Database section at the bottom, select OLE DB as the protocol. If you are working on a 64-bit machine (most likely, you are), then ensure that Force 32 Bit is checked.

3. Click on the Connect button.

4. Select Microsoft Jet 4.0 OLE DB Provider and click Next. (If you can't find this OLE DB provider, try checking and unchecking the Force 32 Bit checkbox. If you don't have the driver, you may need to download it from the Microsoft site and install it on your machine.)

5. Locate the database `Sales.mdb` in the subfolder `\Data\Database`. This subfolder is located in the supporting materials that you downloaded earlier (see "Preparing your Work Environment" in the Introduction).

6. Click the Test Connection button. You should receive a Test Connection Succeeded confirmation message.

7. Click OK to exit the wizard. You will see a long line of settings generated by the wizard:

```
OLEDB CONNECT32 TO [Provider=Microsoft.Jet.OLEDB.4.0;User ID=Admin;Data
    Source=C:\Users\Oleg\Dropbox\QlikView Book\Electronic Materials\
    Data\Database\Sales.mdb;Mode=Share Deny None;Extended Properties="";
    Jet OLEDB:System database="";Jet OLEDB:Registry Path="";
    Jet OLEDB:Database Password="";Jet OLEDB:Engine Type=5;Jet OLEDB:
    Database Locking Mode=1;Jet OLEDB:Global Partial Bulk Ops=2;
    Jet OLEDB:Global Bulk Transactions=1;Jet OLEDB:New Database
    Password="";Jet OLEDB:Create System Database=False;Jet OLEDB:Encrypt
    Database=False;Jet OLEDB:Don't Copy Locale on Compact=False;
    Jet OLEDB:Compact Without Replica Repair=False;Jet OLEDB:SFP=False];
```

There is no need to understand or memorize all the settings. They are always generated by the wizard.

NOTE

Loading a Database Table

Once the database connection is established, you can use the **Select** wizard to load data from the database.

The **Select** wizard (see Figure 6.2) shows all the existing **Tables**, **Views**, **Synonyms**, **System Tables**, and **Aliases** from your database. It's usually enough to select **Tables** and **Views** (A).

- To get started, select a single table from the list of **Database Tables** (B).

- You can ask for all fields (specified by the asterisk symbol *) or select individual fields from the list (C). Use Shift+click to select a range of fields or Ctrl+click to select multiple fields individually.

- The bottom section offers a preview of the script statement that will get generated (D).

- **Column, Row,** and **Structured** are the three possible formats of structuring the script statement (E). We recommend **Column** as the most practical option—with this structure, each column is presented in a separate row, which makes the statement easier to read.

FIGURE 6.2:
The Create Select
Statement window

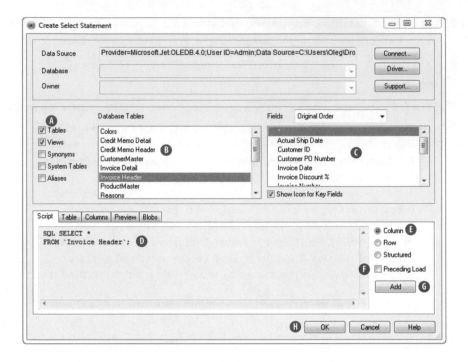

- The **Preceding Load** checkbox (F) offers an important feature of adding a LOAD statement in front of the SQL SELECT statement. At this point, remember that you should always keep it checked. We explain the importance of preceding load later in this chapter.

- Once all the settings are configured, you can click **Add** to generate the script statement and continue creating additional statements for other tables (G), or you can press **OK** and exit the wizard (H).

Exercise 6.3: Load a Database Table

1. Make sure that the cursor is located at the end of the script, in the beginning of a new line.

2. Click the **Select** button.

3. Select the Invoice Header table in the list of tables.

4. Ensure that the **Preceding Load** checkbox is checked. Leave the rest of the default settings unchanged.

5. Click **OK** to exit the wizard. You should see a LOAD statement, followed by a SQL SELECT statement.

Anatomy of a QlikView SQL Select Statement

If you completed the previous exercise, you should be looking at a load script that consists of three statements: the CONNECT statement described earlier and two new statements:

- The LOAD statement.
- The SQL SELECT statement

For readers with a SQL background, the statement should look familiar—it's the standard SELECT statement, with the addition of the word SQL to the beginning.

The syntax of SQL SELECT in QlikView is exactly the same as the standard SQL syntax—it can even include the same conditions and clauses (such as WHERE, GROUP BY, ORDER BY, and SUB-SELECT statements). You can literally copy your favorite SQL SELECT statements from your native database clients and paste them into QlikView, with the addition of the prefix SQL in front of SELECT. These statements will be performed on your database and the results will be passed back to QlikView by the OLE DB provider or ODBC driver.

The LOAD statement in front of the SELECT statement is called a *preceding load*. A preceding load consists of the keyword LOAD and a list of fields, terminated by a semicolon, without any reference to the source of the data. When no source of data is explicitly specified, the LOAD is considered "preceding" and the data is assumed to be supplied by the following SELECT (or another LOAD) statement.

We discuss the merits of preceding loads later, but now let's describe why you need to use a preceding load in front of a SQL SELECT statement.

The SELECT statement belongs to the database. It will be taken by QlikView as is, packaged and sent to your database via the ODBC or OLE DB connection, and it will be evaluated and performed on your database. The syntax of the SELECT statement is the standard SQL syntax that can be understood by your database. None of the QlikView-specific functions or syntax constructions can be included in the SELECT statement, because this statement will be performed on the database and not in QlikView.

Many databases have limitations applied to field names—sometimes field names have to be relatively short, or can only support uppercase letters. You may want to rename the abbreviated codes into human-readable field names using proper case.

Preceding a SELECT statement with LOAD provides an opportunity to rename the fields, independently from the database limitations, and to use any QlikView functions that are not part of the SQL toolset.

Excluding Fields from a Preceding LOAD vs. SELECT

If certain fields are present in a SELECT statement but aren't part of the preceding LOAD, these fields will be extracted from the database and brought into QlikView, and then dropped when the preceding LOAD is being processed. So technically, if you need to exclude certain fields, it's enough to remove them from the preceding LOAD. For large databases, however, it's advisable to remove unnecessary fields from both statements, LOAD and SELECT, in order to avoid wasting your database and network resources processing unused data.

Later, you learn additional benefits of using preceding loads in a QlikView script, but now let's load a few more tables into the data set, using the techniques that you just learned.

Exercise 6.4: Add More Tables from the Database

1. Ensure that your Script Editor is open and your cursor is positioned at the end of the script, in the beginning of a new line.

2. Add the following database tables using the Select wizard:

   - InvoiceDetail

   - ProductMaster

   - Styles

   - Sizes

   - Colors

   - CustomerMaster

   - SalesHierarchy

3. Locate the Reload toolbar button and run the script.

When you run your script, QlikView will interpret it, validate the syntax, and, assuming that everything is correct, load the data into its internal *associative database*. You will see the **Script Execution Progress** dialog, with the details of the load process.

Organizing Your Script

They say that bad habits die hard, which is why we want to introduce you to good habits of QlikView scripting very early. The following material may be considered housekeeping, and yet using or neglecting these simple techniques can set apart a professional from an amateur.

Using Explicit Table Names

Professional programmers always prefer to be explicit in everything they do. While QlikView scripting can hardly be considered "programming," we still believe that the habit of being explicit is a good one.

For starters, let's talk about table names. Each table that you load into QlikView will get a name. If you don't specify one explicitly, QlikView will assign a default name. In most cases, the name of the source table will get assigned. Sometimes it's fine for your needs, and sometimes the names are too cryptic or simply difficult to use. Following the best practice of being explicit, you should always assign table names manually.

To do so, add the desired name of the table, with a colon at the end, directly before the LOAD statement:

```
InvoiceHeader:
LOAD `Actual Ship Date`,
     `Customer ID`,
  . . .
```

Table names, as well as field names in QlikView, typically consist of letters and numbers. If the name should have a space or a special symbol, it needs to be enclosed in square brackets [ ]. The common convention is not to use special characters in the table names, in order to avoid the need for square brackets. It is also quite common to use so-called "CamelCase," which involves capitalizing the first letter of each word in a name that consists of several words—for example, InvoiceHeader.

Exercise 6.5: Add Table Names for All Tables Loaded So Far

Identify the beginning of each LOAD statement and add the corresponding table names in front of the loads, placing a semicolon after the name. Avoid spaces and special characters in the table names. Your tables should be named as follows: InvoiceHeader, InvoiceDetail, Products, Styles, Colors, Customers, and SalesHierarchy.

NOTE You may use the **Search** feature to look for the keyword LOAD. The **Search** functionality is very intuitive; we'll let you discover it on your own.

Using Comments in QlikView Scripts

One of the first things programmers learn about a new language is how to write comments. Comments are extremely useful for many purposes:

- Documenting the logic of your script.
- Keeping track of changes.
- Making certain sections of your script more visible and easily recognizable.
- Disabling segments of your script temporarily.
- Excluding certain fields from the data load, while keeping track of the field name for possible later use.

Like many other scripting languages, QlikView supports the following methods of inserting comments in the script:

```
// Single-line comment — everything from the double-slash
// to the end of the line will be considered a comment

/*
Multi —
line
comment.
Any text between the opening sign "slash-asterisk" and the closing
    "asterisk-slash" will be considered a comment
*/

REM *** any text between the keyword REM (remark) and the following
    semicolon will be considered a comment;
```

Single-line comments are useful for brief annotations in script. Multiline comments are handy when there is a need to disable large fragments of script temporarily, or for large full-page documentation comments. REM can be handy in front of a single LOAD statement—the whole statement becomes a comment.

Now take a look at the script you've created so far. Even though you just started, the script is already getting long, and it looks rather monotonous. If you need to find a specific LOAD statement in the script, it might be quite difficult. You might have to scan your whole script and read it carefully before you find something specific. Adding comments, surrounded by bold lines, may help locate sections of the script more easily:

```
//==========================================
// LOAD Invoice Header
//==========================================
```

Let's enhance the existing script with comments that will make each LOAD more visible. In addition, you will use the technique of commenting to exclude a field or two from the load. When you know in advance that certain fields are not necessary, you can comment out the field.

If you scan the script, you may notice that the field [List Price] exists in two tables—InvoiceDetail and Products. QlikView doesn't deal well with this duplication. To avoid any unnecessary collisions, we will remove one of the two versions for this field. For our purposes, we can use the [List Price] from InvoiceDetail and exclude the field from Products.

When there is a need to disable large blocks of code temporarily, QlikView Script Editor offers nice tools to comment/uncomment multiple lines. Highlight the code, right-click, and select **Comment** or **Uncomment** from the context menu. If you prefer keyboard shortcuts, you can use Ctrl+K+C to comment and Ctrl+K+U to uncomment the highlighted script.

Exercise 6.6: Add Comments to the Script

1. Locate the beginning of each LOAD statement and insert three lines of comments, similar to the example provided earlier in this section. Describe each load in your own words.

2. **Important:** Locate the LOAD statement for Products and comment out the field [List Price], both in the LOAD statement and in the SQL statement.

3. **Save** and **Reload** your script again.

Use **Search** to locate the fields in the script.

Dividing Load Scripts into Tabs

Load scripts can get quite long when all the elements of ETL are added. The QlikView **Script Editor** allows dividing the script into *tabs*. Tabs allow you to separate the script into manageable blocks. The goal of using tabs is to simplify the task of managing long, complicated scripts.

Tabs are managed within the **Tab** menu. You can create, rename, and delete a tab. You can also promote or demote tabs, which means moving the tabs to the left or to the right in the list. The tabs are always executed in the same order—from left to right—hence promoting or demoting a tab will result in changing the logical order of executing the script.

You don't have to separate your script into tabs, but it's extremely useful. Some commonly used conventions:

- The **Main** tab of the script remains reserved for the most basic settings and a database connection string, if there is only one connection in the script.

- Insert a separate tab with the documentation about the script, including the history of changes.

- Each logical unit of the script is presented in a separate tab.

- End the script with a **Cleanup** tab, where all unnecessary tables, fields, and variables can be dropped before the script is finished.

For the current script that you've just created, three tabs would be appropriate:

- The **Main** tab, for the basic settings and the database connection string.

- The **Sales** tab, for the two LOAD statements—Invoice Header and Invoice Detail.

- The **Dimensions** tab, for all other tables.

Exercise 6.7: Separate the Script into Tabs

Using the Tab menu, create two additional tabs—**Sales** and **Dimensions**—and then use Cut (Ctrl+X) and Paste (Ctrl+V) to move the appropriate segments of code into these sections. Make sure that you move both the entire LOAD statement and the entire SQL SELECT statement together.

As an alternative, you can experiment with the menu option Tab ► Insert Tab at Cursor. This option can create a new tab and move the script that is located after your cursor position, eliminating the need for moving the segments of the script manually.

If you end up with a mess, delete all the LOAD statements and repeat the exercises of loading these tables, already within the correct tabs.

NOTE

Structured Look of the Script

Keeping the script structured greatly improves its ease of reading. You can use tabulation to indent certain portions of the script that need to appear as a separate logical unit (for example, the contents of the FOR loop, or the contents of the IF … THEN statement). Similarly, it helps to develop your own preferred "look and feel" for your load scripts and even individual LOAD statements. By default, the QlikView wizard generates the statement in a certain way. For example:

```
LOAD `Invoice Number`,
    `Invoiced Quantity`,
    `Invoiced Quantity STD UM`,
    ...
    `U/M`,
    `Unit Cost`;
SQL SELECT *
FROM `Invoice Detail`;
```

Notice a few distinct issues with this structure:

- Each field on the list appears in a separate line, which makes it convenient to add or remove fields. However, the first field is listed right after the keyword LOAD, which makes that field hard to access.

- The closing semicolon is always attached to the last line in the statement. If you need to make changes or comment out the last line, you may accidentally comment out the semicolon.

Instead, we recommend that you use the following structure:

- All the keywords begin from the beginning of the line.
- All the field names and table names are tabulated, each in a separate line.
- The ending semicolon is always alone on a separate line.

Once you get used to a certain look and feel of a statement, it becomes much easier to spot any problems in the script:

```
LOAD
    `Invoice Number`,
    `Invoiced Quantity`,
    `Invoiced Quantity STD UM`,
    ...
    `U/M`,
    `Unit Cost`
    ;
SQL SELECT
    *
FROM
    `Invoice Detail`
;
```

Extra Credit: Add Structure to the LOAD Statements

If you share our passion for a well-structured look and feel for your script, take a few minutes to rearrange the LOAD and SELECT statements to the unified look presented here.

Basic Anatomy of the Load Script

Since you are now familiar with a few QlikView script statements, this list summarizes some basic facts about QlikView scripts:

- A QlikView script is simply plain text. The QlikView **Script Editor** provides tools and wizards that help generate the syntax, but at the end of the day, it's still just text.

- You can copy snippets of script from one app to another, or you can copy complex SQL statements directly from your database clients, where you can write and debug your SQL directly against your database.

- You probably noticed that script statements always end in a semicolon and therefore multiline statements are allowed, with no need for special line terminating symbols. This rule has a few minor exceptions that you will study later.

- QlikView commands, functions, and other "reserved words" are not case sensitive—you can capitalize your commands in any possible way (LOAD, load, Load, and loaD will all result in the same action). *However, the field names and table names are case sensitive.*

- You may have noticed that some field names are enclosed in square brackets [ ] and some aren't. The rule is to enclose in square brackets any field names that include any special symbols or spaces. So, any field names that consist of multiple words would definitely be enclosed in square brackets. Some ODBC or OLE DB drivers may use double quotes or grave accents instead. These three symbols are accepted in QlikView and they are treated equally. Once the data is in QlikView, it's common to use square brackets for table and field names.

- The script statements are executed sequentially, in the order of tabs, from left to right. Within each section, the script is executed from top to bottom, with the only exception of preceding loads.

  - Since a preceding LOAD statement uses data provided by the next statement, the script will read all the preceding loads until the next non-preceding LOAD or SELECT statement is identified, and then perform all the preceding loads, moving from the bottom up.

  - After that, the script execution will resume the normal top-to-bottom order.

- Each SELECT or LOAD statement includes a list of fields, separated by comma. Notice that each field in the list needs to have a comma after it, except for the last field.

From our experience, the most common "mysterious" syntax errors that beginners experience with QlikView script are:

- A missing or extra comma. Once you begin adding fields to or removing fields from the list, it's common to forget to add a comma when it's necessary, or to leave the comma after the field that just become last in the list.

- A missing semicolon at the end of a statement. This error is relatively easy to spot, unless the semicolon is missing at the end of a tab. In this case, the spell checker can't find the error and the error may appear as an ODBC or OLE DB error coming back from the database.

- A multiline comment that starts with the /* sign but doesn't have the closing */ sign. The **Script Editor** makes it look like the only script that is affected by the comment field is the remaining text in the current tab. In reality, the rest of the script on all remaining tabs becomes commented out.

Using the Table Viewer and Understanding the Data Model

So far, you've developed a very basic script and made it look professional, using the best practices of keeping the script organized. When you ran the script, the data was loaded into QlikView. Now you can look at the results of your work and examine the data model that you just created.

To view data models, QlikView provides a tool called the **Table Viewer**. It displays the graphical representation of the data model that was created by your script.

The graphical diagram in Figure 6.3 shows a number of tables (InvoiceDetail, InvoiceHeader, and so on) with lines connecting them. The linking lines point to the fields in the linked tables that have identical field names, and this is not a coincidence. QlikView builds a link between two or more tables when these tables share an identical field name.

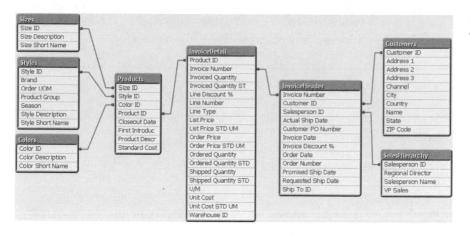

It's important to understand that QlikView doesn't know what fields represent the true "key fields" in your database tables. The linking is only happening due to the identical field names.

Remember that you eliminated the duplication of the field List Price? If you didn't, QlikView would have created extra links based on these identical fields in different tables, and the data model would include wrong associations and could produce unpredictable results.

Let's verify the existing links in the data model:

- InvoiceHeader is linked to InvoiceDetail based on [Invoice Number].

- Products is linked to InvoiceDetail based on [Product ID].

- Styles, Sizes, and Colors are linked to Products by their corresponding ID fields.

- SalesHierarchy is linked to InvoiceHeader based on [Salesperson ID].

- Customers is linked to InvoiceHeader based on [Customer ID].

All of these links appear to be logically correct, which is encouraging. We are likely to get an accurate data model with all the data properly linked and associated. If you saw any links that were based on measures or attributes, such as List Price or Channel, then this could be a warning sign pointing at a possible data structure issue that needs to be resolved.

Using the data model viewer in the process of developing the load script is instrumental for identifying possible problems in the script.

Exercise 6.8: Open the Table Viewer

Select File ► Table Viewer, or press Ctrl+T, or click the Table Viewer toolbar button at the end of the Design toolbar. (It looks like three connected tables.)

What you see might look different than Figure 6.3:

- It might simply be that your arrangement is different. It may take a bit of rearranging to position the tables in a similar way. When you are done rearranging tables, click on the OK button, and your rearrangement will be saved.

- Second, if you are looking at a much more tangled schema, verify that you indeed commented out the field [List Price] in the previous exercise. It could also be that you are loading additional or different tables from the database. Double-check your script and ensure that you are only loading eight tables—InvoiceHeader, InvoiceDetails, ProductMaster, Styles, Sizes, Colors, CustomerMaster, and SalesHierarchy.

Resolving Simple Challenges in Data Load

So far, you loaded a few simple tables while carefully avoiding duplication and eliminating unnecessary fields. QlikView scripting seems very straightforward—the sky is blue and the sun is shining. However, it is not always this easy when dealing with real-life data. Many times, tables may have multiple identical fields, which can cause unnecessary links to be created between tables, producing an extremely tangled data model that may ultimately be incorrect.

In simple cases, when the duplication of identical fields should be avoided, you can use one of a few simple techniques to clean up the data model—renaming or eliminating certain fields from the load. In more complex cases, when keeping multiple identical fields in multiple tables is truly necessary, you have to implement more complex data modeling techniques. You learn about those in Chapters 10 and 14.

Introducing Synthetic Keys and Circular References

Synthetic keys and *circular references* are the two worst enemies of any QlikView developer. Both issues point at existing problems in the data model that QlikView can't tolerate. In other words, synthetic keys and circular references tell you that one of the two basic rules of QlikView data modeling was violated:

- **Rule #1: Any two or more tables cannot share more than one identical field.**

   When two or more tables share two or more fields, QlikView will build composite keys that combine multiple shared keys, to ensure that every link between tables is always based on a single field. These artificial composite keys generated by QlikView are called synthetic keys. QlikView applications with synthetic keys will work, and may even be accurate in some cases.

   Not all synthetic keys are necessarily bad. For example, a synthetic key that is generated as part of the `IntervalMatch LOAD` is necessary in that situation. (You learn about `IntevalMatch` in Chapter 14). It is recommended, however, that you avoid having synthetic keys for a variety of good reasons that will become more evident as you learn more about QlikView.

- **Rule #2: There should be one and only one way to get from any point A to any point B in the data model.**

   When there are multiple ways to navigate from one field to another in a data model, this is called a circular reference. A data model with a circular reference always includes a circle of interconnected tables. QlikView cannot operate with a data model that includes a circular reference since it would lead to ambiguities in logical evaluation. In order to avoid the circle, QlikView will artificially break (the technical term is *loosen*) some of the links. In most cases, the modified data model will produce inaccurate results. Therefore, developers should eliminate circular references explicitly by determining what links should be removed to "break the circle."

NOTE	Circular references often go hand in hand with synthetic keys, but can also occur independently of each other. You may see a circular reference between a number of tables without having a synthetic key, and vice versa—synthetic keys may appear without circular references.

Also, we should repeat that synthetic keys are not always "wrong." However, their existence often is a symptom of another underlying problem.

You will experience the impact of synthetic keys and circular references when you add more tables to your data model.

Exercise 6.9: Add the Warehouses Table to the Data Model

1. Open the **Script Editor**, position your cursor at the end of the script in the **Dimensions** tab, and add one more table to the data model. Follow the process of loading data from a database table and select the table called Warehouses.

2. Remove the unnecessary Address fields and only keep [Warehouse ID], Description, Country, City, and State.

3. After you run the script, you will see an error message informing you about the circular reference. Click **OK** to close it.

4. Navigate to the **data model viewer** (**Table Viewer** in QlikView) and examine the data model. With a bit of rearranging, it should look like the schema in Figure 6.4.

FIGURE 6.4:

The data model with a circular reference

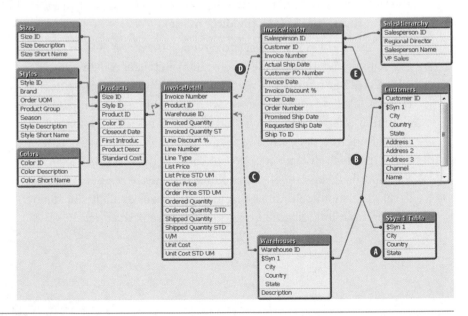

Let's examine the data model in Figure 6.4. In addition to the nine tables that you loaded so far, QlikView added another table called $Syn 1 Table (A). This is the synthetic key that was created because two tables had more than one identical field. The Customers and Warehouses tables have three fields in common—City, Country, and State.

The second problem is the circular reference that was formed in the data model. Four tables are related to each other via multiple paths: Customers is linked to Warehouses via the synthetic key table (B), the Warehouses table is linked to InvoiceDetail (C), which is in turn linked to InvoiceHeader (D), and finally InvoiceHeader is linked back to Customers (E). The links between the four tables create a closed loop, therefore causing the circular reference.

Both problems were caused by the fact that the Warehouses table has fields with the same names as the Customers table. Obviously, these fields have different meanings and they don't need to be named identically—the country, city, and state of a warehouse have nothing to do with the country, city, and state of a customer.

Avoiding Synthetic Keys by Renaming Fields

When different fields are named identically, the solution to the problem described in the preceding section is very easy. You simply need to rename the fields to avoid unnecessary linking. In this case, it's enough to add the word "Warehouse" to the fields Country, State and City in the Warehouses table, to avoid the issue.

The QlikView syntax for renaming fields is the same as in SQL:

```
LOAD
     [Old Field Name 1] AS [New Field Name 1],
     [Old Field Name 2] AS [New Field Name 2],
     . . .
```

Similarly, when loading data from multiple sources, key fields might be named differently in different source tables. In these cases, you can use renaming to enforce data linking for a field that was named differently.

In the following exercise you rename three fields.

Exercise 6.10: Avoid Circular References by Renaming Fields

1. Locate the LOAD statement for the Warehouses table and rename the three fields that are common to the Customers table—Country, City, and State. You do this by adding the word Warehouse in front of the name:

```
Warehouses:
LOAD
        `Warehouse ID`,
        Description as Warehouse,
        City        as [Warehouse City],
        Country     as [Warehouse Country],
        State       as [Warehouse State]
;
SQL SELECT
        *
FROM
        Warehouses
;
```

2. Reload your script and examine the result. There should be no synthetic keys and no circular references in the data model.

Using the QUALIFY and UNQUALIFY Commands

Occasionally, many fields in a given table may need to be renamed to avoid duplication of names. For this purpose, you may find the qualification feature useful. Qualification results in adding the table name in front of the field name for every field that gets loaded, separated by a period. The QUALIFY statement turns qualification on for a list of fields or for all fields, depending on the syntax. The UNQUALIFY statement turns qualification off. For example:

QUALIFY *fieldlist;	Turns qualification on for the list of fields.
QUALIFY *;	Turns qualification on for all fields.
UNQUALIFY *fieldlist;	Turns qualification off for the list of fields.
UNQUALIFY *;	Turns qualification off for all fields.

Naturally, if you need to qualify all attributes of a table, you would turn qualification on for all fields and then turn it off for the *key field*, to facilitate the links to the *key field*. If you don't exclude the *key field* from getting qualified, its name will get modified and it won't link to the corresponding field in other tables, and the table will remain isolated from the rest of the data. At the end of a qualified LOAD statement, you should always turn qualification off to protect the script that comes after the qualified load.

Using QUALIFY May Be Dangerous

Although the QUALIFY statement looks like a handy tool for simple scripts, eliminating the need to rename multiple fields manually, it can become problematic in complex scripts where advanced data modeling techniques are used and tables are joined and concatenated. In these scripts, it might be better to avoid using QUALIFY and instead rename fields manually, only as needed.

Another advantage of renaming fields manually is the format of the resulting field name. A field named Customer City looks much more natural than Customer.City with the dot as a delimiter in the middle. You may save time on scripting, but you will likely have to give it back if you need to re-label the field every time it's used in visualizations.

Nevertheless, let's practice the technique in Exercise 6.11 by adding the ShipTo Master table. This table contains all the shipping addresses that belong to a certain customer (the assumption here is that customers may have multiple shipping destinations). Naturally, the table has many fields in common with the Customers table. In order to load this new table and avoid creating synthetic keys and circular references, you should rename all of the fields or use QUALIFY to rename them automatically.

In addition, the source table ShipTo Master includes the key field [Customer ID] that links it to the Customers table. While this may be beneficial for the needs of the transactional system, you don't need this extra link for analytic purposes. ShipTo locations are linked directly to the InvoiceHeader, and there is no need to also link them to Customers. In Exercise 6.12, you remove the field (comment it out) to avoid another circular reference.

Exercise 6.11: Use QUALIFY for Mass Renaming of Fields

1. Open Script Editor and position the cursor at the end of the Dimensions tab.

2. Add one more database table ShipTo Master, using the same process as before. Name the resulting table ShipTo to keep the qualified names short.

3. Notice all the duplicate address fields in the tables ShipTo and Customers.

4. Add the QUALIFY *; statement in front of the first LOAD statement that was just added. Make sure that you add the new QUALIFY statement before the table label ShipTo.

5. Immediately after QUALIFY, add the UNQUALIFY statement and list the ID field [Ship To ID] to prevent qualifying the key field.

6. Add the UNQUALIFY *; statement after the last SELECT statement.

7. Run the script and examine the result.

Exercise 6.12: Replace QUALIFY with the Manual Renaming of Fields

1. Now, after practicing how to use QUALIFY, scratch it off and rename the fields manually by adding the word ShipTo in front of each attribute field name in the table ShipTo.

2. The field [Customer ID] in the table ShipTo is redundant. To handle this situation, you can comment it out instead of renaming it.

3. To keep consistent naming conventions, rename the same fields in the Customers table by adding the word "Customer" in front of each attribute field name in the Customers table.

 NOTE Remember to use the AS keyword to rename the old field name to the new name, and don't forget to use square brackets [ ] for all the field names that include spaces or other special characters.

Now the load of Customers should look like this:

```
Customers:
LOAD
     `Customer ID`,
     Name          as Customer,
     Channel,
     `Address 1`   as [Customer Address 1],
```

```
         `Address 2`      as [Customer Address 2],
         `Address 3`      as [Customer Address 3],
         City             as [Customer City],
         Country          as [Customer Country],
         State            as [Customer State],
         `ZIP Code`       as [Customer ZIP Code]
    ;
SQL SELECT
         *
FROM
    CustomerMaster
    ;
```

The load of the ShipTo table, after removing the QUALIFY statement, should look like the following:

```
//===================================================================
// Load ShipTo Addresses
//===================================================================
//QUALIFY *;
//UNQUALIFY [Ship To ID];
ShipTo:
LOAD
    `Ship To ID`,
    `ShipTo End Date`,
    `ShipTo Start Date`,
    `Address 1`   as [ShipTo Address 1],
    `Address 2`   as [ShipTo Address 2],
    `Address 3`   as [ShipTo Address 3],
    City          as [ShipTo City],
    Country       as [ShipTo Country],
//    `Customer ID`,
    Name          as [ShipTo Name],
    State         as [ShipTo State],
    `ZIP Code`    as [ShipTo ZIP Code]
    ;
SQL SELECT
         *
FROM
    ShipToMaster
    ;
//UNQUALIFY *;
```

A Few Words About Naming Conventions

You may notice that not all fields were renamed in the same way, which brings us to a brief section about naming conventions. It's advised to develop consistent naming conventions and to follow them across the enterprise. Some of the practical recommendations:

- You and your development team should develop and follow a common approach for naming the fields:
  - Fields that are likely to be used as dimensions in charts and selection fields in list boxes should be called in the most natural way. This is why you renamed `Name` to `Customer` and not `[Customer Name]`. This is also the reason for not renaming the field `Channel`. You will likely prefer to use the label `Customer` in your charts, not `Customer Name`. The label `Channel` looks more natural than `Customer Channel`.
  - There should be a consistent rule about capitalizing multi-word field names. In most cases, developers prefer to capitalize the first letter of each word. Others prefer to use all capital letters or only capitalize the first letter of the first word. For example, `[Product Name]` versus `[PRODUCT NAME]` and `[Product name]`. Keeping the names capitalized in the same way helps avoid confusion and syntax errors caused by misspelled field names. We use proper case (capitalizing every word) in our practice and in the exercises throughout the book.
  - Sometimes developers prefer to signify key fields with a special character, like %, at the beginning of the name.
  - Similarly, sometimes developers like to begin all measures, such as quantities, with a special character, usually a hash sign: #.
- Similar rules should apply to table names.
  - We typically prefer to avoid spaces and special characters in table names, to avoid the need for square brackets.

- When multiple words are combined into a single table name with no spaces, we like to capitalize each word (proper case, or so called CamelCase).

- Sometimes, especially in large environments driven by data warehousing experts, tables are named with special prefixes like FACT_ or DIM_.

- Other developers prefer keeping things simple and natural, avoiding special characters as much as possible.

For the purposes of this book, we use the principle of simplicity for table names, avoiding heavy prefixes. For the field names, we use the following best practices:

- Key fields are named starting with the % sign.

- Measures, such as quantities and amounts, are named starting with the # sign.

- Dimensions and attributes are named in the most natural way, to avoid the need for renaming them at the later stage, when we develop visualizations.

You learn how to implement these changes in a centralized way at the end of this chapter.

Transforming the Data Model

So far, you have learned the basics of using the **Script Editor** and loaded a handful of tables, mostly covering the *extraction* part of the ETL process. This section covers some of the simple scripting techniques that have to do with data *transformation* (cleansing, calculating, and so on) and *load* (forming an efficient data model) concepts:

- First, you learn how to load data from non-database sources, such as Excel spreadsheets or text files.

- You learn how to combine data from multiple tables into a single table, using the JOIN LOAD.

- Then, we will describe the process of calculating derived fields and adding them to existing tables. You will learn the following techniques:
    - Reloading data from previously loaded tables using RESIDENT loads.
    - Dropping and renaming tables and fields.
- You will learn to use conditional flags—a special kind of calculated field that you'll use to simplify conditional aggregation.
- Finally, you will add a common routine for generating a Master Calendar from an external text file, using the INCLUDE function.

Loading Data from a Spreadsheet

Imagine that you've been informed that the sales hierarchy that's recorded in your main database is inaccurate. The only accurate sales hierarchy is stored in a spreadsheet that's maintained by the sales department and you need to replace the sales hierarchy data with the data stored in that spreadsheet. This is quite common—sales people often find it easier to work disconnected from corporate systems and manage their data locally in Excel.

You acquired the spreadsheet from the sales department. It consists of two worksheets. One worksheet lists all the sales persons' names and their regional directors. The other worksheet contains the names of the regional directors and their respective vice presidents.

The goal is to incorporate the different hierarchy into the data model, replacing the original data that was loaded from the Sales Hierarchy table. Note that you still need to load Salesperson ID and Salesperson Name from the original database table, because the spreadsheet doesn't have the IDs. You have to rely on the accuracy of Salesperson Name in order to associate it with the correct director and then use the director's name to associate it with the correct VP. This is not ideal, but common when dealing with data managed by humans.

Loading Data from a Spreadsheet

Spreadsheets and other text files can be loaded into a QlikView associative database using a wizard that's invoked by the **Table Files** button, which is located at the bottom of the **Script Editor**, under the **Data from Files** tab (see Figure 6.5).

Using Relative Path

Notice the **Relative Paths** checkbox in the **Data from Files** section at the bottom of the **Script Editor**. This setting is extremely useful for maintaining your ability to easily transfer your application between computers, servers, and environments. When all local data paths are defined as relative paths, and the same folder structure is maintained on the development machine, on the test server, and on the production server, migrating applications from one server to another becomes easy. Conversely, when absolute paths are used, you may have to revisit your scripts every time the application is installed under a different path.

This is the reason we wanted to save the document before developing any script. The relative path can only be established correctly when the document is saved in the correct folder.

Once the wizard is invoked, it offers a standard **Open File** dialog allowing you to navigate and point to the desired file. After selecting the file, you will see the **File Wizard** dialog that looks like the one shown in Figure 6.5.

The **File Type** section on the left (A) lists all possible formats of text files that can be loaded with this wizard, with the current format detected automatically.

FIGURE 6.5:
File Wizard in QlikView

The **Tables** drop-down box (B) offers a choice of all available tables in the file. In the case of an Excel spreadsheet, each worksheet is considered a separate table and should be loaded separately.

Header Size (C) offers an opportunity to discard a number of lines in the beginning of the file that may be used as "header"—miscellaneous information about the file that is not part of the useful data.

The **Labels** drop-down box allows you to define the field names for the columns. In most cases, spreadsheets and comma-delimited files include field names in the first row of data. In this case, you can select **Embedded Labels** from the list and the first line of data will be treated as labels. Alternatively, you can select **None** and the first line will be treated as data. The wizard will make an attempt to "guess" the right answer, but it's not always possible.

The main area of the screen (E) is used to show a preview of the table that is going to be loaded. The fields can be excluded from the load using the buttons with a little "x," or they can be renamed directly here. You can click on the field heading and override the current field name with the new name.

Clicking on the **Next** button (F) will take you into the transformation parts of the load wizard, which we will describe later. For a simple spreadsheet like this one, it's enough to define these basic settings and click on **Finish** (G) to exit the wizard and to generate the statement.

Let's examine the resulting LOAD statement:

```
Directory;
LOAD Salesperson,
     RD
FROM
[..\Data\Text Files\Sales Hierarchy Override.xlsx]
(ooxml, embedded labels, table is Director);
```

The Directory keyword was created as a result of the **Relative Paths** setting. This setting points at the current folder (directory) that holds the document.

You can reposition all of your file loads to another folder manually by adding the relative path to another folder in the Directory statement. For the most part, this statement is a remnant from the past techniques, and it can be deleted with no harm.

Next, you see a new format for a LOAD statement. This time, there is a FROM clause after the list of fields. The FROM clause describes the source of the data—the file name, including the path, and a set of qualifiers enclosed in parentheses. The qualifiers describe the type of the text file and your various choices that you made in the wizard dialog. There is no need to study them too hard; the wizard always generates them.

Just remember that all text files will be loaded with this kind of LOAD statement:

```
LOAD <list of fields>
FROM <source of data>
```

If you apply the same best practices that were described previously, the previous statement can be reformatted into the following:

```
//=================================================
// Load Directors From the Overriding Table:
//=================================================
Directors:
LOAD
        Salesperson,
        RD
FROM
        [..\Data\Text Files\Sales Hierarchy Override.xlsx]
        (ooxml, embedded labels, table is Director)
;
```

In the following exercise, you will replace some of the previously loaded Sales Hierarchy data with two tables that you will load from an Excel spreadsheet.

Exercise 6.13: Load Data from a Spreadsheet

1. Create a new tab at the end of your script. Name the tab **Sales Hierarchy**.

2. Load the data from the spreadsheet Sales Hierarchy Override.xlsx, located in your book materials in the subfolder \Data\Text Files.

3. Since the spreadsheet contains two tables (two worksheets), repeat the same process for the second worksheet VP.

4. Following best practices, reformat the script to look similar to the previous example. Call the first table Directors and the second table VPs.

5. In order to avoid duplication of data, locate the original load of the Sales Hierarchy table from the database and remove the [Regional Director] and [VP Sales] fields from that load (mind the placement of the commas after you remove the fields).

6. Save and Reload the script.

Reconnecting Broken Links

Your data model should look similar to the one presented in Figure 6.6 (you may need to rearrange your tables to view them clearly).

Notice that the two new tables were created as "islands" in that they are not linked to the rest of the data model. The magic didn't happen…

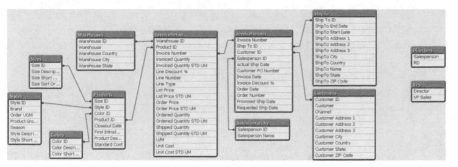

FIGURE 6.6:
Data model with broken links

If Your Picture Looks Different…

If one of the tables appears to be linked to the `SalesHierarchy` table, it may mean that you haven't commented out the original appearance of the two fields in the initial load of `SalesHierarchy`. Verify that your `SalesHierarchy` load from the database includes only two fields—`[Salesperson ID]` and `[Salesperson Name]`.

Well, since you already know that QlikView is linking tables based on the identical field names, let's examine the actual field names in the new tables, compared to the original database.

The original fields were `[Salesperson ID]`, `[Salesperson Name]`, `[Regional Director]`, and `[VP Sales]`. In comparison, the users who provided the spreadsheet used slightly different field names:

`Salesperson` should be called `[Salesperson Name]`

`RD` should be called `[Regional Director]`

`Director` should be called `[Regional Director]`

In order to repair the broken links, you need to rename the fields accordingly in the load script, using the same renaming technique presented earlier with the keyword `AS`:

```
//================================================
// Load Directors From the Overriding Table:
//================================================
Directors:
LOAD
     Salesperson as [Salesperson Name],
     RD as [Regional Director]
```

```
FROM
    [..\Data\Text Files\Sales Hierarchy Override.xlsx]
    (ooxml, embedded labels, table is Director)
;
//===============================================
// Load VPs From the Overriding Table:
//===============================================
VPs:
LOAD
    Director as [Regional Director],
    [VP Sales]
FROM
    [..\Data\Text Files\Sales Hierarchy Override.xlsx]
    (ooxml, embedded labels, table is VP)
;
```

After running the corrected script, the data model will look normal again. All the tables are properly connected, with no island tables. See Figure 6.7.

FIGURE 6.7:
Corrected data model

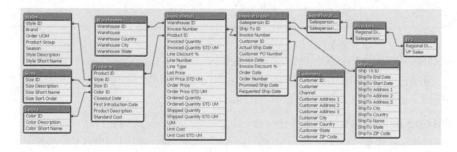

Exercise 6.14: Restore Broken Links

Rename the fields as necessary to restore the links between the newly loaded tables and the existing SalesHierarchy table. Verify that the data model looks like the model presented in Figure 6.7.

Enhancing the Data Model for Online Analytics

The data model that you developed is fine and accurate. You could develop a fully functional QlikView application on top of this data model. However, it's not optimal. There are a few little flaws that may not matter for a small data set, but could become troublesome in a large database.

Advantages of Calculating Measures at the Detailed Level

First, let's examine the main calculation that you will be using. For sales analysis, the most important measure is, of course, sales amount. In this model, the sales amount should be calculated as [Invoiced Quantity] multiplied by [Order Price]. In addition, two discounts need to be applied to the total amount—the line discount, represented by the field [Line Discount %], and the invoice total discount, represented by the field [Invoice Discount %]. Notice that the last field is located in the InvoiceHeader and the rest of the fields are located in the InvoiceDetail. So, the formula for calculating the total sales will be:

```
sum([Invoiced Quantity]*[Order Price]* (1-[Line Discount %]) *
    (1-[Invoice Discount %]))
```

While this is a valid formula, it would be a waste of resources to make QlikView constantly calculate this whole construction during runtime, in front of an impatient user waiting for the chart to recalculate.

In order to help QlikView perform faster, you should precalculate the sales amount for each invoice line. This is helpful for performance, and it's not limiting the flexibility of the analysis in any way, so it's truly a gain with no penalty. You should certainly do it.

The only problem is that you can't perform this calculation on the InvoiceDetail level while the field [Invoice Discount %] is located in a different table, InvoiceHeader. You need to find a way to bring all the necessary fields into a single table in order to perform this calculation.

Avoiding Calculations that Limit Your Flexibility

Sometimes people are tempted to precalculate subtotals at various levels of details. The general recommendation is not to do this, unless absolutely necessary. Precalculating subtotals manually brings you back to the business of building OLAP cubes, and in most cases, it limits the granularity of your analysis. The precalculated totals will only be associated with some dimensions, but not with other, more detailed, dimensions. As a result, the overall association model may become distorted. Stick to best practices of good performance and let QlikView do its job of aggregating on the fly—QlikView does it well.

Advantages of Reducing the Number of Tables and Links

If you recall the discussion about transactional data models versus analytical data models in Chapter 5, we mentioned that the star schema is the best performing model for online analytics.

There are many reasons that explain why the star schema is such a star (no pun intended). Here are the two main reasons:

- All the measures are located in one table. QlikView doesn't need to gather all the measures for a certain calculation, from various tables. Everything is ready in a single spot, and that makes things faster.

- There is exactly one link from the fact table to each one of the dimension tables. When QlikView calculates charts on the fly, it needs to resolve the links between all the necessary tables. Minimizing the number of links helps optimize QlikView performance.

NOTE   We'd like to mention here that from the standpoint of performance, keeping all the measures in a single table is extremely important, especially when working with large data sets. The second improvement listed above offers only marginal performance gains. From this perspective, the performance of a star schema can be only marginally better than the performance of a snowflake. If you have good reasons to keep your data structure in the form of a snowflake, by all means do it. The performance penalty for that is minimal. In our practice, however, we usually try to build a star schema because of its simplicity and scalability.

Keeping the star schema in our minds as the preferable goal, let's examine the data model. Three issues are quite obvious:

- `InvoiceDetail` and `InvoiceHeader` are both in the middle of the schema, and they both kind of look like fact tables. If they could be combined, the data model would get much closer to a star. The reason they are separate is inherited from the structure of the source system—this is how orders and invoices are handled in most transactional systems. Combining the two tables into one would benefit the analytical data model.

- The sales hierarchy, which is now spread over three separate tables, makes the star look like a distorted snowflake. These tables should be brought back together, to support our needs.

- The Styles, Sizes, and Colors tables are connected to Products as separate tables, adding even more of a snowflake look to the picture. While it's very important for the transactional systems to carry these key attributes in separate tables, for our analytical needs it would be better if they could happily join the rest of product attributes in the Products table. This is a good example of stitching a number of source tables into a single dimension table.

To summarize all the issues, you need to combine some of the tables (or de-normalize the structure, using professional lingo). Combining InvoiceDetail and InvoiceHeader will help simplify the calculation of the sales amount. Plus, combining these two tables into a single fact and stitching multiple dimensional tables into a single dimension will transform the snowflake data schema into the proper star schema.

Joining Two Tables into One

The process of combining data from two tables into one is called *joining*, and it's facilitated with the JOIN LOAD statement. The logic and the syntax are very similar to the same technique in SQL, with some subtle differences.

QlikView JOIN versus SQL JOIN

In SQL, we use JOIN within SELECT statements to combine information from two (or more) tables into a resulting data set. The meaning of *joining* on certain join keys is that the values in the join keys are matched and the data with the matching key values are joined together in the resulting data set. The join keys are specified explicitly using the JOIN ON clause.

In QlikView, we use JOIN LOAD to add new fields (columns) from one table into another, through the process of matching identical key fields. The key fields are defined implicitly—all the fields with the same field names that belong to both tables will be considered join keys and therefore will be matched. The difference between a SQL JOIN and a QlikView JOIN is demonstrated in Figure 6.8.

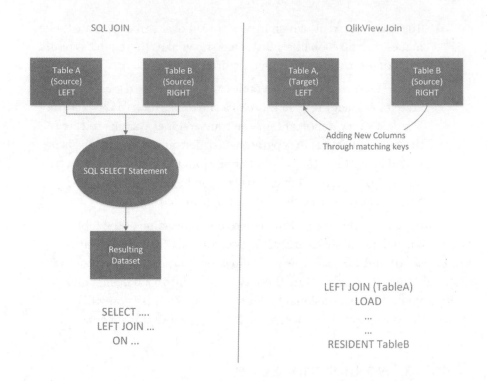

FIGURE 6.8:
Comparing SQL JOIN
with QlikView JOIN

SQL JOIN

Table A (Source) LEFT

Table B (Source) RIGHT

SQL SELECT Statement

Resulting Dataset

SELECT ....
LEFT JOIN ...
ON ...

QlikView Join

Table A, (Target) LEFT

Table B (Source) RIGHT

Adding New Columns
Through matching keys

LEFT JOIN (TableA)
LOAD
...
...
RESIDENT TableB

In SQL, JOIN can be qualified as OUTER, INNER, LEFT, or RIGHT. The table listed first is considered to be LEFT and the other table is RIGHT.

In QlikView, similar qualifiers may apply. The join is OUTER by default. It can also be specified as INNER, LEFT, and RIGHT. The LEFT table is the one that is receiving the end results (target) and the RIGHT table is the one serving as a source.

In SQL, all the source tables remain unchanged and the results are populated in the result set. In QlikView, the results are stored in the "left" table, and even the "right" table may get modified with the INNER JOIN.

In SQL, you can operate with all the fields from both joining tables to calculate new fields. In QlikView, since data from one table (the source) is being added to the data in another table (the target), the only fields that are available at this point are the fields from the source table, but not the fields from the target. Another LOAD statement will be necessary to make calculations using fields from both tables.

OUTER, INNER, LEFT, or RIGHT

If you are not familiar with the notion of OUTER, INNER, LEFT or RIGHT joins, then this sidebar is for you.

When two tables are joined, they can be visualized as two sets of data or two intersecting circles (see Figure 6.9). When the Join Keys are being matched, four possible combinations can be considered:

1. All the key values that belong to the first table, represented graphically by the left circle (LEFT).

2. All the key values that belong to the second table, represented graphically by the right circle (RIGHT).

3. All the key values that belong to both tables, represented by the intersection of the two circles (INNER).

4. All the key values that belong to either one of the two tables, represented by the area that's formed by both circles combined (OUTER).

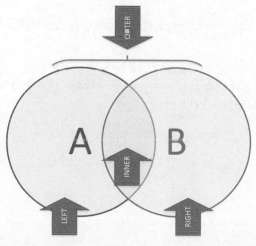

FIGURE 6.9: Understanding OUTER, INNER, LEFT, or RIGHT

These notions are used in SQL and in QlikView JOIN statements to specify what population of matching keys should be included in the result.

Syntax of QlikView JOIN

Any QlikView LOAD statement can be transformed into a JOIN LOAD by adding the JOIN prefix in front of the keyword LOAD. Schematically, it can be presented as following:

```
JOIN (TargetTable)
LOAD
      Key1,
      Key2,
      …
FROM
      <SourceTable>
;
```

The following actions will be performed as a result of this statement:

1. Source table field names and target table field names will be compared, and all identical field names will be considered *join keys*.

2. For all the identified join keys, the field values will be compared and for each combination of matching keys, new rows will be created in the resulting table, with the corresponding values of the non-key fields.

3. When certain rows remain unmatched, the missing values will get padded with NULL values.

When necessary, the keyword JOIN can be qualified by one of the LEFT, RIGHT, or INNER keywords. Remember that the target table is considered the LEFT and the source table is considered the RIGHT:

```
LEFT JOIN (TargetTable)
LOAD
      Key1,
      Key2,
      …
FROM
      <SourceTable>
;
```

In most cases, it doesn't matter what table is used as a source and what table is used as a target—the logic is almost identical, with very subtle differences that are negligible at this point. Let's just mention that it is more common to use a more detailed table (such as a fact table) as a target and join the data from a less detailed table (such as a dimension table), typically using LEFT JOIN. In this case, you will always get your facts right, with or without certain dimensional attributes.

In the following exercise, you use the JOIN LOAD technique to combine data from multiple tables into a single table. The goals of this exercise are:

- Combine InvoiceDetails and InvoiceHeader into a single table. Since the new data model will become a star schema, you will also rename the main table into the commonly used name Fact. In the future, the same Fact table may include other transactions, not just sales invoices.

- Combine sales hierarchy data, spread across three tables, into a single table.

- Combine the Products, Styles, Sizes, and Colors tables into a single dimension table called Products.

Exercise 6.15: Using JOIN LOAD to Combine Two Tables into One

1. In the **Script Editor**, locate the **Sales** tab and verify that InvoiceDetail is loaded before Invoice-Header. If necessary, use cut and paste to move the text around.

2. Replace the table name InvoiceDetail: with Fact:

3. Since the InvoiceHeader table is not going to be created, remove or comment out the table name in front of the InvoiceHeader load.

4. Instead, add the prefix JOIN in front of the InvoiceHeader load:

   ```
   LEFT JOIN (Fact)
   LOAD
   . . .
   ```

5. In the **Sales Hierarchy** tab, where the directors and the VPs are loaded, ensure that the directors are loaded first and VPs are loaded after that. Copy and paste to adjust the order of the load if necessary.

6. Comment out the table names in front of both loads and add LEFT JOIN prefixes to both loads. Specify the SalesHierarchy table as the (TargetTable):

   ```
   LEFT JOIN(SalesHierarchy)
   LOAD
   . . .
   ```

7. Locate the LOAD statements for Products, Styles, Sizes, and Colors. Ensure that the Products table is loaded first and add LEFT JOIN prefixes to the LOAD statements for Styles, Sizes, and Colors. Specify the table Products as the (TargetTable):

```
LEFT JOIN(Products)
LOAD
. . .
```

NOTE Copy and paste table and field names when possible to avoid spelling errors.

8. **Save** and **Reload** your script and examine your data model.

When everything is done correctly, your data model should look like a perfect star (see Figure 6.10).

FIGURE 6.10:

Star schema for sales analysis

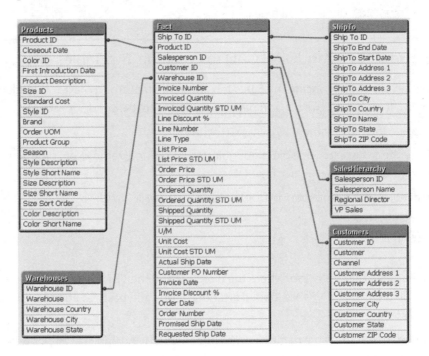

Adding Calculated Fields

At any point in the process of the data load, you can add calculated fields to the loaded tables. In this section, you learn this technique, along with the techniques for reloading data from previously loaded tables (known as *resident tables* and *resident loads*) and for dropping unnecessary tables.

Syntax for Adding Calculated Fields

A new data field can be created by mathematically combining existing fields. This can be performed in any LOAD statement provided the fields that make up the calculation are already present in the source table. For example, the following statement is valid:

```
LOAD
      A,
      B,
      A+B  as  C
FROM
      <Source>
;
```

Here is an example of an invalid statement:

```
LOAD
      A,
      B,
      A+B  as  C,
      A/C  as  D
FROM
      <Source>
;
```

This statement is invalid because the C field is not available in the source table prior to the execution of this load. The C field will only become available after this load is complete.

In order to make this example correct, you need to load this table with fields A, B, and C first, and then use an additional LOAD statement with this table being the source of data, where the C field will be available for the calculation. This type of LOAD statement is called a *resident load*.

Using Resident Load

Resident load is another format of the LOAD statement. It's used to load data from a table that was previously loaded into QlikView (a *resident table*). The syntax is mostly the same, except the FROM keyword is replaced by the RESIDENT keyword.

Continuing with the previous example, fields A, B, C, and D could be loaded into a QlikView data model using the following two LOAD statements:

```
Table1:
LOAD
      A,
      B,
      A+B as C
FROM
      <Source>
;
Table2:
LOAD
      *,
      A/C as D
RESIDENT
      Table1
;
```

After the first load is complete, the C field becomes available and can be used for further calculations. Notice the use of the asterisk in Table2 to signify "all existing fields."

Dropping Temporary Tables and Fields

This example includes one hidden problem. At the end of this script, you end up with two tables—Table1 and Table2. Both tables will have three fields in common—A, B, and C. As you already know, identical fields become key fields in QlikView data models, and multiple key fields result in the creation of synthetic keys.

In other words, Table1 was used as a temporary table and therefore needs to be dropped to avoid duplication of multiple fields. The syntax for dropping tables is simple:

```
DROP TABLE Table1;
```

or

```
DROP TABLES T1, T2, T3;
```

In a similar fashion, you can drop fields—either from specific tables or "globally" from any existing tables that contain the field:

```
DROP FIELD Temp1;
```

or

```
DROP FIELD Field1 FROM TABLE T1;
```

or

```
DROP FIELDS Field1, Field2, Field3 FROM TABLES T1, T2, T3;
```

The data model is now carrying a few fields that are not needed anymore. Examine the Products table in Figure 6.10. The [Color ID], [Size ID], and [Style ID] fields were necessary to facilitate linking relations between the tables. Once the tables are joined, these fields are no longer required. You can safely drop these fields to save on the memory footprint of the data.

Renaming Tables and Fields

Often, a data transformation is added via a resident load in the middle of a complex script. In this case, you might not have the luxury of naming your temporary tables temp1, temp2 temp3, and so on, before loading the final "clean" table with the name Fact. A table with the name Fact may already exist before the addition of this new transformation step.

In this situation, it can be handy to resident load the existing, correctly named table (Fact) into a newly named table (Temp) while creating the added transformation. After the resident load is complete, the source table (Fact) can be dropped and the resulting table (Temp) can be then renamed to the desired title (Fact). The whole construction may look like this (pay attention to the table name in every statement):

```
Fact:
LOAD
        A,
        B,
        A+B as C
```

```
FROM
    <Source>
;
. . .
Temp:
LOAD
    *,
    A/C as D
RESIDENT
    Fact
;
Drop Table Fact;
Rename Table Temp to Fact;
```

In a similar fashion, QlikView allows renaming fields:

```
Rename Field OldName to NewName;
```

The only limitation is that the new field name cannot already exist in the QlikView data model.

In our data model, quite a few fields could use better names. Remember the discussion about naming conventions earlier in this chapter? Recall that we explained that dimension fields that will be utilized in charts should be created using natural names to avoid the need to relabel them when you develop your visualizations.

Let's look at the field names in this data model more closely:

- Warehouse and Customer are named appropriately.
- At the same time, a chart of sales by salesperson would look more natural with the label Salesperson rather than the more formal label [Salesperson Name].
- Similarly, the following fields would look better if they were renamed as follows:
  - [Product Description] to Product
  - [Style Short Name] to Style
  - [Color Short Name] to Color
  - [Size Short Name] to Size

In addition, now would be a good time to implement the naming conventions outlined earlier in this chapter. We will rename all the key fields to begin with the % sign and rename all the measures to begin with a # sign. Here is the full list of fields that need renaming:

- Key Fields:
    - Salesperson ID
    - Ship To ID
    - Customer ID
    - Warehouse ID
    - Product ID
- Measures:
    - Shipped Quantity
    - Line Discount %
    - List Price
    - List Price STD UM
    - Order Price STD UM
    - Order Price
    - Invoiced Quantity STD UM
    - Ordered Quantity STD UM
    - Invoice Discount %
    - Ordered Quantity
    - Unit Cost
    - Unit Cost STD UM
    - Invoiced Quantity
    - Shipped Quantity STD UM

In the following exercise, you rename all these fields. In addition, you learn how to avoid having to key in a long list of existing fields. You can save time by exporting the list of fields to Excel and using an Excel formula to build the renaming statements.

Exercise 6.16: Drop Unnecessary Fields and Rename Fields

1. Create a new tab at the end of your script and call it **Cleanup**. In this tab, you will keep all of the cleanup statements that need to be performed before the script completes. It's good practice to end every script with a **Cleanup** tab to remove any unnecessary fields, tables, and variables.

2. Add a DROP FIELDS statement and list the three ID fields—[Color ID], [Size ID], and [Style ID]—that can be dropped.

3. Add five RENAME FIELD statements and rename the five fields that can benefit from renaming—[Salesperson Name], [Product Description], [Style Short Name], [Color Short Name], and [Size Short Name].

4. Add more RENAME FIELD statements to rename five key fields and 14 measures listed previous to this exercise, to implement the naming conventions. Add a % sign in front of the key field names and a # sign in front of the measure names.

    4.1. This is a long list of fields to type manually. We will offer a "shortcut" that can save you time and spelling errors. You can either follow the "shortcut" directions here or copy and paste the names of the fields manually.

    4.2. To get started, exit the **Script Editor** to return to the Layout view.

    4.3. Right-click on the empty space on the sheet and choose the **Select Fields** option.

    4.4. Check the **Allow System Fields** checkbox at the bottom of the view. Notice the six system fields beginning with the $ sign that appear at the top of the list. Select two fields—$Field and $Table—and click **Add** to add them to the list of the **Fields Displayed in Listboxes**. Click **OK** to exit the **Properties** dialog.

    4.5. Two list boxes will appear in the top-left corner of the screen. Position them next to each other and examine the contents. You will see the list of tables and the list of fields in your data model. Now, you can use QlikView features to help develop your script.

    4.6. Highlight the list of fields and search for the wildcard *ID (all the field names that end with ID). Click Enter, and the five ID fields will get selected.

    4.7. Right-click the list box and select **Copy To Clipboard** ▶ **Possible Values**.

    4.8. Open a new Excel spreadsheet and paste the list in column A.

    4.9. Return to QlikView. Clear all the selections using the **Clear** button in the toolbar.

4.10. In the list of tables, select `Fact`. Notice that all the fields from the `Fact` table are enabled in the list of fields, while all other fields are greyed out.

4.11. Using Ctrl+click, carefully pick all the necessary measures from the list of the fact fields, using the list of 14 measures presented previously to this exercise as a guide.

4.12. Once all 14 fields are selected, copy the possible values to the Clipboard again and paste them to the Excel spreadsheet, below the list of the keys.

4.13. Now you can use an Excel formula to generate the necessary syntax. You need to concatenate the field name with the necessary keywords, square brackets, and semicolons, to produce the desired `RENAME FIELD` statements.

4.14. Here are the formulas for the key fields and for the measures, accordingly (assuming that the field names are stored in column A). For mysterious reasons, unknown to us, the commonly used naming convention requires that the key field names begin with the % sign with no space before the name of the field, while measures begin with the # sign and a space:

```
=CONCATENATE("RENAME FIELD [",A1, "] TO [%", A1, "];")
=CONCATENATE("RENAME FIELD [",A1, "] TO [# ", A1, "];")
```

4.15. Once you copy and paste the formula to all the Excel rows that contain field names, you should see all the necessary `RENAME FIELD` statements that can be now copied and pasted into the QlikView script.

5. **Save** and **Reload** your script. Verify the results in the data model.

Practicing Data Transformations Using Resident Loads

In the next exercise, you practice using resident loads and dropping and renaming tables with the task of calculating additional fields in the `Sales` table. Specifically, you calculate:

- Sales Amount
- Cost of Goods Sold (COGS)
- Margin Amount = Sales Amount – COGS

For the sake of simplicity and convenience, we call the sales amount simply Amount. This measure will be used in chart expressions much more than any others, and it will save designers a lot of time by placing the field name on top of the list.

Exercise 6.17: Add Calculated Fields Using a Resident Load

1. Open your script at the end of the **Sales** tab.

2. Add a Resident Load statement to a new table named Temp1, loading all existing fields (*) from the Fact table, plus two new calculated fields:

    2.1. Since you already know the naming conventions, name the new measure fields accordingly, beginning with the # sign.

    2.2. Notice that the existing fields are still listed with their original names, because their renaming happens later in the script, on the **Cleanup** tab.

    ```
    [Invoiced Quantity]*[Order Price]* (1-[Line Discount %]) *
        (1-[Invoice Discount %]) AS [# Amount],
    [Invoiced Quantity]*[Unit Cost] AS [# COGS]
    ```

3. After this new LOAD, add another RESIDENT LOAD statement in order to calculate the margin amount using the new fields called [# Sales Amount] and [# COGS]. This second load will create another table, called Temp2, with the source data coming from the resident table, Temp1.

4. Drop tables Fact and Temp1.

5. Rename table Temp2 to Fact, to restore the original table-naming structure.

This tab of your script should look like the following:

```
Temp1:
load
      *,
      [Invoiced Quantity]*[Order Price]* (1-[Line Discount %]) *
      (1-[Invoice Discount %]) AS [# Amount],
      [Invoiced Quantity]*[Unit Cost] AS  [# COGS]
Resident
      Fact
;
Temp2:
load
      *,
      [# Amount] — [# COGS] as [# Margin Amount]
Resident
      Temp1
;
drop tables Fact, Temp1;
rename table Temp2 to Fact;
```

Revisiting Preceding Load

The last exercise was an excellent example of the techniques involving the RESIDENT LOAD with dropping and renaming tables. Many mature QlikView developers use these techniques in their practice every day.

In many cases, the sequence RESIDENT LOAD ▶ Drop Table ▶ Rename Table may be replaced with a preceding LOAD. This script technique is more elegant and performs faster.

In this example, the first RESIDENT LOAD cannot be replaced with a preceding LOAD because the Fact table was just created using a JOIN LOAD (as you just learned, only source table fields are available during the JOIN LOAD). The second RESIDENT LOAD , however, could be replaced with a preceding LOAD, making the script a bit cleaner:

```
Temp1:
load
    *,
    [# Sales Amount] — [# COGS] as [# Margin Amount]
;
load
    *,
    [Invoiced Quantity]*[Order Price]* (1-[Line Discount %]) *
    (1-[Invoice Discount %]) AS [# Amount],
    [Invoiced Quantity]*[Unit Cost] AS [# COGS]
Resident
    Fact
;
drop table Fact;
rename table Temp1 to Fact;
```

Extra Credit: Replace Resident Reload with a Preceding Load

Practice replacing RESIDENT LOAD with a preceding LOAD and examine the results. The resulting data model should be identical, while the script should be shorter and execute somewhat faster.

Additional Transformations: Calculating Conditional Flags

At this point, you've learned a few basic transformation techniques that involve using JOIN loads and RESIDENT loads, calculating new fields (sometimes called *derived* fields in the BI lingo), and renaming and dropping fields and tables. In this section, you will use these techniques to further enhance the data model and calculate a few *conditional flags*.

Introducing Conditional Flags

As you learned in Chapter 4, conditional aggregation (used in QlikView chart expressions) means aggregating a subset of the data that satisfies a certain condition. You learned that implementing conditional aggregation using the conditional function IF can cause poor performance and is not recommended as a good practice. For example, to show the current year-to-date sales in a chart, you could use this expression:

```
Sum (If(YearToDate([Invoice Date]),[# Amount]))
```

Although this is a simple expression, it includes an IF conditional function and a YearToDate() date function.

These two functions will get applied to the Invoice Date at every single row in the Fact table, in order to determine if Sales Amount needs to be included in the sum. So, if the Fact table has 1 million rows, the functions will get performed 1 million times. In larger environments, row counts can be in tens or hundreds of millions of rows, and hence the conditional functions will get performed as many times. This is the main reason for the performance degradation when conditional functions are included in the aggregated functions—the heavy conditional calculation will have to be performed many times for each expression.

Instead of calculating heavy IF conditions at runtime, in front of a waiting user, you can extract the heavy load and move it into the load script, which is performed in a batch mode, usually at night when nobody is waiting for the immediate result.

About Functions Used in this Section

Even though you learned about the conditional function IF() in Chapter 4, this is a brief reminder. The IF() function facilitates the commonly used programming logic IF <condition> THEN <do something> ELSE <do something else> ENDIF, which is implemented in a single function that can be used anywhere in QlikView expressions. Here is the syntax:

```
IF(<condition>, <result if true>, <result if false>)
```

The third parameter is optional. When omitted, the function returns a NULL value when the condition is false. Aggregation functions such as sum() treat NULLS as zeroes, so this outcome is perfectly acceptable.

The other function in this example is YearToDate(<date>). This function returns a Boolean value TRUE if the specified date belongs to the current year-to-date period. The function can also evaluate YTD conditions for other years, using a few optional parameters (look it up if you are curious about what those optional parameters are). This is one of many date and time functions available in QlikView. We discuss date and time functions in detail in Chapter 10. At this point, it's enough to know that the function returns TRUE or FALSE, depending on the date.

The idea of moving heavy conditional calculations from the chart expressions to the script has created a special type of data field, called a *conditional flag*. A conditional flag is a numeric field that can hold one of the two possible values. If the condition is true, the flag will be equal to 1; otherwise, the value will be 0 (zero) or NULL.

In this example, a CYTD flag (Current Year-To-Date Flag) will have a value of 1 for the data rows that belong to the current YTD period; otherwise, the value will be 0.

Conditional flags are calculated similarly to the same conditional expressions that they are meant to simplify. For example, we started this section with the following expression:

```
Sum (If(YearToDate([Invoice Date]),[# Amount])
```

Conditional Flags, Flag Fields, or Flags

You might have seen a slightly different terminology in QlikView literature—some authors call those fields "flag fields" or simply "flags." The meaning of all of those definitions is the same. We call them conditional flags to emphasize the conditional nature of those fields. In the following text, we shorten the name and call those fields flags, for simplicity.

Similarly, there are several naming conventions for flags:

- Some developers name their flags beginning with the underscore _, which is short and efficient, but may look confusing to someone who is not used to this convention.

- Others like to begin the fields with the word `flag_`, using underscore as a separator. The advantage is that all flags can be easily found using IntelliSense, when typing the expressions manually in the **Expression Editor.**

- Another acceptable convention is to end the field names with the suffix `_Flag`. This way, the field name sounds natural; however, there are no tangible advantages in terms of finding all available flags.

We suggest a mix of the three naming methodologies that combines all the advantages. We use both a prefix _ (underscore) and a suffix `_Flag`, like this:

    _CYTD_Flag

This way, the name is intuitive and self-explanatory, and the common short prefix helps retrieving all the flag names by entering a single character in the **Expression Editor.**

In order to move the heavy conditional calculation from the chart expression into the script logic, we can calculate the following flag:

```
LOAD
      IF(YearToDate([Invoice Date]),1, 0) as _CYTD_Flag,
      . . .
```

It's helpful to know that conditional functions, such as IF, are Boolean functions in nature, and they operate with Boolean values TRUE and FALSE. In QlikView, these Boolean values can also be treated as numbers—TRUE is represented by -1 (negative one) and FALSE is represented by 0 (zero). When numeric calculations are used as Boolean conditions in QlikView, any non-zero value is interpreted as TRUE, while zero is interpreted as FALSE.

NOTE

It may sound counter-intuitive if you're expecting TRUE to be equivalent to a positive 1. Because of the way the values are stored in binary, many scripting languages use -1 to indicate TRUE (or more precisely, *not false*).

Since a Boolean function already returns a TRUE or FALSE, you don't have to test it with the If( ) statement. Instead, you can use this simplified expression:

```
LOAD
    -1 * YearToDate([Invoice Date]) as _CYTD_Flag
    . . .
```

Notice that we reverse the sign of the Boolean TRUE (which is equal to -1) because positive 1 serves our needs better than negative 1.

In the same way that we used the Boolean nature of the YearToDate( ) function to avoid using an IF statement, we can use the *implied* Boolean result of any Boolean expressions or even numeric calculations. Consider the following:

```
LOAD
    -1 * ([Invoice Date] > Today()-14) as _Last2Weeks_Flag,
```

Notice that the date comparison is going to return a TRUE (-1) or FALSE (0), which you then multiply by -1 to set the value of the flag. It's difficult to understand what this expression is doing unless you know that the date comparison is acting as an implicit Boolean function.

This technique of using the numeric results of conditional expressions directly (where the IF is implied but not explicitly stated) may take some getting used to, but it is considered more elegant among developers, and is believed to perform slightly faster than the explicit IF function.

Once you create the flags in the script, you might wonder how they are used in the front-end. You've seen those expressions before, in Chapter 4, but it might be good to revisit them again here.

You started with a conditional aggregation like this (and we just agreed that this is an expensive expression, in terms of performance):

```
Sum (If(YearToDate([Invoice Date],[# Amount])
```

As an elegant alternative to the IF statement, you can now use the flag created in the script to simplify the expression:

```
Sum ([#Amount]*_CYTD_Flag)
```

In this form of the expression, you simply multiply the sales amount by the flag. The amounts that are associated with the YTD dates are multiplied by 1 and therefore included in the total. Other amounts, which are not associated with YTD dates, are multiplied by 0 and therefore excluded.

Or, you can further improve this expression if you use Set Analysis to reduce the set of available data for this aggregation (we started the discussion about Set Analysis in Chapter 4, and we will talk more about it in Chapters 8 and 12).

```
Sum ({$<_CYTD_Flag={1}>}  [# Sales Amount] )
```

Which Syntax Is Best for Conditional Aggregation?

You've learned three techniques that can be used for conditional aggregation:

- Using the IF() function within the aggregation function.

- Multiplying by the flag within the aggregation, when the flag is precalculated in the script.

- Using Set Analysis with the same flag.

It seems to be evident to most developers that multiplying by the flag is much faster than using the IF function. At the same time, many developers aren't sure how to compare the second and third techniques.

Our testing shows that the aggregated expressions with Set Analysis work faster than the technique of multiplying by the flag when the flag is stored in a dimensional table (such as Calendar) and not in the Fact table.

Conversely, when both the flag and the corresponding measure are stored in the same Fact table, the technique of multiplying by the flag outperforms Set Analysis.

With that, Set Analysis offers significantly more flexibility than the technique of multiplying by the flag; therefore, it remains our recommended choice in most cases.

Despite the less-than-intuitive syntax of Set Analysis, it has become a favorite technique for conditional aggregation, due to its flexibility and superb performance.

We used the simpler `YearToDate()` function here to simplify our explanation of the conditional flags. You may notice that we used another function, `InYearToDate()`, in our scripts. This function requires more parameters and allows calculating the YTD logic compared to any date, not just the current date.

Calculating Conditional Flags for New Products

For analysis purposes, we need to calculate two KPIs that are driven by dates—`% Revenue from New Products` and `New Doors vs. Lost Doors`.

`% Revenue from New Products` is calculated as a ratio between sales revenue associated with new products and the total sales revenue. For analysis purposes, a product is considered new for the first 12 months after its introduction (each company might have its own definition of new products). For the purpose of identifying sales for new products, you can use the `[First Introduction Date]` field in the `Products` dimension table. Comparing the `[Invoice Date]` and the `[First Introduction Date]`, you can determine whether the sales record can be categorized as a "new products" sale. In order to satisfy the condition, `[Invoice Date]` needs to be no later than 365 days after the `[First Introduction Date]`.

Technically, there is a problem. The `[Invoice Date]` is stored in the `Fact` table, and the `[First Introduction Date]` is stored in the `Products` table. If you wanted to verify this condition in a chart expression, the job would be much easier. Since all the data elements are associated in the QlikView data model, the following formula would be accurate as part of the chart expression:

`IF([Invoice Date]<[First Introduction Date]+365, 1, 0)`

In the load script, however, you are operating with data from each table individually. You need to bring the two date fields into a single table, before you can compare between the dates.

Therefore, the process of calculating this particular conditional flag will require the following transformations:

1. Bring `[First Introduction Date]` from the `Products` table into the `Fact` table (you can use `JOIN LOAD` for this purpose). This kind of `JOIN` load should include the key field (`Product ID`) and the necessary attribute

field(s) that need to be populated in the target table—in this case, it's only the field [First Introduction Date].

2. Reload the data from the Fact table into a temporary table using RESIDENT load and calculate the new conditional flag, comparing the two date fields.

3. Drop the original Fact table and rename the Temp table to Fact, to preserve the table names.

4. Drop the [First Introduction Date] field from the Fact table, to avoid an unnecessary link between Fact and Products.

Exercise 6.18: Calculate Conditional Flags: New Product Flag

1. Open the Script Editor.

2. Create a new tab in the script, before the last Cleanup tab. (Since you need to operate with the Fact and Products tables, you need to ensure that these tables exist before this transformation.) Name the new section **New Products**.

3. Perform the four steps described in the preceding section, as follows:

    3.1. Use LEFT JOIN load to copy [First Introduction Date] from the Products table into the Fact table. Don't forget to include the key field [Product ID] to facilitate the JOIN logic.

    3.2. Reload the Fact table data using RESIDENT load and calculate the new flag called _NewProduct_Flag.

    3.3. Drop the Fact table and rename the temporary table to the same name, Fact.

    3.4. Drop the [First Introduction Date] field from the Fact table.

4. Save and Reload your script and examine the result in the Table Viewer. You should find the new flag at the bottom of the Fact table, and you should not see any synthetic keys or broken links.

Your script for this transformation should look like the following:

```
//====================================================
// Calculating NewProduct_Flag:
// Products are considered New for 12 months
// after introduction
//====================================================

// 1. Join the Introduction Date into the Fact:
LEFT JOIN (Fact)
```

```
LOAD
    [Product ID],
    [First Introduction Date]
Resident
    Products
;
// 2. Reload Fact Data into Temp table and calculate the new flag:
Temp:
LOAD
    *,
    -1 * ([Invoice Date] <= [First Introduction Date] + 365) as
        _NewProduct_Flag
Resident
    Fact
;
// 3. Drop table Fact and rename Temp to Fact:
DROP TABLE Fact;
RENAME TABLE Temp to Fact;
// 4. Drop Field [First Introduction Date] from Fact:
DROP FIELD [First Introduction Date] from Fact;
```

Calculating Conditional Flags for New and Lost Doors

The KPI called New Doors vs. Lost Doors helps track sales dynamics in terms of signing up new clients or expanding the client base. This relates to adding new stores (often called *doors* in the professional lingo), versus the inevitable loss of customers or stores. For products sold through retail stores, the number of stores (doors) is an important driver of sales, so it's important to know if the company is "adding doors" or "losing doors" in a given period of time.

The KPI can be presented as a combination of measures—"Doors Added," "Doors Lost," and "Net Doors" per channel—in a period of time.

There are many techniques that can be used for calculating the necessary flags in the script. For the sake of simplicity, we will make the following assumptions about our calculations:

- Any sales recorded within the month of opening the new ShipTo location will be marked with the flag _NewDoor_Flag. We will assume that there will always be sales records in the month of opening the new account.

- Any sales recorded within the month of closing a ShipTo location will be marked with the flag _LostDoor_Flag. We will assume that there will always be sales records in the month of closing the account.

In order to compare the two dates, you use the QlikView MonthStart(Date) function. This function returns the date of the first day of the month that the date belongs to. The conditions can be described as follows:

```
MonthStart([Invoice Date]) = MonthStart([ShipTo Start Date])
MonthStart([Invoice Date]) = MonthStart([ShipTo End Date])
```

The logical process will be very similar to the process that you just used for new products. You need to perform the same four steps that you used in Exercise 6.18. Let's implement these changes in the following exercise.

Is it Better to Combine the Logic or Keep it Separate?

You may notice that this transformation requires another reload of the Fact table and obviously adds to the processing time of the load script. When numerous transformations of this kind are needed, the total length of the process can become much longer. Is it possible and beneficial to combine the logic of several transformations into one?

While it's certainly possible to combine multiple transformations and minimize the number of RESIDENT loads of the Fact table, there are benefits to keeping the calculations separate. The script would be certainly easier to read, understand, and maintain if each transformation was kept separately as a single logical unit. The price is the longer load time.

We recommend combining the transformations and optimizing the load time when dealing with large data sets, when it's important to shorten the script execution time.

Keeping that in mind, we still suggest performing the transformations in separate sequential steps within the script, as long as the impact to the load time is acceptable. Simplicity is worth some extra time in a batch mode, from our perspective.

For the purpose of this book's exercises, we keep the transformations separate.

Exercise 6.19: Calculate Conditional Flags: New and Lost Doors

1. Open the Script Editor.

2. Create a new tab, after the New Products tab. Name the new tab **New and Lost Doors**.

3. Perform the four steps, described in the previous section:

   3.1. Use LEFT JOIN LOAD to copy the [ShipTo Start Date] and [ShipTo End Date] fields from the ShipTo table into the Fact table. Don't forget to include the key field [ShipTo ID] to facilitate the JOIN logic.

   3.2. Reload the Fact data using RESIDENT load and calculate the new flags called _NewDoor_Flag and _LostDoor_Flag.

   3.3. Drop the Fact table and rename the temporary table to the same name, Fact.

   3.4. Drop the temporary fields [ShipTo Start Date] and [ShipTo End Date] from the Fact table.

4. Save and Reload your script and examine the result in the Table Viewer. You should find the new flags at the bottom of the Fact table, and you should not see any synthetic keys or broken links.

Your script for this transformation should look like the following:

```
//===================================================
// Calculating NewDoor_Flag and LostDoor_Flag:
// Marking any Sales in the month of Opening and Closing the location
//
//===================================================
// 1. Join the ShipTo Start and End Date into the Fact:
LEFT JOIN (Fact)
LOAD
     [ShipTo ID],
     [ShipTo Start Date],
     [ShipTo End Date]
Resident
     ShipTo
;
// 2. Reload Fact Data into Temp table and calculate the new flags:
Temp:
LOAD
     *,
     -1 * (MonthStart([Invoice Date]) = MonthStart([ShipTo Start Date]))
          as _NewDoor_Flag,
     -1 * (MonthStart([Invoice Date]) = MonthStart([ShipTo End Date]))
```

```
              as _LostDoor_Flag
Resident
      Fact
;
// 3. Drop table Fact and rename Temp to Fact:
DROP TABLE Fact;
RENAME TABLE Temp to Fact;
// 4. Drop Field [First Introduction Date] from Fact:
DROP FIELD [ShipTo Start Date] from Fact;
DROP FIELD [ShipTo End Date] from Fact;
```

Calculating On Time and Complete Flag

Similarly, we need to prepare a conditional flag that marks order lines that were shipped on time and complete. Logically, this criteria means that the order was shipped on or before the promised ship date, and that the whole ordered quantity was shipped at once.

You are going to follow a similar calculation process in order to generate this flag:

- Reload the Fact table into the temporary table Temp, adding the new calculated field to the LOAD.

- Drop the original Fact table.

- Rename the Temp table to Fact.

Exercise 6.20: Calculate On Time and Complete Flag

1. Open the Script Editor.

2. Create a new tab, after the New and Lost Doors tab. Name the new tab **On Time and Complete**.

3. Perform the three steps that we just described:

   3.1. Reload the Fact data using RESIDENT load and calculate the new flag called _OnTimeAndComplete_Flag.

   3.2. Drop the Fact table

   3.3. Rename the temporary table to the same name, Fact.

4. **Save** and **Reload** your script and examine the result in the **Table Viewer**. You should find the new flag at the bottom of the Fact table, and you should not see any synthetic keys or broken links.

Your script for this transformation should look like the following:

```
//======================================================
// Calculating On Time and Complete Flag
// Marking Order Lines shipped on or before the Promised Ship Date
// and with the Shipped Quantity >= Ordered Quantity
//======================================================
// 1. Reload Fact Data into Temp. table and calculate the new flag:
Temp:
LOAD
     *,
     ([Actual Ship Date] <= [Promised Ship Date]) *
     ([Shipped Quantity] >= [Ordered Quantity])
               as _OnTimeAndComplete_Flag
resident
     Fact
;
// 2. Drop table Fact and rename Temp to Fact:
DROP TABLE Fact;
RENAME TABLE Temp to Fact;
```

Adding a Master Calendar Table Using INCLUDE

As a best practice, every QlikView application that has a Date dimension needs to have a master calendar.

Simply put, a master calendar is a dimension table that describes everything pertaining to the "main" Date dimension.

We've discussed the need for the master calendar in Chapter 5. Since you are just in the beginning of your QlikView education, you don't know all the techniques that need to be used to generate a master calendar. Thankfully, the trusted consultants from Natural Synergies have created a common routine that you can simply use as is. We will describe the process of generating the master calendar in Chapter 10, where you learn more about advanced scripting techniques.

In this section, you learn how to include a commonly used segment of a script (such as a master calendar generator) from an external text file.

How to Determine the Main Date

Most applications include several date fields, and all of them seem to be important. How can you determine which date should play the role of the "main" date? Which date should be selected when your users select a year or a month on the screen? Ask yourself and your users, "When you are selecting January 2014, what do you really mean? Orders that were *invoiced* in January of 2014, orders that were *requested to ship* in January of 2014, or orders that were *issued* in January of 2014?"

Hopefully you can get a single answer to this question. Sometimes you may discover that you have multiple date fields that the user needs to select from. This problem is quite tricky, and the solutions are either fairly complex or not too elegant. For the purpose of this chapter, we will assume a simple case when a single date can be considered the main date and this date will be used for the master calendar.

Including Script Fragments from an External Text File in QlikView

Snippets of script can be included in a QlikView load script using the INCLUDE statement. This statement has a very particular syntax and therefore it's best to use the wizard to generate it instead of typing it manually.

One of the most useful items in QlikView **Script Editor** menus is the **Insert** menu (see Figure 6.11). It offers many goodies, and we encourage you to explore them on your own. At the moment, we are particularly interested in the **Insert ▶ Include Statement** menu item.

FIGURE 6.11:
QlikView Insert menu

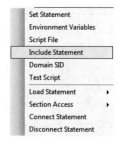

Once **Include Statement** is selected, the standard **Open File** dialog allows you to navigate and point to the desired text file. As a result, a text string similar to the following will be added to the script:

```
$(Include=..\scripts\master calendar.txt);
```

Notice that the `Include` statement is enclosed in parentheses with a dollar sign in front. This syntax is known as a *dollar-sign expansion* in QlikView. Dollar-sign expansion directs QlikView to evaluate the expression inside the parentheses and replace the name with its value. This dollar-sign expansion replaces the name of the included text file with its contents.

All dollar-sign expansions, and the `Include` statement in particular, execute without the possibility of causing a script failure. If certain components are misspelled or missing, the dollar-sign expansion will silently return a `NULL` or an empty string, and the script will continue without an error. This is quite helpful when certain included scripts are optional and may not be present at certain times. On the other hand, sometimes you need to ensure that the script segment is indeed included. For those cases, an alternative form `MUST_INCLUDE` can be used. You'll have to add the `MUST_` prefix manually since it is not available as a configuration option in the wizard:

```
$(Must_Include=..\scripts\master calendar.txt);
```

This form of the statement generates a script error when the file is missing.

When the text file is found, the dollar-sign expansion is replaced with the text stored in the text file. If the contents of the text file change between the two runs of the load script, it's fine. QlikView will evaluate and interpret the new script every time the script statement is encountered. This feature allows transforming portions of the load script dynamically as the situation requires.

It is quite common to save connection strings, basic settings, and configuration values, as well as common script routines, in external files. You can also use `INCLUDE` statements to cause the script segments to be included and evaluated at the time of data loading.

Selecting the Main Date for the Calendar

When using standardized routines stored in text files, it's important to ensure that the field names used in the routines correspond to the specific field names in your script. At times, you may need to add or rename certain fields or tables in order to facilitate all the necessary links.

This is true in this case. The master calendar routine in the text file is using a field called Date. This field doesn't exist in the current data model. Instead, you have a number of different dates that pertain to various stages of the order/invoice lifecycle. You need to decide what field should be used as the main date field that drives the calendar. Most accounting principles prescribe the use of an invoice date field when reporting revenue. If the goal were to analyze booked orders, perhaps the order date would be the appropriate date field to reference instead.

For the current needs, you will add a new field, called Date, into the data model based on the values in the [Invoice Date] field. This field will serve as the link to the Master Calendar:

```
LOAD
    ...
    `Invoice Date`,
    `Invoice Date` as Date,
. . .
```

Exercise 6.21: Add a Master Calendar Using Included Script

1. Open a new script tab before the **Cleanup** tab and name it **Calendar** (always make sure that the **Cleanup** tab remains the last tab in your script).

2. Using the **Insert** ► **Include Statement**, add the statement to include the text file Master Calendar. txt, located in the \Scripts subfolder:

   $(Include=..\scripts\master calendar.txt);

3. Locate the [Invoice Date] field, loaded from the source table Invoice Header. Clone the field and rename the second instance Date, as described in the previous example.

4. Run the script and ensure that the MasterCalendar table was created and properly linked to your data. The final data model after all the recent additions and modifications should look like the one presented in Figure 6.12.

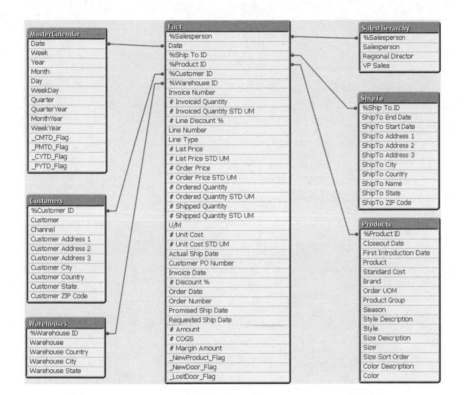

FIGURE 6.12:
Final Data
Model

This exercise completes our discussion of simple scripting concepts in QlikView. You learned how to load database tables and spreadsheets, and we demonstrated simple data modelling techniques. Our discussion of scripting techniques will continue in Chapter 10 and in Chapter 14.

Expanding Your Skill Set: Profitability Analysis

PART

III

7

Defining a Business Scenario for Profitability Analysis

Financial statements are widely used as the "report card" for business. Financial statements follow rules of accounting and are supposed to communicate to the reader a description of results in categories that drive a business. The income statement is a lens for analyzing the earnings of a business. This chapter will examine the income statement in accounting terms and how it falls short of providing critical analytical information to make decisions. You will be introduced to a more detailed analytical approach to understanding the profitability drivers of your business that we call the *direct variable profitability* (DVP) model. The example company information will illustrate data elements to consider when analyzing drivers of profitability and compare that visibility to what you see in the traditional accounting income statements.

The DVP Model will allow you to better understand the drivers of profitability of your business and prioritize resources to manage those drivers. This approach can be used in any business for any reporting period. Use of the DVP model is restricted only by the tools that you have available to access data in your systems.

The Profit and Loss Statement

It's likely that you have seen what is commonly called a *profit and loss statement* (P&L) or an *income statement*. A P&L statement defines profit as being equal to revenue (sales), less all costs and expenses. Seems fairly straightforward; however, it is rarely obvious what action to take just by looking at this financial statement.

Consider a company that has the P&L statement shown in Table 7.1.

TABLE 7.1: Example company P&L statement (in thousands)

		YEAR 1	YEAR 2
Sales		$10,000	$12,000
Cost of Sales		$6,000	$7,200
Gross Profit		$4,000	$4,800
	Percentage of Sales	40.0%	40.0%
Selling Expenses		$2,000	$2,500
	Percentage of Sales	20.0%	20.8%
General & Administrative expenses		$1,000	$1,200
	Percentage of Sales	10.0%	10.0%
Net Income/(Loss)		$1,000	$1,100
	Percentage of Sales	10.0%	9.2%

Based on this statement, can you tell *how the company is doing*? And *what it should do differently going forward?* On the surface, the company seems to have grown sales by 20%, gross profit by 20%, and improved the profits by 10%. Seems like a winning accomplishment. But what does it really mean? For example, a company might grow its sales and profits in the first quarter of year 2 over the previous year and think they are successful. However, it could be that the company is unaware of or does not have visibility into a number of factors that influenced the sales dollars—factors that indicate a problem. Many factors affecting profitability (i.e., the relationship of expenses to sales) are critical to understanding your business and its potential. Those relationships can be defined by the following categories of cost and expenses:

- **Variable costs**—Variable costs vary directly with unit movement. Examples are material costs, volume discounts, labor to make the product, and so on.

- **Fixed costs**—Fixed costs do not vary directly with unit movement. Examples are the cost of your office building, management salaries, security, insurance, and so on.

- **Step variable costs**—These are costs that are fixed in the short term and more variable over the mid term. It is important not to get too hung up on these types of costs. It is better to make some simplifying assumptions. If costs seem relatively fixed in the short term, then classify them as fixed for analysis purposes.

It is important to know how your costs behave relative to the unit movement of your business. The behavior here refers to whether the costs are *variable* (they go up when unit movement goes up and go down when unit movement goes down) or *fixed* (do not move directly with unit movement). This is essentially a contribution margin approach. To illustrate, Table 7.2 shows the example P&L from earlier in the chapter and breaks out some of the underlying data.

TABLE 7.2: Example Company P&L statement (in thousands)

	YEAR 1	YEAR 2	PERCENT CHANGE	TYPE[1]
Gross Sales	$11,000	$13,200		Variable
Customer Returns & Allowances[2]	$1,000	$1,200		Variable
Net Sales	$10,000	$12,000	20.0%	
Direct Material	$3,000	$3,600	20.0%	Variable
Direct Labor	$500	$600	20.0%	Variable
Depreciation	$1,000	$1,000	0%	Fixed
Supervision	$1,500	$1,500	0%	Fixed
Other Manufacturing	$0	$500	N/A	????
Total Cost of Sales	$6,000	$7,200	20.0%	
Gross Profit	$4,000	$4,800		
Percentage of Sales	40.0%	40.0%		
Co-op Advertising	$300	$760	153.3%	Variable
Commissions	$200	$240	20.0%	Variable
Salaries	$1,500	$1,500	0%	Fixed
Total Selling Expenses	$2,000	$2,500	25.0%	
Percentage of Sales	20.0%	20.8%		
General & Administrative Expenses	$1,000	$1,200	20.0%	Fixed
Percentage of Sales	10.0%	10.0%		
Net Income/(Loss)	$1,000	$1,100	10.0%	
Percentage of Sales	10.0%	9.2%		

[1] Type means how the values behave with respect to unit volume.

[2] Customer programs can include returns and allowances for volume, merchandising, seasonal promotions, defectives, shortages, and return to stock.

When you look at the same P&L with a classification of how costs behave, you begin to see a clearer picture of the business. The result is that there is potentially more actionable information that requires further analysis. In this case:

- If the classification of fixed and variable costs within the total cost of sales is correct, there is an unexplained increase in the total of $500K. This could be driven by a number of issues that need to be addressed, such as:

  - Did material prices rise significantly?
  - Did material utilization get worse?
  - Did labor productivity get worse?
  - Did salaries in fixed overhead increase too much compared to the manufacturing activity?

- In selling expenses, why did co-op advertising increase at a rate of 7.5 times the sales increase?

- In general expenses, why did fixed general and administrative expenses increase the same rate as sales?

You get the picture. The existence of these questions does not mean the business is mismanaged. They should not be "I got you" types of questions about the business. They are fundamental questions necessary to understand the business. The answers to these questions lead toward the right actions to take.

The Direct Variable Profitability (DVP) Model

When you define these classifications of fixed and variable expenses in terms of your business, you can begin to analyze your business in more depth. We call this in-depth analytical technique the *direct variable profitability* model (*DVP*). There are three steps to creating this model:

1. Classify revenues and costs as variable or fixed as they relate to unit movement. This will replace the standard classification based on functional P&L lines without regard to how they behave.

2. Group revenues and costs in categories that are directly accountable for them. The activities in these categories directly drive the costs. We call this *direct categories of accountability (DCAs)*. They are:

- **Product**—This includes prices, allowances, deductions, costs, and volume at the unit level that are directly related to the product itself. The profitability measured here can be for a single product or group of products.

- **Customer**—This includes prices, allowances, deductions, costs, volume, and programs for all units directly related to the customer itself. The profitability measured here can be for a single customer or a group of customers.

- **Channel**—This includes a roll-up of variable and fixed revenue/costs directly related to all customers in a given channel of distribution.

- **Region**—This includes a roll-up of information for all customers in a given region.

- **Department**—This includes all costs that relate to expense line items that are in a department or group of departments and are not directly related to unit volume. The activities that cause spending in this DCA will vary depending on expense type.

3. Arrange the information in the P&L starting with data which is directly related to unit movement (variable) at the top and add data which is not directly related to unit movement (fixed) below the variable data until you have completely rearranged the statement. It is important to note that the Net Income line should be the same total as it was before this exercise.

The sample P&L from earlier in this chapter would now look like Table 7.3.

TABLE 7.3: Example Company P&L statement using the DVP Model (in thousands)

	YEAR 1	YEAR 2	PERCENT CHANGE	TYPE [1]
Gross Sales	$11,000	$13,200	20.0%	Variable
Customer Returns & Allowances[2]	$1,000	$1,200	20.0%	Variable
Net Sales	$10,000	$12,000	20.0%	
Co-op Advertising	$300	$760	153.3%	Variable
Direct Material	$3,000	$3,600	20.0%	Variable
Direct Labor	$500	$600	20.0%	Variable
Commissions	$200	$240	20.0%	Variable
Total Direct Cost of Sales	$4,000	$5,200	30.0%	
Direct Contribution Margin	$6,000	$6,800	13.3%	
Percentage of Sales	60.0%	56.7%		
Depreciation	$1,000	$1,000	0%	Fixed
Supervision	$1,500	$1,500	0%	Fixed
Other Manufacturing	$0	$500	N/A	???
Sales & Marketing Salaries	$1,500	$1,500	0%	Fixed
General & Administrative Expenses	$1,000	$1,200	20.0%	Fixed
Total Fixed Costs	$5,000	$5,700	14.0%	
Percentage of Sales	50.0%	47.5%		
Net Income/(Loss)	$1,000	$1,100	10.0%	
Percentage of Sales	10.0%	9.2%		

[1] Type means how the values behave with respect to unit volume.

[2] Customer programs can include returns and allowances for volume, merchandising, seasonal promotions, defectives, shortages, and return to stock.

The analysis now reveals issues that were not visible in the original P&L and were still not obvious in the second version. The questions about the business that are important to understand are:

- Should the business be getting a bigger increase in sales due to their investment in co-op advertising?

- Variable margins are declining and are driven by co-op advertising expenses rising faster than sales. Is the business getting the return they should out of their investment in co-op advertising?

- Why don't they see the impact of productivity and cost reduction programs in the variable costs?

- What is the nature of the "other manufacturing" costs and what is driving it?

- Again, why are fixed general and administrative expenses going up at the same rate as sales?

Each line in the P&L should be linked to someone in your organization who has direct responsibility for the activities that drive those results as well as the actual results. The analysis process should continue as a "deep dive" into a line item that is significantly different than expectations. The ability to build the model and do the deep dive analysis where necessary will likely require locating and extracting data from your system very differently than you do today. The P&L examples shown so far are at the total company level. Figure 7.1 shows how this is built up in the DVP model from the product-level detail.

Deep Dive Example

Sales is an area in which companies definitely benefit from a deep dive analysis! We described a detailed analysis of sales in Chapter 3. In that chapter, we examined the drivers of sales performance. The analysis of sales beyond aggregate sales performance reveals actionable issues about your business that are not visible at an aggregate level. You may recall some of the drivers were price and mix. These drivers had little or no visibility in the traditional analytical reporting of sales results. The same benefit comes from a deep dive into other areas of the P&L. We have demonstrated that the DVP model of a P&L helps to identify less visible areas of the P&L that need further understanding and action.

Product or SKU level:

Revenue
    Less:
        Direct material
        Direct labor
        Product-specific promotions
        Variable manufacturing overhead expenses
        Variable selling expenses
        Product specific volume incentives

Direct variable product margin

Customer level

Direct variable product margin
    Less:
        Customer-specific promotions
        freight
        Variable distribution expenses

Direct variable customer margin

Channel Level

Direct variable customer margin
    Less:
        Channel-specific promotions

Channel-specific distribution expense

Enterprise level

Channel-specific distribution expense

    Less:
        Fixed manufacturing overhead
        Fixed distribution expense
        Fixed selling expense
        Fixed general & administrative expense

Net Income before taxes

FIGURE 7.1:
The Components of the DVP model

In the example case in this chapter we revealed that there are costs that behave differently than expected and have had a negative impact on earnings. One example of this is co-op advertising. Co-op advertising is an investment in advertising with your customer (the customer typically places the ad) aimed at driving sales growth. It should be an expense that is directly variable with sales. In other words, as advertising investment increases, your sales should increase. In the example, the fact that this expense and sales did not behave this way should be a cause for concern:

- Was the timing of the investment correctly made?
- Was the money actually used to place the advertising by the customer?
- Were the ads properly designed to drive sales of the intended product(s)?
- Was a volume increase in fact offset by other pricing actions within the sales line?

This last question can lead to going into more detail on other "investments" in your customers to understand why sales may not have increased more than reported. You might be aware of some of the "investments" in customers to drive your sales. Many of these customer investments are really forms of price adjustments and may not be providing a return to the company making the investment. Some examples other than co-op advertising are:

- Payment term discounts
- Volume discounts back to dollar one each year
- Off-invoice discounts (such as freight, merchandising, and seasonal promotion allowances)
- Foregoing price increases

The effect that these customer investments can have on your business are hidden in a comparison to aggregate lagging indicators. Sales dollars may not be growing as much as expected, but unless you can analyze these investments you may not know why and what it means in terms of how your customers view the real value of your product.

Another area of the example P&L that is shown to require a deeper analysis is the "fixed" departmental spending. Looking at fixed and variable department expenses separately allows you to:

- Identify areas of concern sooner than if they are allocated. When costs are combined (allocated) they tend to lose their identity. It gets further complicated if we combine (allocate) costs that behave differently from one another. For example, costs that are fixed combined with variable cost will make it difficult to understand what is driving those costs—volume activity or a completely different set of activities.

- Identify activities that drive spending more accurately.

- Identify who in your organization is accountable and responsible for these activities and spending decisions more directly.

- Identify when no one has been given the accountability and responsibility for the activities and spending in any area.

Use of Business Intelligence Tools Makes the Data Visible and Available

Based on the DVP model P&L and this example, you should be able to identify who is responsible and determine what corrective action is needed for:

- What, if any, pricing program decisions versus volume are affecting sales.

- What needs to be addressed in terms of the investment in customer co-op advertising.

- Why fixed general and administrative expenses are going up at the same rate as sales.

- The nature of the "other manufacturing costs" of $500K and why they were spent.

- Where are the cost reduction programs showing up in the financials and what is offsetting them.

We believe that speed is the most sustainable competitive advantage in business. This type of actionable reporting and analysis is critical for speed in identifying and correcting problem areas in your business. It is also critical for celebrating the accurate successful results in your business!

In chapters 8, 9, and 10 we describe a simplified profitability model and explain the specific techniques for implementing it in QlikView. For the sake of simplicity and educational value, we focus our technical discussion on the following aspects:

- Analyzing product profitability using variable costs versus total gross standard costs.

- Analyzing customer profitability and how it's impacted by customer allowances, deductions, and returns.

- Analyzing the issue caused by the fact that standard costs are usually set annually and used throughout the same year, but often change dramatically during that year.

8

Visualizing Profitability Analysis in QlikView

In this chapter, you build simple and more advanced visualizations for profitability analysis. In the process of doing so, we introduce you to the following techniques of building advanced QlikView visualizations:

- Creating dynamic dimensions and dynamic expressions through the use of variables
- Combo charts
- Waterfall charts
- Normalized and non-normalized Mekko charts
- Scatter charts
- Heat maps and block charts
- Advanced Set Analysis and advanced search in Set Analysis
- Organizing objects on a sheet using container objects

If you haven't installed the book's electronic materials yet, please revisit the Introduction and follow detailed instructions for preparing your work environment for this book's tutorial. You need to download and install QlikView and Qlik Sense, download our electronic materials and preferably install our font. We describe all the necessary preparations at the end of the Introduction.

Simple Visualizations for Profitability Analysis

In this section, we describe the specific calculations for the various levels of profitability and build a simple P&L report.

You will store those formulas in variables that can be used multiple times within this application. We will describe various aspects of using variables for calculated formulas.

Then you'll develop a few simple charts, mostly based on the material that you learned in the process of developing the Sales Analysis application in Chapter 5.

Preparing the Template for Profitability Analysis

First, let's prepare the environment for developing the new visualizations. You need to create a new document and populate the same template that you used for the Sales Analysis application. You will copy and paste most of the common elements, to save time.

Your documents should follow the same default theme, NS_Flat.qvt, as the Sales Analysis application. This file can be found in the folder \QlikView Your Business\Resources\Themes\. The default theme for new documents can be set in the **User Preferences**, **Design** tab. The default theme for new objects in a document is set in the **Document Properties**, **Presentation** tab.

For the purpose of building visualizations, you use an existing data model: Profitability Data.QVW. You will learn the process of creating this data model in Chapter 13. The data model will be loaded into the document using the BINARY load method.

The BINARY command allows loading the whole data model from one document into another. It can be typed manually, or it can be generated using a simple wizard that is activated by the **QlikView File** button at the bottom of the **Script Editor** (see Chapter 6, Figure 6.1.) Loading entire data models into dashboards using the BINARY command is a very good practice. It allows easy separation between scripting and developing visualizations. There are two limitations that are important to know:

- The BINARY command has to be the first statement in the script.
- There should be no more than one BINARY command in each document. Merging multiple datasets into one is not permitted.

Next, copy the existing template sheet objects from the Sales Analysis application. The easiest way to copy objects from one QlikView document to another is to open both documents side by side. Right-click on the QlikView icon in the taskbar and select QlikView 11 to open a second instance of QlikView. Now it's easy enough to activate all objects (Ctrl+A) and copy them (Ctrl+C) in the existing application and then open the new application and paste (Ctrl+V) all the objects there.

Feel free to prepare your environment on your own, or follow the detailed instructions in Exercise 8.1.

Exercise 8.1: Preparing the Environment for Profitability Analysis

1. Open the Settings ▶ User Preferences, Design tab and verify that the default theme is set to NS_Flat.qvt. If necessary, select this theme file, located in the folder \QlikView Your Business\ Resources\Themes\.

2. Create a new document and save it with the name **Profitability Analysis XX.QVW**, where **XX** is your initials. Open the Script Editor.

3. In the Main tab, load the QlikView file with the data model. Locate the Profitability Data Improved.QVW document in the \Data Models\ subfolder and load it using the BINARY load method. Use the QlikView File button at the bottom of the Script Editor or type the following line manually (remember to place the BINARY command in the first line of the script).

   Binary [..\Data Models\profitability data improved.qvw];

4. Reload the script and close the Script Editor, if necessary.

5. Open the Settings ► Document Properties, General tab and verify that the background color is set to pure white, or RGB(255, 255, 255).

6. Open another instance of QlikView and open the Sales Analysis application.

7. Open the Template sheet in the Sales Analysis document and copy all objects. Navigate to the new Profitability Analysis document and paste all objects here. You may close the second instance of QlikView with the Sales Analysis document.

8. In the Profitability Analysis document, rename the sheet to **Template**. Create a new sheet and call it **P&L**.

9. Copy all objects in the Template sheet and paste them *as links* into the P&L sheet.

10. **Important**: un-link the objects for the sheet heading (the text "Template") and the icon next to it—these two objects need to be different on each page.

11. Save the document. It is now ready for new visualizations.

Preparing the Expressions for Profitability Calculations

Before diving into the process of building visualizations, we first describe the main calculations used throughout this chapter. You will be calculating the different revenue and profit described in Chapter 7. Let's get the terminology out of the way, and then you will use the same calculations throughout the process.

Calculating Various Levels of Profitability

The various revenue and profit will resemble different levels of a simplified profit &loss (P&L) statement. At the top level, you will calculate Sales at List. This is an imaginary revenue number that would be received if all customers paid full list price for all products. This level, which is located above Gross Sales, is used only for analytical purposes. It helps companies understand the level of discounts given for certain products or to certain customers:

Sales at List = `sum([# Amount at List Price])`

The next level of P&L is Gross Sales, which is the common calculation of sales:

Gross Sales = sum([# Amount])

Gross sales are equal to Sales at List minus the total of Discounts. The sum of discounts will also be used in your calculations:

Discounts = sum([# Amount - Discounts])

The next level in the P&L is Net Sales. This is one of the most ambiguous calculations in the P&L, because companies and analysts tend to net out different categories of costs in their calculations of net sales. Most commonly, all returns, chargebacks, and allowances are deducted from gross sales, which is great for reporting purposes at the company level. However, this calculation can't serve your analytical needs quite as well. For your needs, you should get as close as possible to *product* level profitability, and therefore you will only deduct the costs that are associated with products. In reality, many types of customer allowances may be product-specific. In this simplified model, only returns are specified by product. Hence, for the purpose of this analysis, we define Net Sales as Net Direct Product Sales, which is calculated as follows:

Net Direct Product Sales = Gross Sales − Returns

or as a QlikView formula:

Net Direct Product Sales = sum([# Amount]) − sum({<[Reason Description]= {'Return to stock'}>} [# CM Amount])

Next, you deduct all the costs directly associated with products—specifically, material and labor costs. The result of the deduction will represent Direct Product Contribution Margin:

Direct Product Contribution Margin = Gross Sales − Returns − Material Cost − Labor Cost

or as a QlikView formula:

Direct Product Contribution Margin = sum([# Amount]) − sum({<[Reason Description]={'Return to stock'}>} [# CM Amount]) − sum([# COGS - Material]) − sum([# COGS - Labor])

This level of P&L ends the product profitability level of the analysis. Below this level, you subtract customer-specific costs to calculate the customer profitability levels. In reality, any costs that can be tied to a uniquely identified customer should be included here. For example, if a separate sales team is dedicated to a single customer, then all costs attributed to that sales team should be included in the calculation of the customer profitability. In this simplified data model, all credit memos (other than returns) are only customer-specific costs; therefore, the Direct Customer Contribution Margin is calculated as the Direct Product Contribution Margin minus Credit Memos:

Direct Customer Contribution Margin = sum([# Amount]) − sum([# CM Amount]) − sum([# COGS - Material]) − sum([# COGS - Labor])

The next level of profitability analysis is channel profitability. All channel-related costs need to be deducted at this level. These costs may include any channel-specific sales costs, marketing costs, and other costs that can be directly attributed to specific channels of distribution. In this simplified model, we use sales commissions as an example of channel-specific costs. In this model, the percentage of the sales commission is defined at the channel level:

Channel Profit Margin = sum([# Amount] *(1 − [# Commission %])) − sum([# CM Amount]) − sum([# COGS - Material]) − sum([# COGS - Labor])

Next, the total enterprise Operating Profit Margin is calculated by deducting all other costs that cannot be attributed directly to specific products, customers, and channels. These costs include various fixed costs for manufacturing overhead, selling, general, and administrative expenses. Ideally, these costs should be loaded as actual amounts from the general ledger (GL) system. For the purpose of this simplified model, we will only use the manufacturing overhead. Loading the actual costs for the manufacturing overhead from the GL system would be the most accurate method. In this straw man model, we substitute the actual costs with the planned overhead rate applied to the actual quantities, as a proxy. Keep in mind, however, that this method is not recommended for use in real projects, because the calculated costs can vary considerably if actual sold quantities are significantly different from the budgeted quantities.

Operating Profit Margin = sum([# Amount] *(1 − [# Commission %])) − sum({<[Reason Description]={'Return to stock'}>} [# CM Amount]) − sum([# COGS - Material]) − sum([# COGS - Labor]) − sum([# COGS - Overhead])

Note that all these calculations produce the amounts of revenues and profits in dollars (or euros or rubles). It's common to present these numbers in two forms—as amounts and as percentages of the gross sales amount.

In Exercise 8.2, you build a simplified profit & loss (P&L) report that describes all levels of revenue, profit, and the various cost components (see Figure 8.1).

Simple P&L Year over Year

	2013	2014
Sales at List	57,802,563	85,593,861
- Discounts	11,091,930	16,412,111
Gross Sales	46,710,633	69,181,751
- Returns	1,838,885	3,083,431
Net Direct Product Sales	44,871,749	66,098,320
- Material	15,276,600	21,003,063
- Labor	13,313,929	18,421,069
Direct Product Contribution Margin	16,281,220	26,674,187
- Customer Allowances	3,494,150	6,431,135
Direct Customer Contribution Margin	12,787,070	20,243,052
- Channel Related Costs	3,337,489	4,509,708
Channel Contribution Margin	9,449,581	15,733,345
- Manufacturing Overhead	9,556,033	13,232,749
Operating Profit	-106,452	2,500,596

FIGURE 8.1:
Simple profit and loss (P&L) report

This simple P&L report is implemented as a *horizontal* straight table, where Year as a dimension is listed across the top and all the expressions are listed vertically. The **Horizontal** setting can be found in the **Chart Properties** on the **Presentation** tab.

Note that the labels for all the cost calculations are indented and begin with the "minus" sign. Each one of the profit levels can be calculated as the previous level minus the cost line above. In different circumstances, we suggest that you simplify the calculations by referencing previously calculated profit levels; however, in this case, we use each one of those formulas in following exercises. Therefore we ask that each calculation be performed independently of other expressions.

Feel free to build the P&L on your own, using Figure 8.1 as a visual guide and using the formulas listed here. Somewhat detailed instructions are listed in the following exercise. If you prefer to use a shortcut, copy the solution from the \Solutions QlikView\ subfolder. The result of this exercise is instrumental to the rest of the exercises in this chapter.

Exercise 8.2: Building a Simple P&L Report

1. In the newly created P&L sheet, create a new Chart. Select Straight Table as the Chart Type and name it **Simple P&L Year over Year**.

2. Use Year as a dimension.

3. In the Expressions tab, define the 14 expressions described in the following table:

LABEL	DEFINITION
Sales at List	sum([# Amount at List Price])
– Discounts	sum([# Amount - Discounts])
Gross Sales	sum([# Amount])
– Returns	sum({<[Reason Description]={'Return to stock'}>} [# CM Amount])
Net Direct Product Sales	sum([# Amount]) – sum({<[Reason Description]={'Return to stock'}>} [# CM Amount])
– Materlal	sum([# COGS - Material])
– Labor	sum([# COGS - Labor])
Direct Product Contribution Margin	sum([# Amount]) – sum({<[Reason Description]={'Return to stock'}>} [# CM Amount]) – sum([# COGS - Material]) – sum([# COGS - Labor])
– Customer Allowances	sum({<[Reason Description]={*} - {'Return to stock'}>} [# CM Amount])
Direct Customer Contribution Margin	sum([# Amount]) – sum([# CM Amount]) – sum([# COGS - Material]) – sum([# COGS - Labor])
– Channel Related Costs	sum([# Amount]* [# Commission Percent])
Channel Contribution Margin	sum([# Amount] * (1-[# Commission Percent])) – sum([# CM Amount]) – sum([# COGS - Material]) – sum([# COGS - Labor])

LABEL	DEFINITION
– Manufacturing Overhead	sum([# COGS - Overhead])
Operating Profit	sum([# Amount] * (1 - [# Commission Percent])) – sum([# CM Amount]) – sum([# COGS - Material]) - sum([# COGS - Labor]) - sum([# COGS - Overhead])

4. For all the expressions, check the No Totals option under the Total Mode.

5. In the Presentation tab, check Horizontal and center the data for the Year field.

6. In the Number tab, highlight all the numbers and format them as Integer numbers.

7. Your finished chart should look similar to Figure 8.1.

8. Save your work.

A real-life P&L report should also present all the margin levels as a percentage of gross sales. You may add those percentages next to the corresponding amounts, to make your P&L report look more realistic. We decided to keep our chart relatively simple to ease the complexity of the exercises.

Enhancing Calculations with Variables

Building your first P&L report was quite exciting, wasn't it? Now imagine the following scenario: you showed it to your CFO and in response, were asked to show all the numbers in millions. Then, after a bit of hesitation, he added that sometimes it might be helpful to have a similar report in thousands, and that for internal use the existing chart would still be helpful.

You already know that cloning and modifying QlikView charts is easy enough, and yet the prospect of modifying 14 expressions in two separate charts sounds dreadful. Our inner "lazy programmer" protests that there must be a better way!

And of course, there is a better way. You can make your calculations much more flexible with the use of *variables*. In this section, you learn the various uses of QlikView variables in the layout objects.

Introducing QlikView Variables

QlikView variables are quite similar to variables in other scripting languages. Simply put, a variable has a name and holds a single value—in contrast to fields that store many instances of the same type of data.

Variables serve many useful purposes in QlikView, both in the script and in the layout. In this section, we focus on the techniques of creating and using variables in the layout objects. Chapter 10 will continue our discussion about variables and their use in the script.

Creating Variables in the Layout

Variables can be created in many different ways, both in the script and in the layout. In the layout, you can manage all variables in a single place called **Variable Overview**, which is available from the **Settings** menu.

The **Variable Overview** dialog (see Figure 8.2) is quite simple. Existing variables are listed in the **Variables** list. The **Definition** and the **Comment** for the highlighted variable are listed below. The buttons on the right allow you to **Add** or **Remove** a variable.

FIGURE 8.2:
The Variable Overview dialog

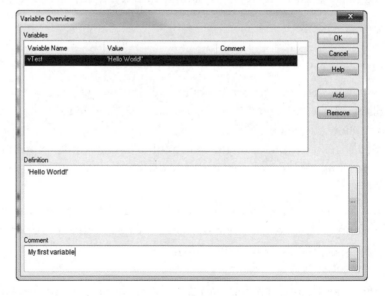

In order to add a variable, click the **Add** button and type the variable name in the window that pops up. In order to assign a value to the variable, highlight the variable in the list and type the value in the **Definition** window. Notice that the newly added variable is not highlighted automatically. You still need to click on the new variable name in order to activate it.

Using Naming Conventions for Variables

A commonly used naming convention requires that all variables begin with a unique prefix, typically with a lowercase letter v. In our practice, we use a number of prefixes to signify variables of different purposes. For example, variables that store expressions begin with the prefix exp_, while variables that store the definitions of colors begin with the prefix color_.

Feel free to experiment with adding and removing variables in the **Variable Overview** dialog. In the next section, we describe another method of working with variables.

Using an Input Box for Creating Variables and Assigning Values

Variables can be used for collecting user input and integrating entered values in calculations. Entered values can be assigned to variables using a special sheet object called the *input box.*

Like any other sheet objects, the input box can be created by right-clicking anywhere on the sheet and selecting the option **New Sheet Object**.

In the **General** tab of the input box **Properties** (see Figure 8.3), you can select what variables out of the **Available Variables** should be displayed in the input box. Once the variable is added to the list, it can be equipped with a nice **Label**, to replace the cryptic variable name. When necessary, a new variable can be added using the **New Variable** button.

The **Presentation** tab offers a few formatting options and can be skipped for now. The next tab, **Constraints**, however, is quite interesting (see Figure 8.4). Here you can define certain rules for the entered values, to guide and validate the user input.

FIGURE 8.3:
Input box properties,
General tab

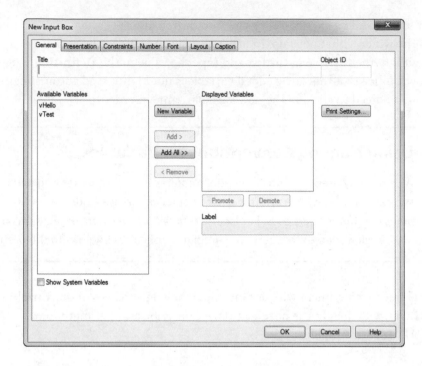

FIGURE 8.4:
Input box properties,
Constraints tab

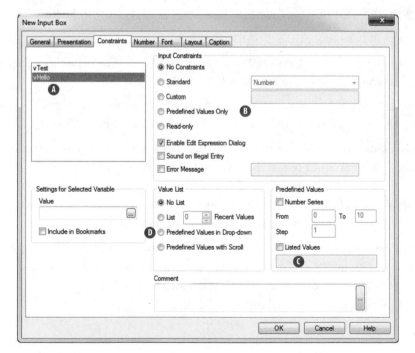

The variables displayed in the input box are listed in the top-left corner (A). All the settings on this tab apply to the variable that's highlighted in this list.

The **Input Constraints** section (B) contains a selection of various constraints, such as applying **Standard** or **Custom** conditions, or limiting the input values to the list of **Predefined Values**. The latter is quite commonly used for any discrete lists of values. For example, we need to show the P&L report in single dollars, in thousands, or in millions. This calls for a variable that can accept one of three values—1, 1,000, or 1,000,000. This condition is perfect for creating a list of predefined values (C) and showing that list in a drop-down list (D).

The **Listed Values** (C) can be entered in a list, separated by a semicolon.

The rest of the input box definitions are quite standard. Overall, we believe that managing variables using the input box object is a bit more convenient than using the **Variable Overview** dialog.

In the following exercise, you create an input box that will host a single variable vUnit (unit of measure). The variable will only allow three predefined values: 1, 1,000, or 1,000,000.

Then, you transform the P&L report that you created earlier, to show information in the required unit of measure.

Feel free to develop these visualizations on your own or follow the detailed directions in Exercise 8.3.

Exercise 8.3: Creating an Input Box

1. Add a new Input Box (right-click, … you know the drill!).

2. Within the Input Box Properties, use the New Variable button to create a new variable. Name it **vUnit**.

3. Highlight the new variable in the list of Displayed Variables and change the Label to **Unit of Measure**.

4. Open the Constraints tab (see Figure 8.5). Make the following changes:

   4.1. Select Predefined Values Only in the list of Input Constraints.

   4.2. Uncheck Enable Edit Expression Dialog.

4.3. Under Value List, select Predefined Values in Drop-down.

4.4. Under Predefined Values, check Listed Values and enter the list of the three values, without commas, separated by a semicolon.

FIGURE 8.5:
Constraint settings for the unit of measure

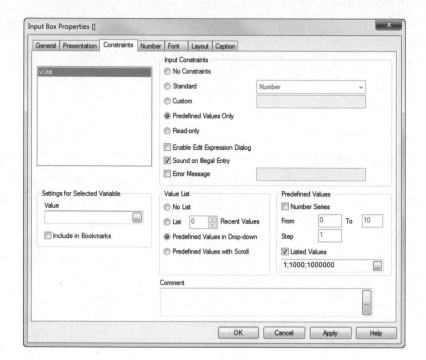

5. In the Number tab, format the number as Integer.

6. Exit the Properties window by clicking on OK and then examine the new object. Resize the object and the individual columns within the object as necessary. Your input box should look like this:

| Unit of Measure | = 1,000,000 | ▼ |

7. Position the new input box in the upper left corner of the sheet, on top of the gray ribbon, just above the Current Selections box.

8. Copy the new input box to the Template sheet and Save your work.

In the next exercise, you integrate the entered value in the P&L report.

Exercise 8.4: Enhancing the P&L Report with a Variable

Open the **Properties** of the P&L report and modify all the chart expressions to reflect the newly added vUnit variable. Enclose every formula in parentheses and divide by vUnit.

Extra Credit:

Transform the chart title into a dynamic calculation that shows the corresponding unit of measure—(in thousands) or (in millions), depending on the current value of vUnit.

Using Variables for a Simple What-If Analysis

In a similar way, you can use variables for a simple form of a What-If simulation. What should happen to the bottom line if sales grow at a certain percent, while material and labor costs change at a different rate?

You can define a few simulation parameters as variables, gather their values using an input box, and include the entered values in chart calculations.

Let's define the logic for this What-If simulation:

- The simulation will be based on three variable parameters—% change in sales, % change in labor cost, and % change in the material cost.

- Labor cost will be affected by both the sales change and the labor cost change factors. Similarly, material cost will be affected by both the sales change and the material cost change factor.

- We assume that discounts, returns, allowances and channel costs will change at the same rate as sales.

- We assume that the general and administrative costs will remain the same, regardless of the other changes.

In order to implement this simulation, you need to create an input box with three new variables—vChangeSales, vChangeMaterial, and vChangeLabor.

In the chart, we will multiply each corresponding component of costs and profits by the corresponding factor of (1+Change%). Material and labor costs will be multiplied by two factors.

For the purpose of this simulation, we will clone the existing **P&L** sheet and make the changes in the new sheet called **What-If**. Feel free to develop this simulation on your own or follow the detailed instructions in Exercise 8.5.

Exercise 8.5: Developing a Simple What-If Analysis

1. Clone the P&L sheet and name the new sheet **What-If**.

2. Create a new Input Box and add three new variables—vChangeSales, vChangeMaterial, and vChangeLabor. Override the labels for all three variables with human-readable descriptions. Type **What-If Parameters** as the input box title.

3. In the Number tab, configure all three variables as Integers, shown as Percentages.

4. Position the new object above the P&L chart (you'll need to move the P&L chart down to make room).

5. Clone the P&L chart and position a new copy next to the original. Change the title to read **Simulated P&L**.

6. Modify the chart expressions based on the logic that we just described:

   - Most of the components of revenues and costs should be multiplied by (1 + vChangeSales).

   - Material and labor costs need to be multiplied by two factors accordingly.

   - General and administrative costs should not change.

   - Your expressions should look like those in the following table:

LABEL	DEFINITION
Sales at List	(sum([# Amount at List Price]) * (1 + *vChangeSales*)) / *vUnit*
– Discounts	(sum([# Amount – Discounts])* (1 + *vChangeSales*)) / *vUnit*
Gross Sales	(sum([# Amount]) * (1 + *vChangeSales*)) / *vUnit*
– Returns	(sum({<[Reason Description]={'Return to stock'}>} [# CM Amount]) * (1 + *vChangeSales*)) / *vUnit*
Net Direct Product Sales	(sum([# Amount]) – sum({<[Reason Description]={'Return to stock'}>} [# CM Amount])) * (1 + *vChangeSales*)/ *vUnit*

LABEL	DEFINITION
– Material	`(sum([# COGS - Material]) * (1 + `*vChangeSales*`) * (1 + `*vChangeMaterial*`))/ `*vUnit*
– Labor	`sum([# COGS - Labor]) * (1 + `*vChangeSales*`) * (1 + `*vChangeLabor*`) / `*vUnit*

Direct Product Contribution Margin	`(sum([# Amount]) -`
	`sum({<[Reason Description]={'Return to stock'}>} [# CM Amount]) -`
	`sum([# COGS - Material]) * (1 + `*vChangeMaterial*`) -`
	`sum([# COGS - Labor]) * (1 + `*vChangeLabor*`)) * (1 + `*vChangeSales*`) / `
	vUnit

– Customer Allowances	`(sum({<[Reason Description]={*} -` `{'Return to stock'}>} [# CM Amount]) ) *(1 + vChangeSales)/ vUnit`

Direct Customer Contribution Margin	`(sum([# Amount]) - sum([# CM Amount]) -`
	`sum([# COGS - Material]) * (1 + `*vChangeMaterial*`) -`
	`sum([# COGS - Labor]) *`
	`(1 + `*vChangeLabor*`)) * (1 + `*vChangeSales*`) / `*vUnit*

– Channel Related Costs	`(sum([# Amount]* [# Commission Percent] ) ) *` `(1 + `*vChangeSales*`) / `*vUnit*

Channel Contribution Margin	`(sum([# Amount]* (1 - [# Commission Percent])) -`
	`sum([# CM Amount]) -`
	`sum([# COGS - Material]) * (1 + `*vChangeMaterial*`) - sum([# COGS -`
	`Labor]) *`
	`(1 + `*vChangeLabor*`)) * (1 + `*vChangeSales*`)`
	`/ `*vUnit*

– Manufacturing Overhead	`sum([# COGS - Overhead])`

Operating Profit	`((sum([# Amount]* (1 - [# Commission Percent])) - sum([# CM Amount])`
	`- sum([# COGS - Material]) * (1 + `*vChangeMaterial*`) - sum([# COGS -`
	`Labor]) *`
	`(1 + `*vChangeLabor*`)) * (1 + `*vChangeSales*`) - sum([# COGS - Overhead]))/`
	vUnit

7. Accept the changes and examine the result. If your new chart shows a lot of NULL values, it means that no values are entered in the input box. Enter all three numbers as percentages and examine the differences between the original P&L and the simulated P&L.

A few closing comments about this exercise. First, notice how percentages are entered into the input box. You may use one of the two formats—either enter the whole number with the percentage sign (20%) or enter the decimal number that represents 20% (0.2 instead of 20%). Entering the number 20 alone results in a value of 2,000%. Keep that in mind when entering percentage values.

Secondly, we owe you an explanation about the unexpected NULLs. When certain values are not assigned, the corresponding fields or variables carry the NULL value. QlikView aggregation functions handle NULL values "graciously," by automatically treating NULLs as zeroes. All other operations, however, are not as smart. Any mathematical operation performed on a NULL value will result in a NULL value. For this reason, these simulated values turn into NULL as soon as any of the components in their calculations are not assigned.

QlikView offers a choice of range functions that can be applied to a number of values. These functions are also smart about NULLs—they will automatically replace NULL values with zeroes. In total, there are 18 range functions. The most commonly used functions are:

```
RangeSum(v1, v2, v3, …)

RangeMin(v1, v2, v3, …)

RangeMax(v1, v2, v3, …)

RangeAvg(v1, v2, v3, …)
```

Their meaning is self-evident—each function calculates the sum, min, max, or average of a number of values. NULL handling may be only a side effect, but it is often a good reason to use RangeSum() instead of a regular addition. For example, the formula

```
(1 + vChangeLabor)
```

will return NULL if the variable wasn't assigned, while the formula

```
RangeSum(1, vChangeLabor)
```

will return 1 as a result, because the missing variable will be treated as zero.

In order to avoid receiving NULL results in your simulated P&L, you may go back into all the expressions and replace all the instances of (1 + vChange…) with the corresponding RangeSum() function.

Should You Use RangeSum() with Multiple Aggregation Functions?

In earlier versions of QlikView, it was even recommended that you use `RangeSum()` to add or subtract multiple aggregated functions, like in this example:

```
RangeSum( sum([# Amount]) , -1* sum([# COGS]))
```

This was in case the data for one of the functions were missing, which would cause the aggregated result to be NULL. In recent versions, however, this issue appears to be solved, and the aggregation functions seem to consistently return zero when the data is missing. However, if you are receiving NULL results with no visible syntax errors, try using `RangeSum()` to resolve a possible problem with NULL handling.

Enhancing Look and Feel with Sliders

While the input box does a fine job of gathering user input, you can use another QlikView object, called *Slider/Calendar*, to spice up the look and feel of the document.

The Slider/Calendar object can serve as a slider or as a calendar. Both styles of the object share many common characteristics. Most notably, both styles serve a similar purpose—they enhance the look and feel of the user input (see Figure 8.6).

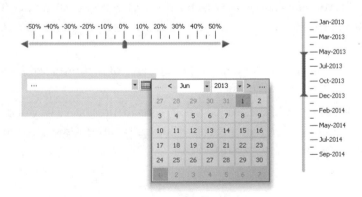

FIGURE 8.6:
Examples of sliders and calendars

The **General** tab of the **Slider/Calendar Properties** window (see Figure 8.7) offers a number of important choices:

- **Input Style** can be **Slider** or **Calendar** (A). We will use the **Slider** style for our purposes.

- The object can be used for a **Field** or **Variable(s)** (B)—when **Field** is selected, the slider is used to make a selection in a field. With variables, it controls the value of a variable.

- The **Mode** setting (C) determines whether the slider can assign a **Single Value** or **Multi Value**. When **Multi Value** is selected, the slider can turn into a range of values with dynamic width. For fields, it means selecting a range of field values. For variables, selecting **Multi Value** unlocks the second choice of a variable (D). In this case, the first variable will receive the lowest value in the selected range and the second variable will receive the highest value in the range.

- **Value Mode** (E) allows working with **Discrete** values (only applicable to fields) or **Continuous/Numeric** values.

- **Min Value** and **Max Value** (F) define the boundaries for the slider.

- The optional **Static Step** (G) can limit user input to certain increments—for example, only allowing whole numbers, tens, or hundreds.

The **Presentation** tab of the properties (see Figure 8.8) allows configuring the colors (A) for all the elements of the slider, setting the **Scroll Orientation** and of the **Label Orientation** (B), as well as configuring the **Scale** settings (C). You can enable and disable displaying the scroll arrows (D) at the ends of the slider. **Slider Style** can be selected between **Solid** and **Shimmer**.

With sliders, you can offer a more appealing way of making selections in fields or assigning values to variables.

In Exercise 8.6, you add three sliders to create an alternative way of defining the three simulation parameters—**Change in Sales**, **Change in Material Cost**, and **Change in Labor Cost**.

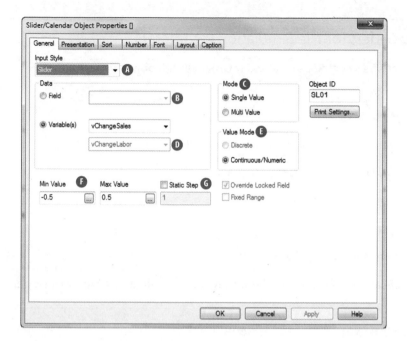

FIGURE 8.7:
The General tab of the Slider/Calendar Object Properties window

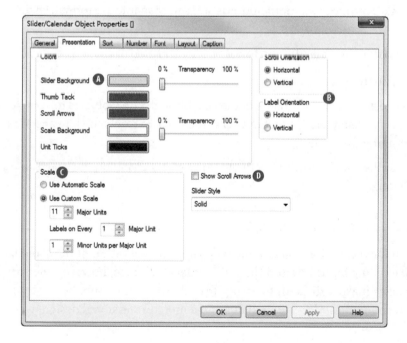

FIGURE 8.8:
The Presentation tab of the Slider/Calendar Object Properties window

Exercise 8.6: Adding Sliders for the Simulation Parameters

1. Create a new sheet object and select Slider/Calendar Object as the object type.
2. On the General tab:

    2.1. Select Slider as an Input Style.

    2.2. Under Data, select Variable and pick vChangeSales from the drop-down list.

    2.3. Leave Single Value and Continuous/Numeric mode.

    2.4. Enter Min Value = **-0.5** and Max Value = **0.5**.

3. On the Presentation tab:

    3.1. Leave the default colors and orientation settings.

    3.2. Select Use Custom Scale, **11** Major Units, Labels on every **1** Unit, and **1** Minor Units per Major Unit.

    3.3. Uncheck Show Scroll Arrows.

4. On the Number tab, check Override Document Settings and select an Integer format. Enable Show in Percent (%).

    4.1 On the Caption tab, assign the Title **Change In Sales**.

5. Exit the wizard and examine the result.
6. Clone the new object twice and replace the name of the variable in the new objects to vChangeMaterial and vChangeLabor, accordingly. Notice that changing the variable resets the Min and Max values, so you have to re-enter the values.
7. Position the sliders next to the input box with the three variables. Try changing the values using the input box and the slider.
8. Save your work.

In the next exercise, you enhance the visual presentation of the screen. The existing input box and the three sliders look nice; however, the varying sizes make it difficult to associate each line in the input box with the corresponding slider. You will develop a more professional design, where each simulation parameter occupies a distinct area on the sheet, with both the input box and the slider available for user input. Figure 8.9 shows the desired look and feel.

Developing the sheet with this look and feel involves the following steps:

- The input box needs to be split into three individual objects, one per variable (see Figure 8.9, A, B, and C).

- The label for each variable should be suppressed by replacing it with a single space.

- The input boxes need to be reformatted with a larger font, without equals signs, and without borders.

- The frame outlining the settings for each variable, as well as the label, should be implemented as a text object that serves as a background behind the slider and the input box (see Figure 8.9, D, E, and F).

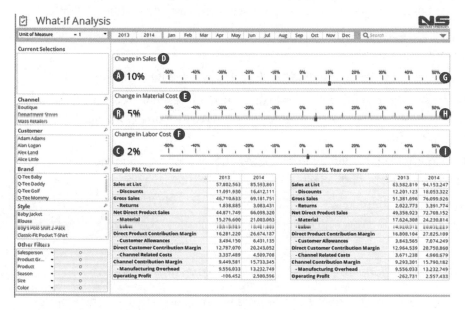

FIGURE 8.9:
An enhanced look and feel of the What-If screen

Feel free to perform those changes on your own or follow the detailed instructions in Exercise 8.7.

Exercise 8.7: Enhancing the Look and Feel of the What-If Analysis

1. Open the Properties of the input box and perform the following changes:

   1.1. On the General tab, replace all three labels by single spaces.

   1.2. On the Presentation tab, uncheck Show Equal Sign.

   1.3. On the Constraints tab, clear the Enable Edit Expression checkbox for each one of the three variables.

   1.4. On the Font tab, increase the font Size to **20**.

   1.5. On the Layout tab, set the Border Width to **0**.

2. Close the properties by clicking OK. Resize the columns of the input box to minimize the size of the label. Split the input box into three separate objects, each one carrying a single variable.

3. Add a Text Object with the transparent background and with the text **Change in Sales**, aligned to the left and to the top.

4. Position the input box and the slider on top of the text object, as presented in Figure 8.9, G.

5. Clone the Text object twice and change the labels to **Change in Material Cost** and **Change in Labor Cost** accordingly. Position all the objects as backgrounds to the corresponding sliders and input boxes, according to Figure 8.9, H and I.

6. Pay attention to the alignment of the different objects. Whenever possible, align the horizontal and vertical borders of the neighboring objects.

7. Save your work when you are done.

Using Variables to Store and Retrieve Expression Formulas

You've seen how variables can be used in expressions to make them more flexible and to perform simple simulations. In addition, variables can be used to store complete formulas that can then be retrieved in multiple expressions.

As you can see, the profitability analysis involves more calculations than the sales analysis, and the calculations get more complex. Entering each of these in various charts would have been tedious and error-prone.

Imagine that you developed this profitability analysis application with a few dozen charts and text objects, all using various combinations of the 14 expressions described in the earlier sections. Then, imagine that in the process of testing the application, you discovered a logical error in one of the expressions. You would need to scan the application for all the objects that use that particular expression and fix the error individually in each of those objects. Doesn't sound like a lot of fun, does it? While QlikView offers a very nice **Expression Overview** (we'll let you explore it on your own; it's available in the **Settings** menu), locating and fixing multiple instances of the same formula sounds like a lot of work. The "lazy programmer" inside wakes up and protests—there must be a better way!

The better way is to use variables to store the definitions of the expressions, and to use the same variable multiple times in different charts and objects.

The first step in this process is to store a formula in a variable. The easiest way to do so is to create and test the expression as part of a chart, and then to copy the text and paste it into the **Value** setting of a variable. This can be done in either the **Variable Overview** or an **Input Box**.

In order to be used in chart expressions, the variable needs to be enclosed in a *dollar-sign expansion*: $(vFormula). The dollar-sign expansion is a special technique that is used for text replacement. When it's applied to variables, the name of the variable is replaced with its contents (this process is called *expansion*) before the chart expression is evaluated.

Using variables within a dollar-sign expansion can be helpful in two cases:

- Using a variable instead of a hard-coded value in a place where the syntactic rules do not allow the use of variables. For example, Set Analysis syntax is not built to accept variables in their "native" form. You can, however, use values stored in variables by enclosing the variable in a dollar-sign expansion. After the text replacement (the "expansion") is done, the result appears to the Set Analysis engine just like a hard-coded value.

- Storing formulas (or parts of formulas) in variables and retrieving the formulas by enclosing the variable in a dollar-sign expansion. After the expansion is done, the expression interpreter treats the result just like a hard-coded formula.

In Exercise 8.8, you create new variables and store all 14 components of the P&L report in the new variables. As a naming convention, we use the prefix exp_ for all the variables that store expressions, in order to differentiate them from all other variables. Also, if the variable name contains multiple words, we will suppress spaces but apply CamelCase—each word begins with a capital letter.

Since we don't know upfront how these formulas will be used in chart expressions (they can participate in subtraction, division, or multiplication), it is advisable to always include all the formulas in an extra set of parentheses, to protect the integrity of each formula.

Exercise 8.8: Storing Expressions in Variables

1. Activate the P&L sheet.

2. Create a new Input Box to the right of the existing P&L report.

3. In the General tab of the input box Properties, use the New Variable button to create 14 variables to match the 14 components of the P&L: exp_SalesAtList, exp_Discounts, exp_GrossSales, exp_Returns, exp_NetDirectProductSales, exp_Material, exp_Labor, exp_DirectProductContributionMargin, exp_CustomerAllowances, exp_DirectCustomerContributionMargin, exp_ChannelRelatedCosts, exp_ChannelContributionMargin, exp_ManufacturingOverhead, exp_OperatingProfit.

4. Press OK to exit the Input Box Properties. Resize and reposition the input box to make it easy to use.

5. For each of the 14 expressions, open the P&L chart properties, copy the formula definition of each expression, then exit the properties and paste the text directly into the value of the corresponding variable in the input box. You may save some time if you open a second instance of QlikView and copy the text side by side, without needing to close and open properties every time. Just don't mix up the two versions of the same document!

6. Include each formula in an extra set of parentheses, to protect its integrity.

7. At the end of the process, your sheet should look like the one presented in Figure 8.10.

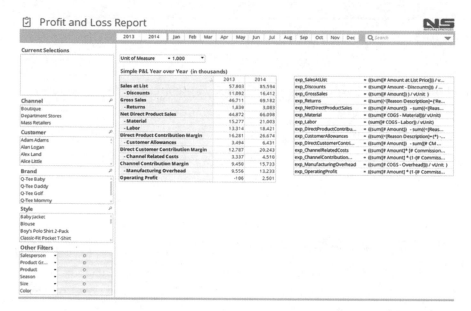

FIGURE 8.10:
Saving formulas in
variables

The next step is to use the newly created variables in chart expressions, including those expressions that already exist. In the simplest form, you should go back to the **Chart Properties** and replace each one of the expression definitions with a dollar-sign expansion and a corresponding variable.

Variable names can be accessed within the **Variables** tab at the bottom of the **Expression Editor**. Alternatively, variable names can be received from the IntelliSense prompt. Unfortunately, IntelliSense does not work well with the dollar-sign expansions. You have to start by typing the name of the variable (luckily, all of the expression variables begin with the same prefix, exp_), then pick the desired variable from the IntelliSense prompt, and only then enclose the variable in the dollar-sign expansion.

Exercise 8.9: Replacing the Existing Formulas with Variables

1. Open the Properties of the P&L chart.

2. Replace the existing formulas in all 14 expressions in the chart by the corresponding variables enclosed in the dollar-sign expansions.

3. Close the Properties and verify that all the lines in the P&L are populated with the same values.

4. Delete the copy of the same chart on the What-If sheet and clone the modified chart once again. This eliminates the need to modify all the expressions again.

Using Formulas that Begin with the Equals Sign

As a reminder of the recently introduced technique: when variables contain formulas, those formulas will get evaluated when the variable is used within the dollar-sign expansion. When such a variable is used in a chart expression, its content is re-evaluated for every line of the chart.

Another technique of storing a formula in a variable involves starting a formula with the equals sign, =. These variables are evaluated immediately, and they get recalculated with every selection and every change in all other variables. When such a variable is used in a chart expression, it is not evaluated in every line of the chart. Instead, the most current value that was calculated with the last selection is used in all chart lines. That means that these variables should only be used for calculations that are not dependent on the dimension values. Adding the equals sign in front of the existing formulas stored within variables will result in the P&L charts showing the overall total numbers, not divided by year. On the other hand, if you wanted to calculate a share of a total, then the total number could be calculated once and stored in a variable, using a formula that begins with the equals sign.

Let's consider the following requirement. Examine the look of the P&L with all three possible units—single dollars, thousands, and millions. The chart looks nice in single dollars and in thousands; however, the presentation in millions looks incomplete. Surely, the users would like to see at least one decimal place when the numbers are listed in millions. That means that this formatting needs to be conditional. If the chart is presenting millions, you want to format all the numbers with one decimal place; otherwise use whole numbers.

Unfortunately, the conventional technique of formatting the numbers in the **Number** tab doesn't allow for conditional formatting. If this is an important requirement, you need to format the numbers "manually," by using the num() function and calculating the format string based on the condition. In this case, it's perfectly fine to start the formula of the formatting string with the equals sign, in order to evaluate the value upfront and avoid calculating it multiple times in the chart expressions.

Following our naming convention, we will name the variable of the formatting string fmt_PL (the format for the P&L). The conditional formula could look like this:

```
=IF(vUnit = 1000000, '#,##0.0', '#,##0')
```

The format string will be recalculated with any selection and any change in any of the other variables. So, if the vUnit variable changes, the new format will be recalculated.

In the expression itself, the formula will look like this:

```
num(
      (sum([# Amount at List Price])) / vUnit
, '$(fmt_PL)')
```

Notice that the dollar-sign expansion is included in single quotes, because the syntax of the num() function expects to see the format string enclosed in single quotes.

Also notice the structured presentation of the expression—the num() function is listed in the first line, then the calculation itself is listed in a separate line and tabulated; and then the format string and the closing parenthesis are listed in a separate closing line. This structured appearance makes it easy to read and understand the formula. When needed, the actual calculation can be easily replaced by another calculation, without affecting the formatting function.

Now you have a decision to make. Should you add the formatting function in the chart expression, leaving the formulas stored within variables unformatted, or should you format the expressions within the formulas?

There are advantages and drawbacks to both options. For our purposes, we decided to format the expressions within the variables. If we have to reformat the same expression later, we can always enclose the variable within another formatting function num().

When you use pre-formatted calculations in chart expressions, you should remember to set the expression format in the **Number** tab to **Expression Default**. It means that no additional number formatting will be done in the chart.

In the following exercise, you create a new variable called fmt_PL with the dynamic formatting string and modify all 14 expression variables, applying the formatting function num() and the dynamic format string.

Exercise 8.10: Adding Dynamic Number Formatting

1. In the input box with the expression variables, create a new variable and name it **fmt_PL**. Use the following formula as the value of the variable (make sure to start the text with the equals sign):

   =IF(vUnit = 1000000, '#,##0.0', '#,##0')

2. Notice how the value displayed in the input box changes when you change the unit of measure. The variable is recalculated with every change in selections and in other variables.

3. Add the formatting function num() and the dynamic format code to all 14 variables that store expressions, as described previously:

   3.1. Insert the first line with the beginning of the num(function.

   3.2. Keep the calculation listed in a separate line (or multiple lines), tabulated.

   3.3. Add another line to the end with the format variable in the dollar-sign expansion, enclosed in a pair of single quotes, and the closing parenthesis for the num():

   , '$(fmt_PL)')

4. In the P&L **Chart Properties**, open the **Number** tab, highlight all the expressions, and select **Expression Default** as the format choice.

5. Examine the result. The numbers in the chart should be formatted as whole numbers when the selected unit of measure is single units or thousands. When the unit of measure is equal to millions, the numbers should be formatted with one decimal place.

Using Variables for Storing Color Definitions

This discussion on variables wouldn't be complete without mentioning colors. In many advanced QlikView applications, all colors are defined using variables. This technique allows developers to stay consistent with their color definitions throughout the application.

In many companies, the Marketing department defines the standard company colors very strictly, using their RGB (Red-Green-Blue) or HSL (Hue-Saturation-Luminance) codes. In QlikView, both code systems are supported, but RGB seems to be more popular. The Marketing department at the fictional company Q-Tee Brands issued a color guide that defines the basic colors that should be used throughout the applications. Table 8.1 lists the RGB values for these colors.

TABLE 8.1: Standard Color Definitions for Q-Tee Brands

COLOR	RGB DEFINITION
Green	RGB(77, 167, 65)
Yellow	RGB(249, 156, 50)
Red	RGB(255, 107, 107)
Blue	RGB(0, 100, 200)
Purple	RGB(143, 68, 173)
Black	RGB(54, 54, 54)
Gray	RGB(200, 200, 200)
White	RGB(255, 255, 255)

If you had to code those numbers every time you needed to use one of those colors, it would be a very tedious task. Moreover, if the branding changes in the future, changing the specific RGB definitions in thousands of objects would be an enormous undertaking.

With variables, you can encapsulate the RGB codes and "hide" them behind the color names, which makes it much easier to use and extremely easy to change.

The process of using variables for color definitions is simple. First, you add a new variable (we usually start the variable name with the prefix color_ in order to differentiate color variables from the rest). Then, you type the RGB formula in the definition of the variable. Quite conveniently, RGB(r, g, b) is one of many color functions supported in QlikView. If you prefer the HSL notation, you can use the function HSL(h, s, l) the same way.

Finally, when the color needs to be specified in the **Color Area** dialog (see Figure 8.11), you simply need to select **Calculated** color instead of **Fixed** and type the color variable name, enclosed in the dollar-sign expansion.

FIGURE 8.11:
Using variables and calculated colors

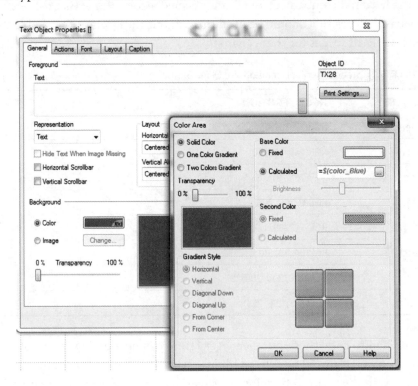

Alternatively, the variables can be used in more complex calculations that return the appropriate color (typically green, yellow, or red) based on a certain metric. For example, the following formula returns one of the three colors, depending on the comparison of the actual Direct Product Contribution Margin percent to its target:

```
if( $(exp_DirectProductContributionMargin) / $(exp_GrossSales)>=
v_TargetProductContribution, $(color_Green),
if( $(exp_DirectProductContributionMargin) / $(exp_GrossSales)>=
v_TargetProductContribution * 0.9, $(color_Yellow), $(color_Red)
))
```

Notice that in all the examples, the color variable name needs to be enclosed in the dollar-sign expansion. At the same time, the target variable v_TargetProductContribution does not need to be enclosed in the dollar-sign expansion, because it carries a simple numeric value that does not need to be evaluated.

In the following exercise, you prepare a set of color variables that will be used for advanced visualizations in the following sections.

Exercise 8.11: Creating Color Variables

1. Create a new **Input Box** on the **P&L** sheet.

2. In the input box **Properties**, use the **New Variable** button to add variables for the eight basic colors listed in Table 8.1. Use the prefix color_ for each variable—color_Red, color_Green, and so on. Once all eight variables are ready, close the **Properties** dialog.

3. Type the RGB formulas for the eight variables, as presented in Table 8.1.

4. In order to test your new variables, create a Text object and define the background as green, using the new variable $(color_Green).

This exercise completes our discussion about using QlikView variables in layout objects. You used variables to add flexibility to your expressions, created a simple What-If analysis, stored and reused repeatable expressions, and arranged dynamic formatting of the same numbers, based on a condition. You also created a number of color variables that you will use for advanced formatting of your objects.

In the following sections, you continue discovering visualization techniques that can help you visualize profitability.

Revisiting Simple Visualization Objects

So far, you have prepared all the expressions for the profit levels and for the different cost buckets, and you've learned the basics of QlikView visualizations when you developed the Sales Analysis application.

Of course, the same simple visualizations remain relevant for the profitability analysis as well. Here are some of the common use-case scenarios:

- You can use gauges and text objects to visualize the main KPIs on top of the dashboard screens.

- You can use bar charts to compare profit contributions among different products, customers, or channels.

- You can use line charts to show profitability trends over time.

- You can use pie charts to show distribution of profits between brands or channels.

Feel free to practice using simple visualizations with the profitability calculations that you learned earlier in this chapter.

In the following exercises, you use some of the simple objects covered earlier in combination with the new techniques that we introduce in this chapter. You will begin developing the **Product Profitability** sheet, which will contain all the aspects of product profitability. The immediate goal is to develop the top portion of the **Product Profitability** sheet, with the three main KPIs that describe product profitability—the **Direct Product Contribution** margin as a measure of outcome, and the two main drivers that affect profitability at this level—the **Discounts** and the **Returns**.

The desired result is presented in Figure 8.12.

FIGURE 8.12:
The top portion of the Product Profitability sheet

Let's describe the elements of this picture:

- Three sections represent the three main KPIs presented on this page—Direct Product Contribution, Discounts, and Returns. The gray lines separate the sections, while a horizontal line separates the top section from the rest of the sheet.

- Each of the three sections contains four objects:

  - The static label with the name of the metric.

  - The calculated Text object with the dollar amount in large font (we used font size 36). The amounts are calculated in the same way as we calculated them in the P&L report, driven by the user-defined unit of measure. Notice the dollar sign in front of the numbers and the symbol, such as M or K, representing the unit of measure. The symbol is calculated as a variable and the dollar sign is appended as a static symbol (when necessary, a dynamic currency symbol can be added the same way).

  - Another calculated Text object with the percentage of gross sales or sales at list that this component comprises.

  - The graphical representation of the same percentage, in relation to budget. This object looks like a gauge, but in fact it's a stacked bar chart that was formatted in a very specific way, in order to obtain this particular presentation.

- The three objects that represent the metrics are colored green, yellow, or red, depending on the actual performance compared to a target number.

- The target percentages are stored in the corresponding variables (in this simplified model, the targets are unified across all brands and all channels; in your real-life applications, you are likely to associate targets with specific brands, categories, or market segments).

The bar chart deserves a separate explanation. As you can see from the appearance of the three charts in Figure 8.12, all the external borders, captions, headings, and axis lines were removed.

The chart is built with two expressions. The first expression, **Actual**, is calculated as the corresponding amount divided by the corresponding sales amount.

The second expression is quite peculiar. When the actual number is below the target, we'd like to show the remaining part as a gray bar, stacked on top of the Actual bar, and the total length of the two bars should exceed the target by 20% (this way, we can show the target using a reference line). If the actual number exceeds the target by more than 20%, then the actual number should cover the whole bar, with no additional gray bar on top. Hence, the expression will be calculated as the higher value between the actual number and the target, multiplied by a factor of 1.2. Then, since the second bar should appear as the stacked bar on top of the actual, we should subtract the actual number:

```
rangemax( Actual, v_TargetProductContribution * 1.2) - Actual
```

where the variable v_TargetProductContribution is one of the new variables that will store the target for the product contribution.

The target number is presented by a **Reference Line** and a **Text in Chart** positioned in the upper-right corner of the chart. You may notice that reference lines can be equipped with their own labels. We still prefer to use a separate **Text in Chart** for this visualization because it's easier to position a separate text in the limited space that's available for this chart. In many other cases, using built-in labels with the reference lines makes more sense.

Try to develop several of these visualizations on your own. The following exercise provides the detailed instructions.

Exercise 8.12: Visualizing Product Profitability KPIs

1. Copy the Template sheet and name the new sheet **Product Profitability**. Replace the icon and the sheet title on top of the sheet.

2. Create the outline of the top section with a long horizontal divider line and two shorter vertical dividers that should separate the available space to three identical sections.

3. Add the three static labels with the names of the metrics—**Direct Product Contribution**, **Discounts**, and **Returns**. Use the color color_Gray as the font color.

4. Create an Input Box away from your main sheet area. Add a new variable called **exp_UnitSymbol** and assign the following formula to the value (beginning with the equals sign). This variable will return the symbol that represents the selected unit of measure:

```
=if(vUnit= 1000000, 'M',    if(vUnit=1000, 'K', ''  ))
```

5. In the same input box, add the three KPI targets as new variables:

```
v_TargetProductContribution = 40%,

v_TargetDiscounts = 15%,

v_TargetReturns = 5%.
```

6. Create the Text Objects with the amounts:

    6.1. Create the Text Object with the calculation of the direct product contribution amount:

    ```
    = '$' &
    $(exp_DirectProductContributionMargin)
    & exp_UnitSymbol
    ```

    6.2. In the Font tab of the Text Object Properties, select font Size=36 and define the color using the following calculated formula:

    ```
    if( $(exp_DirectProductContributionMargin) / $(exp_GrossSales)>=
    v_TargetProductContribution, $(color_Green),
    if(  $(exp_DirectProductContributionMargin) / $(exp_GrossSales)>=
    v_TargetProductContribution * 0.9, $(color_Yellow), $(color_Red)  ))
    ```

    6.3. Test the calculated colors by changing the target value in the input box and verifying that the text turns green, yellow, and red, as expected.

    6.4. Since this color definition will need to be used multiple times, copy the formula and create a new variable called color_ProductContribution, which will store the formula for future use. Replace the font color formula with the new variable.

    6.5. Clone the Text Object with the amount and transform the expression to present discounts. The main expression should look like this:

    ```
    ='$' &
    $(exp_Discounts)
    & exp_UnitSymbol
    ```

    6.6. Create a new variable called color_Discounts and use the following calculation (notice that we reversed the comparisons—we are aiming for higher contribution, but not for higher discounts; therefore, discount numbers are green when they are below target):

    ```
    if( $(exp_Discounts) / $(exp_SalesAtList)<= v_TargetDiscounts, $(color_Green),
    if(  $(exp_Discounts) / $(exp_SalesAtList)<= v_TargetDiscounts * 1.1,
    $(color_Yellow), $(color_Red)  ))
    ```

6.7. Use the new variable called `color_Discounts` as the font color for the discounts amount.

6.8. Create another variable called `color_Returns` with the following calculation:

```
if( $(exp_Returns) / $(exp_GrossSales)<= v_TargetReturns, $(color_Green),
if(  $(exp_Returns) / $(exp_GrossSales)<= v_TargetReturns * 1.1, $(color_Yellow),
$(color_Red)  ))
```

6.9. Clone the Text Object with the amount again and transform the following expression to represent returns. Use `color_Returns` as the font color:

```
='$' &
$(exp_Returns)
& exp_UnitSymbol
```

7. Create the three Text Objects that represent the percentages. Use the corresponding color variables as the font color for each object. Use the following calculations:

7.1. Direct product contribution:

```
=num(
$(exp_DirectProductContributionMargin)/
$(exp_GrossSales)
,'#,##0.0%' ) & ' of Gross Sales'
```

7.2. Discounts:

```
=num(
$(exp_Discounts)
     /
$(exp_SalesAtList)
,'#,##0.0%' ) & ' of Sales at List'
```

7.3. Returns

```
=num(
$(exp_Returns)/
$(exp_GrossSales)
,'#,##0.0%' ) & ' of Gross Sales'
```

8. Create the bar chart that compares actual product contribution percent to the target:

8.1. Create a new Chart. In the General tab, accept Bar Chart as the default and disable Show Title in Chart.

8.2. Skip the Dimensions tab. In the Expressions tab, create two expressions:

LABEL	DEFINITION
Actual	*$(exp_DirectProductContributionMargin) / $(exp_GrossSales)*
Target	rangemax(Actual, v_TargetProductContribution * 1.2) - Actual

8.3. In the Style tab, select Horizontal Orientation and Stacked Subtype.

8.4. In the Presentation tab, uncheck Show Legend and add a Reference Line with the expression **=v_TargetProductContribution** and a separate Text in Chart with this expression:

='Target=' &num(**v_TargetProductContribution**, '#,##0.0%')

8.5. In the Axes tab, choose Hide Axis for the Expression Axes and set both axes' Width to **0**.

8.6. In the Colors tab, replace the definitions of the first two chart colors with the color_ProductContribution and color_Gray, variables accordingly.

8.7. In the Layout tab, set the Border Width to **0**.

8.8. In the Caption tab, disable Show Caption.

8.9. Exit the Properties by clicking OK. Back in the layout, reduce the chart size down to an acceptable size and position it in the corresponding section of the sheet.

8.10. Using Ctrl+Shift, resize and reposition the inner parts of the chart. Enlarge the chart area to take up all the available space and hide the expression labels. Reposition the text in chart to appear in the upper-right corner of the chart.

9. Once you reach the desired look and feel, clone the chart twice and modify all the necessary settings to represent discounts and returns. Remember to revisit the two Expressions, the Reference Line and the Text in Chart on the Presentation tab, as well as the Color calculation for the first color.

10. Arrange and align all the objects to appear like the presentation in Figure 8.12.

11. Save your work.

This exercise completes our discussion of enhancing simple visualization objects for the Profitability Analysis application. In the following section, we introduce more advanced techniques for visualizing profitability.

Learning Advanced Visualizations

In this section, you continue building the Profitability Analysis application and we continue introducing new and more advanced visualization techniques. You will learn how to:

- Visualize components of costs and profits using stacked bar charts, area charts, and block diagrams.

- Build a *waterfall chart*.

- Visualize correlations between sales and profits in a variety of forms, by using combo charts and scatter charts.

- Build a *whale tail chart*—a powerful visualization that demonstrates how your company can make more money with less effort.

Visualizing Components of Costs and Profits

In this section, you learn how to use stacked bar charts and area charts to visualize and compare components of costs and profits. You also learn about Mekko charts and learn how to build *waterfall charts.*

Plotting Components of Costs and Profits Using a Stacked Bar Chart or an Area Chart

It's common to represent various levels of costs and profits in the form of a stacked bar chart, where the whole bar is divided into segments, representing components of the same total amount (see Figure 8.13).

A stacked bar chart is a type of bar chart. When a bar chart is used to visualize multiple dimensions or expressions, the primary dimension values form "groups" of bars and secondary dimension values (or the multiple expressions) are represented by individual bars within the "groups." In this case, the chart can be **Grouped** or **Stacked**. In the **Grouped** bar chart, the individual bars are presented next to each other, and in the **Stacked** bar chart the segments are stacked on top of each other, visualizing the whole amount built from its parts.

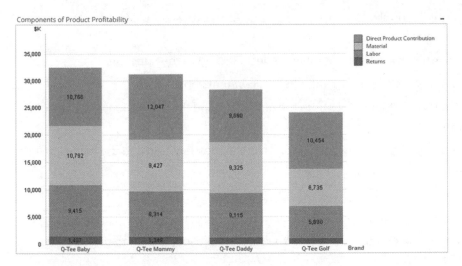

In the case of profitability analysis, the multiple expressions of the costs and the profits represent the stacked bars. The dimension could be time or one of the product-related attributes, or any other field that is usable for this kind of a comparison.

In the following exercise, you create the stacked bar chart presented in Figure 8.13. It shows the four main components of product profitability— returns, material, labor, and direct product contribution, aggregated by brand.

Exercise 8.13: Creating a Stacked Bar Chart

1. Create a new **Bar Chart** on the **Product Profitability** sheet. Select Brand as a dimension and define the following four expressions:

LABEL	DEFINITION
Returns	*$(exp_Returns)*
Labor	*$(exp_Labor)*
Material	*$(exp_Material)*
Direct Product Contribution	*$(exp_DirectProductContributionMargin)*

2. Check **Values on Data Points** for all four expressions.

3. In the **Sort** tab, sort the brands by the **Descending** value of an **Expression**. Use the calculation of gross sales as the expression.

4. In the **Style** tab, confirm **Vertical Orientation** and select **Stacked** as the **Subtype**.

5. In the **Presentation** tab, check the **Plot Values Inside Segments** box.

6. In the **Axis** tab, define **Axis Width** = **1** for both the dimension and the expression, and enable **Show Grid** for the expression.

7. In the **Number** tab, accept **Expression Default** for all four expressions and add the following formula for the symbol:

   ```
   ='$' & exp_UnitSymbol
   ```

8. In the **Caption** tab, allow **Minimize** and **Auto Minimize**.

9. Confirm all the changes and examine the result. You chart should look similar to the chart presented in Figure 8.13.

Let's examine the usefulness of the stacked bar chart together. Some aspects of this visualization are more effective than others. What can you easily learn from observing the chart visually? You can easily see that:

■ Q-Tee Baby is the top brand in sales.

■ For all three brands, the total revenue is split almost equally between material, labor, and contribution, while returns are relatively minor.

■ Q-Tee Mommy is the top brand, based on the contribution amount. We had to look closely and read the actual amounts to determine that, however.

At the same time, many important facts are not easy to spot visually:

■ The shares of material across different brands seem to be comparable, but which one is higher and which one is lower?

■ The contribution amount for Q-Tee Mommy seems to be the highest, but how does it compare in relative terms, as a percentage of sales?

When it's important to emphasize the relative parts of the whole, a different form of stacked bar chart may be more useful (see Figure 8.14). This time, you calculate the percentage of each part to the total. In this case, we will be dividing each amount by the sum of all four expressions.

We could use gross sales as the denominator; however, we'd like to demonstrate another interesting technique to you. We will create another expression that will only serve for the purpose of the calculation and will not be displayed in the chart. The ability to use intermediate expressions that don't have any visual representation in the chart is very useful when the calculations get very complex.

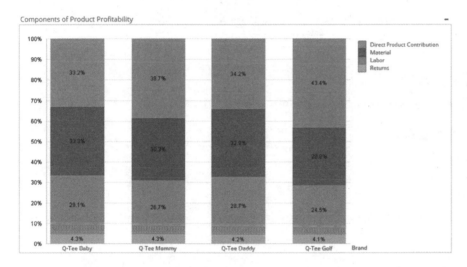

FIGURE 8.14:
Stacked bar chart that shows percentages to total

Exercise 8.14: Building a Stacked Bar Chart with Percentages

1. Minimize the bar chart that you developed in the previous exercise, reposition the minimized icon to the bottom of the page, and clone the icon. Restore the new chart and open its **Properties**.

2. In the **Expressions** tab, create a new expression with the following formula:

```
rangesum(
$(exp_Returns),
$(exp_Labor),
$(exp_Material),
$(exp_DirectProductContributionMargin)
)
```

3. Label the expression **Total**. Uncheck Bar under the Display Options.

4. Divide the existing calculations by Total in all four existing expressions. For example:

   $(exp\_Returns)/Total$

5. In the Number tab, define the number format for all four expressions as Fixed to 1 Decimal, and enable Show in Percent. Remove the formula from the Symbol definition.

6. Confirm all the changes and examine the result. Your y-axis should run up to 120%. This is the result of the automatic axis scaling. While automatic scale is helpful most of the time, in this case it doesn't make sense, because we know that the sum of the parts can never exceed 100%. In these specific cases, we will use the option to set a Static Max value for the Expression Axis Scale. Open Properties, Axes tab, and enable Static Max = **1** for the Expression Axes, as shown in the following figure.

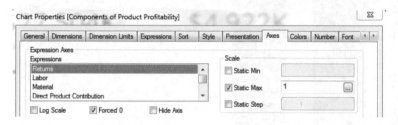

Another useful form for visualizing parts of a whole that's very similar to the stacked bar chart is the area chart (see Figure 8.15).

FIGURE 8.15:
Two area charts

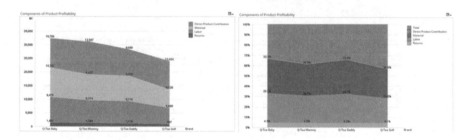

The area chart is one of the styles of the line chart. Both of the stacked bar charts that you developed earlier can be easily converted to the area chart by changing the chart type to **Line Chart** and selecting **Area** as the **Style**. Because of this similarity, the two chart types can be used in the same objects, with the **Fast Change** feature.

Exercise 8.15: Transforming Stacked Bar Charts into Area Charts

For each of the two stacked bar charts developed earlier, perform the following changes:

1. In the General tab, enable Fast Change by selecting Bar Chart and Line Chart as the available Chart Types.

2. Change the "main" Chart Type to Line Chart.

3. In the Style tab, select Area as the Chart Style.

4. In the second chart with percentages, open the Expressions tab. Activate the Total expression and disable Line from the Display Options for this expression (it was assigned automatically when you switched the chart to the Line chart.)

5. Confirm the changes and examine the results. Compare the visualization effect between the bar chart and the area chart.

6. Save your work.

Creating Waterfall Charts

The *waterfall chart* is a type of a bar chart that visualizes changes that happen in the process. Examine the chart in Figure 8.16.

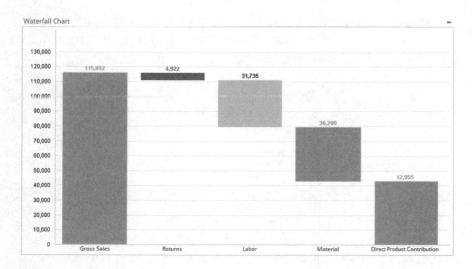

FIGURE 8.16:
The waterfall chart

The company sells products and earns the amount called Gross Sales. Then, some of the sold products are returned, for the total amount of Returns, and that detracts from the revenue. Before the goods could be sold, they had to be manufactured. The costs of Material and Labor are also deducted from the sales revenue. The remaining amount is called the Direct Product Contribution—this is the remaining revenue before other costs are deducted. The waterfall chart helps to visualize this process.

The first bar represents the total revenue of the Gross Sales. The next bar, with the negative amount of returns, begins at the point where the previous bar ends. Then, the Labor bar begins where the Returns bar ended, and so on. The last bar is the positive amount of the remaining contribution margin, begins at zero, and should end where the previous bar ended.

For presentation purposes, however, the negative amounts are typically presented as positive numbers, and hence you need to tweak the calculation of the starting point. Instead of starting the negative bar of Returns from the value of Gross Sales, you are starting the positive bar from the value of Gross Sales minus Returns, or from the sum of the other three components.

The starting point for each bar is called the *Bar Offset* in QlikView and it can be set using one of the optional parameters that are hidden behind every expression.

If you open the **Expression** tab of any **Chart Properties** and click on the plus sign next to any expression (it's called the *expansion icon*), you will see a set of optional attributes (see Figure 8.17).

FIGURE 8.17:
Optional settings for expressions

The attributes appear in a light gray font, as if they are "grayed-out" when their definitions are empty. Once the definition is set, the attribute name appears in black. As you can see in Figure 8.17, four attributes are active for this expression. The following attributes can be set for any expression:

- **Background Color** allows you to calculate the color of the visual element (bar, line, symbol, and so on), thus overriding the settings in the **Colors** tab.

- **Text Color** allows setting the specific color for this expression only, without affecting the axis font colors and other font colors in the chart. Notice how different labels on the waterfall chart in Figure 8.16 appear with the color that matches the corresponding bar.

- **Text Format** allows setting individual formatting tags for each expression. This is done using HTML-style tags, enclosed in single quotes. For example, the tag '<I>' will make the expression text *italicized*.

- **Pie Popout** is only applicable to pie charts. This setting requires an expression that returns zero (as False) or a non-zero value (as True). When the expression returns True, the corresponding pie slice will appear detached from the rest of the pie. For example, profits for a selected brand can appear highlighted, compared to the profits from the other brands.

- **Bar Offset** is the setting that allows the presentation of the waterfall chart. It is used to set the starting point for each bar in the bar chart.

- **Line Style** can be used for modifying the style (solid, dashed, dotted, and so on) and the weight of each line based on a calculation. Like the text format, these settings are also defined using HTML-style tags, enclosed in single quotes. The specific codes are described in detail in the Help article about chart expressions.

- The **Show Value** attribute allows displaying the values on data points based on a condition. When the calculated condition returns True (any non-zero number), the value will be displayed; otherwise, it won't. Using this attribute, it's possible to show only peak values, for instance, and thereby avoid cluttering the view with too many labels.

In the following exercise, you create the waterfall chart displayed in Figure 8.16. You use the **Bar Offset** attribute, along with three other expression attributes. You'll set the **Background Color** to override the default color settings. Then, you'll use the same colors as the **Text Color**. Using **Text Format**, you will turn the label text font into bold.

Exercise 8.16: Creating the Waterfall Chart

1. Create a new Bar Chart and type **Waterfall Chart** in the Title.

2. Skip the Dimensions tab. In the Expressions tab, create five expressions—**Gross Sales**, **Returns**, **Labor**, **Material**, and **Direct Product Contribution**. Use the same variables from the P&L report for each expression.

3. Click on the expansion icon of each expression and enter the corresponding offset formula. The expressions, offset calculations, and colors that will be used in the following steps are listed in Table 8.2.

TABLE 8.2: Waterfall Expression Settings

LABEL	EXPRESSION DEFINITION	BAR OFFSET	BACKGROUND COLOR
Gross Sales	*$(exp_GrossSales)*	None	*$(color_Green)*
Returns	*$(exp_Returns)*	=rangesum(*$(exp_Material)*,*$(exp_Labor)*,*$(exp_DirectProductContributionMargin)*))	*$(color_Red)*
Labor	*$(exp_Labor)*	=rangesum(*$(exp_Material)*,*$(exp_DirectProductContributionMargin)*))	*$(color_Gray)*
Material	*$(exp_Material)*	=rangesum(*$(exp_DirectProductContributionMargin)*))	*$(color_Yellow)*
Direct Product Contribution	*$(exp_DirectProductContributionMargin)*	None	*$(color_Green)*

4. For each of the five expressions, allow Values on Data Points.

5. In the Presentation tab, uncheck Show Legend.

6. In the Number tab, accept Expression Default for all the expressions and enter the following formula as the Symbol:

```
='$' & exp_UnitSymbol
```

7. Accept all the changes and verify that the chart looks like the waterfall chart. Every bar should begin where the previous bar ended. Verify that the expression labels are listed at the bottom and the values are listed on top of the boxes.

8. Now, let's take care of the colors and the formatting. Open the chart Properties, Expressions tab and add attribute expressions for the Background Color, Text Color, and Text Format:

   8.1 Use the color listed in the table above as the Background Color.

   8.2 Use the same color as the Text Color, but use $(color_Black) instead of the gray color (the gray font looks too pale and is not readable).

   8.3 Use the following tag for the Text Format: '<B>'.

9. In the Caption tab, enable Minimize and Auto Minimize.

10. Accept all the changes. Your chart should look similar to Figure 8.16.

11. Save your work.

This exercise concludes our discussion of waterfall charts and the optional expression attributes. You may notice that dimensions can also have optional attributes. Dimension attributes include **Background Color**, **Text Color**, and **Text Format**, and they are defined similarly to the expression attributes. Feel free to experiment with various formatting settings for different dimensions.

Mekko Charts and Synthetic Dimensions

Now we would like to get back to our earlier discussion of visualizing components of costs and profits with stacked bar charts. Recall that you can visualize one of the two main metrics effectively. You can compare absolute numbers, such as amounts, using one sort of a bar chart (see Figure 8.13), but then it's not trivial to compare the relative shares. Using another type of a stacked bar chart (see Figure 8.14), you can compare the relative shares of different components, but then you can't see the total amount.

Introducing Mekko Charts

A *Mekko chart* is a bar chart that allows you to compare both the relative shares of the parts and the total size of the whole between different entities, such as brands, products, etc. In Mekko charts, both the height and the width of the bar can be calculated. Despite their resemblance to bar charts, Mekko charts have a chart type of their own, which is displayed in the list of **Chart Types** with this icon:

Mekko charts (see Figure 8.18) come in two forms, normalized and non-normalized.

In a normalized Mekko chart (see Figure 8.18, left), a single expression is presented over two dimensions. The total expression value for the first dimension determines the widths of the columns. The values of the same expression, aggregated for the secondary dimension level, determine the heights of the individual parts in the columns. As the name suggests, all the values are normalized to 100%.

FIGURE 8.18:
Normalized and non-normalized Mekko charts

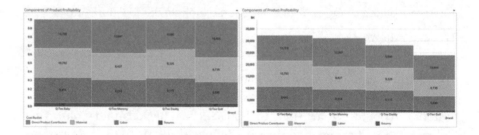

In a non-normalized Mekko chart (see Figure 8.18, right), multiple expressions are presented over a single dimension. Each column represents a single value of the dimension (Brand in our example). The first expression is used to determine the widths of the columns. The rest of the expressions determine the heights of the parts in the columns. All the values are presented as the absolute values, as opposed to being normalized to 100%.

In addition to different sets of dimensions and expressions, the desired Mekko chart style (normalized or non-normalized) is defined in the **Style** tab of the **Properties**.

Developing a Non-Normalized Mekko Chart

As you just learned, a normalized Mekko chart requires two dimensions and a single expression, while a non-normalized Mekko chart works with a single dimension and multiple expressions. Our data contains a single dimension (Brand) and a number of expressions representing various components of costs and profits. Therefore, our data lends itself much more naturally to a non-normalized Mekko chart.

In the following exercise, you develop a non-normalized Mekko chart that looks like the chart in Figure 8.18, presented on the right. Use Brand as a dimension. Gross sales will be used to determine the widths of the columns and to sort the brands on the chart. The four components of product profitability (returns, labor, material, and direct product contribution) will be used as additional expressions to determine the heights of the partial bars. Similarly to the stacked bar charts, you will show values on data points, and the values will be plotted inside the segments.

Exercise 8.17: Creating a Non-Normalized Mekko Chart

1. Create a new Chart. Select Mekko Chart as the Chart Type.

2. Select Brand as a dimension.

3. Add five expressions (the same five expressions that were used in the waterfall chart): **Gross Sales**, **Returns**, **Labor**, **Material**, and **Direct Product Contributions**. Gross Sales will be used to determine the widths of the columns, and the other four expressions will be used for calculating the height of the partial bars. Enable Values on Data Points for all five expressions.

4. In the Sort tab, sort the brands by Descending value of an Expression. Use the calculation of gross sales as the sorting expression.

5. In the Style tab, select Non-Normalized (the second icon) as the Look.

6. In the Presentation tab, check the Plot Values Inside Segments box.

7. In the Colors tab, set specific colors in order to keep consistent colors across the different tabs:

    7.1. The first expression (Gross Sales) is not being plotted, so the color is not important.

    7.2. The second expression represents Returns. Set Color 2 as a calculated color with $(color_Red) as the formula.

7.3. In a similar fashion, use `color_Yellow` for **Labor**, `color_Gray` for **Material**, and `color_Green` for **Direct Product Contribution**.

8. In the **Number** tab, highlight all five expressions and add the following formula as the **Symbol**:

   `='$' & exp_UnitSymbol`

9. In the **Caption** tab, enable **Minimize** and **Auto Minimize**.

10. Accept all changes and examine the result. If you'd like to move the legend to the bottom of the chart, press Ctrl+Shift and drag the red box with the legend to the bottom edge of the chart. Once the red box snaps into place along the bottom edge, release the mouse button and release Ctrl+Shift. Your chart should look like the chart presented on the right side of Figure 8.18.

Pretty nice, huh? Now, what about the normalized Mekko chart? What if your users demand that type of a chart, and they can't understand that the data is not organized properly for it? You don't have two dimensions and a single expression. Are you stuck now? Do you need to re-design your data model to enable such a chart?

Luckily, you don't have to. You can tweak the definitions of the dimensions and the expressions in such a way that allows you to generate a calculated dimension from a set of expressions and collapse multiple expressions into one. In order to do that, you need to learn another cool technique—how to create charts with *synthetic dimensions*.

Using Synthetic Dimensions to Convert a Set of Expressions into a Dimension

You must have noticed the button called **Add Calculated Dimension** in the **Dimensions** tab of the **Chart Properties**, and we are sure you've been eager to learn what it is all about. Calculated dimension is a feature that allows you to create a dimension as you go, rather than from a static database field.

Calculated dimensions are used for many advanced visualizations that require that the dimension values be calculated on the fly, and often they need to be sensitive to current selections.

For the current needs, you need to generate a dimension that can show four "static" values with the names of the main components of product profitability—Returns, Labor, Material, and Direct Product Contribution. Then, you need a way of referring to the same dimension in the chart expression. This can be done using the ValueList() function in a calculated dimension. When used in a calculated dimension, the ValueList() function accepts a set of values in a comma-separated list and generates a synthetic dimension:

```
=ValueList('Returns', 'Labor', 'Material', 'Direct Product
    Contribution')
```

The same function can be referenced in the chart expressions, and it will return the current value of the synthetic dimension for the purposes of calculating the corresponding expression values:

```
IF(ValueList('Returns', 'Labor', 'Material', 'Direct Product
    Contribution') = 'Returns',
$(exp_Returns)
)
```

For the purposes of this example, you could use four nested IF functions (actually, three, if you think about it) to facilitate the task of collapsing the four distinct expressions into a single formula. Alternatively, you can use a combination of the functions Pick() and Match() for a more elegant solution.

The Pick() function receives a number *N* and a set of comma-separated values. The function returns the *N*-th value out of the list. For example, the following function will return the value Green if vNumber = 3:

```
Pick(vNumber, 'Red', 'Yellow', 'Green')
```

The Match() function receives a single value and a number of expressions. It performs a case-sensitive comparison of the value to the list of expressions and returns the number of the expression that fully matched the provided value. For example, the following formula returns 3 if vColor = 'Green':

```
Match(vColor, 'Red', 'Yellow', 'Green')
```

Since your synthetic dimension is built as a list of values, you can use a combination of Match() and Pick() to pick the corresponding calculation from the list of possible formulas.

Imagine that the calculated dimension is built with the following formula:

```
=ValueList(v1, v2, v3)
```

Using `Match()` with the `ValueList()` and the list of the same values for the comparison, you can get the number of the "current" element in the list:

```
=Match(ValueList(v1, v2, v3) , v1, v2, v3)
```

Applying `Pick()` to the same number, you can pick the calculation that's related to the "current" value:

```
=Pick(
Match(ValueList(v1, v2, v3) , v1, v2, v3),
<Expr1>,
<Expr2>,
<Expr3>
)
```

Note that the value list needs to be repeated at least three times—once in the calculated dimension and twice in every expression. In order to simplify maintenance and to avoid spelling errors, it might be beneficial to store the value list in a variable and reference the same variable in all of these instances. For example, if the variable is called `exp_DimList`, then the same expression can be modified like this:

```
=Pick(
Match(ValueList($(exp_DimList)) , $(exp_DimList)),
<Expr1>,
<Expr2>,
<Expr3>
)
```

While this logic takes some getting used to, this syntax appears to be more elegant and easier to maintain than a set of nested `IF` statements. In the next section, you apply these functions in the process of creating a normalized Mekko chart.

Developing a Normalized Mekko Chart

Now, equipped with the techniques for generating a synthetic dimension and for referencing it in expressions, you are ready to develop the normalized Mekko chart. Feel free to follow the general guidelines laid out in the previous section or follow the detailed instructions in the following exercise.

Exercise 8.18: Creating a Normalized Mekko Chart

1. Add a new variable called `exp_DimList` and enter the list of the product profitability components as the value of the variable:

   ```
   'Returns', 'Labor', 'Material', 'Direct Product Contribution'
   ```

2. Create a new Mekko Chart.

3. In the Dimensions tab, select Brand as the first Dimension. Then, click on Add Calculated Dimension and type the following formula:

   ```
   =ValueList($(exp_DimList))
   ```

4. Still in the Dimensions tab, highlight the new Calculated Dimension. Check Show Legend. Enter **Product Profitability Components** in the Label and after that clear the Label checkbox.

5. In the Expressions tab, type the following formula as the single expression:

   ```
   pick(
   match(ValueList($(exp_DimList)), $(exp_DimList)),
   $(exp_Returns),
   $(exp_Labor),
   $(exp_Material),
   $(exp_DirectProductContributionMargin)
   )
   ```

6. Enable Values on Data Points.

7. In the Sort tab, sort brands by the Descending values of an Expression, using the calculation of gross sales as the sorting expression.

8. In the Style tab, select Normalized Look (the first icon of the two).

9. In the Presentation tab, check Plot Values Inside Segments.

10. In the Colors tab, arrange the colors in such a way that the Returns (Color 1) are painted using color_Red, Labor (Color 2) uses color_Yellow, Material uses color_Gray, and Direct Product Contribution uses color_Green.

11. Accept all the changes and examine the result. You may want to move the legend from the right side to the bottom of the chart, in order to maximize the available space.

12. Save your work.

Note that the percentage numbers on the y-axis are presented as decimals and not as percentages. This is the side effect of our desire to show amounts for each one of the segments. Without these amounts, the axis could be nicely formatted as a percentage. Depending on your presentation needs, you can "pick your poison"—either show the actual values and put up with less than perfect presentation on the axis, or hide the numbers and format the axis properly.

This exercise completes our discussion of visualizing components of costs and profits. You learned a number of different visualizations that can help visualize and compare parts of a whole in a number of ways. Next, you learn how to visualize correlations between sales and profits.

How to Visualize Correlations Between Sales and Profits

In this section, you develop the **Customer Profitability** sheet that will host all the new charts that visualize correlations between sales and profits. In preparation, you design the outline of the new sheet and develop the KPI presentation on top of it.

Preparing the Environment for Customer Profitability Analysis

To speed up the process, you will clone the **Product Profitability** sheet and make all necessary modifications.

On top of the new **Customer Profitability** sheet, you will show two KPIs—**Direct Customer Contribution** and **Customer Allowances**—in the same way you presented product-related KPIs in the **Product Profitability** sheet.

You need to create two new variables for the targets and two new color variables, similar to those you created earlier for product profitability.

After that, all expressions, reference lines, and texts in chart need to be modified accordingly.

In addition, list boxes on the left should not include any product-related fields, since customer profitability cannot be calculated for individual products or brands. You will replace all product-related fields with the fields associated with customers, such as VP Sales, Regional Director, and Salesperson.

Feel free to perform all the necessary changes individually or follow the detailed instructions in Exercise 8.19.

Exercise 8.19: Preparing the Sheet for Customer Profitability

1. Copy the Product Profitability sheet and name the new sheet **Customer Profitability**.

2. Replace the Sheet Title and the corresponding icon on top of the sheet with **Customer Profitability**.

3. Delete the four objects that were communicating returns and space out the remaining two groups of objects, to cover the available space.

4. The KPI on the left will be used for Direct Customer Contribution, and the KPI on the right will be Customer Alliances. Modify the labels and the objects accordingly:

   4.1. Modify the Text expression and the Font Color expression for the large-font text box with the amount.

   4.2. Modify the Text expression and the Font Color expression for the smaller font text box with the percentage. Keep in mind that both of those KPIs are calculated by dividing by gross sales (not sales at list).

   4.3. Modify the chart expression, the Reference Line formula, the Text in Chart, and the first Color for the bar chart that's showing actual to target.

5. Delete all the list boxes that contain Brand and Style and the multi box with Other Filters. Instead, add three new list boxes with VP Sales, Regional Director, and Salesperson.

6. Delete all the charts from the main area below the header. Replace all the product profitability variables with new customer-related variables in the input box.

7. Your finished sheet should look similar to Figure 8.19.

FIGURE 8.19:

Customer Profitability sheet

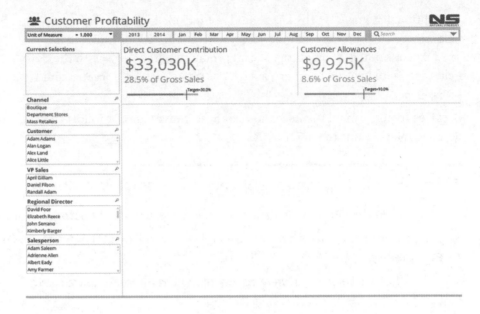

Combo Chart: Charting Sales Volumes and Profits Together

In the process of analyzing sales and profit margins, it's common to visualize the two metrics together, in order to compare the relationship between the two and to spot a potential correlation.

The simplest way of visualizing two different metrics in the same chart is to use the *combo chart*—a combination of a bar chart and a line chart in a single object (see Figure 8.20).

When plotting two different metrics, such as amounts and percentages, we usually try to visualize them with different types of symbols. It's common to present amounts in bars and to use lines for percentages.

Notice that the combo chart has two vertical axes—the y-axis on the left communicates the scale for the amounts, and the y-axis on the right shows percentages. This is done in the **Axes** tab, by assigning **Left** or **Right** axis for each one of the expressions. Optionally, the right axis can also be split, causing the chart to appear as two charts, one on top of the other (see Figure 8.21).

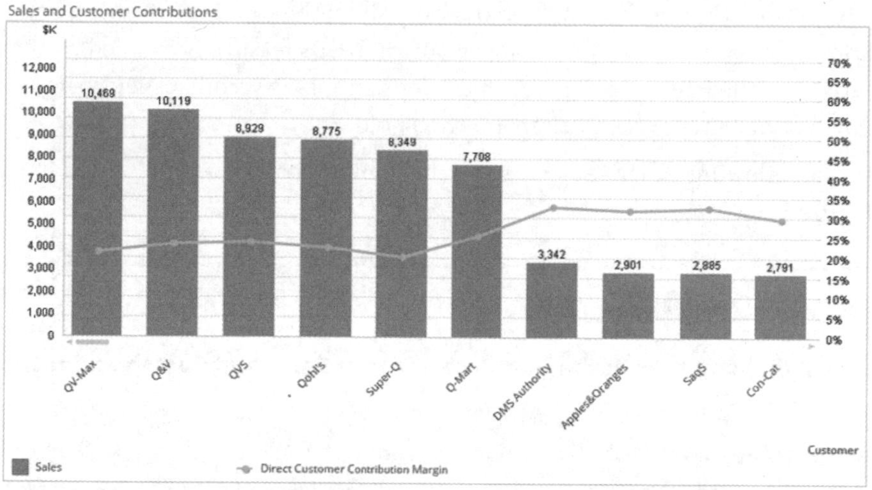

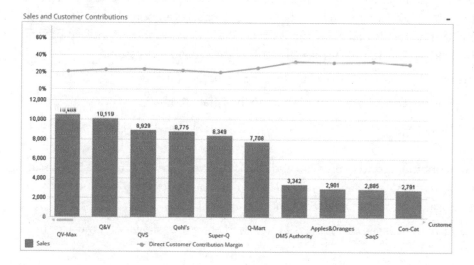

FIGURE 8.20:
The combo chart

FIGURE 8.21:
The combo chart with split axes

In general, combo charts can be used to visualize any two metrics, such as the current profits and the change % from prior year, for instance. Any combination of bars, lines, and symbols can be used for a combo chart.

Also, notice that both combo charts only show the top 10 customers, and there is a horizontal scrollbar at the bottom. This feature is enabled by the setting in the **Presentation** tab that opens an x-axis scrollbar when the number of items exceeds a certain threshold.

In the following exercise, you create the combo chart that's presented in Figure 8.20.

Exercise 8.20: Creating a Combo Chart

1. Create a new Chart, select Combo Chart as the chart type and type **Sales and Customer Contributions** as the Title.

2. Select Customer as a dimension.

3. In the Expressions tab, create two expressions—**Gross Sales** and **Direct Customer Contribution Margin %**. Use the variables with the corresponding expressions that you created earlier. In the second expression, divide the margin amount by the gross sales amount. Notice that by default, the Display Option for the first expression is defined as a Bar, and the second expression is defined as a Line. Add Symbol to the Display Options for the second expression.

4. In the Sort tab, sort the customers by Y-value, in Descending order.

5. Examine the three available Looks in the Style tab. Keep the default Look.

6. In the Presentation tab, enable the box Enable X-Axis Scrollbar and keep 10 as the default Number of Items.

7. In the Axes tab, highlight the second expression and check the Show Grid box. Enable Static Min = **0** for the second ExpressionScale. Select Position as Right (Top). Under the Dimension Axis, select Diagonal (/) position for both the Primary and Secondary Labels.

8. In the Number tab, format the first expression as Integer and enter the following formula as the symbol:

   ```
   ='$' & exp_UnitSymbol
   ```

9. Format the second expression as Fixed to 1 Decimal, Show in Percent (%).

10. Accept all the changes and examine the result. Move the legend from the right side to the bottom of the chart by using the Ctrl+Shift+drag technique.

Scatter Chart: Plotting Customers and Products Based on Sales and Margins

In this section, we introduce a number of techniques related to visualizing multiple measures with the *scatter chart*. You learn how to limit the number of presented data points using *dimension limits*.

Introducing the Scatter Chart

The scatter chart is by far our favorite analytic chart in QlikView! It allows plotting a single dimension (such as products, customers, or salespersons) over two expressions that serve as the bases for the calculated x- and y-axes (see Figure 8.22). In essence, this is your very own Gartner Magic Quadrant, and you can measure any dimensions based on any two expressions of your choosing.

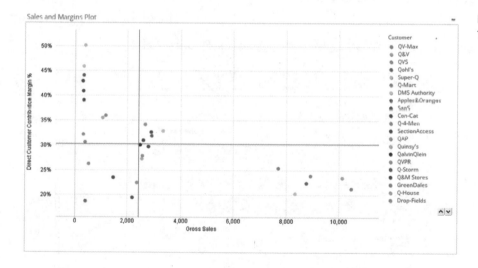

FIGURE 8.22:
The scatter chart

In this example, we are plotting customers in terms of their sales and profit margins. Just like in the Gartner Magic Quadrant, the best customers (those with the highest sales and the best margins) will occupy the upper-right quadrant. The customers in the upper-left corner have high margins but lower sales. Those customers need to be encouraged to buy more. The customers in the bottom-right corner have higher sales but lower margins. Their programs and contracts need to be revisited, with the goal of improving profitability. The customers in the bottom-left corner are the worst—they buy less than others, and they provide lower margins. Those customers need to be dealt with—their business may cost you more than it is worth.

In the following exercise, you develop the scatter chart presented in Figure 8.22 and then continue discovering various features of the scatter charts.

Exercise 8.21: Creating the Scatter Chart

1. Create a new **Chart** and select **Scatter Chart** as the **Chart Type**. The scatter chart is represented by the icon on the left in the following image 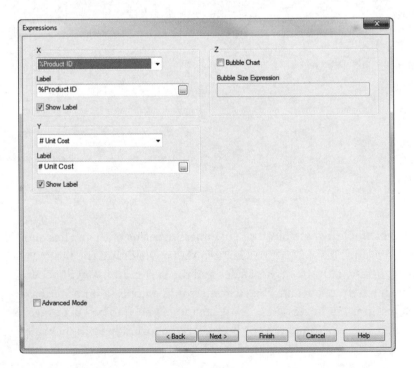.

   It's easy to confuse it with the **Grid Chart** icon located next in the list. Type **Sales and Margins Plot** as the title of the chart. Disable **Title in Chart**.

2. Select **Customer** as the dimension.

3. The **Expressions** tab of the scatter chart looks a bit unusual (see Figure 8.23).

FIGURE 8.23:
The Expressions tab of the scatter chart

4. Paraphrasing Sheldon Cooper from *The Big Bang Theory*, this is too user friendly. We don't like it. Check the box Advanced Mode to revert to the familiar view of the Expressions tab.

5. Back in the Expressions tab, you will see two "random" expressions that the wizard created based on two "random" fields. Delete those expressions and Add two new expressions—**Gross Sales** and **Direct Customer Contribution Margin %**.

6. Next, in the Sort tab, sort Customers based on Y-value, in Descending order.

7. In the Style tab, select the flat (two-dimensional) circles—the second icon from the bottom on the right.

8. In the Presentation tab, add a Reference Line. Accept the location X-axis and Y-axis and select 50% Percentile as the Definition. Use color_Blue as the color for the line. Accept Weight = 1 pt and Solid Line as the Style.

9. In the Axes tab, define the following settings for the x- and y-axes:

    10.1. Uncheck Forced 0

    10.2. Check Show Grid

    10.3. Check Label Along Axis

    10.4. Set the Axis line Width = 1 pt.

10. In the Number tab, enter the same Symbol formula for the first expression, which is formatted as Expression Default:

    ='$' & exp_UnitSymbol

    Format the second expression as a Percentage.

11. In the Caption tab, allow Minimize and Auto Minimize.

12. Accept all the changes and examine the result. Your chart should look similar to Figure 8.24.

13. Save your work.

Notice that the chart looks rather crowded with the majority of the bubbles crowded not far from the y-axis. This is because most of the boutique customers buy small amounts, compared to the larger chains of stores. When the goal is to show the top performers, we will limit the chart to the top X values.

At the moment, however, let's experience the analytical power of the scatter chart and its ability to zoom in quickly and effectively. Let's assume that we wanted to focus on the bottom customers, those with the contribution margin below 10%. We simply highlight them by "lassoing" the desired group of bubbles on the chart (see Figure 8.25) and voilà! The short list of bottom customers is selected. Now we can focus on the short list of problematic customers.

FIGURE 8.24:
The first scatter chart

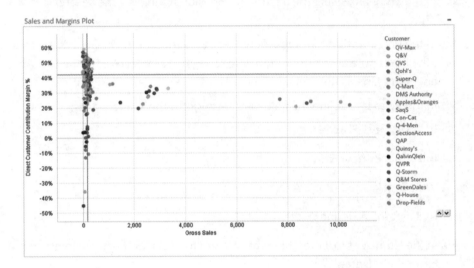

FIGURE 8.25:
Making selections in the scatter chart

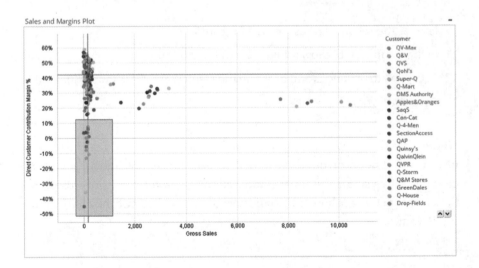

Adding the Third Measure (Size) to the Scatter Chart

Now, let's improve the scatter chart by adding another measure that will determine the size of the bubble. Notice that all the bubbles in Figure 8.25 are equally sized, and you can only examine the x-y location of each bubble. By adding the third measure, you can enhance the visual analysis and differentiate bubbles by size.

Since you are already using sales as the first dimension, it would be redundant to use sales also as a measure of size. You could use the total amount of the contribution margin per customer, or the number of stores, or anything else that defines the size or the importance of the given customer. In the following example, you use the contribution margin amount for this purpose.

Be careful not to allow negative numbers as the results of the third expression. Since the symbol size cannot be negative, customers who have negative contribution margins will simply disappear from the list. In order to avoid this issue, we use the fabs() function, which returns the absolute value of a number.

In addition to the first three expressions, the scatter chart allows additional expressions that can be presented in the popup labels. These labels appear when the user hovers over the data points. For example, if it was important to know the name of the salesperson when assessing their sales and profits, you could present the salesperson as the fourth expression that will be included in the popup text. Keep in mind, however, that those additional expressions need to return fully formatted texts, with the labels included in the expressions. QlikView doesn't perform any additional formatting for these.

Exercise 8.22: Enhancing the Scatter Chart with Additional Expressions

1. Open the **Expressions** tab of the **Scatter Chart Properties** and **Add** two new expressions:

LABEL	DEFINITION
Direct Customer Contribution Margin	fabs(*$(exp_DirectCustomerContributionMargin)*)
Salesperson	='Salesperson: ' & only(Salesperson)

2. For the Salesperson expression, check the Text As pop-up box.

3. Accept the changes and examine the result. The bubbles in the chart should have different sizes. When you hover over one of the data points, the Salesperson information should be visible in the popup label (see Figure 8.26).

FIGURE 8.26:

The enhanced scatter chart

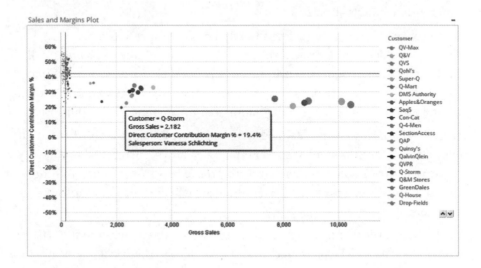

Using Calculated Colors within a Scatter Chart

Next, let's examine the usefulness of the colors for the visual perception of the scatter chart in Figure 8.26. The colors are used to differentiate between the different customers and help connect the names in the legend with the bubbles in the chart. This may be helpful with five to six colored entities, but not when the chart shows hundreds of data points. We should admit that different colors don't do any good to this chart. In order to make color more meaningful, you can assign specific colors based on a certain rule. For example, you could use green for customers who improved their margin contribution since last year and use red for all others. You will use this technique in one of the following charts.

For this example, let's color the customers based on their channel. We will use blue for mass retailers, green for department stores, and purple for boutiques. In order to do that, you will use the familiar technique of assigning a calculated color to the first expression's **Background Color** attribute.

Since the colors can't be used to connect the legend with the bubbles anymore, the legend needs to be replaced with a pseudo-legend, which explains to the users what each color represents. You will implement this pseudo-legend in three individual **Texts in Chart**, each test colored in the same color and the corresponding bubbles. You will use the Unicode symbol ● ('BLACK CIRCLE') to make the text look like the legend. This Unicode symbol can be presented as CHR(9679).

Exercise 8.23: Assigning Specific Colors by Channel

1. Clone the scatter chart and make changes to the new copy.

2. In the Expressions tab, click on the Expansion icon (the little plus sign) next to the first expression (Gross Sales) and enter the following formula for the Background Color:

```
pick(
match(Channel, 'Mass Retailers', 'Department Stores', 'Boutique'),
$(color_Blue),
$(color_Green),
$(color_Purple)
)
```

3. In the Presentation tab, uncheck Show Legend. Add three Texts in Chart, each text with the corresponding Font Color:

```
=chr(9679) & ' Mass Retailers'
=chr(9679) & ' Department Stores'
=chr(9679) & ' Boutiques'
```

4. Accept all changes and exit the Properties. Reposition the three Texts in Chart at the bottom of the chart. You may have to resize the main chart area to make room for the pseudo-legend at the bottom. Your finished chart should look similar to Figure 8.27.

Compare the charts presented in Figures 8.26 and 8.27. With the meaningful colors, the same chart tells much more. The six blue bubbles with the top sales numbers represent the mass retailers, and their average contribution margin % is slightly above 20%. The group of green bubbles in the middle represents the department stores. Their sales are lower than those of mass retailers, and their profitability is slightly higher, with a few exceptions. The cluster of purple dots represents the boutiques—smaller stores that provide lower sales per account, but higher profits, for the most part. The customers at the bottom part of the chart deserve a closer look. Surely we should expect the boutique customers to be at least as profitable as the mass retailers, and preferably much more profitable than that.

Coloring the scatter chart by channel could be done in an easier way—by adding Channel at the second chart dimension. In this case, make sure to select **Only Symbols** in the **Representation** setting on the **Presentation** tab. Feel free to compare the two techniques and pick your favorite.

FIGURE 8.27:
The scatter chart with calculated colors

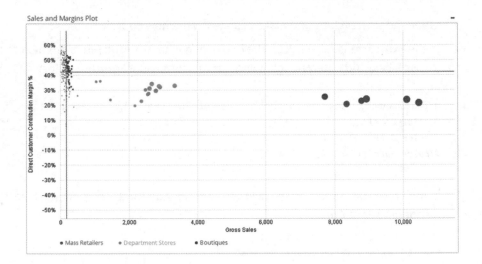

Limiting the Number of Data Points Using Dimension Limits

As you may already have noticed, the scatter charts look rather crowded, with hundreds of data points of various sizes. When the goal is to identify and select the "bottom feeders," then perhaps there is no way around showing all the little dots, even those that don't move the needle at all.

Other times, the goal is to show the "big picture," or focus our attention on customers who buy enough to make a difference. In these cases, it's better to limit the number of data points to those top customers only.

In QlikView, you can do this using the **Dimension Limits** tab of the **Chart Properties** (see Figure 8.28). This tab is located between the **Dimensions** and the **Expressions** tabs; however, it is not included in the sequence of the tabs when you create a new chart. The thought is that developers rarely worry about **Dimension Limits** before the first draft of the chart is ready.

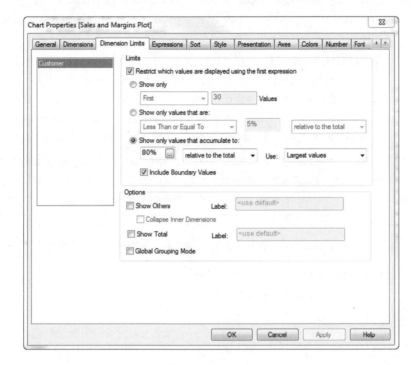

FIGURE 8.28:
Dimension Limits tab

Dimension limits are applied to individual dimensions, and all the conditions are applied using *the first chart expression*. Three types of limits are available:

- Show only a certain number of values (highest, lowest, or first).

- Show only values that are either higher or lower than a certain threshold. The threshold can be defined as an absolute number or as a percent of total.

- Show only values that accumulate to a certain amount, or to a certain percent of total. This type of selection is also called *Pareto* selection. The values that should be included in the aggregated total can be defined as the largest, the smallest, or the first (based on sort order).

Additional options include:

■ The ability to **Show Others** in a single aggregated data point (this is important when there is a need to maintain an overall total of all data points).

■ The ability to **Show Total**. When this feature is used in a straight table chart, it provides an ability to produce subtotals in a straight table.

■ **Global Grouping Mode** can be applied to inner dimensions. When this option is enabled, the dimension limits conditions will be calculated based on this dimension alone, with no regard for the other dimensions. Otherwise, the calculations will be made for the combination of this dimension and all the higher-level dimensions.

In the following exercise, you create another version of the scatter chart that shows the top customers based on the Pareto principle—you will show only the customers who contribute 80% of the sales.

Exercise 8.24: Limiting the Number of Data Points with Dimension Limits

1. Clone the scatter chart that you developed in the previous exercise.

2. Open the Dimension Limits tab of the Chart Properties.

3. Check the Restrict which values are displayed box.

4. Out of the three options, select the third one: Show only values that accumulate to:

5. Type **80%**, relative to total, using Largest values.

6. Make sure that all the Options are unchecked and accept the changes. Your finished chart should look similar to Figure 8.29.

Notice that this version of the chart is much more focused on the most important accounts. As you can see, mass retailers, department stores, and only a dozen boutiques make up 80% of sales. The other 20% are made with hundreds of smaller boutique shops.

In general, dimension limits can be used with any types of charts, except for the pivot table. It's a wonderful technique that allows you to limit the number of data points with a few powerful settings.

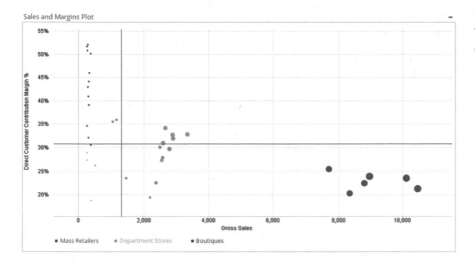

We have to warn you about one pitfall, though. Dimension limits cannot be
used to improve performance of a large data set. For example, if your chart
needs to show consumer data for millions of consumers and you wanted to
limit the list to the first 1,000, dimension limits are not a good choice. The
calculations of the dimension limits are performed on top of the regular chart
calculation. So if you have a very detailed chart that is already slow, using
dimension limits will make it much slower. To resolve this problem, you need
to use an advanced form of Set Analysis search and limit your expressions that
way. This is, however, beyond the scope of this current discussion. Visit our
blog at www.naturalsynergies.com/blog for a detailed explanation of the problem
and the solution.

WARNING

Visualizing Change in a Scatter Chart

We hope you can agree that the scatter chart is one of the most powerful
analytical tools in QlikView. When it's used to measure the productivity
of people, it can certainly serve as a nice conversation starter. Examine the
chart in Figure 8.30, for example.

FIGURE 8.30:

Sales and contribution margins by regional director

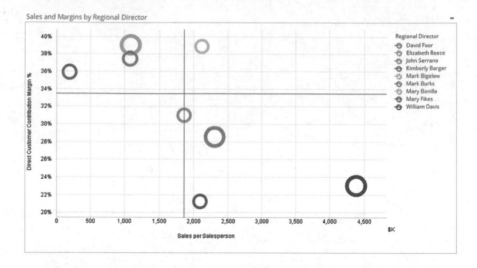

It compares regional directors' performance, measured by sales per salesperson and contribution margins. The size of the ring is determined by the number of salespersons managed by each director. A sales executive could use this chart as the basis of a performance conversation with the sales directors. Based on the chart, one of the directors excels in sales per salesperson, while the average number is around $2M per salesperson. The three directors in the top-left corner lead on profitability, but show low sales per salesperson.

If the goal of the sales organization were to improve on these two KPIs, the conversation could be much more specific if you could also see change from the prior year. Examine the chart in Figure 8.31.

This chart can start a different kind of a conversation. You can see that three directors posted substantial improvements in both KPIs, while four other directors show modest improvements. One of the directors shows a small decline in profitability, and one of the directors is new.

You can see that visualizing performance metrics over time provides even more insight into the story, or may sometimes change the tone of the whole conversation.

This presentation is achieved by adding Year as the primary dimension to the "regular" scatter chart, in addition to the existing dimension (Regional Director in our example). If the existing chart used to be sorted by Y-value, then it's important to verify that the Years are sorted by the **Numeric Value** only.

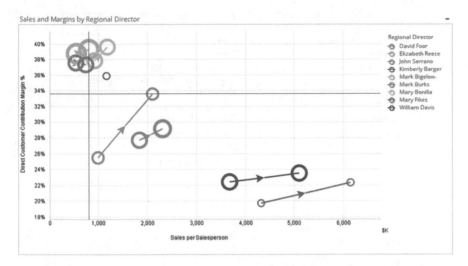

FIGURE 8.31:
The scatter chart
with the change year
over year

The best **Look** for this type of chart is **Rings** (the second icon on the right in the **Style** tab) because it offers a lot of "air" and allows you to see the arrows and the overlapping bubbles in the best possible way.

Several presentation settings need to be tweaked on the **Presentation** tab (see Figure 8.32).

All the settings that are relevant for this transformation are grouped together in the **Representation** section in the upper-left corner.

- **Both Lines and Symbols** should be selected from the drop-down list.

- When the chart shows just a few data points, we recommend increasing the **Max Bubble Size** for better visibility. This is done by unchecking the **Autosize Symbols** box and increasing **Max Bubble Size**.

- Then, the **Show Arrows** box needs to be checked. The default **Arrow Size** is 2, just as the default **Line Width**. This makes the arrows practically indistinguishable from the lines. We recommend increasing the **Arrow Size** to 5 points.

- Four arrow styles are available in the drop-down list **Style**. Feel free to experiment and pick your favorite style.

In the following exercise, you build the scatter chart presented in Figure 8.31.

FIGURE 8.32:
Scatter chart proper-
ties, Presentation tab

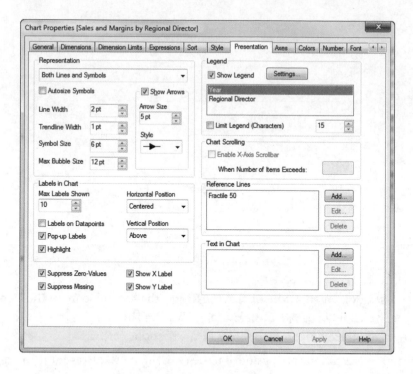

Exercise 8.25: Developing a Scatter Chart with the Time Dimension

Let's start from developing a "simple" scatter chart that is presented in Figure 8.31:

1. Create a new **Scatter Chart**. Name it **Performance by Regional Director**.

2. Use `Regional Director` as a **Dimension**.

3. In the **Expressions** tab, switch to the **Advanced Mode** and **Add** three expressions:

LABEL	DEFINITION
Sales per Salesperson	*$(exp_GrossSales)*/count(distinctSalesperson)
Direct Customer Contribution Margin %	*$(exp_DirectCustomerContributionMargin)* / *$(exp_GrossSales)*
Number of Salespersons	count(distinctSalesperson)

4. In the **Style** tab, select **Rings** (the second icon on the right)

5. In the **Axes** tab, check **Label Along Axis**, **Show Grid**, and **Axis Width=1pt** for both x- and y-axes.

6. In the **Number** tab, format `Sales per Salesperson` as **Integer**, the `Contribution Margin %` as a **Fixed to 1 Decimal**, **Show in Percent**, and `Number of Salespersons` as **Integer**. Then, highlight the first expression `Sales per Salesperson` and add the following calculation for the **Symbol**:

   `='$' & exp_UnitSymbol`

7. In the **Caption** tab, allow **Minimize** and **Auto Minimize**.

8. Accept all the changes and examine the result. Your chart should look similar to Figure 8.31.

Now transform this chart to add the time dimension and to show the change.

1. Open the **Chart Properties** again. In the **Dimensions** tab, add `Year` to the list of dimensions and **Promote** it to the first place in the list.

2. In the **Sort** tab, ensure that `Year` is the first sorting dimension, and that it's sorted by **Numeric Value**.

3. In the **Presentation** tab, make the following changes:

   3.1. Select **Both Lines and Symbols** from the **Representation** drop-down list.

   3.2. Uncheck **Autosize Symbols** and increase the **Max Bubble Size** to **12** pt.

   3.3. Check **Show Arrows** and increase the **Arrow Size** to **5** pt.

4. Accept all the changes and exit the **Properties**. Your chart should be similar to Figure 8.31.

5. **Save** your work.

A Deeper Dive into Set Analysis

We began our conversation about Set Analysis in Chapter 4, and we defined the most basic rules there. Just to remind you of the basics, we said that the Set Analysis condition is inserted in an aggregation function, right after the opening parenthesis. The Set Analysis condition is signified with the pair of curved brackets { } and it consists of the set identifier and the set modifier.

You learned that the set modifier is signified with the pair of angled brackets <> and it includes a comma-separated list of field selections that should override or augment the current user selections. We said that each selection looks like this:

```
FieldName = {values}
```

In this section, you will expand your understanding of Set Analysis and learn how to use variables, calculated formulas, and search conditions.

Using Dollar-Sign Expansions in Set Modifiers

Set Analysis wouldn't be so powerful if it only accepted hard-coded values in set modifiers. In fact, it can do much, much more than that. Let's discover its various capabilities one at a time.

First, you already know that you can use variables with dollar-sign expansions, and the expanded result would look like a hard-coded value. From this perspective, this hard-coded value:

```
Year={2015}
```

can be replaced with the following variable:

```
Year={$(vCurrentYear)}
```

Now your Set Analysis condition doesn't need to be modified every year, which may be bad news for your job security, but is extremely good news for the flexibility of your solutions.

Now, what if you need to select the *previous* year and you haven't prepared a variable for that? Well, one obvious solution is to add a new variable and calculate the previous year there. The other solution is to use another form of dollar-sign expansion that allows you to evaluate any expressions in the boundaries of the expansion and return the result of the calculation. This form of the dollar-sign expansion requires that the formula in the parentheses begins with the equals sign:

```
$(=vCurrentYear-1)    or    $(=max(Year)-1)
```

The two dollar-sign expansions listed here offer two calculations for the previous year. The first calculation evaluates the variable vCurrentYear and subtracts one. The second expression calculates the maximum of the available Year values and subtracts one. Notice that the dollar-sign expansions allow use of aggregated functions (such as max) that will in turn be included in a Set Analysis condition, which in turn participates in another aggregated function. Pretty cool, huh?

Keep in mind that any dollar-sign expansion simply serves for replacing a certain formula with its result. With that in mind, variables with dollar-sign expansions can be used for storing and reusing set analysis modifiers.

For example, you can create a variable called `filter_ThisYear` to store the set modifier (we also call them filters for simplicity):

`filter_ThisYear = Year={$(=max(Year))}`

Then, you can use the same filter in multiple expressions, like this:

`sum({$<$(filter_ThisYear)>} [# Amount])`

The benefit of storing filters in variables is clearly the ease of maintenance. If you find a glitch in your logic and you need to change the definition of the filter, you only need to do it once, as opposed to chasing and modifying multiple expressions.

We will practice the use of variables and dollar-sign expansions with Set Analysis on another flavor of the scatter chart. Many times, analysts are looking for ways of measuring and visualizing *changes in measures*, rather than the measures themselves. In the following example, you will look for a possible relationship between the year-over-year change in **Discounts** and the year-over-year change in **Gross Sales**. You will use the **Current Year Sales** as the third expression, to visualize the difference between bigger accounts and smaller accounts.

Since you are adding new Set Analysis conditions to the calculations, you can't use the existing formulas stored in variables such as `exp_GrossSales`. You will need to develop completely new expressions "from scratch," integrating the set analysis conditions within the aggregation functions.

Exercise 8.26: Analyzing Change Year Over Year in a Scatter Chart

1. Create two new variables and type the following formulas into their values:

VARIABLE	VALUE
filter_ThisYear	Year={$(=max(Year))}
filter_PriorYear	Year={$(=max(Year)-1)}

2. Create a new Scatter Chart. Type **Changes in Sales and Discounts** in the Window Title and disable Show Title in Chart.

3. Select Customer as a Dimension.

4. In the Expressions tab, switch to the Advanced Mode and add three expressions:

LABEL	DEFINITION
Change in Sales	sum({$<$(*filter_ThisYear*)>} [# Amount])/ sum({$<$(*filter_PriorYear*)>} [# Amount]) - 1
Change in Discount %	sum({$<$(*filter_ThisYear*)>} [# Amount - Discounts])/ sum({$<$(*filter_ThisYear*)>} [# Amount]) - sum({$<$(*filter_PriorYear*)>} [# Amount - Discounts])/ sum({$<$(*filter_PriorYear*)>} [# Amount])
Current Year Sales	sum({$<$(*filter_ThisYear*)>} [# Amount])

5. In the Sort tab, sort the chart by Y-value, in the Descending order.

6. In the Style tab, select the Look with the flat (two-dimensional) bubbles.

7. In the Presentation tab, uncheck Autosize Symbols and set the Max Bubble Size to **12**.

8. In the Axes tab, make the following changes for both axes:

   8.1. Check Label Along Axis.

   8.2. Check Show Grid.

   8.3. Use the blue color $(color_Blue) as the Axis Color and set Width to **1**.

9. For X-Axis only, set Static Min = **-0.5** and Static Max = **1**.

10. In the Number tab, format the two Change expressions as Percentages and the Current Year Sales as an Integer.

11. Accept all changes and exit the Properties. Your chart should look similar to Figure 8.33.

Let's examine the chart together. This is another version of the Magic Quadrant. The customers in the upper-right corners received increased discounts and also increased their purchases. The customers in the upper-left corner received higher discounts but decreased their purchases. Something must be done about that. Just by observing the chart, you can conclude that the biggest accounts are located near the x-axis, which means that most of them increased their purchases without any substantial change in discounts.

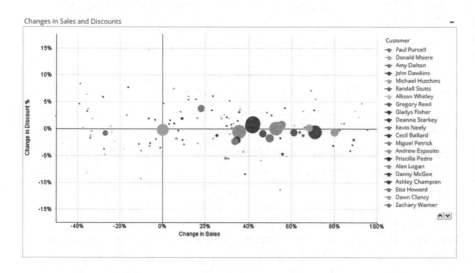

FIGURE 8.33:
Changes in sales and discounts

Using Simple Search in Set Analysis Conditions

Get ready to be amazed by the magnificent power of the next feature! This feature is wide and deep, and not too many QlikView developers understand the full depth of its power.

Since set modifiers, or filters, act like field selections, they support the same features that are supported in a list box with the same field. You can select one or more values or use any type of search to define your selection criteria in a calculated formula.

Simple searches may include wildcards or simple comparisons, as explained in Table 8.3.

TABLE 8.3: Examples of Filters with the Simple Search

FILTER	DESCRIPTION OF A SEARCH
`Color={"*Blue*"}`	Selects all the colors that have the word Blue anywhere in the text
`Year={"201*"}`	Selects all years that begin in 201 (from 2010 to 2019)
`Year={">2013"}`	Selects all years that are greater than 2013

Notice that all search conditions are signified with a pair of double quotes within the curved brackets. In more complex Set Analysis expressions that may involve nested search strings, double quotes need to be alternated with square brackets, to avoid any confusion.

Examine the last filter in this example. Couldn't you formulate the same filter in a more streamlined way, like this:

```
Year > {2013}
```

Unfortunately, this syntax would be incorrect, because the equals sign in the set modifier is not a comparison operator like you might picture at first. Instead, the equals sign means "replace user selections in this field with the following values." You may wonder what other options exist. In order to describe that, we need to introduce set operators.

(If you are wondering where is that magnificent power that we promised to show you, rest assured that it's coming right after the following two sections, when we introduce the *advanced search* in Set Analysis.)

Set Operators

Set Analysis conditions are Boolean expressions. In the end, the Set Analysis condition, as complex as it might be, returns a simple true or false answer that renders each row in the data set as either associated or not associated with the specified set.

As a Boolean expression, a Set Analysis condition can accept the usual Boolean operators, such as union (+), exclusion (-), intersection (*), and symmetric difference (/). They are also called *set operators*, and they can be used in a variety of forms.

Operators can be applied to set identifiers. For example, the set expression {1 - $} selects the inverse of the current selections. When multiple set identifiers are used in the set condition, each set identifier can be equipped with its own set modifier. A combination of two set identifiers can be helpful if the desired selection cannot be made in a single set condition.

For example, imagine that you need to select data for all products that either belong to the brand that contains the word "Golf" in the name or belong to the product group called "Sport." This condition couldn't be easily created in a single set expression, because multiple filters are applied with the logical AND condition, not with the OR. The following combination of the two sets can help in this case:

```
{$<Brand = {"*Golf*"}> + $<[Product Group] = {Sport}>}
```

Another way of using set operators is to apply them to sets of values in a given filter. For example, if you wanted to select all the products that are blue, except for jackets, you could use the following set expression:

```
{$<Product = {"*Blue*"} - {"*Jacket*"}>}
```

Finally, set operators can be used with the equals sign within the set modifier to form so-called *assignments with implicit set operators*. The equals sign in any of these modifiers means that the existing user selection in the field needs to be *replaced* with the given set of values. When a set operator is appended in front of the equals sign, the given values are used to *augment* the existing selection. For example, the following filter selects all currently available (selected or associated) products, except for any blue products:

```
{$<Product -= {"*Blue*"} >}
```

The following filter adds blue products to the set of currently available products:

```
{$<Product += {"*Blue*"} >}
```

Now, with a new understanding of the set operators and the role of the assignment equals signs, you can revisit the question about the correct or incorrect syntax of the year comparison. Now you'll understand why this syntax is correct:

```
Year={">2013"}
```

whereas this syntax is meaningless:

```
Year > {2013}
```

Using Dates in Set Analysis

One of the most confusing issues related to Set Analysis has to do with comparing date fields and date values. As you already know, dates are dual values. They have both the numeric part and the formatted textual part. When you compare dates outside of the Set Analysis, you don't have to be aware of the specific data type of the compared values. QlikView can compare dual fields to numbers and figure out the correct solution. For example, the following expression is perfectly valid:

```
Date>= Max(Date) - 30
```

even though the Date field on the left is dual, while the expression on the right returns a numeric value.

In Set Analysis, the values used in the filters need to be formatted *exactly* the same way as the corresponding field. If dates are stored as numeric values, then numeric values need to be used for the comparison. If dates are stored as dual fields and formatted using the American date standard M/D/YYYY, then the comparison should be done using exactly the same date format. In this case, the following Set Analysis condition will not produce the expected result:

```
{$<Date = {">$(=max(Date) - 30)"}>}
```

In order to ensure that the date values are properly formatted, any calculations involving dates need to be enclosed in the formatting function Date():

```
{$<Date = {">$(=Date(max(Date) - 30))"}>}
```

Alternatively, a *simple search* condition with a date comparison can be replaced with an *advanced search* condition, which is introduced in the following section.

Advanced Search in Set Analysis

If *simple search* can be summarized as applying wildcards and numeric comparisons to the given field's values, then *advanced search* can be defined as applying *any* Boolean condition that can be evaluated for each of the field's values in order to determine which values need to be included. It's best described using practical examples.

Example 1: Format-Free Date Comparison

Let's start from the date comparison presented in the previous section. If you weren't sure what date format to apply, and if you wanted to avoid the whole issue of date formatting, you could replace the *simple search* condition with the following *advanced search* condition:

```
{$<Date = {"=Date>$(=max(Date) - 30)"}>}
```

The Boolean condition in this case is:

```
Date>=$(=max(Date) – 30)
```

This condition is evaluated in the context of the Date field. For each date, the condition returns true or false and that determines the selection. The advantage of using this condition over the simple search condition is that this comparison is not, per se, the direct Set Analysis comparison. Like any other Boolean condition, this comparison isn't dependent on the data type of the operands. You can successfully compare a dual field with a numeric value.

Example 2: Comparing Months Associated with Certain Dates

Sometimes you'll need to compare the month of a given date with the month of another date. You need to create a filter that looks like this:

```
{$<MonthStart(Date) = {"$(=Month(max(Date) - 30))"}>}
```

However, this would be syntactically incorrect because any filter should begin with a field name: Field = {…}. Using an *advanced search* condition, this filter can be formulated as the following:

```
{$<Date = {"=MonthStart(Date)=$(=MonthStart(max(Date) – 30))"}>}
```

It may look like *advanced search* filters should always involve the same fields that they are applied to. In fact, they don't have to. As we said in the beginning, *any* logical condition can be used in an *advanced search* filter.

Example 3: Selecting NULL or Empty Values

It's a known fact that NULL values cannot be selected in QlikView. In Chapter 10, we introduce special NULL handling techniques that allow replacing NULL values with strings. However, if you still have any NULL values, and you need to select all the data rows associated with the NULL value or with an empty string, here is a simple way of achieving that in Set Analysis:

```
{$<RecordID = {"=Len(Trim(Reason))=0"}>}
```

This filter selects records that are associated with any reason codes that are empty or missing or equal to any number of spaces. The Trim() function removes any leading or trailing spaces, and the Len() function returns the length of the resulting text.

Another known solution that allows selecting NULL values in the field itself is the following:

```
{$ - $<Reason={"*"}>}
```

This formula subtracts all possible values of the Reason field from the set of all currently selected data. The remainder is the data that is associated with the Reason = NULL.

Example 4: Selecting Customers Based on Performance

You can use an *advanced search* condition to select only customers who increased their purchases this year, compared to the prior year. Examine the following Set Analysis condition:

```
{$<Customer = {"=sum({<$(filter_ThisYear)>} [# Amount]) >
sum({<$(filter_PriorYear)>} [# Amount]) "}>}
```

This advanced search condition compares the sum of sales for this year to the sum of sales for the prior year. The comparison of the two sums will get evaluated for each customer and the result will determine the selection.

This example concludes our description of the *advanced search* in Set Analysis. In the following exercise, you practice using *advanced search* to clean up the chart presented in Figure 8.33. Notice that the chart looks cluttered with lots of little dots, representing small accounts that don't affect the big picture very much. In order to clean up the chart, you'll limit the number of data points to 30 top accounts based on sales.

You must be thinking, that's easy! You just learned about dimension limits. Surely, you can use dimension limits to show only 30 largest values! Not so fast, grasshopper! If you recall, dimension limits can only restrict values of the *first expression*. If you go back and look at the chart in Figure 8.33, you will see that the first expression is the **Percentage of Change Year over Year**, not the sales amount! You can't use the dimension limits functionality to clean up this chart.

This is where Set Analysis with an advanced search condition helps. You can formulate a filter that selects the top 30 customers based on sales amount and apply the filter to all aggregations in the chart expressions. Since charts don't show missing values and zero values, limiting all chart expressions with the same filter will cause the whole chart to become limited to the same data set.

In order to select top N customers, it's not enough to calculate total sales. You also need to rank the customers based on the sales amount. The function that is used to rank data elements based on aggregated expressions is conveniently called rank(). The rank() function returns 1 for the highest value, 2 for the second highest value, and so forth. Besides the expression itself, the rank() function can accept an optional second parameter that defines how to rank identical results. Feel free to look up the details in the documentation. We will just mention that using the code 4 in the second parameter means that the equal entries should be numbered sequentially, and that's the preferred choice for our purpose. The following expression, when evaluated by customer, returns the rank of a customer based on the total sales:

```
rank(sum([# Amount]), 4)
```

The corresponding Set Analysis filter that selects the top 30 customers looks like this:

```
Customer = {"=rank(sum([# Amount]), 4)<=30"}
```

In order to make this expression more flexible, you can store the desired number in a variable and use the variable in the condition:

```
Customer = {"=rank(sum([# Amount]), 4)<=$(vShowTopN)"}
```

This filter will be used in several aggregated functions within the chart; hence, it's beneficial to store this filter in a variable and reuse it multiple times.

Now you are ready to clean up the chart in Figure 8.33. Feel free to make the changes on your own or follow the detailed instructions in Exercise 8.27.

Exercise 8.27: Selecting Top Performers Using Advanced Search

1. Create two new variables—**vShowTopN** and **filter_TopNCustomers**.

2. Assign **30** to the variable vShowTopN. Enter the following filter as the value of the filter variable:

```
Customer = {"=rank(sum([# Amount]), 4)<=$(vShowTopN)"}
```

3. Locate the scatter chart that you developed in Exercise 8.26 and open its Properties.

4. In the Expressions tab, modify all the expressions by adding the new filter called $(filter_TopNCustomers) to every aggregation function in all three expressions. The new expressions should look like this:

LABEL	DEFINITION
Change in Sales	sum({$<$(filter_ThisYear) , $(filter_TopNCustomers) >} [# Amount]) /sum({$<$(filter_PriorYear) , $(filter_TopNCustomers) >} [# Amount]) - 1
Change in Discount %	sum({$<$(filter_ThisYear) , $(filter_TopNCustomers) >} [# Amount - Discounts])/sum({$<$(filter_ThisYear) , $(filter_TopNCustomers) >} [# Amount]) - sum({$<$(filter_PriorYear) , $(filter_TopNCustomers) >} [# Amount - Discounts])/sum({$<$(filter_PriorYear) , $(filter_TopNCustomers) >} [# Amount])
Current Year Sales	sum({$<$(filter_ThisYear) , $(filter_TopNCustomers) >} [# Amount])

5. Accept the changes and examine the result. The chart should show 30 data points. Experiment with different values of the vShowTopN variable and observe the changes in the chart.

Advanced Visualizations Using Set Analysis

In this section, you will continue practicing advanced Set Analysis concepts that you just learned, and we will introduce two new advanced visualizations—the so-called "whale tail" chart and the so-called "heat map."

Whale Tail Chart: Understanding How Customers and Products Impact Profitability

When companies work on narrow profit margins with many components of costs that are not easy to analyze together, some products or some customers may end up being unprofitable, further eroding slim margins. If this is the case, it's important to identify them and to consider the possibility of discontinuing them.

The *whale tail* chart (see Figure 8.34) is a powerful visualization that demonstrates how a company could produce more profits with less effort.

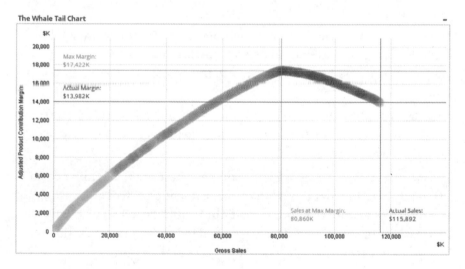

FIGURE 8.34:
The whale tail chart

We will demonstrate the whale tail functionality on the example of product profitability. Similar analysis can be performed at the customer level.

At Q-Tee Brands, Direct Product Contribution Margins are quite high; however, we know that many additional costs will have to be deducted from the revenues before the bottom line. *Just for the purpose of this exercise*, we will assume that an additional 25% of gross sales need to be deducted from each product's profit contribution. So, for this exercise, the calculation of Adjusted Product Contribution Margin will be:

```
<Adjusted Product Contribution Margin> = <Direct Product
    Contribution Margin> — <Gross Sales> * 25%.
```

In the whale tail chart, which is implemented in a specially configured scatter chart, we plot products using the *cumulative* **Gross Sales** as the x-axis and the *cumulative* **Adjusted Product Contribution Margin** as the y-axis. The products are sorted based on the **Product Contribution Margin** percent, in descending order, so the chart starts with the most profitable products on the left and ends with the most unprofitable products on the right.

Four reference lines emphasize the main point of the analysis. The two red lines show the cumulative actuals—the actual sales and the actual profit margins. The two green lines show the maximum profit that would be reached by exiting all the non-profitable products, and the sales amount that corresponds to the maximum margin.

The color-coding of the symbols is optional. In our example, we used green for products with the **Adjusted Contribution Margin %** > 0.25, yellow for products with any positive margins, and red for all the unprofitable products.

Let's describe the main steps of creating the whale tail chart. We start with creating a scatter chart and selecting the dimension of our choice (usually product or customer.)

The two chart expressions are quite simple—these are the familiar calculations of sales and margins (with the adjustment of 25% of gross sales). The only new feature to notice is the **Full Accumulation** setting in the **Expressions** tab, which needs to be applied to both expressions. This is how you can easily calculate cumulative sales and margins.

The sorting of the chart is critical, in order to reach the smooth round shape of the whale tail. The products are sorted by the **Direct Product Contribution Margin** divided by **Gross Sales** (the **Margin %**), in the descending order (!). The 25% adjustment may or may not be applied, since it doesn't affect the sort order.

The reference lines are perhaps the most challenging, especially the green lines. Actual margin and sales are easy to compute; that's not a problem. However, how do you define the horizontal tangent line that's touching the curve at its highest point? Similarly, how do you define the vertical line that's crossing the tangent line? This is one of those situations when it is easier to draw the two lines by hand than to define them in a formula.

Luckily, we have a clearly defined condition that can be used to produce the two green lines. The **Max Margin** and the **Sales at Max Margin** represent the total margin amount and the total sales amount for those products with positive **Adjusted Product Contribution Margin**. This condition can be used as an advanced search condition in a Set Analysis filter to produce the two desired numbers.

Notice that the four reference lines are equipped with labels that explain the meaning of the lines and show the corresponding amounts. We used the CHR(10) function to force these texts into two lines.

You may notice that all three colors are semi-transparent, to produce a distinguished look and to emphasize the areas with higher density of symbols.

In order to generate semi-transparent colors based on conditions, we used the color function ARGB(Alpha, Red, Green, Blue). This function is similar to the familiar RGB() function, with an addition of the Alpha factor that controls the opacity of the color. Alpha = 0 defines a fully transparent color, while Alpha = 255 corresponds to fully non-transparent, solid color. In our example, we used Alpha = 20 to create an almost fully transparent color. The density of the colors in Figure 8.34 is explained by the high density of overlapping symbols in the chart.

In the following exercise, you develop the whale tail chart presented in Figure 8.34.

Exercise 8.28: Creating a Whale Tail Chart

1. Activate the Product Profitability sheet. Create a new variable called **filter_ ProfitableProduct**. Use the following Definition:

```
Product = {"=$(exp_DirectProductContributionMargin) - $(exp_GrossSales) * 0.25>0"}
```

2. Create a new Scatter Chart. Type **The Whale Tail Chart** in the Window Title. Uncheck Show Title in Chart.

3. Select Product as a Dimension.

4. In the Expressions tab, switch to the Advanced Mode and Add two expressions:

LABEL	DEFINITION
Gross Sales	$(exp_GrossSales)
Adjusted Product Contribution Margin	$(exp_DirectProductContributionMargin) – $(exp_GrossSales) * 0.25

5. Still in the Expressions tab, select Full Accumulation for each one of the two expressions. Enter the following formula as the Background Color for the first expression in the list:

```
IF($(exp_DirectProductContributionMargin) / $(exp_GrossSales) - 0.25  > 0.25,
ARGB(20, 0, 255,0) ,
IF($(exp_DirectProductContributionMargin) / $(exp_GrossSales) - 0.25  > 0,
ARGB(20, 255, 128, 0), ARGB(20,255,0,0)  ))
```

6. In the Sort tab, select Sort by Expression in Descending order. Type the following formula as the sort expression:

```
$(exp_DirectProductContributionMargin)/$(exp_GrossSales)
```

7. In the Style tab, select the Look with flat solid bubbles (second icon from the bottom on the right).

8. In the Presentation tab, disable Show Legend and set Symbol Size = **12pt**. Add four Reference Lines with the following Expressions and Labels.

   8.1. Actual Sales (X-Axis, Red line):

Expression:

```
$(exp_GrossSales)
```

Label:

```
='Actual Sales:' &chr(10) & '$' & $(exp_GrossSales) &'$(exp_UnitSymbol)'
```

   8.2. Actual Margins (Y-Axis, Red line):

Expression:

```
$(exp_DirectProductContributionMargin) - $(exp_GrossSales) * 0.25
```

Label:

```
='Actual Margin:' & chr(10) & '$' &
num(
$(exp_DirectProductContributionMargin) - $(exp_GrossSales) * 0.25
, '$(fmt_PL)' ) & '$(exp_UnitSymbol)'
```

8.3. Sales at Max Margin (X-Axis, Green):

Expression:

```
sum( {<Product = {"=$(exp_DirectProductContributionMargin) -
    $(exp_GrossSales) * 0.25 > 0"}>} [# Amount])/vUnit
```

Label:

```
= 'Sales at Max Margin:' & chr(10) & '$' &
num(sum( {<Product = {"=$(exp_DirectProductContributionMargin) -
    $(exp_GrossSales) * 0.25>0"}>} [# Amount])/vUnit,
    '$(fmt_PL)') & '$(exp_UnitSymbol)'
```

8.4. Max Margin (Y-Axis, Green):

Expression:

```
(sum( {<$(filter_ProfitableProduct)>} [# Amount]) * 0.75 -
(sum({<$(filter_ProfitableProduct),[Reason Description]={'Return to stock'}>} [# CM Amount])) -
sum( {<$(filter_ProfitableProduct)>} [# COGS - Labor]) -
sum( {<$(filter_ProfitableProduct)>} [# COGS - Material])
)/vUnit
```

Label:

```
='Max Margin:' & chr(10) & '$' &
num(
    (sum( {<$(filter_ProfitableProduct)>} [# Amount]) * 0.75 -
    (sum({<$(filter_ProfitableProduct),[Reason Description]={'Return to stock'}>}
    [# CM Amount])) -
sum( {<$(filter_ProfitableProduct)>} [# COGS - Labor]) -
sum( {<$(filter_ProfitableProduct)>} [# COGS - Material])
    )/vUnit
, '$(fmt_PL)' ) & '$(exp_UnitSymbol)'
```

8.5. Notice that the two lines with the sales amounts should be defined with the X-Axis Location and the two lines with the margin amounts should be defined with the Y-Axis Location.

8.6. Use `color_Red` for the lines with the Actual Numbers and `color_Green` for the lines with the Max Margin numbers.

9. In the Axes tab, check Label Along Access, Show Grid, and Axis Width=1pt for both axes.

10. In the Number tab, format both expressions as Integers and enter the following formula as the Symbol expression:

`='$' & exp_UnitSymbol`

11. Accept all changes and exit Properties. Your chart should look similar to the Figure 8.34.

12. Save your work.

Creating Heat Maps Using the Block Chart

The *block chart* (see Figure 8.35), also called a *tree map*, looks like a rectangular pie chart, in the sense that it also communicates how a whole number is divided among its parts. In the block chart, bigger parts are located near the upper-left corner, and smaller parts are pushed to the right and down. Smaller "chunks" are aggregated into a single box called **Others**, which can often be one of the biggest boxes in the chart. (This behavior might be different, depending on the Service Release of your QlikView software).

FIGURE 8.35:
A simple block chart

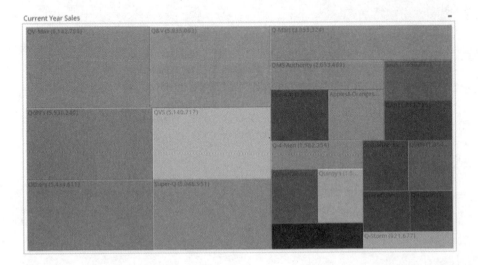

In comparison to the traditional pie chart, the block chart is doing a better job of leveraging the allowed screen space. More importantly, the block chart can visualize a hierarchy of up to three dimensions. For example, sales could be presented by Salesperson, and salespersons could be aggregated into the Regional Director totals, that in turn could be aggregated by VP for Sales.

The block chart is the chart type that's signified by the ⊞ icon. Most of the settings are fairly common, except for the **Presentation** tab (see Figure 8.36).

For the block chart, the **Presentation** properties allow you to configure how **Dimension Labels** and **Numbers** should appear on the screen and on the **Pop-up** label. In addition, **Caption Font** and **Background Color** can be defined for the **Totals** and for the **Intermediate Level Captions**.

In the following exercise, you develop a block chart that shows **Customer Allowances** (the credit memos) for the current year, aggregated by **Customer** and **Channel**.

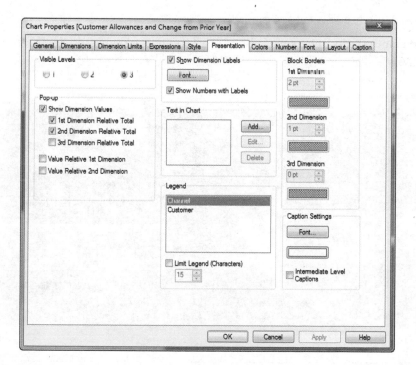

FIGURE 8.36:
Block chart properties, Presentation tab

Exercise 8.29: Creating a Block Chart

1. Create a new **Chart** on the **Customer Profitability** sheet and pick **Block Chart** as the **Chart Type**. Name the chart **Customer Allowances**. Disable **Show Title in Chart**.

2. In the **Dimensions** tab, pick two dimensions —Channel and Customer—in this order.

3. In the **Expressions** tab, create a single expression **Credit Memos**, with the following definition:

    `sum({<$(filter_ThisYear)>}  [# CM Amount])/vUnit`

4. In the **Style** tab, accept the default setting, which is the second icon in the list. Despite our usual preference for flat design, the second **Look** offers better presentation features than the first one.

5. In the **Presentation** tab, repeat all the settings as they appear in Figure 8.36— **Show Dimension Labels**, **Show Numbers With Labels**, and the same **Pop-up** settings. Click on both **Font** buttons and adjust the font color from dark-gray to almost fully black (you will notice that the labels in this chart appear semi-transparent, and you need to make them more pronounced).

6. In the **Number** tab, format the expression as **Integer**.

7. In the **Caption** tab, allow **Minimize** and **Auto Minimize**.

8. Accept all changes and exit the properties. Your finished chart should look similar to the chart presented in Figure 8.37.

FIGURE 8.37:
Customer allowances in a block chart

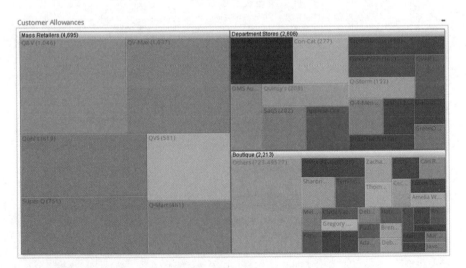

Looking at the chart, you can conclude that mass retailers are responsible for approximately half of all allowances, and the two biggest allowance takers are Q&V and QV-Max.

The wonderful multi-color palette, while looking very festive, doesn't add much to the analytical value of the chart. Replacing the random colors with a meaningful color scheme can make this chart much more informative.

It's common to define the block chart colors based on a certain performance metric or on a comparison. One possible way is to assign colors based on the comparison of the actual **Allowance Percent to Sales**, compared to the **Target**. Another possible way is to compare the **Allowance Percent to Sales** for this year to the prior year number and color all the customers—red if the share of allowances had increased, green if it decreased, or neutral gray if the number remained approximately the same.

The block charts with colors assigned by performance are often called heat maps, in association with the geographical maps colored in a similar way. Elaborate heat maps can have five, seven, or even more shades of each color, based on a certain numeric scale. For the sake of simplicity, we limit our chart to three main colors—positive, negative, and neutral.

In the following exercise, you transform the block chart in Figure 8.37 into the heat map, with the color representing the year-over-year change in customer allowances.

Exercise 8.30: Transforming the Block Chart into a Heat Map

1. Open the Properties for the block chart that you created in Exercise 8.29. In the General tab, add the text **and Change from Prior Year** to the Window Title.

2. In the Expressions tab, add a new expression with the following Definition. Label the expression **Change**:

```
sum( {<$(filter_ThisYear)>} [# CM Amount])/
    sum({<$(filter_ThisYear)>}[# Amount]) -
sum( {<$(filter_PriorYear)>} [# CM Amount])/
    sum({<$(filter_PriorYear)>}[# Amount])
```

3. Click on the Expansion Icon (the little plus sign) next to the main expression Credit Memos and enter the following definition for the Background Color:

```
IF(Change > 0.05, $(color_Red) ,
IF(Change > -0.05, $(color_Gray) ,
$(color_Green)))
```

4. Accept all changes and exit the Properties. Your finished chart should look similar to the chart in Figure 8.38.

FIGURE 8.37:

Heat map of customer allowances and their changes

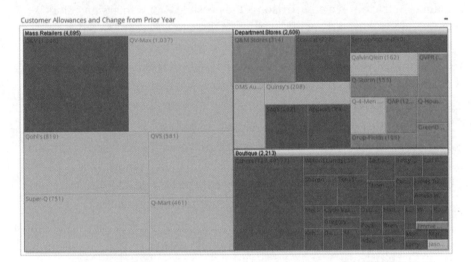

Notice how we added an invisible expression called Change and used it in the calculation of the background color. When the heat map should include many more shades of red and green, this technique becomes even more valuable. The calculation is made once and used multiple times.

Let's examine the new chart. You can learn much more from the same block chart when it's painted in a meaningful way. You can learn that allowances remained mostly flat among the mass retailers. Department stores show improvements in some accounts, and unfortunate increases in four other accounts. Boutiques had posted increases almost by all accounts. If the sales department's goal was to decrease customer allowances, relative to their sales, then the three sales groups should have different kinds of conversations, based on these results.

Using Containers as an Alternative to Auto-Minimized Charts

The heat map and the block chart complete the series of advanced charts that we wanted to explore in this chapter. Before we move on to discussing data modeling and scripting aspects, we want to introduce you to one more technique for arranging multiple charts on the screen.

In Chapter 4, you arranged many charts on the same screen using the Auto-Minimize feature. That technique is quite fine, and yet it could be better in a number of ways:

- Only one group of charts can be managed with the Auto-Minimize feature. If there is a need to show two groups of charts side by side, Auto-Minimize doesn't work.

- All the charts in the Auto-Minimize group need to be equally positioned and sized, in order to ensure a professional look and feel.

- Minimized labels may clutter the sheet, especially if there are too many of them.

- The text of the label has to be the same as the window title, and there is no way of shortening the text for the minimized label.

In this chapter, we introduce a more modern technique that was introduced in QlikView 10.0. This technique involves using *containers* to organize multiple sheet objects on the sheet.

A *container* is a special object type that can host other sheet objects such as charts, table boxes, list boxes, and virtually any other object types, including other containers.

Containers are created in the same way as any other sheet objects. The **General** tab of the **Properties** dialog (see Figure 8.39) describes what **Objects** are **Displayed in the Container**. Objects can be added from the list of **Existing Objects** on the left.

The **Objects Displayed in Container** can be moved up and down the list using the **Promote** and **Demote** buttons. When one of the objects is selected (highlighted), an alternative label can be assigned in the **Label for Selected Object** expression box. This is useful when there is a need to shorten the label.

In the **Presentation** tab (see Figure 8.40), the drop-down list **Container Type** offers a choice between two types—**Single Object** and **Grid**.

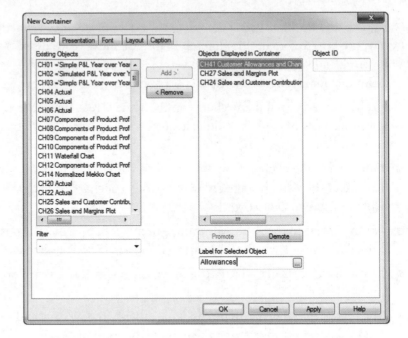

The **Single Object** container (Figure 8.40, left) presents one object at a time in a tabbed view. The tabs can be positioned on the left, on the right, on top, on bottom, or in a drop-down list, and the choice is defined under **Appearance**. You can also set the **Tab Color** here.

The **Grid** container (Figure 8.40, right) presents a number of objects in a grid. The grid can be defined with the number of **Columns** and **Rows**, and the required **Spacing** interval.

While **Grid** containers can be helpful in terms of arranging objects on the sheet, the **Single Object** containers are definitely more commonly used for the purpose of presenting a single chart at a time and providing a choice of charts in a nice tabbed view. With just a few labels, it's common to position the tabs on top. When the number of charts is too high, placing tabs on the left or on the right allows you to fit in many more labels.

When objects are added to a container, QlikView creates a linked object for the original object and places it in the container. If the original object is modified, then its linked clone in the container is modified as well. When the only purpose of the original object was to be included in the container, it can be safely deleted. The object in the container will survive on its own just fine.

Since the objects in the container cannot be minimized, QlikView cancels any **Allow Minimize** and **Auto Minimize** settings. When it happens, all the non-minimized charts appear in the same area on the sheet, overlapping and cluttering the view. Remember to move these charts out of the way prior to adding them to a container.

Once the container is created with only one or two charts, additional charts can be simply dropped into the container by dragging the object onto the tab row of the container. In this case, the object is actually moved into the container, and no linked copy is created. Examine the container in Figure 8.41. This container was created with two charts—the scatter chart and the combo chart—as you can see from the labels on top. The third chart, the allowances heat map, which appears dimmed, is being dragged onto the tab row. Once the object reached the destination, the tab row becomes highlighted with the dashed border.

The same dashed border outlines an important area in the container. As with all other objects, you can access the object's **Properties** by right-clicking anywhere within the object. Containers are different, because they contain other objects within them. Therefore, you need to differentiate two areas within a container—the main area where charts are presented, and the tab row, along with the caption of the container.

Right-clicking in a chart provides access to the chart properties, while right-clicking on the tab row or on the caption provides access to the properties of the container.

FIGURE 8.41:

Dragging and dropping a new chart into a container

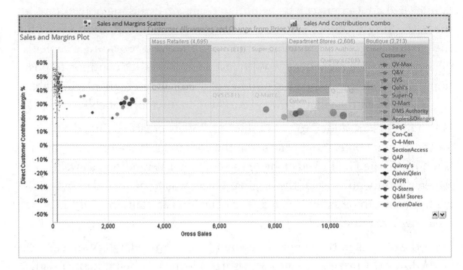

In the following exercise, you create a container on the **Product Profitability** sheet and add the existing charts to the container.

Exercise 8.31: Arranging Charts in a Container

1. Activate the **Product Profitability** sheet.

2. Activate one of the charts and move it away from the central area of the screen, where the new container will be created.

3. Open **Properties** for the same chart and make a note of the **Object ID** (you can find it on the **General** tab of the **Properties**).

4. Create a **New Sheet Object** and select **Container** as the **Object Type**.

5. In the **General** tab, select the **Chart** with the **Object ID** that you just recorded. If needed, enter a shorter label for the chart.

6. In the **Presentation** tab, accept **Single Object** as the **Container Type** and select **Tabs** at top under **Appearance**.

7. In the **Caption** tab, uncheck **Show Caption**.

8. Accept all changes and exit Properties. The new container should be created in the sheet. The chart that was added to the container should be restored and positioned away from the middle, where you relocated it earlier. Delete this copy of the chart; it's not needed any more.

9. Drag-and-drop all the minimized charts onto the tab row of the new container. The new charts should be added to the container and disappear from the sheet.

10. Position and size the container to take up all the available space on the sheet.

11. Right-click on the tab row and open the Container Properties. Give all the charts shorter labels to fit them into the limited space.

12. Your finished container should look similar to the container in Figure 8.42.

Extra Credit

In a similar fashion, use another container to arrange all the charts on the Customer Profitability sheet.

FIGURE 8.42: Product Profitability sheet with the container

Since the container holds linked copies of objects, copying and modifying containers can be dangerous. Sometimes developers fall into a common pitfall, without realizing it until it's too late. Imagine that you developed a number of charts and you add them to a container. Now, you need a similar container with similar charts on your next sheet, with only a few slight changes. You clone the container to the next sheet and you modify the charts based on your needs. After finishing all the modifications, you go back to the original sheet and realize that all your existing objects were modified as well. Now you have two identical containers on both sheets. The reason for this unfortunate situation is that both containers hold links to the same chart objects. Modifying the charts in the second container inevitably leads to modifying the original charts in the first container.

There are two ways to avoid this problem. The best way is to simply avoid cloning containers. Just bite the bullet and create a new container with new charts.

The other way is to **Unlink** each of the objects in the second container, to enable them to be modified independently. This technique was a bit flaky, in our experience, and even lead to crashing QlikView once or twice, so we don't really recommend trying that at home.

This section concludes our discussion about developing advanced visualizations for profitability analysis in QlikView. In the next two chapters, we will discuss the data modeling and the scripting aspects of profitability analysis. Then, we will return to building advanced QlikView visualizations in Chapter 12.

9

Data Modeling for Profitability Analysis

In Chapter 5, we described how to create a dimensional star schema around a single set of business transactions (invoices). We created a single Fact table by loading the rows from the [Invoice Details] table and adding fields from the [Invoice Header] table. Dimension tables were created for Customers, ShipTo (Customers), Warehouses, Products, and [Sales Persons], as well as a [Master Calendar] table of dates. However, to support the more in-depth analysis of profitability, you need more than just invoices. To calculate the profit margins for particular products, a more accurate measure of sales and the cost of goods is needed. In this chapter, we'll introduce several new concepts and discuss data modeling alternatives.

On the revenue side, adding the credit-memo transactions to your model allows you to see not just sales, but also any returns or adjustments. To accommodate the new transactions, we'll compare two modeling techniques: concatenating the Fact table with the new transactions and linking two separate Fact tables together.

On the costing side, we'll bring in labor, material, and estimated overhead costs for each product, by year. This introduces the concept of the *slowly changing dimension* into the model and the modeling challenges that go with it.

The precise way in which you incorporate these new data elements impacts the memory footprint and performance of the application. To better inform your modeling decisions, it's helpful to first understand exactly how QlikView stores the data.

How QlikView Stores Data

QlikView stores data differently from a typical relational database system like Microsoft SQL or Oracle. The most obvious difference is that QlikView uses RAM instead of disk storage. The key difference is that QlikView does *not* store redundant data. In a traditional database, if an Address table had a field for City and 1,000 rows contained the value New York, that string would be stored 1,000 times on disk. In a similar QlikView table, the string New York would be stored only once—each row would instead contain a *pointer* to the value of New York. In this way, QlikView avoids storing redundant data by internally normalizing the data after it's loaded—even if the data model is heavily denormalized!

How does QlikView do this? Let's look at a small example, consisting of a table with four columns and five rows. Figure 9.1 shows the rows from the Customers table as you would normally see them.

FIGURE 9.1:

The Customers table with five rows

[Customers] table with natural values

Customer ID	Customer	Customer City	Channel
101001	Shannon Kemp	Southern Pines	Boutique
101002	SaqS	Pittsburgh	Department Stores
101003	Joan Somers	Espanola	Boutique
101004	Q-Storm	New York	Department Stores
101005	Kacey Hernandez	Adelphi	Boutique

After the data is loaded, it is deconstructed in a two-step process:

1. For each column, QlikView creates a distinct list of values.
2. Data in the tables is replaced with pointers to the associated value in the distinct list.

Figure 9.2 shows a visual example of the lists stored in RAM for this example table.

	Customer ID		Customer		Customer City		Channel
0	101001	0	Shannon Kemp	0	Southern Pines	0	Boutique
1	101002	1	Saq$	1	Pittsburgh	1	Department Store
2	101003	2	Joan Somers	2	Espanola		
3	101004	3	Q-Storm	3	New York		
4	101005	4	Kacey Hernandez	4	Adelphi		

Index   Distinct Value

FIGURE 9.2: Distinct lists for the Customers table

Notice that each distinct value is assigned an index value. For simplicity, the index values shown in Figure 9.2 are in decimal format. Internally, QlikView stores the index as a binary value. Since there are only five rows, the highest pointer value you'll need is 4 (starting with 0). The binary pointer of 100 equates to decimal 4.

After the distinct lists of values for each column are assembled, QlikView replaces the natural values in the tables with the corresponding index (pointer) values. Figure 9.3 visualizes the five rows of the Customers table with the binary pointer values.

[Customers] table with pointer values

Customer ID	Customer	Customer City	Channel
000	000	000	000
001	001	001	001
010	010	010	000
011	011	011	001
100	100	100	000

FIGURE 9.3: Table rows with binary pointer values

So for this small table, QlikView stores the four distinct lists of column values and the logical table of pointers. As you can see, this process boils down to a kind of normalizing. Redundant data is removed, and one-to-many relationships are implemented with pointers, similar to the concept of database foreign-key relationships. Keep in mind that QlikView stores only one list of distinct values for every column in the database. Even a column that appears in more than one table requires only one list. For example, the [Customer ID] column appears in the Customers table as well as in the Fact table. QlikView examines both tables and then creates one list of distinct values. Thus, compared to database storage, the greatest amount of storage efficiency is achieved from a column that has relatively few distinct values, but appears in more than one table with a large volume of rows.

Minimum storage requirements for each field can be calculated by determining the amount of RAM needed to store the actual values (the distinct list) and the pointers to those values. For the distinct values, the math is easy: RAM = (#distinct values * size). For the pointers, you have to do a little work to first figure out the *size* of the pointer you need. In the simple example in Figure 9.3, you only needed a three-bit pointer to point to all five distinct values of the [Customer ID] field. The result (3) is the number to which 2 must be raised to equal at least 5. This logic can be calculated with a binary logarithm (logarithm to the base 2). The binary logarithm of 5 is 3. For a list with 25,000 distinct values, you can calculate the pointer size by asking, "to what power must 2 be raised to at least equal 25,000?" or "What is the binary logarithm of 25,000?" The answer is 15, so you need a 15-bit pointer to represent 25,000 values. Once the pointer size is determined for a particular field, it is multiplied by the number of rows in which it appears. Clearly, a table with 1 million rows of 3-bit pointers requires less storage than 1 million rows of 16-bit pointers. Keep in mind that these calculations are for the minimum storage amounts in RAM— QlikView will carry some overhead to manage the data.

To put it all together, consider a larger example. Assume the Customers dimension table has 50,000 rows and the Fact table has 1 million rows. The storage calculations for the [Customer ID] field are shown in Tables 9.1 and 9.2.

TABLE 9.1: Memory Storage Requirements for [Customer ID] Distinct Values

FIELD	A \# DISTINCT VALUES	B SIZE (BYTES)	(A*B)/1024/1024 VALUE STORAGE (MB)
Customer ID	50,000	8	0.38 MB

TABLE 9.2: Memory Storage Requirements for [Customer ID] Pointers

	C	D	E	(C*E)/1024/1024
TABLE	**# ROWS**	**POINTER LENGTH (BITS)***	**POINTER LENGTH (BYTES)***	**POINTER STORAGE (MB)**
Customers	50,000	16	2	0.10 MB
Fact	10,000,000	16	2	1.91 MB
		* Log2(50,000)	* D/8	

The total RAM required to store the [Customer ID] field is 0.38MB + 0.10MB + 1.91MB = 2.77 MB, with well over 80% going toward storing the pointers. If the [Customer ID] field had 1 million distinct values, a 20-bit pointer would be required to point to every value. The purpose of this exercise is to emphasize that high cardinality contributes significantly to memory usage—even if the data value is small—due to the length of the pointer values.

With Large Data Models, Pay Attention to Cardinality

The cardinality (distinct number of values) of a field is a significant contributor to memory usage, because of the length of the pointer required. Obviously, key fields have high cardinality. It's wise to also keep an eye on other fields—those with long alphanumeric strings or high-precision decimal values often have high cardinality.

While the sheer size of the data model has a direct impact on performance, so does the configuration of the tables. For QlikView to perform aggregation calculations, it must navigate through its system of pointers to find the correct data elements. If the required data elements are stored in many tables, with many hops in between, a certain amount of time is spent just doing pointer lookups. Figure 9.4 illustrates the one-hop relationship between the Fact and Customer tables.

Any chart using fields from these two tables must navigate through one level of pointer-lookup. In the case of snowflaked models, multiple-hop pointer lookups are required to associate the data. If the intermediary snowflaked tables have relatively few distinct values (pointers), then multiple pointer lookups may not impact performance. An intermediary table is a table in the "middle"—one which must be traversed to get to the final destination table. If the intermediary snowflaked tables are relatively large, then the lookup process takes longer. Of course "large" is a subjective term, and is dependent on your available server resources.

FIGURE 9.4:
Table relationship and pointers

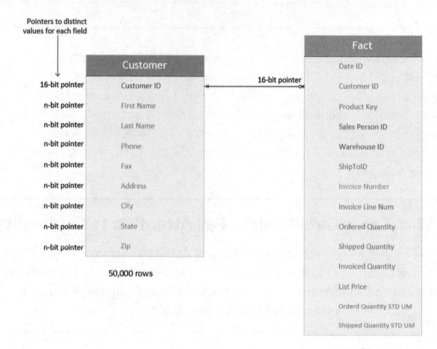

At this point, you might be thinking, "Why have any pointer lookups at all? Why not just denormalize *everything* into one gigantic table?" From Figure 9.4, you could join all eight attributes from the 50,000 row Customer table into the 10 million row Fact table. While this eliminates the time it takes for QlikView to perform pointer lookups, it also requires a huge amount of space for the additional pointer storage—instead of storing pointers to eight attribute values over 50,000 rows, you have to the store pointers to eight attribute values in 10 million rows! Depending on the cardinality of the attributes, the pointers could take up a lot of space.

This drastic increase in memory usage eliminates any benefit that might be gained from removing the hop between tables. This is yet another reason that we prefer using the star schema—especially for large data sets. In reality, some applications perform well with a single denormalized table. Depending on a number of factors, the single table could cause more performance problems than it solves—or vice versa. This is why data modeling remains a bit more of an art than a science.

As you design your data models, keep the following best practices in mind:

- As stated in Chapter 5, we prefer using a star schema, because it can visually communicate the business model, and it's easier to extend. In certain cases, a flat design or a snowflake schema will also perform well.

- When using the star or snowflake schema, make sure to keep all measures in the fact table.

- Aside from overall row count, fields with high cardinality have the biggest impact on memory usage.

- Denormalizing small tables (code tables) into the fact table incurs little penalty.

- Denormalizing wide tables (such as the Customer table) into the fact table can cause slower performance, due to increased pointer storage.

Modeling Multiple Transaction Sources

As you've seen, a basic star schema data model has one Fact table surrounded by one or more dimension tables. Sometimes, requirements dictate the inclusion of facts from several different subject areas. There are two basic approaches to adding facts to the data model. The first involves loading the new facts into a separate Fact table and then creating a table containing keys that *link* the two together. These intermediary key tables are called *link tables* or sometimes *bridge tables*. The other approach is to create a *Concatenated Fact table* by appending the additional transactions into the existing fact table. This section takes a detailed look at both approaches.

Multiple Fact Tables

The main challenge of using multiple Fact tables in a star schema is to maintain the accuracy of data while avoiding circular references and incorrect synthetic keys. One method of expanding the facts included in a data model is to link two or more Fact tables together. A *link table* contains combinations of key fields that associate two or more Fact tables with the dimension tables. In this section, we'll examine how to create a link table and discuss the pros and cons of the technique.

Link Tables

Take a look at a simple example. Figure 9.5 shows a simple star schema with one fact table and two dimensions. Fact2 is from a different transaction source and needs to be integrated into the model somehow.

FIGURE 9.5:
Simple star schema before adding a new set of facts

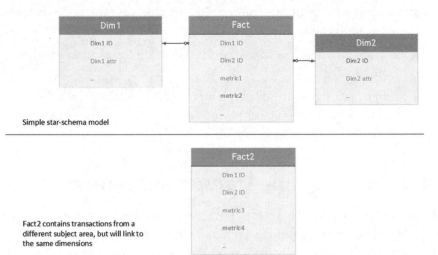

Notice that Fact2 has relationships to both of the dimension tables as well. If you just loaded Fact2 as-is, you would immediately see how QlikView handles two tables with two keys in common. Notice the synthetic key table in Figure 9.6.

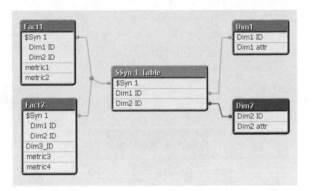

With two common keys between Fact1 and Fact2, QlikView automatically
creates a unique *synthetic key* from the combination of [Dim1 ID] and [Dim2
ID]. In Figure 9.6, this composite key is called $Syn1. Additional synthetic
keys are given sequential names $Syn2, $Syn3, etc. In this simple example,
the synthetic key table acts as a link table, and correctly associates all of
the tables.

When Is It OK to Leave Synthetic Keys In The Data Model?

If the synthetic key results in the correct association of tables in your data model, then it's
technically OK to leave it as-is. As the data modeler, it is up to you to determine the validity of
the associations. Although synthetic keys can work well in many cases, data models with several
synthetic tables can be incorrect, or just difficult to understand and extend. As professionals, we
value the notion of being explicit in everything we do. To that end, we suggest resolving issues
with synthetic keys manually, using your knowledge of the underlying data as your guide.

In addition, we often find more elegant data modeling solutions just by going through the
process of resolving composite keys. As you will learn in Chapter 10, some data modeling
techniques (such as using generic keys) can only be applied through the process of creating
composite keys manually.

So even though the synthetic key table in Figure 9.6 results in a correct
data model, let's go through the steps of manually creating the link table.

To explicitly create the complex associations between fact tables, you can create a table similar to a synthetic key table, called a *link table*. Figure 9.7 shows the basic structure of a link table model.

FIGURE 9.7:
Modified star schema with link table

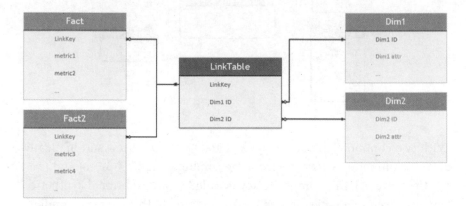

Let's look at each component of the structure separately. First, in the Fact table, notice that the original fields that link to the dimension tables ([Dim1 ID] and [Dim2 ID]) have been removed. Instead, the LinkKey column associates to the LinkTable. To create the LinkKey in the Fact table, you must create a composite key that contains the combination of all the dimension ID values. In the QlikView load script, the LinkKey is created by using the string concatenation operator (&), as follows:

```
Load [Dim1 ID] & '-' & [Dim2 ID] as LinkKey,
```

In this case, we've used a hyphen (-) as the conjunction character to separate the values. Conjunction characters are needed to avoid the accidental matching of keys. For example, a key with the value of 111-1 would incorrectly link to a key with value 1-111 without a conjunction character. Other characters can be used, such as the pipe (|) or underscore (_). It's up to the preference of the developer and the nature of the data. Obviously, you wouldn't want to use a | symbol as a conjunction if this symbol appears naturally in the data itself. Figure 9.8 shows how the resulting rows might look in two rows of the Fact table.

FIGURE 9.8:
LinkKey created from Dim ID fields in the Fact table

FACT				
LinkKey	**Dim1 ID**	**Dim2 ID**	**metric1**	**metric2**
A123-B433	A123	B433	..	..
A229-B698	A229	B698	..	..

The same process is repeated to create the LinkKey in the Fact2 table.

Now that the LinkKey fields exist in both Fact tables, let's look at how to create the LinkTable. The LinkTable is a derived table in that it does not come from a source table in the OLTP system. You can create the table in QlikView by simply loading all the distinct LinkKey and [Dim ID] columns directly from the Fact and Fact2 tables, using a resident load. The contents of the LinkTable would look similar to the rows in Figure 9.9.

LINKTABLE		
LinkKey	Dim1 ID	Dim2 ID
A123-B433	A123	B433
A229-B698	A229	B698

FIGURE 9.9:
LinkTable rows

In the load script, once the LinkTable is created, all of the [Dim ID] fields should be dropped from the Fact tables, to avoid the circular references and synthetic keys.

Generic Keys

Since various business transactions may not share the identical dimensionality or "grain," the LinkKey may contain NULL values for certain dimension IDs. For example, a sales transaction might contain [SalesPerson ID], but a credit memo might not. This could be a problem if Sales Person is used as a filter for reporting. Selecting a particular Sales Person would then associate with only the LinkKeys that included the [SalesPerson ID] as a component of the key. In this case, the credit memos associated with those sales would be unavailable.

Often, the missing ID doesn't indicate a true difference in grain; it is just an effect of normalization. You might have to go through a number of hops to other tables to retrieve an ID. For example, if the credit memo also references an invoice, you could join to the correct invoice and grab the [SalesPerson ID]. QlikView also provides a sort of lookup function called applymap(). This function allows you to retrieve a value from a table without actually executing a join statement. The applymap() technique is described in Chapter 10.

If the missing ID indicates a true difference in grain, you can create *generic keys* that would accommodate for the difference by loosening the relationship between the fact and dimensions. Instead of requiring a strict key composition that includes real keys to all dimensions, you can let some keys slide by inserting what is essentially a fake ID.

Linking Facts Tables with Different Grain

Facts with different levels of granularity (dimensional detail) can make consolidated reporting a bit tricky. In QlikView, when users select an attribute value such as Product or Date, they will expect the chart to display consistent results. If the differences in granularity are left in the data model (LinkKeys with some null components), the user could experience the dreaded 'No data to display' message when a dimension is selected that is outside the granularity of the metric being analyzed.

Let's take a look at an example that illustrates the problem. For example, the Fact3 table shown in Figure 9.10 does not have a [Dim2 ID] column. How would you create the LinkKey without the [Dim2 ID] component? If the second component of the LinkKey is left as NULL, as shown in Figure 9.10, there would be no way for the rows in the other facts to associate to this table.

FACT3				
LinkKey	**Dim1 ID**	**Dim2 ID**	**metric5**	**metric6**
A123-	A123	-	..	..
A229-	A229	-	..	..

With a NULL value as the [Dim2 ID] component of the LinkKey, any selection made on a Dim2 attribute would associate to zero rows in Fact3. Essentially, all the rows in Fact3 would be ignored when a selection is made in the Dim2 table, because there's no key to associate with, and charts may show a 'No data to display' error. While this is technically correct, it does not make for an ideal user experience.

Now let's imagine that Dim2 is a Date dimension. Fact3 contains rows that are not date-sensitive, but you still want to compare the other facts with metric5 and metric6 when any Date is selected. Instead of using a NULL as the

Date component of the LinkKey in Fact3, you could use a generic placeholder that would allow association to all rows of the Date dimension. Figure 9.11 shows how this generic key approach is implemented in the Fact3 table.

FACT3

LinkKey	Dim1 ID	Dim2 ID	metric5	metric6
A123-ALL	A123	ALL	..	..
A229-ALL	A229	ALL	..	..

FIGURE 9.11:
Fact3 using a generic key

For the associations to work, the trick is to add an *extra* row for each key in the LinkTable. Figure 9.12 shows how each unique LinkKey requires an additional generic row to associate Dim2 selections to the Fact3 table.

FACT

LinkKey	metric1	metric2
A123-B433	..	..
A229-B698	..	..

FACT3

LinkKey	metric5	metric6
A123-ALL	..	..
A229-ALL	..	..

LinkTable

LinkKey	Dim1 ID	Dim2 ID
A123-B433	A123	B433
A123-ALL	A123	B433
A229-B698	A229	B698
A229-ALL	A229	B698

Dim1

Dim1 ID	Dim1 attr
A123	East
A229	West

Dim2

Dim2 ID	Dim2 attr
B433	May
B698	June

FIGURE 9.12:
Link table model with generic keys

As you can see in Figure 9.12, selecting May in Dim2 would still allow the inclusion of the rows in Fact3, thanks to the generic key. Using generic keys in a link table model can obviously result in very large LinkTable and could have significant impact on memory usage due to the high cardinality of the LinkKey.

Using the autonumber() Script Function

Using link tables can have some important drawbacks—specifically in regard to performance. In the link table model, a LinkKey field will contain a distinct list of long strings. The link table and each fact table will store a pointer to each LinkKey value. In large data sets, the pointer could be quite long and have a significant impact on memory usage since it is stored in so many tables. Also, aggregation calculations would need to navigate over an additional hop between the dimension and fact tables to find the required data elements. To lessen the impact of this performance hit, the `LinkKey` can be optimized.

Since the `LinkKey` can be a rather long string, shortening it into a more compact value can result in some memory savings. You can achieve this by using the QlikView script function `autonumber()`. During the script load process, the `autonumber()` function can be used to create a unique index value for each string value as follows:

```
Load autonumber(LinkKey) as LinkKey,
```

Each time the string value is encountered in the data load, the integer substitute is stored instead of the string. To use `autonumber()` effectively, keep these tips in mind:

- There is no reverse `autonumber()` function—you cannot retrieve the original value from the generated index value. The script must be run again without using the function to restore original values.

- `Autonumber()` should be used at the end of the development cycle. Keeping the original string keys allows for easier data validation. Since the index values have no intrinsic meaning, it's difficult to investigate any problems with the data.

- Unique values can only be guaranteed in one .qvw file—therefore, `Autonumber()` should not be used on fields that will be stored in .qvd files for future processing.

The `autonumber()` function provides an additional benefit to performance by creating a so-called *perfect key*. Because perfect keys are sequential integers, QlikView uses the actual value as the pointer—thus eliminating the need to keep the list of distinct values. This memory savings can be substantial for a large data set.

Costs/Benefits of Using Link Tables

The primary benefit of using link tables is the ability to preserve the natural relationship among all of the facts and dimensions. With the use of link tables, you can use QlikView's associative functionality to easily see which transactions are related and which are not. For example, if this profitability model is built using a link table, it's easy to calculate all the components of costs and profits associated with a salesperson—even if the field [Sales Person] is only populated in the sales transactions. With the help of generic keys, an indirect relationship between the salesperson and the profitability metrics can be maintained.

The primary drawback is performance. The link key easily consumes more memory than any other field due to its high cardinality. For example, if you combine three fields—Field A with 10,000 distinct values, Field B with 1,000 distinct values, and Field C with 100 values—the combination LinkKey could have up to 1 billion distinct values if all keys are present in all combinations. This huge growth in cardinality causes exponential growth in the memory footprint of the application. With generic keys, the growth is even more dramatic due to the extra rows required.

Another drawback is that metrics are located in multiple Fact tables. As a best practice, metric fields used in aggregation calculations should (ideally) be located in the same table, so that QlikView does not have to navigate multiple tables to execute the calculation. For example, a chart with the expression sum(metricA * metricB) will perform slower if metricA and metricB are in different tables, separated by one or more hops. Within a large data set, this could significantly degrade performance.

The next section describes using one Concatenated Fact table, instead of linking multiple facts together. The single fact table approach has some advantages over the link table technique.

The Concatenated Fact Table

Another approach to adding new transactions into the data model is to create a Concatenated Fact table. Instead of associating multiple fact tables with a link table, we use a much simpler technique by creating a single Fact table that contains all transactions. In QlikView, this type of table is called a *Concatenated Fact table*. In data warehousing terminology, this unified table is sometimes called a *consolidated fact table*. We'll discuss the Concatenated Fact table technique in more detail in Chapter 13.

Working With Dimensions

Most of the time, data elements can easily be identified as either a fact or a dimension. Numeric facts are used in calculations and have an observed time component. Dimensions contain the descriptive attributes of those facts—some of which are used as filters and/or row headers for aggregation reports. However, there are certain data elements that are both descriptive attributes *and* numeric. These elements can be used both in calculations and as filters or grouping headers.

One example of a data element that can be considered both a fact and a dimension is the *lifetime value* for a customer, or LTV. The LTV represents the total dollar value for a particular customer over some historic period. While this value doesn't appear natively in a typical customer table, some businesses pre-aggregate this value over a certain time period (x number of years, or the entire transaction history of the customer) and use it in their sales analysis to characterize customer profiles. This value obviously can be used in numeric calculations to answer the question, "What is the total LTV of the customers who purchased Product A?" It can also be used as a filter to constrain a chart or report—"Show the sales by product of only those customers where the LTV > \$x". So in this case, LTV can be used as both a fact *and* a dimension.

Another example that applies to this profitability application is *product cost*. The cost of a product is a classic example of a data element that is both a fact metric and a dimension attribute. In this application, there are several cost fields for each product: the standard cost (total), as well as the cost components of material, labor, and overhead. These cost values are not actual costs, but rather yearly estimates.

If the costs are intended to be used as headers for grouping totals or to filter reports, the fields should be modeled into the Product dimension. The challenge with that approach is that the costs change every year. To maintain the accuracy of historical reporting, you would need to accommodate the changes in the dimension. In data warehousing terminology, a dimension with attributes that occasionally change is referred to as a *slowly changing dimension* (SCD).

You'll look at how to handle both cases: modeling numeric attributes in both the dimension and fact tables.

Slowly Changing Dimensions Defined

In the field of data warehousing, a *slowly changing dimension* (SCD) is generally defined as a dimension that experiences occasional or irregular changes over time. The name is a bit misleading, in that the dimension doesn't actually change; the *attributes* of the dimension can change. A more generic description of an SCD is "an entity identified by an unchanging natural ID with attributes that change irregularly over time." There are many easy-to-understand examples of an SCD:

- A change of address for a customer or supplier
- An employee transfers to a different department
- A change in the price or cost of a product

Why are SCDs important? A change in certain attributes can have a significant impact on reporting and analysis, especially trend analysis. For example, a change in a customer's ZIP code can impact the results of a sales trend report by ZIP. An analyst running this type of report might notice that last year's sales for ZIP code 63031 has changed since the last time the report was run. What caused this discrepancy? If a customer's ZIP code is changed from 33334 to 63031, then 63031 will inherit the entire sales history of that customer, even though the sales occurred in a different ZIP code. Simply replacing the old ZIP with the new ZIP in the customer record can affect the quality of historical analysis.

There is well-established theory on how to handle changing attributes in a data warehouse or reporting environment. Categorized into *types* (as defined by Ralph Kimball), the most common three methods are described here:

- Type I: The attribute is overwritten with the new value
- Type II: A new row is added with the new value
- Type III: A new column is added to contain the new value

The drawbacks of Type I are obvious—since the original attribute value is overwritten with the new value, all historical context is gone. All rows in the fact tables are associated with the *current* attribute value. Type II allows for rows in the fact table to associate to the dimension row that was current at the time the fact occurred. Since Type III has columns for both current and historical attribute values, the fact row is actually associated with *both*. The advantage here is that you can do a quick compare of current/old values without much effort. Of course adding columns to a database has some limit, so you cannot feasibly track an infinite number of changes by adding columns. Tables that use Type III usually have just two columns for the tracking attribute—one for the current value and one for the previous.

Of the three common types, Type II offers the most flexibility, in that all historical values are preserved. When a new attribute value needs to be stored, a row is added to the table with the new value, and a *version* field is populated. This version field can contain a timestamp (updated date), a version number (1, 2, 3, and so on), or some other value that uniquely identifies the row and its historical order.

Attribute Changes Happen All the Time In the OLTP System. Why Are SCDs Such a Big Deal In Data Warehouse/Reporting Environments?

OLTP systems are designed to efficiently accommodate changes in attributes using normalized techniques. Modeling these changes using a denormalized schema (the star schema) provides the first challenge in the data warehouse. The more difficult challenge occurs when business requirements dictate tracking historical changes that are *not* captured in the source system. In this case, changes must be detected and tracked during the ETL process.

There are several other methods (types) of tracking and many that are hybrids of the common three types. In the next section, we'll describe using the Type II method to incorporate the changing values of product costs into the Product dimension.

Product Costs as Dimension Attributes

Before we discuss modeling, let's take a look at how and where product costs are stored in the source system.

In addition to a total StandardCost, the OLTP Sales database captures the three cost components for each product: material, labor, and overhead costs. The cost values are stored in the StandardCosting table, as shown in Figure 9.13.

Product ID	Year	Standard Cost	Unit Cost - Material	Unit Cost - Labor	Unit Cost - Overhead
110101	2013	4.75	1.82	1.67	1.26
110101	2014	5.29	2.08	1.83	1.38
110102	2013	4.96	2.12	1.65	1.19
110102	2014	5.44	2.25	1.97	1.22
110103	2013	5.23	2.00	1.90	1.33
110103	2014	5.71	2.28	2.04	1.39
110104	2013	5.44	2.20	1.81	1.43
110104	2014	6.02	2.38	2.13	1.51

FIGURE 9.13:
OLTP StandardCosting table

Notice that the Year column allows for tracking the changes in costs for a product on a yearly basis. So, for each product in the ProductMaster table, there can be one or more rows of cost/year values in the StandardCosting table. This normalized relationship between the two OLTP tables is shown in Figure 9.14.

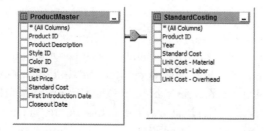

FIGURE 9.14:
OLTP ProductMaster and StandardCosting tables

If the cost values are to be used as report filters or column headers for reports, then the fields could be modeled as attributes in the Product dimension. In this case, it might be tempting to bring in the StandardCosting table just as it is and allow it to associate to the Product dimension table with the [Product ID] field. However, the values in the StandardCosting table vary by year, and solely linking to [Product ID] would not allow you to see that variance in the reporting. The best approach is to join the cost fields from StandardCosting into the Product dimension table. This will create a Product dimension that can have multiple rows for each product—one for each Year that has different cost values. In this way, we've implemented the Type II method of tracking the changing attributes of a product, while maintaining the star schema design. Figure 9.15 shows the Product dimension with the new columns.

FIGURE 9.15:
Product dimension with
cost values

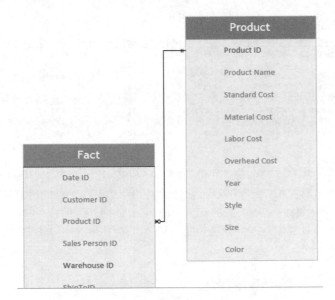

Notice that the Fact table is still associated with the Product table on the natural key [Product ID]. You haven't created the link between the timeframe of the invoice (in the Fact table) and the timeframe of the cost (in the Product dimension). The best way to make sure that a time-sensitive fact lines up with a time-sensitive dimension is to embed a time element into the key that links the two.

Since the uniqueness of each row in the Product table is now defined by [Product ID] and Year, you can incorporate the two fields to create a *composite* key. For example, the unique values of 110101-2013 and 110101-2014 identify the first two rows of the table shown previously in Figure 9.13.

We'll use these composite values to populate a new column named [Product Key]. As this column is now the primary key of the Product dimension, the rows in the `Fact` table must also contain [Product Key] in order to correctly associate the two tables. Figure 9.16 shows the data model with the addition of [Product Key].

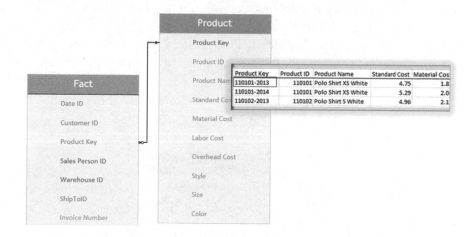

FIGURE 9.16:
Product dimension
using [Product Key]

These cost columns can now be used as report constraints (filters) to answer questions such as, "What are the total sales for products with a material cost > $x." Also, aggregate reports can answer questions such as, "What are the total $sales for Product A, broken down by labor cost?"

For the aforementioned report types, the expression of the report is still `sum ([# Sales Amount])`, and the cost columns are used as report dimensions or filters. To use the cost values in expressions, best practices suggest that you model the values as facts as well.

Product Costs as Fact Metrics

In the previous section, we showed how to model the costs in the `Product` dimension, while keeping the yearly variance. For this profitability application, you primarily need the product cost values to determine profit (sales costs). Without changing the model, you could create charts that use expressions such as `sum([# Sales Amount])-sum([Standard Cost])`, but it would go against one of the best practices for the star schema model: metrics used for aggregation should be in one table. Remember that aggregations in QlikView perform best when the targets of the aggregations are located together in the same table.

The business requirements for this profitability application only require that you use the costs for profit calculations, not for report filters. For this reason, we'll bring the values into the Fact table only and not model them as Product attributes. Although it will cost memory space to accommodate the additional field pointers in the Fact table, having the metrics located in the same table should more than make up for it. Now, instead of joining the cost metrics into the Product table, they are joined into the Fact table, as shown in Figure 9.17.

FIGURE 9.17:
Product costing fields in the Fact table

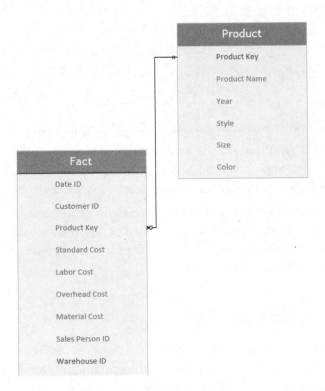

The technique for creating the [Product Key] field is the same as described in the previous section—the [Product ID] is combined with Year to create a composite key.

If the requirements dictated that product cost be used as both facts and dimensions, you could include them in both tables. However, remember that QlikView will create associations on fields that have the identical name—so the fields must be named differently to avoid synthetic keys and/or circular references. In the Product table, you could use the field names Product.Standard Cost, Product.Labor Cost, and so on, to distinguish the columns from those in the Fact table.

Using the Cost Columns in the Fact Table as Dimensions

Technically, the product cost columns in the Fact table can be used as filters or as column headers for aggregation charts. Why load the same fields more than once? If you use the fields in the Fact table as dimensions, just be aware that the values would be limited to the entities captured in the Fact table (you couldn't see a cost value for a product that hasn't been sold).

Chapter 10 presents the detailed instructions for creating link tables and resolving slowly changing dimensions.

10

Developing a Data Load Script for Profitability Analysis

In this chapter, you'll learn how to build the data model for the Profitability Analysis application. In the process of doing so, the chapter continues to describe QlikView data load scripting. Building on the foundation laid out in Chapter 7, this chapter describes more advanced scripting techniques. You will learn how to:

- Use QlikView Data (QVD) files in a separate data layer.
- Use variables and script control statements.
- Create and use a library of common routines.
- Use mapping for data cleansing and to fetch a single field from another table without joining.
- Create a Master Calendar.
- Deal with slowly changing dimensions.

Creating a QVD Data Layer

This section introduces QVD files and describes various techniques for loading database tables and storing them as QVD files. In the process of building the QVD Generators, we describe how to use QlikView variables and script control statements.

Why Do You Need a Separate Data Layer?

At our fictional company, Q-Tee Brands, the QlikView development team was celebrating. The Sales Analysis application was a huge success, and that is why the business immediately requested the team to develop the next dashboard—the Profitability Analysis.

In the process of gathering data for the Profitability Analysis, the team discovered that many of the same tables used for the Sales Analysis will be needed for the new dashboard. They will have to load Sales data, Products, and Customers, and even repeat most of the same calculations! Now, this discovery causes a number of concerns:

- Reading the same data repeatedly will extend the extra load on the back-office databases and networks.

- With every new QlikView application, the nightly processing will take longer and longer, and the documents may not be available on time.

- Repeating the same logic in several QlikView applications is a waste of resources and a future maintenance nightmare. Any future changes will have to be repeated identically in several load scripts.

The team needs a solution that will allow them to extract from source databases only once and provide a fast and efficient source for multiple QlikView applications. They were told that the solution is to use QVD files. Let's explore this solution.

Exercise 10.1: Preparing the Environment for the QVD Generator

1. Create a new QlikView document and store it in the subfolder \Data Loaders, with the name QVD Generator XX.QVW where XX represents your initials.

2. Connect to the same MDB database—\Data\Database\Sales.MDB, using the Connect button in the Script Editor.

Introducing the QVD File Format

QVD is a proprietary file format that stores data in a way that is optimized for a super-fast load into QlikView. Each QVD file contains a single table. In essence, a QVD file is similar to a conventional comma-separated file, only we can't easily see the data unless we load the QVD file into QlikView.

As a proprietary data format, QVD can only be created and utilized within QlikView. What makes it special is the speed of loading a QVD file into QlikView. Loading a large database table may take several hours. Loading the same amount of data from the QVD file may take only a few seconds.

QVD files provide the magical solution to the problem described in the previous section.

- Large database tables can be extracted once and stored in a set of QVD files.

- Multiple QlikView applications can read the same data multiple times and load the data very fast into QlikView.

- Business logic can be processed once and the results can be stored in a QVD file, to be used in multiple QlikView applications.

Loading Data from a QVD File

Data from QVD files is loaded in the same way we load data from any other flat files, such as Excel spreadsheets and comma-separated files. We use the **Table Files** wizard to generate the corresponding LOAD statement.

Once the wizard is invoked and the desired QVD file is selected from the corresponding folder, the **File Wizard** dialog comes up and shows the contents of the QVD file (see Figure 10.1). There is no need to make any definitions—we can sit back and relax because QlikView already knows what to load. The picture in Figure 10.1 presents the **File Wizard** dialog for a QVD file.

When loading all the fields from many QVD files, it may be easier to type the LOAD statements manually, using the following notation:

```
LOAD * FROM [..\Data\QVDs\Colors.QVD] (qvd);
LOAD * FROM [..\Data\QVDs\Sizes.QVD] (qvd);
LOAD * FROM [..\Data\QVDs\Styles.QVD] (qvd);
```

FIGURE 10.1:
File Wizard dialog

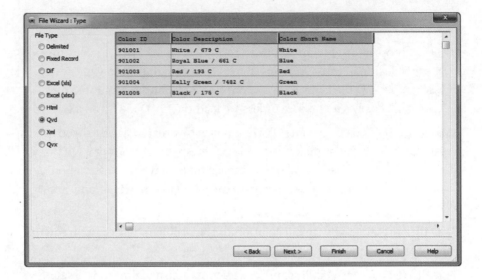

Feel free to use this manual technique if you prefer, but don't forget to add the qualifier (qvd) at the end of each statement. This little detail is commonly overlooked, and the error message that QlikView throws in this case is rather cryptic.

Depending on the transformations that you add to the QVD load, it may be loaded in an *optimized mode* or in a *not-optimized mode*. Optimized loads are significantly faster than not-optimized loads. The load can be kept optimized if the data is loaded pretty much "as is," with no transformations. Here is a list of some of the main rules related to optimized loads versus not-optimized loads:

- Renaming fields is okay, but adding new fields makes the load not optimized.

- The only possible WHERE condition is WHERE Exists(). Any other WHERE condition makes the load not-optimized.

- Any sorting (ORDER BY) or grouping (GROUP BY) logic will make the load not-optimized.

The difference between optimized and not-optimized loads may not be evident on smaller data files; however, it's very significant for large QVD files. In large data environments, developers always go the extra mile to preserve the optimized mode of their QVD loads. In the exercises in this chapter, you will be loading QVD files with no transformation and performing transformations in subsequent RESIDENT loads.

Creating QVD Files

Creating QVD files is equally simple. Any table that was loaded into QlikView can be stored into a QVD file, and the syntax is almost written in plain English:

STORE *<TableName>* INTO *<FileName>*;

Or an extended format (which is less common):

STORE *<FieldList>* FROM *<TableName>* INTO *<FileName>*;

This is it, folks. End of story. Now you know how to load and store QVD files.

To wrap up the description of the STORE command, we will just mention that you can store comma-separated text files with the same STORE command, using the optional qualifier (txt) at the end of the statement. This is useful when the data that was extracted, cleansed, and transformed in QlikView needs to be consumed by another reporting tool (shhh, we won't tell Qlik that you want to do it!):

STORE *<TableName>* INTO *<FileName>* (txt);

In addition to the option of storing QVD files manually, QlikView offers a "buffer" technique that allows developers to create and maintain QVD files automatically, based on the age of the data. This technique isn't commonly used, and therefore we decided to leave it out of the discussion. Feel free to explore this feature in the online documentation.

In the following exercise, you practice the technique of generating QVD files manually, one table at a time.

Exercise 10.2: Storing QVD Files Manually

1. In the new document called QVD Generator.QVW, open the Script Editor.
2. Create a new script tab and call it **Single Table Load**.
3. Load the table CustomerMaster from the database, the same way you did before.
4. Store the table in a new QVD file ..\Data\QVDs\CustomerMaster.QVD.

5. Drop the table `CustomerMaster`. Your script should look like the following:

```
CustomerMaster:
SQL SELECT *
FROM CustomerMaster;
store CustomerMaster into ..\Data\QVDs\CustomerMaster.QVD;
drop table CustomerMaster;
```

6. Repeat Steps 3-5 for the table `ProductMaster`.

7. Save and Reload your script. Verify that the files `CustomerMaster.QVD` and `ProductMaster.QVD` were created with the current date.

In Case of an Error...

If you script generates a "General Script Error" message, that means the ..\Data\QVDs folder is not found. Check your spelling or adjust your relative path reference as necessary to match the location of your QVW.

Variables and Script Control Statements

This section continues developing and enhancing the QVD Generator. In order to do so, we need to introduce two new concepts—using variables and using script control statements, such as IF, FOR, and other scripting language commands that help us control and organize our scripts.

QlikView Variables

QlikView *variables* are quite similar to variables in other scripting languages. Simply put, a variable has a name, and it holds a *single value*—in contrast to fields that store *many instances* of the same type of data.

Variables serve many useful purposes in QlikView, both in the script and in the UI. This section focuses on the techniques of creating and using the variables in the script.

You may notice in the following examples that all variable names begin with the lowercase letter v. This is not a requirement, but rather a commonly used naming convention. It helps developers differentiate between variables and fields.

Creating QlikView Variables

Variables can be created in many different ways, both in the script and in the UI. In the script, we use one of the two commands to assign values to new or existing variables—LET and SET:

```
SET vPath='..\Data\QVDs\';
LET v1 = 1;
SET v2 = v1 + 1;
LET v3 = v1 + 1;
```

With the LET statement, the assigned value is being evaluated immediately. When SET is used, the text to the right of the equal sign will be stored as is and used as a value when the variable is used. Following these rules, these statements will produce the results shown in Table 10.1.

The SET statement is used to assign string literals or constants to a variable. If the string literal happens to define a formula, the variable can be used later in the script to evaluate the formula. In contrast, the LET statement is used to immediately assign the results of a formula to a variable. You can use this simple trick for remembering the difference—S is for string and L is for live.

TABLE 10.1: Variables and Their Stored Values

VARIABLE	STORED VALUE
vPath	..\Data\QVDs\
v1	1
v2	v1 + 1
v3	2

There is a number of ways to review the variables that exist in the document. While working on the load script, the easiest way is to open the **Variables** tab at the bottom of the **Script Editor**. All the existing variables are listed in the drop-down list. The value for the currently selected variable is displayed in the text box. See Figure 10.2.

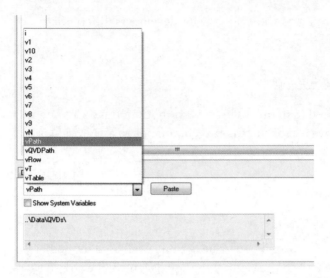

For temporary variables that are created in the script, it's considered good practice to destroy them at the end of the script execution. The following syntax can be used to destroy unnecessary variables:

```
let v1=;
let v2=;
let v3=;
```

When you try creating and destroying variables, you may notice that the variables may not get destroyed if you already ran your script at least once before adding the clean-up statements. QlikView assigns more "respect" to variables that made it all the way to the UI than to variables that were just created in the script. After the variables were promoted to the UI status, they can only be deleted manually in the UI. This is done using the menu option **Settings ▶ Variable Overview**. Delete all the unwanted variables there, and then you can safely create and destroy variables in the script, before they get promoted.

Using the Variables in the Script

The variables can be used in a number of ways, but the following two formats are the most common:

- Simply calling the variable by name will result in using the stored value of the variable. It is accepted in all of the script control statements, and while calculating values for other variables in the SET and LET commands:

```
LET v4 = v2;
```

- Enclosing the variable name in a *dollar-sign expansion* $(variable) will result in evaluating the contents of the variable and substituting the dollar-sign expansion with its value before the statement is parsed:

```
LET v5=$(v2);
```

Let's continue the example started earlier (see Table 10.1). The variable v2 was holding a string 'v1 + 1'. The two previous statements will produce the results shown in Table 10.2.

TABLE 10.2: Variables and Their Stored Values, Continued

VARIABLE	STORED VALUE
v1	1
v2	v1 + 1
v4	v1 + 1
v5	2

The variable v4 will get assigned the same value v1 + 1 as v2. The variable v5, however, will get the value 2 as the evaluated result of the calculation. This is due to the use of the dollar-sign expansion.

It's important to remember when you can use simple variable names, as opposed to the dollar-sign expansions. Variable names alone are not acceptable in any LOAD or SQL SELECT statements. It's fair to say that using dollar-sign expansions is more universal. We don't recommend using them at all times (that would clutter the view too much), but as a rule of thumb, it's safe to say, "When in doubt, use the dollar-sign expansion." Even if it isn't necessary, in most cases it won't hurt.

Here is one of a few uncommon examples when dollar-sign expansion needs to be used with caution. Consider the following sequence of statements:

```
let v6 = today();
let v7 = $(v6);
```

The first LET statement assigns the current date to the variable v6 and the second LET statement assigns the value of v6, evaluated through the dollar-sign expansion, to the variable v7. Try to guess the results of those statements before you look at Table 10.3. Do you expect the two variables to store the same value?

TABLE 10.3: Variables and Their Stored Values, Continued

VARIABLE	STORED VALUE
v6	7/22/2014
v7	0.00015798501399296

Can you explain the unexpected result of v7? Here is what happened—the dollar-sign expansion performed an evaluation of the value of v6 as a mathematical expression. The number 7 was divided by the number 22 and then divided by 2014, and that's what caused such a strange result.

You must be wondering what we should do in this case, if we need to use a variable that stores a date in a LOAD statement, especially since LOAD statements can't accept variables without the dollar-sign expansions. The way to use the variable as is and avoid the unwanted evaluation is to include the dollar-sign expansion in a set of single quotes:

```
let v8 = '$(v6)';
```

Common Use Cases for Variables in the Script

Here are a few common use cases for script variables:

- Variables are used as counters and parameters in all the loops and script control statements (it will get clearer when we describe those commands in the next section).

- It's common to store the paths to the various data folders and to replace the hard-coded paths in each LOAD statement with the variable enclosed in a dollar-sign expansion. Those variables are typically assigned in the beginning of the script, in the Main tab. In the future, if data needs to be loaded from a different folder, the change is rather easy, compared to scanning the whole script and replacing the path in multiple places.

- It's common to assign the current date to a variable vToday and to use it in all calendar-related calculations. This way, the current date can be easily assigned as needed. For example, if your test data ends on December 31, 2014, you can freeze your current date at the same day and test your application as if today were December 31, 2014.

- Variables can be very helpful for passing the information from one LOAD or SQL SELECT statement to another. For example, you may load historical data from a QVD file up to a certain date/time. Then, the next SQL SELECT statement needs to load newer data from the database, with the condition that the transaction timestamp is higher than the previously loaded date/time. The highest value can be fetched from the first table into a variable and then the same value can be used in the subsequent SQL SELECT statement, through the use of a dollar-sign expansion.

Passing Data Between Tables, Variables, and LOAD Statements

Even though we can use variables to pass data stored in tables between the different LOAD statements, we can't access this data directly. We need to use special functions to fetch the field values from tables before we can assign them to variables.

In order to fetch a single value from a given row in a table, we can use the Peek() function. The Peek() function can be used with up to three parameters: the 'FieldName', the row number, and the 'TableName'. Notice the single quotes — the field name and the table name are expected to be enclosed in single quotes:

```
let vDate = Peek('Date', -1, 'Facts');
```

Row number -1 refers to the last row in the table, while the first row is numbered as row 0.

Another possibility is to fetch a value from the list of field values, using the function FieldValue('FieldName', ElementNumber).

```
let vDate = FieldValue('Date', 1);
```

This function, which deals with a list of field values and not with table rows, starts the numbering from 1.

With these functions, any single value can be fetched from any table or any field and then stored in a variable.

The Dreaded Silent Fail

Many functions in QlikView receive table names and field names as string parameters, listed in a pair of single quotes. If one of the names should be accidentally misspelled, don't expect an error message or a warning. The function will fail silently and return a NULL value, with no visible indication of a problem. We recommend verifying the results of Peek(), FieldValue(), ApplyMap(), and other functions that accept field or table names as string parameters. All of them will fail silently.

On the other hand, variables can be included in any LOAD or SELECT statements, but *only* through the use of dollar-sign expansions. Depending on a specific need, a variable can pass a numeric value, a string value (enclosed in a pair of single quotes), or even a fully formatted fragment of a LOAD statement that needs to be included in the statement.

We will be using variables for several purposes in the following sections. For now, we will replace the hard-coded path to the subfolder ..\Data\QVDs with a variable that we will assign at the beginning of the script.

Exercise 10.3: Using a Variable to Define Folder Locations

Before you add too many STORE statements, replace the hard-coded folder path with a variable that you can assign in the beginning of the script.

1. In the Script Editor, open the Main tab and create a new variable called vQVDPath that will hold the path to the QVD files:

   ```
   SET vQVDPath ='..\Data\QVDs\';
   ```

2. Replace the hard-coded path in the existing STORE statements with the new variable, enclosed in the dollar-sign expansion:

   ```
   store CustomerMaster into $(vQVDPath)CustomerMaster.QVD;
   ```

3. Save and Reload your script.

> ## Those Cryptic Error Messages!
>
> If your script (that stores QVD files) fails, verify that the path is spelled correctly. QlikView can't store QVD files in a folder that doesn't exist. You won't get any specific errors, except for the general failure message, "**Execution of script failed. Reload old data?**" at the end of the script.

Special Variables in QlikView Script

In addition to variables that are created by developers, QlikView has a number of *system variables* that are pre-defined with their own default values. Those variables serve as settings for various tasks, such as number formatting, error handling, and so on. The following short list explains the most notable special variables (the full list can be found in the documentation, or in the Help section, in an article called "Script Variables"):

Error Variables:

> `ErrorMode`—This action defines what should happen in case of an error during script execution.
>
> `ScriptError`—Returns an error code of the last executed statement.

System Variables:

> `HidePrefix` and `HideSuffix`—Those two variables allow hiding fields that begin or end with a certain string. The fields with the specified prefix or suffix will be considered as system fields and hidden from the users.

These are just a few of the most commonly used special variables, but there are many more. Feel free to explore other special variables in the documentation.

Script Control Statements

This section describes *script control statements* that allow developers to perform parts of the script based on conditions, to repeat some of the logic in a loop, or to extract some of the repeating sections of the script into subroutines.

Using IF … THEN … ELSE … END IF for Conditional Operations

When parts of the script need to be performed based on a certain condition, we can use the IF statement:

```
IF Condition THEN
     statements;
     statements;
     statements;
ELSE
     statements;
     statements;
     statements;
END IF
```

Notice that the IF statement doesn't end with a semicolon (this exception is common for all script control statements). For this reason, the first line of the statement, which includes the keywords IF and THEN, needs to be written in a single script line (even if your condition is very complex).

Let's examine our recently developed script that generates QVD files. We load the data from the database and then store the data in a QVD file, replacing the previous version of the same file. If the database load should fail for any reason, we could override the previously stored QVD file with an empty table. In order to protect our data, we can add a condition that will allow storing the file only if the previous statement finished successfully, or if the row count of the data table is greater than zero.

We can verify the success of the previous LOAD statement by testing the condition ScriptError=0. Alternatively, we can verify the number of rows in the loaded table using the table function NoOfRows('TableName'). Look up other useful table functions in the Help article "Table Functions."

Exercise 10.4: Using the IF Statement for Conditional Processing

Add the IF condition to the script developed in the previous exercises to ensure that the QVD files are stored only if the row count of the same tables is greater than zero.

To conclude this discussion about conditional processing, we will mention that QlikView supports another conditional statement that allows selecting one of many choices, based on the value of an expression. The command is SWITCH…CASE…DEFAULT…END SWITCH, and you can find it in the Help article "Script Control Statements."

Using Subroutines for Repetitive Logic

You may have noticed that the script that reads two database tables and generates two QVD files is quite repetitive. You should be able to count five places in the script where the table name CustomerName is used, and five similar places where the name ProductName is used.

If we had to repeat the same logic for additional 10 tables, we'd have to copy the same logic 10 times and replace the table names in 50 places. This gets a bit too tedious, and our chances of making a mistake grow.

We can use a *subroutine* to avoid repeating the same logic over and over again. The concept is very similar to other scripting languages, and the syntax is as follows. The subroutine is declared by the statements SUB … END SUB. The subroutine is defined by its name and an optional set of *parameters*:

```
SUB RoutineName(Parameter1, Parameter2, …)
    statements;
    statements;
    statements;
END SUB
```

After the subroutine is declared, it can be called anywhere in the script using the command CALL.

```
CALL RoutineName(P1, P2);
```

The parameters declared in the SUB statement are called *formal parameters* while the parameters listed in the CALL statement are called *actual parameters*.

Formal parameters are used in the subroutine as local variables. The rest of the script variables are also available in the subroutine as global variables.

Actual parameters can be variables, fields, or any expressions. Any hard-coded values should be provided as strings, enclosed in single quotes, even for numeric values. Actual parameters with numeric values without quotes still work, but this technique will result in creating an extra variable with the numeric value as the variable name.

In the following exercise, you create a generic subroutine that loads a database table and stores it into a QVD file, in order to avoid repeating the same logic many times.

Exercise 10.5: Creating a Subroutine

1. In the Script Editor, create a new tab at the end of the script. Name it **Generic Subroutine**.

2. Copy one of the two repeating segments of the existing script and paste it into the new tab. Then, comment out the contents of the old tab Single Table Load.

3. Add the control statements SUB and END SUB to the beginning and at the end of the script segment. The new subroutine should be called **GenerateQVD** and it should have two parameters—**TableName** and **FilePath**.

4. Replace the path to the QVD file with the name of the new parameter called FilePath. Replace all five instances of CustomerMaster with the name of the parameter TableName, enclosed in a dollar-sign expansion.

5. Since this is going to be a generic subroutine that can be used with any table names, you should prepare it for a possibility of having a space or a special character in the table name. For this purpose, you need to add a pair of square brackets [ ] to all the table names and file names. For that same reason, the name of the table in the SQL SELECT needs to be enclosed in a pair of double quotes " " or grave accents ` `, to fit the syntax that's accepted by MS Access database. Your complete script in this tab should look like the following:

```
sub GenerateQVD(TableName, FilePath)
    [$(TableName)]:
    SQL SELECT *
    FROM `$(TableName)`;
    IF NoOfRows('$(TableName)')> 0 THEN
        store [$(TableName)] into [$(FilePath)$(TableName).QVD];
    END IF
    drop table [$(TableName)];
end sub
```

6. Create another new tab after the Generic Sub tab and name it **Call Subroutine**. Call the new subroutine twice, to generate QVD files for the same two tables—CustomerMaster and ProductMaster.

7. Clone the same subroutine call three more times and add three more tables—Styles, Sizes, and Colors. Notice how easy it is to add another table to the list:

```
call GenerateQVD('CustomerMaster', vQVDPath);
call GenerateQVD('ProductMaster', vQVDPath);
call GenerateQVD('Styles', vQVDPath);
call GenerateQVD('Sizes', vQVDPath);
call GenerateQVD('Colors', vQVDPath);
```

8. Save and Reload your script. Verify that five QVD files were generated in the folder.

   Notice that you are using the variable vQVDPath that you defined in Exercise 10.3.

Using FOR Loops for Repeating the Same Logic a Number of Times

In the last section, we simplified the task of adding another table to the QVD Generator, and yet copying the same subroutine call so many times, just to replace the table name, sounds like a tedious job. There must be a better way of doing the same thing. Fortunately, there is.

Similarly to other scripting languages, QlikView offers a few ways of repeating the same logic in a loop. There are three formats of loop statements:

- **FOR … NEXT** statements perform the same logic a number of times, based on a counter.

- **FOR EACH … NEXT** statements perform the same logic for each item in the specified list of items.

- **DO … LOOP** statements perform the same logic based on a condition—either WHILE or UNTIL the specified condition is true.

Feel free to explore the complete syntax of each command in the Help article called "Script Control Statements." For the purpose of enhancing the QVD Generator, you use the FOR EACH … NEXT format in the following exercise.

Exercise 10.6: Using a FOR EACH … NEXT Loop

1. Comment out the contents of the tab `Call Subroutine`.

2. Create a new tab at the end of your script and call it **FOR Loop**.

3. In the new tab, create a loop that calls the subroutine `GenerateQVD` for each table in the list of tables. Your script should look like this (make sure that the first line remains intact as a single line):

```
FOR EACH vTable in 'CustomerMaster', 'ProductMaster', 'Styles', 'Sizes', 'Colors'
    call GenerateQVD(vTable, vQVDPath);

NEXT
```

4. Save and Reload the script. Wouldn't you agree that this syntax is much more elegant than the previous version?

Automating the Process of QVD Generation for All Tables in a Database

Ultimately, it would be nice to automate the process once and forever, to be free from the task of adding new tables every time the new need arises. In this section, we will build a universal QVD Generator that always loads all the tables in a given database and generates QVD files for all of the tables. This approach might not be useful in your database environment, depending on the size of your databases, so please apply caution when implementing this logic in your own environment.

The automated process consists of multiple steps:

1. We need to query the database and get the list of all tables. Different databases have different tools to achieve that; however, most of them support the ODBC command SQLTABLES. If the SQLTABLES command is not supported on your database, you may need to find an alternative solution and possibly modify some of the field names in the following logic.

2. We will create a FOR loop based on the number of rows in the list of tables. Each iteration of the loop will process a single row from the table.

3. For each row in the list of tables, we will verify that this is in fact a TABLE (as opposed to other table types such as system tables, views, and so on).

4. For each table that satisfied the condition, we will fetch the table name and call the subroutine GenerateQVD.

Practice implementing this multi-step process in the following exercise.

Exercise 10.7: Creating a Universal QVD Generator

1. Comment out the script generated in the **For Loop** tab in the previous exercise. Keep the declaration of the subroutine.

2. Create a new tab at the end of the script. Name it **Universal Generator**.

3. Start the new tab with the ODBC command SQLTABLES. Name the new table **Tables**.

```
Tables:
sqltables;
```

4. Reload your script and examine the contents of the new Tables table. In order to view the contents, create a **Table Box** on the sheet and include all fields in it. You should see that table names are stored in the field called TABLE_NAME and that the field TABLE_TYPE shows the type of the table. We are only interested in the tables of the TABLE_TYPE = TABLE.

5. Type a FOR … NEXT statement that will run with the counter variable i from 0 to the number of rows in the Tables table (subtracting 1 to compensate for starting from 0):

```
FOR vRow = 0 TO NoOfRows('Tables') - 1
NEXT
```

6. Within the FOR Loop, add an IF statement that verifies the TABLE_TYPE. Use the Peek() function to fetch the required value from the row number vRow in the table:

```
IF peek('TABLE_TYPE', vRow, 'Tables') = 'TABLE' THEN

END IF
```

7. Within the IF statement, fetch the name of the table into the new variable vTable and call the subroutine GenerateQVD() to load the table and create the QVD file:

```
let vTable = peek('TABLE_NAME', vRow, 'Tables');
call GenerateQVD(vTable, vQVDPath);
```

Your complete script in this tab should look like the following:

```
Tables:
sqltables;
FOR vRow = 0 TO NoOfRows('Tables') - 1
    IF peek('TABLE_TYPE', vRow, 'Tables') = 'TABLE' THEN

        let vTable = peek('TABLE_NAME', vRow, 'Tables');
        call GenerateQVD(vTable, vQVDPath);

    END IF
NEXT
```

8. **Save** and **Reload** your script. Verify that new QVD files were generated for all 14 database tables from the `Sales.mdb` database.

Congratulations! You created the universal QVD Generator! With this simple script that hardly exceeds a dozen lines, you can load all tables from any database, assuming that the database of your choice supports the SQLTABLES ODBC command.

Creating a Library of Common Routines

The routines that we generated in the previous sections are quite generic and universal, in the sense that they are likely to be reused in multiple applications. These commonly used routines are best kept in external text files that can be included in other scripts and reused without the need for copying and pasting.

At this point, you start the library of common routines that will be used for similar tasks in future applications.

Exercise 10.8: Creating a Library of Common Routines

1. Copy the subroutine `GenerateQVD()` from the script tab Generic Subroutine.
2. Create a new text file in the \Scripts subfolder and name it **CommonRoutines.txt**. Open the file with the text editor of your choice and paste the copied text. Save and close the file.
3. Return to QlikView and comment out the contents of the Generic Subroutine tab.

4. In the Main tab, add the INCLUDE statement (choose Insert ▶ Include Statement) to include the CommonRoutines.txt text file. Manually add the prefix Must_ before the keyword Include, to ensure that the desired file can be found:

$(Must_Include=..\scripts\commonroutines.txt);

This little known feature helps developers ensure that the included file was indeed found. If the file doesn't exist, the script execution fails with an error.

5. Save and Reload the script. The end result should be the same, now with the use of the external library of common routines.

Extra Credit

Create another subroutine based on the script that generates QVD files for all database tables (you created this script in the Exercise 10.7). Add this new subroutine **StoreAllDatabaseTablesIntoQVD** to the library of common routines. If you do, add the CALL statement to the end of the Main tab and call the new subroutine there:

```
call StoreAllDatabaseTablesIntoQVD(vQVDPath);
```

Ensure that all previously create script is commented out in all other tabs.

For convenience, we can open external script files in QlikView Script Editor, using the Script Editor's **File ▶ Open External Script File** menu option. We can edit the file using all QlikView development tools, and then we can save our changes using the **File ▶ Save External Script File** menu option.

Creating Transformed QVDs

The QVD files that we generated in the previous sections are often called *raw QVDs*, as an indication of the fact that no transformation was performed on the data. The data was loaded in its "raw" format, just as it was stored in the source database. It's common to use raw QVD files in the *transformation layer* of the data load process and to create another set of so-called *transformed QVDs*, as a result of the transformations.

The benefit of implementing a transformation layer is the ability to perform common transformations once and use them many times. For example, consider all the transformations we did in Chapter 6 to create a "clean" set of tables for the Sales Analysis dashboard. We combined Order Header and Order Details, calculated a few derived fields, and calculated several conditional flags. It's likely that most of the same transformations will be required for every new application that needs the sales data. Specifically, the new Profitability Analysis application will require all or most of the same transformations.

The transformation layers of QVDs and the corresponding load scripts may be organized in many different ways. Sometimes, a number of transformed QVD files are generated in a single script, and sometimes the scripts are separated for individual QVD files.

For the current needs, we try to keep things relatively simple. We reuse the same script we created for the Sales Analysis as our combined transformation script. In order to differentiate our transformed QVDs from the raw QVDs, we keep them in a separate folder called \Data\Transformed QVDs\ and name the transformed files using the prefix T_.

Repurposing Sales Analysis Script as the Sales Transformation Script

In this section, you create a new Sales Transformation script that will be mostly based on the Sales Analysis Data load script that you developed in Chapter 6.

The process involves the following logical steps:

1. Store the existing script in the external text file. In QlikView, this is done in the **Script Editor**, using the **File ▶ Export To Script File** menu option.

2. Create the new QVW document that will host the Sales Transformation script. Insert the script from the external script file using the **Insert ▶ Script File** menu option.

3. Search the document for the text SQL SELECT and replace all the SELECT statements with LOAD statements, selecting the corresponding raw QVD with the same name as the database table name. Since we already have the preceding LOAD statements that process all the transformation logic, it's sufficient to load all fields (using the asterisk *) and not list all the fields again.

4. Comment out or delete the database connection statement in the **Main** tab of the script.

5. At the end of the script, add logic to run through the list of the existing tables—using the table functions `NoOfTables()` and `TableName('TableIndex')`—and generate transformed QVDs for each one of the tables. After the QVD files are generated, the tables need to be dropped, in order to save space.

Should You Wait to the End of the Script?

We suggested the process that includes storing and dropping all tables at the end of the script. When your data size is manageable, it's certainly convenient to perform these tasks together in one spot at the end of the script. For larger datasets, however, this technique may cause wasting too much memory. Every time a table is dropped, QlikView releases the memory that was occupied by the table. Hence, it's more efficient from the performance standpoint to store and drop tables as early as possible.

For the purpose of our conversation, we will keep the process simple and drop all tables at the end. Consider the other alternative if your data tables require too much memory.

If you feel comfortable performing these steps individually, please do. Exercise 10.9 provides detailed instructions for the same logic.

Exercise 10.9: Creating a Sales Transformation Script in QlikView

1. Open the `Sales Analysis Data` document that you developed in Chapter 6. If you don't have a finished load script from Chapter 6, copy the solution file called `06.21 Sales Analysis Data.QVW` from the `\Solutions QlikView` subfolder and save the file in your `\Data Models` subfolder.

2. Open the Script Editor. Export the script into an external script file called **`\Scripts\Sales Transformation.txt`** using the File ▶ Export To Script File menu option.

3. Close the `Sales Analysis Data` document and open a new QlikView document.

4. Save the new document in the `\Data Loaders` subfolder, under the name **`Sales Transformation Script.QVW`**.

5. Open the Script Editor. Use the Insert ▶ Script File menu option to insert the same file that was created in Step 2. Close and reopen the Script Editor again.

6. After reopening the **Editor**, you should see all the new tabs, copied from the script that we developed in Chapter 6. Notice that there are two tabs named **Main**. The first **Main** tab is the default tab from the new document, and the second **Main** tab came from the inserted script file. Activate the first tab and remove it, using the menu option **Tab ▸ Remove**.

7. In the remaining **Main** tab, do the following:

   7.1. Remove or comment out the database connection statement.

   7.2. Include the external script file called `CommonRoutines.txt` using the `Must_Include` command:

   ```
   $(Must_Include=..\scripts\commonroutines.txt);
   ```

   7.3. Copy and paste the same `vQVDPath` variable definition from the QVD Generator that you created earlier:

   ```
   LET vQVDPath='..\Data\QVDs\';
   ```

   7.4. Copy the statement once again, but this time change the variable name and the folder name to reflect **Transformed QVDs**:

   ```
   LET vTransformedQVDPath='..\Data\Transformed QVDs\';
   ```

8. Search the script for SQL SELECT statements and replace each statement with a corresponding LOAD command, using raw QVD files with the same names as the database tables. Delete the Directory commands that are generated by the wizard.

9. Add a new tab at the end of the script and name it **Generate QVDs**. Add the following logic:

   ```
   let vNoOfTables = NoOfTables();
   FOR vTableNum = vNoOfTables - 1 to 0 step -1
       let vTable = TableName('$(vTableNum)');
       store [$(vTable)] into [$(vTransformedQVDPath)T_$(vTable).QVD];
       drop table [$(vTable)];
   NEXT
   ```

10. **Save** and **Reload** your script. Verify that the seven new QVD files, beginning with the prefix T_, were generated in the \Data\Transformed QVDs subfolder.

At this point, we should stop and explain a few things about the script snippet that we've just added in Exercise 10.9:

- We used two new table functions: NoOfTables() returns the number of tables that were loaded and TableName('Index') returns the name of the table, based on its number in the list of tables. Notice that the index appears in single quotes, because this function requires a string data type as a parameter. Read full details about those and other table functions in the Help article called "Table Functions."

- Notice that we added the prefix T_ between the path and the table name within the STORE command. This was done to differentiate between transformed and raw QVD files.

- Examine the structure of the FOR loop—it starts with the number of tables minus one and moves down to zero with the negative step -1:

  - We need to subtract 1 from the number of tables because the list of tables starts with 0. The first table in the list carries the index 0, and therefore the last table in the list carries the index that's equal to the number of tables minus 1.

  - This example shows that the FOR loop can accept a STEP that's different from the default value 1—the step can be positive or negative.

  - We need to start from the highest number in the list and move down to the lowest number in the list because we drop tables as part of the process, and therefore the list of existing tables gets shorter with each iteration of the loop. This is also why we had to calculate the number of tables before the beginning of the loop and to store the number in the variable. Within the loop, NoOfTables() would return a smaller number with each iteration, causing unexpected logical issues.

This little snippet of code looks generic enough, just like other common routines that we've added before. With this routine, we can always scan all the existing tables in any QlikView application and store them into QVD files. In the next exercise, you transform this routine into one of the common routines and add it to the library of common routines. In order to make this routine even more flexible, you add two new parameters—the customizable prefix that can be different from the hard-coded prefix T_ and a flag (0/1) that enables or disables the DROP TABLE command.

Exercise 10.10: Creating a Generic Routine that Stores All Tables Into QVD Files

1. Transform the snippet of script that you created in the Step 9 of Exercise 10.9 into a subroutine. You do this by adding the SUB command at the beginning and the END SUB command at the end of the snippet.

2. Name the new subroutine StoreAllTablesIntoQVDs(). The subroutine will have three parameters—path, custom prefix, and the drop tables flag.

3. Replace the hard-coded prefix T_ with the new custom prefix variable.

4. Enclose the DROP TABLE statement in an IF statement with the new DropTables flag used as a condition.

5. Add clean-up statements at the end of the subroutine, to destroy temporary variables.

6. Add the CALL statement to execute the subroutine.

7. Add clean-up statements at the end of the script in order to destroy the two path variables. Your complete script for this tab should look like the following:

```
SUB StoreAllTablesIntoQVDs(QVDPath, Prefix, DropTables)
    let vNoOfTables = NoOfTables();

    FOR vTableNum = vNoOfTables - 1 to 0 step -1

        let vTable = TableName('$(vTableNum)');
        store [$(vTable)] into [$(QVDPath) $(Prefix)$(vTable).QVD];
        IF DropTables THEN
            drop table [$(vTable)];
        END IF
    NEXT
    let vNoOfTables =;
    let vTableNum =;
    let vTable =;
END SUB
CALL StoreAllTablesIntoQVDs(vTransformedQVDPath, 'T_', '1');
LET vQVDPath=;
LET vTransformedQVDPath=;
```

8. Save and Reload your script. Verify that all the tables were in fact stored as QVD files.

9. Copy the subroutine definition into the CommonRoutines.txt text file created in Exercise 10.8. Comment out the definition of the same subroutine in the body of your script.

10. Verify that the text file named `CommonRoutines.txt` is included with the command `MUST_INCLUDE` in the `Main` tab of your script.

11. `Save` and `Reload` again. You should see the same results, performed with the externally stored subroutine.

Extra Credit

Replace the hard-coded path in all the new `LOAD` statements with the variable `$(vQVDPath)`. Make sure to use the variable `vQVDPath` when loading raw QVD data and to use `vTransformedQVDPath` when storing transformed QVD files.

This exercise completes the section that describes the logic and the techniques of creating and using QVD files. In the process, you learned about variables and script control statements. From the project standpoint, you've accomplished the following:

- You minimized the data load time and the impact on the back office database by creating a layer of raw QVD files.

- You unified the transformation logic and avoided unnecessary duplication of efforts by creating a layer of transformed QVD files and a single transformation script that generates the files.

- You started a library of reusable common routines that can be used in multiple applications and therefore can save developers' time in the future.

To conclude our discussion about QVD files, we'd like to mention that QlikView offers a set of five QVD-related functions that allow you to extract metadata information from QVD files. The most practical example is extracting the timestamp of the QVD file creation. This is important when you need to show the users how old the data in your app is:

```
let vQVDRefreshTime = QvdCreateTime('Orders.qvd');
```

Feel free to explore other QVD-related functions in the Help article "File Functions in Script."

In the next section, you learn various ways of troubleshooting complex scripts that you may need to use in order to isolate and find problems in your scripts. After that, you add two more transformed QVD files to your library. Make sure to finish reading the following sections in order to build a complete data set.

Troubleshooting QlikView Load Scripts

We've reached a respectable level of complexity, where many things in the script can go wrong. In this section, you learn about the tools that can help developers troubleshoot issues in QlikView scripts.

The Syntax Check and the Table Viewer

You may have noticed that the QlikView **Script Editor** performs an interactive syntax check while you create your script. The statements that are deemed incorrect are underlined with a curvy red line, similarly to other spell checkers.

In addition, you can initiate **Syntax Check** by clicking on the little ⬚ button at the end of the **Script Editor** toolbar, or by using the **Tools ▶ Syntax Check** menu option. QlikView will run through the script and stop at the point that looks "suspicious". With the use of complex expressions and dollar-sign expansions, the syntax checker is not always 100% accurate, but it can still prevent you from overlooking simple syntax errors, like a missing comma (by far the most common error among new developers).

Another easily available troubleshooting tool is the **Table Viewer**. The **Table Viewer** is available from both the **Script Editor** and from the main Layout window. The corresponding toolbar icon ⬚ resembles the table structure. The **Table Viewer** helps examine the end result of the data load:

- Have we created the desired data structure?
- Are all tables linked with the expected key fields?
- Do we see the expected row counts?

Two valuable metrics are available when we hover over the field names in the **Table Viewer**:

- *Information density* tells us the percentage of the table rows that have non-null values in this field. Information density that is less than 100% may point out at a possible problem.
- For key fields, the *subset ratio* tells us what percentage of the total number of values for the field exists in the current table.

- When the subset ratio is less than 100% for a key field in a fact table, it means than some of the dimension values are not present in the fact table, and therefore may not be needed.

- When the subset ratio is less than 100% for a key field in a dimension table, it means that some of the key values in the fact table don't have the corresponding definitions in the dimension table.

Since our QVD Generator scripts drop tables after storing them, our table structure will be empty in those documents. The **Table Viewer** is best examined on a fully loaded data model, such as `Sales Analysis Data`.

The Script Execution Progress Dialog, the Log, and the TRACE Command

The **Script Execution Progress** dialog provides a decent troubleshooting tool—it shows an interactive log of all the tables that were loaded and the counts of rows for each table.

With that, the usefulness of the **Script Execution Progress** dialog is limited. Developers can gain more insights from the log file that can be generated during the script execution. This is enabled in the **Document Properties, General** tab, with the **Generate Logfile** checkbox. The subsequent checkbox, **Timestamp in Logfile Name**, enables generating a unique log file name with each run—the log file names will be stamped with the timestamp. This may be helpful for keeping the history of log files, but watch the number of logs grow like mushrooms!

The log files are generated in the same folder where the QVW document is stored. In the log file, each script statement is listed with the timestamp of its execution. You can learn a lot from the log file—the execution times of individual commands and any possible errors that may happen along the way.

Two important settings in the **User Preferences** pertain to log files:

- In the **General** tab, the **Flush Script Log After Each Write** checkbox causes the log to be written out after each statement. This is important in case of any possible crashes. If the log is not flushed until the end, the log file may not get generated at all if QlikView should crash in the middle of the process.

- In the **Design** tab, the **Always Use Logfiles for New Documents** checkbox allows enabling log files by default, which is very useful. The log file will be ready for you when you realize the need to see it.

Developers can enhance the information available in the **Script Execution Progress** dialog and in the log file, with the use of the TRACE command. For example:

```
TRACE Generating the Table $(vTable)...;
```

With TRACE, you can add any custom information that will appear both in the **Script Execution Progress** dialog and in the log file. This information may include the names of the tables that are being loaded, row counts, the values of temporary variables, and so on. Keep in mind that the TRACE command expects a hard-coded text, so any variables need to be enclosed in a dollar-sign expansion, and any functions and expressions need to be pre-calculated and stored in variables before they can be used in TRACE.

Feel free to experiment with the TRACE commands throughout your load scripts. Examine the results on the **Script Execution Progress** dialog and in the log file.

Using the Debugger to Solve Problems in the Script

The ultimate troubleshooting tool for QlikView scripts is of course the **Debugger** (see Figure 10.3). Using the **Debugger**, developers can run the script in a controlled fashion, stop in the middle of script execution, and examine the logic as it's being processed.

The **Debugger** dialog is activated with the **Debug** toolbar button, which is located next to the **Reload** button. Let's examine the various parts of the **Debugger** dialog, displayed in Figure 10.3.

The main window (A) hosts the read-only copy of the load script. The red dots next to the line numbers (C) represent the breakpoints (for any non-technical readers, breakpoints are the intermediate stops where the script execution should pause per our request, so we can examine the script). Breakpoints can be added or removed by clicking on the line number.

You can scan the script visually to find the required statement, or you can initiate a search in the script by pressing Ctrl+F. This fact is little known because Search is not offered in any of the toolbars, and therefore it's assumed to be unavailable.

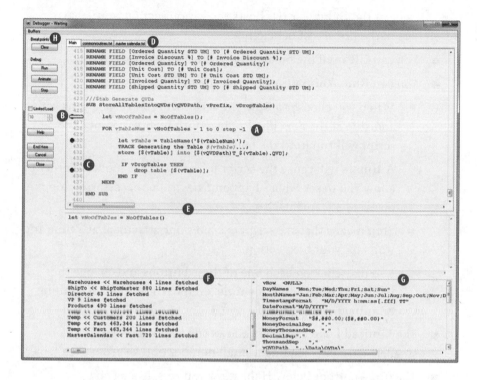

FIGURE 10.3:
The Debugger

Notice that the external script files included in the script get added in separate tabs (D). This feature enables debugging the script even if it's stored externally.

The yellow bar (B) signifies the next line that is going to be executed. The same statement, fully formatted, is presented in a smaller window below the script window (E). This is handy when script statements contain variables and dollar-sign expansions. In this window, we can see the fully formatted statement after all the variables and dollar-sign expansions were resolved.

The small window in the lower-left corner (F) shows the familiar **Script Execution Progress** dialog. Next to it, another small window (G) shows all the script variables and their assigned values. When another variable is assigned a new value, it is displayed at the top of the list. Don't be alarmed by the red color of the variables. This is not a sign of a problem, just a poor color choice.

The left side of the **Debugger** (H) hosts the various actions available to developers in the process of debugging:

- You can **Clear** all the breakpoints with a single click.
- You can **Run**, **Animate**, or **Step** through the script:
  - When you choose to **Run**, the script will run through the script and stop at the next breakpoint. With no breakpoints, the script will run until the end.
  - **Animate** will cause the script to run in a slow mode, in order to allow you to see what's happening, without necessarily stopping on every statement.
  - **Step** means that the script executes one statement at a time and waits for your next action.
  - You may click on each one of these buttons and change the mode of execution at any time, even in the middle of running or animating.
- The **Limited Load** checkbox allows you to process the script on a smaller scale, only loading a small number of rows from each table.
- The three buttons below **Help** allow you to exit the debugger window at any stage in the script execution. Different options are available at different stages, so try all three if you need to get out in the middle. One of them will open the exit door for you.

Exercise 10.11: Using the Debugger

If you already faced any problems in your scripts, try to use the debugger to diagnose the problems. Otherwise, make an intentional mistake in the script and find it using the debugger.

For example, misspell the path in the variable vQVDPath and use the log file and the debugger to isolate and find the problem.

Creating Transformed QVD Files for Profitability Data

In addition to the sales data that you addressed earlier in this chapter, you need to prepare additional data elements that are specific to profitability analysis. In this section, you prepare transformed QVD files for `Credit Memos` and `Product Costing` tables.

Loading and Transforming the Credit Memos

As QlikView developers, we may not be intimately familiar with the structure of the Credit Memo tables that we received from our financial systems. This is a very common challenge—we need to analyze data that we are not familiar with. The best way to understand the data is to load it into QlikView and to examine what we have on our hands.

Exercise 10.12: Loading Credit Memos from the Raw QVD Files

1. Create a new QlikView document. Store the document in the `\Data Loaders\` subfolder with the name **Profitability Transformation Script XX.QVW**, where XX is your initials.

2. In the Script Editor, create a new script tab and name it **Credit Memos**.

3. Generate LOAD statements to load data from three table files located in the subfolder `\Data\QVDs\`— `Credit Memo Header.QVD`, `Credit Memo Detail.QVD`, and `Reasons.QVD`, in that order. Reload your script.

4. Next, validate the data that you loaded. Create three individual Table Boxes. In each one of the boxes, select all fields from one of the three tables. This way, one Table Box should show all the data from `Credit Memo Header`, the other Table Box will show all the data from `Credit Memo Detail`, and so on.

Now you can examine the data visually and make some initial conclusions.

You probably noticed that the table structure includes a synthetic key that consists of two fields—[Credit Memo Number] and [Reason Code]. Apparently, `Reason Code` is stored in both the `Header` and the `Detail`. Now you need to decide which one of the two fields should be used. You can create a chart and calculate the number of distinct `Reasons` per `Credit Memo` and determine this way if the reason should stay at the header level or at the detailed level. In this case, however, you are going to combine the two tables, so the problem is solved rather easily. Keep the Reason from the Details table and avoid loading the same field from the Header.

Now, examine the Credit Memo Header. It includes references to Customers, Ship To, and even to the Order Number. Apparently, Order Number is populated for all rows, which means that all Credit Memos can be safely attributed to specific Orders. This is a huge advantage, which is rarely available in real life (we made this little assumption for the educational value of this discussion).

The Header includes three date fields—the Credit Memo Header, the Due Date, and the Ship Date. While all three dates might be important, only one of the fields can be associated with the Master Calendar. In other words, we need to pick one date out of three to be used as the main date field for this data. We will use the Ship Date as the main date, to attribute all the costs to the date of the sale.

What Date Should Be Used as the Main Date?

When analyzing profitability of sales, it's preferable to attribute all the costs and allowance payments to the date of the sale, as much as possible. That means that if we shipped product in January and we issued the invoice in January, then the sales are attributed to January. Then, later in the year, we might receive a credit memo in May and pay it in June. Still, these costs need to be attributed to January, in order to represent profitability of the sales in January. This is why it's desirable to know the original ship date for each credit memo.

The Credit Memo Details table contains the reference to the product; however, not all of the rows are populated with the Product ID. Actually, only rows with the Reason Code = 701010 ("Return to Stock") show a Product ID that's not empty. So, in the process of data modeling we should be aware of the fact that Product ID may or may not be available in the credit memo data.

At this point, you are ready to prepare the credit memos for being stored as transformed QVDs. In the process of transformations, you will address the following:

1. Avoid loading duplicate fields, such as [Reason Code]. Also avoid loading unnecessary fields, such as [Due Date], [Credit Memo Date], and [Line Number].

2. Apply the naming conventions:

   2.1. Rename all the key fields to begin with the % sign.

   2.2. Rename all the metrics to begin with the # sign. Also, add the abbreviation CM to fields like Quantity and Amount, in order to differentiate them from sales quantities and amounts.

3. Denormalize the structure and join all three tables into a single fact table that we will call CreditMemos.

4. Rename the main date field [Ship Date] to [Date].

Feel free to make these changes on your own, using this list as a guide. More detailed instructions can be found in Exercise 10.13.

Exercise 10.13: Transforming Credit Memos

1. Ensure that the Credit Memo Header table is loaded first. Perform the following changes:

   1.1. Name the table **CreditMemos**. Delete the Directory statement.

   1.2. Comment out the [Credit Memo Date], [Due Date], and [Reason Code] fields. Make sure that the last remaining field in the LOAD statement doesn't have an unnecessary comma.

   1.3. Rename the ID fields [Customer ID] and [Product ID] to include the % sign in front of the name.

```
CreditMemos:
LOAD
     [Credit Memo Number],
     [Customer ID]          as [%Customer ID],
     [Ship To ID]           as [%Ship To ID],
     [Order Number],
     [Customer PO Number],
//   [Credit Memo Date],
     [Ship Date]            as Date
//   ,
//   [Due Date],
//   [Reason Code]
FROM
[..\Data\QVDs\Credit Memo Header.QVD]
(qvd);
```

2. Ensure that the Details table is loaded next. Perform the following changes:

    2.1. Delete the Directory statement. Add the LEFT JOIN (CreditMemos) prefix in front of the LOAD.

    2.2. Rename [Product ID] to [%Product ID]. Also rename the metric fields according to the following resulting script:

```
LEFT JOIN(CreditMemos)
LOAD
     [Credit Memo Number],
//     [Line Number],
     [Reason Code],
     [Product ID]           as [%Product ID],
     Quantity               as [# CM Quantity],
     [U/M],
     [Unit Price]           as [# CM Unit Price],
     Amount                 as [# CM Amount]
FROM
[..\Data\QVDs\Credit Memo Detail.QVD]
(qvd);
```

3. Add the same LEFT JOIN prefix in front of the LOAD for the Reasons table.

4. Save and Reload your script. In the Table Viewer, you should see a single table with all the fields renamed as planned.

Loading and Transforming the Costing Data

Standard costing data is another component of the profitability model that needs to be loaded and transformed. In reality, standard costing data is extremely complex and includes many components that can be dynamically created and classified. In our case, we are loading a simplified "flat file" extract that was created in our back office system specifically for our analysis.

The transformation of the costing data is much simpler, since it's already stored in a single table. You simply need to rename the key fields and the metrics according to the naming conventions.

Feel free to develop this simple transformation script on your own or follow detailed instructions in Exercise 10.14.

Exercise 10.14: Transforming the Costing Data

1. Create a new tab in the script and name it **Costing**.

2. Load the data from the table file called StandardCosting.QVD.

3. Delete the Directory statement and name the table **StandardCosting**.

4. Rename the [Product ID] and the measure fields according to the naming convention:

```
StandardCosting:
LOAD
     [Product ID]              as [%Product ID],
     Year,
     [Standard Cost]           as [# Standard Cost],
     [Unit Cost - Material]    as [# Unit Cost - Material],
     [Unit Cost - Labor]       as [# Unit Cost - Labor],
     [Unit Cost - Overhead]    as [# Unit Cost - Overhead]
FROM
[..\Data\QVDs\StandardCosting.QVD]
(qvd);
```

Generating New Transformed QVDs

Now you just need to create new transformed QVDs for the profitability and the costing data that you just transformed. You could do it manually, or you can leverage the common routine that we developed earlier.

In order to use the common routine, you need to Include the external text file in the beginning of the script and then call the routine StoreAllTablesIntoQVDs at the end of the script. The easiest way of accomplishing this task is to copy those statements from the Sales Transformation Script and paste them here.

Feel free to add this logic on your own or follow the detailed instructions in Exercise 10.15.

Exercise 10.15: Generating New Transformed QVDs

1. In the **Main** tab of the script, assign the path variable that will be used as a parameter to the common routine.

2. Still in the **Main** tab, add the `Must_Include` statement to include the text file with the common routines:

   LET *vTransformedQVDPath='..\Data\Transformed QVDs\';*
   $(Include=..\scripts\commonroutines.txt);

3. Add a new tab at the end of the script and name it **Generate QVDs**.

4. Call the common routine to store all tables into QVD files, with the following parameters:

   CALL StoreAllTablesIntoQVDs(vTransformedQVDPath, 'T_', '1');

5. Add another LET statement at the end to destroy the variable `vTransformedQVDPath`.

6. **Save** and **Reload** your script. You should see that two new transformed QVD files are generated in the `\Transformed QVDs` subfolder.

Extra credit: replace all references to the QVD path with the variable `vQVDPath`.

This exercise completes the process of creating the QVD data layer. The next step is to use the transformed QVD files in the process of building an efficient data model for the profitability analysis.

Building the Data Model for Profitability Analysis

Let the fun go on! We are ready to build the data model for the Profitability Analysis application. Let's take a look at the data that we need to include in the model. We have two fact tables—Sales and CreditMemos—plus a handful of dimension tables, and one slowly changing dimension (StandardCosting).

As you learned in Chapter 9, multiple fact tables can be combined into a single model using one of the two main techniques—*Link Tables* or *Concatenated Facts*. The Profitability model can be built with either one of the two techniques. Even though our personal preference is to use Concatenated Facts, especially for large data models, the discussion in this chapter focuses on building the Link Table model—mostly because this book wouldn't be complete without a discussion of this technique. We will describe the process of building Concatenated Facts in Chapters 13 and 14.

An Overview of the Process

Here is what we know from the business requirements and from our understanding of the data:

- The analysis needs to be done at the monthly level; therefore, there is no need to store details at a more granular level.

- The main dimensions for the analysis are Customer, Product, and Salesperson. There is no need to analyze profitability by other attributions such as Ship To and Warehouse.

- Sales data needs to be enhanced with a summary of the standard costing information.

- The field Salesperson is not available for credit memos, but it can be fetched from the Order Header and populated in credit memos.

- Some credit memos are listed by Product ID and some are not. This means that some of the credit memos won't link to the sales data if the link between sales and credit memos includes the Product ID.

With this knowledge in mind, we will build our data model using the following series of steps:

1. Load the sales data and aggregate it to the level of Customer, Product, Salesperson, and Year/Month.

2. Populate data from the product costing in the summarized sales data and pre-calculate the basic components of cost of goods sold.

3. Load the credit memos data and aggregate it to the level of Customer, Product, Salesperson and Year/Month. The Salesperson information will be fetched from the Order Header, within the aggregated load of credit memos (kids, don't try this at home!).

4. Build the LinkTable with the common keys from the two fact tables.

5. Load dimension tables for Customers, Products, and SalesHierarchy.

6. Generate a new Calendar table.

In the process of building this quite complex data model, we will of course continue discovering various techniques and features of QlikView scripting.

Aggregating Data in QlikView

Since profitability only needs to be analyzed at the monthly level, we can aggregate all the transactions to that level. By doing so, we can improve performance.

The syntax of *aggregating data* in QlikView is very similar to the syntax of aggregating data in SQL. Any LOAD statement can be enhanced with the GROUP BY clause, with the list of aggregation keys that define the level of aggregation:

```
LOAD
      Key1,
      Key2,
      Key3,
      sum(Measure1) as Sum1,
      min(Measure2) as Min2
RESIDENT
      Tab1
GROUP BY
      Key1,
      Key2,
      Key3
;
```

The rules of QlikView aggregation are the same as the SQL rules—the only fields that are allowed in the list are the aggregation keys (the same fields that are listed in the GROUP BY clause) or measures included in aggregation functions. Even if you know for sure that a certain attribute is unique for the combination of keys, the only way to include it in the aggregation load is to declare it either as a key or as an aggregated measure. If you break that rule, the consequence is imminent—your load script will fail with an extremely cryptic message (in most cases, the message will state "**Unknown error**").

As you will see in the exercises, QlikView allows calculated expressions to be used as aggregation keys, as long as the expression is listed the same way in both lists.

Remember that a GROUP BY clause can be added to any LOAD, including preceding LOADs (the LOAD statements that draw data from the following LOAD or SQL SELECT statement).

In the following exercise, you load the sales data from the transformed QVD T_Fact.QVD file and then reload the same data using RESIDENT LOAD, with the aggregation GROUP BY clause. Since there is no wizard for the RESIDENT LOAD, the easiest way to create one is to clone the script of the initial QVD load and transform it manually to fit your needs.

We will remove many unnecessary fields, except for the following:

- Keep the ID fields for Customer, Product and Salesperson.

- Calculate MonthStart() for the field Date and call the result with the same name Date.

- Summarize Invoice Quantity into the field [# Quantity] and summarize Amount into the field [# Amount].

- Multiply Invoice Quantity by List Price and summarize the result into the field [#Amount at List Price].

- The GROUP BY clause will include four key fields—[%Customer ID], [%Product ID], [%Salesperson ID], and MonthStart(Date).

We encourage you to try to develop this step on your own, if you can. Detailed instructions, if needed, are listed in Exercise 10.16.

Exercise 10.16: Aggregating Sales Data

1. Create a new QlikView document. Store the document in the \Data Loaders\ subfolder with the name **Profitability Data XX.QVW**, where XX is your initials.

2. In the Script Editor, add a new script tab and name it **Sales**.

3. Load the data from the transformed QVD file called \Transformed QVDs\T_Fact.QVD. Name the new table **Temp_Sales**.

4. Add new script tab and name it **Sum Sales**. Copy the LOAD statement from the Sales tab and paste it in the new tab.

5. Transform the LOAD statement into the following:

```
Sales:
LOAD
      [%Customer ID],
      [%Product ID],
      [%Salesperson ID],
      MonthStart(Date)                as Date,
      sum([# Invoiced Quantity])      as [# Quantity],
      sum([# Invoiced Quantity]  *  [# List Price])
                                      as [# Amount at List Price],
      sum([# Amount])                 as [# Amount]
RESIDENT
      Temp_Sales
GROUP BY
      [%Customer ID],
      [%Product ID],
      [%Salesperson ID],
      MonthStart(Date)
;
drop table Temp_Sales;
```

Notice that we used the MonthStart(Date) function as an aggregation key in the GROUP BY list. This degree of flexibility is quite remarkable.

Next, we need to add standard costing data to the sales data—we'd like to know the components of the standard cost for each aggregated row of sales. We could simply join the Costing table to the Sales table, using JOIN LOAD as demonstrated in Chapter 6. Since costing data is defined by the product ID and year, we'd have to calculate the Year field in the Sales table, join the costing data, and then drop the Year field again.

There is nothing wrong with that approach, but we would like to use this opportunity to introduce you to another very powerful feature of QlikView, called mapping.

How to Use Mapping in QlikView Script

Mapping was introduced for the purpose of data cleansing. Imagine that you need to load data from two data sources, and the same data element is coded differently in the two systems. For example, two sales systems (old and new) have their own customer master tables, with their different ways of coding the same customers.

In order to load their data into a single analytic application, you have to cross-reference the codes and replace the old code with the new code during the data load process.

This process is called *mapping*, and the cross-reference table that holds pairs of old and new values, is called a *mapping table*. Mapping is a two-step process:

1. First, we need to create the mapping table, using a *mapping load*.

2. Then, we can map certain field values using the mapping table.

The mapping process had proven to be fast, clean, and robust. Once QlikView developers got used to the idea, they began using mapping for other purposes, not just for cleansing or cross-referencing data. With mapping, you can fetch any data element from any data source and make that data element readily available in another LOAD statement. For example, if you need to use the field Standard Cost in the process of loading sales, you can create a mapping table that converts a combination of product ID and year to the corresponding cost value.

In essence, mapping has become a viable and often preferable alternative to joining tables when only one or a few values need to be fetched. Using mapping tables instead of joining tables offers a number of important advantages:

- Mapping can never cause duplication of data, while JOIN loads can produce duplicate results if one of the data sources should accidentally have duplicate values. This issue has been a source of many developers' frustrations.

- With mapping, missing or mismatched values can be replaced with a value, such as 'Missing' or 'No Match'. The same can't be easily done with joining.

- In most cases, mapping performs faster than joining; however, this is not always the case.

Creating Mapping Tables

Mapping tables always store two fields—the old value and the new value, in that order (by the way, this is one of the few places in QlikView where the order of fields in a LOAD statement is significant). Any form of a LOAD statement can be used as a MAPPING load with the use of the prefix MAPPING in front of the keyword LOAD. In earlier versions of QlikView, optimized QVD loads couldn't be used for MAPPING loads; however, this limitation was removed in version 11.

Since mapping tables are inherently temporary, they are dropped automatically at the end of the script execution. For the same reason, the field names are ignored—only the order of the two fields is important.

It's important to keep in mind that mapping tables need to be distinct, and there should always be only one new value for each old value. When the same old value can be mapped to multiple new values, the mapping process returns the first found new value.

Mapping tables need to be created before they can be used. For this reason, it's good practice to add a special **Mapping** tab in the script and to place it very early in the process—usually next to the **Main** tab. This way, you will always have a single address for any issues related to mapping.

In the following exercise, you create four mapping tables for the four metrics related to the standard costing data—the product cost and the three cost components (material, labor, and overhead). The old value for the mapping will be the combination of the fields [%Product ID] and Year, with the pipe symbol '|' as a delimiter.

Exercise 10.17: Creating Mapping Tables

1. Open Script Editor and create a new tab next to the Main tab. Name the new tab **Mapping**.

2. Load data from the transformed QVD file called T_StandardCosting.QVD. Name the new table **Temp_Costing**.

3. Next, type the MAPPING LOAD statement that loads two fields from the resident Temp_Costing table. The first field is calculated as [%Product ID] concatenated with Year, with the pipe symbol '|' as a delimiter, and the second field is [# Standard Cost]. Name the mapping table **Cost_Map**:

```
Cost_Map:
MAPPING LOAD
    [%Product ID] & '|' & Year,
    [# Standard Cost]
Resident
    Temp_Costing
;
```

4. Clone the same mapping statement three times and change the field names and the map names to create mapping tables Material_Map, Labor_Map, Overhead_Map for the fields [# Unit Cost - Material], [# Unit Cost - Labor], and [# Unit Cost - Overhead], respectively.

5. At the end of the tab, drop the temporary costing table.

Mapping Data Using Mapping Tables

Once the mapping tables were created, they can be used in the process of mapping. There are two main methods that can be used for mapping—one is easier and the other is the method that you should use, for the most part.

The first and the easier method is the MAP command:

```
MAP <FieldList> USING <MappingTable>;
```

When the MAP command is used, the listed fields will be mapped using the listed map anywhere in the load. Sounds wonderful and easy to use. The caveat is that the mapping is done last in the order of operations between loading, calculating, and storing the data. The mapping will happen when a certain field is stored with the specified name, but not when the field is used in other calculations, or needs to be used in WHERE, GROUP BY, or ORDER BY clauses.

For these reasons, our recommendation is to make it a good habit to use explicit mapping with the ApplyMap() function:

```
ApplyMap('<MappingTable>', <expression> [, <DefaultValue>])
```

With the `ApplyMap()` function, the mapping happens immediately where specified. Notice that the mapping table name is enclosed in a pair of single quotes—it's provided as a string. The *expression* can either list a certain field name, or it can be any calculated expression. The resulting value of the calculation will be verified against the mapping table and replaced with the corresponding new value, if the value is found in the table. If the value is not found in the mapping table, the function will return the default value, which can be listed as an optional third parameter. When no default is provided, the original unmapped value will be returned as a result. This is preferable in the process of data cleansing. When fetching a piece of data from another table (like `StandardCost`, for example), it's preferable to set a default value (zero or `NULL`) when the product ID cannot be found in the table.

Keep in mind that the `ApplyMap()` function won't throw an error if the mapping table doesn't exist or when no match was found (it will fail silently and all the mapped values will be stored with the `NULL` value). Always take steps to verify that the script generates the expected results.

In the following exercise, you add a preceding LOAD statement to the aggregated load of sales and load the four costing measures, using the four mapping tables that you created earlier. After that, you add another preceding LOAD that will be used to calculate a number of derived fields. You will calculate amounts for the total standard cost of goods sold (COGS) and for the three components (material, labor, and overhead). In addition, you will calculate the amount that was given as a discount by subtracting the sales amount from the amount at list price.

You can develop this addition to the script on your own or follow the detailed instructions in Exercise 10.18.

Exercise 10.18: Using Mapping Tables to Fetch Data from the Costing Table

1. In the script tab **Sum Sales**, add a preceding LOAD right after the table name `Sales:`.

2. In the preceding LOAD, request to load all the existing fields (asterisk *) and four new costing measures, using the `ApplyMap()` function with the four maps that you created in the Exercise 10.17. The maps should be applied to the same concatenated value used in the mapping load:

```
LOAD
    *,
    ApplyMap('Cost_Map', [%Product ID] & '|' & Year(Date), 0)
                as [# Unit Cost],
    ApplyMap('Material_Map', [%Product ID] & '|' & Year(Date), 0)
                as [# Unit Cost - Material],
    ApplyMap('Labor_Map', [%Product ID] & '|' & Year(Date), 0)
                as [# Unit Cost - Labor],
    ApplyMap('Overhead_Map', [%Product ID] & '|' & Year(Date), 0) as
                [# Unit Cost - Overhead]
;
```

3. **Save** and **Reload** your script. Verify that the Sales table was loaded with the four new costing fields. In the **Table Viewer**, use the **Preview** feature to validate that the costing data is populated with non-zero numeric values.

4. Add another preceding load in front of the previous one, right after the table name Sales:. This preceding load will use the costing measures that we just added, to calculate the following amounts:

```
LOAD
    *,
    [# Amount at List Price] - [# Amount]      as [# Amount - Discounts],
    [# Unit Cost]            * [# Quantity]    as [# COGS],
    [# Unit Cost - Material] * [# Quantity]    as [# COGS - Material],
    [# Unit Cost - Labor]    * [# Quantity]    as [# COGS - Labor],
    [# Unit Cost - Overhead] * [# Quantity]    as [# COGS - Overhead]
;
```

5. **Save** and **Reload** the script. Examine the new measures that we've just added.

In the next section, we will use aggregation and mapping again to load the Credit Memos into the data model.

Using Aggregation and Mapping to Load the Credit Memos

The next step is to load the Credit Memos data into our data model. If you recall from our earlier description, three data modeling challenges were related to Credit Memos.

First of all, the detailed data needs to be aggregated to the monthly level by Customer, Product, and Salesman. As you will see, Credit Memos include other levels of detail that also need to be preserved, such as the Reason Code, Description, and Category.

Secondly, Salesperson is not part of the credit memos data. We need to fetch it from the Order Header file. We will use the mapping technique that you just learned to bring the Salesperson ID into the Credit Memos.

Lastly, Product ID is only available for some of the Credit Memos. We will learn how to replace undesired NULL values in key fields, using the special null handling techniques.

Loading and Aggregating Credit Memos

In this section, we will use the same aggregation technique used for sales, to aggregate the data from the transformed QVD file called T_CreditMemos.QVD.

Credit Memo Quantity and Credit Memo Amount need to be aggregated by Product, Customer, Salesperson (which is missing for now), Month, Reason Code, Reason Description, and Reason Category.

Feel free to add this logic to your script, or follow the detailed instructions in Exercise 10.19.

Exercise 10.19: Aggregating the Credit Memos

1. Add a new tab at the end of your script and name it **Credit Memos**.

2. Load the data from the transformed QVD file called T_CreditMemos.QVD. Name the table **Temp_CM**.

3. Clone the same LOAD statement and transform it into an aggregated RESIDENT LOAD:

```
CreditMemos:
LOAD
      [Reason Code],
      [%Customer ID],
      [%Product ID],
      [Reason Description],
      [Reason Category],
      MonthStart(Date)        as Date,
      sum([# CM Quantity])    as [# CM Quantity],
      sum([# CM Amount])      as [# CM Amount]
```

```
RESIDENT
     Temp_CM
GROUP BY
     [Reason Code],
     [%Customer ID],
     [%Product ID],
     [Reason Description],
     [Reason Category],
     MonthStart(Date)
;
drop table Temp_CM;
```

Fetching the Salesperson ID from the Order Header Using Mapping

Our aggregated LOAD is still missing the Salesperson ID. In the following exercise, you create the mapping table and use it in the ApplyMap() function within the aggregated LOAD.

Exercise 10.20: Fetching the Salesperson ID Using Mapping

1. Open the script in the Mapping tab. At the bottom, add a comment with the explanation of the following logic (e.g. Loading the Salesperson Map).

2. Load two fields from the raw QVD file called Invoice Header.QVD—[Order Number] and [Salesperson ID]. Ensure that the fields appear in this order.

3. Add the MAPPING prefix in front of the LOAD. Name the table **Salesperson_Map**:

```
//----------------------------------------------------------
// Create a Map for Salesperson
//==========================================================
Salesperson_Map:
MAPPING LOAD
     [Order Number],
     [Salesperson ID]
FROM
[..\Data\QVDs\Invoice Header.QVD]
(qvd);
```

4. In the script tab **Credit Memos**, add another field to the aggregated load, using the `ApplyMap()` function and applying the new mapping table on the field `[Order Number]`:

```
ApplyMap('Salesperson_Map', [Order Number],'N/A') as [%Salesperson ID],
```

5. Add the same `ApplyMap()` function to the `GROUP BY` list of aggregation fields, to satisfy the rules of `GROUP BY`:

...

```
ApplyMap('Salesperson_Map', [Order Number],'N/A'),
```

...

6. **Save** and **Reload** the script. Verify that the `Salesperson` field is populated in the `CreditMemos` table. At this point, you don't need to worry about the synthetic key that was created between `Sales` and `CreditMemos`. You will learn how to resolve it in the following sections of this chapter.

Notice that you were able to fetch the `Salesperson ID` from another table and use it as an aggregation key in the `GROUP BY` clause. We can't stop being fascinated by the enormous flexibility of QlikView scripting logic!

> **NOTE**
>
> You may be wondering, "Why couldn't we use `ApplyMap()` in the QVD load, and then use it in the aggregated load as a field?" We could, of course. We had two reasons to do it the way we did it—one real and one educational. In reality, if it were important to keep the QVD load optimized, then we should avoid adding new fields in that load. Placing the `ApplyMap()` function in the subsequent aggregated load allows us to keep the QVD load optimized. The second reason is to give you the opportunity to experience this wonderful ability of using `ApplyMap()` in a `GROUP BY` clause—in our opinion, this is truly remarkable!

Handling NULL Values

NULL values are considered "bad news" in many database environments. In those environments, NULLs cause an unnecessary waste of space, performance degradation, and other issues. Database administrators go to lengths just to avoid having too many NULL values in their tables.

In QlikView, NULL values don't cause any issues. Since NULL values are not stored or indexed, there is no performance penalty for having many NULL values in the data set.

The only problem related to having NULL values is caused by the fact that NULL values cannot be linked, or associated, with other NULL values. Hence, having a key field with possible NULL values may lead to potential issues with table linking. Similarly, NULL values can't be selected in a list box, which is sometimes necessary.

QlikView offers a technique of substituting a NULL value in certain fields with a certain string. The specific fields that need to be treated this way should be listed in the command NullAsValue. For example:

```
NullAsValue [%Product ID];
```

NULL values in the field [%Product ID] will be converted to the empty string (that's the default value) in all the subsequent LOAD statements. When needed, the conversion can be stopped with the command NullAsNull:

```
NullAsNull;
```

The default value (the empty string) can be replaced with any other text, using the special variable NullValue:

```
Set NullValue = '*ALL*';
```

Here is an interesting little-known fact about NULL conversion. Because NULL conversion happens at the single row level, it's not going to happen in an optimized QVD load, where data is loaded in a super-fast mode that does not allow single row operations. This is another feature that fails silently. There is no error message to warn you that something is wrong. You just need to be aware of the problem and know how to avoid it. The trick is to force the corresponding QVD load into a non-optimized load. The easiest and the commonly used technique is to add a simple WHERE clause with the condition 1=1.

Another caveat to keep in mind about NULL handling has to do with the NULL values that are created by JOIN and CONCATENATE LOAD statements. These NULL values cannot be substituted by the NullAsValue statements. If you need to substitute these values, you will have to reload the same data once again using RESIDENT load and to take care of these values manually.

Why Not Get Rid of All NULLs?

Some developers may have a desire to convert all NULLs to text values just because of their general animosity toward the NULL values. We advise that doing this for all fields would be counterproductive. Unlike NULLs, the text values *will be* stored and indexed, hence increasing the memory footprint of the data.

In addition, converting NULL values to strings impacts the counting function. The Count() function will now include NULL values in the count, which is incorrect.

It's best not to convert NULL values to strings, unless you have a good reason to do so. Our exercise is an example of such a reason.

In Exercise 10.21, you use the *NULL handling* techniques to avoid NULL values in the key field [%Product ID]. Feel free to read more about NULL handling in QlikView in the Help article called "Null Value Handling."

Exercise 10.21: NULL Value Handling

1. In the main **Layout** view (exit the **Script Editor** if needed), create a **Straight Table** chart. Use the key field [%Product ID] as a dimension and the sum of [# CM Amount] as the expression:

   sum([# CM Amount])

2. Scroll down to the bottom of the list and verify that a large amount is attributed to the Product "-" (the dash is the default sign for NULLs and missing values). We will use the same chart at the end to verify that the NULL handling techniques worked properly.

3. Open the **Script Editor** and activate the **Main** tab of the script.

4. Add the two NULL handling statements for the field [%Product ID]:

   NullAsValue [%Product ID];
   Set *NullValue* = '*ALL*';

5. **Save** and **Reload** the script. Do you notice any difference in the chart? If everything went as planned, you should see no difference—the NULL value is still listed at the bottom of the chart.

This is because the [%Product ID] is loaded using an optimized QVD load. Locate the QVD load of the CreditMemos in the **Credit Memos** tab and add the following WHERE clause:

```
...
FROM
[..\Data\Transformed QVDs\T_CreditMemos.QVD]
(qvd)
WHERE 1=1
;
```

5. **Save** and **Reload** the script again. Verify that the NULL value is now replaced with the text '*ALL*', which is now listed on top of the list.

Building the Link Table

Our two fact tables are now ready to be linked with the Link Table. If you examine the current table structure presented in Figure 10.4, you may notice the synthetic table with the synthetic key that consists of the four key fields that are common between the two fact tables—Customer, Product, Salesperson, and Date.

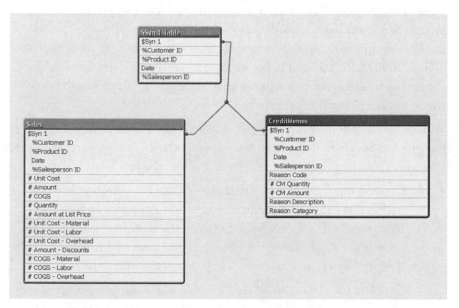

FIGURE 10.4:
Two facts with a synthetic key

This Is Easy!

We have to admit that this case is relatively easy—all four keys are populated in both tables, and there are no more tangled links to worry about.

Imagine that you had to load a budget table into this structure. The budget may be managed at the level of channel (as an aggregation of customers), brand (as an aggregation of products), and quarter (as an aggregation of months). None of these three fields is stored directly in `Sales` or in `Credit Memos`. Before you could link the budget data, you would have to fetch and populate all those keys in all fact tables.

Well, this is why you are in a protected educational environment. You learn the concepts that you will later apply to much more complex problems in your real applications.

The Process of Building the Link Table

There is a controversial opinion in the developer community that claims that a synthetic key of this kind can be used rather efficiently in data structures like ours. Technically, this might be true, and yet we are following the "traditional school" that requires avoiding synthetic keys as possible symptoms of underlining data modelling issues. Most of all, we believe in the good habit of being explicit in every way. Furthermore, by the end of this chapter, you will see that in this particular case, the synthetic key simply couldn't do the job.

What's helpful about this particular synthetic key is that it helped us easily identify the common fields between the two tables. Now we can get to the process of building the `LinkTable`, which involves the following steps:

1. Create a combined `LinkKey` that includes all the common key fields between the two tables. Notice the subtle difference in terminology. Out of all *common fields* between the tables, we only need to include the *key fields* in the `LinkKey`. If you have a common attribute field that can't be considered a key, it doesn't need to be included.

2. Populate the `LinkKey` in all the fact tables by adding the corresponding calculation to all the `LOAD` statements that loaded the data into the facts.

3. Load the `LinkTable` from each one of the fact tables, with the new `LinkKey` and all the common fields (including the attributes). This is done using a DISTINCT RESIDENT LOAD, from each one of the fact tables, into the `LinkTable`.

4. Drop the common fields from all the fact tables.

In our case, all four common fields are key fields, so all of them will need to be included in the `LinkKey`. We will concatenate all the key values, using the pipe symbol '|' as a delimiter:

```
[%Customer ID] & '|' & [%Product ID] & '|' & [%Salesperson ID] & '|' &
    Date as %LinkKey
```

Feel free to implement the described process in your script, or use the detailed instructions in Exercise 10.22.

Exercise 10.22: Building the Link Table

1. Open the **Script Editor**. Activate the script tab **Sum Sales**. Add the calculation of the %LinkKey, listed previously, to the first of the preceding loads (counting from the top).

2. In the **Credit Memos** tab, add a new preceding LOAD in front of the aggregated load for CreditMemos, and load all existing fields, and the new %LinkKey:

```
CreditMemos:
LOAD
    *,
    [%Customer ID] & '|' & [%Product ID] & '|' & [%Salesperson ID] & '|' & Date as %LinkKey
;
```

3. Create a new tab at the end of the script and call it **Link Table**. In the new tab, type the LOAD statement to load the %LinkKey, along with all the common fields, into the new table called **LinkTable**:

```
LinkTable:
LOAD DISTINCT
    [%Customer ID] & '|' & [%Product ID] & '|' & [%Salesperson ID] & '|' & Date as
%LinkKey,
    [%Customer ID],
    [%Product ID],
    [%Salesperson ID],
    Date
RESIDENT
    Sales
;
```

4. Clone the last statement and repeat the same `LOAD` from the `CreditMemos` table.

5. At the end, drop the common fields from both fact tables:

```
DROP FIELDS
        [%Customer ID],
        [%Product ID],
        [%Salesperson ID],
        Date
FROM
        Sales,
        CreditMemos
    ;
```

6. **Save** and **Reload** your script. Examine the data model in the **Table Viewer**. You should see that the new Link Table replaced the synthetic table, and that the link key had replaced the synthetic key.

Validating the Logic and the Associations

The new structure looks nice and yet it hides a serious issue that you will discover with a simple data validation exercise. When linking multiple facts, it's important to verify that your logic works properly by comparing the measures from the different facts aggregated by the various dimensions.

In the following exercise, you create two charts that compare sales amounts and credit memo amounts, aggregated by `Product ID` and `Reason Description`. Can you spot the problem before we describe it in the book?

Exercise 10.23: Verifying the Data Associations

1. In the **Layout** view (exit the **Script Editor** if necessary), create a new **Straight Table** chart. Use [%Product ID] as the dimension.

2. Add two expressions—the sum of the field [# Amount] and the sum of the field [# CM Amount]. Format the two numbers as **Money** in the **Number** tab.

3. Clone the chart and replace the dimension in the second chart by `Reason Description`.

Examine the two charts (presented in Figure 10.5).

%Product ID	Sales Amount	Credit Memos Amount		Reason Description	Sales Amount	Credit Memos Amount
	$117,385,889	$11,214,005			$117,385,889	$11,214,005
ALL	$0	$10,926,551		Advertising	$0	$1,235,004
110101	$217,595	$212		Annual volume all...	$0	$1,338,241
110102	$227,580	$218		Defective allowance	$0	$980,054
110103	$239,187	$215		Freight allowances	$0	$627,155
110104	$249,113	$231		Late shipments	$0	$943,185
110105	$254,310	$220		Merchandising	$0	$1,024,606
110106	$284,446	$262		Payment terms al...	$0	$951,287
110107	$266,873	$246		Return to stock	$1,744,133	$287,454
110201	$217,427	$199		Shortages	$0	$1,403,081
110202	$229,942	$203		Specific seasonal ...	$0	$1,166,494
110203	$244,007	$208		Wrong warehouse	$0	$1,257,444
110204	$244,545	$219		-	$115,641,756	$0

FIGURE 10.5:
Verifying the associations

Notice that the first line in the first chart shows the Product ID '*ALL*' with a substantial amount of credit memos and no associated sales. Apparently, these credit memos are not associated to any sales records. The second chart shows the problem from a different angle. Out of all Reason Descriptions, only one reason, "Return to stock," shows both the sales amounts and the credit memo amounts, while the rest of the reasons are not associated with sales. At the end of the list, most of the sales amount is listed with the reason " ," which means "missing" or "no value."

While our table structure looks perfectly valid, the actual associations between the data elements are, in fact, broken! We could get to the bottom of the issue by creating a detailed list of all LinkKey values that are not associated with sales; however, the problem is quite evident at the high level.

Our Link Table is associating sales and credit memos based on the combination of the four keys—Customer, Product, Salesperson, and Date. All the sales records are populated with a specific Product ID. However, most of the credit memos, except for the "Return to Stock," are not associated with a Product ID. We replaced the NULL value with the text "*ALL*," but we did nothing special to associate all the Product IDs from Sales to the generic value "*ALL*" on the CreditMemos side.

So, despite the Link Table, most Sales rows are not associated with most CreditMemo rows!

Restoring the Missing Associations with Generic Values

In order to restore the missing associations, we need to ensure that the specific product from the sales records get associated with all relevant credit memos that are not listed by product.

In order to do so, we need to split our %LinkKey into two key fields—%SalesKey and %CMKey.

- %SalesKey will represent the sales data and will always include the specific Product ID.

- %CMKey will represent the credit memos and will have two versions— one version will include the specific Product ID when it's available, and the other version will include the generic value '*ALL*' instead.

- The sales data will only contain the %SalesKey and the credit memo data will only contain the %CMKey.

- The Link Table will store both fields. In addition to the existing calculations, another LOAD statement will populate the missing associations between the sales keys and the corresponding CM keys that contain the generic value '*ALL*'. This additional LOAD will be based on the data from Sales, because this is where we always have the specific Product ID values.

In the following exercise, you make the necessary adjustments to the process, in order to restore the missing associations.

Exercise 10.24: Restoring the Missing Links

1. Open the **Script Editor**.

2. In the **Sum Sales** tab, replace the field name %LinkKey with %SalesKey.

3. In the **Credit Memos** tab, replace the field name %LinkKey with %CMKey.

4. In the **Link Table** tab, clone the calculation of the %LinkKey and calculate both %SalesKey and %CMKey in both existing statements.

5. Clone the first LOAD statement that populates the Link Table from Sales, and replace the [%Product ID] field in the calculation of %CMKey with the generic value '*ALL*.' Your third LOAD statement should look like this:

```
LOAD DISTINCT
    [%Customer ID] & '|' & [%Product ID] & '|' & [%Salesperson ID] & '|' & Date as
  %SalesKey,
    [%Customer ID] & '|' & '*ALL*' & '|' & [%Salesperson ID] & '|' & Date as %CMKey,
    [%Customer ID],
    [%Product ID],
    [%Salesperson ID],
    Date
RESIDENT
    Sales
;
```

6. Save and Reload your script.

Notice that many more sales amounts are now associated with various Reason Descriptions. On the flip side, most of the credit memo amounts are now associated with each and every product. We will have to find a work-around in our expressions to circumvent this side effect.

Using AutoNumber() to Reduce Wasted Space

You probably noticed that the newly created key fields store long textual values, built by concatenating four original key values—Customer, Product, Salesperson, and Date. This is one of the known performance drawbacks of the Link Table technique—the long alphabetic key values require a lot of space.

While the application is being verified and tested, it's helpful to be able to trace the individual key values for troubleshooting needs. However, once the application is tested, verified, and is ready for production, it's recommended to replace long alphabetic keys with shorter numeric values. This can be easily done with the use of the AutoNumber() function. This function performs an automatic indexing of the text values that are provided as the input parameter. The AutoNumber() function is guaranteed to return the same number for the same text, *within the boundaries of a single QlikView document*. It's important to fully understand this limitation. The internal logic of the AutoNumber() function consists of creating a distinct list of text values and returning a numeric index for each value. Text values are indexed in the order of their load in the specific document. The same texts may be indexed in a different order in another document. Therefore, we shouldn't use AutoNumber() if we are planning to store the resulting data into a QVD file for further processing. The only place where it's safe to use AutoNumber() is at the very last stage of building the data model.

If you need to create more than one index in the same script, you can add an index ID as an optional second parameter to the AutoNumber() function:

```
AutoNumber(text, ID)
```

In our application, we will use the AutoNumber() function to create two different keys—one key for sales and another key for credit memos. In order to ensure that both keys are generated as sequential integers, we will use different IDs for their AutoNumber() calculations. The benefit of generating sequential integers is saving space that is otherwise used for the list of distinct values. Since sequential integers' values are identical to their pointer values, QlikView doesn't need to store the list. The savings can be quite substantial in applications with large data sets.

In order to apply AutoNumber() in our load script, we need to search for all the places in the script where we concatenated fields into link keys and enclose the expression inside the AutoNumber() function, along with the ID string. We will use 'Sales' and 'CM' as the IDs for the %SalesKey and the %CMKey, respectively.

Exercise 10.25: Applying AutoNumber() to the Link Keys

1. You may want to save a separate copy of the QlikView document, to be able to compare the results at the end of this exercise.

2. Locate all the instances in the script where the link keys are being built as concatenated strings. There should be one instance in the **Sum Sales** tab, one instance in the **Credit Memos** tab, and several instances in the **Link Tables** tab. Enclose each one of the concatenated strings inside the function AutoNumber() and add either 'Sales' or 'CM' as the ID.

```
AutoNumber([%Customer ID] & '|' & [%Product ID] & '|' &
   [%Salesperson ID] & '|' & Date, 'Sales') as %SalesKey,
```

2. Save and Reload your script. Save the document one more time after reloading. Compare your document with the saved copy of the same document. You should be able to see that the document lost about 13% of its original size, just as a result of applying the AutoNumber() function.

Loading the Dimensions

Most of the heavy lifting is behind us. To complete the data model, we need to load the necessary dimension tables and to generate a new calendar table.

With the transformed QVD files being prepared up-front, loading all the dimensions is a breeze. We simply need to load data from the three transformed QVD Files—Customers, Products, and SalesHierarchy.

Exercise 10.26: Loading the Dimension Tables

1. Open the Script Editor. Add a new script tab at the end of the script and name it **Dimensions**.

2. Load the data from three transformed QVD files—T_Customers.QVD, T_Products.QVD, and T_SalesHierarchy.QVD. Name the tables **Customers**, **Products**, and **SalesHierarchy**, respectively.

3. Save and Reload your script. Verify the table structure. Your tables should form a structure resembling a star schema with the Link Table in the middle.

Building the Master Calendar

The last remaining step in our data-modeling project is to generate the Master Calendar for our aggregated data model. In Chapter 6, we promised to teach you how calendars are generated in QlikView, and now is the time to do so.

Before we get to it, you need to know how dates are handled in QlikView.

How Dates Are Handled in QlikView

Dates are different from text fields and numeric fields in the way they are presented, sorted, and processed. For example, the same date can be presented as 01/04/2014, 'January 4th, 2015', or 2014-01-04. At the same time, dates need to be sorted chronologically. Jan 4th, 2014 should appear before Feb 1st, 2014—even though "F" appears before "J" alphabetically.

The Dual Nature of Date Fields

In order to accommodate these different needs of formatting and sorting, dates are managed as *dual* values in QlikView. A dual value has two parts—a text and a number. The textual part is used to present the data, while the numeric part is used for sorting, summing, and performing other math operations.

A Side Note About Dual Values

Generally speaking, dual values serve many purposes in QlikView, in addition to serving as dates. For example, a Yes/No field can be defined as a dual value. Yes and No can be displayed in charts and list boxes, while the numeric part of 1 and 0 could be used for counting the number of "Yes" values, or even for color-coding the presentation of Yes and No using visual cues.

In order to create a dual value manually, you can use the `Dual()` function:

```
Dual(Text, Number)
```

In essence, even regular numbers are, in fact, dual. The same number 5 can be presented on the screen as 5, as 5.000, or as $5.00. All these different formatted presentations represent the textual part of the dual value, while the number 5 is the numeric part.

Try typing various QlikView functions in the **Expression Editor** or in the **Script Editor**. Type the name of the function and the opening parenthesis. QlikView will show a little yellow sticky note with the definition of the function. Notice the return data type, which is listed in front of each function name. For example, the `num()` function that we used to format numbers appears as dual. Most data casting and formatting functions (such as `num()`, `num#()`, `date()`, `date#()`, and so on) also appear as dual. Conversely, all aggregation functions, such as `sum()`, `avg()`, `min()`, and `max()`, appear with the type `num`. In the process of discovering new functions, pay attention to the data type of the function, as it may be important in many cases, especially when dealing with dates.

The numeric part of the date follows the same logic as the Microsoft tools. The numbers are sometimes called serial values, and they represent the number of days since December 30, 1899. The serial value of January 1st, 2015 is 42,005, because this is the number of days that have passed since December 30, 1899.

Since dates are stored as numbers, it's easy to perform math calculations with date fields. For example, the date that represents "one week ago" can be easily calculated by subtracting seven from the current date.

Timestamps are stored as the decimal parts of the date fields' serial values. If the whole day is equal to 1, then:

1 Hour = 1 / 24

1 Minute = 1 / 24 / 60

1 Second = 1 / 24 / 60 / 60

Converting a full timestamp into a whole date field is very simple—the serial value needs to be rounded down (using the Floor() function) and the result needs to be formatted as a date (using the Date() function).

Loading Date Values from Various Systems

Different databases and software systems manage dates differently. Microsoft systems are the easiest from this standpoint, because the date format is the same, and we don't need to perform any additional transformations in order to load dates from SQL Server, MS Access, or Excel. Here is the list of some common exceptions that we need to deal with:

- **Microsoft Excel for Mac**—in MS Excel for Mac, dates are managed on a similar calendar that begins from 1904. If you need to load data from an Excel spreadsheet that was originated on a Mac, your dates may appear four years off. You need to add four years to offset the difference in the calendars. The best way to do that is using the AddMonths() function or the AddYears() function:

    ```
    AddMonths(Date, 48)
    AddYears(Date, 4)
    ```

- **Julian dates**—some ERP systems manage dates using a format called Julian format, which stores dates as five-digit numbers that consist of the two-digit year number and the three-digit sequential number of the day within the year (despite being called "Julian," this format is different from the Julian date used in astronomy). The most popular example is the JD Edwards ERP system (currently owned by Oracle). One of the earlier QlikView templates for JD Edwards offered a VBScript function that converted Julian dates to the standard date fields. This practice, however, proved to be extremely slow, especially for large databases. Later on, it was replaced by a faster approach—loading a static conversion table from a QVD file and mapping dates using pre-calculated field values.

- **Eight-digit date numbers**—many other systems, including SAP, store dates as eight-digit numbers, typically in the YYYYMMDD format. Those numbers can be easily converted into date fields using a combination of the casting function Date#() and a formatting function Date(). The casting function Date#() evaluates the given string as a date, based on the specified format string:

  ```
  Date#(LegacyDate, 'YYYYMMDD')
  ```

  However, the textual presentation of the date remains the same (YYYYMMDD). In order to reformat the value into the default date format, the result of Date#() needs to be formatted using the formatting function Date():

  ```
  Date(Date#(Date, 'YYYYMMDD'))
  ```

- **Time_t format**—some systems, especially those developed in C/C++, manage the dates internally using the time_t format. This format stores dates as the number of seconds since January 1st, 1970. In most cases, the internal date will get converted into the standard formatted date before it gets to you, but if it doesn't, then it's not too hard to calculate the QlikView timestamp from the time_t number:

  ```
  set vUnix2Date = 'TimeStamp((UnixDate/86400)+25569)';
  ```

  where TimeStamp() is another formatting function, 86,400 = 24 * 60 * 60, or the number of seconds in a day, and 25569 is the serial value of January 1st, 1970.

You may encounter other ways of storing dates, but these are the most commonly used. Perhaps the most universal method to create a date field in QlikView is to use the `MakeDate()` function with the separate fields for year, month, and day:

```
MakeDate(Year, Month, Day)
```

A similar function `MakeTime()` allows you to create a time value from hours, minutes, and seconds.

Using Dates with Date Functions and Numeric Functions

QlikView offers over 60 date/time functions. You'd likely get really bored if we tried to describe all of them, so we recommend that you refer to the Help article "Date and Time Functions" to look up specific functions when you need them. This section lists just a few of the most useful functions:

- We already discussed **casting and formatting functions**, such as `Date#()`, `Date()`, `Timestamp#()`, `MakeDate()`, and `MakeTime()`.

- **Date and time math functions**, such as `AddMonths()` and `AddYears()` can be used for precise date calculations that take into account leap years. Similar to those are functions like `MonthStart()`, `MonthEnd()`, `WeekStart()`, `WeekEnd()`, and a few similar functions that return the date of the beginning or the end of the corresponding period.

- Functions such as `Year()`, `Month()`, `Week()`, `Day()`, and a few more **date parsing functions** return the corresponding parts of the date value.

- **Date comparison functions,** such as `InYearToDate()`, `InMonth()`, and several other similar Boolean functions return True or False based on the comparison of the date to the base date. For instance, the function `InYearToDate()` returns True if the date belongs to the year-to-date period defined by the base date.

- **Current date functions**, such as `Now()` and `Today()`, can provide the "current date" based on a few different scenarios. The function `Now()` is known to consume a lot of CPU resources when it's used in the layout, because it polls the operating system every second.

In addition to date/time functions, date values can participate in the numeric functions and arithmetic expressions. In aggregated loads, we can calculate the lowest and the highest dates using Min and Max. We can add and subtract number of days, hours, or minutes, and so forth.

When dealing with dates and timestamps, it's important to be aware of the resulting data format of a given expression. When comparing dates or using dates in Set Analysis, incorrect date format may easily break the logic of your search.

All the date functions that return date values will return results of the dual data type. Conversely, all math functions will return numeric results. Compare the examples in Table 10.1.

TABLE 10.1: Comparing Data Types Returned by Different Functions

FUNCTION	DATA TYPE
Today()	Dual
Today() - 1	Number
AddMonths(Date, 1)	Dual
Date + 30	Number
Only(Date)	Dual
Min(Date)	Number

In order to ensure consistency, you should decide on a consistent format of storing and managing dates—dates can be stored as numbers or as dual dates. Applying the Num() function to a date field allows retrieving the numeric value. Conversely, applying the Date() function to a number converts it to a dual date.

Another issue that developers need to be aware of is dealing with the timestamp part of the date value. Because of the slightly different timestamp values and the rounding issues, it might be difficult to compare dates or times calculated in different ways.

For example, the following condition is relatively safe:

```
IF MonthStart(OneDate) = AnotherDate THEN …
```

because MonthStart() returns the date of the first day of the month, at midnight, and therefore the numeric representation of the date is a whole number. Conversely, this similar statement is likely to produce incorrect results:

```
IF MonthEnd(OneDate) = AnotherDate THEN …
```

because `MonthEnd()` returns the timestamp of the *last millisecond* of the last day of the month, and therefore the serial value carries a non-zero decimal part that is unlikely to match the other date. The better way of comparing those two dates is to round both dates down:

```
IF Floor(MonthEnd(OneDate)) = Floor(AnotherDate) THEN …
```

Another peculiar example was first described in a wonderful blog post by Rob Wunderlich, a good friend and colleague at the Masters Summit for QlikView. It involves comparing timestamps generated by QlikView. The following calculation:

```
time(MakeTime(8) - MakeTime(1))
```

produces a display value of 7:00:00 AM. At the same time, if we compared it to the value of `MakeTime(7)`, the comparison would return false. Due to rounding issues, `MakeTime(8)` - `MakeTime(1)` is not equal to `MakeTime(7)`. Visit Rob's blog at `qlikviewcookbook.com` for detailed explanations and suggested solutions.

Generating Data Within the QlikView Script

The next section uses many of the date and time functions that you just learned in the process of generating the Master Calendar. But first we need to describe how to generate data within the QlikView script. Using the opportunity, we are going to present a number of different techniques of generating data within the script.

INLINE Load

The `INLINE Load` provides an ability to enter hard-coded values into a data table in the QlikView Script. This can be handy if certain fixed values are not expected to change and therefore can be entered in the script. For any values that are likely to change, we recommend avoiding the `INLINE Load` and loading the values from a text file or a spreadsheet.

For example, imagine that we need to calculate fiscal periods that are different from the calendar months. Many companies use other calendars for their financial reporting (those calendars are called fiscal calendars). For the purpose of this discussion, our fictional company Q-Tee Brands starts their fiscal year on April 1st, and the fiscal periods begin and end on the same dates as the calendar months, but they are numbered differently (April is numbered as Period 1, May is Period 2, and so on). There are many ways of defining the relation between calendar months and fiscal periods. One of them could be implemented using the INLINE Load.

The INLINE Load wizard is initiated from the **Script Editor** menu option **Insert ▶ Load Statement ▶ Load Inline**. The wizard resembles a simplified spreadsheet (see Figure 10.6).

FIGURE 10.6:
Inline Data wizard

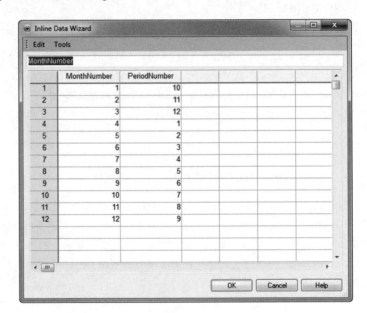

You can enter values in the cells of the table. Double-click the field headers in order to change the field names. You can add as many columns and rows as necessary.

The resulting script will look like the following:

```
LOAD * INLINE [
    MonthNumber, PeriodNumber
    1, 10
    2, 11
    3, 12
    4, 1
    5, 2
    6, 3
    7, 4
    8, 5
    9, 6
    10, 7
    11, 8
    12, 9
];
```

Notice that this statement is another form of a LOAD statement and it supports all the features of any LOAD statements—it can be turned into a MAPPING LOAD, a JOIN LOAD, and so on.

Exercise 10.27: Using the INLINE Load

1. Open the Script Editor. At the end of the Mapping tab, add the INLINE LOAD statement listed previously. Use the INLINE LOAD wizard or type the statement manually.

2. Add the prefix MAPPING in front of the LOAD statement and name the table **FiscalPeriod_Map**.

Generating Data Using AutoGenerate Load

Generating data with the INLINE LOAD is fairly easy, and yet it's pretty clear that it has a very limited use. Typing 12 rows of hard-coded values was only a little annoying, but what if we had to generate 120 rows? Every time we need to type more than just a few rows of data, the "lazy programmer" deep inside all of us wakes up and protests. There must be a better way!

In fact, there is. We can generate any number of data rows using AutoGenerate LOAD. The contents of the automatically generated data can be calculated based on the row number, which can be retrieved with the function RowNo(). AutoGenerate LOAD statements are typed manually in the script. The following is the alternate way of loading the relation between months and periods using AutoGenerate:

```
Load
      RowNo() as MonthNumber,
      if(RowNo() < 4, RowNo() + 9, RowNo() - 3) as PeriodNumber
AutoGenerate 12
;
```

The simple IF function defines the logic of assigning the period number based on the month number. The number 12 following the keyword AutoGenerate provides the number of rows that need to be generated.

Exercise 10.28: Using the AutoGenerate Load

1. Open the Script Editor. At the end of the Mapping tab, comment out the INLINE LOAD statement that we generated earlier and replace it with the new AUTOGENERATE statement.

2. Add the prefix MAPPING in front of the LOAD statement and name the table **FiscalPeriod_Map**.

Generating Data Using the WHILE Clause

Sometimes there is a need to generate a certain number of rows based on a condition. In these cases, the number of rows may not be initially known. We can generate data based on a logical condition using a LOAD statement with a WHILE clause:

```
LOAD
      <Some calculations involving IterNo()>
RESIDENT
      Table1
WHILE
      <A condition involving IterNo()>
;
```

QlikView will continue generating new rows as long as the condition that's listed in the WHILE clause remains true. Each iteration of this process is numbered, and the number can be retrieved with the IterNo() function.

Notice that the WHILE clause generates new data for each row in the source table, and the iteration number IterNo() restarts from 1 for each new source row.

As an example, if we had to track promotions, and each promotion was listed with start and end dates, we could use WHILE to generate a list of all dates that were impacted by various promotions.

We will defer exercising the WHILE logic until the next section, where you use it in the process of building the calendar.

The Logic of Building the Master Calendar

The process of building the Master Calendar is fairly common among all QlikView books and training manuals. In a nutshell, it boils down to the following steps:

1. Determine the lowest and the highest dates in the fact table. This is typically done using an aggregated load with the Min() and Max() functions.

2. Fetch the MinDate and MaxDate field values into variables, using the Peek() function.

3. Generate the temporary list of dates for the whole range between the MinDate and the MaxDate. This is usually done using either the AUTOGENERATE LOAD or using the WHILE clause. The temporary field that's being generated is usually called TempDate.

4. Reload the temporary list of values into the Calendar table, applying several date functions to the TempDate field, in order to generate the necessary date-related fields.

5. Drop all the temporary tables and variables.

We will use a similar process, in a slightly more elegant form, which was suggested by Rob Wunderlich in his lecture on Advanced Scripting at the Masters Summit for QlikView (www.masterssummit.com). With Rob's permission, we are presenting this technique to you. The process involves calculating the same steps as listed previously, with one subtle difference. Instead of loading and reloading temporary tables and using temporary variables, the whole process is implemented as a set of preceding loads.

At the end of the process, there are no temporary tables to drop and no temporary variables to destroy. Very clean and elegant, indeed:

1. The first step is the same—calculate the lowest and the highest dates in the fact table (in our case, in the LinkTable).

2. In the preceding load with a WHILE clause, generate all the daily date values in the range between the min date and max date.

3. In another preceding load on top of the previous one, reload the temporary list of values into the Calendar table, applying a number of date functions to the calculated TempDate field.

As you can see, the logic seems to be much simpler and more elegant. Feel free to script it on your own or follow the instructions in Exercise 10.29.

Exercise 10.29: Building the Master Calendar

1. Open the **Script Editor**. Add a new tab at the end of the script. Name it **Calendar**.

2. First, type the aggregated LOAD that calculates MinDate and MaxDate based on the Date field in the LinkTable:

```
Load
      min(Date) as MinDate,
      max(Date) as MaxDate
resident
      LinkTable
;
```

3. Next, type a preceding LOAD *above* the previously entered LOAD that loads both existing fields and creates a new field TempDate using the WHILE clause. Usually, you would generate Calendar records for every single day by adding IterNo() to the MinDate. In this case, since the resolution of the analysis is monthly, you only need to generate one date for every month. Therefore, you use the AddMonths() function to iterate over months. Since the first value of IterNo() is 1, you subtract 1 to compensate. This way, the first date in the list will be the MinDate and not "one month after MinDate."

```
Load
      *,
      AddMonths(MinDate, IterNo() -1) as TempDate
WHILE
      AddMonths(MinDate, IterNo() -1) <= MaxDate
;
```

4. Next, add another preceding LOAD above the previous one and type the following Calendar calculations:

```
LOAD
        Date(TempDate) AS Date,
        Year(TempDate) AS Year,
        Month(TempDate) AS Month,
        'Q' & ceil(month(TempDate) / 3) AS Quarter,
        Year(TempDate) & '-' & 'Q' & ceil(month(TempDate) / 3) AS QuarterYear,
        Date(MonthStart(TempDate), 'MMM-YYYY') AS MonthYear,
        InMonthToDate(TempDate, MaxDate, 0) * -1 AS _CMTD_Flag,
        InMonthToDate(TempDate, MaxDate, -12) * -1 AS _PMTD_Flag,
        inyeartodate(TempDate, MaxDate, 0) * -1 AS _CYTD_Flag,
        inyeartodate(TempDate, MaxDate, -1) * -1 AS _PYTD_Flag
    ;
```

5. Now you can add logic to calculate Fiscal Period, Fiscal Year, and Fiscal Quarter. Type the following two preceding LOAD statements above the previously entered ones:

```
LOAD
        *,
        'Q' & ceil([Fiscal Period] / 3) AS [Fiscal Quarter],
        [Fiscal Year] & '-' & 'Q' & ceil([Fiscal Period] / 3)
                        AS [Fiscal QuarterYear]
    ;
LOAD
        *,
        ApplyMap('FiscalPeriod Map', num(Month), 'Error') as [Fiscal Period],
        IF(Month<4, Year, Year + 1) as [Fiscal Year]
    ;
```

6. Add the table name **Calendar:** in front of the top load. If you got lost in the multiple preceding LOAD statements, you can verify your script with the solution file \Solutions QlikView\10.29 Profitability Data.QVW.

7. **Save** and **Reload** your script. In the **Layout** view, add a **Table Box** and include all Calendar fields. Verify that the logic worked correctly and that you created monthly records with all the Calendar fields populated as expected.

A few comments about the logic in this exercise:

- We had to use so many preceding loads because each load used fields that were calculated in the previous preceding load. Remember that the preceding loads are calculated from the bottom to the top.

- We calculated the quarter number as the month number divided by 3 and rounded up using the `Ceil()` function (ceil stands for ceiling).

- We calculated all the flags using the `MaxDate` as our "current date". We do it this way because our data is frozen at a certain point in time, and we need all the YTD flags to reflect that "frozen" point in time. In your own applications, you should be using the actual current date, which is calculated using the `Today()` function.

A Few Words About Link Tables

Whew, that was fun, wasn't it? Let's examine our data structure (see Figure 10.7) and make a few final conclusions.

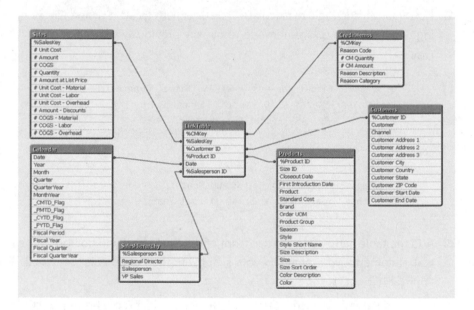

FIGURE 10.7:
Profitability data structure

As you can see, our data model resembles a star schema, with the `Link Table` positioned in the middle and facts and dimensions positioned no further than one link away. And the data modeling process wasn't way too complicated.

Link Tables can serve us quite well, when the number of fact tables is small and the volume of data is relatively low.

At the same time, Link Tables carry a number of inherent issues that can become problematic in more complex environments or with larger data volumes.

In order to demonstrate one of the key issues, we invite you to open the QlikView menu **Settings ▶ Document Properties** and display the **Tables** tab (see Figure 10.8).

In the **Tables** tab of **Document Properties**, we can gather basic information about the tables and fields that we loaded into the document. Highlighting a specific table can narrow the list of fields down. For our discussion, let's highlight the LinkTable.

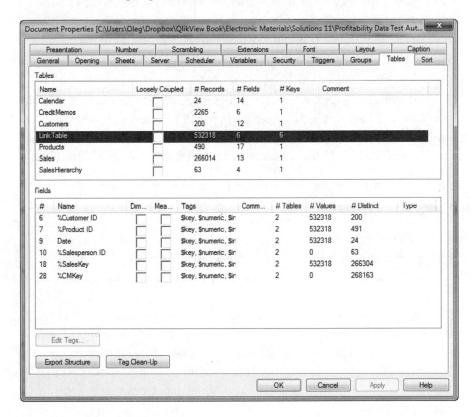

FIGURE 10.8:
Document Properties, Tables tab

For starters, let's look at the # **Records** column in the list of tables. The Sales table contains 266,014 rows. The LinkTable is nearly twice as long—this is the result of our "generic value" solution to the problem of the missing Product ID values in some of the credit memos. If we didn't have that problem, the LinkTable would have had the same size as the biggest fact table. Adding another table of that size can be very "expensive" with large data sets.

Next, let's look at the list of fields, specifically focusing on the column # **Distinct**. This column shows the number of distinct values for each field, which is very important for the memory footprint of your data. As you know from Chapter 9, the number of distinct values determines the size of the pointer that will be stored in the fact tables and in the LinkTable. Examine the fields in the LinkTable. 200 customers, 491 products, 24 dates, 63 salespersons, and—wait for it—266,304 sales keys and 268,163 credit memo keys! The cardinality of our new keys is more than 500 times higher than the longest of our original key fields! This is a *huge* difference, and it will have a huge bearing on the memory footprint of a large data set.

The pointer that covers our longest key, the Product ID, will be 9 bits long ($2^9 = 512$, which covers 491 values). The pointer for our new keys will be 18 bits ($2^{18} = 262,144$), and this longer pointer will have to be stored in two of our longest tables. This is the performance penalty that we need to pay for the convenience of linking multiple fact tables using the Link Table model.

Issue #1: Link Keys Are Heavy!

Link keys, created by listing all possible combinations of several keys, are inherently heavy. The cardinality of those fields exceeds the cardinality of the original key fields by a lot.

The other major issue with the Link Table models is less evident and you'll have to take our word for it. Since our two fact tables Sales and CreditMemos are stored separately, the measure fields in those tables are located far from each other. To be exact, there are two links (or hops between tables) that need to be processed in order to combine data from those facts into a single calculation.

> ## Issue #2: Measures in Different Tables
>
> Calculations and charts that involve measures coming from different tables will take much longer to calculate than the same calculations performed with fields from the same table. This is the biggest advantage of the star schema with a single fact table containing all the measures in one place.

You must be wondering: "Why did you have to teach me how to build Link Tables, and how do we do it better?" Well, Link Tables can still be helpful and quite convenient to use with relatively small data sets. With large data sets, the preferred solution is to implement single (or concatenated) fact tables.

You learn the concept of Concatenated Fact tables in Chapter 13, and the practical implementation of the concept in Chapter 14, where you build the data model for the next project, the Inventory Analysis.

A Round of Improvements

After developing the data model for the Profitability Analysis app, developers at the fictional company Q-Tee Brands asked the key users to test the data, to verify that all the data elements were loaded as expected, and that the data model is ready for analysis.

The users came back with the following observations and requirements:

- While the idea of linking sales and credit memos by date and summarizing by month sounded right in the beginning, the granularity of the association between sales and the corresponding credit memos got tampered with. It would be better to link the two data elements by the order number.

- Since the charges associated with the credit memos need to be attributed to the date of Sales, we can ignore the dates from the credit memos and just use the dates from the sales side.

- Our data model doesn't include another category of costs—the commissions. Those costs are not stored in any of the available databases. The commissions are calculated as a percentage of gross sales (we are using a simplified example here), and the rates differ by channel. The company changed the commission rates twice in the last two years; hence, the rates need to be loaded for a combination of channel and year/month. The data is available from a spreadsheet that is maintained by the finance group.

In this section, you perform the necessary improvements in the data model and load the additional information from the commissions spreadsheet. In the process of doing so, you learn how to load data from complex spreadsheets, including crosstable spreadsheets that contain one of the dimensions that runs across from left to right.

Modifying the Data Model to Restore Missing Associations

The first task is to modify the load script and to restore the associations between sales and credit memos. We will need to perform the following changes:

- Sales data needs to be summarized by the same GROUP BY fields plus [Order Number] as the new aggregation key.

- Credit memos data needs to be summarized by the same fields, except for the field Date, and with the field [Order Number] as the new aggregation key.

- [Order Number] needs to replace Date in all the concatenated keys and as an individual key in the LinkTable.

- The logic of generating the calendar needs to be based on the field Date coming from the Sales table instead of the LinkTable.

Feel free to make the changes on your own, following this list as a guide, or use more detailed instructions in Exercise 10.30.

Exercise 10.30: Modifying the Script to Restore Missing Associations

1. Save your QVW document with a new name **Profitability Data Improved XX.QVW**, where *XX* is your initials.

2. In the **Sum Sales** tab, add [Order Number] to the list of fields and to the list of GROUP BY fields. Replace Date with [Order Number] in the composite key.

3. In the **Credit Memos** tab, replace the field `Date` with the field `[Order Number]` in the list of fields, in the list of GROUP BY fields, and in the composite key.

4. In the **Link Table** tab, replace all appearances of the field `Date` with `[Order Number]`. (Hint: Use the **Find & Replace** feature to replace all the instances at once.)

5. In the **Calendar** tab, replace the table name `LinkTable` with the name `Sales`.

6. **Save** and **Reload** your script. Your resulting data model should look similar to the one presented in Figure 10.9.

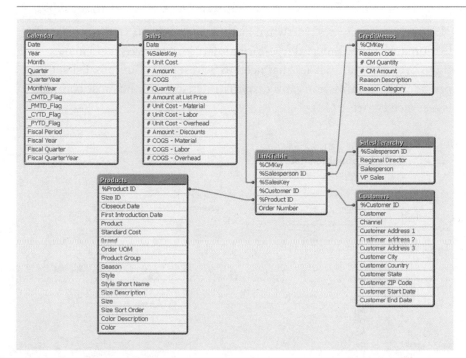

FIGURE 10.9:
Improved data model

As bad as it looked at first, this change wasn't too hard, was it? In our experience, QlikView is a very flexible tool that makes even significant structural changes quite easy to make.

Loading Complex Spreadsheets

In this section, you load the new table with the commissions data from a complex spreadsheet. You learn various techniques of cleansing and transforming spreadsheet data. You also learn how to load crosstable spreadsheets.

Data Cleansing Challenges of Loading Data from Spreadsheets

When we load data that was generated by computer systems, the data is usually clean—it's organized in a nice tabular form, with columns representing the fields and rows representing the different instances of the data. If the same value should be duplicated in multiple rows, it will be populated consistently in all rows. We typically don't expect any values to be missing and we don't expect any unnecessary data to be in the table.

The same is not always true when loading spreadsheets that are created by humans. The wonderful free-format nature of spreadsheets makes them prone to many issues that need to be resolved. The spreadsheet that provides the commission rates demonstrates some of the most common issues (see Figure 10.10).

FIGURE 10.10:

Data cleansing issues in a spreadsheet

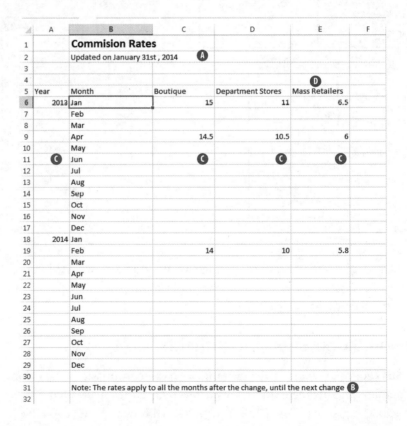

On top of the spreadsheet (A), there might be a header with the title of the table and a lot of information that might be relevant for humans, but totally irrelevant to our needs. We call this section of the spreadsheet the *header*.

Throughout the spreadsheet, there might be several lines that contain comments, subtotals, and other data elements that need to be excluded from the load (B). We call those lines the *garbage lines*.

When the same value needs to be populated in multiple rows (C), humans have a ridiculous habit of stating the value in the first line and assuming that the value applies to all underlying lines, until the new value is entered. For our needs, the missing values need to be *filled*, or populated in every line.

Many spreadsheets contain a *crosstab*—a table with one of the dimensions listed across. In those spreadsheets, the values that are listed in the *body* of the table, typically represent a single data field that's associated with the combination of the *regular* dimensions that are listed top to bottom, and the crosstable dimension listed across. In our example (Figure 10.10, D) the field `Channel` is listed across and the data in the body of the spreadsheet represents the `Commission Rate` values. Loading such a spreadsheet the usual way would result in creating five columns—`Year`, `Month`, `Boutique`, `Department Stores`, and `Mass Retailers`. This of course is not ideal for data processing. For our needs, we'd like to load a table with the structure that looks like the table in Figure 10.11.

Year	Month	Channel	Commission
2013	Apr	Boutique	14.5
2013	Apr	Department Stores	10.5
2013	Apr	Mass Retailers	6.0
2013	Aug	Boutique	14.5
2013	Aug	Department Stores	10.5
2013	Aug	Mass Retailers	6.0
2013	Dec	Boutique	14.5
2013	Dec	Department Stores	10.5
2013	Dec	Mass Retailers	6.0

FIGURE 10.11:
Resulting table after resolving the crosstab

Compare the two tables in Figures 10.10 and 10.11:

- The first two fields Year and Month remained unchanged. Those fields listed from top to bottom are called *qualifying fields* in QlikView terminology.

- The three values listed across from the Channel field. The field that is listed across is called the *attribute field*

- The values listed in the body of the table, are transformed into the field Commission. This field is called the *data field*.

In the following two sections, we will review the process of cleansing the data and resolving the crosstable in QlikView.

Loading Complex Spreadsheets in QlikView

We begin the process by activating the **Table Files** wizard. After selecting the desired spreadsheet, we land on the **Type** tab of the **File Wizard** (see Figure 10.12).

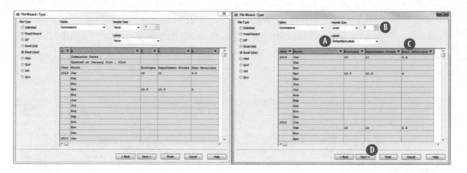

At first, the data in the table preview looks strange, because our spreadsheet begins with a number of the header lines that don't contain structured data (see the image on the left). Our first task is to get rid of the
header lines and to help QlikView recognize the field headings as labels.
It's not always easy to guess how many header lines need to be suppressed;
therefore we will follow this process (Figure 10.12, right):

1. First, select **Embedded Labels** from the **Labels** drop-down (A).

2. Then, select **Lines** from the **Header Size** drop-down and start
   increasing the number of lines in the field next to it (B).

3. Watch the labels in the table preview, while increasing the number
   of header lines. Once you see that the field names snap into place as
   labels (C), you can stop increasing the number of lines. In this case,
   the necessary number of lines is 2.

4. In previous exercises, we usually finished the wizard at this point.
   Now, since we need to perform additional transformations, we will
   click on the **Next** button and proceed to the next screen.

The next screen displays a brief explanation about the transformation step
and a single button that allows us to **Enable Transformation Step**. We
use the transformation step every time we need to cleanse the spreadsheet
data—remove garbage, fill in missing data, and so on.

Next, after enabling the transformation step, the **Transform** tab opens
(see Figure 10.13). QlikView offers five types of transformations, and the
first two are the most commonly used—**Garbage** allows deleting some of
the lines based on a condition and **Fill** allows filling in missing data, based
on the data in one of the neighboring cells (above, below, left, or right). The
other three options are less common. **Column** allows copying the contents

of one column into another column. **Unwrap** is used when the spreadsheet contains repeating sets of columns listed next to each other. **Rotate** can be used when the data in the table is listed in an unusual direction and needs to be rotated.

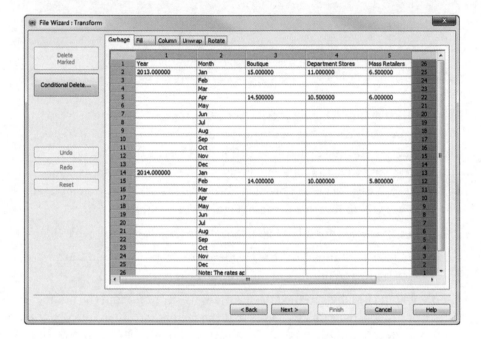

For our needs, we will use the first two transformations. On the **Garbage** tab, which opens first by default, we will click on the button **Conditional Delete** to activate the **Garbage** wizard (see Figure 10.14).

Our goal is to eliminate the line at the bottom that contains a comment that begins with the word "Note." You can see it in line 26 in Figure 10.13. Notice that the comment is entered in the second column.

As you can see in Figure 10.14, the **Conditional Delete** wizard offers four types of conditions—you can compare a value in a certain column with:

- Another value
- Another column
- Select a range of rows
- Select all rows

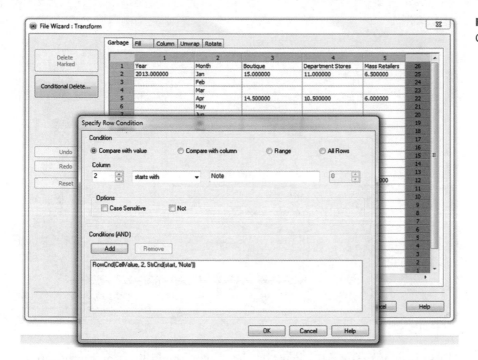

For our purposes, we will use the first condition. We will specify **Column** number **2**, then select the comparison operator **starts with** and specify the value **Note**. When necessary, we can use the optional settings **Case Sensitive** and **Not** (a logical reversal of the condition). We add the condition to the list by pressing on the **Add** button.

The resulting condition looks rather cryptic, but we don't need to worry about it. We will always use this wizard to generate conditions of this kind. At this point, we are ready to close the **Conditional Delete** wizard by pressing **OK**. Back in the **Transform** dialog, the garbage line should disappear from the table preview.

Next, we will open the **Fill** tab (see Figure 10.15). Our goal here is to fill missing values in columns 1, 3, 4, and 5. In all cases, the value is supplied from the cell above.

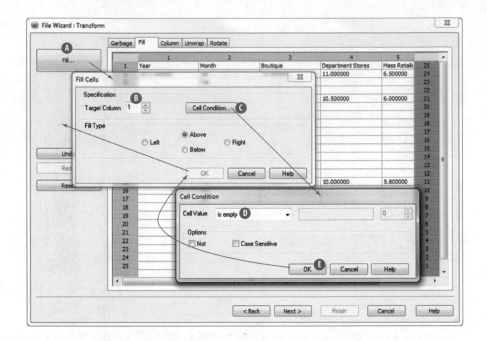

We will activate the **Fill** wizard by clicking on the **Fill** button on the left (A). The **Fill Cells** dialog opens. Here, we specify the **Target Column** (B) and click on the **Cell Condition** button (C). In the **Cell Condition** dialog, we need to select and confirm the condition. The most common condition is to fill the value when the cell is empty (D), so it's enough to accept the default by clicking on the **OK** button. Back in the **Fill Cells** dialog, we should specify the **Fill Type**. Again, the default value is **Above**, and it's the most commonly used value. Accept the default with **OK** (F) and verify the changes in the table preview.

We need to activate the **Fill** wizard four times, in order to fill missing values in four columns. As a result, you should see that correct values are populated in all five columns and in every row of the table. Notice that you can **Undo** the last transformation or **Reset** all transformations and start from scratch, using the buttons on the left.

Once we're ready, we can click **Next** to proceed to the next screen. On the next dialog, **Options** (Figure 10.16), additional wizards allow adding a **Where** clause or adding one of the two available prefixes—**Crosstable** or **Hierarchy**. At the moment, we are interested in the **Crosstable** wizard.

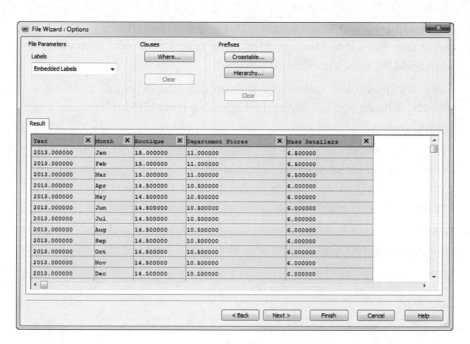

FIGURE 10.16:
File wizard: Options

Clicking on the **Crosstable** button opens the **Crosstable** wizard (see Figure 10.17). This wizard provides a color-coded guide that helps us define the **Qualifier Fields**, the **Attribute Field**, and the **Data Field**.

As a reminder, the **Qualifier Fields** (color-coded with the magenta background) represent the regular data fields that are listed from top to bottom. In our spreadsheet, we have two **Qualifier Fields**—Year and Month. Increasing the number of **Qualifier Fields** (A) to **2** results in the first two columns being highlighted with magenta.

 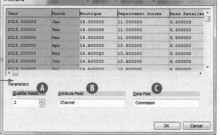

FIGURE 10.17:
The Crosstable wizard

The **Attribute Field** (color-coded with the green background) is the dimension that's listed on top of the table, from left to right. Our **Attribute Field** (B) needs to be named `Channel`.

The **Data Field** (color-coded with the turquoise background) is the measure that's listed in the body of the table. Our **Data Field** (C) needs to be named `Commission`.

Pressing **OK** results in returning to the **Options** dialog, where the table preview should already reflect the crosstable transformation. Instead of the five original columns, we now have the four columns that we wanted to have from the beginning—`Year`, `Month`, `Channel`, and `Commission`.

Now we can close the **File Wizard** with the **OK** button and examine the `LOAD` statement that was generated in the script:

```
Directory;
CrossTable(Channel, Commissions, 2)
LOAD Year,
     Month,
     Boutique,
     [Department Stores],
     [Mass Retailers]
FROM
[..\Data\Text Files\Commissions.xlsx]
(ooxml, embedded labels, header is 2 lines, table is Commissions,
   filters(
Remove(Row, RowCnd(CellValue, 2, StrCnd(start, 'Note'))),
Replace(1, top, StrCnd(null)),
Replace(3, top, StrCnd(null)),
Replace(4, top, StrCnd(null)),
Replace(5, top, StrCnd(null))
));
```

Notice that the `LOAD` statement is similar to other `LOAD` statements that we've created before, with a few new elements. The filters at the end of the statement reflect all the transformations such as garbage removal and filling the missing values.

Notice the `CrossTable` prefix in front of the load. It lists the names of the attribute field and the data field, as well as the number of the qualifier fields. It's helpful to remember this syntax, in case you need to make any changes to the number of qualifier fields, or if you decide to apply the

CROSSTABLE LOAD logic to another type of LOAD that cannot be created with the wizard.

In the list of fields, the values of the attribute field (the channel names, in our case) are listed as field names. The CROSSTABLE logic will transform these column names into the values of the attribute field. However, this syntax is not very flexible. If another column needs to be added in the future, this script needs to be revisited. For this reason, we recommend replacing the list of fields with a single asterisk to signify all fields. This way, the statement will remain valid even if new columns should be added to the spreadsheet.

In the following exercise, you will practice all the transformations described in this section.

Exercise 10.31: Loading a Complex Spreadsheet

1. Create a new QlikView document and store it with the name Commissions Transformation.QVW in the folder \Data Loaders\.

2. Using the wizards described in this section, load the data from the Commissions.xlsx spreadsheet, which is stored in the \Data\Text Files\ subfolder. Use the Transformation tools Fill and Garbage and the Crosstable wizard.

3. Name the new table Temp_Commissions.

4. Save and Reload your script. Examine the results.

Transforming the Commissions Data

In the previous section, we cleansed the data coming from a spreadsheet, and we resolved a crosstable. Now, our data table contains four fields— Year, Month, Channel, and Commission. We need to perform a few additional transformations before we can use this data in our data model.

First, we need to transform Year and Month into a proper date field. Notice that the month is listed as a three-character string. What could we do in this case? One way would be to map month names to month numbers, using a mapping table, and then to build a Date field using the MakeDate(Year, Month, Day) function. Sounds like too much trouble, though.

The easier way is to use the existing data to form a string that contains a date in a certain format and then convert that string into a date using the `Date#()` casting function. The following expression creates a string that corresponds to the first day of the month/year:

```
num(Year, '0000') & '/' & Month & '/1'
```

Notice that we are formatting the `Year` into a four-digit number. This is necessary because the values in the field `Year` were loaded with several decimal digits (see Figure 10.16 as an example). Formatting the `Year` this way ensures that we only use the four digit numbers.

Enclosing this expression in the `Date#()` function, with the proper formatting string, results in converting the string into the date field:

```
date#( num(Year, '0000') & '/' & Month & '/1', 'YYYY/MMM/D')
```

Finally, the latter needs to be enclosed in the `Date()` function, in order to reformat the date field to the default date format:

```
date(date#( num(Year, '0000') & '/' & Month & '/1', 'YYYY/MMM/D'))
```

A Few Side Comments About Date Formats

You might be wondering about the specific date formats and what should be used where—why three characters in MMM and why only one D character? Here are a few basic rules about date formatting:

- Year is typically presented with either four or two characters—YYYY or YY

- Month can be presented in one, two, three, or four M characters:

  - M—Month numbers with no leading zeroes, such as 1, 2, 3, ... 12.

  - MM—Month numbers with leading zeroes, such as 01, 02, 03, ... 12.

  - MMM—Month names in three letters, such as Jan, Feb, Mar, ...

  - MMMM—Month names in full words, such as January, February, March, ...

- Day can be presented in one or two characters—with or without the leading zeroes.

- Date formats are always described with upper case letters, while timestamps are described with lower case letters (because the letter "m" is being used in both).

This transformation solves the need to create a proper date field from a year and a textual month name.

The second transformation that's needed in this table is the commission rate itself. Notice that the percentages have been entered into the spreadsheet as whole numbers. We should divide those numbers by 100 in order to enable using them as percentages in all the calculations.

The CROSSTABLE LOAD that we used to load the spreadsheet is quite quirky when it comes to transformations. Most of the transformations that are available in regular loads don't quite work in a CROSSTABLE LOAD . Similarly, PRECEDING LOAD on top of a CROSSTABLE LOAD will not work as expected. For this reason, we usually load the crosstable data as is and then add any necessary transformations in the subsequent RESIDENT LOAD.

Feel free to perform the described transformations on your own or follow the detailed instructions in Exercise 10.32.

Exercise 10.32: Transforming the Commissions Data

1. Continue the script that you started in Exercise 10.31.

2. Add the following RESIDENT LOAD after the CROSSTABLE LOAD that you generated earlier:
   ```
   Commissions:
   Load
        Channel,
        date(date#( num(Year, '0000') & '/' & Month & '/1', 'YYYY/MMM/D')) as Date,
        Commission/100 as [# Commission Percent]
   Resident
        Temp_Commissions
   ;
   ```

3. Drop the temporary table Temp_Commissions:
   ```
   drop table Temp_Commissions;
   ```

4. Store the table Commissions into a transformed QVD file in the \Transformed QVDs folder:
   ```
   STORE Commissions into ..\Data\Transformed QVDs\T_Commissions.QVD;
   ```

5. Save and Reload your script. Verify that the transformed QVD file was generated in the requested folder.

Adding Commissions Data to the Data Model

The only remaining piece of the puzzle is to add the new data into our data model. While it sounds fairly simple, it's actually not too obvious.

The commissions' data needs to be joined to the sales data, since the percentage rate needs to be applied to the gross sales. Commissions are defined per Channel and Date. The Channel field, however, doesn't exist in the Sales table. It's currently part of the Customers table. See the problem? We can't join commissions by Channel if Channel doesn't exist in the Sales table.

However, we already know all the techniques necessary for this data transformation.

1. The Channel field needs to be populated in the Sales table. This can be done either through joining or using mapping. Our preference is to use mapping.

2. The new Commissions table can be joined into Sales by Channel and Date.

3. The Channel field needs to be dropped from Sales to avoid unnecessary links and circular references.

Feel free to perform these transformations on your own or follow detailed instructions in Exercise 10.33.

Exercise 10.33: Adding Commissions to the Data Model

1. Open the Profitability Data XX.QVW document that we worked with earlier in this chapter. Open the Script Editor.

2. In the Mapping tab, create a Mapping LOAD from the transformed QVD file T_Customers.QVD. Load [%Customer ID] and Channel. Name the map Channel_Map:

```
Channel_Map:
MAPPING
LOAD
     [%Customer ID],
     Channel
FROM
[..\Data\Transformed QVDs\T_Customers.QVD]
(qvd);
```

3. In the **Sum Sales** tab, add the following line to the first (from the top) preceding load, in order to add `Channel` to the `Sales` table:

```
ApplyMap('Channel_Map', [%Customer ID], '') as Channel,
```

4. At the bottom of the **Sum Sales** tab, add a `JOIN LOAD` to join the `Commissions` data into `Sales`:

```
LEFT JOIN (Sales)
LOAD
      Channel,
      Date,
      [# Commission Percent]
FROM
[..\Data\Transformed QVDs\T_Commissions.QVD]
(qvd);
```

5. Drop the `Channel` field from `Sales`:

```
Drop Field Channel from Sales;
```

6. Save and Reload your script. Verify that the [# Commission Percent] is populated in 100% of the Sales rows.

This exercise completes the process of building the data model for the Profitability Analysis app.

Explaining the Multi-Tier Data Architecture

At this time, let's step back and describe everything we've done in this chapter at a high level. In essence, we described how QlikView professionals typically perform the three steps of the ETL process—*Extraction, Transformation,* and *Load*. Another common name for the same process is the *multi-tier data architecture*. In this section we describe each step in detail (see Figure 10.18).

First, in Exercises 10.1–10.11, we described the various techniques you can use to simplify and automate the *Extraction* process—reading the raw data and storing it into a set of raw QVD files. This is the Tier 1 of the multi-tier process, commonly referred to as the "Raw QVD" tier. These QlikView scripts, commonly called "QVD Generators," were stored in the \Data Loaders subfolder, and the resulting QVD files were stored in the \QVDs subfolder. The goal of this step is to extract the data from the source databases as quickly as possible. At this stage, incremental loads are often used to speed up the process of loading large data tables.

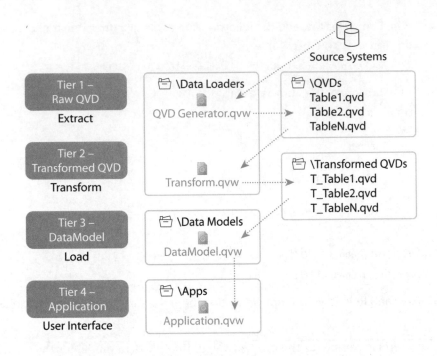

Then, in Exercises 10.12–10.15 and 10.31–10.32, we described the *Transformation* process—loading the data previously stored in raw QVDs or in other text files, and performing various transformations to make the data more useable for analytic needs. This is the Tier 2 of the multi-tier process, commonly referred to as the "Transformed QVD" tier. These QlikView scripts, also called "QVD Generators" or "Transformation Scripts," were stored in the \Data Loaders subfolder, and the resulting QVD files were stored in the \Transformed QVDs subfolder. The goal of this step is to transform the raw data in the consistent manner and to apply business rules that need to be followed in multiple analytical applications.

After that, in Exercises 10.16–10.29 and 10.33, we described the *Load* process—we loaded the data into a specific data model (sometimes referred to as "data mart" or "QlikMart") that will be used for the Profitability Analysis dashboard. Here we used QlikView data modelling techniques to resolve any structural issues in our data model. This is the Tier 3 of the multi-tier process, commonly referred to as the "Data Model" tier. These QlikView scripts and the resulting data sets, combined in the same QVW document, were stored in the \Data Models subfolder. The goal of this step is to load all data tables that are necessary for the specific application and to arrange them in error-free efficient data structure, such as a star schema or a snowflake.

The resulting data model is then loaded into the final analytical application using the BINARY load (we described that in Chapter 8, for educational purposes). This is the fourth and the final tier in the multi-tier process. The final applications were stored in the \Apps subfolder. Keeping this step separate allows QlikView teams to split responsibility between developers and business analysts. When necessary, different people can be responsible for each one of the four tiers of the data load process.

This is a typical example of implementing a multi-tier data architecture in a mature QlikView environment.

This brief overview of the process completes Part III, "Expanding Your Skill Set: Profitability Analysis," and our discussion of Profitability Analysis. In Part IV, "Mastering Advanced Techniques: Inventory Analysis," we continue introducing advanced QlikView techniques, demonstrating them on the business requirements for the Inventory Analysis dashboard.

Mastering Advanced Techniques: Inventory Analysis

Defining a Business Scenario for Inventory Analysis

This chapter describes the common business challenges related to inventory management. It describes what inventory is and how it should be analyzed in order to optimize your company's cash flow and operational results.

What Is Inventory—Asset or Liability?

Inventory: What does it mean to you and your business? Inventory means something different depending on your perspective:

- **Owner of a business**—it is a headache that must be managed to service the customer. The worry is that it will take up all the cash needed to invest properly in the business.

- **Investor in a company and the chief financial officer**—it is a drain on cash flow that is a necessary investment to service customers. The worry is: can it be converted into enough cash to pay the bills and make money?

- **The lender to a business**—it is a use of cash. The worry is: can it be converted into enough cash to pay the bills?

- **Vice president of sales**—it is required to service the customer. The worry is that there will not be enough of what the customer wants when the customer wants it.

- **Chief operating officer**—it is something required to meet production/shipping schedules. The worry is that the COO will be blamed if there is not the right amount on hand at any point in time.

- **Employees who have to handle it**—it is necessary to service customers. The worry is finding the asset that they need. Can I find what I am supposed to move?

- **The financial statements**—it is described as an asset.

It appears that deep down, everybody knows that inventory is something needed to attract and retain customers. Paying customers keep the business running and the paychecks coming! Therefore, inventory is a good thing, right? On the other hand, if some of the worries mentioned here are familiar to you, then you might wonder sometimes if inventory and all that goes into managing it really is a good thing.

The mix and amount of inventory you have on hand at any time is a significant worry regardless of your perspective. In addition to what is on hand, the flow (timing) of inventory is also a significant worry. Both mix/amount and flow affect the value of your inventory. Think about your blood. There is a need for blood cells to replenish on a regular basis and flow relatively uninterrupted or the quality (its value to you) of your blood is diminished. Inventory is the lifeblood of a business. If it does not replenish and flow properly, you will have significant business health problems. Having too much or too little inventory can be equally detrimental.

Having inventory means you must pay for, protect, and handle it. That investment takes cash. When you have more inventory than you need, it requires using cash that could be used for investments in other parts of the business. The cost (cash) of *excess* inventory does not earn any return on your investment because there is no revenue or earnings on inventory when it remains unsold. Inventory that does not sell is in fact a liability, not an asset. On the other hand, not having enough inventory results in lost revenue and is equally as bad as too much inventory.

The reality is that the right amount of inventory at the right time allows a company to maximize its revenue while minimizing its costs. The result is making the highest return on investment possible.

Consider the following example. The financial statements of a business show inventory valued at $17 million dollars. That fact by itself does not tell you if $17 million is good or bad. Without more information, you don't know if that business should do anything differently. Let's add another fact: The inventory balance in dollars is equal to the annual sales of the company. Again the facts don't give you enough information to make decisions to change what the company is doing. Perhaps one turn of inventory per year is appropriate for that business. If the company is in the business of manufacturing heavy machinery and the production cycle takes a year, the one turn per year might be acceptable.

Factors to Consider When Measuring Inventory

Your inventory of course needs to be accurate. With this in mind, there is a number of factors to consider when measuring and analyzing inventory.

- Customer and operationally driven factors include:
  - **The demand for the product**—this is critical because it is referring to who wants your product, when they want it, and how much they want. Timing of demand is frequently referred to as a *forecast*.
  - **The manufacturing cycle time**—this involves how long it takes to manufacture, assemble, package, and ship the products.
  - **The supply chain lead time for raw materials and components**—this is the time that it takes to get the raw materials and/or components to your place of manufacturing and assembly, in order to build new inventory when it's needed.
  - **The shelf life of the products**—how long the product will last after it's made. For example, a cake may have a shelf life of four days, while a knife may have an indefinite shelf life because it

does not go bad after a period of time. Shelf life may refer to the ingredients, as in the previous example; however, it may also refer to the life of a style or trend.

- **The age of the inventory**—this can be referred to as days on hand using a forward-looking forecast. It can also refer to how long you kept the inventory on hand, using the receipt date. This is related to shelf life factors as well as valuation.

- Financially driven factors include:

  - **The carrying cost of the inventory**—the cost of carrying inventory includes:

    - The cost of locations you need to keep it in (warehouses and so on).

    - The costs to move the inventory (forklifts, trucks, people, and so on).

    - The cost to finance the difference between the time you pay for the inventory and the time you convert it into cash.

    - Cost of insurance against loss.

  - **The cost of the inventory**—the actual cost of the components and finished products. It is related to the carrying cost and the cash flow factors of inventory.

  - **The company's requirement for timing of cash flow**—the timing of cash flow in and out of a business is heavily dependent on inventory movement. You need to know if the timing of converting inventory into cash meets your requirements to make cash payments.

  - **Valuation**—this is the net value reported in your financial statements. It is equal to the amount you paid for the item less any reserve you may have taken against the amount paid for various reasons.

We have described the major factors when measuring and analyzing inventory. Analyzing these factors can require a lot of information, processes, systems, and human resources. That said, *perfect information always costs too much*!

The reason we describe them as factors to consider is because you don't want to spend more money on addressing some of the factors than the benefit of doing so. Consider a product that involves some sort of fastener like a bolt. Let's also consider that this bolt cost 2 cents each and that the manufacturing cycle time for the bolt is 2 months. The effort of hand counting every bolt you receive and every bolt in inventory probably costs more than it would be to use other techniques to manage that item in inventory. In this example, you could avoid the cost and effort of counting the individual bolts by estimating the count by weight. In addition, you could keep a "safety stock," or a minimum amount of bolts in excess of demand, to cover any inaccuracies of the weight mechanism. The cost of extra bolts at 2 cents a piece is far less than stopping production because you ran out due to an inaccurate count. In this example, the factors of *cost of the product*, *timing of demand*, and *carrying costs* are not as important to consider in light of interrupting the factor of *production cycle time*.

The Definition of Inventory Analysis

With all of this in mind, let's go back to the business case discussed earlier that has inventory value equal to the annual sales value. That company did not know enough information about the factors that relate to their inventory to know how good or bad the inventory was.

The priorities for understanding your inventories are, in order of importance:

1. Demand for the inventory
2. Lead times
3. Shelf life of the inventory
4. Costs

These four critical factors lead to the determination of cash flow requirements, valuation, and your ability to meet the service demands of your customers.

> **NOTE**
>
> Earlier in this chapter, we said that inventory is the lifeblood of your company and can be likened to the blood in your body. Your blood is best measured and analyzed at the cellular level. The cellular level is the lowest unit of measure. Likewise, inventory is best measured and analyzed at the lowest unit of measure.

Commonly Used Metrics for Inventory Analysis

In order to go deep into managing and analyzing the lifeblood of your business—your inventory—you must be able to access data at the individual item level (sometimes referred to as SKU—stock keeping unit). The ability to analyze your inventory at the item level will allow you to make decisions that are critical to the health of your business. Consider these questions:

- How much inventory do you need to service your customer demand?
- When do you need that inventory?
- How much cash flow do you need to invest in inventory?
- When do you need that cash?
- Are your inventories valued properly?

These are all forward-looking questions that require a good forecasting methodology for customer demand. These critical questions can also be reviewed with respect to the inventory you have on hand at any moment. Even if you had good answers to these questions in the past, things change. Customers change, products and their components change, and production and sourcing methods change. Because of the ongoing changes, the best in class companies have analytical methods to review inventory on a regular basis. This ongoing review helps you understand and address the potential effect on inventories brought about by ongoing changes in your business. You can then be in a position to answer the critical questions:

- Do your business processes result in having the right inventory at the right time to service your customer demand?
- Are your inventories valued properly?
- Are you managing cash as effectively as possible?

The following is the list of the quantitative metrics that are commonly used for analyzing inventory and answering those critical questions.

- **What items in inventory have less than the forecasted demand**—this, along with lead time information, will allow you to calculate when you can service the customer and communicate with the customer accordingly. The metrics here include:

- Inventory on hand less historical or future forecasted demand. A negative result in this calculation represents a shortage of inventory to meet requirements.
- Analyzing the timing and quantities of inventory that will be received or manufactured.

- **What inventory is in excess of demand**—this will allow you to look at specific actions to turn that inventory into cash as quickly as possible. Metrics here include:
  - **Days on hand**—this metric tells you how many days it will take to use up the inventory you have on hand at any point in time. Ideally, the inventory should be compared to future demand (forecast and orders). When future demand is unknown, historical sales may be used instead. The inventory balance is divided by the average daily demand. It's important to determine the appropriate time frame when calculating the average demand. This may include considerations of seasonality, promotions, and so on.
  - **Inventory turns**—this metric shows how many times a year the inventory is turned into cash. Higher turns lead to higher profits on the same inventory investment. The metric is calculated as annual cost of sales divided by annualized average inventory.
  - **Inventory in excess of demand**—this metric is calculated as on hand balance minus the future demand. A positive result represents an excess of inventory to meet requirements. In absence of future demand, this calculation can be replaced by calculating inventory in excess of X months of historical sales. The desired number of months may be tied to the product lead time for more accurate evaluation.
  - **Inventory aging**—this metric displays inventory balances identified by age buckets. Ideally, the age is determined by the receipt date of each inventory lot (when inventory is managed in lots). When lot data is not available, the age can be calculated manually, using the first-in-first-out (FIFO) logic. The FIFO

method assumes that the most recently received inventory is the current one on the shelf.

- **Inventory by ABC class**—many companies use ABC codes to classify their products. When available, ABC classification can be used to analyze inventory in terms of velocity and value.

- **What is the current recorded cost of excess inventory**—if the cash you can get for the item is less than its current recorded cost, you have a valuation issue that must be addressed. The metric used here is:

  - **Lower of cost or market test**—this is the difference between the cost you paid for an item in inventory based on the invoice and what you could sell that item for in the market. If the market value is less than the recorded value, you have overstated the value of the inventory (your asset). The market value can be one of several possibilities:

    - Zero, because you have to throw away the item. This case would clearly be below your recorded value.

    - Some scrap value. This case would also clearly be below your recorded value.

    - The price you could sell the item for.

Common Data Elements Required for Inventory Analysis

To perform this type of ongoing analysis, you need to access the following data:

- On-hand quantities and costs
- Inventory history in monthly buckets
- Inventory transactions in units and dollars, by date
- Shipments history, in the most detailed form (usually the same as invoice history)
- Demand forecast in units, when available

- Lead times for products and materials
- Units of measure and conversion rates
- For raw materials inventory analysis, bills of materials are used to calculate demand

Some of the more advanced analytic applications may also include analysis of future receipts from purchasing and manufacturing.

For raw materials inventory analysis, forecasted demand in units must be derived from product forecasts (usually by customer) that are bumped up against the bill of materials to give you demand extended at the item level.

Admittedly, inventory analysis requires building a complex data structure involving many different data elements. However, implementing inventory analysis can be extremely beneficial to the cash flow of your business.

The Benefits of Advanced Inventory Analysis

With the proper analysis, I believe that most businesses can achieve 20% to 30% reduction in inventory investment, thus improving their cash flow by that same amount.

NOTE

The fictitious company in our example, which had $17 million in inventory, had not analyzed its inventory in many years. Their time was consumed with trying to meet customer order requirements.

They had the following issues:

- Their existing systems were not used as an ERP or MRP tool.
- They didn't know what the demand going forward was for their product.
- Service levels (product delivered on time and complete) had dropped to 40%.
- Sales had been declining at a rapid rate.

As a result of all these issues, it was all hands on deck just to try to meet the existing customer orders. They knew they had problems with their inventory, but they didn't have analytical information to determine what action to take. Does this sound familiar?

They were able to begin with some basic information and processes. They took steps available to most any business regardless of IT systems.

Initial actions taken:

- Took steps to get their inventory accurate and measure accuracy with a combination of cycle counts and physical inventories.

- Began to forecast the demand by product and customer.

- Turned demand into material requirements.

- Began to analyze inventory in terms of demand excesses or shortages at the item level.

- Began to analyze days on hand.

- Implemented an advanced Inventory Analysis dashboard using QlikView.

As a result of their analysis, they discovered:

- Over half of their inventory was significantly in excess of demand.

- A full third of the inventory was obsolete.

- Critical raw materials and components for products were not ordered within the lead times to meet customer demand for the finished product.

- Their cash flow was significantly retarded because of poor inventory management.

With proper implementation of some basic processes like forecasting and tying purchasing decisions to demand and lead time, the company was able to achieve significant results. Those results were:

- Inventory required to run the business was reduced, freeing up cash flow.

- Existing obsolete inventory was turned into cash.

- Critical raw materials and components were ordered on time to meet customer demand.

- Service levels rose to 98%.

- Excess and obsolete inventory was minimized going forward, identified sooner in the product life cycle, and turned into cash more quickly.
- Inventory was valued properly.
- *Sales began to grow again!*

The following chapters describe the process of building a simplified Inventory Analysis dashboard. Developing a similar dashboard at your company could help you identify and realize as much as 20% to 30% savings in inventory investments.

For the sake of simplicity and educational value, this simplified model focuses on the following aspects:

- Analyzes the existing inventory in comparison to historical sales, without including future demand. The goal of this analysis is to identify excess inventory and report on it at various levels of detail.

- Limits the analysis to finished goods inventory, in comparison to sales history. For the purpose of this simplified model, we are not going to load bills of materials that are typically used to calculate true demand for raw materials.

- Doesn't perform an advanced inventory valuation since this exercise requires manual data input from the sales and marketing management of the company.

12

Visualizing Inventory Analysis in QlikView

In this chapter, you build the visual part of the Inventory Analysis solution in QlikView. In doing so, we will introduce advanced QlikView visualization techniques. In the process, you will learn how to:

- Use dollar-sign expansions with parameters.
- Present performance as of a past date, using the As of Date technique.
- Use Advanced Aggregation (AGGR) for a number of analytic purposes, including nested aggregation, building histograms, and more.

Developing the Key Measures for Inventory Analysis

This section covers all the preparations and develops some of the basic visualizations that you are already familiar with, only this time within the context of inventory analysis.

Preparing the Environment for Inventory Analysis

Before we delve into the task of building visualizations, let's describe the main measures that will be used in inventory analysis, walk through the data model, and get a general understanding of the task ahead.

Key Measures for the Inventory Analysis

Chapter 11 described the key metrics that are typically used for Inventory Analysis. Now, let's define those metrics included in the educational sample and get more detailed in our definitions.

We will be using the following measures for the Inventory Analysis application:

- **Current or Historical On Hand Balance**—this is a simple sum of the On Hand Balance amount, presented for the current date or for a historical date. We will use date-related conditional flags and filters to select the appropriate time frame.

- **Days On Hand**—we will calculate Days On Hand using historical sales. We will divide the current inventory balance by the average daily sales for the last 12 months.

- **Average Daily Sales**—since our data model is aggregated on the monthly level, we will divide the sum of the Rolling 12 Months of Sales by the Number of Days since the First Date of Sales for the Product within the Last 12 Months.

- **Inventory Turns**—to remind you, this KPI shows the velocity of the product's turnaround. It shows how many times a year the inventory is sold out and replenished. We will calculate turns by dividing the 12 Months Cost of Sales by the 12 Months Average of On Hand Balance.

- **12 Months Average of On Hand Balance**—this will be calculated as a sum of On Hand Balance history records for 12 months, divided by the number of months in the same period.

- **Excess Inventory**—we will calculate Excess Inventory as the portion of the On Hand Balance that exceeds a certain number of Months of Sales.

- **Inventory Aging**—aged balances are presented as On Hand amounts divided into separate buckets by age.

Note that many of these metrics have to be calculated by product and only then aggregated at a higher level. Measuring these metrics at the total level would be as effective as measuring the average temperature across all of the patients in a hospital.

Let's clarify with an example. Imagine that you are managing three products. Two of them are top sellers. They sell out very quickly, and you can't replenish the inventory fast enough. Based on the sales and on the average inventory, the two products show over 12 inventory turns a year. The third product never took off, and the sales have been sluggish. The initial forecast never materialized, and now you are sitting on an on hand balance that can cover 12 months of sales. The product made less than one annual turn. On average, you would see three products with decent annual turns (approximately 5-6). However, in reality you know that you have two excellent products and one product that needs to be discontinued, with an inventory balance that needs to be liquidated one way or another.

In this chapter, you learn how to calculate metrics that need to be aggregated at a specific level of detail and how to visualize such metrics more effectively than by simply showing the averages.

Describing the Inventory Data Model

In Exercise 12.1, you start by creating a new QlikView document and loading the data model. After that, we describe the data model.

Exercise 12.1: Loading the Inventory Data Model

1. Create a new QlikView document. If necessary, cancel out of the New Document wizard.

2. Save the document in the subfolder \Apps with the name **Inventory Analysis** and add your initials at the end of the document name. Saving this document in the proper location is important. If you choose to save your document elsewhere, some of the included scripts in the following exercises may not work properly.

3. Open Settings ▶ Document Properties and make the following choices:

   3.1. In the General tab, ensure that Styling Mode is defined as Simplified, and Sheet Object Style is Transparent. Change the Background Color to pure white.

   3.2. In the Presentation tab, ensure that NS_Flat.qvt is selected as the Default Theme for New Objects. If needed, navigate to the subfolder \Resources\Themes\ to select the file.

4. Open the Script Editor. Activate the QlikView Files wizard and select the file Inventory Data.QVW from the subfolder \Data Models\. You should see that the BINARY statement is added to the beginning of the script.

5. Save and Reload the document. Open the Table Viewer and examine the data model.

The data model should look similar to Figure 12.1.

In the data model you just loaded, we implemented the Single Fact technique. The Fact table contains slices of data combined from multiple fact tables. The field FactType qualifies each "slice" with its own name—Sales, OnHand, and Aging.

FIGURE 12.1:
Inventory data model

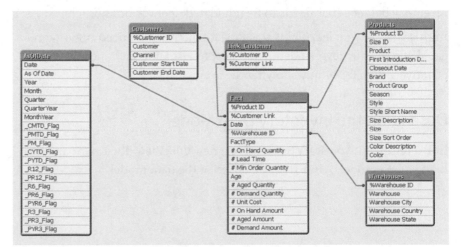

Three main dimensions are linked to the Fact table — Warehouses, Products, and Customers. As you can see, the Customers table is linked to the Fact table indirectly. A special link table Link_Customer connects the two tables. This is called a *Generic Link Table*. We describe this technique in Chapters 13 and 14. For now, let's just say that the Generic Link Table restores the missing association between Customers and On Hand balances for the Products that they purchased. This association was lost when the two tables (Sales and On Hand balances) were concatenated into the same Fact table.

Another table that deserves your attention is called the AsOfDate table. In this data model, this table replaces the traditional Master Calendar. We describe it in the following section.

What the As of Date Table Is and How to Use It in Visualizations

The AsOfDate table is needed when there is a requirement to report performance not only for the current date, but also for other dates in the past (hence the name As of Date).

For example, we used the calendar flags to calculate Current YTD Sales, compared to Prior YTD Sales. The YTD flags were calculated in the Master Calendar, based on the Current Date. Now, the users request that we calculate YTD Sales compared to Prior YTD Sales, as of May 1st, or as of July 1st, or as of any date in the past that the application can support.

Now, it's not enough to calculate the YTD flag based on the Current Date only. We need to calculate all date-related flags for all possible values of the As of Date.

Once again, the essence of the As of Date solution is described in Chapters 13 and 14. For now, you need to understand how to work with the AsOfDate table when building visualizations.

As you can see, there are two date fields in the AsOfDate table—the usual Date field and the field [As Of Date]. The Date field is linked to the Fact table. This is the transactional date and it should not be used directly in sheet objects.

The [As of Date] is the date that needs to be selected by the user. The essence of the [As of Date] analysis requires that a single [As of Date] be selected at all times. This selection drives the associated `Date` values through the use of conditional flags. For example, if the calculation requires the `Date` values that belong to the same month as the selected [As of Date], then the corresponding Set Analysis condition should be:

```
_CMTD_Flag = {1}
```

If we need to include rolling 12 months of sales, the condition should be:

```
_R12_Flag = {1}
```

The unfortunate aspect of the As of Date solution is that it requires that almost every expression in the document be equipped with a Set Analysis condition that includes one of the date-related filters.

Take another look at the `AsOfDate` table in Figure 12.1. Notice the 13 date-related flags that describe various relations between the two date fields. Each chart expression in our application will need to be equipped with a Set Analysis filter that involves one of those flags. Following the same best practices that you learned in Chapter 8, we should store these 13 filters in variables for future use.

Since you already know how to use the input box for storing formulas and filters in variables, there wouldn't be much value in entering 13 new variables manually. Instead, we will load the variables from a text file. For now, just sit back, relax, and enjoy the ride. In Chapter 14, you will learn how to develop the script that generates variables using their definitions loaded from a text file.

Exercise 12.2: Loading Variables from a Text File

1. Open the Script Editor.

2. Create a new tab and name it **Variables**.

3. Using the Insert menu, add an INCLUDE statement to include a snippet of script from the file \Scripts\Load Expressions.txt:

   `$(Include=..\scripts\load expressions.txt);`

4. Save and Reload the document. Open Settings ▶ Variable Overview and verify that a number of new variables, including the 13 filters, were created in the document.

Now you can use the 13 filters for chart expressions as necessary. For example, if you need to calculate YTD Demand (Sales), you would use the following:

```
sum({<_CYTD_Flag={1} >} [# Demand Amount])
```

On the other hand, if you needed to aggregate demand for the rolling six months, you would use the following:

```
sum({<_R6_Flag={1} >} [# Demand Amount])
```

"Wait a minute!" you should be thinking at this point, "Are you telling me that I need to prepare *13* versions of each expression? That is way too much to maintain!" And we totally agree. Maintaining 13 versions of each expression is certainly way too much. There must be a better solution!

As usual, there is. And, to everyone's relief and convenience, it's coming up in the next section.

Using Dollar-Sign Expansions with Parameters

So far, we've used two forms of dollar-sign expansions—with a variable and with an expression. Now, we introduce another form of variable expansion. You can use formal parameters in the variable definition and then call the variable expansion with specific values that will replace the formal parameters.

The formal parameters are presented as $1, $2, $3, and so on. The actual parameters are listed similarly to any function parameters—in a comma-separated list, enclosed in a pair of quotes.

For example, you can add a new variable vGreeting and enter the following as the variable definition:

```
'Hello, ' & $1 & '!'
```

Now, you can use this variable with actual parameters to generate different outcomes:

```
=$(vGreeting('World'))
```

We admit, this is not the easiest way of saying "Hello, World!" Perhaps the benefits of this feature become more evident when you use it with the expressions.

Examine the two Demand formulas in the previous section. Both formulas aggregate Demand, with the Set Analysis filter being the only moving part. You can store the definition of the formula in a variable `exp_Demand`, using this format:

```
Sum ( {<$1>}  [# Demand Amount])
```

Now, you can expand the variable `exp_Demand` with different actual parameters:

```
= $(exp_Demand('_CYTD_Flag={1}'))
= $(exp_Demand('_R6_Flag={1}'))
```

Or, you can take it a step further and replace the filters with the corresponding variables that are in turn represented by dollar-sign expansions:

```
= $(exp_Demand($(filter_CYTD)))
```

Now you can eliminate the need to maintain 13 copies of the same expression. Using this technique, you can keep only one copy of each expression and apply the necessary filters as parameters.

Exercise 12.3: Creating Formulas Using Variables with Parameters

1. In the layout view, add a new sheet and name it **Variables**.

2. Create a new **Input Box**. Open the input box's **Properties** and add two new variables: `exp_OnHand` and `exp_Demand`.

3. Enter the following expression as the definition of the variable `exp_OnHand`:

```
sum({<$1>} [# On Hand Amount])
```

4. Enter the following expression as the definition of the variable `exp_Demand`:

```
sum({<$1>} [# Demand Amount])
```

5. Create a new **Straight Table** chart. Select `[As Of Date]` as a dimension.

6. Add two expressions. Leave the **Labels** empty and only enter the following **Definitions**:

   6.1. The On Hand Balance in the month of the `As of Date`:

```
=$(exp_OnHand($(filter_CMTD)))
```

   6.2. The Demand for rolling 6 months:

```
=$(exp_Demand($(filter_R6)))
```

7. In the **Number** tab, format both numbers as integers.

8. Accept all changes and examine the result.

We'd like to point out the technique of leaving the expression Label empty. Notice that the column headers show fully expanded definitions of the formulas. This is helpful when developing expressions using dollar-sign expansions with parameters. You can examine the end result of the expansion and troubleshoot any possible problems here.

Preparing the Template for Inventory Analysis

It's time to prepare the template for the new Inventory Analysis document. In the interest of time, in Exercise 12.4, you will use the same screen layout as you did in your previous applications. Therefore, you will copy the common layout elements from the Profitability Analysis document and tweak a few elements.

The biggest difference is in the date-related objects. Since inventory is a snapshot taken at a point in time, there is not much value is selecting Years and Months. Instead, you need to allow users to select a single As Of Date.

You could add a list box with the field [As Of Date] in it. However, we believe that a single selected value will look better in a multi box, where it only takes a single row and where the values can be selected from a drop-down list, enabled on demand.

Due to the nature of the As of Date solution, a single value for the [As Of Date] should be selected at all times. If more than one value of [As of Date] becomes available, most of your expressions will show incorrect results. It's possible to configure a list box or a field in a multi box to have **Always One Selected Value**. This setting is located in the **Presentation** tab of the multi box (for list boxes, it's the **General** tab). Most of the time, this checkbox is disabled. It becomes enabled when a single value is selected in the field. Once **Always One Selected Value** is enabled, QlikView will guard that single selection. It becomes impossible to **Clear** that selection. It's also impossible to make another selection that may cause this selection to disappear. Notably, this setting is managed for the field, not for the specific list box or multi box. Therefore, it's enough that one list box in the whole application is configured with **Only One Selected Value**, and the rest of the list boxes for the same field will share the same behavior.

Beware of Reducing Data!

The feature Always One Selected Value is used when it's critically important that one and only one value is selected at all times. However, if you need to reduce all data in your QlikView document and then you restore all data later, the setting disappears. It's only available when a single value is selected, and it can't be available if the document contains no data. Remember to restore this setting if you have to reduce data in your documents.

For the same reason, you need to restore this setting if you ever copy our solution from the folder \Solutions QlikView\. Our solutions are saved with no data, in order to save disk space, therefore the Always One Selected Value setting has to be restored after you reload the data again.

Other minor changes involve the list boxes along the left edge of the sheet. We will replace Channel with Warehouse and remove Salesperson, which is not available anymore, from the multi box with **Other Filters**. The rest of the filters can remain the same.

Exercise 12.4: Preparing a Template for Inventory Analysis

1. You should already have the Inventory Analysis XX document opened. Right-click on the QlikView icon in the task bar and select **QlikView 11** to open another instance of QlikView. Open the document Profitability Analysis XX, so that both documents are available side by side. If you haven't developed your own version of the Profitability Analysis app, you can copy one from the \Solutions QlikView\ subfolder.

2. Copy the contents of the **Template** sheet from the Profitability Analysis document into an empty sheet in the Inventory Analysis document. Name the sheet **Template**.

3. Remove the **List Boxes** for Year and Month from the top of the sheet.

4. Add a new **Multi Box**. Select As Of Date as the only field displayed in the multi box.

5. Select a single value from the As Of Date list. Open the Multi Box Properties, under the Presentation tab. Highlight the As of Date field in the list of fields on the left and enable the Always One Selected Value checkbox.

6. Position the multi box on top of the gray ribbon, in the top-left corner of the sheet.

7. Replace Channel with Warehouse in the list box on the left.

8. In the multi box Other Filters, remove the Salesperson field that is unavailable now.

9. Your finished template sheet should look like Figure 12.2.

10. Open a new sheet and name it **Inventory Dashboard**.

11. Copy the contents of the Template sheet (Ctrl+A, Ctrl+C).

12. In the new sheet, right-click on the sheet and use the Paste Sheet Object as Link option to create linked objects for all template elements.

13. Unlink the icon and the heading label Template on top of the screen, since these two objects need to be different on different sheets.

14. Modify the label and the icon on the new sheet and verify that each sheet has its own title and its own icon. This step completes the preparation of the template for Inventory Analysis. Remember to Save your work periodically.

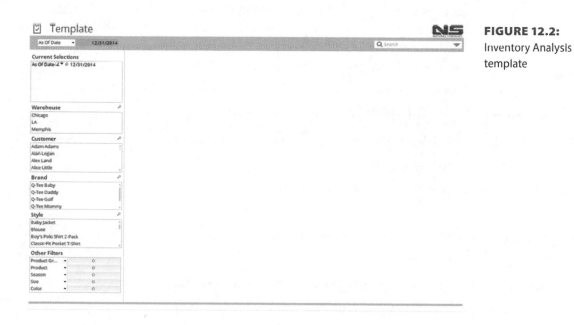

FIGURE 12.2:
Inventory Analysis template

Using Advanced Aggregation (AGGR) for Inventory Measures

This section introduces the concept of Advanced Aggregation (AGGR) and describes how it can be used for complex inventory analysis measures.

Introducing the Case for Advanced Aggregation

Let's examine the key measures for inventory analysis described earlier in this chapter. Many of these measures involve comparing on-hand balances to sales volumes. Calculating these measures using simple aggregation may lead to deceiving results.

We will demonstrate the issue based on the example developed in Exercise 12.3. In this exercise, you will create a chart that demonstrates calculating excess inventory. For the purpose of this exercise, you will calculate excess inventory as the sum of inventory balances in excess of six months of sales. In order to visualize this calculation, you transform the straight table chart that you developed in Exercise 12.3. We already have two expressions that calculate the current on hand balance and rolling 6 months of demand. We will simply add the third expression that calculates the difference between the two columns, only taking into account positive results. We will also replace the existing dimension with Brand, so the chart will calculate excess inventory by brand.

Exercise 12.5: Calculating Excess Inventory by Brand

1. Open **Properties** of the straight table on the **Variables** sheet. You added this chart in Exercise 12.3.

2. Replace the existing dimension by Brand.

3. Add the third expression with the following calculation:

   `column(1) - column(2)`

4. Enclose this calculation in the `RangeMax()` function to ensure that only positive results are included:

   `RangeMax(0, column(1) - column(2))`

5. Label the three expressions as **On Hand**, **Demand**, and **Excess Inventory**.

6. Format all three numbers as **Money** with no decimals and exit the **Properties**.

If everything worked as expected, you should see zeros in the third column for all the brands and in the total line. If this were true, it would be phenomenal! No excess inventory whatsoever! Hold the champagne, though, and let's drill down to the product level. Let's see how the same chart looks like when it's aggregated by Product.

Exercise 12.6: Calculating Excess Inventory by Product

1. In the same chart, replace the existing dimension with Product.

2. Sort the chart by the third expression, Excess Inventory, in descending order.

3. Examine the result.

Now you should see that many products have non-zero Excess Inventory numbers (see Figure 12.3).

Excess Inventory

Product	On Hand	Demand	Excess Inventory
	$7,767,979.96	$20,613,779.81	$0.00
Women's V-Neck T-Shi...	$31,123.47	$0.00	$31,123.47
Women's V-Neck T-Shi...	$30,735.54	$0.00	$30,735.54
Crew T-Shirt 3-Pack XL...	$22,705.68	$0.00	$22,705.68
Crew T-Shirt 3-Pack L ...	$21,697.20	$0.00	$21,697.20

FIGURE 12.3:
Excess Inventory by product

When the same calculation is performed at the Product level, it produces completely different results! Now, many products show on-hand balances that are higher than demand, and therefore their calculated excess inventory is greater than zero. Let's look at the total line, though. In total, we still show zero. While it looks counterintuitive that the total of many non-zero lines produced zero, technically this is the correct outcome of *Simple Aggregation*. The **Total** line is being evaluated at the total level. The total Demand is far higher than the total On Hand balance; hence, in total, there is no excess inventory.

To work around the problem in this particular chart, we can change the way totals are calculated. Instead of using **Expression Total** under the **Total Mode** settings in the **Expressions** tab (see Figure 12.4), we can use **Sum of Rows**.

If you change the **Total Mode** in your chart to **Sum of Rows**, you should see the expected amount of total Excess Inventory in the **Total** line.

Now, if you add Warehouse to the list of your chart dimensions, you will see that the total number becomes even higher. Now we have two possible results. Which one of the two is the accurate result?

FIGURE 12.4:

Expressions tab, Total Mode settings

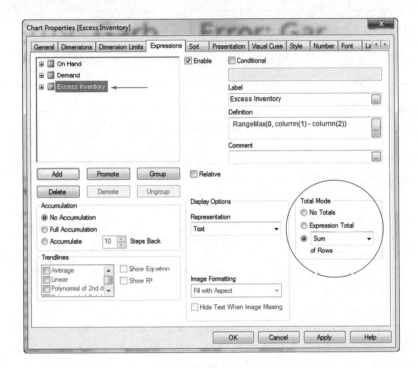

More importantly, how can we satisfy our initial requirement to show excess inventory by Brand if we have to calculate the number by Product and possibly by Warehouse in order to get it right? At the moment, we seem to have more questions than answers...

In order to produce an accurate measure of excess inventory by Brand, we'd need to perform a two-step calculation:

1. Aggregate On Hand balances and Demand at the level of Product and Warehouse; then calculate the Excess Inventory as the positive difference between the two aggregated numbers.

2. Aggregate (summarize) the results of Step 1 to the level of `Brand` and display the results in a chart expression.

This two-step process is called *nested aggregation*, and it can't be implemented using the tools that you've learned so far.

The main conclusion of this exercise is that *some expressions need to be pre-aggregated at a certain level in order to produce accurate results.* These advanced metrics cannot be calculated with simple aggregation. It's time to introduce the concept of *Advanced Aggregation*.

Defining Advanced Aggregation

Advanced Aggregation is one of the most advanced analytical techniques in QlikView. It allows performing an aggregation at a specific level of detail. The pre-aggregated results are kept in memory and can be aggregated again or serve as an array of values, such as in a dimension.

Advanced Aggregation is implemented using the `AGGR()` function. The syntax of the `AGGR()` function is the following:

```
AGGR(expression, Dim1, Dim2, Dim3, …)
```

The *expression* contains the actual formula with an aggregation function, and the list of dimensions defines the desired level of aggregation.

As a result, the `AGGR()` function produces a virtual array of aggregated values that are associated with the specified dimensions. These can be used in another aggregation function, to form a nested aggregation formula.

Let's continue with the example from the previous section. The calculation of excess inventory, combined in a single formula, can be defined as this:

```
RangeMax(0,
     sum({<_CMTD_Flag={1}>} [# On Hand Amount]) -
     sum({<_R6_Flag = {1}>} [# Demand Amount]))
```

Or, using the expression variables introduced in Exercise 12.3, the same expression can be defined like this:

```
RangeMax(0,
     $(exp_OnHand($(filter_CMTD))) -
     $(exp_Demand($(filter_R6))))
```

Now, we can enclose this formula in the AGGR() function and aggregate this formula by Product and Warehouse:

```
AGGR(
        RangeMax(0,
                $(exp_OnHand($(filter_CMTD))) -
                $(exp_Demand($(filter_R6)))        )
, Product, Warehouse)
```

This expression produces an array of aggregated results, associated with the dimensions Product and Warehouse. Now we can aggregate this array to any dimension that is at a higher hierarchical level (or less granular, in other words) than the two AGGR dimensions. Since Brand is less granular than Product, it's safe to aggregate these subtotals by Brand. The outer aggregation level doesn't need to be specified in the expression. Instead, it's defined by the chart dimension. All we need to specify here is the aggregation function that should be applied to the pre-aggregated subtotals:

```
sum(
        AGGR(
                RangeMax(0,
                        $(exp_OnHand($(filter_CMTD))) -
                        $(exp_Demand($(filter_R6)))            )
        , Product, Warehouse))
```

Exercise 12.7: Correcting the Calculation of Excess Inventory

1. In the same **Straight Table** chart that we developed earlier, add a new **Expression** and enter the nested aggregation formula listed previously. Format the expression as **Money** with no decimals.

2. Verify that Product and Warehouse are still used as the chart dimensions.

3. Accept all changes and examine the result.

4. Your chart should now include two calculations of excess inventory—one using simple aggregation and the other using Advanced Aggregation. The two expressions should return the same result.

5. Clone the chart and replace Product and Warehouse by Brand as a single dimension. Compare the two columns now. The expression with the simple aggregation shows zero, while the expression with Advanced Aggregation returns the accurate result. See Figure 12.5.

Excess Inventory

Brand	On Hand	Demand	Excess Inventory (Simple)	Excess Inventory (AGGR)
	$7,767,979.96	**$20,613,779.81**	**$0.00**	**$381,933.88**
Q-Tee Mommy	$2,014,215.01	$6,295,326.73	$0.00	$182,371.19
Q-Tee Daddy	$2,011,407.39	$5,858,324.61	$0.00	$98,174.62
Q-Tee Baby	$2,312,722.64	$5,278,943.37	$0.00	$90,253.74
Q-Tee Golf	$1,429,634.91	$3,181,185.09	$0.00	$11,134.33

FIGURE 12.5:
Comparing results of simple aggregation vs. Advanced Aggregation

Formulating Inventory Measures Using AGGR

Now that you know and understand Advanced Aggregation, we can formulate more complex measures that are commonly used for inventory analysis.

For example, let's analyze the measure Days On Hand. For each Product/Warehouse, we need to divide the current On Hand balance by the average daily sales (usually calculated over a 12-month period). These intermediate results are aggregated again using either a simple average or a weighted average, with On Hand balance as a weight. While both average calculations are technically valid, using weighted average is more common.

Next you build the formula for calculating Days On Hand using weighted average, one step at a time.

We need to divide the current (or As of Date) On Hand Balance by the average Daily Demand for a 12-month period of time. In order to calculate the average Daily Demand, we will summarize the demand for rolling 12 months and divide that by the number of days between the first and the last day of sales within the last 12 months. Let's formulate each component of this calculation:

The number of sales days in the 12-month period is calculated as the difference between the first month of sales and the last available month in the rolling 12 months period. Note that for the first month of sales, we need to apply filter that only selects *sales dates*, and for the last available month in the period, the same filter is not needed. We are not interested in the last month of sales, but rather in the last available month:

```
Max({<_R12_Flag={1}>} Date) -
Min({<_R12_Flag={1}, FactType={Sales}>} Date) + 1
```

Building the Expression Inside-Out

In the following explanation, we will be building the expression step by step, adding new components to the same formula in every step. In each formula, we highlighted the new elements with bold font, to focus your attention on the new additions.

Average Daily Demand is calculated as the total Demand for 12 months divided by the same Number of Sales Days:

```
sum({<_R12_Flag={1}>} [# Demand Amount]) /
(Max({<_R12_Flag={1}>} Date) -
Min({<_R12_Flag={1}, FactType={Sales}>} Date) + 1)
```

Days on Hand are calculated as the Current On Hand Balance divided by the Average Daily Demand:

```
sum({<_CMTD_Flag={1}>} [# On Hand Amount])/
(     sum({<_R12_Flag={1}>} [# Demand Amount]) /
      (Max({<_R12_Flag={1}>} Date) -
      Min({<_R12_Flag={1}, FactType={Sales}>} Date) + 1))
```

The same result is multiplied by the Current On Hand Balance one more time for the purpose of calculating weighted average:

```
sum({<_CMTD_Flag={1}>} [# On Hand Amount])*
sum({<_CMTD_Flag={1}>} [# On Hand Amount])/
(     sum({<_R12_Flag={1}>} [# Demand Amount]) /
(     Max({<_R12_Flag={1}>} Date) -
      Min({<_R12_Flag={1}, FactType={Sales}>} Date) + 1))
```

Now, this calculation should be enclosed in the AGGR() function by Product and Warehouse:

```
AGGR(
      sum({<_CMTD_Flag={1}>} [# On Hand Amount])*
      sum({<_CMTD_Flag={1}>} [# On Hand Amount])/
      (    sum({<_R12_Flag={1}>} [# Demand Amount]) /
      (    Max({<_R12_Flag={1}>} Date) -
           Min({<_R12_Flag={1}, FactType={Sales}>} Date) + 1)        )
, Product, Warehouse)
```

The results of the AGGR() need to be summarized and divided by the total Current On Hand Balance, to complete the calculation of the weighted average:

```
Sum(
    AGGR(
        sum({<_CMTD_Flag={1}>} [# On Hand Amount])*
        sum({<_CMTD_Flag={1}>} [# On Hand Amount])/
        (   sum({<_R12_Flag={1}>} [# Demand Amount]) /
        (   Max({<_R12_Flag={1}>} Date) -
            Min({<_R12_Flag={1}, FactType={Sales}>} Date) + 1))
    , Product, Warehouse)
) / sum({<_CMTD_Flag={1}>} [# On Hand Amount])
```

Wow, this was fun, wasn't it? It felt like peeling the onion, only in reverse. This is our recommended way of creating complex calculations—"inside-out." We start with the inner calculation, then enclose it in another function, and then add another function, until we get the whole expression ready. This way, the calculation makes sense at every step of the process. To understand why we do it this way, try typing it straight, left to right, and see how soon you lose track of parentheses, brackets, and the overall logic of the calculation.

In a similar way, we can formulate the expression for the Inventory Turns. We calculate Inventory Turns by dividing the 12 Months Cost of Sales by the 12-Month Average of On Hand Balance. This definition is good if all of our products have been selling for at least 12 months. This is almost never true. Each company has some new products that were introduced in the last 12 months. Hence, the more accurate calculation would be this: the 12-Month Average of Monthly Cost of Sales, multiplied by 12 and divided by the 12-Months Average On Hand Balance. Both 12-month averages are calculated as the sum of the measure for the last 12 months, divided by the distinct number of months within the last 12 months (filtered for the same type of data).

Admittedly, these calculations get more and more complex, and some of you might consider jumping ship at this point. Before that happens, let's introduce a simplified approach that can help encapsulate some of the complexities in smaller building blocks that you can store in variables and use when needed. Instead of formulating the whole formula for Inventory Turns, let's build it from smaller blocks stored in variables.

Formulating the Same Measures Using Variables with Parameters

You already created two major building blocks, `exp_OnHand` and `exp_Demand`, in Exercise 12.3. Now, let's create additional building blocks for our calculations.

You need a variable that counts the Days of Sales in a certain period of time (parameter `$1`):

```
exp_SalesDaysCount=
(Max({<$1>} Date) - Min({<$1, FactType={Sales}>} Date) + 1)
```

Now, using this variable and the two variables created earlier, we can formulate the raw calculation of Days On Hand like this:

```
exp_DaysOnHandRaw =
$(exp_OnHand($1)) /
($(exp_Demand($2))/$(exp_SalesDaysCount($2)))
```

In this formula, the formal parameter `$1` represents the Current Date filter and the formal parameter `$2` represents the Rolling 12 Months date filter.

After we apply the Advanced Aggregation function `AGGR()` and calculate weighted average, the final expression looks like this:

```
exp_DaysOnHand =
Sum(
      AGGR(
          $(exp_OnHand($1))*
           $(exp_DaysOnHandRaw($1, $2))
      , Product, Warehouse)
 )/ $(exp_OnHand($1))
```

Now, this formula is much simpler than the fully expanded expression listed in the previous section. However, most developers need to gain some experience and proficiency before they can write these formulas with parameters from scratch. In the beginning, it's safer to build a simple expression in a temporary chart, verify its accuracy, and only then transform the expression into the generic formula with parameters.

In order to allow you to focus on the QlikView features, we saved you the trouble of creating these complex expressions on your own, by including them in the text file that we loaded earlier in the chapter. You should already have all the necessary expressions loaded into the document. If you are interested specifically in the Inventory Analysis metrics, take the time to dissect the expressions, following the explanations in this section as an example.

> ## Verify the Variable Names exp_OnHand and exp_Demand
>
> The formulas that you loaded from the text file were built on the assumption that the two variables that you created in Exercise 12.3 are named and calculated exactly the same way as we described them. It is important for the rest of the exercises in this chapter that these two variables exist with the same names and the same definitions. Please take a minute to verify that.

Creating the Top Section of the Inventory Dashboard

Now you are ready to develop your new visualizations. With the formulas that you loaded from a text file, you will develop these advanced visualizations quickly and effectively. The expressions listed in Table 12.1 are used frequently throughout this chapter.

TABLE 12.1: Most Common Inventory Measures

DESCRIPTION	EXPRESSION (PARAMETERS MAY VARY)
Current or Historical On Hand Balance	$(exp_OnHand($(filter_CMTD)))
Historical Demand	$(exp_Demand($(filter_R12)))
Excess Inventory	$(exp_Excess($(filter_CMTD), $(filter_R6)))
Days On Hand	$(exp_DaysOnHand($(filter_CMTD), $(filter_R12)))
Inventory Turns	$(exp_Turns($(filter_CMTD), $(filter_R12)))

In the following exercise, you develop the top section of the Inventory Dashboard. Four KPIs will be presented at the header level—Total Inventory, Excess Inventory, Inventory Turns, and Days on Hand. For each one of the four KPIs, you will display the current measure, the change from prior year, and the chart that compares the actual number to the target. See Figure 12.6.

FIGURE 12.6:
Four KPIs on top of the Inventory Dashboard

These objects are very similar to the ones that you developed for Profitability Analysis in Chapter 8. We will ask you to develop these objects on your own, using the variables and the expressions described in Exercise 12.8.

Exercise 12.8: Creating the Top Section of the Inventory Dashboard

1. Open the Inventory Dashboard sheet.

2. You may create the new objects from scratch or copy them from the Profitability Analysis.QVW document. If you decide to copy the existing objects, resize and reposition the objects as necessary to fit four KPIs in the same space where three KPIs used to be.

3. You will need the variables, expressions, and settings shown in Table 12.2 to replicate the objects presented in Figure 12.6. For your convenience, the variables were added to the external text file that you loaded in Exercise 12.2. You can simply add them to a new Input Box and examine their contents.

4. Use the same techniques described in Chapter 8, Exercise 8.12, to develop the top section of the Inventory Dashboard sheet.

5. Save your work.

TABLE 12.2: Variables and Expressions for the Top Section of the dashboard

DESCRIPTION	NAME	DEFINITION
Formatting Variables		
Arrow Up	vUp	=CHR(9650)
Arrow Down	vDown	=CHR(9660)
Formatting string for % change	format_ChangePercent	=*vUp* & '#,##0.0%;' & *vDown* & '#,##0.0%'
Formatting string for change, integer	format_ChangeInteger	=*vUp* & '#,##0;' & *vDown* & '#,##0'
Formatting string for change, with 1 decimal place	format_Change1Decimal	=*vUp* & '#,##0.0;' & *vDown* & '#,##0.0'
Target Numbers		
Target for Total Inventory	v_TargetTotalInventory	**8,000,000**
Target for Excess Inventory	v_TargetExcessInventory	**500,000**
Target for Days On Hand	v_TargetDaysOnHand	**60**
Target for Inventory Turns	v_TargetTurns	**5**
Expressions for the Main KPIs		
Total Inventory		= num($(exp_OnHand($(filter_CMTD))) / 1000000, '$#,##0.0M')
Excess Inventory		= num($(exp_Excess($(filter_CMTD), $(filter_R6))) / 1000000, '$#,##0.0M')
Days On Hand		= num($(exp_DaysOnHand($(filter_CMTD), $(filter_R12))), '#,##0')
Inventory Turns		=num($(exp_Turns($(filter_CMTD), $(filter_R12))), '#,##0.0')
Expressions for Changes from Prior Year		
Total Inventory		=num($(exp_OnHand($(filter_CMTD))) / $(exp_OnHand($(filter_PMTD))) - 1 ,'$(format_ChangePercent)') & ' from PY'
Excess Inventory		=num($(exp_Excess($(filter_CMTD), $(filter_R6))) / $(exp_Excess($(filter_PMTD), $(filter_PYR6))) - 1 ,'$(format_ChangePercent)') & ' from PY'
Days On Hand		=num($(exp_DaysOnHand($(filter_CMTD), $(filter_R12))) - $(exp_DaysOnHand($(filter_PMTD), $(filter_PR12))) ,'$(format_ChangeInteger)') & ' days from PY'

(continues)

(continued)

DESCRIPTION	NAME	DEFINITION
Inventory Turns		=num($(exp_Turns($(filter_CMTD), $(filter_R12))) - $(exp_Turns($(filter_PMTD), $(filter_PR12))), '$(format_Change1Decimal)') & ' turns from PY'
Bar Chart Expressions		
Total Inventory	Actual	$(exp_OnHand($(filter_CMTD)))
	Target	rangemax(Actual, v_TargetTotalInventory * 1.2) - Actual
	Reference Line	=v_TargetTotalInventory
	Text in Chart	='Target=' & num (v_TargetTotalInventory/1000000, '$#,##0M')
Excess Inventory	Actual	$(exp_Excess($(filter_CMTD), $(filter_R6)))
	Target	rangemax(Actual, v_TargetExcessInventory * 1.2) - Actual
	Reference Line	=v_TargetExcessInventory
	Text in Chart	='Target=' & num(v_TargetExcessInventory/1000000, '$#,##0.0M')
Days On Hand	Actual	$(exp_DaysOnHand($(filter_CMTD), $(filter_R12)))
	Target	rangemax(Actual, v_TargetDaysOnHand * 1.2) - Actual
	Reference Line	=v_TargetDaysOnHand
	Text in Chart	='Target=' & num(v_TargetDaysOnHand, '#,##0')
Inventory Turns	Actual	$(exp_Turns($(filter_CMTD), $(filter_R12)))
	Target	rangemax(Actual, v_TargetTurns * 1.2) - Actual
	Reference Line	=v_TargetTurns
	Text in Chart	='Target=' & num(v_TargetTurns, '#,##0.0')
Calculated Color Variables		
color_InventoryChange	IF($(exp_OnHand($(filter_CMTD)))< $(exp_OnHand($(filter_PMTD))), $(color_Green), $(color_Red))	

(continues)

(continued)

DESCRIPTION	NAME	DEFINITION
	color_Inventory2Target	IF($(exp_OnHand($(filter_CMTD))) < $(v_TargetTotalInventory), $(color_Green), $(color_Red))
	color_ExcessChange	IF($(exp_OnHand($(filter_CMTD), $(filter_R6)))< $(exp_OnHand($(filter_PMTD), , $(filter_PYR6))), $(color_Green), $(color_Red))
	color_Excess2Target	IF($(exp_Excess($(filter_CMTD), $(filter_R6))) < $(v_TargetExcessInventory), $(color_Green), $(color_Red))
	color_DaysOnHandChange	if($(exp_DaysOnHand($(filter_CMTD), $(filter_R12))) < $(exp_DaysOnHand($(filter_PMTD), $(filter_PR12))), $(color_Green), $(color_Red))
	color_DaysOnHand2Target	if($(exp_DaysOnHand($(filter_CMTD), $(filter_R12))) < $(v_TargetDaysOnHand), $(color_Green), $(color_Red))
	color_TurnsChange	IF($(exp_Turns($(filter_CMTD), $(filter_R12))) >= $(exp_Turns($(filter_PMTD), $(filter_PR12))) , $(color_Green), $(color_Red))
	color_Turns2Target	IF($(exp_Turns($(filter_CMTD), $(filter_R12))) >= $(v_TargetTurns) , $(color_Green), $(color_Red))

Enhancing Visual Analysis with Advanced Aggregation

Communicating the big picture with totals and averages is an important part of any analytical application, but the overall picture wouldn't be complete if we only calculated our KPIs at the total level. This section explores advanced techniques of analyzing inventory at the detailed level, using the Advanced Aggregation function AGGR().

Developing Histograms

So far, we aggregated data using the default simple aggregation. That allowed us to answer straightforward questions, such as "What are our sales by brand?" or "What is the total inventory by brand?" With the use of nested aggregation, we learn how to answer more complicated questions, such as "What are our average inventory turns by product category?"

Now, let's turn the questions around. For example, we know that our average turns measure is approximately four turns a year. It's likely that some products are turning much faster and some products are turning much slower. Can we calculate how many products are turning less than once a year? Twice a year? Twelve times a year? Or, an even more interesting question—how much money is tied up in inventory balances for products that turn slowly, versus products that turn fast?

We could create a straight table by product, calculate turns by product, and equip every user with a calculator to manually count products by turns. That wouldn't be too advanced, would it?

Using statistics lingo, we need to visualize distribution of products and on-hand balances by turns (or by days on hand). This type of a chart is similar to a statistical histogram, only it can be plotted over any calculated measures, not necessarily over probability numbers.

In QlikView, histograms can be developed with the use of calculated dimensions and Advanced Aggregation.

Recall the initial description of Advanced Aggregation. The AGGR() function returns a virtual array of aggregated numbers, temporarily stored in memory and associated with the specified dimensions. So far, we always enclosed the AGGR() within another aggregated function (nested aggregation) and calculated a single result. We are now ready to formulate the First Law of AGGR():

The First Law of AGGR()

Any time we need to nest two aggregation functions, there *must* be an AGGR() function between them. For example:

`sum(sum(Measure))`	Incorrect!
`sum(AGGR(sum(Measure), Dim1, Dim2, ...))`	Correct

Another way of implementing AGGR() is using the array of aggregated results to form a calculated dimension for a histogram.

The virtual association of the aggregated results to the AGGR() dimensions allows us to calculate and display associated measures that pertain to these dimensions. For example, if we used AGGR() to calculate turns by product and warehouse, now we can count products that are associated with the results of the AGGR(). We can also sum inventory balances associated with those products. Using the power of QlikView associative logic, we can calculate any measures that are associated with products and warehouses and present them as associated with the results of AGGR().

Using AGGR() in calculated dimensions is the second common use of Advanced Aggregation. In fact, AGGR() is the only way to use aggregated functions in chart dimensions. Let's explain the reason for that.

By definition, chart dimensions provide the aggregation level for the whole chart. Now, if we decide to use an aggregation function, such as sum(), within the chart dimension, it would be unclear at what level of detail our sum() should be aggregated. In order to clarify that, we are required to use the AGGR() function. The dimensions of the AGGR() define the level of detail for the aggregation function within the chart dimension, and the aggregated results define the level of aggregation for the whole chart.

The Second Law of AGGR()

Any time we need to use an aggregation function in a chart dimension, the function *must* be enclosed in the AGGR() function. For example, when used in a calculated dimension:

sum(Measure)	Incorrect!
AGGR(sum(Measure), Dim1, Dim2, ...)	Correct

In the following exercise, you build a histogram that shows the distribution of products by turns. Use the saved formula exp_TurnsRaw in combination with the AGGR() function in the calculated dimension. In order to produce buckets of products for each whole number of turns, round the calculated number of turns. In the expression, calculate the distinct count of products.

Exercise 12.9: Building a Histogram of Products by Turns

1. Create a new bar chart in the Inventory Dashboard sheet. Type **Distribution of Products by Turns** as the Window Title and disable Show Title in Chart.

2. In the Dimensions tab, click on the Add Calculated Dimension button and type the following formula as the Definition:

   ```
   =AGGR(Ceil($(exp_TurnsRaw($(filter_CMTD), $(filter_R12)))), Product)
   ```

3. Label the dimension Turns.

4. In the Expressions tab, enter the following formula as the Definition for the Expression. Label the Expression **# of Products**.

   ```
   count(DISTINCT Product)
   ```

5. In the Sort tab, check Numeric Value, Ascending. Note that no sorting method was defined by default. Calculated dimensions don't have the default sorting method, hence the sorting method must be specified explicitly.

6. In the Axis tab, enable Show Grid and set Axis Width=1 for the expression. Define the Dimension Axis as Continuous.

7. In the Number tab, format the number as Integer. Accept all changes and examine the results. Your chart should look similar to Figure 12.7.

FIGURE 12.7:
Distribution of products by turns

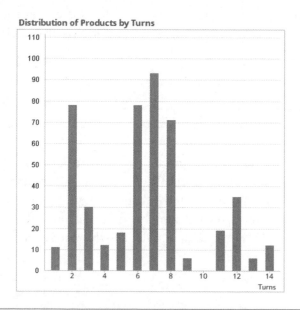

Distribution of Products by Turns

Let's discuss the results presented in the chart. We can see that the distribution of products is nearly normal—the majority of products falls in the middle of the curve, except for the atypically large number of products that have two turns. In a classical normal distribution, the shape of the curve resembles a bell. For this reason, histograms are often called bell curves. Our bell curve is somewhat distorted by a large group of products with unusually low annual turns.

The shape of our bell curve suggests that most products posted an impressive five-seven turns a year, and yet the weighted average on top of the screen shows approximately four. Perhaps this anomaly can be explained with a similar histogram that shows the distribution of on-hand balances by turns.

Exercise 12.10: Building a Histogram of On-Hand Balances by Turns

1. Resize the existing bar chart in such a way that it takes up about half of the available space. Clone the chart and position two bar charts side by side, as presented in Figure 12.8.

2. Modify the Properties of the second bar chart to produce the histogram of on-hand balances:

   2.1. In the General tab, change the Window Title to **Distribution of On Hand Balances by Turns**.

   2.2. In the Expressions tab, change the expression to show the current on-hand balance:

   `$(exp_OnHand($(filter_CMTD)))`

   2.3. In the Number tab, format the expression as Money and enter the four symbols to scale the chart to single **$, $K, $MM**, or **$Bn**, accordingly.

3. Accept all changes and examine the result. Your complete sheet should look similar to Figure 12.8. Save your work.

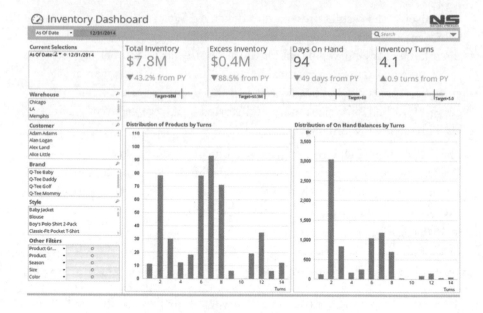

Visualizing Parts of Totals and Subtotals

In Chapter 8, you learned how to visualize parts of a whole, using pie charts, stacked bar charts, and block charts. In this section, you learn how to calculate a share of a total, or a share of a certain subtotal, using the keyword TOTAL. This section also introduces grid charts that can be used for visualizing distribution of a single measure between two dimensions.

Aggregating Data Using the Keyword TOTAL

You just learned that the AGGR() function allows developers to modify the default behavior of simple aggregation. While simple aggregation always aggregates all available data to the level defined by chart dimensions, Advanced Aggregation allows us to alter the level at which the aggregation is performed.

In a similar way, the keyword TOTAL, when added to the aggregation function before the expression like in the following example, allows us to aggregate the data at a different level. When TOTAL is used in its most simple form, like this:

```
=sum(TOTAL expression)
```

the expression is evaluated at the total level, disregarding all chart dimensions. In a more advanced form, the keyword TOTAL may be equipped with a list of dimensions in angled brackets:

```
=sum(TOTAL <Dim1, Dim2, Dim3> expression)
```

In this case, expression is evaluated at the total level for the specified dimensions.

The syntax of AGGR() and TOTAL may look somewhat similar, perhaps because both functions use dimensions to specify the level of aggregation; however, the two functions work quite differently. The data for the AGGR() calculation is supplied directly from the associative database. Conversely, the data for the TOTAL calculation is taken from the virtual "mini-cube" that is created for each chart. For this reason, only existing chart dimensions can make up the list of the TOTAL dimensions. Any other dimensions listed will be simply disregarded.

The keyword TOTAL is commonly used to calculate the share of the particular element in the overall total, or in a category's total. We will illustrate the technique of using the keyword TOTAL in the process of analyzing the aging data.

In addition to inventory history, we calculated estimated aged balances, based on the history of goods receiving. In Chapter 14, we describe the process of calculating the aging balances. At the moment, it's sufficient to understand that aged balances are stored for each product, warehouse, and age. The aged quantities and amounts are stored separately from the on-hand quantities and amounts, in the fields [# Aged Quantity] and [# Aged Amount].

Because of the special method of calculating the aging data, it's not designed to follow the same As of Date logic. It would be much more complicated and resource-intense to calculate aging for each As of Date. Therefore, aging data is only calculated for the current date, and the selection of As of Date needs to be disregarded for the purpose of presenting aged balances.

In the following exercise, you develop a pivot table that shows Aged Balances by Brand and Age. For each Brand and Age, you will calculate the Aged Amount and the percent of that amount to the total amount by Brand.

Exercise 12.11: Using the Keyword TOTAL

1. Copy the sheet Inventory Dashboard and name the new sheet **Aging**. Delete the two bar charts to make room for the new objects.

2. Create a pivot table and name it **Aging by Brand**.

3. Use Brand and Age as Dimensions.

4. Enter the following expression and label it as **Aged Amount**:

   sum({<[As Of Date]=>} [# Aged Amount])

5. Add another expression with the following formula and label it **% of Total by Brand**:

   sum({<[As Of Date]=>} [# Aged Amount])/
   sum({<[As Of Date]=>} total <Brand> [# Aged Amount])

6. In the Presentation tab, check Wrap Header Text to **2** Lines and Center the Label for both expressions. Also center Label and Data for the Age dimension.

7. In the Number tab, format the first expression as Money with no decimals. Format the second expression as Integer, Show in Percent (%).

8. Accept all changes and examine the results.

9. At first, you should see that Brand is the only visible dimension. The additional dimension(s) need to be expanded in order to be displayed. Right-click on the Brand column and select Expand All from the context menu.

10. Now you should see both dimensions side by side. Pivot the Age field by dragging its label to the right and up. Drop it above the expressions labels. The end result should look like the chart in Figure 12.9.

FIGURE 12.9:

Aging by brand

Aging by Brand

Age	60		91		121		1 5
Brand	Aged Amount	% of Total by Brand	Aged Amount	% of Total by Brand	Aged Amount	% of Total by Brand	A g
Q-Tee Golf	$204,453	14%	$361,221	25%	$64,490	5%	
Q-Tee Baby	$322,975	14%	$657,507	28%	$49,874	2%	
Q-Tee Mommy	$436,158	22%	$445,312	22%	$207,053	10%	
Q-Tee Daddy	$309,917	15%	$606,071	30%	$94,217	5%	

With the pivot table like this, we can compare the summarized aging data by Brand and see what dollar amount and what relative share fall in a certain aged balance by Brand. While this chart is certainly informative, its analytical value is somewhat limited. We have to read and comprehend every single number before we can understand what's going on. This information could be enhanced with a graphical representation that could help comprehend the big picture pre-attentively. The following section introduces the grid chart—another chart type that can be used to visualize parts of a whole, distributed over two dimensions.

Using Grid Charts

The **Grid Chart** icon is located next to the **Scatter Chart** icon in the list of chart types, and the two charts are often mistaken for similar, or even the same. Both could be loosely called "bubble charts"; however, their use and purpose are completely different.

While the scatter chart plots a single dimension over two or more calculated measures, the grid chart (see Figure 12.10) does exactly the opposite. The grid chart plots a single measure over two (or three) dimensions. The X and Y axes are discrete. The symbol location is determined by the crossing of the two dimension values. In this sense, the grid chart somewhat resembles a graphical representation of a pivot table.

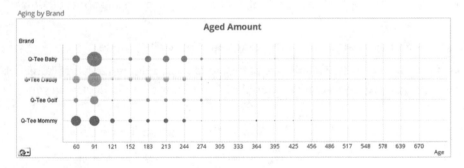

FIGURE 12.10:
The grid chart

The size of the symbol is determined by the value of the expression. The optional third dimension can transform solid symbols into mini pie charts that further divide each symbol into parts.

In the following exercise, we will clone the pivot table that we just created and transform the clone to a grid chart. Since our pivot table has two expressions and the grid chart can only visualize one expression at a time, we should either **Disable** one of the expressions or **Group** them. Each one of the two expressions can be useful for answering different questions. When the emphasis should be placed on comparing the dollar amounts between brands, then the On Hand Amount is more useful. When it's important to understand the share of aged inventory for each age bucket within its brand, then the second expression becomes more insightful. Grouping the two expressions sounds like a good idea.

Exercise 12.12: Creating a Grid Chart

1. Clone the pivot table created in Exercise 12.11 and position the copy below the original. Open the Chart Properties of the new chart and make the following modifications.

2. In the **General** tab, change the **Chart Type** to **Grid Chart** (second icon in the bottom row). Enable **Show Title in Chart** and leave the title empty.

3. In the **Dimensions** tab, **Promote** the Age dimension to appear first between the two dimensions.

4. In the **Expressions** tab, **Group** the two expressions. Highlight the second expression and click on the **Group** button.

5. In the **Sort** tab, make sure that Age is sorted by its **Numeric Value**, *not* by its **Y-value**.

6. In the **Style** tab, select the flat **Look** with variable size of the symbols (see Figure 12.11, first icon on the right). Alternatively, you may choose the 3D bubbles, if you enjoy the built-in glare in your charts.

7. In the **Axes** tab, set **Axis Width** =1 and enable **Show Grid** for the **X-axis** and the **Y-axis**.

8. Accept all changes and examine the result. Your fully formatted sheet should look similar to Figure 12.12.

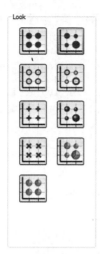

Look

FIGURE 12.11:
Look options for grid charts

FIGURE 12.12:
The aging sheet with two charts

We think you'll agree that the grid chart allows much more effective visual perception of this information, compared to the textual pivot table.

Other Ways of Visualizing Aged Data

Perhaps a better way of visualizing the aged data could be using the good old bar chart, in combination with the Accumulation function.

Before we do that, let's improve the two existing aging charts by modifying the Age dimension. We will replace the "static" dimension Age with the **Calculated Dimension**, to achieve the following two improvements:

- The actual age numbers that were generated from our aging calculation look quite obscure and confusing. We'd like to round the numbers to identical 30-day buckets.

- Since it's evident that the aged amounts beyond 300 days are extremely small, we'd like to combine all these small amounts into the 300 days bucket, to make the charts smaller and more focused.

The first transformation can be achieved by simply rounding the number to the nearest 30:

```
=Round(Age, 30)
```

The second transformation can be done in a number of ways. We like using the RangeMin() function to limit a number to a specific boundary:

```
=RangeMin(300, Round(Age, 30))
```

For all the values of Age that are below 300, the RangeMin() will pick the lower Age number. For all the ages above 300, the number 300 will be selected as the lowest.

We will save this formula (without the equals sign) in a variable, since we are going to use it in multiple charts.

Exercise 12.13: Enhancing the Aging Charts

1. Create a new variable exp_AgeDim and enter the following formula into its **Definition**:

   ```
   RangeMin(300, Round(Age, 30))
   ```

2. Open chart **Properties** and perform the following changes in both of the existing charts:

   2.1. Edit the definition of the Age dimension. Replace the field name Age with the new variable, enclosed in a dollar-sign expansion:

   ```
   =$(exp_AgeDim)
   ```

2.2. Type **Age** in the Label definition for the same dimension.

2.3. Verify that the new dimension is still sorted by Numeric Value, Ascending.

3. Examine the results. The two charts should be showing fewer age buckets, and all age buckets should be rounded to 30 days.

4. Make the grid chart narrower, to make room for another chart.

The goal of the new chart is to show accumulated values of the on-hand balances by Age. This chart can help us answer questions like, "How much of our inventory is more recent than X days?" or "How much of our inventory is older than X days?"

Exercise 12.14: Creating the Cumulative Aging Chart

1. Clone the grid chart and perform the following changes in the Properties.

2. In the General tab, change the Window Title to **Cumulative Aged Balances** and disable Show Title in Chart. Change the chart type to Bar Chart.

3. In the Dimensions tab, Remove the dimension Brand from the list.

4. In the Expressions tab:

   4.1. Ungroup the two expressions and Delete the Percent to Brand Total.

   4.2. Select Full Accumulation under the Accumulation section for the Aged Amount expression.

5. In the Axes tab, set Width = 1 and enable Show Grid for both Axes.

6. In the Number tab, enter the four Symbols at the bottom—**$, $K, $MM**, and **$Bn**.

7. Accept the changes and examine the results. Your finished aging sheet should look like Figure 12.13. Save your work.

Now, with this new bar chart, it's quite easy to see that over $5M worth of inventory is no more than 180 days old. When the emphasis should be placed on the older inventory, it might be helpful to sort the same chart in the descending order of age buckets (see Figure 12.14).

FIGURE 12.14:

The Aged Balances chart in reverse order

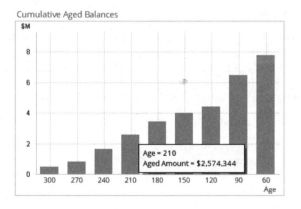

Now it's easy to gather, for example, that over $2.5 M are older than 210 days. The yellow sticky note appears when the user's mouse hovers over the individual bar.

Using the Chart Inter-Record Function Above()

Perhaps the cumulative bar chart that we just created could be improved even more if we could make it similar to the waterfall chart, which was introduced in Chapter 8. If you recall, the waterfall chart shows individual bars that represent cost components, and each bar begins where the previous bar ends.

If we could present individual bars for each age bucket, and start each bar from the point where the previous bar ended, we could communicate both the size of each age bucket and the total cumulative balance at every level.

The problem here is that it's easier said than done. In the Profitability model, each bar was defined as a separate expression, and each expression had its own **Bar Offset** attribute that was calculated individually for each cost component. Here, we are dealing with a single expression, and different bars represent different dimension values. Now, in order to calculate the offset value for each bar, we need to refer to the cumulative total for the previous bar. At the same time, we need to calculate the new cumulative total to supply the offset for the next bar.

In QlikView, when we need to refer to other values in the same chart, we use the *Chart Inter Record Functions*. There are a number of specialized functions, including Above(), Below(), Top(), Bottom(), and a few others. You can look up the full details about these functions in the Help article called "Chart Inter Record Functions."

We will use the Above() function for our purposes. The function evaluates the specified expression in the context of the row that is *above* the current row in the chart data. For graphs, the term *above* refers to the straight table equivalent of the same chart. You can think of it as "the previous value in the chart." When more than one dimension is involved, you may need to use the keyword TOTAL in combination with Above() because by default this function operates within a single *segment*, or within a single value of the major dimension.

The Above() function is a bit tricky when it's used for accumulating balances. The logic for accumulating any aggregated balance looks like this:

```
[Cumulative Balance] = Above([Cumulative Balance]) + sum(Value)
```

We fetch the previous value of the balance, and we add the current value to it. Sounds pretty simple, doesn't it? Here is a little secret about Above(): for the first row in the chart, the function returns NULL, since there is nothing above the first row. As we all know, adding any value to a NULL value results in NULL, and therefore the formula listed previously can never work. We have to use the RangeSum() function instead of simple addition to take care of the first NULL value:

```
rangesum(
        above([Cumulative Balance]),
        sum(Value))
```

With this new knowledge, we are now equipped to make our cumulative bar chart look similar to the waterfall chart.

Exercise 12.15: Transforming the Cumulative Aging Chart

1. Open the chart Properties for the cumulative bar chart created in the previous exercise.

2. In the Expressions tab:

    2.1. Select No Accumulation for the Aged Amount expression.

    2.2. Add the following expression and label it **Cumulative Balance**:

    ```
    rangesum(
    above([Cumulative Balance]),
    [Aged Amount])
    ```

    2.3. Note that this formula refers to two expressions by their labels—Cumulative Balance and Aged Amount. If you named your expressions differently, adjust the formula accordingly.

    2.4. Uncheck Bar under the Display Options for the new expression—this expression will be used only for calculating the cumulative balance.

    2.5. Click on the Expansion Icon (the little box with a plus sign +) next to the Aged Balance and enter the following formula into the definition of the Bar Offset attribute:

    ```
    rangesum(above([Cumulative Balance]))
    ```

3. Sort the chart by the Numerical Value of Age, in Descending order.

4. Accept all changes and examine the result. You chart should look similar to Figure 12.15.

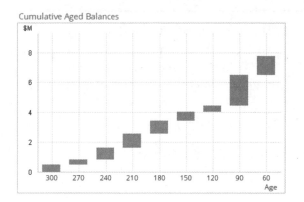

Now we can see both the size of the pile for each age bucket and the cumulative balance on the same chart. When we hover over the bars with our mouse, we can only see the value of the individual balance, but not the cumulative balance (see Figure 12.16, left). It would be very nice if we could see both numbers there.

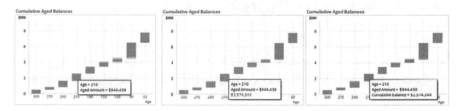

The simple solution is to enable the checkbox **Text as Pop-up** at the bottom of the **Expressions** tab, for the expression Cumulative Balance. That, however, leads to a rather obscure result. The number is presented in the pop-up window with no description for it (Figure 12.16, center). We've been wondering for years about this mystery—who needs to see the number without knowing what it means? Anyway, our idea of showing **Text as Pop-up** is displayed in Figure 12.16 on the right. That, however, will have to be achieved manually, through hard work, sweat, and tears.

Exercise 12.16: Adding Text to the Pop-Up Sticky Note

1. Open the Properties for the cumulative bar chart.

2. In the Expressions tab, modify the Cumulative Balance expression as follows:

```
Dual(
    'Cumulative Balance = ' &
    num(
        rangesum(above([Cumulative Balance]),[Aged Amount])
    , '$#,##0')
,
    rangesum(
    above([Cumulative Balance]),[Aged Amount])
)
```

3. Enable the checkbox Text as Pop-up at the bottom of the tab. Disable Expressions as Legend for both expressions.

4. In the Number tab, ensure that Cumulative Balance is formatted as Expression Default.

5. Accept all changes, Save your work, and examine the results.

Note that any text can be added to the pop-up sticky note by adding more expressions to charts, with **Text as Pop-up** as the only enabled **Display Option**.

The Trellis Chart

You must be excited about the chart that we just finished improving, and you share your excitement with your key user, perhaps the Inventory Manager. He likes the chart, and at the same time he declares that he absolutely has to see this information by brand, without the need to select one brand at a time. He needs to compare the aging picture between brands, and for that he needs to see all four brands at once.

If this happened a few years ago, you'd have no choice but to build four separate charts and limit each chart to a specific brand. Ever since version 9.0, QlikView offers a feature called the *Trellis Chart*. The trellis chart is in essence an array of charts that occupy the same object and share the same set of properties. The trellis chart implements the idea of *small multiples* that was popularized very nicely by Edward Tufte.

The array is built based on the chart's first dimension. Optionally, we can build a grid based on two dimensions. In this case, the values of the first dimension will be listed in columns while the value of the second dimension will be listed in rows of the grid.

The process of configuring the trellis chart is amazingly simple (see Figure 12.17).

Once you have a chart that you'd like to turn into the trellis chart, you add the desired dimension(s) in front of the existing dimension of the chart (A) and click on the button **Trellis** (B) at the bottom-left corner of the **Dimensions** tab. The **Trellis Settings** dialog (C), which opens next, allows you to configure the look of the trellis chart.

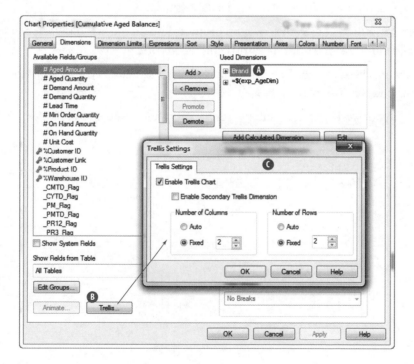

FIGURE 12.17:
Configuring the Trellis Chart

There are four **Trellis Settings**:

- The checkbox **Enable Trellis Chart** turns the feature on.

- The checkbox **Enable Secondary Trellis Dimensions** does exactly what the name says. It's used to form a two-dimensional grid of charts.

- The **Number of Columns** and the **Number of Rows** can be set to a fixed number or defined as **Auto** for automatic positioning of charts.

In the following exercise, you are going to create the trellis version of the cumulative aging chart that you created in the previous exercise. Since your **Aging** sheet is full, you will create the new chart in a new sheet.

Exercise 12.17: Creating the Trellis Chart by Brand

1. Clone the **Aging** sheet and name the new sheet **Trellis by Brand**.

2. Remove the unnecessary charts, only keeping the cumulative bar chart that you created in the previous exercise. Resize the chart to take up all of the available space.

3. Open **Chart Properties**, **Dimensions** tab. Add Brand and promote it to be the first dimension in the list. Click on the **Trellis** button at the bottom of the **Dimensions** tab.

4. In the **Trellis Settings** dialog, check the box **Enable Trellis Chart** and select **Fixed 2** for both the **Number of Columns** and the **Number of Rows**.

5. Confirm all changes, **Save** your work, and examine the result. Your sheet should look similar to Figure 12.18.

FIGURE 12.18:

The Trellis chart by brand

The ability to compare the four brands side by side in the trellis chart opens up additional analytical possibilities. If one of the brands develops any signs of a problem, it could be spotted easily in a chart like this.

Similarly, any fashion analysis always revolves on three main dimensions of a product—style, size, and color. To this day, we haven't yet invented an effective way of visualizing three-dimensional analysis. Let's agree that the three-dimensional chart options offered by most modern software tools can't be called "effective" visualizations. For this reason, the fashion data is usually presented by style, in a matrix of sizes and colors.

QlikView allows us to go further and analyze a matrix of sizes and colors for multiple styles aggregated together. Using the two-dimensional capabilities of the trellis chart, we can create a grid of aging charts by size and color, to help our users spot trends related to individual sizes and colors.

Exercise 12.18: Creating the Trellis Chart by Size and Color

1. Copy the Trellis by Brand sheet and name the new sheet **Trellis by Size and Color**.

2. In the new sheet, open the Properties of the Aging Chart in the Dimensions tab.

3. Remove the Brand from the list of Used Dimensions and add Size and Color. Promote both new dimensions to appear in the list before the calculated Age dimension.

4. Click on the Trellis button.

5. In the Trellis Settings dialog, check the box Enable Secondary Trellis Dimension and change both the Number of Columns and the Number of Rows to Auto.

6. In the Sort tab, sort Size by Expression. Use the field [Size Sort Order] as the sorting expression.

7. In the Caption tab, check the box Allow Maximize (this chart could certainly use as much space as possible).

8. Accept all changes and examine the result.

9. You may find that the font for the Size/Color titles is too big for the small size of each little chart. The font for this title is governed by the Title Settings for the Title in Chart. Follow the steps in Figure 12.19 to reduce the title font size.

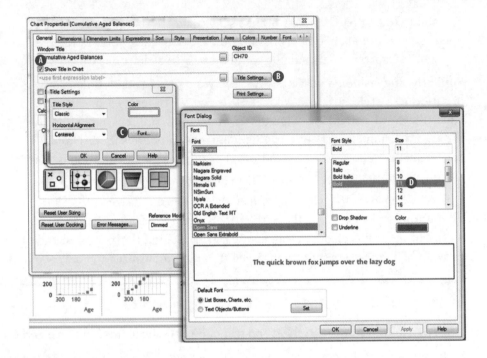

9.1. Navigate to the General tab of the Properties chart.

9.2. Enable Show Title in Chart (A). This enables the Title Settings button (B). Click on this button.

9.3. In the Title Settings dialog that opens next, click on the Font button (C).

9.4. In the Font Dialog, change the size of the font to 11. Click OK twice to accept the Font and the Title Settings.

9.5. Back in the General tab, disable Show Title in Chart again.

10. Save your work. Your finished chart should look similar to Figure 12.20.

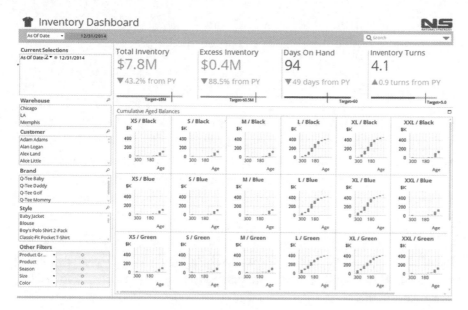

FIGURE 12.20:
Trellis chart by size
and color

Let's examine the chart together. Each row of the grid contains charts for
an individual color, while each column of the grid represents a specific size.

Comparing the patterns for various sizes and colors, we can clearly see
that the aged curves are much longer and taller for two sizes, large and
extra-large, across all colors.

We wouldn't go as far as declaring that Americans finally won the fight for
healthy living, especially when sizes XXL and XXXL show no signs of aged
inventory. More likely, our forecasting software might be configured in
such a way that L and XL are always forecasted higher than they should be.

We can't solve this problem in QlikView; however, we were able to spot
the problem in a matter of seconds, thanks to the wonderful visualization
power of the trellis chart!

This exercise completes this section, in which we explored many ways
of visualizing aging data. This was quite an eclectic section. We learned
about the keyword TOTAL and about the Inter Record Functions. We introduced grid and trellis charts. In the following sections of this chapter, you

will continue learning more about Advanced Aggregation, the use of the keyword TOTAL, and other advanced analytic techniques.

Bucket Analysis

Sometimes data scientists analyze large numbers of data elements by dividing them into equally sized buckets and comparing the performance traits of each bucket. This is mostly applicable when analyzing large groups of people—consumers, prescribers, insurance members, or insurance agents. Bucket analysis helps analysts understand what characteristics are common to the best performers and what can be done better about the bottom performers.

In our example, we will apply bucket analysis to products. This may not be as powerful as analyzing human behavior; however, it's good enough to demonstrate the mechanics of bucket analysis based on our data set.

Let's first describe the logic of assigning a bucket number to each data element—in our example, to each product. To begin, we need to decide how many buckets should be created. We typically leave that decision for the user, partly to be nice, but mostly for the benefit of delaying the decision to a later time. Hence, the number of buckets will be defined in a variable that can be modified by the user.

Next, we need to know the total number of products that are currently available (selected or associated with selection). Usually we calculate the number of values by producing a distinct count:

```
=Count(DISTINCT Product)
```

Keep in mind that this calculation will likely be used in a chart expression or in a calculated dimension. Then the formula will always return the count of products associated with each single line in the chart. In order to get the total number, we should add the TOTAL keyword after DISTINCT:

```
=Count(DISTINCT TOTAL Product)
```

Next, we need to rank our products based on the metric that we decided to use for our buckets. For example, if we decided to divide products into buckets based on Days On Hand, then we should rank the products based on each product's Days On Hand. If you remember, we use the `Rank()` function for ranking dimensions based on a measure. Following the logic that claims that "bigger is better" (in most cases), the `Rank()` function assigns number 1 to the highest value of the metric. For our metric, we'd like to assign number 1 to the lowest value of Days On Hand, and therefore we need to reverse the calculation. Multiplying by -1 does the job quite nicely:

```
=Rank( -1 * $(exp_DaysOnHandRaw), 4)
```

Note that we used the saved formula for the "raw" calculation of Days On Hand. The optional second parameter of the `Rank()` function defines how to deal with equal values. Option 4 means that the items with identical values should be numbered sequentially, and that's the best option for our needs. Feel free to explore other options in the Help section.

Now we know the total number of products, the rank of each product in the list, and the total number of buckets that we want to create. In order to calculate the bucket number, we will divide the product's ranking by the total number of products. This will give us the percentile of each product in the list. Then, we will multiply the result by the number of buckets and round up the result. For example, if we wanted to create 10 buckets, the first 10% of the products end up with number 1, the next 10% will get assigned number 2, and so on:

```
=Ceil(
    Rank( -1 * $(exp_DaysOnHandRaw($(filter_CMTD), $(filter_R12))), 4)/
    Count(DISTINCT TOTAL Product) *v_Buckets)
```

If we were going to create a chart by product and display the corresponding bucket number, we could use this formula as the expression for the bucket. Our goal, however, is to create a chart with `Bucket` as a dimension. Remember *The Second Law of AGGR()* that we introduced earlier in this chapter? The only way to use an aggregated formula in a calculated dimension is to enclose it in the `AGGR()` function.

Now, the million-dollar question—what dimension should be used in the `AGGR()` function? Well, since we are ranking products, we should use `Product` as the dimension of the `AGGR()`. The aggregated results will be associated with `Products`, and therefore we will be able to calculate any product-related metrics in this chart. Here is how this formula should look like in a chart dimension:

```
=AGGR(
    ceil(
        Rank( -1 * $(exp_DaysOnHandRaw($(filter_CMTD), $(filter_R12))), 4)/
        Count(DISTINCT TOTAL Product)
        *v_Buckets
    )
, Product)
```

In a way, the chart by buckets resembles a histogram—we calculate an aggregated measure as a dimension, and then we calculate other metrics that are associated with the aggregated results of the dimension.

In the following exercise, you build a combo chart that plots Average Days On Hand and total Demand by bucket, when the buckets are calculated based on Days on Hand. We will also add a new variable v_Buckets that will be used to store the desired number of buckets and the input box that will allow our users to alter the value.

Exercise 12.19: Bucket Analysis of Products by Days on Hand

1. Copy the Inventory Dashboard sheet and name the new sheet **Days On Hand**.

2. You can either remove the two existing charts, or keep and modify them to fit our needs. We'll leave the choice to you.

3. Create a new Input Box.

4. In the Input Box Properties, add a New Variable v_Bucket. Highlight the name in the list of Displayed Variables and enter the label **Number of Buckets**.

5. In the Constraints tab, configure the following settings (see Figure 12.21):

   5.1. Under the Input Constraints, select Predefined Values Only (A) and uncheck Enable Edit Expression Dialog (B).

   5.2. Under the Value List, select Predefined Values in Drop-down (C).

   5.3. Under Predefined Values, select Number Series, From **2** To **100** (D).

   5.4. Enter **10** as the Value (E).

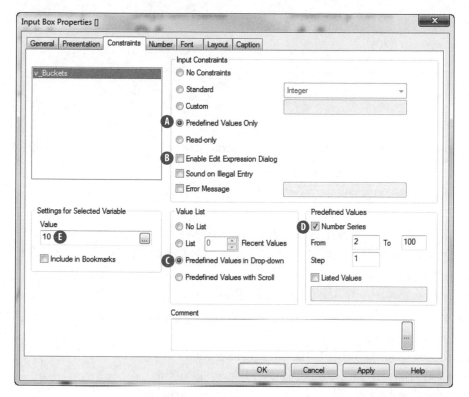

FIGURE 12.21:
Input Box properties,
Constraints tab

6. In the Caption tab, clear the Show Caption checkbox.

7. Accept all changes. Resize and reposition the input box. Place it on top of the screen next to the As Of Date multi box, using the gray banner as the background. Use Figure 12.22 (shown after Exercise 12.20) as a visual guide.

8. Create a new Combo Chart or modify the existing chart on the left. Name the chart **Average Days On Hand by Bucket**. Select Combo Chart as the Chart Type.

9. Create the following Calculated Dimension. Label it **Days on Hand Bucket**:

```
=AGGR(
     ceil(
          Rank( -1 * $(exp_DaysOnHandRaw($(filter_CMTD), $(filter_R12))), 4)/
           Count(DISTINCT TOTAL Product) *v_Buckets)
, Product)
```

10. In the Expressions tab, create two expressions:

    10.1. Avg Days, displayed in Bars:

```
avg(AGGR($(exp_DaysOnHandRaw($(filter_CMTD), $(filter_R12))), Product))
```

    10.2. Demand, displayed in Lines and Symbols:

```
$(exp_Demand($(filter_R12)))
```

11. In the Sort tab, sort the dimension by Numeric Value, Ascending.

12. In the Axes tab, highlight Demand and change its Position from Left to Right. Check Continuous for the Dimension Axis. This setting will allow better scaling of the X-axis when the number of buckets is high.

13. In the Number tab, format Avg Days as Integer and type **Days** as the Symbol. Format Demand as Money with no decimals and enter the four Symbols for automatic scaling—**$, $K, $MM,** and **$Bn.**

14. Accept all changes and examine the result. Notice that the legend takes up a lot of valuable space. Using Ctrl-Shift, move the legend to the top edge of the chart.

15. As an extra visual aid, we can color-code the bars based on the comparison of the average days to the target number for "Days On Hand." Open Properties, Expressions tab, and navigate to the Background Color attribute for the Avg Days expression. Enter the following formula for the Background Color (note that we are using the expression label in the formula):

```
if ([Avg Days] <= v_TargetDaysOnHand, $(color_Green), $(color_Red)   )
```

16. Similarly, use *$(color_Blue)* as the Background Color expression for Demand.

17. Save your work. Your formatted chart should look like the chart on the left in Figure 12.22.

Next you create the chart on the right. It will be a bar chart that shows the on-hand balances for each one of the 10 buckets. The balances are divided into Excess and Non-Excess and presented in a stacked bar chart. This chart uses the same calculated dimension as the first chart, so it probably makes sense to clone the chart on the left and modify it to our needs.

Exercise 12.20: Bucket Analysis of Products: Chart 2

1. Clone the chart on the left and position the second copy next to it on the right. Make the following changes in the Properties of the second chart.

2. Name the chart **Distribution of On Hand Balances by Days Buckets**. Select Bar Chart as the Chart Type.

3. In the Expressions tab, replace the existing expressions with the following two expressions:

   3.1. Excess:

   ```
   $(exp_Excess($(filter_CMTD), $(filter_R6)))
   ```

   3.2. Non Excess (note that we refer to the label of the other expression here):

   ```
   $(exp_OnHand($(filter_CMTD)))   - Excess
   ```

4. Promote the Non Excess expression to the first place. Add Background Color attributes to both expressions, to color Non Excess inventory using color_Green and Excess inventory using color_Red.

5. In the Style tab, select Stacked as the Subtype.

6. In the Number tab, format both expressions as Money with no decimals and enter the four symbols for automatic scaling—**$, $K, $MM,** and **$Bn**.

7. Accept all changes and examine the result. If necessary, move the legend to the top edge of the chart again. Your finished sheet should look similar to Figure 12.22. Save your work.

FIGURE 12.22:
The Days On Hand sheet

Let's discuss our findings. Understandably, more inventory belongs to products with higher days on hand. Fortunately, the last bucket, which can be called obsolete, has relatively low inventory balance. That is a pleasant surprise. Also, notice that only the last two buckets show any excess inventory. This means that over 80% of our products don't have any excess inventory at all. These observations could not be made from any of the previous visualizations that we've learned so far.

Does It Get Any More Advanced with Advanced Aggregation and Advanced Set Analysis?

This section does not cover any dazzling visualization techniques. Instead, we will have a detailed discussion about the intricacies of Advanced Aggregation and advanced Set Analysis. We truly hope that at the end of this section, you will have more answers than questions, but surely you will have plenty of both.

We will cover the following topics:

- Using the TOTAL keyword versus AGGR()—which one to use when?
- DISTINCT and NODISTINCT AGGR()
- *The Third Law of AGGR()*—safe versus unsafe use of AGGR() in chart expressions
- Set Analysis with implicit field value definitions—functions P() and E()
- Set Analysis with a combination of several conditions

Comparing TOTAL with AGGR()

We introduced two techniques that serve a somewhat similar purpose—the keyword TOTAL and the Advanced Aggregation function AGGR(). Developers often ask which technique is better and how they compare. Just to remind you of the basics, we'll repeat the most common definitions.

The TOTAL keyword can be used in chart expressions in order to "break out" of the dimensional structure and produce a total—either the total for all possible values, or a total for some of the dimensions:

```
Sum(TOTAL Value)
```

or

```
Sum(TOTAL <Dim1, Dim2> Value)
```

The data for the TOTAL calculation is provided from the mini-cube that was created for the same chart; therefore, only existing chart dimensions can make up the list of the TOTAL dimensions.

AGGR(), on the other hand, is free from this limitation, at least technically. The data for the AGGR() function is provided from the associative database and isn't limited to chart dimensions. Let's explore how it works in detail.

Examine the straight table in Figure 12.23.

TOTAL vs. AGGR()

Style	Size	Color	count (Product)	count(TOTAL Product)	count(TOTAL <Size> Product)	count(TOTAL <Color> Product)	sum(AGGR (count (Product), Size))	sum(AGGR (count (Product), Color))
			490	490	490	490	490	490
Polo Shirt	XS	White	1	490	70	98	70	98
Polo Shirt	XS	Red	1	490	70	98	0	98
Polo Shirt	XS	Green	1	490	70	98	0	98
Polo Shirt	XS	Blue	1	490	70	98	0	98
Polo Shirt	XS	Black	1	490	70	98	0	98
Polo Shirt	L	White	1	490	70	98	70	0
Polo Shirt	M	White	1	490	70	98	70	0

FIGURE 12.23: TOTAL vs. AGGR()

All six expressions count products by Style, Size and Color in different ways:

1. The first expression is the simple count of products.

2. The second expression is the count of products with the TOTAL keyword. For every line in the chart, it returns the total number of all products.

3. The third expression counts products with the TOTAL by Size. For every line in the chart, it returns the count of products by the corresponding Size. Don't be surprised by the fact that every line shows exactly the same count. In our company (or rather because of the way we generated the data set), all styles are produced in the same colors and the same sizes.

4. Similarly, the fourth expression returns the count of products by Color. Again, the total per Color appears in every line.

5. In the fifth expression, the same count by Size is calculated using AGGR()—the products are counted by Size, and then the aggregated results are summed. Notably, the result of the AGGR() is the same as the result of the TOTAL, only it appears once for each Size.

6. In the sixth expression, the total by Color is calculated using AGGR() in a similar way. Similarly, the aggregated results only appear once for each Color.

The difference between the results of TOTAL and AGGR() may look confusing at first. However, the reason for such strange behavior by the AGGR() function can be found in the basic definition of AGGR() in the Help file. The calculation will produce a single result for each distinct combination of the dimension values.

From the same definition in the Help article, we learn that AGGR() can be equipped with the keywords DISTINCT or NODISTINCT. Contrary to the other aggregation functions, AGGR() is considered DISTINCT by default. Now we can understand the unexpected results that we saw in Figure 12.23. The AGGR() results appeared only once per Size or per Color, because the AGGR() function is DISTINCT by default. Let's see the same chart, produced with the NODISTINCT version of AGGR(), in Figure 12.24.

FIGURE 12.24:
TOTAL vs. NODISTINCT AGGR()

TOTAL vs. AGGR() - NODISTINCT

Style	Size	Color	count (Product)	count(TOTAL Product)	count(TOTAL <Size> Product)	count(TOTAL <Color> Product)	sum(AGGR (NODISTINCT count (Product), Size))	sum(AGGR (NODISTINCT count (Product), Color))
			490	490	490	490	34,300	48,020
Baby Jacket	L	Black	1	490	70	98	70	98
Blouse	L	Black	1	490	70	98	70	98
Boy's Polo ...	L	Black	1	490	70	98	70	98
Classic-Fit ...	L	Black	1	490	70	98	70	98
Crew T-Shirt...	L	Black	1	490	70	98	70	98

Note that the NODISTINCT AGGR() produced consistent results in the chart lines; however, the total numbers are now way out of line. This is because the aggregation was repeated for each detailed row. Therefore the totals got duplicated many times. If we wanted to use this AGGR() for some sort of a line calculation, we'd have to do something different at the total level.

At this point, we are ready to draw our first conclusion about using TOTAL vs. AGGR().

> ## Using TOTAL vs. AGGR() in Charts
>
> When we need to summarize data to the level of an existing chart dimension, TOTAL produces more accurate results more predictably and more efficiently. The only reason to use AGGR() in chart expressions is for its ability to use dimensions that are outside of the scope of the chart.

Using TOTAL and AGGR() with Dimensions Outside of the Chart Data

Let's explore what happens when TOTAL and AGGR() are used with dimensions that are outside of the chart's scope. Figure 12.25 shows the same straight table, with Size as the only dimension (no Style and no Color).

TOTAL and AGGR() - with Dimensions Outside of the Chart

Size	count (Product)	count(TOTAL Product)	count(TOTAL <Size> Product)	count(TOTAL <Color> Product)	sum(AGGR (count (Product), Size))	sum(AGGR (count (Product), Color))	sum(AGGR (count (Product), Style, Color, Size))	sum(AGGR (count (Product), Product))
	490	490	490	490	490	490	490	490
XS	70	490	70	490	70	490	70	70
S	70	490	70	490	70	0	70	70
M	70	490	70	490	70	0	70	70
L	70	490	70	490	70	0	70	70
XL	70	490	70	490	70	0	70	70
XXL	70	490	70	490	70	0	70	70
XXXL	70	490	70	490	70	0	70	70

FIGURE 12.25:
TOTAL and AGGR() with dimensions outside of the chart's scope

The TOTAL calculation by Size produces the expected results, because Size is the chart dimension.

The TOTAL calculation by Color, however, produces incorrect totals, because Color is not one of the chart dimensions. The "wrong" dimension is simply ignored.

Well, you could say—repeating the GEICO commercials—everybody knows that! What about the AGGR() calculations?

The AGGR() by Size produced the correct results, as expected.

The AGGR() by Color, however, produced incorrect totals. Instead of the total by Color, it produced the overall total, populated in one of the chart lines. Let's try to visualize the process, in order to understand why.

The AGGR() function by Color aggregated the detailed data by Color. So, now we have a virtual table in memory with the pre-aggregated totals by Color. Now, we are trying to present those pre-aggregated totals by Size. This is simply impossible—our data is pre-aggregated at a different level, which cannot be presented by Size. Hence, the total of all colors is presented at one of the chart rows.

So, when we use AGGR() to pre-aggregate data at a certain level, we should be careful about presenting that data at a different level of aggregation. We can always aggregate *up*, but never *down* and never *sideways*, so to speak.

Let's continue reviewing the chart expressions in Figure 12.26. We added two more columns at the end to demonstrate the correct use of AGGR() in chart dimensions. In the seventh expression, the AGGR() is defined with Style, Color, and Size as the AGGR dimensions. This expression produces the correct results, because Size is one of the chart dimensions. If we have subtotals by Style, Size, and Color, we can always aggregate them up by Size.

AGGR() and Chart Dimensions

Conclusion: You can secure the accurate calculation of AGGR() by adding the chart dimensions to the list of the AGGR() dimensions (when it's possible without changing the logic of the AGGR() function).

Now, let's take a look at the last expression in the chart. It aggregates the calculation by Product. The expression returns accurate results, even though Product is not one of the chart dimensions, and the chart dimension Size was not included as one of the AGGR() dimensions. Why would this formula work, if the same formula by Color didn't work?

The answer is hidden in the logical relations between these fields. Size can be considered one of the attributes of a Product. Therefore, multiple products can be aggregated up to the Size level. Colors, on the other hand, are not related to sizes in the same way. Each color can be associated with multiple sizes and vice versa. Using technical lingo, sizes and products have a one-to-many relation (one size relates to many products), while sizes and colors have a many-to-many relation (many sizes relate to many colors). It is safe to use AGGR() with dimensions that can be aggregated up to the chart dimensions.

Now we are ready to formulate *The Third Law of AGGR().*

The Third Law of AGGR()

With very few exceptions, it is unsafe to use AGGR() with dimensions that don't include the chart dimensions and cannot be aggregated up to the chart dimensions. In other words, it's only safe to use AGGR() if:

- The AGGR() dimensions include all of the chart dimensions, or

- The AGGR() dimensions are more detailed than the chart dimensions and therefore the AGGR() subtotals can be aggregated up to the chart dimensions.

Here are some examples of "safe" versus "unsafe" uses of AGGR() in chart expressions:

CHART DIMENSIONS	AGGR() DIMENSIONS	SAFE OR UNSAFE	COMMENTS
Channel and Year	Customer and Date	Safe	Customers can be aggregated to channels and dates can be aggregated to years.
Channel and Year	Product and Date	Unsafe	Products cannot be aggregated to channels (many-to-many).
Style and Month	Product Category and Week	Unsafe	Product categories cannot be aggregated to styles and weeks overlap with months.
Product Description	Product Short Name	Unsafe	Even though both attributes describe Products, there is a possibility of having multiple Product Description values per single Product Short Name, which makes this AGGR unsafe.

In very few specific implementations, developers may use the AGGR() function in an unsafe manner intentionally. This is done when a certain aggregated total needs to appear only once per dimension. For example, the order discount needs to appear only once per order, even if the chart displays detailed order lines.

More About Advanced Set Analysis

We talked about Set Analysis several times throughout the book, and we introduced several examples from very simple to very advanced. You must be wondering—does it get any more advanced than that? Actually, it can.

The most complex Set Analysis scenarios can happen when a number of different conditions need to be combined in a variety of ways.

Ranking Products with an Additional Condition

In Chapter 8, you learned how to use Set Analysis and ranking to limit charts to a certain number of top performers (see Exercise 10.27).

Now, let's implement the same logic to ranking products. Let's create a chart that shows the current on-hand balance for the top 20 products. For the purpose of this exercise, we will not use the dimension limits feature. Instead, we will use Set Analysis and ranking to limit the chart to 20 entries.

To refresh your memory, the calculation of the current on hand balance, with the As of Date filter, looks like this:

```
sum({<_CMTD_Flag={1}>} [# On Hand Amount])
```

In order to limit the list to top 20, we should add another Set Analysis filter that limits the Rank() of the same expression to the first 20 entries:

```
Product = {"=rank(sum({<_CMTD_Flag={1}>} [# On Hand Amount]), 4) <=20"}>}
```

The complete expression looks like this:

```
sum(
  {<_CMTD_Flag={1},
     Product = {"=rank(sum({<_CMTD_Flag={1}>} [# On Hand Amount]), 4) <=20"}
  >}   [# On Hand Amount])
```

You'll create this chart in Exercise 12.21 before continuing any further.

Exercise 12.21: Ranking Products by Inventory

1. Copy the Inventory Dashboard sheet and name the new sheet **Total Inventory**.

2. Remove the two existing charts in the new sheet and create a new straight table.

3. Name the new chart **Top 20 Products**.

4. Use Product as a dimension.

5. Create a single expression with the following formula. Label the expression **On Hand**:

```
sum(
    {<_CMTD_Flag={1},
        Product = {"=rank(sum({<_CMTD_Flag={1}>} [# On Hand Amount]), 4) <=20"}
    >}   [# On Hand Amount])
```

6. Format the number as Money with no decimals.

7. Accept all changes, Save your work, and examine the result.

You should be able to see the list of exactly 20 products and their on-hand balances. Now, let's complicate the requirement. One of our product attributes is Season. This field should be available in the multi box that we named **Other Filters**. If you select **Summer** as a season, you will see a list of top 20 products that belong to the summer season.

Now, let's imagine that we need to calculate *Top 20 On Hand Balances for Summer Products* in an expression, without the need to select the Season manually. This means that we need to add the necessary filter to our Set Analysis modifier.

Well, this is easy. Everybody knows that. We simply add the filter for the field Season to the Set Analysis expression. There is nothing advanced about it!

Exercise 12.22: Ranking Products by Inventory, Continued

1. Clone the chart that you just created and place the copy next to the original.

2. Modify the expression to include the filter for Season:

```
sum(
    {<_CMTD_Flag={1},
      Season={Summer},
      Product = {"=rank(sum({<_CMTD_Flag={1}>} [# On Hand Amount]), 4) <=20"}
    >}   [# On Hand Amount])
```

3. Change the title of the chart to **Top 20 Summer Products**.

4. Accept all changes, Save your work, and examine the result.

Count the lines of the chart now. Do you still see 20 lines? If everything worked as expected, you should see about 10 lines now. How can we explain it? When we selected the Season manually, we definitely saw 20 products. When we do the same thing in Set Analysis, the list of products is much shorter! How is this possible?

The explanation is based on the way Set Analysis filters work. When we selected the Season manually, our Set Analysis expression applied the current MTD flag and ranked the *available* products by their on hand balances. Hence, only summer products participated in the process of ranking.

On the other hand, when we applied the same condition as a Set Analysis filter, the two filters are evaluated independently and the end result is the intersection of the two filters. This time, *all* products (assuming that no other selections were made) are ranked and the top 20 on-hand balances are selected. Then, the set of these 20 products is intersected with the set of data associated with summer. Apparently, only 10 out of 20 top products are associated with summer.

Hence, our Set Analysis condition answered a different question—what summer products made it to the list of top 20 products? The result could contain any number of lines between 0 and 20. How can we get back to our original question and compile a list of top 20 summer products? We need to ensure that we limit the scope of the ranking to the summer products only. Hence, the same Set Analysis filter needs to be included in the sum() function that's being ranked. In Exercise 12.23, you fix the expression in the chart accordingly.

Exercise 12.23: Ranking Products by Inventory: Final

1. Open the chart properties and modify the expression to include the filter for Season in the sum that's being ranked:

```
sum(
    {<_CMTD_Flag={1},
      Product = {"=rank(
          sum({<_CMTD_Flag={1}, Season={Summer}>} [# On Hand Amount])
      , 4) <=20"}
    >}   [# On Hand Amount])
```

2. Accept all changes, **Save** your work, and examine the result.

Now you should see 20 lines again.

> ## Combining Multiple Conditions in Set Analysis
>
> Conclusion: When multiple conditions must be combined in Set Analysis, it's not always obvious where certain filters need to be placed. Some of the conditions may need to be nested in other advanced search conditions in order to produce the expected results.

Implementing Multiple Conditions with Boolean OR and AND

Sometimes we need to implement several set conditions and apply Boolean operations, such as intersection (AND) or union (OR), differently from their default function.

By default, when we specify a list of values for a single field, the different values are added using the Boolean union (OR). For example, the set condition Year = {2013, 2014, 2015} translates to the following logical condition: "Year should be equal to 2013, OR to 2014, OR to 2015."

Conversely, different filters that are listed in the comma-separated list are combined with an AND operation. For example, the following condition:

Size = {L}, Color = {Blue}

translates to the logical condition "Size is equal to L and Color is equal to Blue."

Sometimes we need to elicit the opposite effect. For example, select products that were sold in both years 2013 and 2014. Or select products where either one of two different conditions is true—either large or blue (admittedly, this particular example doesn't make any sense).

There are several ways to implement these tricky combinations using Boolean math. The most robust method, however, is to use so-called *implicit field value definitions*. The name is a bit quirky, and it came up as an opposite to the *explicit* field values that we specify in simpler Set Analysis conditions. We could argue that any advanced Set Analysis condition could be classified as implicit field *values definitions*, but in this particular case, the term refers specifically to using two functions—P() and E(). P stands for *possible* values and E stands for *excluded* values. Both functions produce a list of values (possible or excluded) of a certain field, with a certain Set Analysis condition. The syntax of the Set filter is this:

```
Field1=P({Set} Field2)
```

Functions P() and E() can be very helpful any time there is a need to make a selection in one field based on certain conditions applied to another field (or even to the same field, when necessary).

The specific advantage with multiple conditions is caused by the ease of combining multiple functions P() and E() in one filter. For example:

```
Field1=(P({Set} Field2) + P({Set} Field3)) * E({Set} Field4)
```

Let's develop a chart that displays the most problematic products—those that have both Days On Hand above target and Annual Turns below target. Both conditions need to be applied to the Product field and the results need to be combined with the Boolean AND operand (intersection, or Boolean multiplication).

Let's build this Set Analysis condition step by step. Using the expression variables that we created earlier, the condition for the Days On Hand comparison needs to be enclosed into the advanced Set Analysis filter for the Product field:

```
Product={"=$(exp_DaysOnHand($(filter_CMTD), $(filter_R12)))
>=$(v_TargetDaysOnHand)"}
```

This filter will be used in the inner Set for the P() function and applied once again to the Product field:

```
P( {<Product={"=$(exp_DaysOnHand($(filter_CMTD), $(filter_R12)))
>=$(v_TargetDaysOnHand)"}>} Product)
```

In a similar way, the second P() function, representing the Turns condition, can be formulated like this:

```
P( {<Product={"=$(exp_Turns($(filter_CMTD), $(filter_R12)))
<$(v_TargetTurns)"}>} Product)
```

Now, the two P() functions can be multiplied and the result can be applied as a filter to the Product field. Here is the full expression:

```
sum({<_CMTD_Flag={1},
Product=P( {<Product={"=$(exp_DaysOnHand($(filter_CMTD), $(filter_R12)))
                      >=$(v_TargetDaysOnHand)"}>} Product) *
        P( {<Product={"=$(exp_Turns($(filter_CMTD), $(filter_R12)))
                      <$(v_TargetTurns)"}>} Product)
>} [# On Hand Amount])
```

In Exercise 12.24, you develop a straight table chart that implements this expression. Since you will use the same Set Analysis filter several times, save the filter in a variable and reuse it when needed.

Exercise 12.24: Combining Multiple Conditions in a Set

1. Delete the earlier two versions of the Top 20 Products chart, to make room for new charts.

2. Create a new straight table and name it **Products with High Days On Hand and Low Turns**. Use Product as a dimension.

3. In the Expressions tab, use the formula that we just built step by step as the expression. Label the expression **On Hand**. Format the number as Money with no decimals.

4. Accept all changes and examine the result.

5. Once you are satisfied with the result, create a new variable and name it **filter_ProductsWithHighDaysLowTurns**.

6. Copy and paste the filter definition from the chart expression to the definition of the new variable:

   ```
   Product=P( {<Product={"=$(exp_DaysOnHand($(filter_CMTD), $(filter_R12)))
                          >=$(v_TargetDaysOnHand)"}>} Product) *
           P( {<Product={"=$(exp_Turns($(filter_CMTD), $(filter_R12)))
                          <$(v_TargetTurns)"}>} Product)
   ```

7. Modify the chart expression, replacing the same filter with the new variable enclosed in the dollar-sign expansion:

   ```
   sum({<_CMTD_Flag={1}, $(filter_ProductsWithHighDaysLowTurns)>}
   [# On Hand Amount])
   ```

You should see a straight table that lists products and their on-hand balances. The total on-hand value for the chart should be approximately $4M, or about a half of the company total. We don't truly know if the products in the list satisfy our condition. In order to verify the logic, and to make the chart more informative for the users, let's add two more expressions—Days On Hand and Turns.

Exercise 12.25: Adding Days On Hand and Turns to the Straight Table

1. Open the Properties of the straight table and add two new Expressions:

    1.1. Days on Hand:

    $(exp_DaysOnHand($(filter_CMTD), $(filter_R12)))

    1.2. Turns:

    $(exp_Turns($(filter_CMTD), $(filter_R12)))

2. In the Presentation tab, Center labels for all three expressions and Wrap Header Text to 2 Lines.

3. In the Number tab, format Days on Hand as Integer and Turns as a Fixed to 1 Decimal.

4. Accept all changes, Save your work, and examine the result. Your chart should look similar to Figure 12.26.

FIGURE 12.26:
Products with High
Days On Hand and Low
Turns

Products with High Days On Hand and Low Turns

Product	On Hand	Days On Hand	Turns
	$4,072,168	58	4.0
Baby Jacket L Black	$28,560	101	2.1
Baby Jacket L Green	$35,666	120	1.7
Baby Jacket L Red	$30,625	108	1.9
Baby Jacket L White	$30,989	108	1.9
Baby Jacket M Black	$0	32	6.8
Baby Jacket M Green	$0	32	6.7
Baby Jacket M Red	$0	38	5.6
Baby Jacket M White	$0	32	6.7

As you can see, the list of products in the chart is now longer, and some products have zeros in their on-hand balances. It happened because the first expression in the chart applied a Set Analysis condition that allows only certain products into its calculation. The second and the third expressions, however, don't have the same condition and therefore they produce their results for all products.

In order to ensure that the whole chart is limited to the same condition, we should replicate the same Set Analysis modifier in all aggregated functions across all chart expressions. That is a lot of work!

An easier workaround is to condition all other expressions, based on the value of the first expression. We can add an IF condition that will return a value only if the [On Hand] expression returns a positive value. Since QlikView charts suppress zero values and missing values by default, the chart will not show a line for a product when all of the expressions return zeros or nulls (when necessary, this setting can be modified in the **Presentation** tab of the chart's **Properties**).

Exercise 12.26: Adding Conditions to All Other Chart Expressions

1. Open the chart **Properties** and add the new IF conditions to the second and the third expression. Each condition should test the value of the first expression. For example, here is the formula for Days On Hand (assuming that you labeled the first expression as **On Hand**):

```
IF([On Hand] >0,
    $(exp_DaysOnHand($(filter_CMTD), $(filter_R12)))
)
```

2. Accept all changes, **Save** your work, and examine the result.

The chart is now back to the shorter list of products, and we can validate visually that each one of the products has Days On Hand that are higher than the target of 60 days, and Turns that are lower than the target of five turns. You may notice that the total values of Days On Hand and Turns are not quite correct, because they represent the company total values, without the special Set Analysis condition that we applied to the first column. In our case, it's sufficient to remove total values. If totals were important, then our easy workaround wouldn't be helpful. We'd have to replicate the same Set Analysis condition in all chart expressions.

This exercise completes the discussion of advanced Set Analysis. The following section introduces comparative analysis using *Alternate States*.

Comparative Analysis Using Alternate States

The introduction of Set Analysis in QlikView 8.5 was revolutionary. It equipped QlikView developers with a robust tool that allowed them to define a specific set of data for each individual aggregation. In a similar way, the introduction of Alternate States in QlikView 11.0 enabled developers to take comparative analysis to the next level.

Prior to Alternate States, developers were able to perform simple comparisons—for example, comparing this year's performance to the same for the prior year. Sometimes, the needs of the business analysis require more than that. You may need to compare one set of selected products, customers, and locations, with another set of products, customers, and locations.

Alternate States allow defining and maintaining multiple sets of user selections that are independent of each other. In the QlikView Server environment, every user can have a unique set of selected values and multiple users can navigate the same document independently at the same time. Similarly, each Alternate State can hold its own set of selections.

This section describes the various ways of using Alternate States for comparative analysis.

Declaring Alternate States

Alternate States need to be created (or, as it is sometimes called, "declared") before they can be used in objects. This is done in the **Alternate States** dialog, which is available from the **General** tab of the **Document Properties** dialog (see Figure 12.27, A).

The **Alternate States** dialog is extremely simple. It allows you to add and remove Alternate States. In order to add a new Alternate State, click on the **Add** button (B) and enter a name for the new Alternate State. That's it, folks. It's that simple.

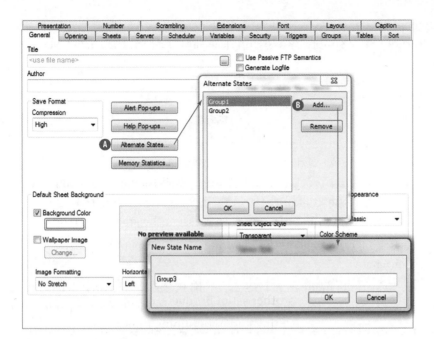

Exercise 12.27: Declaring Alternate States

Locate the Alternate States button in the General tab of the Document
Properties dialog and Add two Alternate States—**Group1** and **Group2**.

Assigning Objects to Alternate States

Once at least one Alternate State is declared, a new drop-down box
Alternate State becomes available in the **General** tab of all sheets' and
objects' **Properties** dialogs (see Figure 12.28). This drop-down box allows
you to select which state should be associated with the object.

By default, all objects belong to the <**inherited**> state. This means that the
state is inherited from the higher-level object in the hierarchy of objects.
This hierarchy (from top to bottom) includes sheets, containers, and

objects. It is possible to associate all objects on a given sheet with an Alternate State simply by assigning the same state at the sheet level.

FIGURE 12.28:

The Alternate State drop-down box

The standard state that we've been using before introducing Alternate States is called the **<default state>**. By default, the **<inherited>** state points at the **<default state>**, until we reassign the state manually.

Perhaps we should explain the meaning of assigning objects to different states.

- Selections made in list boxes, multi boxes, and in any charts affect the specific state that the corresponding object is assigned to.

- The **Current Selections Box** shows selections made in the state that the box is assigned to.

- The data that's aggregated in chart expressions reflects the state that the chart is assigned to, unless the data set was altered in Set Analysis.

Typically, when we use Alternate States to compare two groups of items, we create two sets of list boxes and two identical charts, associating one of each with each state. Visually, it helps to clearly divide the screen in two parts and to emphasize the difference using contrasting colors, to avoid any confusion.

In the following exercise, we use Alternate States to compare on-hand trends between two groups of products. We will duplicate the same group of list boxes that we use throughout this application and assign each group to one of the two Alternate States that we declared earlier. Then, we will add two charts that show a 12-month trend of the on hand balance. We will associate each chart with one of the two Alternate States. Feel free to develop these visualizations individually, or follow detailed instructions in Exercise 12.28.

Exercise 12.28: Assigning Objects to Alternate States

1. Copy the Template sheet and name the new sheet **Alternate States**.

2. In the new sheet, highlight all the objects on the left side of the screen related to selections—beginning with the Current Selections Box, all the way to the Other Filters multi-box at the bottom. Unlink the objects (right-click and choose Linked Objects ▶ Unlink This Object). It's important to unlink these objects from the rest of the linked instances; otherwise, the changes will affect the rest of the document. Make sure you get this right.

3. Clone the same group of objects and position the second copy at the right edge of your sheet.

4. Modify the Caption Text Color for all new objects on the right, using the color variable $(color_Purple). Make sure that no objects on the left change their caption color (if they do, then you didn't Unlink these objects properly—undo your changes and repeat Step 2).

5. Open Properties, General tab, for all selection objects on the left and assign them to Alternate State Group1. Similarly, assign all the objects on the right to Group2. Make different selections in the two groups and notice how they are presented in the two Current Selections Boxes.

6. Add a line chart in the upper-left part of the screen. Name the chart **On Hand Trend - Group 1**. Use Date as a dimension. Use the following formula as the expression:

   `sum( {<_R12_Flag = {1}>}[# On Hand Amount])`

7. Format the Number and the Axes to make your chart look like the chart on the left in Figure 12.29. Assign the chart to the Alternate State Group1.

8. Clone the chart and position the new copy next to the original, side by side. Assign the second chart to the Alternate State Group2 and modify the title accordingly. Change the Caption Color, as well as the main chart Color 1, using the color variable $(color_Purple).

9. Examine the behavior of the two charts when different selections are made in the two Alternate States. The upper half of your sheet should look similar to Figure 12.29. Save your work.

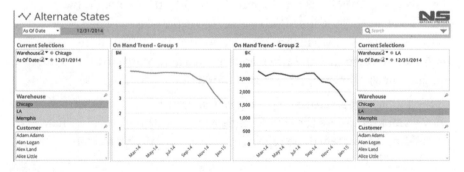

FIGURE 12.28:
Comparing two charts side by side

Using Alternate States in Combination with Set Analysis

Comparing charts assigned to different states is quite easy, but it's not always enough to get the job done. Sometimes you'll need to get more granular in your comparison and combine multiple Alternate States in a single chart.

This is done using Set Analysis with the Alternate State name serving as a set identifier. Any chart expression can be easily modified to become a state-specific expression by adding the State Name as the set identifier. For example:

- On-hand amount in the **inherited** state:

  ```
  sum( {<_R12_Flag = {1}>}[# On Hand Amount])
  ```

- On-hand amount in the **default** state:

  ```
  sum( {$<_R12_Flag = {1}>}[# On Hand Amount])
  ```

- On-hand amount in the state **Group1**:

  ```
  sum( {Group1<_R12_Flag = {1}>}[# On Hand Amount])
  ```

- On-hand amount in the state **Group2**:

  ```
  sum( {Group2<_R12_Flag = {1}>}[# On Hand Amount])
  ```

Notice that the meaning of the *default* set identifier changes with the introduction of Alternate States. Prior to Alternate States, there was no tangible difference between the first two expressions listed previously. When no set identifier was specified, the default set identifier $ was assumed implicitly. With the introduction of Alternate States, specifying (or not specifying) the $ as a set identifier is no longer a matter of good housekeeping. When the $ is specified explicitly, the expression will always use the default state. Otherwise, the expression will be applied to the inherited state, which might not point at the default state. This is important to keep in mind when adding Alternate States to an existing application with existing Set Analysis conditions.

In the following exercise, you create a similar on-hand trend chart that allows you to compare the two Alternate States within the same chart. Each Alternate State will be represented in a separate expression.

Exercise 12.29: Using Alternate States in Set Analysis

1. Clone one of the existing line charts and position the new copy below the two charts. Resize the new chart to take up all available space.

2. Assign the new chart to the <inherited> Alternate State and modify the title to end with the word **Comparison**.

3. Modify the chart expression to represent On Hand Amount for Group 1, as specified in the formula listed previously. Label the expression **Group 1**.

4. Clone the expression and modify the new copy to represent Group 2, with the corresponding Label.

5. Save your work. Your chart should look similar to the chart in Figure 12.30.

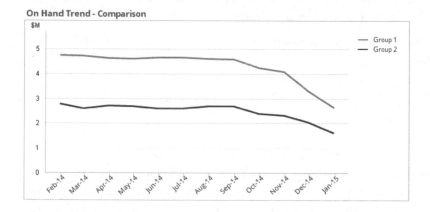

FIGURE 12.30:
Comparing two Alternate States within a single chart

Combining Selections from Multiple States

Many times, certain selections that are made in a certain state need to be combined with selections made in another Alternate State. For example, it's common to keep the date selections in the default state and to use them universally across all Alternate States.

In our application, notice the field As of Date. The selection made in the default state was also populated in both Alternate States, as a result of the restrictive setting **Always One Selected Value** that we applied on the field. At the same time, if we modify the selection on top of the screen, the selected values in the Alternate States will not change. Therefore, our comparison is not sensitive to the selection of the field As Of Date, because this field belongs to the default state.

In order to fix this problem, we need to *synchronize* selections in the As Of Date field between all states, using the default state as the base. This can be done in a couple of ways, using Set Analysis modifiers. We can refer to the *selected* field values from a certain state as follows:

```
Field=$::Field
```

or

```
Field=Group1::Field
```

Note that the Alternate State's name is used as a prefix to the field name, with the double colon (::) as a delimiter.

Alternatively, we could synchronize possible values using already familiar syntax:

```
Field = P({$} Field)
```

or

```
Field = P({Group1} Field)
```

Here, the Alternate State name is simply used as a set identifier in the P() function. Notice the subtle difference between the two formats. The first modifier brings over the *selected* values, while the second modifier brings over the *possible* values. When no selections are made, both formulas produce similar results—all possible values are brought over.

However, if other selections should limit the possible values of the field, the second formula brings only *possible* values, while the first formula still brings the full list of *selected* values (even if they are not possible due to other selections). You should pick your preferred syntax based on the needs of your analysis. Use the second form in the following exercise, in which you fix all three charts to synchronize the selections in the field As of Date across all states.

Exercise 12.30: Synchronizing Selections Across Multiple States

In all three charts, add the following set modifier to the beginning of each Set Analysis condition:

    [As Of Date]=P({$} [As Of Date]),

Verify that all three charts present the rolling 12-month period for the selected As of Date.

This exercise completes the discussion of Alternate States.

Getting Advanced with Straight Tables

Let's take a break from all the complexity of Set Analysis and AGGR() and have some fun with our straight table. If you are chuckling at the prospect of "having fun" with a straight table, we understand. Straight tables (often referred to as *reports*) are those boring textual tables that we have to read line by line in order to get any clues about the data. These are so-called "details," and most people don't like spending too much time at the detailed level.

In this section, we explore some of the visualization techniques that can help us make the straight table a bit less boring. All these different visualizations are defined in the **Representation** drop-down list on the **Expressions** tab as shown in Figure 12.31.

FIGURE 12.31:
Expressions settings, Representation Options

In addition to **Text** (the default), other **Representation** options include:

- **Image**
- Four types of **Gauges**
- **Mini Chart**
- **Link**

In this section you learn how to use these representations in a straight table.

Using Gauges in Straight Tables

Some of the same gauges that you learned about earlier as single charts can be incorporated in a straight table. As you can see in Figure 12.28, four types of gauges are available—Circular Gauge, Linear Gauge, Traffic Light Gauge, and LED Gauge.

To configure an expression to be presented as a gauge, select the desired gauge option from the **Representation** drop-down list (see Figure 12.32). After doing so, a new **Gauge Settings** button becomes available below to the drop-down list.

FIGURE 12.32:
Configuring an Expression as a Gauge

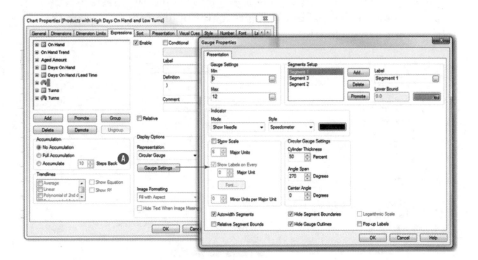

The **Gauge Settings** button opens the **Gauge Properties** dialog, which is nearly an exact copy of the **Presentation** tab for a free-standing gauge chart (with the exception of **Reference Lines** and **Texts in Chart**). The settings here are exactly the same as the settings of the gauge chart.

The gauge size is substantially smaller when it is enclosed in a straight table cell, so we rarely use **Show Scale**. For the same reason, the settings **Hide Segment Boundaries** and **Hide Gauge Outlines** become increasingly helpful. They help reduce the amount of "noise" that the black boundaries and outlines generate.

The **Linear Gauge** (one of the four available gauge types) can be used in a few ways. Traditionally, it can present the same "speedometer" look, only in a horizontal line instead of a circle. Alternatively, when it's used with the **Fill to Value** mode, it can create a horizontal bar chart embedded in a straight table. See Figure 12.33 for an example.

In the following exercise, you continue enhancing the same straight table that we developed for Exercise 12.26. You will add another helpful measure that represents the ratio of the Days on Hand over the Lead Time.

We will present the new measure in two columns—once as a text and then as a **Circular Gauge**, next to the text. We will also add another gauge to help visualize the number of Turns.

Exercise 12.31: Adding Gauges to the Straight Table

1. On the Total Inventory sheet that you developed in Exercise 12.26, open the Properties of the straight table Products with High Days and Low Turns. Make the following changes.

2. In the Expressions tab, clone the Days On Hand expression. (Right-click on the expression, select Copy, then right-click on the empty space in the list and select Paste).

3. In the second copy of the expression, divide the existing Days On Hand calculation by the average Lead Time:

```
IF([On Hand] >0,
    $(exp_DaysOnHand($(filter_CMTD), $(filter_R12))) / avg([# Lead Time])
)
```

4. Label this expression Days On Hand / Lead Time.

5. Clone the new expression and define the following settings:

   5.1. Replace the Label for the expression with a single space to suppress the automated labeling.

   5.2. Under Display Options, select Circular Gauge as the Representation.

   5.3. Click on the Gauge Settings button that appears next.

6. In the Gauge Properties dialog that opens next, configure the following settings:

   6.1. Min = **0**, Max = **12**.

   6.2. Configure three Segments—green, yellow, and red. Keep the default Autowidth Segments setting on.

   6.3. Under Indicator, keep the default settings Show Needle and Speedometer.

   6.4. Disable Show Scale.

   6.5. Check boxes Hide Segment Boundaries and Hide Gauge Outlines.

   6.6. Accept the Gauge Properties and return to the Expressions tab.

7. Clone the Turns expression and promote the new expression to appear next to the original.

   7.1. Replace the label of the new expression with a single space.

   7.2. Select Linear Gauge as the Representation for the new expression.

   7.3. Press the Gauge Settings button that appears next.

8. In the Gauge Properties dialog that opens next, configure the following settings:

   8.1. Min = **0**, Max = **5**

   8.2. Configure a single Segment and paint it blue.

   8.3. Under Indicator, select Fill to Value as a Mode.

   8.4. Disable Show Scale.

   8.5. Check boxes Hide Segment Boundaries and Hide Gauge Outlines.

   8.6. Accept the Gauge Properties and return to the Expressions tab.

9. Select No Totals for *all* expressions in the chart.

10. Continue to the Presentation tab.

    10.1. Center both the Label and the Data for all expressions.

    10.2. Under the Multiline Settings, define Header Height as 3 Lines and Cell Height as 2 lines.

11. Accept all changes and examine the result. Your chart should look similar to Figure 12.33.

Product	On Hand	Days On Hand	Days On Hand / Lead Time		Turns	
"Boy's Polo Shirt 2-Pack XL Blue"	$91,328	126	9		1.8	
"Boy's Polo Shirt 2-Pack XL Green"	$89,785	127	9		1.8	
"Boy's Polo Shirt 2-Pack L Green"	$84,662	127	9		1.8	
"Boy's Polo Shirt 2-Pack XL Black"	$83,118	120	9		1.9	
"Boy's Polo Shirt 2-Pack XL White"	$81,498	113	8		2.0	

Products with High Days On Hand and Low Turns

FIGURE 12.33:
The straight table with two gauges

Mini Charts (Sparklines)

Mini charts, just like trellis charts, were inspired by Edward Tufte. Mini charts implement and extend the concept of sparklines—tiny charts that can be embedded in text, to enrich the visual perception of the information.

In QlikView, mini charts cannot be embedded in any text. Instead, they can be incorporated into a straight table chart as an expression.

Similar to gauges, mini chart configuration starts by selecting **Mini Chart** as a **Representation** for the specified expression (see Figure 12.31). Once **Mini Chart** is selected, a new **Mini Chart Settings** button appears next to the **Representation** drop-down. See Figure 12.34 (A).

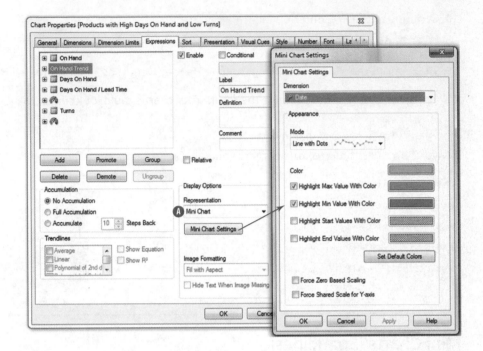

Clicking on the button opens the **Mini Chart Settings**. The first and most important setting is the **Dimension**. Each mini chart will be rendered in the context of the straight table chart dimensions. At the same time, one more dimension is needed to produce the mini chart. Since mini charts are often used to visualize trends, it's common to use one of the calendar fields, such as MonthYear, as the mini chart **Dimension**. In our case, since our data is aggregated into monthly buckets, we can use Date as the dimension.

The rest of the settings define the **Appearance** of the mini chart. The **Mode** drop-down offers five visualization options (see Figure 12.34, on the right)—**Sparkline, Line with Dots, Dots, Bars**, and **Whiskers**.

Then we can configure the colors for the mini chart. Gray is traditionally used as the main color, to keep the color intensity down. Four optional colors can be used to highlight the **Max** and **Min** values, as well as **Start** and **End** values (these are less commonly used, and they are unchecked by default).

Two checkboxes at the bottom define the scaling of the charts. The first checkbox, **Force Zero Based Scaling**, when enabled, makes the mini chart always start the Y-axis scale from zero. This is helpful when proportions within the chart are important. On the other hand, if all of the numbers are relatively high and close to each other, the mini chart with this setting will look like a horizontal line with no movement.

The second checkbox, **Force Shared Scale for Y-Axis**, when enabled, causes all mini charts across all values of the straight table dimensions to share the same scale. It helps when the comparative size of the different lines needs to be preserved. However, when some of the line items in the chart have values that are considerably smaller than others, the mini charts for the smaller items will not produce any pronounced trend patterns.

Both check boxes should be disabled when it's more important to visualize the pattern of the trend than to compare values between different items.

In the following exercise, we will add two mini charts to our straight table. The first mini chart, presented as a **Line with Dots**, will show the 12-months trend of the On Hand Balance.

The second mini chart, presented as **Bars**, will show the Aging pattern of the inventory. For this mini chart, Age will be used as the dimension.

The expressions for these two mini charts deserve a bit of explanation. Generally speaking, the expression for a mini chart is no different than the expression that calculates the total number. For example, if this was a Sales Analysis application, the same expression Sum(⌊# Amount⌋) would do just fine. In our case, however, we need to take into considerations some of the complications related to our As of Date logic, and related to the fact that our straight table is limited to those products that have high Days On Hand and low Turns.

For the On Hand Trend, we will use the date filter based on a rolling 12 months flag, in order to produce a 12-Month trend. The limitation of products have to be done within the Set Analysis. Unfortunately, mini charts can't work with our quick work-around with the IF() function. Since this expression needs to be evaluated over another dimension and presented as a mini chart, we have to spell out the whole condition within the aggregation itself. Using the saved variable with the product filter, we can formulate this expression like this:

```
sum({< _R12_Flag={1}, $(filter_ProductsWithHighDaysLowTurns) >}
[# On Hand Amount])
```

For the Aging calculation, we need to disregard the selection of As Of Date, since Aging data is not associated with this field. Also, we need to add the same product filter, to limit the set of products for the chart in the same way:

```
sum({<[As Of Date]=, $(filter_ProductsWithHighDaysLowTurns)>}
[# Aged Amount])
```

Exercise 12.32: Adding Mini Charts to a Straight Table

Using the explanation provided above, add two mini charts to the same straight table that you enhanced in the previous exercise. Your end result should look like the chart in Figure 12.35.

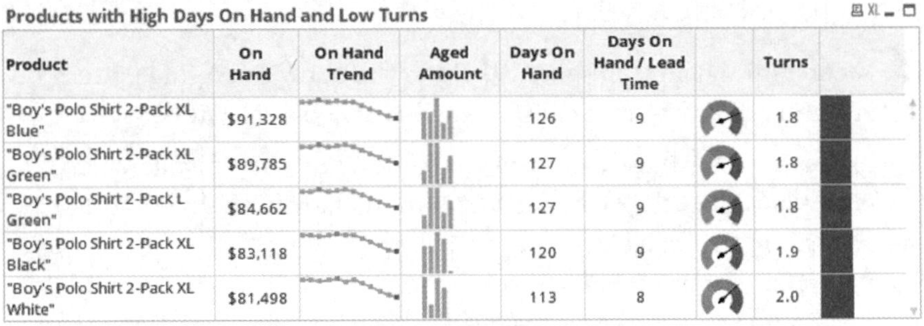

FIGURE 12.35:
The straight table with two mini charts

Products with High Days On Hand and Low Turns

Product	On Hand	On Hand Trend	Aged Amount	Days On Hand	Days On Hand / Lead Time		Turns	
"Boy's Polo Shirt 2-Pack XL Blue"	$91,328			126	9		1.8	
"Boy's Polo Shirt 2-Pack XL Green"	$89,785			127	9		1.8	
"Boy's Polo Shirt 2-Pack L Green"	$84,662			127	9		1.8	
"Boy's Polo Shirt 2-Pack XL Black"	$83,118			120	9		1.9	
"Boy's Polo Shirt 2-Pack XL White"	$81,498			113	8		2.0	

Adding Images to Straight Tables

Images can be used in QlikView in a variety of different ways. They can be presented within text objects, in list boxes, and also in straight tables.

In order to configure a chart expression as an image, we begin by creating an expression. In the **Expression Editor**, we need to create an expression that points at an image. Specifically for this purpose, the **Expression Editor** offers a special **Image** tab among other tools at the bottom (see Figure 12.36, A).

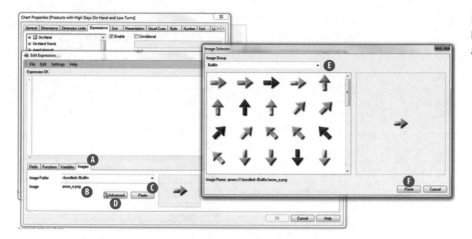

FIGURE 12.36:
Defining an expression
as an image

Image Folder (or **Image Group**) represents different collections of images that you may have in your application. By default, each application is equipped with the **<bundled>** folder and **BuiltIn** group. Additional folders and groups can be created through use of the load script statement BUNDLE INFO LOAD. This topic is outside of our scope, but feel free to explore it in the Help article "Bundle."

The **BuiltIn** group, which is loaded into QlikView automatically, contains a variety of images that can be used for communicating good or bad news—arrows, smileys, and even thumbs up and down.

The desired **Image Name** can be selected from the drop-down list **Image** (B). Once the image is selected, it can be included in the expression definition by clicking on the **Paste** button (C).

For a visual guide, we recommend clicking on the **Advanced** button (D), which opens the **Image Selector** dialog (E). This dialog offers the icons of all available images. Once the image is selected, it can be added to the expression with the same **Paste** button (F).

Obviously, just adding a static image wouldn't be very insightful. We aren't just trying to add colorful pictures to our charts. We use images to draw attention to exceptionally good and exceptionally poor performance. Therefore, the image names need to be combined with the IF() functions in order to produce a meaningful, insightful visualization that involves images.

Once we are done formulating an expression, we need to define this expression as an image by selecting **Image** in the **Representation** drop-down list (Figure 12.37).

When the expression is defined as **Image**, two additional options become available. The **Image Formatting** drop-down offers four choices for stretching the image to fit in the available space: **No Stretch**, **Fill**, **Keep Aspect**, and **Fill with Aspect**. In our experience, **Keep Aspect** is the most practical setting for most images. The checkbox **Hide Text When Image Missing** does just what it says.

This is it; pretty simple indeed. In the following exercise, you calculate the weighted average of Age for each Product in the chart. Then you add another expression that will show a yellow warning sign if the average age is over 200 days, and a red warning sign if the average age is over 365 days.

Exercise 12.33: Adding an Image to a Straight Table

1. Open the Properties of the straight table chart in the Expressions tab.

2. Add a new expression. Label it **Avg Age**. For the expression definition, copy the expression from the Aged Balance mini chart and transform it to our needs:

```
sum({<[As Of Date]=, $(filter_ProductsWithHighDaysLowTurns)>}    [# Aged Amount] * Age)/
sum({<[As Of Date]=, $(filter_ProductsWithHighDaysLowTurns)>}    [# Aged Amount])    ,
```

3. Add another expression. Label it **Age Warning**. Create the expression in the following way:

   3.1. Type the first IF condition, referencing the [Avg Age] expression by name:

   ```
   IF([Avg Age] > 365,
   ```

3.2. Then, open the Images tab at the bottom (see Figure 12.36)

3.3. Click on the Advanced button.

3.4. Scroll down to the image with the red exclamation sign.

3.5. Double click on the image. The name of the image should be added to the expression:

```
IF([Avg Age] > 365, 'qmem://<bundled>/BuiltIn/exclamation_r.png'
```

3.6. Add a comma at the end of the line and add the second `IF` condition in the second line:

```
IF([Avg Age] > 365, 'qmem://<bundled>/BuiltIn/exclamation_r.png',
IF([Avg Age] >= 200,
```

3.7. Click on the Advanced button again. This time, navigate to the yellow exclamation sign and include that image in the expression.

3.8. Add two closing parentheses at the end, to finish the two `IF()` functions. Here is the complete expression:

```
IF([Avg Age] > 365, 'qmem://<bundled>/BuiltIn/exclamation_r.png',
IF([Avg Age] >= 200, 'qmem://<bundled>/BuiltIn/exclamation_y.png'
))
```

3.9. Click OK to exit the Expression Editor and return to the Expressions tab.

4. In the Expressions tab, select Image in the Representation drop-down.
5. In the Presentation tab, center the label and the data for the two new expressions. At the bottom of the tab, replace Null Symbol and Missing Symbol with a single space. It will help eliminating the dash signs in all the lines that don't need an image.
6. In the Number tab, format the Avg Age expressions as Integer.
7. Accept all changes and examine the result. Your chart should look similar to Figure 12.38.

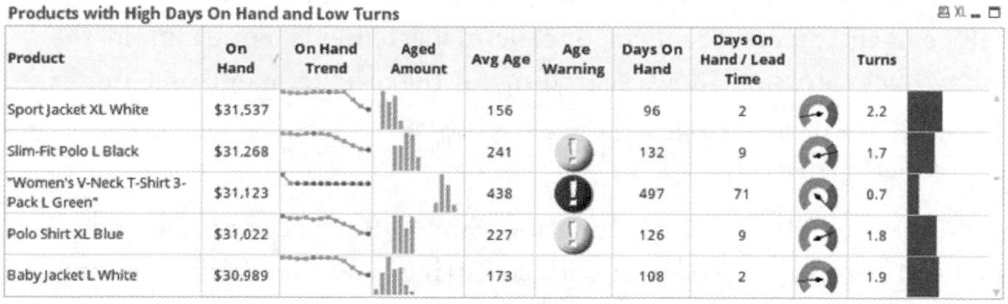

Products with High Days On Hand and Low Turns

Product	On Hand	On Hand Trend	Aged Amount	Avg Age	Age Warning	Days On Hand	Days On Hand / Lead Time		Turns	
Sport Jacket XL White	$31,537			156		96	2		2.2	
Slim-Fit Polo L Black	$31,268			241		132	9		1.7	
"Women's V-Neck T-Shirt 3-Pack L Green"	$31,123			438		497	71		0.7	
Polo Shirt XL Blue	$31,022			227		126	9		1.8	
Baby Jacket L White	$30,989			173		108	2		1.9	

FIGURE 12.38: The straight table with a warning image

Adding Links (URLs) to Straight Tables

This type of expression representation may not add much visualization, but it can make our analytical application a bit more actionable.

An expression in a straight table can be declared as a **Link** and work like any other hyperlinks that we know. The best part is that the link can be built with the information that is associated with the chart dimensions or other expressions.

For example, if your chart shows credit scores by customer, you could build a link that could take you directly to the customer profile in your back office system. Or, you could search for additional information about the customer on a web site of your choice.

The syntax of the **Link** expression is very simple. The expression should produce a text that is built from three parts:

1. The *Display Text*
2. The keyword <URL> enclosed in angled brackets (URL stands for Universal Resource Locator).
3. The URL itself (the web address) that needs to be opened.

The three parts are concatenated together and appear as a single text. For example:

```
='Read Our Blog Here' & '<URL>' & 'www.naturalsynergies.com/blog'
```

In this example, since this is a static text that doesn't depend on any dimension values, the concatenation wasn't necessary. The following simplified expression would work just as well:

```
='Read Our Blog Here<URL>www.naturalsynergies.com/blog'
```

In a more complex implementation, the URL could include concatenated values of customers, products, or other data elements. For example, the following expression allows searching for the product name on Google:

```
='Search the Product<URL>www.google.com/#q=
    ' & Replace(Product, ' ', '%20')
```

Note the use of the Replace() function. Since URL syntax disallows spaces, we need to replace each space with the string '%20'. Generally speaking, a number of reserved characters may need to be replaced in order to make any text ready to be included in a URL. If you have a specific need for that, look up the subject of "Percent Encoding of URL characters" and use a nested `Replace()` statement to build a URL-safe string.

An even more interesting implementation of the Link feature is using the *mailto: URL scheme* to simplify the task of sending a context-specific e-mail directly from the QlikView application. For example, your inventory analysis may call for a certain action that should be taken by a planner. You may need to e-mail the planner and provide all necessary measures that you see in the chart—the on-hand balance, the days on hand, and so on. Similarly, if you are using QlikView in a call center environment, you could format a `tel:` URL and automate the process of dialing the numbers of customers, suppliers, etc.

In the following exercise you add a Link expression that prepares a draft of an e-mail to the planner. In the body of the e-mail, you inform the planner about a specific product, the On Hand Balance and the Days On Hand. This simplified e-mail will look like this:

```
To: Planner@QTeeBrands.com|
Subject: Product AAAAAAAAAAA
Dear Planner,


The Product AAAAAAAAAAA has a balance of
$N,NNN or NNN Days On Hand.


Please stop sourcing this Product.
```

While the full description of the `mailto:` syntax is outside of our scope, we need to explain a few elements that we used in the process of constructing this URL:

- The subject line is defined by the keyword `Subject:`
- The body of the e-mail is defined by the keyword `Body:`

- The parts of the URL, such as Mailto, Subject, and Body, are separated by an ampersand sign '&'
- The space character should be replaced with the code '%20'
- The dot character should be replaced with '%2E'
- The comma character should be replaced with '%2C'
- A new line can be forced with '%0A'

If you feel up to the challenge, go ahead and add this expression on your own, or use the instructions in the following exercise.

Exercise 12.34: Adding a Link Expression

1. Open the **Expressions** tab for the **Properties** of the same straight table you used in the previous exercise.

2. Add the following expression:

```
= IF([On Hand] > 0,
      'Mail the Planner <URL>mailto:Planner@QTeeBrands.com&' &
      'subject=Product%20' & replace(Product, ' ', '%20') & '&' &
      'body=Dear%20Buyer' & '%2C' & '%0A' & '%0A' &
      'Product%20' & replace(Product, ' ', '%20') &
      '%20has%20a%20balance%20of%20' & num([On Hand], '$#,##0') &
      '%20or%20' & num([Days On Hand], '#,##0') &
      '%20Days%20On%20Hand' & '%2E' &  '%0A' & '%0A' &
      'Please%20stop%20sourcing%20this%20Product' & '%2E'
)
```

3. Label the expression **Mail the Planner**.

4. Under **Display Options**, select **Link** from the **Representation** drop-down list.

5. Accept all changes and examine the result. You should see a new column with the underlined text Mail the Planner in every line. Click on one of the links. You will get a message asking for your approval to launch the mail application.

6. If your mail client is properly configured on your machine, you should see your default mail client with the New Mail Dialog popping up. The corresponding data should be already populated in the message. See Figure 12.39.

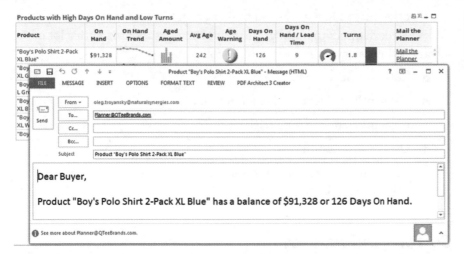

This exercise completes our discussion of the advanced visualization features that can be added to straight tables. Let us mention in conclusion that most of these features, except for mini charts, are also available for pivot tables.

Advanced Presentation Features—Buttons, Actions, and Triggers

The majority of QlikView applications are well served with the standard QlikView navigation features, such as the Tabrow for selecting sheets, auto minimize options or containers for arranging multiple charts on the sheet, and so forth. Sometimes there is a need in more sophisticated look and feel, or in more advanced interactivity that allows the users to commit certain actions by clicking buttons or other sheet objects.

Many times, these special needs are driven by the requirements of mobile environments. As mobile BI gains more and more popularity, developers need to make their dashboards suitable for mobile users. Mobile clients may not have access to all of the menus that are available to computer clients; hence, certain menu options may have to be available directly on the screen.

This section introduces advanced presentation features that allow QlikView developers to build exquisitely sharp dashboards with a lot of advanced interactivity. It describes the following features:

- Buttons and actions
- Using other objects to invoke actions
- Invoking actions using triggers
- Using show conditions
- Using buttons, actions, and show conditions for developing advanced navigation features

Buttons and Actions

The button is a special object type in QlikView that allows you to add a standard-looking button on the sheet. Once clicked, the button triggers a set of actions that can perform some of the standard interactive functions such as activating a sheet, minimizing an object, making a selection, or setting a value of a variable.

Adding a Button

As any other sheet objects, a new button can be added by right-clicking on the screen and selecting **New Sheet Object** from the context menu (see Figure 12.40, left).

FIGURE 12.40:
Adding a button

The Button object is defined in two tabs of **Properties—General** and **Action**. In the **General** tab (Figure 12.40, middle), you can define the following properties:

- The **Text** that the button will carry and the alignment options for it.
- The style of the **Background**, with three choices:
  - **Aqua**—Conjures up memories of Windows Vista
  - **Plain**—Reminiscent of Windows 3.11
  - **Image**—Allows developers to choose a background image
- The **Transparency** option allows you to make the background fully or partially transparent, which can be the best option in some cases.
- The **Enable Condition** can be used to specify in what conditions the button should be enabled. When the specified condition is not met, the button will appear grayed-out, or disabled, and it won't be clickable.

The **Actions** tab (Figure 12.40, right) contains the list of actions that should be performed when the button is clicked. You can **Add**, **Delete**, **Promote**, and **Demote** actions in the list. Clicking on the **Add** button reveals the **Add Action** dialog, which provides the choice of all available actions, grouped into five **Action Types**—**Selection**, **Layout**, **Bookmark**, **Print**, and **External**. Each of the **Action Types** holds a collection of actions that are associated with its name. When needed, certain parameters that are required for certain actions become available next to the list of actions. Feel free to explore all five action types on your own. We will practice using some of the actions in the exercises that follow the next section.

Before we continue, let's take a brief history detour. Buttons existed in QlikView from very early stages. Initially, buttons were used to invoke macros (VBScript or JScript) that allowed performing certain commands that are not easily available to the end users. Using macros and the QlikView API set, advanced developers can perform virtually any commands that are available in QlikView.

A Few Words About Buttons, Macros, and Actions

While versatile, macros are unstable and negatively affect performance. For these reasons, macros were always frowned upon, but they remained the "necessary evil" until the introduction of actions in Version 9.00.

While actions are not nearly as versatile as macros, they cover the most common needs without the negative impact on performance. When absolutely necessary, macros can still be invoked using the special action **Run Macro**, which is a part of the **External** action type.

With the introduction of actions, buttons lost their exclusivity in terms of allowing interactivity. Many other sheet objects can now function as buttons and invoke actions—text objects, line/arrows, and gauge charts.

Considering the modern flat design trends, text objects offer better design capabilities, and they contain almost all the features that buttons have to offer (everything except for the **Enable Condition**, to be exact). Because of the preferred look and feel, and because text objects work more consistently than buttons in various mobile environments, many developers abandoned buttons and use text objects instead. Likewise, we will use text objects in all future exercises. At any future mention of a button, we will be referring to a text object that acts like a button.

In the following exercise, you add three buttons that are commonly included in QlikView applications. The three buttons allow end users (including the various mobile clients) to **Clear Selections**, as well as move **Back** and **Forward** in the selections stack. They are typically positioned below the **Current Selections** box.

Exercise 12.35: Adding Selection Buttons

1. Activate the Template sheet.

2. Highlight all the objects that are located below the Current Selections box and move them downward, to create some empty space between the Current Selections box and the Warehouse list box. Resize some of the objects if necessary, to make more space. While all these objects are still selected as a group, right-click on the group and select the Linked Objects ▶ Adjust Position of Linked Objects menu option in order to reposition all instances of the same linked objects in other sheets.

3. Create three text objects that look like the buttons in Figure 12.41. Use $(color_LightGray) as the Background Color and $(color_Blue) as the Font Color. Assign the following actions to the three buttons, accordingly (all three actions belong to the Selection action type): Back, Clear All, and Forward.

4. Align and position the three buttons below the current selections box. Once you are happy with the presentation, Copy the three objects and Paste Sheet Object as Link in all other sheets.

5. Save your work.

FIGURE 12.41: Adding selection buttons to the template

Invoking Actions Using Triggers

Actions can also be invoked based on certain application events, or *triggers*, that can be associated with the whole document or with a single sheet. Document-level triggers are managed in **Document Properties**. Sheet-level triggers are managed in **Sheet Properties**. Locate the **Triggers** tab in both **Properties** dialogs to examine the available triggers.

At the document level, **Triggers** can be linked to document events such as **OnOpen** or **OnPostReload**. In addition, **Field Level Triggers** can invoke certain actions when selections were made or modified in one of the fields. Similarly, **Variable Event Triggers** can invoke actions when a value in a certain variable was entered or changed. At the sheet level, actions can be invoked upon activating or leaving the sheet.

The actions that can be assigned to various triggers are no different from those that can be assigned to buttons. While a more detailed discussion of triggers is outside of the scope of this book, we offer a warning regarding a hidden pitfall. Since triggers and actions are assigned at multiple levels independently from each other, it could be relatively easy to get into trouble and create a never-ending cycle of actions. In order to protect us from ourselves, QlikView won't perform certain triggers in certain cases. For example, the sheet trigger **OnActivateSheet** works nicely when the user opens the sheet using the **Tabrow**; however, it won't be activated if the user arrived at the same sheet as a result of another action.

We recommend using actions and triggers in moderation, keeping the number of actions and their relative importance to the overall application experience at bay, in order to avoid costly troubleshooting when things don't work as expected.

Using Show Conditions and Calculation Conditions

Now, let's examine another important presentation feature in QlikView—*Show Conditions*. You probably noticed by now that every sheet object in QlikView can be equipped with a **Show Condition** (**Object Properties**, **Layout** tab). Similarly, sheets can be equipped with the same **Show Condition** (**Sheet Properties, General** tab).

Show Conditions can accept any Boolean expression that renders TRUE or FALSE, or simply any numeric condition that can return any non-zero value as TRUE or a zero value as FALSE. When the condition is false, the object is not visible. These conditions can be useful in a number of ways. In combination with security settings, they allow us to hide certain objects from certain users. Sometimes, certain charts may only be relevant in a certain context, and therefore they are kept invisible until they are needed.

The next session describes another common use of Show Conditions, one which allows arranging objects in a tabbed view that resembles the Container functionality, but is free from the limitations of Containers.

Before we go there, we must also mention **Calculation Conditions** that can be assigned to charts (**Chart Properties, General** tab). Calculation Conditions work somewhat similarly to Show Conditions, with a subtle difference. When the Calculation Condition renders FALSE, the object is still visible on the screen, but the calculation is not being performed. Instead, an error message, **Calculation condition unfulfilled**, is presented in the middle. This default error message can be altered using the **Error Messages** dialog that can be activated with the **Error Messages** button on the **General** tab.

Calculation Conditions can be used to enforce certain logical procedures—for example, a certain chart will be calculated only when certain selections are made. They are extremely important when straight tables and pivot tables are used to produce detailed reports, under the premise that the user should make selections to narrow down the volume of available data. When these detailed charts are opened with a full data set, they require an enormous amount of resources. For this reason, it's strongly advised that all detailed straight tables and pivot tables carry calculation conditions with the requirement that the volume of data is reduced to an acceptable threshold level.

In the following self-guided exercise, you will equip the three charts on the **Alternate States** sheet with the calculation condition that requires that any selections be made to reduce the number of products in each group. It would be meaningless to calculate three charts that show exactly the same picture for both groups.

Exercise 12.36: Using Calculation Conditions

1. Add Calculation Conditions to the three charts on the Alternate States sheet. The condition should request that the number of products be reduced by any selections. We suggest the following condition that needs to be adjusted accordingly for each Alternate State. For the comparison chart, we suggest an "OR" condition that requires that the number of products is reduced in at least one of the Alternate States.

   ```
   count( Product) < Count({1}  Product)
   ```

2. Locate the Error Messages button on the General tab and replace the default error message Calculation condition unfulfilled with a more informative Custom message.

3. Test your results.

Using Buttons, Actions, and Show Conditions to Develop Advanced Navigation Features

So far you learned two techniques of arranging multiple charts in a limited space. In Chapter 4, we used the **Auto Minimize** feature that allowed one chart to be visible at a time, with the rest of the charts minimized as icons. In Chapter 8, we introduced containers that allowed a similar functionality within a single object with a tabbed view.

Both techniques are somewhat limited in their presentation options. We'd like to introduce another technique that allows advanced navigation within sheets, and can be also used to arrange navigation between sheets. This technique may require a bit more time and skill to develop; however, it offers the best and most flexible presentation capabilities when exquisite presentation is required. For the purpose of the book exercise, we will keep things relatively simple; however, you can use the same technique to spice up your presentation in any imaginable way.

This presentation technique begins with adding a number of buttons (usually text objects) that are formatted as tabs (see Figure 12.42). One button appears as active at a time. In a simple form, the effect is achieved with simple texts and conditional colors for the **Background** and the **Text Font**. In more sophisticated designs, the desired effect can be achieved with alternating images that highlight the necessary tab.

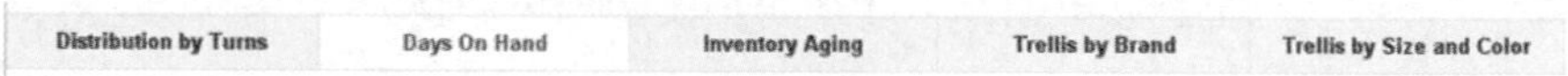

FIGURE 12.42:
Five buttons arranged as tabs

| Distribution by Turns | Days On Hand | Inventory Aging | Trellis by Brand | Trellis by Size and Color |

The whole presentation model is driven by a single variable. We typically call it vChart. When five different views are needed, the variable can be assigned values from 1 to 5. Each one of the five buttons carries the following attributes (we will specify all the expressions for the first button):

- **Actions**—when the button is pressed, the variable vChart is set to **1**.
- **General** tab, **Background Color**—when vChart = **1**, use the highlight color (white in this example); otherwise, use the neutral light-gray color:

  if(vChart=1, $(color_White), $(color_LightGray))

- **Font** tab, **Color**—when vChart =**1**, use the highlight color (blue in this example; otherwise, use the neutral black color):

  if(vChart=1, $(color_Blue), $(color_Black))

These three settings need to be populated in each one of the buttons, and the number 1 in each setting needs to be replaced with the corresponding number for each button. Once fully populated, these settings take care of the tabs and their presentation. Clicking on any tab makes it highlighted with the blue text on a white background, compared to the neutral black/gray presentation of the other four tabs.

Now, the same variable vChart is used for showing and hiding the charts that belong to each view. In our application, the two charts that show Distribution of Products and On Hand Balances by Turns need to be equipped with the same **Show Condition**:

vChart=1

Similarly, the charts that provide analysis of days on hand need to be copied into the same sheet and equipped with the similar **Show Condition**:

vChart=2

You get the idea. The rest of the charts need to be copied from the **Inventory Aging, Trellis by Brand**, and **Trellis by Size and Color** sheets. Each chart needs to be equipped with the corresponding **Show Condition**. Voilà! We replaced five static sheets with a single sheet and a handful of buttons that determine the on-screen navigation. The result is presented in Figure 12.43.

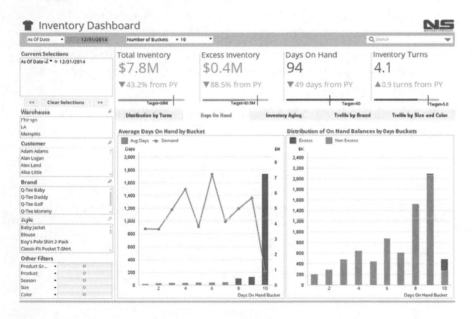

FIGURE 12.43:

The complete Inventory Analysis dashboard

In a similar way, we could also arrange navigation between sheets. This time, one of the actions would have to activate the desired sheet and the other action would set a value of another variable, such as vSheet, that could regulate the presentation of the buttons in a similar way. While this exercise is outside of the scope of this book, we invite you to experiment and to develop this solution on your own.

Now we'll point out the advantages of this technique, compared to the auto minimize and the container techniques:

- Any number of sheet objects can be displayed or hidden at a time. The other two techniques allowed you to show only one chart at a time.

- The buttons can be formatted freely, using any colors or images. With the other techniques, the presentation of the minimized icons, as well as the container buttons, is tightly regulated by QlikView.

- The buttons can be positioned anywhere on the sheet and given any shape or form.

- Similar actions can be easily triggered from other related objects on the sheet. For example, the same action can be assigned to the text boxes that communicate the main KPIs' numbers on top. The user can switch the view to **Days on Hand** by clicking on the number on top of the screen. The same would be more difficult to implement with the **Auto Minimize** feature, and practically impossible to do with a container.

Without further delay, let's practice developing the view presented in Figure 12.43.

Exercise 12.37: Arranging the Tabbed View Using Buttons and Actions

1. Activate the Inventory Dashboard sheet and make room between the top section and the two charts in the middle.

2. Create a new vChart variable.

3. Add a new text object with the following attributes:

   3.1. Text: **Distribution by Turns**.

   3.2. Background Color: Calculated

   ```
   if(vChart=1, $(color_White), $(color_LightGray))
   ```

   3.3. Actions: Set Variable. Variable = vChart, Value = **1**

3.4. Font Color: Calculated

```
if(vChart=1, $(color_Blue), $(color_Black))
```

3.5. Position the button at the horizontal line that divides the top section of the screen and the main chart area. Allow an approximate height of 35 pixels and a width of 195 pixels.

4. Clone the text object four more times and position the five objects next to each other, with no extra room between the borders. Modify the width of the objects to cover all available space. Use Figure 12.43 as a visual guide.

5. Modify the other four buttons with the corresponding text. Replace the chart number **1** with the corresponding number from **2** to **5** in the three attributes—the Background Color, the Action, and the Font Color.

6. Test the presentation features of the five buttons by clicking each button and observing the color changes.

7. Once you're satisfied, assign Show Conditions to the corresponding charts (use the Layout tab of the chart Properties):

   7.1. Assign the following Show Condition to the two Distribution by Turns charts:

   ```
   vChart=1
   ```

   7.2. Click on the second button and verify that the two charts disappeared. Now, copy the Days On Hand charts from the corresponding sheet. If necessary, resize and reposition the charts to fit in the available space. Assign a similar Show Condition, using the number 2 instead of 1. Verify that the charts are displayed when the second button is clicked and that they disappear when any other button is activated.

   7.3. In addition to the two charts, copy the Input Box with the Number of Buckets from the Days On Hand sheet and equip it with the same Show Condition.

   7.4. Using the same logic, copy all other charts from the sheets Inventory Aging, Trellis by Brand, and Trellis by Size and Color. Equip each set of charts with the corresponding Show Condition. Verify that the Show/Hide logic works as expected.

8. The other four sheets can now be removed, or you may keep them for your reference. The development of the Inventory Dashboard is now complete. Remember to Save your work.

This exercise completes our discussion of advanced visualization techniques in QlikView. In the following two chapters we discuss the advanced data modelling and scripting techniques that we used to build the Inventory Analysis data model. One of the sections in Chapter 14 presents yet another advanced Set Analysis technique that can be used as an alternative to building Generic Link Tables—make sure to check it out!

13

Data Modeling for Inventory Analysis

In this chapter, we discuss advanced modeling techniques that will be used to build the data model for the Inventory Analysis application.

You will learn the data modeling concepts that lie behind the following techniques:

- Calculating running balances
- Building data models with Concatenated Fact tables
- Advanced date-handling techniques

Calculating Running Balances

In this section, we introduce the logic of calculating running balances and how it applies to inventory and inventory aging.

The Logic of Calculating a Running Balance

Imagine a traditional bank statement. It starts with a beginning balance, followed by a list of transactions—deposits and withdrawals. An intermediate balance is presented next to each transaction. We usually call it a *running balance*. Running balances are not always stored with the transactions. Instead, they are calculated on the fly. The logic of calculating a running balance is relatively simple. Each running balance is equal to the previous value of the same balance, plus the value of the current transaction. The running balance in the next line will use the current balance as its base and so on. This logic is very easily implemented in an Excel formula.

In QlikView, however, calculating running balances on the fly could be too costly from the performance standpoint. It is much better if we could precalculate running balances and store them in the data.

The overall logic is still the same. However, there is an additional degree of complexity because we need to calculate running balances for multiple accounts. Now our logic has to be more sophisticated. We should add the current transaction to the previous balance *only if* the previous balance belongs to the same account as the current transaction. Otherwise, we need to restart the calculation from a different beginning balance.

Hence, the calculation of the running balance in the data model involves the following steps:

1. Load the beginning balances and the transactions into the same table, sorted by the transaction date.

2. For each line, check if the previous row of data belongs to the same account.

    2.1. If it does, add the transaction value to the previous value of the running balance and store the result in the same running balance field.

    2.2. If it does not, use the beginning balance as the running balance.

This common logic can be used in many applications that involve running balances. In the next section, we discuss how this process can be applied to inventory analysis.

How Running Balances Apply to Inventory and Inventory Aging

The same logic can be applied to calculating inventory balances. In this case, `Product ID` may be used in place of the account. Sometimes, when location is important, a combination of `Product ID` and `Warehouse ID` may serve as the account.

In many systems, historical inventory balances may not be stored in the database. In these situations, all we are given is the current on-hand balance and the table with all inventory transactions. When needed, historical inventory balances can be created using a similar approach. In our sample database, we provide the `Inventory History` table for your convenience.

A very similar logic can be used to calculate *inventory aging*. When inventory is managed in lots, each lot is recorded with its own manufacturing date. In this case, calculating inventory age is rather simple. Conversely, when lots are not managed and different batches of inventory are co-mingled, calculating the estimated age requires certain initial assumptions and a very particular logic.

The assumption we have to use is that the older inventory is consumed before the newer inventory. This principle is called *first in, first out* (FIFO). Using the FIFO principle, we will assume that the inventory on the warehouse shelf was supplied in the most recent batch(es) that were received by the warehouse.

The calculation logic begins with the current balance as the starting point. Then, the program needs to read all the *goods receiving* transactions, starting from the most recent transaction, and moving back in time toward earlier transactions. For each transaction, the running balance needs to be depleted by the transaction `Quantity` and the corresponding part of the current balance becomes *aged*. Consider the aging example in Figure 13.1.

Description	Date	Quantity
Current Balance	Dec 31st, 2014	1000
Goods Receiving	Dec 1st, 2014	500
Goods Receiving	Nov 1st, 2014	300
Goods Receiving	Oct 1st, 2014	400
Goods Receiving	Sep 1st, 2014	450

Based on this example, we can conclude that the 1,000 pieces in the current balance can be divided into three Aging records—500 pieces were received one month ago, 300 pieces were received two months ago, and the remaining 200 pieces were received three months ago.

It was quite easy to make this conclusion intuitively. Now, let's formulate the expressions that allow us to calculate the same result programmatically. Figure 13.2 explains the calculation logic.

FIGURE 13.2:

Aging: calculation logic

Description	Date	Quantity	Aged Quantity	Running Balance
Current Balance	Dec 31st, 2014	1000		1000
Goods Receiving	Dec 1st, 2014	500	500	1000 - 500 = 500
Goods Receiving	Nov 1st, 2014	300	300	500 - 300 = 200
Goods Receiving	Oct 1st, 2014	400	200	200 - 400 = -200
Goods Receiving	Sep 1st, 2014	450	0	-200 - 450 = -650

Two expressions need to be calculated in order to calculate the Aged Quantity.

- **Running Balance** is the previous value of the Running Balance minus the received Quantity.

- **Aged Quantity** is the lower value between the previous value of the Running Balance and the received Quantity. Aged Quantity cannot be negative, so we should add another transformation to the previously calculated quantity. Aged Quantity will be the higher value between that calculated number and zero. When the calculated Aged Quantity becomes negative, the end result will be replaced with zero.

Let's keep in mind that this calculation needs to be performed separately for each Product and Warehouse. Hence, we can formulate our calculations in the following pseudo-algorithm:

1. Load current balances and receiving transactions into the same table.

2. Run through the records, which are sorted by Product, Warehouse, and descending Date.

3. If this is the first row of data for a `Product` and a `Warehouse`, then assign `Running Balance = Quantity`. Otherwise, assign `Running Balance = <previous value of Running Balance> - Quantity`.

4. Within the same load, assign `Aged Quantity =` the higher between zero and (the lower between the <previous value of the `Running Balance`> and the `Quantity`), only for goods receiving transactions, but not for on hand balances.

5. Reload the same data again, this time only loading the receiving transactions (disregarding the on hand balances) with positive `Aged Quantity`.

We described almost all of the QlikView techniques that are needed for implementing this algorithm, except for the following:

- We need to know how to determine if the current row in the loaded table is the first row for a certain set of key fields.

- We need to know how to fetch a previous value for a certain field from the previous row.

Both of those questions will be answered in Chapter 14, when you learn about the inter-record functions `Peek()` and `Previous()`.

The Concatenated Fact Table

In Chapter 9, you learned how Link Tables can be used to connect multiple fact tables in a data model. With QlikView's associative functionality, the Link Table model provides an easy way to see the relationships among the transactions. However, the primary drawback to using Link Tables is performance. The high cardinality of the link keys can cause the Link Table to grow to an untenable size.

Introducing the Concatenated Fact Table

An alternative approach to combining different types of transactions into the data model is to create a data model with a single fact table. Instead of linking multiple fact tables with a Link Table, we simply create a single fact table containing all transactions. In QlikView, we call this type of table a *Concatenated Fact table*. In data warehousing terminology, this unified table is sometimes called a *consolidated fact table*. The Concatenated Fact table provides a way to "drill across" business processes, with better performance than a model with multiple fact tables. Figure 13.3 illustrates the concept of the Concatenated Fact.

FIGURE 13.3:
Concatenated fact model

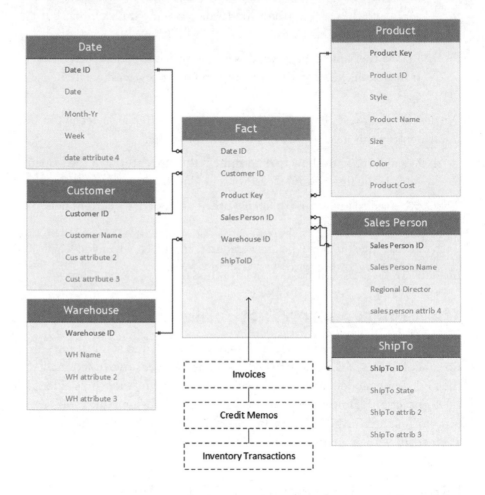

The concatenation process works by loading the rows from each transaction source into a single fact table using the QlikView keywords `concatenate load`, as shown in Figure 13.4.

```
Fact:
Load
    dim1,
    dim2,
    dimN,
    metric1
From Process1;

concatenate (Fact)
Load
    dim1,
    dim2,
    dimN,
    metric2
From Process2;

concatenate (Fact)
Load
    dim1,
    dim2,
    dimN,
    metric3
From Process3;
```

With this technique, metrics from various business processes are stored in one table, allowing for easy cross-process (or drill-across) analysis. Each transaction row (ideally) has a key to the dimension tables. In SQL, the UNION ALL statement can be used to combine the results of multiple queries into one table, but each query must have the exact same fields. In QlikView, data from multiple sources can be *concatenated* together into one table, even if the sources do not have the same columns (as illustrated in Figure 13.3).

To identify the data entity from which the row is sourced, we also can include a new field such as [FactType], and manually populate it with some qualifier value, like Sales, PO, and so on.

Storing all transactions together in one table is the perfect employment of the star schema. The model is fast, easy to understand, and extensible. With one fact table, expressions such as sum(metric1*metric2) + sum(metric3) allow cross-process analysis and benefit from not having to hop among different tables to execute. In addition to the sales and inventory transactions shown in Figure 13.4, it wouldn't be hard to imagine adding transactions (and dimensions) from other related business processes such as finance or marketing. Any process can be added to this model, as long as it makes sense from an analytical perspective. If you're faced with a process that has attributes that will only be analyzed in isolation, then it probably doesn't make sense to store it alongside the others—a separate model and a separate application would be more efficient.

Based on your requirements, choose the greatest possible granularity (highest level of detail) with which to build the concatenated fact. The strength of QlikView is being able to quickly perform aggregations at runtime, so go for the most detail possible within your constraints. Most often, this means loading the rows from a line-level table when faced with transactions stored in a header/detail table duo. This technique was described in Chapter 5, so we won't repeat the details here.

After loading transactions from several processes into the fact table, you'll start to see some holes—missing keys or attributes. Sometimes, due to normalization in the source database, transactions can have certain attributes or keys missing, even though they have a valid, logical relationship to all dimensions.

Null values in key columns cause the rows in the fact table to appear disconnected from the dimension tables. In some cases, the missing values can easily be found by retrieving the key from associated tables.

Let's walk through an example.

Resolve Missing Associations

Figure 13.5 shows what a row for a `Purchase Request` and a `Purchase Order` might look like in separate source tables. (For the purposes of this example, only a few of the typical fields are shown for these transactions.)

FIGURE 13.5:
Example data before concatenation

Purchase Request	Date ID	Employee ID	Request Amount	Request Number			
	20140101	678	500.00	R34821			

Purchase Order	Date ID	Employee ID	Request Amount	Request Number	Vendor ID	PO Number	PO Amount
	20140115	678		R34821		567 P928374	486.26

After the rows are concatenated, the resulting table contains all of the columns from both sources. Figure 13.6 shows the same two rows in a concatenated table.

FIGURE 13.6:
Example data after concatenation

	Date ID	Employee ID	Request Amount	Request Number	Vendor ID	PO Number	PO Amount
Purchase Request →	20140101	678	500.00	R34821			
Purchase Order →	20140115	678		R34821		567 P928374	486.26

In order to identify the source data entity, we add a new field [FactType] and manually populate it with the qualifier value. In Figure 13.7, we use PO or PR as values for [FactType] to indicate purchase order or purchase request as the source process.

FactType is manually added to identify the source process ↓

	Date ID	Employee ID	Request Amount	Request Number	Vendor ID	PO Number	PO Amount	FactType
Purchase Request →	20140101	678	500.00	R34821				PR
Purchase Order →	20140115	678		R34821	567	P928374	486.26	PO

FIGURE 13.7:
A new column to indicate the row source

Notice that each row has null values in the columns that did not originally exist in the source for that transaction type. Figure 13.7 shows a null value for [PO Amount] on the Purchase Request row, because that column does not exist in the Purchase Request process.

In a database environment, best practices for table design dictate that empty columns should be avoided for optimal performance and efficiency. We deal with empty columns differently in QlikView.

Since QlikView does not use any storage in RAM for nulls, the impact of loading these empty columns is trivial. Null values for metrics behave nicely in fact tables, since the common aggregate functions (SUM, MIN, MAX, and so on) will simply ignore them.

But what about the missing key? The Purchase Request row is missing a Vendor ID. If a chart is used to show both PO and PR metrics together (perhaps for a procurement audit), and a user selects a particular vendor from a list box, all of the expressions containing PR will be excluded from view. If this is undesirable, we need to make sure that a Vendor ID is associated with the Purchase Request rows.

In Figure 13.8, the Vendor ID is added to the PR row. If this vendor was selected by a user, both the PR and PO metrics would be available for analysis.

Resolve missing associations ↓

	Date ID	Employee ID	Request Amount	Request Number	Vendor ID	PO Number	PO Amount	FactType
Purchase Request →	20140101	678	500.00	R34821	567			PR
Purchase Order →	20140115	678		R34821	567	P928374	486.26	PO

FIGURE 13.8:
Vendor ID is populated

In this example, you could join to the PO table to retrieve the Vendor ID, using Request Number as the join key. Another technique is to use the

`ApplyMap()` function, which is similar in concept to Excel's `vlookup()` function. Depending on the size of the tables involved, using `ApplyMap()` can offer a significant reduction in load time compared to a `JOIN` statement, as well as eliminate the risk of duplicating records.

Using similar techniques, you may need to fill in missing *attributes* as well as keys, depending on your analysis requirements.

Forcing Alignment with Link Tables and Generic Keys

In our inventory application, we confront a trickier problem: some transactions have entirely different granularity. Up until now, our `Fact` table has included sales transactions such as invoices and credit memos, which involve products, customers, and dates. However, inventory transactions do not involve a customer at all. If we concatenate the inventory transactions into the Fact table, the key field for `Customer ID` will be missing, and therefore filled with `NULL` values.

Again, the missing relationship in itself is not a problem. The problem arises when a user is analyzing a chart of inventory metrics, and then selects a value for the `Customer` field. Since none of the inventory rows are associated with the `Customers` table, the chart does not have any metrics to display.

The business requirements for the application indicate that it would be helpful to see inventory balances related to products that a customer has purchased. For example, if product P1 is experiencing shortages, we'd like to inform the customers who are likely to purchase product P1 (based on their history). How can we do this? We create a special type of a link table that associates inventory balances to customers who have purchased those products. This link table should not be confused with the Link Table data models, where the Link Table plays a central role in the data model. In order to avoid confusion, we like to call this type of link table a *Generic Link Table*, since it is also associated with *generic keys*. Let's explain this technique based on the following example.

Figure 13.9 displays the contents of a very simple Concatenated Fact table. The first two rows are inventory transactions, and the next rows are sales transactions.

	Date ID	Customer ID	Product ID	# On Hand Quantity	# Sales Quantity
Inventory Transactions	20140131		P1	100	
	20140131		P2	1	
Sales Transactions	20140115	C1	P1		10
	20140115	C1	P2		50

FIGURE 13.9: Concatenated Fact including inventory and sales transactions

To associate the inventory transactions to the `Customer` table, we need *something* to substitute for `Customer ID`. The initial requirement was to associate customers with the products that they purchased. Therefore, the natural choice for this substitution is the `Product ID`. We'll use the `Product ID` as the artificial "link" to the `Customers` table.

In Figure 13.10, the `Customer ID` field is dropped and replaced by `CustomerLink`. This new field will contain some artificial generic values that will be linked to the `Customer ID`. For inventory transactions, the `Product ID` is used; for sales transactions (or any other transactions where `Customer ID` is available), the `Customer ID` is used.

New Generic Key

Date ID	Customer ID	Product ID	# On Hand Quantity	# Sales Quantity	CustomerLink
20140131		P1	100		P1
20140131		P2	1		P2
20140115	C1	P1		10	C1
20140115	C1	P2		50	C1

FIGURE 13.10: Generic key added to the Fact table

Figure 13.11 shows how the link table associates the inventory rows with the `Customer` table.

To create the Generic Link Table, the combinations of keys are loaded in two steps:

- First, the `Customer ID` is loaded into both fields, to facilitate the original link between the `Customer ID` and the corresponding `CustomerLink`.
- Then, all distinct combinations of `Customer ID` and `Product ID` are loaded from the `Sales` records, in order to generate the association between customers and the products that they purchased.

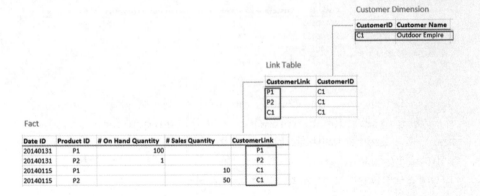

FIGURE 13.11:
Inventory rows associated with the Customer table

To help identify the `CustomerLink` values as "artificial" and to avoid any possibility of duplication, a unique prefix (such as P or C) can be used along with the key value. For example, if your system should have a `Product ID = 12345` and a `Customer ID = 12345`, this may create an erroneous link. By adding a prefix, we ensure that the two values are unique—the `CustomerLink` value for the `Product ID` will be `P12345`, and the same value for the `Customer ID` will be `C12345`.

While the Generic Link Table is a clever solution, it's not ideal. We have introduced an additional hop between tables, and depending on the size of the data set, the extra table can take up a lot of memory. With the use of Set Analysis, charts can use expressions to loosen the relationships between transactions, instead of using link tables. We will introduce this alternative to Generic Link Tables in Chapter 14.

Link Tables or Concatenated Facts?

We are often asked by our students, "What data modeling technique is better? The Link Table (not to be confused with the Generic Link Table) or the Concatenated Fact?" As always, the answer is "it depends."

With mid-sized data models and relatively simple data structures, Link Table models offer simplicity and native associations. On the other hand, Concatenated Fact models are clearly better for performance, especially with larger data models and more complex data structures.

The benefits of the Concatenated Fact model are summarized here:

- Expressions are calculated much more quickly with all of the operands in the same table.

- The application will take up less storage in RAM without a giant Link Table.

- The star schema is kept intact, which makes the model:
  - Easier to understand
  - Easier to extend

We'll use the Concatenated Fact model going forward as our application development continues in Chapter 14.

Advanced Date Handling

To support the analysis of metrics that are typically aggregated or compared over various time periods, we can build *date flags* into the data model to make the chart expressions more efficient. In this section, we'll look at the pros and cons of storing date flags in the Master Calendar vs. the Fact table, and also introduce a concept to support a more flexible As Of Date logic.

Should Date Flags Reside in the Master Calendar or in the Fact Table?

In Chapter 10, we described how to create a Calendar dimension based on the dates that exist in the Fact table. In Figure 13.12, notice that the date flags for current/previous month-to-date, as well as current/previous year-to-date are included in the table.

How should these conditional flags be used in the application? The fact that they exist in a *dimension* table suggests that they should be used in dimensional calculations. One such use could be to limit the dimensions shown in a chart. For example, if you create a bar or line chart to display a sales metric by month, but only want to present the months that are YTD, you could create a calculated dimension : if(_CYTD_Flag=1,Month). Of course, the Calendar table shown in Figure 13.12 shows only a few of the possible data flags required by the application. Other examples include time periods such as quarter-to-date, last three months, last six monts, last three months previous year, and so on.

FIGURE 13.12:
The Master Calendar table

However, we have to point out that Calculated Dimensions are very costly in terms of application performance and should be avoided whenever possible. Calculated Dimensions with an IF() function are even worse.

To avoid a Calculated Dimension with an expensive IF() function, you could add another non-flag field to the Calendar called CYTD_Month. Using a similar expression to the one that created _CYTD_Flag, you would store the month name instead of a 1 or 0. This new field could be used as a usual dimension in any chart that should display months in the current year-to-date. Since this technique is rather limited in its flexibility, it is most useful when there are specific requirements dictating which time spans are to be used for analysis. In other words, the technique is best suited for guided analysis, not necessarily ad-hoc discovery.

From the performance standpoint, it's much better to use flags as modifiers within a Set Analysis expression. For example, the following expression

```
sum({<_CYTD_Flag={1}>}[# Sales Amount])
```

can be used to calculate the sum of sales only for those rows flagged as CYTD.

Note that this expression seems to be contrary to best practices, which suggest that fields used in calculations should all reside in the same table. However, this is not the case here. Fields that are used in Set Analysis modifiers do not need to reside in the same table. Since Set Analysis leverages the QlikView associative logic, the modifiers are processed in a different way than the regular formula operands.

Keeping the flag fields in the dimension table (instead of the fact table) saves memory (less pointer storage), and using Set Analysis mitigates the usual performance cost incurred when QlikView must hop between tables to calculate an expression.

The other technique of using conditional flags in chart expressions is multiplying the aggregated value by the flag. Before Set Analysis was introduced, the use of flags as multiplication operands was common. The expression sum([# Sales Amount] * _CYTD_Flag) returns the same results as the Set Analysis expression shown previously.

Unlike with Set Analysis modifiers, when measures are multiplied by flags directly, the need to collect the fields from multiple tables causes significant slow-down. When using this multiplication, it's best to store the flags in the fact table, along with the metrics.

When it comes to performance benchmarks, the following conclusions are believed to be true with the recent versions of QlikView:

- Set analysis usually outperforms multiplication by flags when the flags are stored in the dimension table.
- Multiplication by flags commonly outperforms Set Analysis when the flags are stored in the fact table.

Hence the choice of the solution becomes more specific—either keep the flags in the dimension tables and use Set Analysis, or move the flag into the fact table and use multiplication.

Our recommendation is conditional:

- In most applications with manageable data sets, keep the flags in the dimension tables and use Set Analysis.
- In truly huge data sets, when performance savings are critical, consider saving the flags in the fact table and using the multiplication technique instead, for better performance.

WARNING Sometimes developers take the idea of conditional flags to an extreme and generate dozens or even hundreds of flags for every possible logical condition. Such proliferation of flags becomes counterproductive in large applications with a lot of data. Storing and indexing a huge number of flags takes a lot of memory, and the extra overhead outweighs the benefits of pre-calculating logical conditions. We advise that you use common sense in determining what conditions are worth storing in conditional flags, and what conditions are better to be verified on the fly, using Set Analysis.

Supporting Flexible "As Of" Dates

The standard date flags shown so far in this chapter are used to indicate whether a date is within a certain time span, based on a single "as of" date. The commonly used base date is today(), or the last posting date of your data set. In addition to simplifying expressions, these flags allow the developer to create guided analysis. This means that charts can be pre-baked to show metrics within YTD, previous YTD, current quarter, and so on. The limitation of this technique is that the user can only see the time spans relative to a single base date. While this is sufficient in most applications, sometimes the requirements are more sophisticated. In some applications, the user wants the ability to pick the base date to answer questions such as, "What were the YTD sales as of October 31st?" or "What were the previous YTD sales, as of March 31st?"

To support time-span analysis as of *any* date, we can create a link table of sorts, which includes flags for each transaction date relative to *all other "as of" dates*. This is called the *As of Date* technique and this special kind of link table is an *As of Date* table.

Logically, we split a single Date field into two. The *transactional* date is the date that's attached to the transactions stored in the Fact table. The *display* date, or the As of Date, is the date displayed on the screen. The As of Date table defines the relationship between each As of Date and each transactional Date.

That requires creating a Cartesian join of all transactional dates with the list of all display dates. The relationship between the two dates is then defined in a number of conditional flags, very similarly to the conventional calendar flags.

Realistically, this technique is best used when the number of dates in the data model is relatively small (two or three years). Data models that contain a long history of transactions are not well suited for this technique. Also, creating a table of relative months is more realistic than a table of individual dates. To illustrate, let's start by taking another look at the basic date flags.

In Figure 13.13, the [_Rolling_3MO_Flag] was created by comparing the Transaction_Date to the base date of 8/31/2014.

Flag calculated as of 8/31/14

FIGURE 13.13: Rolling three-month date flag as of 8/31/14

Fact table

fact col3	fact col2	Date ID
x.x	x.x	20140801
x.x	x.x	20140701
x.x	x.x	20140601
x.x	x.x	20140501
x.x	x.x	20140401

Master Calendar

Date ID	Month	_Rolling_3MO_Flag
20140801	August	1
20140701	July	1
20140601	June	1
20140501	May	0
20140401	April	0

As we've seen previously, using the flag as a modifier within a Set Analysis expression offers a convenient way to quickly calculate a metric within the current rolling quarter. Without this flag, a user would have to manually select the relevant dates to get the same result.

```
sum({<_Rolling_3MO_Flag={1}>}[# Sales Amount])
```

However, this limits the user to analyzing only the current rolling quarter, as of the base date of 8/31/14. We can implement a special kind of a link table to allow the user to analyze a rolling quarter based on any selected as of date. We called this table the As Of Date table. Figure 13.14 shows the contents of the As Of Date table, using one transaction date and its relationship to all of the other possible dates. The flags are moved from the Master Calendar into the As Of Date table.

Master Calendar

As of Date	Month
20140801	August
20140701	July
20140601	June
20140501	May
20140401	April
20140301	March
20140201	February
20140101	January
20131201	December
20131101	November
20131001	October
20010901	September

As Of Date Table

Date ID	Rolling_3MO_Flag	CYTD_Flag	As of Date
20140601	1	0	20140801
20140601	1	0	20140701
20140601	1	1	20140601
20140601	0	1	20140501
20140601	0	1	20140401
20140601	0	1	20140301
20140601	0	1	20140201
20140601	0	1	20140101
20140601	0	0	20131201
20140601	0	0	20131101
20140601	0	0	20131001
20140601	0	0	20130901

Fact

fact col3	fact col2	Date ID
x.x	x.x	20140801
x.x	x.x	20140701
x.x	x.x	20140601
x.x	x.x	20140501
x.x	x.x	20140401

The same chart expressions can be used with this data structure, but the user must select an As Of Date. If a date is not selected, the expression needs to be modified so that it uses the last date of the calendar as the default As Of Date.

Notice that the As Of Date table is very similar in its look to a generic link table. And, once again, it adds another link to be resolved in the runtime. This time, however, we can eliminate the extra link by merging the Master Calendar data with the As of Date data. The price to pay is some duplication of the Calendar attributes. Depending on the size of the data set and the number of dates in the application, this idea can be more or less beneficial to the performance of your application.

This concludes our discussion of advanced data-modeling techniques in QlikView. In Chapter 14, we will use the data-modeling concepts described here to build the Inventory Analysis data model.

14

Developing a Data Load Script for Inventory Analysis

In this chapter, we develop the Data Model for our Profitability Analysis application. In doing so, we describe how to:

- Generate a running balance, using the Inter-Record functions Peek() and Previous().

- Distribute a single inventory balance into buckets by aging date.

- Use IntervalMatch to match distinct dates with continuous periods.

- Combine multiple fact tables into a single *Concatenated Fact.*

- Populate missing attributes across multiple slices of the Concatenated Fact.

- Add a generic key with a Generic Link Table to create or restore a missing association.

- Use advanced Set Analysis as an alternative to Generic Link Tables.
- Allow advanced date analysis with the As of Date table.
- Use the load script and text files to manage expression definitions stored in variables.

Review of the Business Requirements and the Data Sources

Before we get to the task of building the data model, let's summarize the business requirements and the data sources for this application. The main goal of this particular implementation of Inventory Analysis is to analyze which products have excess balances in the inventory, in comparison to historical sales. The business sponsors of the project outlined the following required features. The application should include:

- Detailed drill-down analysis of the current on-hand balances, as well as a 12-month history of inventory.
- Calculations of months on hand and inventory turns, made by comparing current on-hand balances with the historical sales.
- A special logic of adjusting historical sales quantities for the periods of promotions. During promotions, sales volumes were inflated beyond the norm due to promotional pricing and incentives. All sales quantities that were recorded during promotion periods need to be divided by a special factor.
- A detailed analysis of inventory aging. The inventory balances need to be divided into age buckets. The age needs to be calculated based on the current balances and the history of receiving transactions.
- A historical analysis of inventory and months on hand. The same KPIs need to be produced for the current date, as well as for any month end in the 24-month history.
- An easy way to understand the relationship between the inventory balances and the customers who purchased the corresponding product in the past. The application should allow users to select a customer and to see the list of products that the customer purchased in the past, along with the current inventory balances for

the same products. On the other hand, it should be possible to select a product and see the list of customers who purchased the same product, along with their sales history.

In order to build all these features, you need to load the following data elements:

- Current inventory balances, by product and warehouse
- The history of inventory balances, saved at every month end
- Sales history by product, customer, warehouse, and month
- The history of goods receiving transactions by product, warehouse, and month
- Unit costs per product
- Promotions data: dates, styles, and volume factors

We should first say a few words about quantities, units of measure, and cost amounts. Sales and inventory quantities may be managed using different units of measure (U/M). For example, inventory may be managed in cases, while sales may be managed in pieces or in two-pack or three-pack quantities. For the purpose of our analysis, we will be using all quantities in the standard unit of measure that is determined for each product. In our example, the standard U/M is always a single piece.

You learned from the Profitability Analysis example in Chapter 10 that standard cost can be modified from one year to another. Specifically for the purpose of inventory analysis, it's preferable to "dollarize" all quantities using the same cost amount per product. Imagine reporting the same inventory balance that didn't change at all from one year to another, and yet the inventory value had changed. Even though this is accurate from the accounting standpoint, it wouldn't help the analytic purposes. Similarly, the value of sales needs to be calculated using the same cost amount, not using the sales amount that is based on the sales price.

With that in mind, it's important to understand that these numbers will likely be different from any official reports of sales and inventory history. The sales quantities are adjusted for promotions, the sales amounts represent the current standard cost of goods sold, and the history of inventory is calculated using the current standard cost, not the standard cost at the time of recording the historical balance. It's important to communicate this caveat to your users and to explain why you opted to analyze inventory this way.

Note that aging information doesn't exist in any of the existing data sources. The following section describes the process of generating the aging data based on the current balance and the history of goods receiving transactions.

Transforming Inventory Data

In this section, you will create transformed QVD files for the Inventory Analysis data model that will include the transformed inventory tables, aging data, and transformed sales data.

In the process, you will learn and implement the technique of calculating running balances using *inter-record functions*. In addition, you will learn the IntervalMatch technique for joining data based on matching distinct values to intervals of numeric values.

The Process of Generating the Aging Data

Chapter 13 described the logic of calculating running balances and a specific implementation of this logic for calculating inventory aging. In this chapter, you learn the practical implementation of this technique with the Peek() and Previous () functions.

Using the Inter-Record Functions Peek() and Previous()

The Inter-Record functions Peek() and Previous() look very similar to each other and are often considered interchangeable.

The Peek() function receives up to three parameters:

```
Peek('Fieldname', Row, 'TableName')
```

It returns the value of the specified field from the specified row of the specified table. When no table is specified, the current table is assumed. When no row is specified, the last loaded row is assumed. Row numbering begins with 0 for the first record, 1 for the second record, and so on. Negative row numbers allow you to retrieve values from the last row in the table (row -1), or the second last row (-2), and so on.

The data for the `Peek()` function is loaded from the previously loaded table in the associative QlikView database.

The `Peek()` function can be used in a load to retrieve data from the same table or from another table. It can also be used outside of a load, in which case the table name and the row number are mandatory.

Notice that both the field name and the table name need to be provided as strings, enclosed in single quotes.

Conversely, the `Previous()` function only accepts a single parameter:

`Previous(expression)`

The *expression* is evaluated using data from the previous input record. The data is drawn directly from the input source, *not necessarily from the QlikView database*. This means that the expression can include fields that may not be stored in QlikView, as long as they are available in the source table. On the other hand, newly calculated fields that are created in QlikView in the same load cannot participate in this expression.

In most cases, the expression simply consists of a single field, and that's where `Previous(Field)` looks similar to `Peek('Field')`. Notice that the field name does not need to be enclosed in quotes for the `Previous()` function, because the parameter is not a string, but rather an expression or a direct field reference.

Both functions can be used in a LOAD that involves calculating a running balance of any kind, but not in the same way. Just to remind you, any calculation of a running balance by one or a few *key dimensions* consists of two steps:

1. Check if the current record is the first for the set of the key dimensions. This is done by comparing a set of key dimension values from the current row with the same values from the previous row.

2. If this is the first record, restart the `Balance` from the current quantity (or from the beginning balance); otherwise, add the current quantity to the previous value of the `Balance` (depending on a specific scenario, you may be adding to or subtracting from the balance).

In the first step of this process, either one of the two functions can be used successfully. We recommend using Previous() to enable comparing expressions such as concatenated key dimension values, as opposed to always comparing distinct fields. Another benefit is that unlike the Peek() function, the Previous() function will not fail silently. If any field names are misspelled, you will know about it.

In the second part of the process, the Previous() function cannot be used, because the Balance field is likely to be a new field that is being created in the same load. Since the field didn't exist before the statement was executed, the syntax checker wouldn't allow its use in the expression for the Previous() function. In this case, the Peek() function wins, because of its string parameters and because of its silent fail. The field Balance may not exist at the beginning of the LOAD; however, it will be perfectly valid when it needs to be used for the Peek() function in the second row of the loaded table.

So, remember the following schema for any calculations of running balances:

```
IF Previous, THEN Peek()
```

This means use Previous() in the IF condition and then use Peek() to calculate the running balance.

Generating Aging Data

Now you are ready to generate the aging data and to store it in a transformed QVD file that will be loaded later into the Inventory data model. The data for this transformation script will be provided in raw QVD Files located in the \Data\QVDs\ subfolder.

Here is the logical description of the process:

1. As a first step, load and concatenate receiving transactions and current balances into a single concatenated fact.

    1.1. For the current on hand balances, assign the "current date" as the Date. Since the data in this sample database ends in December 2014, we will assign Dec 31st, 2014 as our "current date."

    1.2. Add a new field RowType that will serve as a qualifier of the data type. For on hand balances, RowType = 'OH'. For receiving transactions, RowType = 'RT'.

2. Reload the same table in memory, sorted by Warehouse, Product, and Date in descending order. In the process of this load, calculate two new fields—Balance and [# Aged Quantity], based on the logic described in the previous sections.

   2.1. Check if the combination of Warehouse and Product is identical to the previous value of the same combination (using the Previous() function).

   2.2. If the combination of keys is different from the previous row, which means that this is the first row for Product and Warehouse, then assign Balance = Quantity. This should be the current on-hand balance loaded in Step 1 of this process.

   2.3. If the combination of the keys is the same as in the previous row, assign Balance = <the previous Balance> - Quantity. We will use the Peek() function to retrieve the previous Balance value.

   2.4. For the row type 'RT' only, calculate the value of [# Aged Quantity]. This calculation is described in a few steps:

      a. First, calculate the lower value between the *current* Quantity and the *previous* Balance.

      b. Then, calculate the higher value between the previously calculated value and zero. In other words, we are only interested in positive numbers here.

      c. Again, use Peek() to determine the previous balance and RangeMin/RangeMax functions to determine the lower and the higher values.

3. Finally, reload the resulting table once again, only selecting RowType= 'RT' and only including rows with positive [# Aged Quantity].

   3.1. In this load, calculate the new field Age as the difference between the "current date" and the Date. The Age field will replace the Date field. The aging data can only pertain to the current date, so keeping the Date field would lead to an unnecessary link between aging data and other historical records like sales and inventory history.

   3.2. Rename all the key fields according to the naming conventions—adding a percent sign (%) in front of the key field name.

We encourage you to develop this script on your own, following this logic. Detailed instructions are provided in the following exercise.

Exercise 14.1: Generating Aging Data

1. Create a new QlikView document and store it in the subfolder \Data Loaders with the name **Inventory Transformation Script XX.QVW**, where *XX* is your initials. Open the Script Editor.

2. In the **Main** tab of the script, create the variable *vToday* and assign the date of Dec 31st, 2014 as the value:

   ```
   let vToday = MakeDate(2014,12,31);
   ```

3. Create a new tab and name it **Aging**.

4. In the new tab, load the following fields from the QVD file Receiving Transactions.QVD:

   ```
   Receiving:
   LOAD
           'RT'                          as RowType,
           [Transaction Date]            as Date,
           [Warehouse ID],
           [Product ID],
           [Transaction Quantity STD UM]   as Quantity
   FROM
   [..\Data\QVDs\Receiving Transactions.QVD]
   (qvd);
   ```

5. Using CONCATENATE, load the following fields from the QVD file On Hand.QVD to the same table:

   ```
   Concatenate (Receiving)
   LOAD
           'OH'                          as RowType,
           '$(vToday)'                   as Date,
           [Warehouse ID],
           [Product ID],
           [On Hand Quantity STD UM]       as Quantity
   FROM
   [..\Data\QVDs\On Hand.QVD]
   (qvd);
   ```

6. Type the following statement (copy and paste as much as possible) to load the temporary Aging_Temp table with the following calculations of the new fields Balance and [# Aged Quantity]:

```
Aging_Temp:
Load
      RowType,
      Date,
      [Warehouse ID],
      [Product ID],
      Quantity,
      if( Previous([Warehouse ID] & '|' & [Product ID]) =
                     [Warehouse ID] & '|' & [Product ID],
          Peek('Balance') - Quantity, Quantity)           as Balance,
      if( RowType = 'RT',
          RangeMax(0, RangeMin(Peek('Balance') , Quantity)))  as [# Aged Quantity]
Resident
      Receiving
Order By
      [Warehouse ID],
      [Product ID],
      Date DESC
;
drop table Receiving;
```

7. Reload the result, but load only the *receiving* records with positive quantities. Add the age calculation:

```
Aging:
Load
      '$(vToday)' - Date   as Age,
      [Warehouse ID]       as [% Warehouse ID],
      [Product ID]         as [% Product ID],
      [# Aged Quantity]
Resident
      Aging_Temp
WHERE
      RowType = 'RT'
And
      [# Aged Quantity] > 0
;
drop table Aging_Temp;
```

8. **Save** and **Reload** your script. Preview the Aging table that was generated as the result. Verify that the Age field is populated with reasonable non-zero values.

Extra Credit

Do you remember why you had to enclose the date variable $(vToday) in single quotes? What would happen if you don't do this?

Transforming Sales Data for Inventory Analysis

As described earlier, we will use the historical sales records as a representation of demand for the inventory. For this purpose, we will be using the same sales data (Invoice Header and Invoice Detail), but the data needs to be transformed in a slightly different way.

Required Transformations for the Sales Data

The only sales dimensions that are relevant for this inventory analysis are Product, Warehouse, Customer, and Date. The only measure that we need is the sales quantity. Since we are using sales as a measure of demand, we will use the Requested Ship Date, not the Invoice Date that was used for Sales Analysis. For the same reason, we will use the Ordered Quantity (in the standard U/M) rather than the Invoiced Quantity. For the purpose of estimating demand, the original requirement is much more valuable than the end result that may have been affected by product availability and other factors.

Based on the business requirements, the sales quantities need to be adjusted for promotions. During promotions, the sales activity may be inflated beyond the norm. Using inflated sales quantities for inventory analysis or for forecasting may lead to inflating the estimated demand for the inventory and therefore distorting the true picture.

In order to avoid using inflated numbers, we need to match sales records by date with the promotion periods that are defined by the pairs of start and end dates. This technique is described in the next section.

Lastly, since our inventory analysis only needs to be performed at the monthly level, we can aggregate all monthly sales for the same Product,

Warehouse, and Customer. In most cases, we use MonthStart() as the representing date for the month. However, we know that inventory history is stored at month end; therefore, using MonthStart() date would be counter-intuitive. For this reason, we will use the MonthEnd() function for both the sales and inventory history dates. If you remember the earlier discussion about dates, using the MonthEnd() function can be dangerous because this function returns *the last millisecond of the last day of the month*. We will apply the Floor() function to round the number down and then use the formatting function Date() to format the resulting number as a date:

```
Date(Floor(MonthEnd([Requested Ship Date]))) as Date
```

In the next section, you learn how to join distinct numbers (or dates) to continuous ranges of numbers (or dates) using the IntervalMatch load.

Introducing the IntervalMatch Load

IntervalMatch is a technique that allows QlikView developers to match distinct numbers (or dates or timestamps) to continuous ranges of numbers (or date periods).

The tables that contain the distinct numbers and ranges need to be loaded before performing the IntervalMatch load. Then, the IntervalMatch load is used to load the pairs of start and end values and to match them to the distinct value:

```
IntervalMatch (DistinctNumberField)
LOAD
      Start,
      End
Resident
      Ranges
;
```

This is the syntax of the IntervalMatch Load in its most simple form. As a result, two extra tables are created in the database (see Figure 14.1). The first table contains the synthetic key that combines two keys Start and End into a single key (remember, QlikView can only link tables based on a single key). The second table contains the links between the ranges and the distinct values.

FIGURE 14.1:
The simplistic data
structure with the result
of IntervalMatch

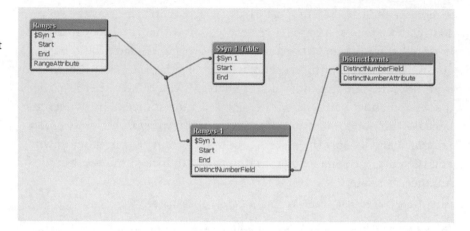

You can imagine that we are not particularly happy with this kind of a data structure, knowing our general dislike for synthetic keys and our tendency to minimize the number of unnecessary links between tables.

The extra links and the synthetic key can be eliminated by joining the IntervalMatch table back into the Ranges table:

```
INNER JOIN (Ranges)
IntervalMatch(DistinctNumberField)
LOAD
     Start, End
Resident
     Ranges
;
```

The resulting data structure is much simpler and cleaner (see Figure 14.2). The synthetic key and the extra link tables are gone, and the two tables are linked directly. Note, however, that the table of Ranges now includes more rows, based on the number of distinct events from the other table. When the table with the Ranges is merely used as a dimension table, this is not a problem. In rare occasions when this table includes measures, watch for duplicate values!

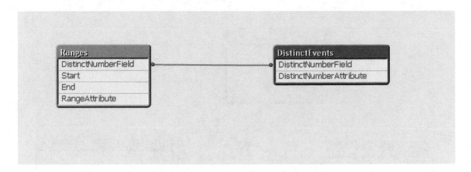

If the goal of the whole exercise is to fetch the value of the RangeAttribute, then the Ranges table can be joined into the table of DistinctEvents, eliminating the last extra link. Before joining the tables, however, check for the possible duplication of data. You can join the two tables only if the ranges don't overlap. In other words, there should be only one Range associated with each one of the distinct events. If multiple ranges can correspond to the same event, then joining might cause duplication of event data, and therefore should be avoided.

In certain cases, it's not enough to just match distinct values to ranges of values. Sometimes the match needs to include one or more other keys. For example, sales promotions may be tracked by the style of the product and a date range. In this case, sales dates need to be matched to the promotional ranges in combination with matching styles.

This form is called the *extended syntax of* IntervalMatch. The extra keys are added to the IntervalMatch load statement like this:

```
INNER JOIN (Ranges)
IntervalMatch(DistinctNumberField, Key1, Key2)
LOAD
     Start, End, Key1, Key2
Resident
     Ranges
;
```

In this case, the key field(s) must exist in both tables. Because of the multiple link keys, even the streamlined data structure, comparable to Figure 14.2, will now involve a synthetic key (see Figure 14.3). In this case, it's preferable to join the two tables, provided that joining doesn't cause any duplication of data.

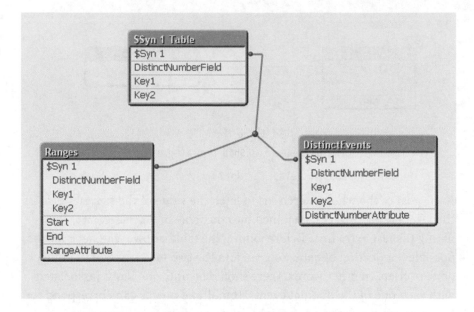

If the ranges could overlap and duplication is possible, then the data in
the Ranges table needs to be de-duplicated before joining. Aggregating the
ranges data by the distinct number and the keys and selecting the min, the
max, or the average of the RangeAttribute could do the job.

In the next section, we will use IntervalMatch to load promotions and to
match them to the sales dates.

To Join or Not to Join—That's the Question!

In all fairness, we have to admit that despite our personal dislike for synthetic keys, they don't
have to be eliminated and in some cases can even deliver slightly better performance. Many
respectable QlikView experts will tell you that the IntervalMatch is the perfect example of a
valid synthetic key that doesn't need to be eliminated.

Furthermore, in some data models, joining the IntervalMatch table into the Ranges table may
create more problems than it solves. As an alternative, this table can be joined to the fact table
DistinctEvents or left as is, not joined.

We will teach you the techniques and leave the final decision in your hands.

Performing the Transformations of the Sales Data

Transforming sales data involves the following logical steps:

1. Create a `Mapping` table that will allow you to map `Product` to `Style`. This is necessary in order to match the promotions data by `Date` and `Style`.

2. Load the data from the `Invoice Header.QVD`—[Invoice Number], [Customer ID], and [Requested Ship Date] from the `Invoice Header.QVD`.

3. Join (into the same table) the data from the `Invoice Detail.QVD`— [Invoice Number], [Product ID], [Warehouse ID], [Ordered Quantity STD UM], and the `Style` as the result of `Mapping`.

4. Load `Promotions` from the `Promotions.xslx` spreadsheet. This load involves using the `Crosstable` technique that you learned in Chapter 10.

5. Using the extended `IntervalMatch` syntax, match [Requested Ship Date] to [Start Date] and [End Date] of the promotions, including the field `Style` in the match. Use an `INNER JOIN` to avoid the unnecessary link table.

6. Join the table of `Promotions` to the `Sales` table, in order to avoid another synthetic key and eliminate an extra link.

7. Reload sales data, aggregating by [Customer ID], Date, [Product ID], and [Warehouse ID].

   7.1. In the process of summarizing quantities, divide the [Ordered Quantity STD UM] by the `PromoFactor`, when the latter is greater than zero.

   7.2. Aggregate all dates to the monthly buckets by using the `EndMonth()` function. Round the result down and format it as a `Date` again. Name the result `Date`.

   7.3. Name all keys and measures according to our naming conventions.

We encourage you to write this script on your own. The detailed instructions are provided in Exercises 14.2a through 14.2c.

Exercise 14.2a: Transforming the Sales Data, Part 1

1. At the end of the `Inventory Transformation Script`, add a new script tab and name it **Sales**.

2. Load `[%Product ID]` and `Style` from the transformed QVD file `T_Products.QVD` and transform the LOAD into a MAPPING LOAD:

```
Style_Map:
MAPPING
LOAD
    [%Product ID],
    Style
FROM
[..\Data\Transformed QVDs\T_Products.QVD]
(qvd);
```

3. Load the following fields from the raw QVD `Invoice Header.QVD`. Name the temporary table Sales_Temp:

```
Sales_Temp:
LOAD
    [Invoice Number],
    [Customer ID],
    [Requested Ship Date]
FROM
[..\Data\QVDs\Invoice Header.QVD]
(qvd);
```

4. Load the following fields from the `Invoice Header.QVD` and join the results into the same temporary table. Use the `ApplyMap()` function to retrieve the `Style` for each `[Product ID]`.

```
Left Join (Sales_Temp)
LOAD
    [Invoice Number],
    [Product ID],
    ApplyMap('Style_Map', [Product ID], '') as Style,
    [Warehouse ID],
    [Ordered Quantity STD UM]
FROM
[..\Data\QVDs\Invoice Detail.QVD]
(qvd);
```

5. Using the Table Files wizard with the Crosstable wizard, load the Promo table from the spreadsheet Promotions.xlsx, which is stored in the \Data\Text Files\ subfolder. You will have two Qualifying Fields. Name the Attribute Field `Style`. Name the Data Field `PromoFactor`. Replace the list of all fields with a single asterisk:

```
Promo:
CrossTable(Style, PromoFactor, 2)
LOAD
    *
FROM
[..\Data\Text Files\Promotions.xlsx]
(ooxml, embedded labels, table is Promotions);
```

6. Create an `IntervalMatch` link between the tables `Sales_Temp` and `Promo`:

```
IntervalMatch ([Requested Ship Date], Style)
Load
    [Start Date],
    [End Date],
    Style
Resident
    Promo
Where
    PromoFactor >0
;
```

7. At this point, we'd like to stop and assess the results before we continue. In order to eliminate any unnecessary linking with the aging data, we will temporarily disable that part of the script:

   7.1. Promote the Sales tab, positioning it before the Aging tab.

   7.2. At the end of the Sales tab, add the following statement. As you can guess from its name, this statement will stop executing the script and exit the process at that point. The rest of the script will be disregarded.

   ```
   exit script;
   ```

8. Save and Reload your script. Examine the resulting table structure.

Your table structure should look similar to Figure 14.4.

FIGURE 14.4:
The intermediate result
of the IntervalMatch

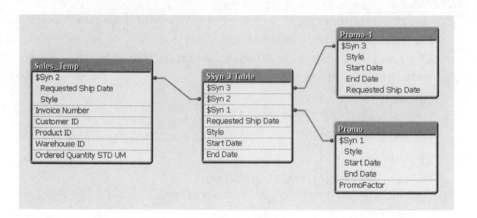

This is the result of the IntervalMatch load when it's not joined back to one
of the tables. Three synthetic keys were created to account for all possible
combinations of link keys. This result certainly has too many synthetic
keys and too many tables for our needs. Remember, the goal is to assign a
corresponding PromoFactor to every row of Sales.

In order to simplify the structure, you will add an INNER JOIN prefix, joining
the Link Table back into the Promo table.

Exercise 14.2b: Transforming the Sales Data, Part 2

1. Add the following prefix in front of the IntervalMatch load:

```
Inner Join (Promo)
```

2. **Save** and **Reload** your script. Examine the resulting table structure.

Your data structure should look similar to Figure 14.5.

As you can see, the structure is much simpler now. We are down to a
single synthetic key. This one is inevitable—the two tables share two
common fields, and QlikView has to combine them into a single link key.

The only way to eliminate the synthetic key completely is to join the two tables. Joining, however, could cause data duplication if the Promo table was not distinct.

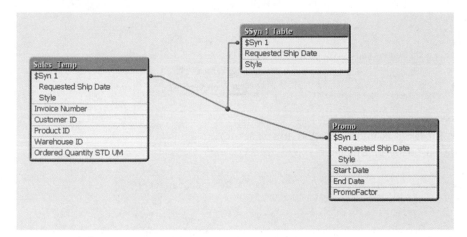

FIGURE 14.5:
Streamlined data structure resulting from IntervalMatch

In our case, we know for a fact that our promotion periods do not overlap, and that there is no more than one row for each combination of Style and Date. With that in mind, it is safe to join the Promo data into Sales_Temp, without causing any duplication. You will complete the process of transforming the sales data in Exercise 14.2c.

Exercise 14.2c: Transforming the Sales Data, Part 3

1. Delete the temporary statement Exit Script.

2. At the bottom of the script tab **Sales**, add the following load statement:

```
left join (Sales_Temp)
load
    *
Resident
    Promo
;
drop table Promo;
```

3. Now we should have a single table `Sales_Temp`, with the `PromoFactor` populated in some, but not necessarily all, rows. We will need to check for the value of the `PromoFactor` before using it. At the end of the **Sales** tab, add the following aggregated load statement:

```
Sales4Inventory:
LOAD
     [Customer ID]                                   as [%Customer ID],
     Date(Floor(MonthEnd([Requested Ship Date])))    as Date,
     [Product ID]                                    as [%Product ID],
     [Warehouse ID]                                  as [%Warehouse ID],
     sum(
         IF(PromoFactor>0,
             ceil([Ordered Quantity STD UM]/PromoFactor),
             [Ordered Quantity STD UM]
         )
     )                                               as [# Demand Quantity]
Resident
     Sales_Temp
GROUP BY
     [Customer ID],
     Date(Floor(MonthEnd([Requested Ship Date]))),
     [Product ID],
     [Warehouse ID]
;
DROP TABLE Sales_Temp;
```

4. **Save** and **Reload** your script. Examine the table structure. You should see two tables, `Aging` and `Sales4Inventory`, linked with a synthetic key. No need to worry about this synthetic key. By the time we finish the exercise and store the individual tables into QVD files, it will be gone.

Transforming On-Hand Balances and On-Hand History Data

The rest of the transformations for the inventory data are straightforward. We simply need to load the raw data and rename the fields based on our naming conventions. The following exercise is a necessary step in the process of creating the Inventory data model, even though it doesn't present any new scripting techniques.

Exercise 14.3: Transforming On-Hand Balances and On-Hand History Data

1. Add a new tab at the end of your script and name it **On Hand**.

2. Load the on-hand balances from the QVD file On Hand.QVD. Rename the fields and comment out some of the fields as follows:

```
OnHand:
LOAD
        [Warehouse ID]              as [%Warehouse ID],
        [Product ID]                as [%Product ID],
//      [On Hand Quantity],
//      [Inventory U/M],
        [On Hand Quantity STD UM]   as [# On Hand Quantity],
        [Lead time]                 as [# Lead Time],
        [Order Quantity]            as [# Min Order Quantity]
FROM
[..\Data\QVDs\On Hand.QVD]
(qvd);
```

3. In a similar way, load the data from the QVD File On Hand History.QVD:

```
OnHandHistory:
LOAD
        Date,
        [Warehouse ID]              as [%Warehouse ID],
        [Product ID]                as [%Product ID],
//      [On Hand Quantity],
//      [Inventory U/M],
        [On Hand Quantity STD UM]   as [# On Hand Quantity]
FROM
[..\Data\QVDs\On Hand History.QVD]
(qvd),
```

Storing the Transformed QVD Files

Now we need to store the four transformed data tables into QVD files. We could do it manually or we can leverage the library of common routines that we developed earlier. You can copy the necessary snippets of code from the Profitability Transformation script developed in Chapter 10.

Exercise 14.4: Storing the QVD Files

1. Copy the following snippets of code from the `Profitability Transformation` script that you developed in Chapter 10.

   1.1. In the **Main** tab of the script, add the following:

   ```
   LET vTransformedQVDPath='..\Data\Transformed QVDs\';
   $(Include=..\scripts\commonroutines.txt);
   ```

   1.2. Add a new tab at the end of the script and name it **Generate QVDs**. Add the following line in the new tab:

   ```
   CALL StoreAllTablesIntoQVDs(vTransformedQVDPath, 'T_', '1');
   ```

2. **Save** and **Reload** your script. Verify that the four new QVD files were created in the `\Transformed QVDs\` subfolder.

This exercise completes the transformations that we had to perform on our raw data before building our data model.

Building the Concatenated Fact Table

In this section, we will practice the techniques that are necessary to build the Concatenated Fact data model:

- Combining multiple fact tables into a single table
- Propagating missing attributes to all the slices of the Concatenated Fact
- Adding a generic key and a Generic Link Table in order to restore a missing association.

Combining Multiple Facts in a Single Table

Let's start by examining our main data elements and their relations. The following facts need to be combined into a cohesive data model:

- `Current On Hand` balances, stored by `Product` and `Warehouse`
- `Inventory History`, stored by `Product`, `Warehouse`, and `Date`

- Aging data, stored by Product, Warehouse, and Age
- Sales History, stored by Product, Warehouse, Customer, and Date

In a real-life inventory analysis scenario, the list of fact tables could be much longer, including Open Orders, Forecasts, Manufacturing Orders and Purchase Orders, Raw Materials data, Bills of Materials, and more. Our list of four fact tables, believe it or not, is a major simplification of real-life needs. Even then, the structure is complex enough to discard the option of building a Link Table and handling all of those different combinations of common keys. As you learned in Chapter 13, the "Single Fact" (or Concatenated Fact) data model is a more viable alternative for a complex data structure like this one.

If you recall, the essence of the Concatenated Fact data model is that all different facts are concatenated together into a single table. Each type of fact data is qualified by a unique qualifier value in a new field that we will call FactType. For example, we will assign FactType = 'Sales' for all the sales records. Since Current On Hand data and On Hand History data play a similar role in this application, it would be easier to select them together if they had the same FactType. For this reason, we will qualify both of those fact types with the same FactType = 'OnHand'.

The identical fields will be populated with the corresponding values across all "slices" of the Concatenated Fact, and missing fields will get populated with NULL values, unless an alternative value is specified.

Similar measure fields can be named either identically or differently, depending on the needs of your analysis. For example, all slices of the Concatenated Fact will include some sort of a Quantity field. We could call all of these fields by the same field name Quantity. If we did, it would be easier to sum up quantities from all the slices together. At the same time, we would have to use Set Analysis filters when we need to aggregate a particular kind of quantity.

Considering the various options, we should probably name the quantity fields differently, because we cannot imagine the expression that would benefit from adding up on-hand balances with aged balances and sales quantities. All of our calculations will involve separate quantities, always gathered from one individual fact type. The only exception would be the on-hand balance vs. the on-hand history. These two fact types complete each other. They store on-hand snapshots. The current on-hand is the snapshot as of the current date, while the on-hand history stores earlier snapshots. These two fact types should have their quantity fields named identically.

In the following exercise, you will load the four fact tables from the transformed QVD files into the new document Inventory Data.QVW, while adding a unique qualifier value in the new field FactType. Develop this script on your own if you can or follow the detailed instructions in Exercise 14.5.

Exercise 14.5: Combining Multiple Facts into a Single Table

1. Create a new QlikView document and name it **Inventory Data XX.QVW**, where *XX* is your initials. Save the document in the subfolder \Data Models.

2. Open the Script Editor. In the Main tab of the script, assign the value to the variable vToday. As we did before, we use the date of December 31, 2014 as our current date because our tutorial data ends then:

   let *vToday* = makedate(2014,12,31);

3. Add a new script tab and name it **OnHand**.

4. Using the Table Files wizard, load the data from the transformed QVD file T_OnHand.QVD.

   4.1. Add a new field FactType and assign the hard-coded value **'OnHand '** to it.

   4.2. Add the Date field and assign the value from the variable vToday to it. As always, you need to use a dollar-sign expansion with a variable that's used in a LOAD statement.

   4.3. Name the new table Fact.

   ```
   Fact:
   LOAD
           'OnHand'                    as FactType,
           '$(vToday)'                 as Date,
           [%Warehouse ID],
           [%Product ID],
           [# On Hand Quantity],
           [# Lead Time],
           [# Min Order Quantity]
   FROM
   [..\Data\Transformed QVDs\T_OnHand.QVD]
   (qvd);
   ```

5. Add another tab and name it **History**. In the new tab, add the following statement to load inventory history data from the T_OnHandHistory.QVD file. Use the Concatenate prefix to add this data to the Fact table:

```
Concatenate (Fact)
LOAD
    'OnHand'                    as FactType,
    Date,
    [%Warehouse ID],
    [%Product ID],
    [# On Hand Quantity]
FROM
[..\Data\Transformed QVDs\T_OnHandHistory.QVD]
(qvd);
```

6. Next, add another tab and name it **Aging**. Add the following statement to load data from the file T_Aging.QVD.

```
Concatenate (Fact)
LOAD
    'Aging'                     as FactType,
    Age,
    [%Warehouse ID],
    [%Product ID],
    [# Aged Quantity]
FROM
[..\Data\Transformed QVDs\T_Aging.QVD]
(qvd);
```

7. Add one more tab and name it **Sales**. Add the following statement to load the data from the file T_Sales4Inventory.QVD:

```
Concatenate (Fact)
LOAD
    'Sales'                     as FactType,
    [%Customer ID],
    Date,
    [%Product ID],
    [%Warehouse ID],
    [# Demand Quantity]
FROM
[..\Data\Transformed QVDs\T_Sales4Inventory.QVD]
(qvd);
```

8. **Save** and **Reload** your script. Examine the resulting data structure. You should see a single table named Fact.

This is it, folks. Your Concatenated Fact is ready. Well, almost. In the following sections, you learn a few additional techniques that need to be used to make this fact table operational.

Propagating Missing Attributes to All the Slices of the Concatenated Fact

If you are accustomed to developing data structures where all related entities are linked between them, then there is one adjustment that you need to get used to, and it is not obvious at first.

Now we'll demonstrate this concept using an example. Examine the load statement for the on-hand data. It includes two fields that are not available in any other facts—[Lead Time] and [Min Order Quantity]. Those data elements typically come from the MRP system and are commonly defined for each product and warehouse. For this reason, the two fields were included in the on-hand data extract that is also defined by product and warehouse.

It is possible that those two data elements become necessary in calculations that involve other facts' data—for example, historical balances. If different facts were kept in separate tables and linked one to another, then the data would be associated, or obtained through the links. In the Concatenated Fact, however, the different facts are merely the different slices of the same table. When a certain data element is missing in some of the slices, the field value is simply padded with NULL.

> ### True Facts About Concatenated Facts
>
> *In the Concatenated Fact model, the different facts are not directly associated.*
>
> This means that in contrast to all other data models, an attribute that belongs to one of the facts is not available when another fact data is being analyzed.
>
> *All attributes that may be needed across multiple facts need to be populated in all related facts.*
>
> As part of the process of building the Concatenated Fact model, we need to identify all attributes that may be needed in other facts and populate them manually across all related facts.

What Are Lead Time and Minimum Order Quantity?

Lead Time is the number of days needed to receive or produce a certain product. It tells the MRP system when an order needs to be placed for each product, based on its future demand.

Minimum Order Quantity means just that—vendors establish the minimum order quantity for each product. Manufacturers define the minimum batch size for producing the product. It's not economical to run the manufacturing cycle just to produce a few shirts. Therefore, when a new order is placed, the quantity has to comply with the established minimums.

We need those two fields in order to assess the on-hand balance and the calculated measure of Days On Hand, in comparison to Minimum Order Quantity and Lead Time.

For example, if we had 800 units in stock, while the Minimum Order Quantity was 200, it would mean that we ordered way too much. On the other hand, if Min Order Quantity was 1,000, the balance of 800 wouldn't look as bad.

Similarly, if we concluded that we had enough inventory for 100 days of sales (we call this measure *Days On Hand*) and the Lead Time was 20 days, it would mean that we have way too much inventory. If the Lead Time was 120 days, however, we would not have enough and we would need to order immediately.

In order to enable all necessary data elements in all related slices of the fact table, you need to populate the missing data in each slice manually. This can be done using joining or mapping techniques. Our preference is to always use mapping, which is a more flexible solution that never causes data duplication.

In the following exercise, you create two mapping tables that map the combination of Warehouse and Product to the Lead Time and the Min Order Quantity. Then, you use the mapping tables to propagate Lead Time and Min Order Quantity across all slices of the Concatenated Fact table.

Exercise 14.6: Propagating Missing Attributes

1. Add a new tab after the `Main` tab of the script and name it **Mapping**.

2. Copy the `Load` statement of the `On Hand` table and paste it twice in the new tab. Transform the two load statements into the following `Mapping Load` statements:

```
LeadTime_Map:
MAPPING
LOAD
    [%Warehouse ID] & '|' & [%Product ID] as Warehouse_Product,
    [# Lead Time]
FROM
[..\Data\Transformed QVDs\T_OnHand.QVD]
(qvd);
MinOrder_Map:
MAPPING
LOAD
    [%Warehouse ID] & '|' & [%Product ID] as Warehouse_Product,
    [# Min Order Quantity]
FROM
[..\Data\Transformed QVDs\T_OnHand.QVD]
(qvd);
```

3. Open the **History** tab and add the following two lines at the end of the load of the history data (don't forget to add the comma after the last field):

```
ApplyMap('LeadTime_Map', [%Warehouse ID] & '|' & [%Product ID], 0)
                                as [# Lead Time],
ApplyMap('MinOrder_Map', [%Warehouse ID] & '|' & [%Product ID], 0)
                                as [# Min Order Quantity]
```

4. Copy the same two lines and add them at the end of the aging data load and at the end of the sales data load.

5. Save and Reload your script.

6. In order to validate the results, build a **Table Box** on the **Main** sheet and select all the fields in their **Load Order**. Add **List Boxes** for the major fields, such as `FactType`, `[%Warehouse ID]`, and `[%Product ID]`. Navigate the data and verify that the `[Lead Time]` and `[Min Order Quantity]` fields are populated consistently for all fact types.

Adding Dimension Tables and Calculated Fields

The next step in our data modeling process is to add the dimension tables for warehouses, products, and customers. This step is no different from any of the other data-modeling exercises. We simply load the dimension tables from the transformed QVDs.

When we load dimensions and facts from our back office systems, there is a possibility of loading more dimensional values than needed for the specific application. Our application, for example, only loads 24 months of sales and inventories. Your master tables may store customers, products, and warehouses that have no activity in the last 24 months.

Loading unnecessary dimension values is not terribly wrong, and yet it can be wasteful in large data environments. In addition, showing irrelevant data items in list boxes may cause unnecessary confusion.

For these reasons, we usually prefer to load only those dimensional values that exist in the fact table (except for the specific type of analysis that highlights customers who made no purchases, or what products were not sold in a certain period of time).

There are two ways of limiting dimensional values to those that already exist.

We can use the prefix KEEP in front of the LOAD, which works very similar to the JOIN prefix, only the two tables are not joined together. The tables remain separate, but the populated data in one or both tables is reduced based on matching the values of the identical fields. Just like the JOIN prefix, the KEEP prefix needs to be preceded by one of the the INNER, LEFT, or RIGHT prefixes. For our needs, we will be using the LEFT KEEP prefix with the Fact table in the LEFT position:

```
LEFT KEEP(Fact)
LOAD
...
```

The other technique involves using the Exists() function. The Exists() function validates if the given field value already exists in the list of field values. The function has two possible formats. In its simplest form,

```
Exists(Field)
```

the function verifies the current value of the field with the list of previously loaded values in the same field. In a more elaborate form,

```
Exists(Field, expression)
```

the function verifies the result of the *expression* against the list of the existing values in the field. In this form, it's possible to compare a value of one field with existing values of another field, which comes in handy in certain logical conditions. For our purpose of limiting dimension values to those loaded in the Fact table, the simple form is sufficient:

```
LOAD
        Fields
RESIDENT        Table
Where
        Exists(%Key)
;
```

The two techniques, the KEEP prefix and the Exists() function, work nearly identically in terms of their functionality and performance. The differences are very subtle.

The KEEP Load compares all identical fields between the two tables, not necessarily just one key. You need to specify the table name, but you don't have to worry about the specific key field name(s).

Conversely, the Exists() function verifies the value of a single field; however, the field values may exist in multiple tables. In complex data structures, where the same key field might exist in multiple tables, it's convenient to verify the new key value against all existing tables at once. You need to specify the field name, but you don't need to worry about the specific table name(s).

In most cases, the comparison is done versus a single field in a single fact table, and then the two solutions are virtually identical. In our practice, we use Exists() more often than KEEP, but feel free to pick and choose the solution that looks better to you.

Exercise 14.7: Loading Dimension Tables

1. Add a new tab at the end of the script and name it **Dimensions**.

2. Add three LOAD statements for the three dimension tables—Warehouses, Products, and Customers. Comment out some of the fields that are not going to be required for the inventory analysis. Add

the Exists() function at the end of each load, in order to limit the key fields to those that were previously loaded in the Fact table:

```
Warehouses:
LOAD
      [%Warehouse ID],
      Warehouse,
      [Warehouse City],
      [Warehouse Country],
      [Warehouse State]
FROM
[..\Data\Transformed QVDs\T_Warehouses.QVD]
(qvd)
WHERE
      Exists([%Warehouse ID])
;
Products:
LOAD
      [Size ID],
      [%Product ID],
      Product,
//    [# List Price],
//    [Standard Cost],
      [First Introduction Date],
      [Closeout Date],
      [# Unit Cost STD UM],
      Brand,
//    [Order UOM],
      [Product Group],
      Season,
      Style,
      [Style Short Name],
      [Size Description],
      Size,
      [Size Sort Order],
      [Color Description],
      Color
FROM
[..\Data\Transformed QVDs\T_Products.QVD]
(qvd)
WHERE
      Exists([%Product ID])
;
Customers:
```

```
LOAD [%Customer ID],
     Customer,
     Channel,
//     [Customer Address 1],
//     [Customer Address 2],
//     [Customer Address 3],
//     [Customer City],
//     [Customer Country],
//     [Customer State],
//     [Customer ZIP Code],
     [Customer Start Date],
     [Customer End Date]
FROM
[..\Data\Transformed QVDs\T_Customers.QVD]
(qvd)
WHERE
     Exists([%Customer ID])
;
```

3. **Save** and **Reload** your script. Verify the resulting table structure. Our data model is becoming a proper star, with a single Fact in the middle and three dimensions around the Fact.

If you recall, earlier we explained that all product quantities that participate in the inventory analysis need to be dollarized based on the same unit cost, for the sake of consistency. Even though our historical balances may not match the official inventory reports, for analytical purposes we have to compare apples to apples. For this reason, this Fact table stores quantities only and no amounts.

The unit cost for the standard unit of measure was loaded in the Products table. Logically, this is the right place for a measure that needs to be distinct per product. However, from the performance standpoint, this field should be populated in the Fact table.

When we introduced the Concatenated Fact model, we mentioned that one of the biggest benefits of the Concatenated Fact is its ability to keep all measures in the same table. Having all measures in the same table saves a lot of valuable time when QlikView collects all of the necessary fields for a given chart. Keeping the unit cost in the Products table would be counterproductive for the application's performance.

In addition, we should pre-calculate the extended amounts for all the quantities in our Fact to eliminate the need to multiply the same fields over and over again. Remember that any calculation that does not affect the granularity of your analysis, and can therefore be performed in the script, can save valuable run-time when users are waiting for the results in front of their screens.

In the following exercise, you create another mapping table that will map each [%Product ID] to the corresponding value of [Unit Cost STD UM] and then reload the Fact table once again, adding the calculation of all extended amounts for all different quantity fields in the Fact table.

Exercise 14.8: Adding Calculated Fields to the Fact

1. In the Mapping tab, load a new mapping table from the transformed QVD file T_Products.QVD:

```
Cost_Map:
Mapping
LOAD
     [%Product ID],
     [# Unit Cost STD UM]
FROM
[..\Data\Transformed QVDs\T_Products.QVD]
(qvd);
```

2. In the Dimensions tab, locate and comment out the line within the Products load, where the field [# Unit Cost STD UM] was loaded.

3. Add a new tab at the end of the script and call it **Cost**.

4. You need to reload the data from the Fact table into a temporary table, while adding the new field [# Unit Cost], and then drop the Fact table and rename the temporary table to Fact:

```
Temp_Fact:
Load
     *,
     ApplyMap('Cost_Map', [%Product ID], 0) as [# Unit Cost]
Resident
     Fact
;
drop table Fact;
rename table Temp_Fact to Fact;
```

5. Add another preceding load on top of this load, right after the table name `Temp_Fact`:

```
Load
    *,
    [# On Hand Quantity]     * [# Unit Cost] as [# On Hand Amount],
    [# Aged Quantity]        * [# Unit Cost] as [# Aged Amount],
    [# Demand Quantity]      * [# Unit Cost] as [# Demand Amount]
;
```

6. Save and Reload your script. Verify the resulting data model.

Restoring Missing Associations

In this section, we will discuss the requirement that pertains to the association between customers, products, and their inventories. The users would like to see which customers are buying which products. For example, if they saw that certain product had an insufficient inventory balance, they would like to see which customers might be affected by the shortage.

You will learn how to solve the problem using data modeling and then we'll present an alternative to that approach that may be better from the performance standpoint.

Adding a Generic Key to Restore a Missing Association

The problem is somewhat similar to the problem with the missing attribute discussed earlier. If you were using a Link Table model, the Sales table would be linked to the Inventory table, and all the associations would work perfectly. Selecting a Customer would lead to selecting the On-Hand balances for the Products that the Customer is buying. Selecting a Product would lead to selecting all Customers who ever bought this Product.

With the Concatenated Fact, nothing like that is possible. The Customer field is only available for sales records. Selecting a Customer will make the rest of the data excluded, or unavailable. In order to facilitate the same association logic, you need to create an artificial ("generic") link that would associate all customers with all of the products that the customer ever purchased.

Let's visualize the problem. In the following exercise, you build a straight table chart that displays the total on-hand amount by brand. You will add two list boxes with the Customer and Channel fields. Then you will examine what happens when a single channel and/or customer is selected.

Exercise 14.9: Visualizing the Problem with the Missing Association

1. In the Layout view (if necessary, close the Script Editor), add a new Sheet and name it **Customer**.

2. Select two Fields to be displayed in List Boxes—Customer and Channel.

3. Create a new Straight Table chart. Use Brand as a dimension and a sum of the On Hand Amount as an expression. Format the number as Currency.

4. Back in the Layout view, you should see the chart that displays on-hand balances for the four brands (If necessary, Clear Selections).

5. Select **Boutique** in the list of Channels and any of the names from the list of Customers. The chart will become empty. Try selecting different channels and customers. The chart will remain empty.

Now you can see the problem visually—the customers are not associated with the on-hand balances for their products. After we solve the problem, we will revisit this chart and examine the difference.

We described the solution to this problem in Chapter 13. The solution is to add a *Generic Link Table* between the Fact table and the Customers table, and to describe the necessary associations between customers and products in the Generic Link Table. As part of this solution, the original Customer ID field in the Fact table needs to be replaced with a new generic key.

In the following exercise, you solve the problem by adding a Generic Link Table between the Fact and the Customers table:

- Replace the key field [%Customer ID] in the Fact table with the new field [%Customer Link].

- For the sales records, the [%Customer Link] will be populated with the original [%Customer ID] values, with the addition of the prefix 'C|'.

- For all other slices of the Fact table, the [%Customer Link] will be populated with the [%Product ID] values, with the addition of the prefix 'P|'.

- Create a new table Link_Customer with the two key fields—the original [%Customer ID] and the new [%Customer Link].
- The Generic Link Table will be loaded from two sources:
  - From the Customers table, load the association of the [%Customer ID] to itself, with the addition of the prefix 'C|'. This link will serve the sales records.
  - From the transformed QVD file T_Sales4Inventory.QVD, load the association of the [%Customer ID] to the [%Product ID], with the addition of the prefix 'P|'. This link will serve all other facts.

Exercise 14.10: Adding a Generic Link Table

1. Save a backup copy of the document and name it **Inventory Data With No Generic Link XX.QVW**, where XX is your initials. Save the document in the subfolder \Data Models.

2. Re-open the original document Inventory Data XX.QVW. In the **Script Editor**, open the tab **Sales**. Copy the line that loads the [%Customer ID] and transform the copied line as follows. Notice that you need to keep the original [%Customer ID] field because it's used in the Exists() function for the purpose of validating the customers loaded into the Customers table. See the Customers load in Exercise 14.7 for a refresher.

   ```
   [%Customer ID],
   'C|' & [%Customer ID] as [%Customer Link],
   ```

3. Open the **On Hand** tab. Add the following line to the load of the On Hand records:

   ```
   'P|' & [%Product ID] as [%Customer Link],
   ```

4. Copy the same line and add it to the History load and the Aging load.

5. Add a new tab at the end of the script and name it **Link Customer**.

6. Type (or rather copy and paste as much as possible) the following statement:

   ```
   Link_Customer:
   LOAD
       [%Customer ID],
       'C|' & [%Customer ID] as [%Customer Link]
   Resident
       Customers
   ;
   ```

7. Add the following LOAD statement, based on the load from the transformed QVD file T_Sales4Inventory.QVD: Notice the keyword Distinct that needs to be added after the keyword LOAD. This is important, in order to avoid many duplicate rows from multiple sales records for the same customer and product:

```
Concatenate(Link_Customer)
LOAD Distinct
     [%Customer ID],
     'P|' & [%Product ID] as [%Customer Link]
FROM
[..\Data\Transformed QVDs\T_Sales4Inventory.QVD]
(qvd);
```

8. At the end of this tab, drop the original field [%Customer ID] from the Fact table. It was needed temporarily, as a comparison base for the Exists() function. At this point, you can drop the field as it's redundant:

```
drop field [%Customer ID] from Fact;
```

9. Save and Reload your script. Examine your table structure.

Your table structure should look similar to the one in Figure 14.6.

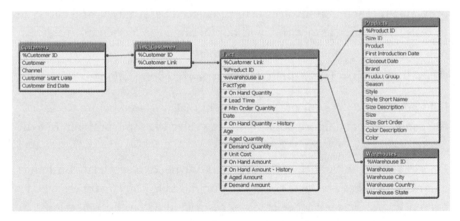

FIGURE 14.6:
The data structure with the Generic Link Table

Take a look at the straight table that you added in Exercise 14.9. If you made all the changes properly, the chart will show on-hand balances even when specific channels and customers are selected. The association was restored! Don't get confused if the balances do not change too much when you select individual customers. In our randomly generated database, almost all customers buy almost all products. This is just the way we generated the data (which is a separate story that deserves to be published in a separate book, or at least in a blog post).

Well, now we have good news and bad news. On the bright side, we've restored the missing association between customers and on-hand balances. On the other hand, our star schema is not quite the same anymore. In the classic star schema, there should be no more than one hop between the fact and any of the dimensions. In our data model, there are two hops between the Customers and the Fact tables.

This is the price we have to pay for the benefit of associating customers and on-hand balances. In a truly huge data set, the performance penalty might be so high that it makes this solution impossible, but in a reasonably sized data set the performance penalty is acceptably small.

Okay, you must be wondering, now what? What solution do we suggest? Well, sometimes the only possible answer is the quote from the favorite song of all DBAs and system administrators in the world. The Rolling Stones' song, "You Can't Always Get What You Want..." Other times, we can find alternative solutions.

In the following section, we will review an alternative solution to the same problem. This solution involves using advanced Set Analysis and allows us to restore the same association without building a Generic Link Table.

An Alternative to Building a Generic Link Table

Let's get back to the copy of the document that we saved before we added the generic key and figure out how we can solve the same problem in a different way.

Let's examine the essence of the problem. We need to aggregate on-hand balances for those products that were purchased by the customers who are currently *available* (either selected or associated with other selections). So, what seems to be the problem here? Well, two problems, actually:

- Since on-hand records are not directly associated with sales records, we have no direct way of knowing what products are associated with those *available* customers.

- Since the Customer field is not populated within the on-hand records, selecting any customers or any customer-related fields makes all on-hand records disabled, or *not available* (grayed-out).

Both of these problems can be solved with advanced Set Analysis.

To solve the first problem, we need to formulate a Set Analysis filter that selects those Product ID values that are *available* (or *possible*) within the 'Sales' fact type—those are the products that are associated with the *available* customers, right? This filter looks like this:

[%Product ID]=P({<FactType={Sales}>} [%Product ID])

The function P() returns the set of *(P)ossible* values of the field [%Product ID]. The inner Set Analysis filter defines the scope for the possible values— in our case, FactType= 'Sales'. We are only interested in those products that are currently *possible* within the sales records.

This filter solves the first problem. Now we know the set of products that should be included in the aggregation. Now, the solution to the second problem is even simpler than that. If selecting a customer disables the on-hand records, then this selection needs to be disregarded. We know the syntax for disregarding field selections:

Customer=

This little set modifier will disregard the Customer selection. This is it; problem solved!

Wait a minute! Is that really it? What if the Channel is selected? Hmm, true. We should disregard the Channel, too:

Customer-, Channel=

Here we go. Got it right this time. Can we wrap it up now? Well, technically any field from the Customers table can be selected, and any of those selections will disable the on-hand records, so we should disregard all of them.

The simple solution to this problem is to list all customer-related fields in the Set Analysis modifier, to ensure that no customer-related selections can break this logic.

There is a universal formula that can help you automatically disregard all field selections from a number of tables. The credit for this solution goes to our good friend and QlikView veteran Phil Bishop.

This solution involves using the QlikView function Concat(), which can take a set of values and concatenate them into a single string using a delimiter of your choice. One day, we will write a separate book about our love of the `Concat()` function. Until then, check it out in the Help section. We will just briefly describe the format of the function:

```
Concat ([{set_expression}]  [ distinct ] expression [, delimiter [,
   sort-weight]])
```

`Concat()` is a string-aggregation function. Like any other aggregation function, it can have its own Set Analysis expression. When it's applied to repeating values, you may use the prefix DISTINCT to de-duplicate the list of values that are going to be concatenated together. The *expression* describes *what* needs to be concatenated. Two other optional parameters provide the delimiter that should be used in the process of concatenation, and the `sort-weight` expression that should be used for sorting the components prior to concatenating them. The `Concat()` function is truly wonderful for the multitude of advanced solutions that it can provide.

Here is the formula that builds the universal set modifier. This set modifier includes the list of all the fields that should be disregarded by the Set Analysis expression.

```
$(='[' & CONCAT({<$Table={Table1, Table2, Table3}>} $Field,']=,[') & ']=')
```

Let's describe the components of this wonderful formula:

- The formula uses two system fields that are managed automatically by QlikView—$Field and $Table. These fields hold the lists of existing tables and fields in your QlikView database. Moreover, the fields and the tables are associated in QlikView metadata, so we can derive the information about fields that are associated with certain tables.

- In the heart of this formula is the CONCAT() function that lists $Field values. The Set Analysis condition limits the $Field values to only those associated with certain tables (listed here as Table1, Table2, Table3).

- The second parameter of the function CONCAT() provides the delimiter that should be used for concatenating the field names. The delimiter in this case is ']=,[' which provides the closing and the opening brackets that need to be used with the field names, as well as the equal sign and the comma that should separate the list of set modifier filters. Since the order of filters is not important, the optional sort-weight parameter is omitted.

- In front of the CONCAT, the opening bracket is appended to the list on the left. At the end, the closing bracket and the last equals sign are appended on the right.

- The whole calculation is enclosed in a dollar-sign expansion that turns the formula into a solid string that lists all the necessary fields that need to be disregarded, in the following format:

`[Field1]=, [Field2]=, [Field3]=`

We color-coded the text to emphasize its different parts—the brown Field names are concatenated into a single list with the blue delimiters and are surrounded by the green opening bracket on the left and the green closing bracket with the equals sign on the right.

If this is a bit too much to process, don't worry. It's perfectly fine to list all the related fields manually and not worry about the complex CONCAT() calculation.

One way or another, you now know the solutions to both problems that you started with. In the following exercise, you add a Set Analysis condition to the straight table chart that you created in Exercise 14.9, as an alternative to building the Generic Link Table.

Exercise 14.11: Adding a Set Analysis Condition as an Alternative to the Generic Key

1. Open the document **Inventory Data With No Generic Link XX.QVW** that you saved in the previous exercise.

2. Locate the straight table chart that you developed in Exercise 14.9 and open the Chart Properties.

3. Open the definition of the expression and add the following Set Analysis condition to the existing formula:

```
Sum (
    {$<[%Product ID]=P({<FactType={Sales}>} [%Product ID]),
        Customer=, Channel=
    >}  [# On Hand Amount]
)
```

4. Accept all changes and exit the properties. Try making selections of customers and channels. Verify that the chart shows the numbers in the same way as it did in the version of the document with the generic key.

5. Clone the same chart and open the properties again.

6. In the Expressions tab, modify the definition of the expression in such a way that any selections in the Customers table are disregarded, using the universal formula that we brought up earlier:

```
Sum (
        {$<[%Product ID]=P({<FactType={Sales}>} [%Product ID]),
        $(='[' & concat({<$Table={Customers}>}$Field,']=,[') & ']=')
        >}   [# On Hand Amount]
)
```

7. Accept all changes and verify that the two charts show identical results.

8. Open Sheet Properties and add the [%Customer ID] field to be displayed in a List Box.

9. Make a selection in the [%Customer ID] field and observe the difference between the two straight tables.

This exercise concludes the discussion of generic keys and the Set Analysis alternatives. You may be wondering which solution is better. As always, the answer is "it depends."

In a mid-size data set, where performance is not an issue, adding a Generic Link Table may not be so bad. The obvious benefit is that the association between the data elements is encoded in the data model, keeping the chart expressions relatively simple.

In a large data set, the performance penalty of adding a generic link may be too heavy, forcing the developer to opt for more complex Set Analysis conditions. While this solution is fast, slick, and elegant, it requires that the corresponding Set Analysis filters be added to each and every expression in your application. That adds a lot of complexity to many chart expressions. The problem becomes increasingly more difficult when multiple dimensions need to be linked this way.

So pick your poison, folks! What will it be in your application? The generic link key, the Set Analysis solution, or ... "you can't always get what you want"?

Building the As Of Date Table

The *As of Date* table is a very particular solution that's required in situations when users need to assess performance as of an earlier date.

In essence, the As of Date solution is similar to the generic link solution. We disconnect the direct association between the Fact table and the Master Calendar by splitting the single Date field into two fields. The date field in the Fact table is still called Date, while the date field in the Master Calendar is now called [As Of Date].

The new link between the Fact and the Calendar tables will now be facilitated by another link table. This table will contain all possible combinations of the original Date and the new [As Of Date], and a set of conditional flags that describe the relation between the Date and the [As Of Date].

For example, Table 14.1 displays a partial list of flags, calculated for the combination of Date = April 1, 2014 and [As Of Date] = May 1, 2014:

TABLE 14.1: Examples of Conditional Flags in the As Of Date Table

FLAG/METRIC	VALUE	COMMENT
_CMTD_Flag	0	The date does not belong to the same current month as the [As of Date]
_CYTD_Flag	1	The date belongs to the same YTD
_PYTD_Flag	0	The date does not belong to the prior YTD
_R12_Flag	1	The date belongs to the rolling 12 month period
_PR12_Flag	0	The date does not belong to the prior rolling 12 months

Generating the conditional flags for the AsOfDate table is very similar to the process of generating the flags for the Master Calendar. The only difference is that the [As of Date] field is used instead of the current date variable vToday.

Let's describe the logical process of building the AsOfDate table, tailored for our scenario of managing all of the data in the monthly buckets with month end date serving as the representative date for each month.

1. Make a distinct list of all Date values. Name the resulting field Date, using the same name that is used in the Fact table.

2. Determine the lowest and the highest dates in the list.

3. Generate a list of month-end dates for all the months that fall between the lowest and the highest dates. Name the resulting field [As Of Date].

4. Join the list of [As of Date] values with the list of Date values. This will be a Cartesian join, generating a list of all possible combinations between the two fields. This is one of a few instances when we cause the Cartesian join intentionally. This is also the reason for our earlier comment about this solution only being feasible when the number of possible dates is relatively small.

5. Reload the resulting list, only including those pairs of dates where [As of Date] is greater or equal than Date. This is because our application is only looking back into history, never forward. In other situations, when you may be trying to predict future inventory balances, you would not limit the list with such a condition.

Should We Keep a Separate Calendar or Should We Combine It with a Link Table?

As usual, it depends. If you can't stand the thought of storing values for fields like Year, Month, and Quarter multiple times, then by all means keep a separate distinct calendar that ensures that these attributes are only stored once.

If you don't mind a little duplication of data, then the question boils down to performance gains versus losses. In a huge data set, every extra table and link takes up a lot of valuable time in the process of rendering charts. In these environments, reducing the number of links is better, even with some manageable increases in memory requirements.

On the flip side, in smaller applications, the benefit of reducing a link may not be as high. At the same time, if you have many dates to work with, then the overhead of storing many attributes in a more detailed table may be substantial. For example, if your calendar consists of 10 years' worth of single days, then its size is approximately 3,650 rows. The corresponding AsOfDate table may have as many as 3,650 x 3,650 = 13,322,500 rows! Duplicating many fields by such a huge factor can be very costly. That is a huge overhead, especially for a mid-size data set.

When performance matters, you should try both models and determine which one works best in your situation. And when performance doesn't matter, simply pick the solution that looks nicer to you; why bother comparing?

6. In the process of this reload, calculate all the conditional flags that describe the relation between the two dates.

7. Calculate all the date-related attributes, such as Year, Month, Week, and so on. These attributes can be created in the table with the distinct list of [As Of Date] values, thus forming the MasterCalendar table. Alternatively, the same fields can be created in the newly created link table that we will call Link_AsOfDate. In this case, the attribute values will be stored multiple times, causing a slight waste of memory. At the same time, eliminating the need for a separate Calendar table and saving another link generate significant performance benefits to make up for the use of extra memory.

In addition, we'd like to introduce here another little technique that helps with generating the list of dates for the calendar in the most efficient way. Step 1 in the process described above requires making a distinct list of all existing Date values. Conventionally, this is done by loading the values from the Fact table. Aggregating a large Fact table, however, can be a heavy procedure that takes up valuable time and resources. In QlikView, it is much faster to generate the necessary table directly from the list of field values. This can be done using an AutoGenerate LOAD, with the use of the FieldValue() and FieldValueCount() functions. We will let you discover all the details about these functions individually, and only provide the following sample here:

```
LOAD
     FieldValue('Date', RecNo()) as Date
AutoGenerate
     FieldValueCount('Date')
;
```

The FieldValueCount() function provides the number of rows that need to be generated by the AutoGenerate LOAD. The FieldValue() function, applied to the RecNo() function, retrieves the sequential value of the Date field for each row. This technique is proven to be much faster than the conventional method of extracting the field values from the Fact table.

In Exercise 14.12, you will build the As of Date table following the logical process described previously. You will use preceding loads whenever possible, to simplify the flow and to reduce the number of temporary tables. Note that we are adding the logic to the original Inventory Data XX.QVW document, not to the separate copy that we diverted to in the previous exercise.

In our data model, we opted to combine the Calendar table with the AsOfDate table, to save on the number of tables in the data set. Since we are only managing monthly totals, our AsOfDate table will be small.

Exercise 14.12: Building the As Of Date Table

1. If you still have the side copy of the document opened from Exercise 14.11, close it and open the document named Inventory Data *XX*.qvw.

2. Open the Script Editor. Add a new tab at the end of the script and name it **As Of Date**.

3. Load a distinct list of Date values into a temporary table:

```
Temp_Dates:
LOAD
     FieldValue('Date', RecNo()) as Date
AutoGenerate
     FieldValueCount('Date')
;
```

4. Calculate the lowest and the highest dates on the list and calculate the corresponding MonthEnd dates:

```
Load
     Date(floor(MonthEnd(Min(Date)))) as MinDate,
     Date(floor(MonthEnd(Max(Date)))) as MaxDate
Resident
     Temp_Dates
;
```

5. Add a Preceding Load in front of the last load statement to generate all the month end dates between the min and the max using the WHILE clause:

```
Load
     Date(floor(MonthEnd(AddMonths(MinDate, IterNo() -1)))) as [As Of Date]
WHILE
     Date(floor(MonthEnd(AddMonths(MinDate, IterNo() -1)))) <=
     Date(floor(MonthEnd(MaxDate)))
;
```

6. Join the results of the preceding load back into the Temp_Dates table. Add the Join prefix in front of the preceding load:

```
Join (Temp_Dates)
Load
...
```

7. As a result of the previous steps, you generated the temporary table with all possible combinations of Date and AsOfDate. Now, reload this temporary table into the resulting table AsOfDate, only including those rows where AsOfDate >= Date. In the process, calculate all the attribute fields and the conditional flags. At the end, drop the temporary table:

```
AsOfDate:
Load
    Date,
    [As Of Date] ,
    Year([As Of Date] )                          AS Year,
    Month([As Of Date] )                         AS Month,
    'Q' & ceil(month([As Of Date] ) / 3)         AS Quarter,
    Year([As Of Date] ) &'-'& 'Q' & ceil(month([As Of Date] ) / 3)
                                                 AS QuarterYear,
    Date([As Of Date] , 'MMM-YYYY')              AS MonthYear,
    InMonth(Date, [As Of Date] , 0) * -1         AS _CMTD_Flag,
    InMonth(Date, [As Of Date] , -12) * -1       AS _PMTD_Flag,
    InMonth(Date, [As Of Date] , -1) * -1        AS _PM_Flag,
    InYearToDate(Date, [As Of Date] , 0) * -1    AS _CYTD_Flag,
    InYearToDate(Date, [As Of Date] , -1) * -1   AS _PYTD_Flag,
    (AddMonths(Date, 12) > [As Of Date] ) * -1   AS _R12_Flag,
    (AddMonths(Date, 12) <= [As Of Date] ) *
    (AddMonths(Date, 24) > [As Of Date] )        AS _PR12_Flag,
    (AddMonths(Date, 6) > [As Of Date] ) * -1    AS _R6_Flag,
    (AddMonths(Date, 6) <= [As Of Date] ) *
    (AddMonths(Date, 12) > [As Of Date] )        AS _PR6_Flag,
    (AddMonths(Date, 12) <= [As Of Date] ) *
    (AddMonths(Date, 18) > [As Of Date] )        AS _PYR6_Flag,
    (AddMonths(Date, 3) > [As Of Date] ) * -1    AS _R3_Flag,
    (AddMonths(Date, 3) <= [As Of Date] ) *
    (AddMonths(Date, 6) > [As Of Date] )         AS _PR3_Flag,
    (AddMonths(Date, 12) <= [As Of Date] ) *
    (AddMonths(Date, 15) > [As Of Date] )        AS _PYR3_Flag
Resident
    Temp_Dates
Where
    Date<=[As Of Date]
;
drop table Temp_Dates;
```

8. Save and Reload your script. Examine the resulting data structure. In order to verify that all the conditions were processed as expected, create a Table Box and include all fields from the AsOfDate table. Examine the pair of dates and the corresponding flags and validate that they were calculated correctly.

Perhaps we should explain a few points about this exercise.

- As a reminder, we use the `Date(Floor(Monthend()))` construction to truncate the timestamp portion that's returned by the `MonthEnd()` function, and to format the numeric result of truncating as a date.

- Most of the calendar logic here is no different from the calendar logic you learned in Chapter 10.

- We added flags for rolling 12 months, rolling 6 months, and rolling 3 months, to demonstrate how to handle these date comparison options. Different companies may use different periods to compare between dates, and our logic can accommodate that. For each one of these periods, we are also calculating the "previous" flag—for example, "previous rolling 6 months"—and "same period prior year" flag, such as `_PYR6_Flag`, representing the same six months in the prior year.

This exercise completes our discussion of the advanced date handling with the As of Date table. In conclusion, remember that this solution applies a specific requirement to our chart expressions. Every expression in the application that includes date-related metrics now has to be equipped with the appropriate Set Analysis filter that defines the desired relationship between the transactional `Date` and the `As Of Date` that is selected.

For example, the current on-hand balance is not date-sensitive, but the historical on-hand is, and so is the historical demand, based on the sales history. All of these expressions need appropriate Set Analysis filters in order to produce accurate results.

This requirement, along with the increasing complexity of analysis, surely makes the task of creating and maintaining chart expressions much more difficult. In the following section, we will review various techniques that developers can use to simplify and standardize their approach to managing chart expressions.

Generating Chart Expressions in the Script

In this section, we will discuss various techniques of creating script expressions, which are stored in variables, from the load script. QlikView offers a number of techniques that can be used for this purpose. In this section, you will learn:

- How to create expression variables manually and how to assign them values.

- How to deal with special characters, such as quotes.

- How to generate variables programmatically, using dollar-sign expansions.

- How to load expressions from an external text file and generate the corresponding variables automatically.

Creating Expressions Stored in Variables in the Script

In Chapter 8, you learned how to use formulas stored in variables, but you assigned those formulas in the **Layout** view, using either input boxes or a **Variable Overview**. While this method is fast, convenient, and doesn't require reloading your data with any change in expressions, there are some disadvantages to keeping your formulas created in the **Layout** view.

- If your document should become corrupted because of an unexpected failure, there is no way of restoring your valuable formulas, other than restoring a previously saved backup version of your document.

- If you gave your document to another developer and he made a number of changes in the variables, there is no easy way to find the differences.

- If you need to perform a global change across a large number of expressions, there is no tool that could help you find and replace texts across multiple variables.

- If your IT group uses source control for its applications, expressions should be stored in such a way that makes it easy to be checked in and out of the source control tool.

All of these issues point in the same direction—in a complex analytic application, expressions should be stored in variables and variables need to be assigned in the script. Preferably, the script should be managed using external text files for easy backup/restore, global change, analysis of changes, and source control.

The simplest method of creating expression variables in the script is the manual method. The corresponding formula is simply assigned as a value to the variable:

```
SET exp_Demand = 'Sum ([# Demand Amount])';
SET filter_CYTD = '_CYTD_Flag = {1}';
```

If you recall, the SET command stores the text as is, without trying to evaluate it. Note that the formulas are provided as strings—that is, enclosed in single quotes.

In a similar way, color definitions can be created in the script:

```
SET color_Blue = 'RGB(0, 100, 200)';
```

For the most part, storing formula definitions in script variables is very similar to entering the same definitions into the variable values in an input box. The biggest difference may occur if your expression should include special characters, such as a single quote. Since single quotes are used to define the boundaries of text values, having a single quote symbol inside the text makes it difficult for the script interpreter to evaluate the expression correctly. Let's examine the following example.

Imagine that we need to create a filter that selects all products that contain the text "Women's" in the name. It's quite simple to create such a filter in the layout. We simply type the following as the value of the filter variable in the input box:

```
Product = {"*Women's*"}
```

The same is not as simple in the script. The following syntax wouldn't work, because of the single quote in the middle of the text:

```
set filter_Womens = 'Product = {"*Women's*"}';
```

There are two ways of dealing with this problem. In simple cases like ours, with only one single quote in the text, the easy way out is to omit the outer pair of quotes. Since the SET command always stores the text as is, the outer quotes are optional (the same would not be true with the LET command):

```
set filter_Womens = Product = {"*Women's*"};
```

This statement looks a bit quirky, especially with the two equals signs next to each other, and yet it produces the correct result. The text to the right of the first equals sign is taken as is and is stored in the filter.

The more universal method is to build the string from its parts, replacing the single quote with the ASCII code CHR(39). In this case, we have to use the LET statement instead of the SET statement, because we need QlikView to evaluate the formula and perform the concatenation:

```
let filter_Womens = 'Product = {"*Women' & CHR(39) & 's*"}';
```

In this example, the first part of the text, which appears before the single quote, is concatenated with the function CHR(39) that replaces the single quote, and then the ending part of the text is concatenated on the right. Admittedly, this expression is more difficult to code and is hard to maintain. We are trying to avoid them as much as possible. You will soon learn an alternative technique for creating and storing expression variables, which eliminates this issue.

Now, let's try to estimate how many different expressions we should create, to cover the potential needs of the visual analysis. Ironically, because of the reversed order of presenting this material in our book, you already know what should happen in the phase of developing visualizations—you read about it in Chapter 12. If this was a real project, you would only be planning your future needs at this stage.

As we mentioned earlier, the As of Date solution requires that all date-driven calculations include Set Analysis filters that define the relationship between the selected As Of Date and the transactional Date in the Fact table. Take a look at our calendar table AsOfDate. It includes 13 conditional flags, describing various date-related conditions. Therefore, we will need 13 versions of each expression that involves inventory history or sales history. That sounds like too many expressions to handle.

You already know the solution from Chapter 12. Instead of repeating each expression 13 times, we used another form of the dollar-sign expansion, which allows parameters to be used in the formula. For example:

```
SET exp_Demand = 'Sum ( {<$1>}  [# Demand Amount])';
```

When a dollar-sign expansion with parameters gets expanded, the parameter placeholders such as $1, $2, and $3 are replaced by the actual parameters specified in the expression that's using the formula. In our example, the following expression could be used for calculating Current YTD Demand:

```
$(exp_Demand($(filter_CYTD)))
```

`$(filter_CYTD)` serves as a parameter for the `Demand` expression. When this formula is fully expanded, it is identical to the following "static" formula:

```
Sum ({<_CYTD_Flag={1}>}  [# Demand Amount])
```

Now our task is somewhat simplified. We need to create a single formula for each specific calculation and a list of 13 filters. Each filter has the same structure. For example:

```
SET filter_CYTD = '_CYTD_Flag = {1}';
SET filter_PYTD = '_PYTD_Plag = {1}';
```

You can surely see the commonality. It would probably take us just a few minutes to copy and paste one of these expressions thirteen times and modify each line to represent another conditional flag. However, we'd like to use this opportunity to show you how to generate these statements automatically using dollar-sign expansions.

This technique would be useful in a case where many similar expressions need to be created, following the same pattern.

For our example, we will use the FOR EACH … NEXT loop statement to repeat the logic for each one of the 13 conditional flag names, such as CYTD, CMTD, and so on. Within the loop, we will calculate the name of the corresponding filter variable and the corresponding definition of the filter. Then, we will use those two calculated variables in a SET statement that will generate our filter variable.

Before we get to build our first expressions in the script, let's discuss one more topic. Where would be the best place to generate the expression variables? Should we add this logic to our data model documents, or to the final UI documents? We recommend placing this logic in the final UI documents, primarily for the sake of speed. If you need to make changes to your expressions or add new expressions, you will only need to reload the final UI document, rather than wait for the whole data model to get refreshed.

Another good reason to create variables in the final document is the fact that variables are not passed with the BINARY load. The BINARY load only loads the database— tables and fields—not variables. Even if you created your variables before, you'd have to recreate them in the UI.

For these reasons, you will open a new document that could become the beginning of your new UI document, if you haven't developed one already. You will use this document for all the exercises related to variables.

Exercise 14.13: Generating Filter Variables for Conditional Flags

1. Save and close the Inventory Data *XX*.QVW document. Create a new QlikView document and name it **Inventory Expressions *XX*.QVW**, where *XX* is your initials. Save the document in the subfolder \Data Loaders. You will use it solely for the purpose of practicing various techniques of creating expressions in the script.

2. Open the **Script Editor**. In the Main tab, activate the **QlikView Files** wizard and select the Inventory Data document that you just saved. When you are done, you should see the new BINARY statement added as the first line in the script:

   Binary [inventory data.qvw];

3. Add a new tab and name it **Generate Expressions**.

4. In the new tab, add the FOR EACH … NEXT loop statement and list the 13 flag names. Terminate the loop with the NEXT statement. We had to break the FOR line into two, because of printing limitations. You should keep everything related to the first line of the FOR statement in a single line.

   ```
   FOR EACH vFilter IN 'CYTD', 'PYTD', 'CMTD', 'PM',
    'PMTD', 'R12', 'PR12', 'R6', 'PR6', 'PYR6', 'R3', 'PR3', 'PYR3'
   NEXT
   ```

5. Within the loop, calculate two new variables—the name of the future filter variable and its definition. The name should begin with the prefix 'filter_' and end with the name of the flag vFilter. The definition should form the Set Analysis filter that has the corresponding flag name and the condition '={1}':

   ```
   LET vFilterName = 'filter_' & vFilter;
   LET vFilterDefinition = '_' & vFilter & '_Flag = {1}';
   ```

6. Next, add the SET statement that assigns the value of the definition to the filter name. Note that the filter name doesn't require single quotes, since it's the name of the future variable, while the definition is enclosed in single quotes as a string value. As you already learned, these quotes are optional:

   ```
   SET $(vFilterName) = '$(vFilterDefinition)';
   ```

7. Add three LET statements at the end of the script, to destroy the temporary variables vFilter, vFilterName, and vFilterDefinition.

8. Your complete script in this tab should look like this:

```
FOR EACH vFilter IN 'CYTD', 'PMTD', 'CMTD',
'PMTD', 'R12', 'PR12', 'R6', 'PR6', 'R3', 'PR3'
    LET vFilterName = 'filter_' & vFilter;
    LET vFilterDefinition = '_' & vFilter & '_Flag = {1}';
    SET $(vFilterName) = '$(vFilterDefinition)';

NEXT
LET vFilter = ;
LET vFilterName = ;
LET vFilterDefinition = ;
```

9. **Save** and **Reload** your script. Verify that 13 new variables have been created in the document.

So far, you learned how to create script variables and store expression definitions in them, either manually or with some automation. These techniques serve some of the requirements that we laid out in the beginning of this section. Now our expressions can easily be recreated. You can search and replace across multiple variables. You can even create many similar expressions by copying and modifying a source expression many times.

There are a few things you still cannot do. You cannot share similar expressions across multiple QlikView documents. You cannot easily track changes between different versions, nor can you easily use a source control tool to manage these expressions as an asset.

In order to meet these needs, you can externalize the relevant sections of the script into externally stored text files, and include them in your scripts using the INCLUDE statement. You may remember using the INCLUDE statement in Chapter 6. This time, we skip practicing this technique again.

Loading Expressions from External Text Files

Our favorite method of managing expressions in variables is to store the variable names and their definitions in a comma-separated text file and then load the variables into the application using a simple universal script that you can copy and use in your own environment as needed.

Let's describe the process of developing our expressions. Simple expressions can be entered into any text editor manually, without any special helper tools such as syntax check. Conversely, more complex expressions that may involve complex Set Analysis conditions would be too tough to author outside of QlikView **Expression Editor**. We need to let QlikView validate our syntax and calculate the results, as a confirmation of our expressions' validity and accuracy.

So, the first step is established. We begin by creating and testing our expressions in QlikView, usually within the corresponding charts that use the same expressions.

When we are ready to store the expression in a variable, we usually create the variable in the UI using an input box and copy the definition of the variable from the chart into the input box. We continue this process, creating new expressions and storing them in variables. It's a fast and convenient way to make changes without leaving the same QlikView sheet.

At some point, we are ready to organize the variables and store them in an external text file. That can be done in a number of ways and using an input box, once again, is the most convenient of all.

We usually create a new input box and select all color, filter, format, and expression variables to be displayed in the input box. Then, we can use the **Export** function from the right-click context menu to export all the variables and their definitions to an external text file. We can choose between several formats, including comma-separated files, HTML, XML, Excel, and a few others. Our preference is to use comma-separated text files. They are easy to work with and easy to modify, compare, copy, and paste.

Excel would have been a good option, if not for the two following issues. First, Excel has its own way of processing the quoting around our text definitions—it may add or remove the outer double quotes based on its internal logic that's outside of our control. Secondly, Excel spreadsheets are not text files, so they cannot be easily compared side by side using advanced text editors or commonly used diff tools. Because of these two issues, we prefer to use comma-separated text files, and we edit them using an advanced text editor. There are many excellent text editors, and you may use the editor of your choice. Our preferred editor is Notepad++ (`http://notepad-plus-plus.org/`), which is free to use and offers many advanced features.

In the following exercise, you will export the expressions from the existing `Inventory Analysis XX.QVW` document that you built in Chapter 12.

Exercise 14.14: Exporting Existing Variables into an External Text File

1. Open the `Inventory Analysis XX.QVW` document that you developed in Chapter 12. It should be stored in the `\Apps` subfolder.

2. Open the **Variables** sheet. Add a new **Input Box** and select all color, filter, format, and expression variables. You may select all variables, if you'd like to manage all of them in a text file.

3. In the **Presentation** tab of the input box **Properties**, clear the **Show Equals Sign** checkbox.

4. **Save** the document before proceeding to the next step.

5. Verify all the values and determine the variables that contain formulas that begin with equals signs. You may promote all these variables to the top of the list, to make it easier to remember. Remove the equals signs manually and remember what variables require their equals signs to be restored later.

6. Right-click on the **Input Box** and select the **Export** option.

7. In the **Save As** dialog that opens, select **Comma Delimited (*.csv, *.txt)** in the **Save as type** drop-down list.

8. Name the text file `Inventory Variables XX.txt`. Save the file in the `\Metadata\` subfolder.

9. In QlikView, restore the equals signs at the beginning of those formulas that were modified in Step 3. Alternatively, close the QlikView document without saving to preserve the earlier configuration.

10. Open the newly created text file using the text editor of your choice (do not use Excel!) and enter the opening equals signs in all the variables that need them. Save the text file after the change.

Examine the contents of the text file, while you have it open (see the example in Figure 14.7).

```
1  exp_UnitSymbol,"=if(vUnit= 1000000, 'M',    if(vUnit=1000, 'K', '' ))"
2  fmt_PL,"=IF(vUnit = 1000000, '#,##0.0', '#,##0')"
3  color_Black,"rgb(54,54,54)"
4  color_Blue,"rgb(0,100, 200)"
5  color_CustomerAllowances,"if( $(exp_CustomerAllowances) / $(exp_GrossSales) <= v_TargetCustomerAllowances, $(color_Green),
6  if( $(exp_CustomerAllowances) / $(exp_GrossSales) <= v_TargetCustomerAllowances * 1.1, $(color_Yellow), $(color_Red) ))"
7  color_CustomerContribution,"if( $(exp_DirectCustomerContributionMargin) / $(exp_GrossSales) >= v_TargetCustomerContribution, $(color_Green),
8  if( $(exp_DirectCustomerContributionMargin) / $(exp_GrossSales) >= v_TargetCustomerContribution * 0.9, $(color_Yellow), $(color_Red) ))"
9  color_Discounts,"if( $(exp_Discounts) / $(exp_SalesAtList) <= v_TargetDiscounts, $(color_Green),
10 if( $(exp_Discounts) / $(exp_SalesAtList) <= v_TargetDiscounts * 1.1, $(color_Yellow), $(color_Red) ))"
11 color_Gray,"rgb(200,200,200)"
12 color_Green,"rgb(77,167,65)"
```

FIGURE 14.7:
Example of expressions stored in a text file

Each line in the text file stores a variable name and its definition, separated by a comma. Some definitions span across multiple lines. This should not be a problem when the variables are loaded back into QlikView.

However, if you should experience any issues with multi-line expressions, you may want to invest some time in housekeeping and combine all the multi-line expressions into single lines. If you are using Notepad++, all you need to do is highlight all the lines that should be combined and press Ctrl+J to join all the lines into one.

Next, you are going to learn how to load these variables from the text file back into QlikView, and how to create variables based on those definitions.

The process involves two steps. First, we load the external text file just like we load any other data file. The result of this load is a table with two fields that represent the name of the variable and the expression definition. We usually name them Var and Expression.

The second step is processing the new table in a FOR … NEXT loop, one line at a time. For each line, we do the following:

- Fetch the name of the future variable from the Var field into a new vVar variable.

- Then we assign the formula definition that we fetch from the Expression field, to the variable with the name $(vVar) using the LET command.

Exercise 14.15 provides detailed instructions for developing the script for this process.

Exercise 14.15: Generating the Variables Stored in the External Text File

1. If necessary, close the `Inventory Analysis XX.QVW` document and open the `Inventory Expressions XX.QVW` document. Open the **Script Editor**.

2. Add a new tab at the end of the script and name the new tab **Load Variables from File**.

3. Using the **Table Files** wizard, load the text file that you created in Exercise 14.14. Specify **Comma** as the delimiter and accept all other default settings. Rename the first field **Var**. Rename the second field **Expression**. Name the table **Variables**:

```
Variables:
LOAD
        @1 as Var,
        @2 as Expression
FROM
[..\Metadata\Inventory Variables.txt]
(txt, utf8, no labels, delimiter is ',', msq);
```

4. Add a `FOR` loop to process all the rows of the new table one by one:

```
FOR i = 0 TO NoOfRows('Variables') - 1
NEXT
```

5. Within the loop, fetch the value of the `Var` field into the temporary variable:

```
let vVar = peek('Var', i, 'Variables');
```

6. Then, generate the new variable using the following `LET` command:

```
let $(vVar) = peek('Expression', i, 'Variables');
```

7. After the end of the loop, drop the `Variables` table and destroy the two temporary variables:

```
drop table Variables;
LET i=;
LET vVar =;
```

8. **Save** and **Reload** your script. The new expressions should be created in the document as variables. Validate that your most complex expressions were generated as expected.

9. Your complete script for this exercise should look like this:

```
//=================================================================
// Load Variables from the text file
//=================================================================
Variables:
LOAD
     @1 as Var,
     @2 as Expression
FROM
[..\Metadata\Inventory Variables.txt]
(txt, utf8, no labels, delimiter is ',', msq);
// Loop through all rows and assign variables:
FOR i = 0 TO NoOfRows('Variables') - 1
     let vVar = peek('Var', i, 'Variables');
     LET $(vVar) = peek('Expression', i, 'Variables');
Next
Drop Table Variables;
LET i=;
LET vVar =;
```

It's important to fetch the expression definition using the peek() function and to assign it to the new variable in one step, avoiding the intermediary variable. Otherwise, we'd have to deal with special characters, such as quotes and dollar signs, that would get in the way. While the value is being retrieved using the peek() function, those special characters don't cause any harm.

Note that this routine is quite universal, except for the text file name. It would be nice to package it as a common subroutine and store it in the external text file with all common routines. We will leave it for you, as an extra-curricular activity.

In your environment, you may choose to organize separate layers of text files with different variables definitions. For example, color definitions could be shared between multiple applications, as well as some of the expressions. Other expressions might be specific to each analytic application.

What if you need to override a variable that is set among common variables for a specific application? Actually, QlikView variables are a perfect choice for implementing *common* versus *local* definitions. If you generate all common variables first, and then generate local variables next, any new values will override the older values; so local definitions of the same variables will override the common definitions that might have been loaded earlier.

Now, you'll complete the circle and create the external text file included in the `Inventory Analysis XX.QVW` document in Chapter 12.

Exercise 14.16: Creating an External Text File that Loads Variables from Another External Text File

In this exercise, you export the script segment that you developed in Exercise 14.15 and store it in an external text file.

1. Copy the contents of the script tab that you developed in the previous exercise.

2. Using a text editor of your choice, create a new text file and save it with the name `Load Expressions XX.txt` in the subfolder `\Scripts`.

3. Paste the copied script there and save the file.

4. Back in QlikView, comment out the copied script. Add a new `INCLUDE` statement that replaces the same script:

    `$(Include=..\scripts\load expressions XX.txt);`

This exercise completes our discussion of generating expression definitions as variables in the script. You learned two methods for doing this—one method involved creating the variables manually or automatically and externalizing segments of script in an external text file, and the other method involved exporting variable definitions into an external text file and loading the same definitions back into the script. Let's briefly compare and contrast the two methods.

While both methods involve external text files, several differences separate them. In the first case, the text file stores a script segment that needs to be included in the load script using the INCLUDE command. In the second case, the text file stores metadata and it's loaded into QlikView script as a data file, which gets processed in order to generate the variables described in the file.

Special characters such as single quotes, double quotes, and dollar signs are processed differently. With the first method, the single quotes need to be avoided by using string concatenation and the ASCII code CHR(39). With the second method, the special characters don't present any problems.

Pick your favorite method for your own applications. Our favorite is the second method, which involves exporting and loading the expression definitions.

A Few Words in Conclusion

This section concludes both our discussion of the Advanced Inventory Analysis and our description of QlikView features. Before we move on to describe Qlik Sense, we'd like to mention that we couldn't possibly include the full-fledged implementations of Sales Analysis, Profitability Analysis, and Inventory Analysis in the framework of a single book. We hope that our straw man models gave you a taste of these complex solutions and a direction that you can further develop in your real-life projects.

Similarly, we couldn't possibly cover all of the wonderful features available in QlikView with the same level of depth as we tried to achieve in our discussions. Some of the features that we opted to omit are less commonly used. Other features are covered so well in the Reference Guide that we didn't think we could add any extra value by including our own description in the book.

The following section contains a list of the most important features that were not described in this book.

Presentation Features Not Covered in the Book

Here are the most important features that were not described in this book, but you might want to investigate:

- **Radar Charts**—these sophisticated charts resembling spider webs are not common in our experience. Similarly to bar charts and line charts, radar charts visualize one or more expressions over a single dimension. They are fairly easy to configure.

- **Animations**—this feature looks very cool in a demo presentation, but perhaps isn't as helpful in practical analysis. **Animation** features are available from the **Dimensions** tab, next to the **Trellis** button, and the settings are somewhat similar to those of the **Trellis** chart.

- **Reports**—while Qlik is not in the business of competing with full-fledged report writers, a simple report writing utility is included with the tool. In a nutshell, this utility allows you to drag and drop QlikView objects onto an empty white page. Each report can contain multiple pages of two types—Single Paper Page and Multi Paper Page. A Single Paper Page can contain multiple graphs that fit together on a single piece of paper. Conversely, a Multi Paper Page can only contain a single object such as a straight table or a pivot table, which can possibly run through multiple pages. The Report Editor is quite basic, and getting things right can become quite frustrating. In our experience, many customers opt for affordable add-on solutions that are available from several Qlik Partners. One of the more popular solutions, NPrinting, was recently purchased by Qlik and now it's available as one of Qlik's products.

- **Bookmarks and the Bookmark Object**—bookmarks are extremely helpful and widely used by developers and users. They are extremely easy to pick up on your own, so please don't overlook this functionality. We tend to treat bookmarks mostly as an advanced user tool that helps users navigate their data effectively. We hear that many developers use bookmarks as an integral part of their solutions. We consider that to be unsafe, since users may accidentally delete or override the contents of an important bookmark, possibly breaking the initial logic that the developer had in mind.

For this reason, we don't cover bookmarks as part of the developers' curriculum.

- **Alerts**—QlikView allows the developer to send alert messages to users, based on certain conditions in the data. As cool as it sounds, we haven't seen too many production implementations of the alerts functionality.

- **Themes**—QlikView is shipped with a number of pre-defined themes that can be used for applying consistent design elements to your applications. In addition, developers can create their own themes when needed. As much as the idea is wonderful, our experience shows that most developers opt for creating a template for their documents and don't take the extra step of creating a theme. You can experiment with themes using the button **Theme Maker** in the **Layout** tab of any object **Properties** dialog.

Scripting Features Not Covered in the Book

We tried to cover most of the common scripting techniques in the book, and yet some of them remained outside of our scope.

- **Security**—this is perhaps the most important topic that we left out. Security is described wonderfully in the Reference Manual and in the online Help section. Feel free to explore and learn the basics of the Section Access there. In addition, security is closely related to Server and Publisher Management, which is a whole different area that requires a separate book of its own.

- **Incremental (Delta) Loads**—the techniques for implementing Incremental Loads using QVD files is described extremely well in the Reference Guide and in the Help section. The Help article "Using QVD Files for Incremental Load" describes the four typical scenarios for incremental loads, with detailed script examples for each of them. We couldn't describe this topic any better.

- **Hierarchy Load**—QlikView offers two special load prefixes called Hierarchy and HierarchyBelongsTo that allow building unbalanced hierarchies. This topic is quite complex and at the same time the requirement is not very common. If you find a need to load an unbalanced hierarchy with unknown number of nodes, please look up these keywords in the Reference Manual. In addition, this topic is covered in a number of blogs, beginning with the Qlik Design Blog by Henric Cronström (https://community.qlik.com/blogs/qlikviewdesignblog/2013/11/11/unbalanced-n-level-hierarchies).

- **Metadata Commands**—QlikView offers a set of commands for adding comments and tags as metadata attributes of fields and tables. This functionality is quite easy to pick up on your own.

- **Direct Discovery**—this is a whole new discipline that became available in QlikView since Version 11.2. Targeted at extremely large data sets, this technology allows developers to keep the bulk of the facts in a database and only retrieve aggregated totals when they are needed in a chart. These techniques are extremely advanced and perhaps deserve a separate book that will surely be written one day.

There are a few other commands that we haven't covered in the book; however, we believe that they carry only marginal importance to your education. For a full list of the script statements, visit the Help article called "Script Statements and Keywords."

Qlik Sense

15

Loading Data in Qlik Sense

In this chapter, you'll learn the basic steps for creating a new Qlik Sense app and techniques for loading data. By the end of the chapter, you will have loaded data into an app that we will expand on in Chapter 16. You won't learn anything new regarding data modeling or script functions, since Qlik Sense uses the same scripting engine as QlikView, and these topics were thoroughly covered in previous chapters. Instead, we'll describe the key concepts necessary to begin developing in Qlik Sense:

- The Hub
- Data connections
- Loading data
- Developer tools

Before we get started, it's helpful to remember that Qlik Sense is not the "new" version of QlikView—it's an entirely new product. You can think of QlikView and Qlik Sense as two different interfaces of the same analysis engine. Whereas QlikView offers an interface for skilled developers to deliver apps with well-thought-out design, Qlik Sense offers an interface for non-technical users to create self-service apps that are more ad hoc in nature.

Another important concept to remember is that Qlik Sense is available for two different environments, the single-user desktop as well as the global enterprise. As a desktop product, Qlik Sense provides self-serve visualizations and analysis for the single user. Qlik Sense is also available in a server-based environment, which adds security, governance, and deployment options for Qlik Sense applications.

For the purposes of this book, we'll focus on content creation using Qlik Sense Desktop.

Getting Oriented with Qlik Sense

If you're accustomed to consuming or developing QlikView apps, the Qlik Sense environment can take a bit of getting used to at first. With just a little guidance, we'll help you get oriented with the layout, and you'll soon be able to explore for yourself. You'll find that tasks that took 10 mouse clicks in QlikView may only require five (or fewer!) in Qlik Sense. As Qlik Sense was intended to be an intuitive, self-explanatory tool for non-technical users, its goal is to allow you to create beautiful and powerful data visualizations with very little effort.

Introducing the Desktop Hub

Before we begin loading data, let's get acquainted with the general workflow of using Qlik Sense. The *Desktop hub* is the centralized portal for all interactions with Qlik Sense Desktop. To open the Hub, simply run the Qlik Sense Desktop program from your application menu. By default, QlikSense.exe is installed in the following folder location:

%UserProfile%\AppData\Local\Programs\Qlik\Sense

Since Qlik Sense is inherently web-based, the **Desktop hub** is a web browser in a shell application. The full Qlik Sense product offers access to the Hub from any browser, while Qlik Sense Desktop requires that you use QlikSense.exe.

From the Hub, you'll create, manage, and use Qlik Sense apps. A QlikView developer can think of the Hub as a combination of the QlikView Access Point and the desktop client, all rolled into one. It might be hard to imagine, but all of your development work will happen through this portal.

Figure 15.1 shows the Hub with a few apps and identifies the key navigation features by number.

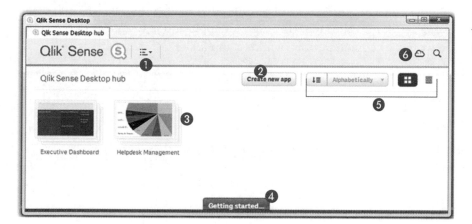

FIGURE 15.1:
The Qlik Sense Desktop hub

1. **Global menu**—always includes Help and About.

2. **Create new app**—click to create and name a new app.

3. **Application icons**—click on an app to view and use content, as well as to edit the visualizations and load scripts.

4. **Getting started**—link to a product support page containing tutorials and videos to help you get started (Internet access required).

5. **Organize apps**—change sort and view options for app icons.

6. **Qlik Cloud**—link to Qlik's Cloud platform. Create an account and access your Qlik Sense applications from anywhere. As of the writing of this book, you can also share with up to three other users for free.

When working with the Hub, you'll notice that the icons and menus automatically realign, change shape, or even disappear, depending on the size of the window. This auto-sizing, or *responsive* behavior, is a major design difference between Qlik Sense and QlikView.

 NOTE

Qlik Sense apps use QVF as the file extension (QlikView apps use QVW). In Qlik Sense Desktop, the default folder location for QVF files is `%UserProfile%\Documents\Qlik\Sense\Apps`. To change the location of the app folder, edit the `Settings.ini` file in the `%UserProfile%\Documents\Qlik\Sense` folder and add the `DocumentDirectory=<new path>` key.

To open and edit Qlik Sense files from other folders, simply drag and drop the QVF file into the Hub. However, for applications to appear in the Hub, they must be copied into the working app folder.

Exercise 15.1: Experiencing the Desktop Hub

1. Open Qlik Sense Desktop.
2. Explore the Hub using different window sizes. Note that some objects may disappear entirely if the window becomes too small.

Create a New App

Qlik Sense makes it easier than ever before to create applications for discovering and analyzing data. In this section, you will create a new app and use the new **Quick data load** wizard to load data from a flat file. Exercise 15.2 walks you through the steps of creating a new app.

Exercise 15.2: Creating a New App

1. Open the Qlik Sense Desktop.
2. From the Hub, click the Create new app button.
3. Enter **Sales Analysis** as the name for the new app and click Create.
4. Click Close to exit the wizard.

In the Hub, you should now see the icon for the new app **Sales Analysis**. Click on the icon to enter the **App overview**. For newly created apps, the main area of the **App overview** will show large shortcut icons for the **Quick data load** wizard and the **Data load editor**. Once data is loaded in the app, the main area is used to view and manage the GUI objects and bookmarks within the app. Figure 15.2 shows the **App overview** for the new **Sales Analysis** app.

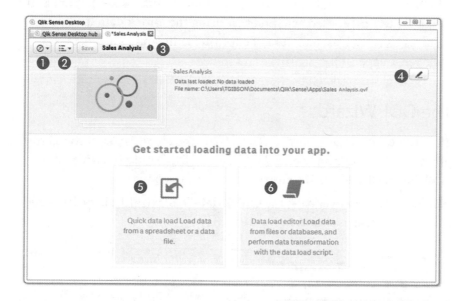

FIGURE 15.2:
App overview

The features identified by number in Figure 15.2 are described next.

Main Toolbar:

1. **Navigation menu**—links for the **App overview**, **Data load editor**, **Data model viewer**, and **Hub**.

2. **Global menu**—while in **App overview**, the **Global Menu** also includes the link to **Quick data load**, as well as to **Help** and **About**.

3. **Save**—this button may appear inactive if there are no changes to be saved.

4. **App info**—click to show/hide the app info panel.
   - **Edit info**—edit the app name or description, or add a thumbnail image.

Main Area:

5. **Quick data load wizard**—Click to launch the wizard.

6. **Data load editor**—Click to enter the **Data load editor**.

Using Quick Data Load

Qlik Sense makes loading data from a text file (or other flat file) simple and fast. Non-technical users will find that using the **Quick data load** option requires using the least amount of effort in loading or adding data to a Qlik Sense app.

The QDL Wizard

The **Quick data load** wizard, or *QDL*, leads you step-by-step through the process of loading data from a flat file. The QDL feature is currently only available in Qlik Sense Desktop (not the full version).

While in the **App overview**, the **Quick data load** wizard can be launched from two places, as shown in Figure 15.3.

FIGURE 15.3:

Quick data load

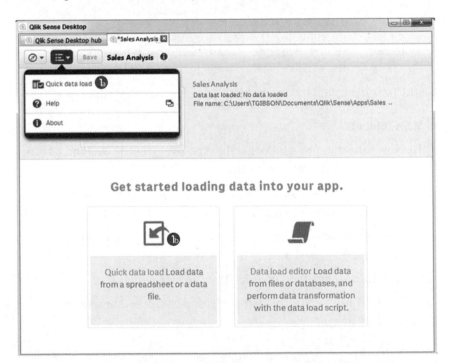

1a. From a link from the **Global menu**

1b. From the main area of **App overview** (if the app is empty)

Once launched, the **Quick data load** wizard requires just two more steps, displayed in Figure 15.4.

FIGURE 15.4:
Quick data load wizard

2. Select the flat file for import.

3. Map the columns and click **Load data**.

In Step 3, make sure that the column names are mapped correctly. Confirm that delimiter settings, header size, and other mapping options are correct. You can rename the columns simply by clicking in the orange header area and typing an alias.

Drag and Drop

The step of browsing for and selecting the file can be avoided altogether by just dragging and dropping a data file into the App overview, as shown in Figure 15.5.

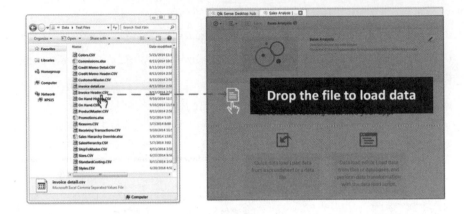

Exercise 15.3: Using Quick Data Load

1. From the Hub, click on the **Sales Analysis** app.

2. Open Windows Explorer.

3. Browse to the \Data\Text Files\ folder and drag the [invoice detail.csv] file onto the App overview screen.

4. Review the fields to be imported and click Load data.

5. You should see a popup that confirms the data was loaded successfully. Click Close to return to the App overview.

Now that the app has been loaded with data, the **App overview** page contains more options, as shown in Figure 15.6 and described in the following list.

Main Toolbar:

1. Navigation Menu—Options appear for **Data load editor, Data model viewer,** and **Open Hub.**

Main Area:

2. Category icons to show 🔲 Sheets, 🔖 Bookmarks, and 🖵 Stories in the main area.

3. Click this icon to edit an existing sheet.

4. Click these buttons to create new sheets.

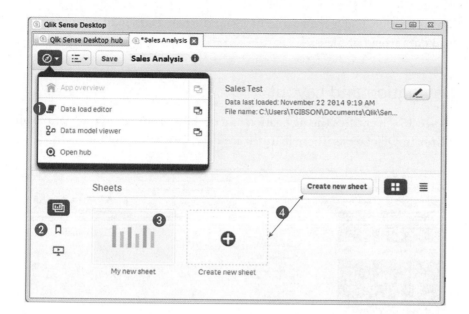

FIGURE 15.6:
App overview after
data load

Designed for a single-user environment, Qlik Sense Desktop does not
contain features related to security or publishing. As such, some menus
and options that appear in the Hub and App overview of the full-version
Qlik Sense are not visible in Qlik Sense Desktop.

Apps created with Qlik Sense Desktop can be exported and used by the full
version of Qlik Sense, where enterprise features are available. See the Qlik
Sense product page on Qlik.com for a full description of available features.

NOTE

Using the Data Load Editor

Similar to QlikView's script editor, the *Data load editor* is where you manage connections and the data load script. Along with the newly designed
interface, the advanced usability features simplify the effort of writing and
managing the script.

The script function library available in Qlik Sense is the same as that in
Qlik View (with a few additions related to geo-mapping and derived fields);
therefore, scripts written in QlikView can be run in Qlik Sense with only
minimal adjustment.

In this section, you learn how to navigate the new **Data load editor** and load data from flat files.

Navigation and Layout

Figure 15.7 identifies the navigation and usability features of the **Data load editor** in Qlik Sense. These features are described in the following list.

FIGURE 15.7:

Data load editor

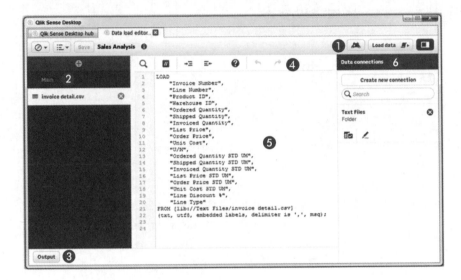

Main Toolbar:

1. **Debug, Load data**, and **Show/Hide Data connections**—these icons appear on the right side of the main toolbar.

Script Sections Panel:

2. **Add/Edit Sections**—organize your script by creating separate **Sections** (we used to call them **Tabs** in QlikView).

3. **Output**—button to show/hide the reload log window. This becomes part of the **Debug panel** when in debug mode.

Editor Toolbar:

4. Usability features:

🔍 Find/Replace.

▥ Comment/Uncomment selected text.

⁌≡ Indent/Outdent selected text.

❷ Help Mode—while in Help Mode, the keywords in the script display as hyperlinks. Click to open the relevant help page on `help.qlik.com`. The script cannot be edited in Help Mode.

↰ Undo/Redo.

Main Area:

5. Text editor—write and edit script code. Includes the **IntelliSense** (auto-complete) feature to assist with spelling of keywords.

Data Connections Panel:

6. Data connections—create and manage connection library.

Perhaps the biggest material difference between scripting in Qlik Sense and scripting in QlikView is the concept of the **data connection**. In the next section, we'll look at how to create and use **data connections** in Qlik Sense Desktop.

Introducing Data Connections

If you're familiar with the concept of creating ODBC database connections in MS Windows, you understand why it's convenient to configure a link to a source only once—and subsequently refer to it using a "nickname"—instead of configuring it over and over. This nickname, or **Data Source Name**, can be configured to allow other users or programs to use it as needed. Similarly, Qlik Sense provides centralized management of all types of data sources.

Using the **Data connections** panel of the **Data load editor**, developers can create and manage connections for folders, databases, web files, and custom connections. Figure 15.8 shows a **Data connections** panel containing connections to a database and two folders. Once these connections are created, the developer clicks the **Select data** icon to select columns from the source and insert them into the script.

FIGURE 15.8:
Data connections panel

In contrast to QlikView, managing data sources in Qlik Sense is much more transparent, simple, and secure. With the improved visibility offered by the **Data connections** panel, it's easy to see which data sources are being used by a particular application, without paging through each tab of a script. Also, when used in a Qlik Sense server environment, data connections can be secured, shared, and managed by administrators, thus ensuring that only users with authorization are allowed access to use the connection.

Custom Connectors

Connectors to other data sources can be acquired from Qlik (for salesforce, SAP, and others) or from third-party developers and data providers.

Let's take a look at the script created from the **Quick data load** wizard that we ran in Exercise 15.2. Figure 15.9 shows the **Data connections** panel on the right, and an example of how a data connection is used in the script. The numbered features in the figure are described in the following list.

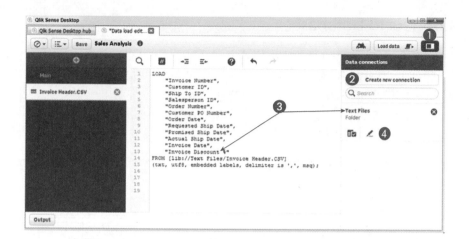

FIGURE 15.9:
Data load editor show-
ing the use of a data
connection

1. **Show/Hide** the **Data connections** panel.

2. **Create new connection**.

3. Notice the existing connection named **Text Files**. The **Quick data load** wizard created this automatically in Exercise 15.2. The FROM clause in the script shows the syntax of referencing a data connection.

4. Click the icon 🖥 to select data from the exiting connection and then click ✐ to edit the name or reconfigure the connection.

By default, Qlik Sense is configured to reload data using so-called "StandardMode," which requires the use of data connections within the script. This results in a bit of extra work if you're copying a script created in QlikView—the script must be edited to replace the standard folder paths with data connection library syntax. To enable Qlik Sense to reload scripts using standard paths (legacy mode), edit the %UserProfile%\ Documents\Qlik\Sense\Settings.ini file and set StandardMode=0.

However, if you plan to publish your app on the server version of Qlik Sense, you should instead change your data connections to use the Qlik Sense library, since legacy mode isn't fully supported in the full version.

Connect to Databases

For database sources, create ODBC- or OLEDB-based connections. If you're connecting to an enterprise database, make sure you have the proper permissions and the drivers before you start.

In Exercise 15.4, you'll create a connection to the Sales.mdb database from the chapter download materials.

Exercise 15.4: Creating a Database Connection

1. Open the Sales Analysis app in the Hub.

2. From the Navigation menu, open the Data load editor.

3. Create a new data connection for the **Sales.mdb** Access database.

   3.1. Click Create new connection.

   3.2. Select OLEDB.

   3.3. From the Select provider drop-down, select Microsoft Jet 4.0 OLE DB Provider (32-bit).

   3.4. Copy and paste the name of the .mdb file, with its full path, into the Data source input box.

4. Click Test Connection to verify.

5. Name the connection **Sales db** at the bottom, then click Save.

To browse the database and select data, click on the **Select data** icon on the connection link. Figure 15.10 shows the **Select data** dialog for the Sales.mdb database.

The newly styled layout of the **Select** dialog, along with the ability to immediately see a preview of the data, makes loading data even more intuitive and simple. For added efficiency, multiple tables can be selected in the left pane.

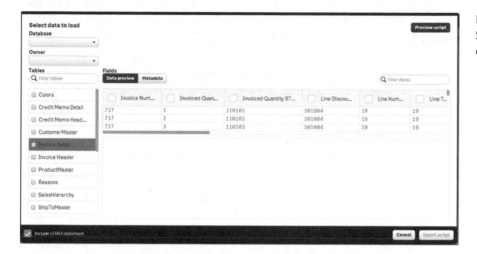

FIGURE 15.10:
Select data dialog for a
database connection

Connect to Folders

Folder connections allow for quick access to load flat files. Connectors are
available for the usual flat-file types, spreadsheets, as well as HTML, KML,
XML, QVD, and QVX files.

To manually load data from flat files, first create the data connection by
following these steps:

1. In the **Data load editor**, click **Create new connection** in
   the right pane.

2. Browse to the folder containing the files you want to load.

3. Give the connection a **Name** at the bottom and click **Save**.

The connection should now appear in the right pane. To open the data
files, click the **Select data** icon, shown in Figure 15.11.

FIGURE 15.11:
Select data from
connection

At the bottom of the **Select file** dialog, you can choose from a number of file types. Each has its own configuration properties. The connector for Excel files includes a helpful new feature: select from multiple sheets at once. In Figure 15.12, you'll see that the connector wizard gives you the option to check both the **Director** sheet and the **VP** sheet in the left pane. Selecting more than one sheet at a time will result in multiple LOAD statements when inserted into the script.

FIGURE 15.12:
Selecting data from
Excel files

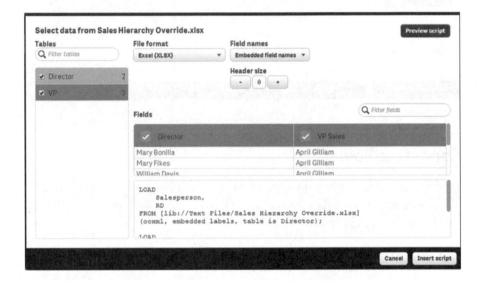

Let's create a data connection to the \Transformed QVDs\ folder that we'll use to load data for our Sales Analysis app.

Exercise 15.5: Creating a Connection to the QVD Folder

1. Open the **Sales Analysis** app from the **Hub**.

2. From the **Navigation** menu, open the **Data load editor**.

3. Create a new data connection to the QVD folder:

   3.1. Click **Create new connection**; select **Folder** from the list.

   3.2. Browse to the \Data\Transformed QVDs\ folder.

   3.3. Name the connection **Transformed QVDs** and click **Save**.

4. The connection should now appear in the **Data connections** panel.

Loading Data from QlikView into Qlik Sense

There are several options available when you need to use a data model that was originally created in QlikView:

- Use *Binary Load* to import the data model from a QVW file.
- Create the proper data connections, import the script from a QVW file, and then edit each LOAD statement to use the data connection syntax.
- Store the tables from the QlikView data model into QVD files and load them into Qlik Sense.

Binary Load

The *Binary* statement is a type of LOAD statement that uses a QVW file as its source. Upon reload, the QVW file is opened, and its entire data model is extracted and loaded into the RAM of the new app. This process is done *very* quickly, because the source file is already in the format that the Qlik data engine uses to arrange data in RAM.

Figure 15.13 shows an example of how to use the Binary data load.

FIGURE 15.13:
Binary load

Create a data connection to the folder that contains the QVW (or QVF) and then manually type the Binary statement (there currently is no wizard in Qlik Sense).

```
Binary [lib://path/filename]
```

The same rules apply to the `Binary` statement whether you're using Qlik Sense or QlikView: only one `Binary` statement is allowed in a script, and the statement must be on the first line of the first script tab.

After the data model is loaded into Qlik Sense, additional transformations can be made here.

Open a QlikView File in Qlik Sense

Qlik View files can be opened in Qlik Sense, but only the script is reusable. All graphic objects as well as layout variables are ignored and must be recreated using Qlik Sense objects. To reuse a QlikView script, follow these steps:

1. Copy the QVW file into the Qlik Sense apps folder.

2. From the Hub, open the QVW file.

3. In the **Data load editor**, create the required data connections.

4. Edit the script and replace the older connection strings or FROM clauses with the new data connection library paths.

5. Reload the data.

6. The QVW will be converted to a QVF file upon saving.

Drag and Drop a QlikView File into Qlik Sense

QlikView files that are not stored in the working Apps folder for Qlik Sense can be opened by dragging and dropping the file into the Hub (or any Qlik Sense page). The file opens with no GUI objects, but the script may be edited. Upon saving, the file extension is changed to QVF, and a backup copy of the QVW is stored in the original folder.

Loading Data for Sales Analysis

To prepare for the exercises in Chapter 16, the data model that was created in previous chapters must be recreated for Qlik Sense. In this section, you'll load data from QVD files stored from QlikView, and learn how the new derived fields in Qlik Sense can be used to create calendar attributes.

Loading QVD Files

In previous chapters, we stored tables from the Sales Analysis QlikView data model into QVD files. We'll use these files to recreate the data model in Qlik Sense. Exercise 15.6 walks you through the steps of using the **Data load editor** to load data from QVD files.

Exercise 15.6: Loading Data from Transformed QVD Files

1. Open the Sales Analysis app and then open the Data load editor window.

2. Delete any sections of the script that you created in earlier exercises.

3. Click to place your cursor on a blank line in the text editor.

4. Load data from the Transformed QVDs connection to recreate the data model.

    4.1. Click the Select data icon on the Transformed QVDs data connection.

    4.2. Select T_Customers.qvd and confirm that all columns are checked.

    4.3. Click Insert script and then place your cursor on a blank line beneath the inserted text.

    4.4. Repeat these steps for the following files:

    - T_Fact.qvd

    - T_MasterCalendar.qvd

    - T_Products.qvd

    - T_SalesHierarchy.qvd

    - T_ShipTo.qvd

    - T_Warehouses.qvd

5. In the LOAD statement created for the T_Products.qvd table, comment out the following fields: [# Unit Cost STD UM] and [# List Price].

6. From the main toolbar, click Save then click Load data.

7. As a best practice, explicitly name each table (Fact, Product, Customer, and so on).

Using Derived Fields

The data model of the Sales Analysis application contains a `Master Calendar` table, associated to the `Fact` table via the `Date` field. The `Date` field was originally created based on `[Invoice Date]`, so fields such as `Week`, `Year`, and `Month` are all attributes of `[Invoice Date]`. What if we need to report on the `Week`, `Year`, and `Month` of the `[Order Date]`? One of the traditional solutions would be to create another calendar table and then link it to the `Fact` table via another key field based on the `[Order Date]`. For users who do not have calendar tables available in their data warehouse, or who in general find the scripting to be a little daunting, Qlik Sense offers an alternative.

Introduced in Qlik Sense 1.1, *derived fields* provide a mechanism to calculate attributes associated to a particular "base" field, which can then be used as a dimension in the application. A common use for derived fields is to calculate the many calendar attributes related to a base date. Instead of being stored in a table in memory, fields like `Week`, `Month`, and `Quarter` can be calculated on the fly. Derived fields are defined in the script, but are calculated at runtime.

To create derived fields, define a calculation template using a `DECLARE FIELD DEFINITION` statement and invoke the calculation using the `DERIVE FIELDS` statement. In the sample code that follows, the field definition is given the name `Calendar`. Although the code looks similar to a table definition, it does not create a table in memory.

```
Calendar:
Declare Field Definition
    Parameters
        fiscal_start_month='7'
    Fields
        Month($1)                                    as
  MonthName,
        Year($1)                                     as Year,
        if(Month($1)<fiscal_start_month,
            Month($1)+fiscal_start_month-1,
                Month($1)-fiscal_start_month+1)      as
  FiscalPeriod;

Derive Fields from Fields "Order Date" Using Calendar;
```

There are two main sections in this DECLARE statement:

1. **Parameters (optional)**—here you can define local variables to be used within the template. In the example code, the parameter fiscal_start_month is set to 7, indicating that the fiscal year starts in July. Multiple parameters may be defined using a comma-separated list.

2. **Fields**—this section is where you define the fields to be derived. In this case, four fields are defined. Notice that the ($1) parameter is used as the operand for the functions. When executed, the DERIVE statement will pass a field name as an argument, and the template receives it as ($1).

The Qlik Sense Help pages provide a complete definition of the DECLARE syntax, including the following features:

■ Automatically tag derived fields in the field definition.

■ Create new field definitions by re-using existing ones using the DECLARE.. USING syntax.

After the template is defined, the DERIVE statement invokes these calculations by passing fields to the Calendar template, one by one. The resulting field names are in this form:

```
[source_field_name.definition_name.derived_field_name]
```

In the example code, only one field is passed. You could use the DERIVE statement to send multiple fields through to the field definition:

```
Derive Fields from Fields "Order Date", "Actual Ship Date" Using
    Calendar;
```

This would create four derived fields for each of the passed arguments:

```
[Order Date.Calendar.MonthName]
```

```
[Order Date.Calendar.Week]
```

```
[Order Date.Calendar.Year]
```

```
[Actual Ship Date.Calendar.FiscalPeriod]
```

```
[Actual Ship Date.Calendar.MonthName]

[Actual Ship Date.Calendar.Week]

[Actual Ship Date.Calendar.Year]

[Actual Ship Date.Calendar.FiscalPeriod]
```

As you can see, this is an efficient way to perform date functions on fields—you only have to type the function once. Similarly, you can define multiple field definitions (templates) with different functions, and a field can be passed to more than one.

Qlik Sense provides new system variables that allow you to fine-tune the behavior of certain date functions. Consult the Help pages for details on `BrokenWeeks`, `ReferenceDay`, and `FirstWeekDay`.

In Exercise 15.7 you will add derived fields based on `[Order Date]` to your application.

Exercise 15.7: Using Derived Fields, Create Additional Calendar Attributes Based on [Order Date]

1. Open the Sales Analysis app that you've been working on and open the Data load editor window.

2. Add another sheet: Click the + above the Main sheet in the left pane. Name the sheet **Field Definitions**.

3. Type or paste the following code.

```
Calendar:
Declare Field Definition
    Parameters
        fiscal_start_month='7'
    Fields
        Year($1)                                as "Year",
        Month($1)                               as "Month",
        Month($1)&'-'&Year($1)                  as "MonthYear",
        QuarterName($1)                         as "Quarter",
        'Q'&ceil(Month($1)/3)&'-'&Year($1)      as "QuarterYear",
        Week($1)                                as "Week",
        Week($1)&'-'&Year($1)                   as "WeekYear",
        if(Month($1)<year_start_month,
            Month($1)+year_start_month-1,
                  Month($1)-year_start_month+1) as "FiscalPeriod",
```

```
            if(Month($1)<year_start_month,
                Year($1)-1,
                        Year($1))                        as "FiscalYear";

    Derive Fields from Fields "Order Date" Using Calendar;
```

4. Click the Load data button.

In Chapter 16, you'll learn how to use these derived fields on the dashboard.

Using Developer Tools

In addition to basic script management, the Data load editor includes the following features:

- An enhanced **Data model viewer**
- A new **Debug panel**

Data Model Viewer

The **Data model viewer** is used to view the results of loading data into a Qlik Sense app. Tables are shown as vertical lists of fields, with linked fields identified by a key. While its purpose is the same (to graphically display the tables in memory), the **Data model viewer** in Qlik Sense allows the developer some significant usability improvements from the Table viewer in QlikView, including:

- New options to control the display of the tables on the screen
- New **Preview** panel allows viewing table metadata, data values, and adding fields as dimensions or measures

To open it, click the **Data model viewer** option from the **Navigation** menu.

Figure 15.14 displays the layout of the **Data model viewer** in Qlik Sense.

FIGURE 15.14:
The Data model viewer

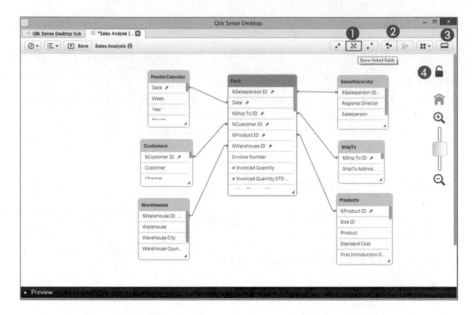

The main features of the **Data model viewer** are indicated by number in Figure 15.14.

Data Model Viewer Toolbar:

1. Table sizing options, which include [ ] fully collapsed, [×] show linked fields only, and [ ] show full table.

2. Show internal (RAM) or source tables.

3. Show/hide **Preview** panel.

Main Area:

4. Lock current view.

Notice in Figure 15.14, the tables are shown with the **Show linked fields** option selected. This option automatically resizes the tables in the display, to show only the key fields in each table. In Figure 15.15, the tables are shown with the **Expand all** option selected.

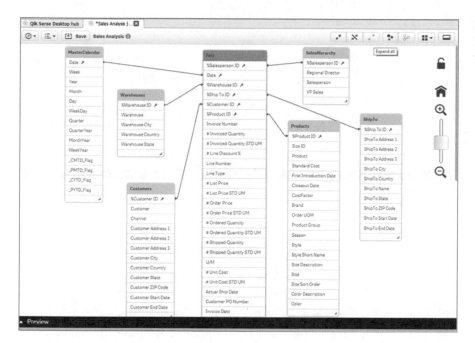

A touch-friendly zoom control appears on the right to allow quick resizing of the model. After rearranging or resizing the table display, make sure to click **Save** to retain the table layout.

Figure 15.16 shows the **Preview** panel with the Fact table selected. Metadata is displayed on the left, and the **Preview of data** appears on the right.

In Figure 15.17, the Brand field is selected from the Products table.

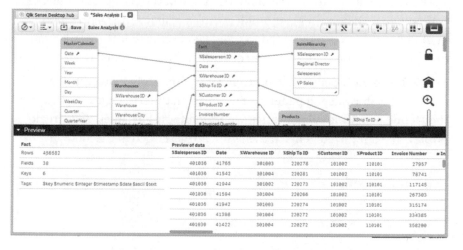

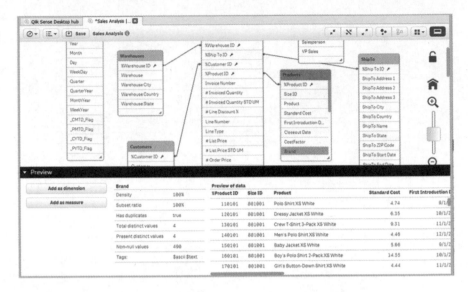

When a single field is selected in the data model, the **Preview** panel displays the field's metadata and offers options to **Add as dimension** or **Add as measure**. These options launch a simple dialog to add the field to the **Library of Master items** in the application. (You'll learn more about the **Library of Master items** in Chapter 16.)

Debug Panel

To help identify bugs or performance problems in the script, **Debug** mode allows the developer to step through each line of the script, examine the contents of variables, and load small samples of data. The **Debug panel** in Qlik Sense has been designed to offer easy access to features that you need, as well as the ability to hide the features that you don't need.

The **Debug panel** opens in the bottom pane of the **Data load editor** by clicking the **Show debug panel** icon in the main toolbar. Figure 15.18 shows the **Debug panel** with windows shown for **Output**, **Variables**, and **Breakpoints**. The numbered items in the figure are described in the following list.

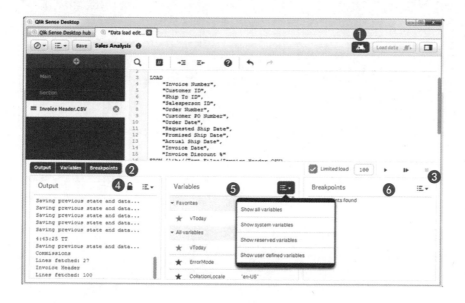

Main Toolbar:

1. Toggle button to show/hide the **Debug panel**.

Debug Panel:

2. Toggle buttons to show/hide windows within the **Debug panel**.

3. **Debug toolbar—Limited load** option, and **Run, Step, End here** buttons.

4. **Output window**—shows the progress of the script and any errors.

5. **Variables window**—the Variables menu controls which types are visible.

6. **Breakpoints window**—breakpoints are set by clicking on a line number in the text editor while in Debug mode.

Also notice in Figure 15.18 that the **Variable** window has an area to display **Favorites**. This is a handy way to quickly determine the status of certain important variables during debugging. To identify a variable as a **Favorite**, simply click the star next to the variable's name.

Up next in Chapter 16, you'll learn how to create visualizations in Qlik Sense using data from the Sales Analysis model created in this chapter.

16

Developing Visualizations in Qlik Sense

In this chapter, we will continue exploring Qlik Sense and describe the basics of developing applications in Qlik Sense. We will also demonstrate how to prepare a Qlik Sense self-service environment for users.

We will develop a Qlik Sense Sales Analysis app that is somewhat similar to the QlikView Sales Analysis Dashboard that we developed in Chapter 4. In the process, we will introduce the following concepts:

- Exploring the chart types available out-of-the-box in Qlik Sense
- Using and building the library of reusable objects
- Placing and resizing objects on a grid
- Navigating object properties

- Managing selections in Qlik Sense
- Creating and using stories (Storytelling)
- Developing geo-visualizations in Qlik Sense
- Integrating Qlik Sense apps

Exploring the Qlik Sense Visual Environment

Qlik Sense was developed as an intuitive self-explanatory tool for non-technical users, so not every step in the process may need to be described in a great detail. We encourage you to navigate the tool on your own and discover additional features when you perform our simple exercises.

NOTE In case you haven't built the dataset for your Qlik Sense app in Chapter 15, you can copy the 15.xx Sales Analysis.qvf file from the \Solutions Sense\ subfolder and store it as Sales Analysis.qvf in the standard folder that holds all Qlik Sense apps:

%userprofile%\Documents\Qlik\Sense\Apps

Once you do this, the app should become available in Qlik Sense Hub.

Navigation in Qlik Sense

Navigating the various screens and menus is perhaps one of the features that may take some getting used to, especially if you are accustomed to the traditional QlikView navigation.

In Chapter 15, we described the Hub and the first steps in navigating the Qlik Sense desktop environment. Here, we continue navigating Qlik Sense:

- When you open Qlik Sense Desktop, you arrive at the Hub, where you can open one of the existing applications or **Create a new app**.
- When you open an existing application, Qlik Sense opens the **App overview** in a separate tab. In the **App overview**, the following navigation options are available:
  - Edit the **Title** and the **Description** of the app.

- Open one of the existing sheets or **Create new sheet**.
- Review existing **Bookmarks**.
- Open or create a **Story**.

- When you open or create a sheet, Qlik Sense opens the **Analysis** view. Here, you can start analyzing the data in your application. From the **Analysis** view, the same navigation options are available with the **Navigation menu** and the **Global menu** toolbar buttons. You can drag and drop sheet icons to rearrange the sheets.

- In addition, you can switch between sheets or create a new sheet, using the toolbar buttons in the upper-right corner of the sheet.

- Next to it, you will find the **Edit** button, which allows you to enter the **Edit** mode. Note that unlike in QlikView, the **Analysis** mode and the **Edit** more are separate.

- Next to the **Edit** button, three buttons allow access to **Snapshots**, **Stories**, and **Bookmarks**. We will describe these features later in this chapter.

Without further delay, let's start developing our Sales Analysis dashboard in Qlik Sense. At this point, you should already have your Sales Analysis app, loaded with data, that you developed in Chapter 15. Or, you should have the same app copied from the \Solutions Sense\ subfolder into your Apps folder (see "Obtaining a Copy of the App" at the beginning of this chapter).

Exercise 16.1: Creating a New Sheet and Entering Edit Mode

1. From the Hub, open the Sales Analysis app and create a new sheet.
2. Name the new sheet **Sales Analysis**.
3. Click on the sheet icon to open it and click on the Edit button to enter the Edit mode.
4. Reach for the "Staples Easy button."

Building Simple Charts

If you follow our exercises, you should be looking at a picture that's similar to Figure 16.1.

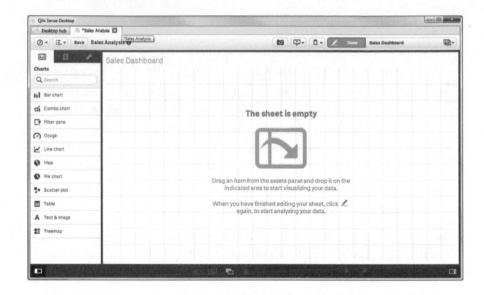

The main area of the sheet is defined by the fixed 24x12 grid. This is where all sheet objects reside. The grid offers an easy way of sizing the objects without counting pixels. On the left, the **Assets pane** offers a choice of 13 chart types that are currently available in Qlik Sense.

In order to add a new chart, we simply drag the corresponding icon onto the grid. Once we do, the frame of the new object snaps into the grid and Qlik Sense prompts us what to do next. Figure 16.2 shows the look of a bar chart right after it was dropped onto the grid.

This chapter was written based on the Version 1.1.0 of Qlik Sense, which was released in February 2015. Qlik plans to release a new version three times per year, so it is likely that a more current version has been released by the time the book reaches your hands. You may see more available objects and possibly more navigation features. The essence of the tool, however, should remain the same, so don't get confused if the pictures are slightly different.

In the middle, the two buttons suggest that we need to add a dimension and a measure. The label on top of the chart suggests that we should add a title by clicking on the text.

When we click on the **Add dimension** button, we get a list of all available fields, with a **Search** box that can be used to narrow down the list of fields (Figure 16.3, left). Typing a few first letters of the dimension narrows the list down to a few relevant fields. Selecting the field from the list completes the task of adding a dimension.

FIGURE 16.3:
Adding a dimension
and a measure

Similarly, when we click on the **Add measure** button, we get a list of fields (Figure 16.3, middle). Since our numeric fields are conveniently named with the hash sign (#) in front of the name, narrowing the list down is rather easy. After selecting a field, we are presented with the choice of the five most common aggregations—Sum, Count, Avg, Min, and Max (Figure 16.3, right).

After the dimension and measure are defined, Qlik Sense creates the first draft of the chart and opens its **Properties** in a separate panel on the right (Figure 16.4).

If you compare your first chart created in Qlik Sense with the first chart you created in QlikView, you will probably notice two major differences. First, the chart is much more beautiful (notice that the long labels are already angled and the amounts are already scaled without us doing anything for it). Secondly, when you navigate the **Properties** panel, you will discover that there are far fewer properties and settings. You may decide if the glass is half-full or half-empty. On one hand, you don't get full control over your chart's look and feel. On the other hand, you have fewer settings to worry about.

FIGURE 16.4:
First draft of a bar chart
with the Properties
panel

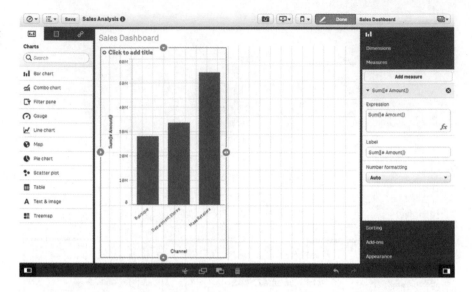

All **Properties** for a bar chart are presented in four tabs: **Data**, **Sorting**, **Add-ons** and **Appearance**.

- The **Data** tab contains the lists of dimensions and measures with very few related settings, such as labels and a number format.

- The **Sorting** tab defines the sort order for the chart.

- The **Add-ons** tab allows defining **Data handling options** and **Reference lines**.

- Under **Appearance**, there are five sub-tabs: **General**, **Presentation**, **Colors and legend**, **X-axis** and **Y-axis**.

The **Properties** panel conveniently opens on the **Data** ▶ **Measures** tab, probably because we should label our measure to make the chart more presentable.

We will let you explore the various chart settings on your own. Notice that you can add either another dimension or another measure using the **Add data** button (but not both, since you can't visualize both multiple dimensions and multiple expressions with a bar chart).

In the following exercise, you create two simple bar charts: Sales by Salesperson and Sales by Channel Year over Year.

Exercise 16.2: Developing Two Bar Charts

1. Create a **Bar chart**. Use `Salesperson` as a dimension. Use the usual formula of Sales `sum([# Amount])` as a measure.

2. Create a similar **Bar chart** with `Channel` as a dimension. Add `Year` as a second dimension. If necessary, clear the **Show null values** checkbox to avoid showing null values.

3. Add all necessary labels and titles.

4. Resize each chart to cover 11x6 cells of the grid (nearly a quarter of the sheet). Leave a two-cell-wide empty space along the left edge of the screen for later use.

Introducing the Library of Master Items

The process we just went through was quite easy, perhaps a bit easier than the same process in QlikView. However, it wasn't substantially different from the traditional QlikView process—we picked the chart type, selected a dimension from the list of fields, then entered a measure, and so on.

What makes Qlik Sense truly different is the **Library** of **Master items**. Let's examine the panel on the left side of the screen (see Figure 16.5). This panel is called the **Assets** panel while the app is in development (once the app is published, the **Assets** panel is replaced with a similar looking **Library** panel).

The **Assets** panel consists of three sections. So far, we used the first section (Figure 16.5, A) that contains the list of available chart types (the list is called **Charts** on the screen).

The second section contains the list of **Fields** (Figure 16.5, B). This list contains two sub-sections—**All fields** (C) and **Date & time fields** (D). Under **All fields**, you can access all available database fields in your application. The list can be trimmed down by selecting a single table or by searching for the field name in the **Search** box. The list of **Date & time fields** (new in Sense 1.1.0) contains the short list of the *derived fields* that we described in Chapter 15. As a reminder, derived fields are declared in the script in a special way. They are not stored in the dataset. Instead, they are calculated on the fly.

FIGURE 16.5:
The Assets panel

Admittedly, the title **Date & time fields** is a bit deceiving. Generally speaking, derived fields don't always have to be related to date and time. Conversely, calendar fields don't always have to be defined as derived fields. However we expect that future developments in the area of smart calendars will make derived fields a natural choice for all calendar features.

Both field lists offer similar functionality. Clicking on any of the fields allows three choices: **Create dimension**, **Create measure**, or **Add to visualization** (when no visualization is selected, this option is replaced with **Add to sheet**). The same three options are available upon right-click.

The topic of creating dimensions and measures brings us to the third section of the **Assets** panel (Figure 16.5, E). This section, with an icon that looks like a chain link, contains the list of **Master items**, divided into three tabs—**Dimensions**, **Measures**, and **Visualizations**. Here we can create and manage our reusable dimensions, measures, and visualizations as Master items. These Master items will be available to us and to our users as building blocks of the future discoveries.

Adding Dimensions and Measures to the Library of Master Items

Let's start exploring the **Master items** from the **Dimensions** section. While our list of available dimensions is empty, the only option is to **Create new**. Clicking on this button opens the **Create new dimensions** dialog (see Figure 16.6).

FIGURE 16.6:
The Create new dimensions dialog

Here we can create a new dimension in a variety of ways—as a single field, as a drill-down group, or as a calculated dimension. Each dimension is described with its definition and it can be given a **Name**, a **Description**, and a set of optional **Tags**.

For a drill-down group, the setting **Field** accepts multiple field entries. Overall, the process is very intuitive and self-explanatory.

The process of creating a new measure is very much similar, and we will let you explore it on your own.

The Benefit of Adding Tags

Adding tags may not be our first priority at the moment, but remember to use tags in your real-world applications. Tags are searchable in all Search boxes that are used across Qlik Sense to narrow down the list of fields, which is quite handy. In a large application with hundreds of fields, using tags can substantially improve your ability to keep things organized.

There are several other ways of creating new dimensions and measures. From the **Fields** tab of the **Assets** panel, right-click on the field and you will get a choice to **Create dimension** or **Create measure**. From the **Table Viewer**, select the desired field and open the **Preview** panel. Two buttons in the **Preview** panel allow you to add the field as a dimension or as a measure.

In the following exercise, we will create a few dimensions and measures as Master items.

Exercise 16.3: Creating Dimensions and Measures as Master Items

1. Create several dimensions for the most commonly used attribute fields, such as Channel, Customer, Salesperson, Brand, Style, Size, Color, Product, Year, and MonthYear. Experiment with the various ways of creating dimensions—from the list of Master items, from the list of Fields, and from the Table Viewer.

2. Create a drill-down group for a product hierarchy, using the fields Brand, Style, and Product.

3. Create a new measure with the usual Sales calculation: sum([# Amount]).

4. Create another measure for Gross Margin %:

   sum([# Margin Amount])/sum([# Amount])

Building Charts Using Dimensions and Measures from the Library

When dimensions and measures are defined in the library, the process of creating new charts becomes even easier. The existing dimensions and measures are listed before the list of all available fields, and they can be easily selected from the list. Alternatively, dimensions and measures can be dragged directly from the **Assets** panel and dropped onto any visualization on the sheet. For new visualizations, the dimension or measure is simply added to the chart. If other dimensions or measures already exist at this point, you will be given a choice of replacing the existing item or adding the new dimension or measure to the chart (only if the chart can support an additional dimension or measure).

Since the names are already defined for the Master items, there is hardly anything left to be configured for the new chart.

When dimensions and measures are added to a chart from the library of **Master items**, they appear differently in the chart properties. Instead of the usual **Definition** and **Label** settings, dimensions and measures simply show the link to the Master item, with the link icon next to the name. It is possible to unlink the item by clicking on the icon, when there is a need to alter the definition or the label for a particular visualization.

This section is embarrassingly short, but this is indeed how easy it is.

In the following exercise, you build a pie chart that shows Sales by Brand. You will configure the chart to be presented as a donut.

Exercise 16.4: Creating a Pie Chart Using Master Items

1. In the Edit mode, drag the icon of a Pie chart onto the grid.

2. Open the Master items list in the Assets panel. Open the Dimensions tab and drag the Brand dimension onto the new chart.

3. Open the Measures tab and drag the Sales measure onto the new chart.

4. Click in the title area of the chart and type **Sales by Brand**.

5. Admire the work of art that you've just created. As an optional improvement, open the Appearance ▶ Presentation tab in the Properties panel and switch the style of the chart from Pie to Donut.

6. Explore other settings that are available here. For example, you can switch the appearance of the values from Share to the actual Values.

Your pie chart should look similar to the chart in the upper-right corner in Figure 16.7. While we are at it, let's create a combo chart that shows Sales and Gross Margin % by Style. We will display Sales with bars and Gross Margin % as a **Line Marker**. If you remember, in QlikView we used bars, lines, and symbols. In Qlik Sense, the symbols are called **Markers**. Markers can be presented as **Circles**, **Squares**, **Diamonds**, **Triangles**, and **Lines**. The line marker, which is new in Qlik Sense, appears in the form of a short horizontal line plotted at the corresponding height (see the combo chart in Figure 16.7).

Exercise 16.5: Creating a Combo Chart Using Master Items

1. Drag the icon of the Combo chart onto the grid.

2. Drag the corresponding Master items from the Assets panel and drop them onto the new combo chart—Style as the dimension, Sales and Gross Margin % as the measures.

3. Locate the setting (under Measures) that allows changing the default Circle marker to a Line.

4. Locate the Number Formatting setting for the Gross Margin % measure and replace the Default format with the Number format that shows numbers as whole percentage points.

At this point, your Sales Analysis sheet should look similar to Figure 16.7.

You can click on the **Done** button in the toolbar on top to see the end result and to analyze your data. Click on the **Save** button to save the results of your work.

FIGURE 16.7:
The Sales Analysis sheet with four charts

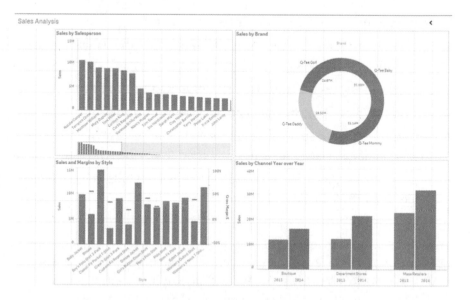

Adding Visualizations to the Library of Master Items

Once you create visualizations that can be useful in the future, you can add them to the library of Master items. Once again, we use dragging and dropping, only in the opposite direction this time. Dragging an object from the sheet and dropping it onto the **Assets** panel causes the object to be added to the list of **Master items**. These can be used later by other users.

Once an object is added to the library, it becomes linked to the Master item. It can't be edited unless it's unlinked from the Master item. Alternatively, Master items can be edited from the **Assets** panel. Clicking on a chart in the list of **Master items** opens a callout panel (Figure 16.8) with a small image of the chart and three icons that allow developers to **Delete**, **Edit**, or **Add to Sheet**.

FIGURE 16.8:
Working with visualizations as Master items

Exercise 16.6: Adding Visualizations to the Library of Master Items

1. Add all four charts to the list of Master items in the Assets panel.

2. Modify the pie chart as a Master item in such a way that it displays actual amounts instead of the relative share percentages (under Appearance ▶ Presentation).

Developing the Sales Analysis Dashboard in Qlik Sense

While Qlik Sense is primarily a self-service discovery tool, it can also be used for developing dashboards and professionally crafted analytical apps. In this section, we develop a Sales Dashboard that resembles the one that we developed in Chapter 4 using QlikView. In the process, we will introduce **Gauges**, **Text and Image Charts**, and **Tables** in Qlik Sense.

Creating Gauges

Gauges in Qlik Sense are largely similar to the gauges in QlikView, with a more modern look and more streamlined configuration process. We need to configure the following:

- If needed, create a new measure as a Master item.

- Create the gauge by dropping the **Gauge** icon onto the grid.
- Add the measure from the library of Master items.
- Format the number for the measure.
- In the **Appearance** tab, define the range of **Min** and **Max** values for the gauge.
- Define segments and limits (see Figure 16.9).
- Configure **Labels and title**—by default, both the value of the measure (the label) and its title are presented within the gauge. Depending on the available space, you may not want the title to be presented.

In the following exercise, you configure the same four gauges you created for the Sales Analysis dashboard in QlikView. This time, you will be using the library of **Master items** and will leverage the presentation capabilities of Qlik Sense.

FIGURE 16.9: Appearance settings for a gauge

Exercise 16.7: Developing Gauges for the Sales Dashboard

1. Create new sheet and name it **Sales Dashboard**. Enter the **Edit** mode.

2. Add the following four measures to the library of Master items:

NAME	DESCRIPTION
Sales YTD vs PYTD Change %	`(sum({<Year=, Month=, Quarter=, _CYTD_Flag={1}>}  [# Amount])/` `sum({<Year=, Month=, Quarter=, _PYTD_Flag={1}>}  [# Amount])) - 1`
Sales MTD vs Same Month Prior Year Change %	`(sum({<Year=, Month=, Quarter=, _CMTD_Flag={1}>}  [# Amount])/` `sum({<Year=, Month=, Quarter=, _PMTD_Flag={1}>}  [# Amount])) - 1`
Unit Sales YTD vs PYTD Change %	`sum({<Year=, Month=, Quarter=, _CYTD_Flag={1}>}  [# Invoiced Quantity])/` `sum({<Year=, Month=, Quarter=, _PYTD_Flag={1}>}  [# Invoiced Quantity])-1`

ASP YTD vs PYTD Change %	`((sum({<Year=, Month=, Quarter=, _CYTD_Flag={1}>}  [# Amount])/`
	`sum({<Year=, Month=, Quarter=, _CYTD_Flag={1}>}  [# Invoiced Quantity]))/`
	`(sum({<Year=, Month=, Quarter=, _PYTD_Flag={1}>}  [# Amount])/`
	`sum({<Year=, Month=, Quarter=, _PYTD_Flag={1}>}  [# Invoiced Quantity]))) - 1`

3. Create the four gauges by dropping the Gauge icons onto the grid. Drop the four new measures to the gauges accordingly.

4. In the Data ► Measures ► Number formatting section of the gauge's Properties, format the measures as a percentage with a single decimal digit.

5. In the Appearance tab:

   5.1. Under General, disable Show titles.

   5.2. Under Appearance ► Presentation, set Range limits to Min=-1, Max = 1.

   5.2. Enable Use segments and add two limits. Assign the first limit at -0.1 and the second limit at 0.1. Use Red, Yellow, and Green colors for the three segments. Define all colors as Gradient.

   5.3. Under General ► Measure axis ► Labels and title, select Labels only.

6. Size each of the four gauges to 3x2 grid sections.

Creating Text and Image Charts

The good old QlikView Text object got a major promotion in Qlik Sense. It is now called the **Text & image** chart, and for a good reason. This new type of chart can now combine text, measures, and images in a single object. Each segment of text can now be sized and formatted individually, while their composition and alignment can be managed as a whole.

For example, in our QlikView dashboards we had to create three individual objects if we wanted to have a black heading (font 20), then a blue measure (font 36), and then a gray text comparing This YTD to Prior YTD for the same measure (font 12). In Qlik Sense, all of it can be accomplished in a single **Text & image** chart (see Figure 16.10).

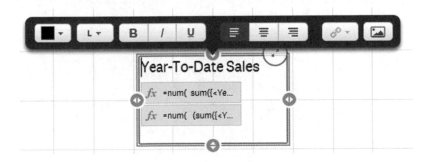

FIGURE 16.10:
Configuring the Text & Image chart

As soon as the **Text & Image** chart is activated, Qlik Sense opens an **Edit** panel, which offers several editing options for the new object. Each segment of text within the chart can be formatted as follows:

- Colored with one of the twelve standard colors.
- Assigned one of the five standard sizes—XS, S, M, L, or XL (as fashion specialists, we surely understand this terminology).
- Formatted as **Bold**, **Italicized**, or **Underlined**.
- Aligned to the **Left**, **Center**, or **Right**.
- Configured as a hyperlink.
- An image can be added from the **Edit** panel and aligned accordingly.

In addition to these options, measures can be added to the same object, in a variety of ways—dragged as a **Master item** from the library; dragged as a field from the list of **Assets** and added as a measure; or added using the **Add measure** button in the **Properties** panel. Once added, each measure can be formatted using the same formatting options listed previously.

Qlik Sense does not offer an object type that is similar to the QlikView Line/Arrow object. If there is a need to add any separating lines to a Qlik Sense Dashboard, they can be implemented with the **Text & image** chart that uses an image with the separating line as a background. This kind of an object needs to be at least one cell wide (or tall). Hopefully, the next versions of Qlik Sense offer a more elegant solution, like for example an ability to make some of the grid lines visible when needed.

In the following exercise, you develop the top part of the Sales Dashboard, as displayed in Figure 16.11. The calculations in this dashboard are identical to those that we used for the Sales Analysis dashboard in Chapter 4. Some of the actual formulas are described in detail in Chapter 4, in the section entitled "Building Dashboards." Others are quite easy to come up with, following a similar example.

FIGURE 16.11:
The top part of the Sales Dashboard

Exercise 16.8: Creating the Top Part of the Sales Dashboard

1. Create four Text & Image charts for the four main KPIs: YTD Sales, MTD Sales, Unit Sales (including change to prior YTD), and Average Selling Price.

2. Configure the size of the heading labels as L, the KPI numbers as XL, and the change to previous period as M.

3. Position each Text & image chart to the left of the corresponding gauge.

4. Configure another Text & image chart to communicate the Sales Drivers in the top-right corner.

5. Use two vertical dividers and one horizontal divider as separators between the groups of KPIs and between the top and the bottom portion of the sheet. Use the Background image, rather than adding an image to the object. Locate the rule and vertical rule images in the list of all available images.

Creating KPIs

Qlik Sense ver. 1.1.0, which was released in February 2015, introduced a "new kid on the block"—a KPI. You can think of it as a hybrid between a text chart, formatted in a particular way, and a textual form of a gauge.

A KPI (see Figure 16.12) shows a single measure, with an optional secondary measure that can be added as a reference. For example, when communicating Year-To-Date sales, you may want to add the prior Year-To-Date sales, or percent change versus prior Year-To-Date.

FIGURE 16.12:
A KPI

Year-To-Date Sales

69.18M 48.1% ▲
vs. Prior Year-To-Date

A KPI is a good example of reducing flexibility in exchange for ease of use. Generally speaking, the Text & image chart is more versatile and allows constraint-free composition of the different measures and labels within the object. On the other hand, a KPI is much easier to configure and it helps to ensure a greater consistency across multiple KPI objects. Here are some of the highlights:

- The composition of a KPI is fixed—the main measure is presented on the left in a larger font. Its label is always positioned above. It can be aligned to the left, right, or centered.

- The secondary measure is presented on the right, in a smaller font, and its label is always below the measure itself.

- Unless you decide to unlink the measures from their Master items, the names of the measures have to be spelled exactly the same as the desired labels. For example, the secondary measure in Figure 16.12 has to be called "vs. Prior Year-To-Date." We found it a bit quirky; however, the ability to unlink the measure and to customize the label to the needs of the particular KPI is a reasonable compromise.

- Numbers can be formatted using the standard formatting choices—no need to tinker with the num() function anymore. Notably, the automated number formatting, especially when applied to amounts and quantities, can now scale the number presentation automatically and show the numbers in thousands or millions when appropriate. This feature is extremely handy for high-level dashboards.

- Measures can be equipped with **Conditional colors**, defined with sectors and limits, just like the gauge limits (see Figure 16.13). In addition to colors, each segment can be associated with a *glyph* (a fancy name for a simple icon) that can serve as a graphical sign of increase, decrease, good or bad news, or a warning.

FIGURE 16.13:
The conditional color settings for a KPI

An additional nice touch is hiding under the section **General ▶ Presentation**. The **Link to sheet** checkbox allows specifying another sheet from the same app that should be open when the user clicks on the KPI object.

Bottom line—the ease of use of the new KPI object is certainly going to make it popular among Sense developers and will surely shape up the way we communicate KPIs on the Sense dashboards.

Exercise 16.9: Replacing Text & Image Charts with KPI Objects

Replace all or some of the four Text & image charts that we used for communicating our KPIs in the dashboard with the KPI objects. Use Conditional colors and Limits to color the secondary measures (% change). Compare the look and feel of the two object types, along with the ease of use.

Creating Tables

Tables in Qlik Sense are very similar to QlikView straight table charts. Similarly to other charts, you can create tables by dragging and dropping the icon onto the grid, and then dragging and dropping dimensions and measures onto the table. Tables offer very little configuration options. For the most part, Qlik Sense is supposed to make it "genius and gorgeous" out of the box.

The **Properties** of the table include three main groups—**Columns, Sorting,** and **Appearance. Columns** include **Dimensions** and **Measures**.

A dimension is defined by its **Field** and **Label**. In addition, we can apply a **Limitation** to limit the dimensional values to a fixed number of **Top/Bottom** values, or to certain thresholds (a simplified implementation of QlikView dimension limits).

A measure is defined by its **Expression** and **Label**. The values can be formatted using the standard **Number formatting** options. In addition, the optional **Background color expression** and **Text color expression** formats can be defined to color-code the results based on performance conditions. We noted a nice touch here—when the calculated background color is dark, Sense automatically changes the default text color from black to white.

In the following exercise, you complete the bottom part of the dashboard as displayed in Figure 16.14. In our effort to match the look and feel of the Sales Dashboard that we developed earlier in QlikView, you will add the table and two bar charts that communicate Mix by Channel and by Brand.

Exercise 16.10: Creating a Table and Two Bar Charts

1. Create the **Top 10 Customers** table as presented in Figure 16.14.

   1.1. Use Customer as a dimension. Limit the chart to the top 10 values.

   1.2. Add the following measures—YTD Sales, Prior YTD Sales, YTD vs. PYTD Change %, Gross Margin %, and Number of Stores. Use the same expressions as we used for our QlikView Sales Dashboard.

2. Create two similar Bar charts that communicate Mix by Channel and by Brand.

   2.1. Use Channel and Brand as the dimensions, respectively.

   2.2. Create two measures in each chart—Current YTD Mix and Prior YTD Mix (use the same expressions as we used for the QlikView Dashboard).

   3.2. Format the charts as Grouped, Horizontal.

Examine the responsive behavior of the table when the screen size gets smaller. When the table can't be wide enough to display all columns, it automatically adds the **Column picker**—a vertical bar on the right side, with the three dots signifying that there is more to see. Clicking on the bar opens the list of all available columns. The columns that fit into the table are displayed above the line, and the hidden columns are displayed below the line. Users can rearrange the columns in such a way that the most important columns can be displayed in the available space. Ultimately, users can maximize the table to see maximum available information, utilizing the full size of the screen.

A Few Words About Responsive Behavior

One of the most notable visual improvements in Qlik Sense is its responsive layout. The tool will always show all or most of the sheet objects, and it will adapt itself to different resolutions and screen sizes. You can experience the responsive behavior when you resize the Sense window, making it smaller than your full screen. You will notice that some of the elements, such as legends and labels, may disappear when available space gets too tight. Some charts may automatically turn on scrollbars as needed. When the screen becomes very small (about the size of a smartphone screen), Sense presents all sheet objects one at a time, allowing the user to scroll down in order to see more.

With this in mind, it's important to avoid adding too many elements and settings so that the user doesn't lose the overview in the responsive logic. For example, the divider lines that we added to our dashboard may look nice on the computer screen, but they might unnecessarily clutter smaller mobile screens.

Similarly, keeping most presentation settings at their default values (such as Auto) can help you preserve the default responsive behavior of the charts.

Building More Advanced Analytics in Qlik Sense

In this section, we add **Scatter plots**, **Treemap** charts, and **Pivot tables** to our Qlik Sense app.

Creating Scatter Plots

The **Scatter plot** in Qlik Sense is quite similar to its QlikView predecessor, with a simplified configuration process. The chart is defined by a single dimension and a set of two or three measures. The first two measures are used as X and Y coordinates for the symbols. The optional third measure can be added to determine the size of each symbol.

The properties of the **Scatter plot** include three major tabs—**Data**, **Add-ons**, and **Appearance**.

The **Data** tab consists of dimensions and measures and is no different from any other charts. The **Add-ons** section allows you to configure X-axis and Y-axis reference lines. These lines are similar to QlikView **Reference Lines**, only they appear to be much smarter—the numbers and the texts are formatted automatically and they manage to avoid overlapping quite nicely.

The **Appearance** tab opens five sections (see Figure 16.15).

- Under the **General** section (A), we can enable and enter the **Title**, the **Subtitle**, and the **Footnote**.

- The **Presentation** section (B) provides access to **Navigation, Bubble Size, Labels,** and **Grid Line Spacing**.

- Under **Colors and Legend** (C), the configuration of colors is available. There are three color choices—**Single Color, By Dimension**, or **By Expression**. With **Single Color**, all bubbles will be plotted with the same color. Coloring **By Dimension** means that the chart will be painted like a rainbow. That may be festive, but not too informative. The last choice offers the ability to calculate the color based on certain conditions, and that can be quite useful.

- The two **Axis** sections (D and E) offer similar properties related to the chart axes—**Labels and Title, Position, Scale,** and **Range**. All of these properties have their default settings, and you may never need to configure them explicitly, unless you need to be very particular about the appearance of your chart.

FIGURE 16.15:
The Appearance properties of a scatter chart

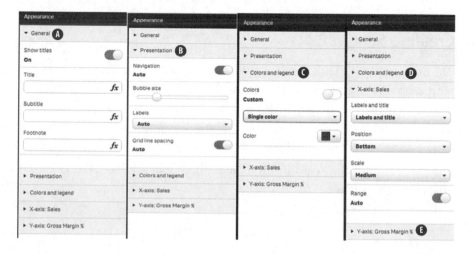

Very few settings, indeed! If it was simple enough to create powerful scatter charts in QlikView, the process in Qlik Sense looks like a child's play! In the following exercise, you develop a scatter plot of Products based on their Sales and Margins. You will add "low" and "high" reference lines for both Sales and Margins (use Figure 16.16 as a visual guide).

Exercise 16.11: Creating a Scatter Plot

1. Create a new sheet and name it **Sales and Margins**.

2. If necessary, add two new measures to the library of Master items:

   YTD Sales:

   ```
   sum({<Year=, Month=, Quarter=, _CYTD_Flag={1}>}  [# Amount])
   ```

   YTD Gross Margin %:

   ```
   sum({<Year=, Month=, Quarter=, _CYTD_Flag={1}>}  [# Margin Amount])/
   sum({<Year=, Month=, Quarter=, _CYTD_Flag={1}>}  [# Amount])
   ```

3. Create a new Scatter plot.

4. Using the library of Master items, add Product as a dimension. Add the two newly created measures.

5. Format the number for YTD Gross Margin % as a percentage.

6. Under Add-ons, add four reference lines using hard-coded values, as presented in Figure 16.16.

7. In the Appearance ▶ General sub-section, enter the Title.

8. In the Presentation sub-section, allow Navigation.

9. In the X-axis subsection, set Range = Custom, select Min = **0**. This is to prevent the X-axis from extending into the negative territory (even if some smaller customers should have negative sales).

Your finished **Scatter plot** should look similar to Figure 16.16.

We encourage you to spend some time and navigate the data in the scatter plot. You can zoom in and out using a pinching gesture (if you have a touch screen) or by rolling the mouse wheel up and down. You can move the picture left, right, up, and down by dragging it using the mouse. Press the little **Home** button in the upper-right corner of the chart to get back to the initial view. Also, explore the process of making selections in the **Scatter plot**—by dragging the mouse along the X-axis, or the Y-axis, or both; or by switching to the **Lasso** mode and enclosing a cluster of dots to select the corresponding values.

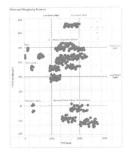

FIGURE 16.16:
The scatter plot

Creating Treemaps

Treemap is the new and improved name for the good ol' block chart that we've known from QlikView. The **Treemap** looks very similar and it fulfills the same need—visualizing a distribution of a whole among its parts by using nested rectangles.

The possible number of dimensions was increased from 3 to 15. However, it may be hard to visualize a hierarchy that's more than 2-3 levels deep.

Just like all other charts in Qlik Sense, the **Treemap** can be configured with very few basic settings. Two groups of properties describe the **Treemap**—**Data** and **Appearance**. The **Data** tab includes dimensions and measures and is no different from other charts. Under **Appearance**, three subsections are available—**General**, **Presentation**, and **Colors** (see Figure 16.17). The settings include **Titles**, **Headers and Labels**, and the **Colors**.

In the following exercise, you will create a **Treemap** of YTD Sales by Brand and Style. As an optional addition, you can also color the elements of the chart based on the Gross Profit Margin % (use Figure 16.16 as a visual guide).

Your chart should look similar to Figure 16.18.

FIGURE 16.17:
The Treemap properties

Exercise 16.12: Creating a Treemap

1. Drag the Treemap icon from the Assets panel and drop it onto the grid.

2. Drag Brand and Style from the list of Master items and drop them onto the chart as dimensions.

3. Drag the YTD Sales measure from the list of Master items and drop it on the chart as a measure.

4. Click on the chart title and type **Sales by Brand and Style**.

5. Under General ▶ Presentation, enable Show Values.

Extra Credit

Configure the Colors based on the YTD Gross Margin %. If you do this, add a Footnote describing the colors and the thresholds.

Creating Pivot Tables

The pivot table is another recent addition in Qlik Sense ver. 1.1.0. It allows you to present a table with one or more dimensions and one or more measures that can be rearranged in a variety of ways, including "pivoting" (moving some of the dimensions from rows into columns).

It may sound at first that the pivot table in Qlik Sense is no more than the new implementation of the good ol' pivot table that we know from QlikView. However, if you look closer, you will see that this is not your grandfather's pivot table (see Figure 16.19).

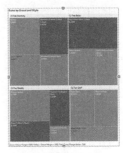

FIGURE 16.18:
The Treemap

FIGURE 16.19:
The pivot table

YTD Sales by Brand and Channel

Brand	Channel Measures					
	Boutique		Department Stores		Mass Retailers	
	YTD Sales	Change vs Prior YTD	YTD Sales	Change vs Prior YTD	YTD Sales	Change vs Prior YTD
Totals	**$16,160,335**	**36.6%**	**$21,361,355**	**75.2%**	**$31,660,061**	**39.5%**
Q-Tee Baby	$3,951,251	4.8%	$5,903,956	51.2%	$7,962,314	15.6%
Q-Tee Daddy	$3,904,698	37.1%	$5,113,427	60.7%	$7,736,392	48.0%
Q-Tee Golf	$3,244,534	19.2%	$3,912,077	58.7%	$6,145,374	17.8%
Q-Tee Mommy	$5,059,852	183.5%	$6,431,895	156.0%	$9,815,981	183.2%

For starters, the process of pivoting has become much easier and more intuitive. Dimension labels appear as buttons that are easy to grab and move around. When more than one measure exists, a similar button with the label **Measures** appears in the chart. Both dimensions and measures can be rearranged in any possible way, vertically or horizontally.

The best part is—the default placement of dimensions and measures in rows and columns can now be defined explicitly in the **Pivot table** properties. This has been a dream of many QlikView developers for many years.

Let's explore the properties of the **Pivot table** (see Figure 16.20). All the properties are presented in three major tabs—**Data, Sorting,** and **Appearance**.

The **Data** tab (Figure 16.20, A), which typically lists dimensions and measures, is divided here into **Rows** (B) and **Columns** (G). Dimensions specified in the **Rows** section will appear in the chart vertically (the dimension values are listed in rows) and the dimensions specified in the **Columns** sections will appear in the chart horizontally (the dimension values are listed in columns).

The properties related to each dimension include:

- The definition of a dimension—either a link to a **Master item** (C) or the **Field** and **Label** settings.

- The checkbox that allows you to **Show null values** or hide them (D).

- The **Limitation** settings (E)—that's right, the dimension limits that weren't available for Pivot tables in QlikView are now available here!

- The switch that allows to **Show totals** (F).

In the **Measures** section (I), one or more measures can be configured with the following properties:

- The definition of a measure—either a link to a **Master item** (J), or the **Definition** and **Label** settings.

- **Number formatting** options (K).

- **Background** and **text color expressions** (L).

When multiple measures exist, the label **Measures** (H), which represents all the measures as a group, appears among **Rows** or **Columns**. Similar to dimensions, measures can be pivoted; however, all measures have to move as a group.

In the **Sorting** tab (M), each one of the dimensions can be sorted using **Auto** (N) or **Custom** (O) sorting options. **Custom** sorting options include **Sort by expression**, **Sort numerically**, and **Sort alphabetically**. The sorting order can be **Ascending** or **Descending**.

The **Appearance** tab is relatively slim. The **General** section (Q) allows configuring titles and subtitles. The **Presentation** section (R) offers two options—**Fully expanded** and **Indent Rows**.

As you can see, pivot tables can be simple! We are sure that the better pivoting capabilities and the ability to set dimension limits creates a lot of excitement among QlikView developers who explore the new features of Qlik Sense.

In the following exercise, you will create the pivot table displayed in Figure 16.19. It communicates YTD Sales and the Change to Prior YTD by Brand and Channel.

Exercise 16.13: Creating a Pivot Table

1. Create a new sheet and name it **Reports**.
2. Create a new Pivot table by dragging the icon to the grid.
3. Add two dimensions, Brand and Channel, from the library of Master items.
4. Add two measures, YTD Sales and Sales YTD vs PYTD Change %, from the library of Master items. Format the numbers appropriately.
5. In the pivot table properties, arrange the dimensions and the measures into Rows and Columns. Experiment with the different combinations of rows and columns and examine the look and feel of the pivot table.
6. Enable Show Totals for one or both dimensions and examine the result. Notice that the totals appear in bold font when the Presentation option Indent Rows is cleared.
7. Save your work.

Extra Credit

Create additional pivot tables of your choice. For example, display sales and/or margins by Style, Color, and Size.

Selections in Qlik Sense

Without a doubt, selections are the heart of any Qlik application. The user's ability to make selections in the data and to see the associated results instantly is what made Qlik products so popular. Qlik Sense takes the business of making and managing selections to the new level. In this section, we explore various features and objects that can help Sense users to make, view, and manage selections.

Keep in mind that selections can be made and managed in the **Analysis** mode only. Since we are spending most of our exercise time in the **Edit** mode, you may need to press the **Done** button in order to switch between the two modes.

Making Selections in Charts

The process of making selections in charts is more intuitive and intelligent in Qlik Sense. You can make selections by dragging the mouse over the values along the axes (X-axis or Y-axis), or by lassoing the visual symbols on the chart. Once the selection is identified, it remains tentative until it's either **Confirmed** or **Rejected** (see Figure 16.21).

FIGURE 16.21:
Making selections
in charts

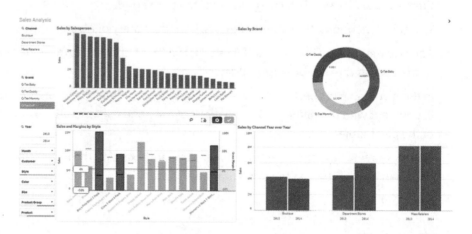

Examine the selection made in Figure 16.21. Our task was to find the three least profitable styles and to analyze their sales and margins. In order to do so, we made a selection in the **Sales and Margins by Style** chart, by dragging the mouse from the bottom of the Margin % axis (the right Y-axis in this chart) up, until we saw three styles being selected. Notice that the chart displays all the alternative values in a lighter color, which allows us to see the impact of our selection in the context of all other values. At the same time, all other charts recalculate their totals and show the associated data only.

At this point, we can still edit our selection—we can add or remove selected items or clear the selection. Once the selection is confirmed by pressing the green **Confirm selection** button, the chart is reduced to showing only selected values.

Feel free to make selections in the charts that you have developed, and explore all the features of the new selection process.

Working with Current Selections

Qlik Sense adopted many features that were recommended in QlikView as best practices and turned them into permanent features of the tool. For example, we always recommended that developers include the Current Selections box in every QlikView application, but the specific implementation was up to each developer. In Sense, the Current Selections box is called the **Selections bar** and it appears as a dark-gray ribbon above the charts (see Figure 16.22).

FIGURE 16.22:
Working with current selections

Each field that has a current selection appears on the **Selections bar** automatically as a little label. It provides the name of the field and some basic information about the selected values. From here, the selection can be easily cleared by using the little "X" icon on the right. Clicking on the label itself opens a drop-down box with the list of all field values (see Figure 16.23). From here, you can modify the list of selected values. Users can also **Search** for values, **Lock** and **Unlock** the selection, or use the **Selections menu**, which offers a list of less common options, such as selecting **Possible** and **Alternative** values. Feel free to explore the **Selections menu** on your own.

FIGURE 16.23:
Modifying a selection

The current selection labels are equipped with tiny narrow bars at the bottom. These bars are color-coded to show the relative share of the field values that were selected (green) or excluded (dark gray). You may also notice that some of the bars are colored in light gray. These are **Alternative** values, a state that you can enable also in QlikView. In Qlik Sense, this display mode is on by default. These values could have been **Possible** if not for the current selection in the same field (see more about selection states later in this section).

Three icons are permanently placed in the left corner of the **Selections bar**. They allow to navigate **Back** and **Forward** in the selections stack and to **Clear all selections**.

The Search and Selections Tools

On the right side of the **Selections bar**, there are two permanent buttons that implement two other features that used to be best practices in QlikView—the **Search tool** and the **Selections tool**.

The **Search tool** in Qlik Sense is an upgraded version of the QlikView **Search Object** (see Figure 16.24).

FIGURE 16.24:
The Search tool

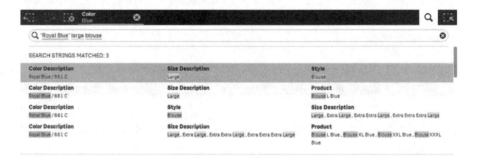

Just to remind you, the QlikView **Search Object** allows users to search across multiple fields, but in the end, the actual selection has to be made in a single field. The **Search tool** in Sense allows searching *and selecting* in multiple fields, while offering suggestions of all possible combinations. In our example, we searched for three strings—**"Royal Blue"**, **large**, and **blouse**. In response, the **Search tool** suggests a number of combinations with all three strings matched. Additional matches of two strings or a single string can be viewed by scrolling down the list. When the user clicks on the highlighted line, the combination of fields listed in that line gets selected.

The **Selections tool** implements another QlikView good practice of adding a separate sheet (or sometimes a hide-away panel) that is fully devoted to making selections. In this separate sheet, QlikView developers place list boxes and multi boxes for all the fields that could not fit in dashboards and analysis sheets. In Qlik Sense, this functionality is available out of the box, implemented within the **Selections tool** (see Figure 16.25).

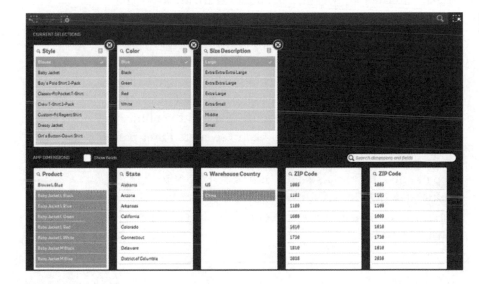

FIGURE 16.25:
The Selections tool

In the **Selections tool**, all **App Dimensions** are listed in the bottom part of the sheet, while the **Current Selections** are listed on top. When needed, all fields in the app can be displayed using the **Show fields** checkbox. When the number of dimensions or fields is large, users can narrow the list down by using the **Search Dimensions and Fields** box. Current selections can be modified or cleared, and new selections can be made with this extremely easy-to-use tool.

You can close the **Selections tool** and return to the previous sheet by clicking on the icon in the upper-right corner.

Introducing the Filter Pane

You must be wondering what happened to the good ol' QlikView list box? In Qlik Sense, both the list box and the multi box are implemented in a new control called the **Filter pane**.

The **Filter pane** can accept one or more fields to be displayed and available for selections. When multiple fields are selected and the screen space permits, the last field in the list is fully expanded. The rest of the fields appear as labels, and the list of values becomes available after the user clicks on the label.

With this behavior in mind, we recommend you create a separate **Filter pane** for a single field when there is a need to present an expanded list of values. When it's enough to just display the label, multiple fields can be combined in a single **Filter pane**. For example, Figure 16.26 shows three **Filter panes**—Channel and Brand are defined in separate **Filter panes**, while the rest of the filters share one common **Filter pane**.

Keep in mind that the actual presentation of the objects may be altered by the responsive design. On smaller screens, even a single-field **Filter pane** may get reduced to a label, subject to available space.

FIGURE 16.26:
Three Filter panes

Exercise 16.14: Creating Filter Panes

1. Open the Sales and Margins sheet. Resize the existing charts to free up a two-cell wide area along the left edge of the sheet.

2. Drag and drop the Filter pane icon onto the empty area of the grid. Drag the Channel field onto the Filter pane.

3. Resize the Filter pane to be three cells tall.

4. Repeat the same steps to create the second Filter pane for the Brand field.

5. Add the third Filter pane with the following dimensions: Year, Month, Customer, Style, Color, Size, Product Group, and Product.

6. Click on the Done button on top of the sheet and practice making selections in the new Filter panes.

7. Repeat the same on the Sales Analysis sheet.

The complete sheet should look similar to Figure 16.27.

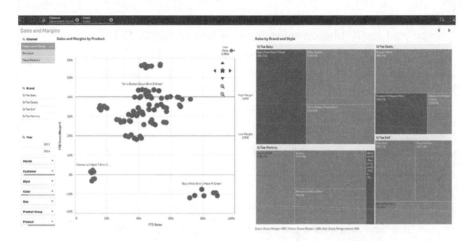

FIGURE 16.27:
Qlik Sense sheet with filters and selections

Storytelling

Storytelling is a way to put our visualizations in context by adding annotations, special highlights, and symbols to communicate the hidden stories that the data is telling us.

In Qlik Sense, *Stories* contain *Slides* that can be either static or dynamic. Static slides are built using *Snapshots*, and the data in these slides will never change. Dynamic slides are built by adding full sheets to the story, along with the necessary comments and insights. These slides can be interactive—users can make selections and have full interactive experience. The data in dynamic slides gets modified with each data reload.

Taking Snapshots

Before we can create our first story, we need to take a few snapshots. The **Take snapshots** toolbar icon (see Figure 16.28, A) opens a special snapshot-taking mode, in which all sheet objects are enclosed in orange frames (B).

FIGURE 16.28:
Taking snapshots

Clicking within an object results in creating a snapshot of the object. After that, a new **Snapshot** icon appears in the upper-right corner of the object (C), along with the number of existing snapshots for the object. Clicking on this icon opens the ability to edit the list of existing snapshots and to delete old snapshots that are not needed anymore.

In order to exit the snapshot-taking mode, click again on the **Snapshot** icon in the toolbar (A).

Now we are ready to create our first story.

Exercise 16.15: Taking Snapshots

1. Open the Sales Dashboard sheet and take snapshots of the YTD Sales, Unit Sales, and Average Sales Price KPIs and the corresponding gauges, along with the two bar charts called Mix by Channel and Mix by Brand.

2. Navigate to the Sales and Margins sheet.

3. Using the scatter plot, make a selection of all products with low margins.

4. Take a snapshot of the treemap Sales by Brand and Style and of the Sales and Margins by Product scatter plot.

Creating Stories

The **Stories** toolbar button (Figure 16.29, A) is located next to the **Snapshots** button. It opens the **Stories** dialog, which offers a list of the existing stories and the ability to create a new story (B). A new story is created with the default **Title**, which can be replaced with the title of your choice.

The thumbnail icon on the left (C) allows you to assign a custom image as the story thumbnail.

Once you are done editing the **Title** and the **Description**, click anywhere on the screen. The new story is added to the list of stories as a new icon. Clicking on the story icon allows you to enter the **Storytelling view** and begin the creative process.

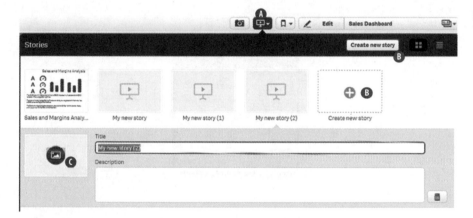

FIGURE 16.29:
The Stories dialog

The **Storytelling view** (Figure 16.30) allows you to create and edit the slides of the story.

The sidebar on the left contains the list of all existing slides. The toolbar on the right offers access to **Snapshots**, **Texts**, **Shapes**, **Highlights**, and **Images**. All these visual elements can be added to the slide by dragging and dropping.

New slides can be created using the **Add Slide** button (Figure 16.31) at the bottom of the left sidebar.

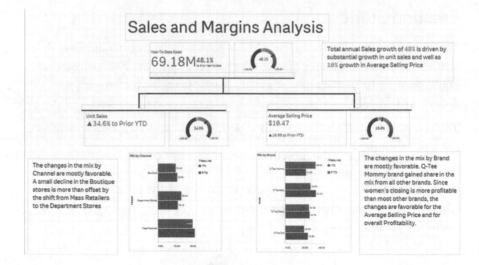

Three types of slides are available:

- A **Blank** slide is a new empty slide that can contain the five types of static elements described previously.

- A **Sheet** slide includes an image of an existing sheet. In this case, the sheet will be used dynamically. It allows users to interact with the data from within the story presentation. It's important to keep in mind that the content on these sheets gets refreshed with each data reload.

- A **Sheet left-aligned** slide is similar to a **Sheet** slide, but it allows for an empty space on the right, where additional annotations and images can be added to complete the message in the story.

Using the **Storytelling** view is extremely intuitive, and we will let you explore all the little elements on your own.

Exercise 16.16: Creating a Story

1. Create a new **Story** and name it **Sales and Margins Analysis**.

2. In the first **Slide**, explain the drivers that impacted the YTD Sales growth. The growth is driven by the volume growth and the growth in Average Sales Price. Explain the impact of the changes in Brand Mix and Channel Mix.

3. Add a new **Blank** slide and describe the impact of the low margin products on profitability. Make a suggestion for an improvement (Discontinue some of the products? Raise the price?) Use your imagination to come up with a creative solution.

4. Add a new **Sheet** slide to allow users to interact with the Sales Analysis sheet.

Using Story Playback

Once the story is created, it can be played with the green **Play the story** button in the upper-left corner of the **Storytelling** view. Slides can be navigated by swiping to the left and to the right (a gesture that we're used to, thanks to tablets and smartphones). From the first glance, you may get the impression that Qlik Sense Storytelling is no more than an embedded PowerPoint feature. In reality, that's far from true.

The beauty of Storytelling is in its close ties with the original app. During playback, users can right-click on any chart in the story and choose **Go to source** in the original app. This functionality is even available for static snapshots. When the user selects the **Go to source** option, Sense opens the appropriate sheet with all the selections made at the time the snapshot was taken.

Picture yourself making a presentation at the executive meeting and conveying your findings using the Qlik Sense story. At any point in time, you may be asked a clarifying question that may require digging deeper into the data. Being able to quickly access the source makes your presentation more dynamic, and your story appears more trustworthy.

Once you are done interacting with the original app, you can get back to the story by pressing the **Storytelling** button on the toolbar. This time, you will be taken back to *the same slide in the story where you left it off*. This is pretty cool, huh?

Similar interaction is available from the dynamic slides that contain full sheets. You can navigate the data and make selections in the story, then choose **Go to source**, continue navigating the data in the app, and get back to the story to pick up your presentation where you left it off.

This section completes our discussion of storytelling. In the next section, we will describe how to build geo-visualizations in Qlik Sense.

Geo-Mapping in Qlik Sense

Geo-visualizations are widely used in analytics, specifically where there is a known or an expected spatial relation between geographic locations and measure outcomes. In simple English, a well-crafted geo-visualization might help us to find out that certain colors are more popular in the Midwest, and other colors are more popular in the South, which will in turn impact the placement of our products in different regions.

In this section, we demonstrate the basics of creating geo-visualizations in Qlik Sense. You will learn the following concepts:

- Understanding how geographical objects are defined in the data.
- Loading geographical objects, such as *area* and *point*, into Qlik Sense dataset.
- Building **Map** charts using *area* and *point* dimensions.

Loading Geography Data

Before you can build your first map, you need to add descriptions of the geographic objects to your data. In this section, we describe the methods in Qlik Sense for defining geographical objects, and the scripting techniques that we can use to load geographic data into Qlik Sense. Don't worry if you are not a hard-core developer—these concepts are very simple and don't require any deep knowledge of scripting. Tag along, and you will be rewarded with the ability to create beautiful maps in your Qlik Sense applications.

How Geography Is Defined in the Data

Different geographies can be represented by *points, polygons, multi-polygons* and other objects. The most complete and detailed definition of the encoding format is called *GeoJSON*, and it can be found at `www.geojson.org`.

We will describe these concepts in a much more simplified way, so you have an overall understanding of the data that we will be using for geo-mapping.

A point is the most basic geographical object. It is defined by its geographic coordinates—*latitude* and *longitude*. Using the GeoJSON format, a point is defined like this:

```
[lat, long]
```

A polygon is defined as a collection of points that together define its outline. The notion for multiple points is the following:

```
[Point1, Point2, Point3]
```

or, in the fully expanded form,

```
[[lat1, long1], [lat2, long2], [lat3, long3]]
```

When multiple polygons are needed to describe a certain geographical object, they are enclosed in another comma-delimited list within square brackets:

```
[Polygon1, Polygon2, etc.]
```

In Qlik Sense, the multitude of different geographic objects is simplified and reduced to two main objects—*point* and *area*. An area can be represented by a polygon or by any combination of polygons.

In order to be used in geo-visualizations, points and areas need to be loaded into the dataset and associated with the data fields that are related to geography, such as states, ZIP codes, and so on.

Once the data is properly loaded, points can be used to create a bubble chart that can be presented on top of a map, and areas can be used to create an area chart (sometimes called the *Heatmap*), where corresponding geographic areas (countries, states, and so on) can be colored based on certain measures.

Loading Area Definitions from KML Files

The most commonly used format for geographic data is .KML (KML stands for Keyhole Markup Language). KML is an XML-based file format used for displaying geographical objects on a map. A variety of commercial and free sources of KML files exist that describe common geographies such as countries, states, counties, ZIP codes, and more. In the United States, several detailed KML files can be found on the official US Census website.

A typical KML file contains the commonly used codes describing the geography (country, for instance) and a definition of a point or an area (or both) associated with the geography. It's common to use points for placing markers on the map, while areas are used to define boundaries for the geographies. For this reason, point information is usually empty in the KML files that describe geographic areas, and we typically exclude it from the load.

Loading a KML file is no different from loading any other text file. You add a new **Data Connection** in the **Data Load Editor** and load the data from there, or simply drag and drop the file onto your Qlik Sense app.

The best part about loading area information is that the rest happens auto-magically (in the Qlik environment, this is an accepted technical term). Qlik Sense auto-magically classifies the area data based on the content. From this point on, any dimensions associated with the area can be plotted on an area map.

The only changes that we recommend to make here are purely cosmetic:

- When point information is empty, comment-out the point field.
- Rename the table and the area field to make the names more user-friendly.

Sometimes, there is a need to load additional cross-reference data in order to create the association between the existing fields in your dataset and the geographic codes supplied in the KML files. For example, countries and states may need to be translated from their fully spelled out names to the abbreviated codes that are commonly used in data systems (California vs. CA). ZIP codes may have to be consistently truncated to the first five digits, and so on.

In the following example, we are loading a KML file with U.S. state information. Then, we load a conversion table to translate state names to their two-letter abbreviations and associate states with larger regions.

Exercise 16.17: Loading a KML File

1. Open the Data load editor and create a new section called **Mapping** at the end of your load script.

2. Create a new Data connection to the folder \Data\Mapping. Name the new connection **Mapping Data**.

3. Load the KML file cb_2013_us_state_5m.kml, using the new data connection.

4. Rename the field cb_2013_us_state_5m.Name to State. Similarly, rename the cb_2013_us_state_5m.Area field to be simply called Area. Your complete LOAD statement should look like this:

```
States:
LOAD
    cb_2013_us_state_5m.Name as State,
    cb_2013_us_state_5m.Area as Area
FROM 'lib://Mapping Data/cb_2013_us_state_5m.kml'
(kml, Table is [cb_2013_us_state_5m/cb_2013_us_state_5m]);
```

5. Next, you need to translate the fully spelled out state names to their two-letter abbreviations. For that matter, you will use a spreadsheet that contains both the state names and the state IDs, along with the regions that different states belong to.

   5.1. Load the US Regions State Boundaries.csv spreadsheet using the same data connection.

   5.2. In the wizard, Sense doesn't always recognize the field names in the first row. Select Embedded field names instead of No field names, and watch the labels snap into their places as field names.

   5.3. Rename the field ID to [ShipTo State], in order to associate the geographical information with the ShipTo locations.

   5.4. This information can be joined into the previously loaded table of states, in order to avoid an unnecessary link in the data model:

   ```
   left join (States)
   LOAD
       Region,
       State,
       ID as [ShipTo State]
   FROM [lib://Mapping Data/US Regions State Boundaries.csv]
   (txt, codepage is 1252, embedded labels, delimiter is ',', msq);
   ```

6. Save the script and click on the Load data button. Examine the results in the Data model viewer.

Loading Point Definitions from Text Files

Sometimes you may have geographical coordinates stored separately as latitude and longitude, either in a database table or in a text file. These definitions can be used for geo-mapping as well, after a small transformation.

The table with lat-long information is loaded as usual. In order to convert a pair of coordinates into a proper *point* object, we use the following function:

```
GeoMakePoint(latitude, longitude)
```

This function creates a proper GeoJSON definition of the point, and it lets Qlik Sense know that point maps should now be enabled in the app.

Similarly, the key field that identifies the geography and the corresponding key field in your existing data model need to be conformed to a consistent coding standard. In our example, we are loading point definitions for the U.S. ZIP codes that will be linked to the ZIP codes from our ShipTo locations. In order to facilitate the link, we need to create a separate field ZIP5 that contains the first five digits of the [ShipTo ZIP Code].

Exercise 16.18: Loading Point Definitions from a Text File

1. Open the **Data Load Editor** at the end of the **Mapping** section.

2. Load the `zip_codes_states.csv` text file, using the same **Mapping Data** connection.

3. Rename the `zip_code` field to ZIP5.

4. Add the `GeoMakePoint()` function in order to generate the point field. Your complete script should look like this:

```
ZIP:
LOAD
    zip_code as ZIP5,
    latitude,
    longitude,
    GeoMakePoint(latitude, longitude) as ZIP_Point
FROM 'lib://Mapping Data/zip_codes_states.csv'
(txt, codepage is 1252, embedded labels, delimiter is ',', msq);
```

5. Locate the `LOAD` statement for the `ShipTo` information earlier in the script, and add an extra line to generate the field `ZIP5`:

```
...
    "ShipTo ZIP Code",
    left("ShipTo ZIP Code", 5) as ZIP5,
...
```

6. Save your script and choose Load data. Examine the results in the Data model viewer.

Creating Maps

Once geographical data is loaded into a Qlik Sense app, mapping becomes possible. In this section, we explore the techniques that can be used for building *area maps* and *point maps* in Qlik Sense.

Creating Area Maps

Like with any other Sense charts, creating a map begins with dragging the **Map** icon onto an empty area of the grid.

The new object frame is created, and Sense suggests adding a title and dimension (see Figure 16.32).

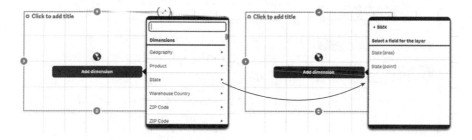

FIGURE 16.32:
Creating a map, step 1

After you click the **Add Dimension** button and select a dimension from the list, Sense offers a choice of plotting the selected dimension as an **area** or as a **point**. This choice is available because we loaded both the area and the point data into our dataset. Since ver. 1.1.0, it's possible to load multiple sets of area and point definitions, and the different available options are suggested in this window.

Technically, any dimension or field can be used as a map dimension, but not every dimension can be a good logical choice. For an area map that presents states, for example, it would not be logical to use anything less than a state as a dimension. Therefore, we will select the field that represents the same geography that was loaded from the KML file. In our example, this is the new State field that is linked to the original [ShipTo State].

Once the dimension is selected, it's being added as a **Layer** to the map. The **Layer** can now be equipped with an expression (see Figure 16.33). For an area map (also called the *Heatmap*), the expression can be used to determine the area color.

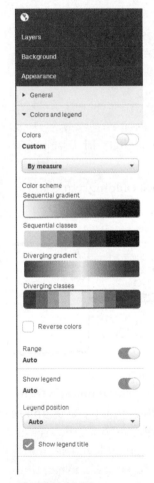

After entering the expression, we need to configure the **Colors** options under the **Appearance** tab. The default **Auto** color scheme is **Single Color**, which is rarely the desired option (Figure 16.34). Other options include **By Dimension** and **By Measure** (in this case the expression is treated as the measure).

Since painting the map **By dimension** creates a meaningless rainbow-colored chart, the most useful option is to paint it **By measure**. Four main color schemes are available here— **Sequential gradient**, **Sequential classes**, **Diverging gradient**, or **Diverging classes**. No promises, but we were told that more color options are on the way in future releases.

In addition, we can choose to **Show legend**, which can be used to communicate the meaning of different colors in numbers.

In the following exercise, you create an area map that communicates the Number of Stores per State. This may not be the most brilliant example of visualizing spatial relationships; however, it is simple enough to practice the technique of Qlik Sense mapping for the first time.

FIGURE 16.33:
Configuring an area layer

FIGURE 16.34:
Defining map colors

Exercise 16.19: Creating an Area Map

1. Add a new Sheet and name it **Mapping**.

2. Create a new Map by dragging the icon to the sheet. Type **Number of Stores per State** in the Title.

3. Create a new dimension in the library, using the field State. Use State(area) as the dimension for the Map.

4. Enter the following expression for the distinct number of stores:

   count(distinct [ShipTo Name])

5. Under Appearance, use the Custom color, By measure, Sequential gradient. Enable Show legend and keep the rest of the settings as the defaults.

6. Click on the Done button in the main toolbar to switch from the Edit mode to the Analyze mode.

7. Don't worry if your map looks too small. It happened because some of the small islands that belong to Alaska cross over to the Eastern hemisphere, causing the map to cover the whole world, instead of being focused on North America. You can zoom in and move the center of the map as needed in order to focus the map on the continental United States. A permanent solution to this problem involves excluding some of the geographic locations from the data load. Figure 16.35 shows the initial look of the map on the left and the same map after zooming in, on the right.

FIGURE 16.35:
The area map, before and after zooming in

Area maps offer another nice capability—you can aggregate geographic areas to bigger regions, and the map will be colored based on the aggregated results. For example, state information can be aggregated up to the region level, and the area map will show the aggregated data by region. More than that, we can create a drill-down dimension with regions and states and create a geographical drill-down map that can start at the level of regions and drill down to the state level.

Our data is already prepared for such a map. All we need to do at this point is create a drill-down dimension in the library.

In the following exercise, you create a drill-down map that displays average sales per store and allows drilling down from the region level to the state level. Analyzing sales per store, as opposed to total sales, helps to overcome the size differences between different states.

Exercise 16.20: Creating a Drill-Down Area Map

1. Create a new Drill-Down dimension in the library, using the Region and State fields. Name the dimension Region/State.

2. Create a new map by dragging the Map icon onto the grid. Type **Average Sales per Store** in the Title.

3. Use Region/State(area) as the dimension for the map.

4. Enter the following expression for the average Sales per Store:

   `sum([# Amount]) / count(distinct [ShipTo Name])`

5. Under Appearance, use the Custom color, By measure, Sequential gradient. Enable Show legend and keep the rest of the settings as default.

6. Click on the Done button in the main toolbar to switch from the Edit mode to the Analyze mode. Zoom in and move the map as needed.

Figure 16.36 shows the resulting map. On the left, you can see that even though the states are plotted separately, they are colored according to the aggregated results by region. The central region is displayed with the darkest color, which means that it is the best in sales per store. If we click on the central region and **Confirm** the selection, the chart becomes colored at the state level, with the central region being selected (Figure 16.36, right).

FIGURE 16.36:
The drill-down map, before and after selecting a region

Now, we have a choice of three different geo-visualizations based on this area map:

- Using `Region` as the dimension, we can get an aggregated chart by region.
- Using `State` as the dimension, we allow comparison between all states.
- Using the drill-down dimension, we get the drill-down chart, but the state comparison is limited to a single region.

Creating Point Maps

Creating a point map is quite similar to creating an area map. It begins with dragging the **Map** icon onto the empty area on the grid. Next, we select the dimension for the point map. This time, we select the (**point**) version of the desired dimension.

Once the dimension is selected, the draft of the map is created and the **Point layer** is being added to the map (see Figure 16.37).

The next step is to add an expression. We can use the regular `Sales` expression to determine the size and the color of the bubbles:

```
sum([# Amount])
```

The next setting is **Use size**. It defines whether the expression should be used to size the bubbles. When it's enabled, we get to choose the approximate range of the bubble sizes. Narrowing the range down helps prevent very large bubbles that can clutter the map and distort the view.

The next settings tab, **Background**, is optional for area maps, but is very important for the point map—this is, in fact, what makes it a map. This setting determines what kind of a map should be used as a background behind the bubbles.

As of version 1.1.0, a default map, provided by Mapbox, can be used with Qlik Sense charts.

Alternatively, a custom **Slippy map (XYZ)** can be used if necessary. We simply need to point Qlik Sense at the URL of our choice and provide the attribution (since these services are free, their providers would like to be recognized at least by mentioning them properly and pointing at their website).

FIGURE 16.37:
Configuring the point map

Since most of us don't know the URLs and the attribution strings for the publicly available tile servers, the link **URLs and attributions** is conveniently provided here, and it takes us to the section in the online help that lists several available options. All we need to do is copy and paste the two strings into the corresponding settings.

The rest of the settings in the **Appearance** tab are exactly the same. If your visual message is mostly conveyed by the bubble size, you may opt for a single color. Otherwise, the same four color schemes are available here (see Figure 16.34).

In the following exercise, we create two point maps that show Sales and Profit Margins by ZIP code.

Exercise 16.21: Creating Point Maps

1. Resize the two maps that you developed earlier, to make room for two more maps.

2. Create a new **Map** and type **Sales by ZIP Code** as a title.

3. Use ZIP5 (point) as a dimension.

4. Type the following expression for Sales:

   sum([# Amount])

5. Limit the Bubble size to approximately 50% of the maximum.

6. In the Background tab of the Settings, use the default map (Auto).

7. Color the map By measure, using Sequential gradient, with the Legend. Position the legend on the right.

8. Resize the new map to a quarter of the screen size (12x6 grid cells).

9. Copy the newly created Map object (right-click and select Copy) and paste it in the remaining empty quarter of the screen (right-click and Paste).

10. Change to title to read **Profit Margins by ZIP Code**.

11. In the Layers tab, replace the expression with the following:

    num(
            sum([# Margin Amount]) /
            sum([# Amount])
    , '#,##0%')

12. Click Done to switch from the Edit mode to the Analyze mode. Examine the results.

The bottom half of your sheet should look similar to Figure 16.38.

Note that you can make selections in the map itself and also in the legend. Click on top of the range and drag your mouse down to select ZIP codes with top sales. Accept your selections. Now both maps show sales and profit margins for the top sales ZIP codes.

Obviously, we wouldn't suggest creating four maps side by side in your real-life applications. Use maps in combination with other visualizations, and only when you have a good reason to use geographical maps as opposed to bar charts or scatter plots. The map examples in this chapter were used solely for the purpose of learning the technique.

Integrating Qlik Sense Apps

Perhaps the most significant advantage of Qlik Sense is its extensibility. In this section, we introduce the basics of Qlik Sense extensions and mashups and demonstrate a simple example of using an extension in your Qlik Sense App.

Defining Qlik Sense Integration Terminology

Since the term *integrating* may mean many different things to different people, we'd like to clarify our terminology. For the purpose of this discussion, we describe two main forms of Qlik Sense integration:

- Using external objects in Qlik Sense apps (in Qlik terminology, we call them *Extensions*).

- Using Qlik Sense objects on a web page or embedded in another web application (we call this scenario a *Mashup*).

Extensions and mashups have both been available in QlikView for years; however the process of building and using these features is relatively difficult and usually requires more technical skills than most QlikView developers can demonstrate. For this reason, we couldn't even dream of including this sort of a discussion in our description of QlikView.

In Qlik Sense, these two types of integration become extremely easy and seamless. You still need to know JavaScript and CSS in order to develop a new extension. However, if you obtained an existing extension that does what you need, it is extremely easy to include it in your Qlik Sense environment.

In Qlik Sense, all "standard" sheet objects are implemented as extensions, using the same protocol and the same set of APIs. This allows for a seamless integration of new sheet objects, brought into Qlik Sense as extensions. As you will see shortly, the main properties and the behavior of Extension objects are exactly the same as those of the standard Qlik Sense objects.

Integrating Extensions in Qlik Sense

Extensions are developed using JavaScript and CSS (Cascading Style Sheets). If you are a hard-core Web developer, you probably know exactly what we mean by that. For the rest of us, it's enough to know that each extension is stored in a folder that contains a few text files with file extensions such as .js, .css, .qext, and .wbl, along with some other resources such as images, and so on (see Figure 16.39).

FIGURE 16.39:
An example of an Extension folder

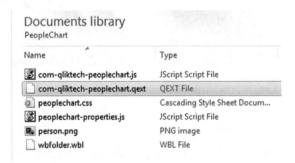

All extension subfolders are stored in the Extensions folder:

```
%userprofile%\Documents\Qlik\Sense\Extensions
```

To help us get started with extensions, Qlik Sense is shipped with a number of examples. These are stored in the `Examples\Extensions` subfolder:

`%userprofile%\Documents\Qlik\Examples\Extensions`

In the version 1.1.0 that we currently use, the examples include seven extensions that are stored in the following folders: `AngularChart`, `HelloWorld`, `helpdesk`, `HorizList`, `PeopleChart`, `SimpleTable`, and `ToolBar`. For the purpose of our discussion we will use the `People Chart` extension.

In order to be used in Qlik Sense, the examples need to be copied from the *Extensions Examples* folder to the *Extensions* folder. This is about as technical as it gets—we need to copy a subfolder from one location into another.

After copying the extensions and restarting Qlik Sense, we can see that the new extension(s) appear in the **Assets** pane on the left, next to the standard Qlik Sense charts (see Figure 16.40).

Note that **People Chart** appears in the list of default **Charts** as equal among equals. Now it can be dropped onto the grid in the same way as any other charts. And, just like any other charts, it will suggest to add a dimension and a measure. The extension behaves exactly the same way as the standard Qlik Sense charts!

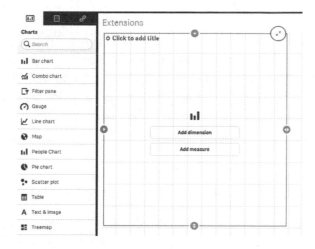

FIGURE 16.40:
The People Chart extension behaves like any other chart

In the following exercise, you add the **People Chart** extension to your Qlik Sense Desktop environment and create a pictogram of `Sales by Brand`.

Exercise 16.22: Adding an Extension to Your Environment

1. Do the following to add a new extension into your Qlik Sense Desktop environment:

    1.1. Copy the `PeopleChart` folder from the *Extensions Examples* folder to the *Extensions* folder.

    1.2. In the Qlik Sense Desktop, **save** your previous work and restart the Desktop.

2. Now, add a new chart using the new extension:

    2.1. Open your **Sales Analysis** app and create a new **Sheet**. Name the new sheet **Extensions**.

    2.2. You should see the new chart type called **People Chart** in the list of available chart types on the left. Drag the icon onto the grid to add a new **People Chart**.

    2.3. Add **Brand** as the dimension and **Sales** as the measure.

    2.4. You should see the pictogram that looks similar to Figure 16.41. Examine the **Properties** in the toolbar on the right. All of the familiar settings apply to the extension object, very similarly to the default chart types.

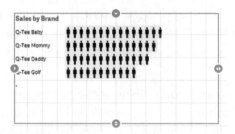

FIGURE 16.41:
The finished People Chart pictogram

Extra Credit: Replace the Image

A People Chart pictogram would be more relevant if you were showing counts of people, not sales amount. For these purposes, a picture of a T-shirt or a dollar sign could be more appropriate. Locate the picture file called `person.tif` in the `\Extensions\PeopleChart\` folder and replace the image with one of the icons from the `\Icons\` subfolder (you need to rename the original image file and then rename the new image file as `person.tif`). Restart Sense Desktop and examine the result in the chart.

Exploring the Feature of Converting Charts

The feature of converting charts is not specific to extensions, but it helps us emphasize how seamlessly all sheet objects work together in Qlik Sense.

You may have figured out that any chart in Qlik Sense can be easily converted to another chart type by dragging one chart type over an existing chart. For example, a bar chart icon can be dragged onto a pie chart on the sheet, and Qlik Sense will offer three options—**Replace** the chart with a Bar chart, **Convert** it to a Bar chart, or to **Cancel** the operation (see Figure 16.42).

Replacing the chart results in scratching off the old object and starting from a new bar chart. **Converting** to **bar chart** results in changing the chart type while preserving all the properties of the original object. This operation is very smart. It preserves even those properties that are not relevant for the new object, in case the user wants to convert back to the original. When necessary, new dimensions or expressions may be required. All these properties will be saved and used as necessary in the future, in case the users want to convert the chart again.

FIGURE 16.42:
Converting a pie chart to a bar chart

Now, what about extensions? Well, Extension objects can participate in the same process, exactly in the same way. A bar chart can be converted to a People Chart, which can in turn be converted to a pie chart, and so on.

In a similar way, users can replace dimensions and measures by dragging a corresponding Master item onto an existing chart, and extensions share the same features.

The only exception to the overall conversion ability is a **Map**. Due to its slightly different structure, a **Map** cannot be replaced with another chart, and **Map** dimensions cannot be replaced by dragging (at least, currently).

We encourage you to practice converting charts into different chart types, including the extensions, and to replace dimensions and measures by dragging and dropping.

Where to Find More Extensions and More Information

Such an easy extensibility of Qlik Sense opens the door for a wide community of developers to contribute their unique creations to the initial set of visualizations available in Qlik Sense. You can find additional extensions and information in many places. We will mention just a few here:

- **Qlik Community** (community.qlik.com) is the main forum of Qlik developers and users, where developers, analysts, and users can ask questions, get answers, and share their ideas and apps. Here you can find more information and more examples of just about anything related to QlikView and Qlik Sense, including extensions.

- **Qlik Market** (market.qlik.com) is the Qlik solution exchange where Qlik partners and customers exchange information about their solutions. Most of the presented apps here are demos of commercially available solutions, but some solutions and extensions may be free.
- **Qlik Branch** (branch.qlik.com) is the collaborative workplace and open exchange, primarily for developers. This is where developers can find tutorials, white papers, examples, and ready-to-use extensions. All the information here is free to use and follows the principles of open source. Anyone who is serious about extending and integrating Qlik Sense should certainly register and become a member at Qlik Branch.

What About Mashups?

As we promised in the beginning of this section, developing mashups—that is, integrating Qlik Sense objects in external web pages—is also quite simple. Yet, this topic is slightly outside of the scope of our book. We will just point you in the right direction and let you explore this fascinating material on your own.

QlikView integrations are developed using a tool called *Workbench*. Conveniently, it's bundled with Qlik Sense Desktop and doesn't require a separate license, so you already have it. All you need is to know how to use it.

The best way to get started is to follow the tutorials that are available on Qlik Community and Qlik Branch. At the time when this chapter was written, the best starting point is this thread on Qlik Community:

http://community.qlik.com/thread/140982

It points at a number of video tutorials that can be found on YouTube by searching for **Qlik Mash-Up APIs**.

We'd like to wish you the best in your Qlik Sense integration journey, and we hope to see your contributions to the growing collection of wonderful Qlik Sense visualizations!

This section completes our discussion of Qlik Sense and it's also the end of our curriculum. We hope that you enjoyed the time that we spent together as much as we did, and we'd like to hear from you.

In the following appendix, we suggest sources of additional information that can help you ramp up your career as a Qlik data scientist.

What's Next?

If this is your first QlikView book and you completed the
tutorials, we assure you that you know more about QlikView
and Qlik Sense than the average beginner. In this appendix,
we describe additional educational opportunities that can
help you and your company successfully ramp up your
QlikView knowledge.

***QlikView Your Business* in the classroom**. If you'd like us to teach your
team the contents of this book in a classroom environment, please contact
us at Natural Synergies (www.naturalsynergies.com). You can invite one of
the authors or one of our certified instructors to deliver this curriculum to
your team in a classroom setting.

Private *QlikView Your Business* courses. Many times, business analysts
need to see their company's data and their company's problems in order
to connect with a new technology like QlikView. In all fairness, it can be
difficult to learn how to apply QlikView in healthcare, for example, by
going through tutorials such as those in this book, which are based on

sales of fashion products. If this is the case for your company, contact us at Natural Synergies (www.naturalsynergies.com). Our team can develop and deliver a customized *QlikView Your Business* course that will be based on your own data and your own business analysis problems.

Masters Summit for QlikView. Most of the existing training classes are geared toward teaching beginners the basics of QlikView development. Masters Summit for QlikView (www.masterssummit.com) is the only advanced technical venue available for QlikView developers with some experience. This three-day hands-on event features four recognized QlikView experts (including one of the authors of this book) who teach the most advanced topics in QlikView Data Modeling, Scripting, Visualizations, and Advanced Expressions (Set Analysis and Advanced Aggregation). Additional sessions include Performance Tuning, Tips and Tricks, Server Administration, and more. If you are looking to expand your skills beyond the topics discussed in this book, definitely inquire if Masters Summit is a good fit for you.

In addition to these educational opportunities, make sure to leverage the multitude of available free resources:

- Join Qlik Community to participate in the forums and to read Qlik blogs: community.qlik.com.

- If you are planning on extending Qlik applications, join Qlik Branch: branch.qlik.com.

- If you are looking for QlikView solutions, visit Qlik Market: market.qlik.com.

- Follow QlikView bloggers. The list of active bloggers grows every day. We will refer you to a nice summary of all currently available blogs here: www.askqv.com/blogs/.

- Check out QlikView Components and QlikView Cookbook by Rob Wunderlich: http://qlikviewcookbook.com/.

When it's time to call for help. Sometimes QlikView implementations can present challenges. There can be many possible reasons, but the most common issue we've seen is a gap between the complexity of the project and the QlikView toolbox of the project team. If you feel that your QlikView team may need expert help, contact us at naturalsynergies.com. Whether it's performance tuning, advanced training, or application review, our QlikView experts can help your team overcome the issues and get back on track.

Let us know how we did. We'd like to hear back from you! If you liked our book, leave us a comment, tweet about your learning experience, blog about it, and so on. If we can improve the experience, send us an e-mail and let us know! We will try to incorporate your feedback in the next release.

Most of all—enjoy your Qlik journey and don't forget to have fun! See you around the community!

Index